大学翻译学研究型系列教材

总主编　张柏然

语言学与翻译研究导引

Selected Readings of Translation and Translation Research from Linguistic Perspectives

编　著　孙会军　郑庆珠

南京大学出版社

图书在版编目(CIP)数据

语言学与翻译研究导引 / 孙会军,郑庆珠编著. ——
南京 :南京大学出版社,2012.11
大学翻译学研究型系列教材 / 张柏然总主编
ISBN 978 - 7 - 305 - 10630 - 9

Ⅰ. ①语… Ⅱ. ①孙… ②郑… Ⅲ. ①翻译学—高等
学校—教材 Ⅳ. ①H059

中国版本图书馆 CIP 数据核字(2012)第 227031 号

出版发行　南京大学出版社
社　　址　南京市汉口路 22 号　　　　邮　编　210093
网　　址　http://www.NjupCo.com
出 版 人　左　健
丛 书 名　大学翻译学研究型系列教材
总 主 编　张柏然
书　　名　**语言学与翻译研究导引**
编　　著　孙会军　郑庆珠
责任编辑　裴维维　罗思遥　　　　　编辑热线　025 - 83592123
照　　排　南京南琳图文制作有限公司
印　　刷　江苏凤凰通达印刷有限公司
开　　本　787×1092　1/16　印张 23.5　字数 586 千
版　　次　2012 年 11 月第 1 版　2012 年 11 月第 1 次印刷
ISBN 978 - 7 - 305 - 10630 - 9
定　　价　48.00 元

发行热线　025 - 83594756　83686452
电子邮箱　Press@NjupCo.com
　　　　　Sales@NjupCo.com(市场部)

* 版权所有,侵权必究
* 凡购买南大版图书,如有印装质量问题,请与所购
图书销售部门联系调换

大学本科翻译研究型系列读本
大学翻译学研究型系列教材

顾　问（按首字母排序）

黄国文　中山大学

廖七一　四川外国语学院

潘文国　华东师范大学

王宏印　南开大学

王克非　北京外国语大学

谢天振　上海外国语大学

许　钧　南京大学

仲伟合　广东外语外贸大学

总　序

张柏然

　　到了该为翻译学研究型系列教材说几句话的时候了。两年前的炎炎夏日,南京大学出版社责成笔者总揽主编分别针对高等院校翻译学本科生和研究生学习与研究需求的研究型系列读本和导引。俗话说,独木难撑大厦。于是,笔者便千里相邀"招旧部",网罗昔日在南大攻读翻译学博士学位的"十八罗汉"各主其事。寒来暑往,光阴荏苒,转眼两年过去了。期间,大家意气奋发,不辞辛劳,借助网络"上天",躲进书馆"入地",上下求索,查阅浩瀚的文献经典,进而调动自己的学术积累,披沙拣金,辨正证伪,博采众长,字斟句酌,终于成就了这一本本呈现在读者面前的教材。

　　众所周知,教材乃教学之本和知识之源,亦即体现课程教学理念、教学内容、教学要求,甚至教学模式的知识载体,在教学过程中起着引导教学方向、保证教学质量的作用。改革开放以来,我国各类高校组编、出版的翻译教材逐年递增。我们在中国国家图书馆网站上检索主题名含有"翻译"字段的图书,检索结果显示,1980 至 2009 年间,我国引进、出版相关著作 1800 余种,其中,翻译教材占有很大的比重。近些年来,翻译教材更是突飞猛进。根据有关学者的不完全统计,目前,我国正式出版的翻译教材共有 1000 多种。* 这一变化结束了我国相当长一段时间内翻译教材"一枝独秀"的境地,迎来了"百花齐放"的局面,由此也反映了我国高校翻译教学改革的深化。

　　但是,毋庸讳言,虽然教材的品种繁多,但是真正合手称便的、富有特色的教材仍属凤毛麟角。教材数量增多并不足以表明教学理念的深刻转变。其中大多都具有包打翻译学天下的纯体系冲动,并没有打破我国既往翻译教材编写从某一理论预设出发的本质主义思维模式和几大板块的框架结构。从教材建设看,我国翻译理论教材在概念陈设、模式架构、内容安排上存在着比较严重的雷同化现象。这表明,教材建设需要从根本上加以改进,而如何改则取决于我们有什么样的教学理念。

　　有鉴于此,我们组编了"大学翻译学研究型系列教材"和"大学本科翻译研究型系列读本"这两套系列教材。前者系研究生用书,它包括《中国翻译理论研究导引》、《当代西方翻译理论研究导引》、《当代西方文论与翻译研究导引》、《翻译学方法论研究导引》、《语言学与翻译研究导引》、《文学翻译研究导引》、《汉语典籍英译研究导引》、《英汉口译理论研究导引》、《语料库翻译学研究导引》和《术语翻译研究导引》等 10 册;后者则以本科生为主要读者对象,它包括《翻译概论读本》、《文化翻译读本》、《文学翻译读本》、《商务英语翻译读本》、《法律英语翻译读本》、《传媒英语翻译读本》、《科技英语翻译读本》、《英汉口译读本》、《英汉比较与翻译读本》和《翻译资源与工具读本》等 10 册。这两套教材力图综合中西译论、相关学科(如哲学、美学、文学、语

---

　　* 转引自曾剑平、林敏华:《论翻译教材的问题及编写体系》,《中国科技翻译》,2011 年 11 月。

言学、社会学、文化学、心理学、语料库翻译学等)的吸融性研究以及方法论的多层次研究,结合目前高校翻译教学和研究实践的现状进行创造性整合,编写突出问题型结构和理路的读本和导引,以满足翻译学科本科生和研究生教学与研究的需求。这是深化中国翻译学研究型教材编写与研究的一个重要课题,至今尚未引起翻译理论研究界和教材编写界的足够重视。摆在我们面前的这一课题,基本上还是一片多少有些生荒的地带。因此,我们对这一课题的研究,也就多少带有拓荒性质。这样,不仅大量纷繁的文献经典需要我们去发掘、辨别与整理,中西翻译美学思想发展演变的特点与规律需要我们去探讨,而且研究的对象、范畴和方法等问题,都需要我们进行独立的思考与确定。研究这一课题的困难也就可以想见了。然而,这一课题本身的价值和意义却又变为克服困难的巨大动力,策励着我们不揣浅陋,迎难而上,试图在翻译学研究型教材编写这块土地上,作一些力所能及的垦殖。

这两套研究型系列教材的编纂目的和编纂特色主要体现为:不以知识传授为主要目的,而是培养学生发问、好奇、探索、兴趣,即学习的主动性,逐步实现思维方式和学习方式的转变,引导学生及早进入科学研究阶段;不追求知识的完整性、系统性,突破讲授通史、通论知识的教学模式,引入探究学术问题的教学模式;引进国外教材编写理念,填补国内大学翻译学研究型教材的欠缺;所选论著具有权威性、文献性、可读性与引导性。具体而言,和传统的通史通论教材不同,这两套系列教材是以问题结构章节,这个“问题”既可以是这门课(专业方向)的主要问题,也可以是这门课某个章节的主要问题。在每个章节的安排上,则是先由“导论”说明本章的核心问题,指明获得相关知识的途径;接着,通过选文的导言,直接指向“选文”—— 涉及的知识面很广的范文,这样对学生的论文写作更有示范性;“选文”之后安排“延伸阅读”,以拓展和深化知识;最后,通过“研究实践”或“问题与思考”,提供实践方案,进行专业训练,希冀用“问题”牵引学生主动学习。这样的结构方式,突出了教材本身的问题型结构和理路,旨在建构以探索和研究为基础的教与学的人才培养模式,让年轻学子有机会接触最新成就、前沿学术和科学方法;强调通识教育、人文教育与科学教育交融,知识传授与能力培养并重,注重培养学生掌握方法,未来能够应对千变万化的翻译教学与研究的发展和需要。

笔者虽说长期从事翻译教学与研究,但对编写教材尤其是研究型教材还是个新手。这两套翻译学研究型教材之所以能够顺利出版,全有赖各册主编的精诚合作和鼎力相助,全有仗一群尽责敬业的编写和校核人员。特别值得一提的是,在这两套系列教材的最后编辑工作中,南京大学出版社外语编辑室主任董颖和责任编辑裴维维两位女士全力以赴,认真校核,一丝不苟,对保证教材的质量起了尤为重要的作用。在此谨向他(她)们致以衷心的感谢!

总而言之,编写大学翻译学研究型教材还是一项尝试性的研究工程。诚如上面所述,我们在进行这项“多少带有拓荒性质”的尝试时,犹如蹒跚学步的孩童,在这过程中留下些许尴尬,亦属在所难免。作为教材的编撰者,我们衷心希望能听到来自各方的意见和建议,以便日后再版修订,进而发展出更好更多翻译学研究型教材来。

是之为序。

二〇一二年三月二十七日

撰于沪上滴水湖畔临港别屋

前　言

　　翻译是从源语到目的语的语码转换过程,因而翻译首先是一种语言现象。语言学作为一门研究语言的科学,在翻译实践以及在对翻译实践的描述、总结和探究中至关重要,甚至可以说是不可或缺的,语言学对于翻译研究的重要性是显而易见。

　　在历史上,翻译研究逐渐发展成为一个较为系统的学科,可以说始于语言学,并在一定程度上依赖于语言学的研究成果。有关翻译的研究曾经一度是语言学研究中的一个组成部分,或被看成是语言学的一个分支。到了二十世纪中叶,语言学的发展及其对于翻译理论研究的介入,使翻译理论得以摆脱以往点评式、印象式的特点,变得越来越科学、系统。美国的奈达,英国的卡特福德、纽马克,以及加拿大的维内和达贝尔内,都尝试借助语言学的研究成果,对翻译进行学理上的思考和系统的研究,并取得了具有里程碑意义的研究成果。

　　从二十世纪八十年代后期开始,文化批评和文化研究在西方学术界崛起,并逐渐上升到主要地位,学者们开始从文化角度切入翻译研究,语言学途径的翻译研究因为其"唯科学主义"的嫌疑受到质疑。借用张柏然教授的话说,"翻译的语言学范式给人们带来了理性思维,破除了原来与文学研究范式的神秘性和主观直觉的研究方式,从主观性走向客观性,使翻译研究取得了很大进展。但由于语言学范式使译者过多依赖于语言的规律性,忽视主体的主观能动性,排除言语活动的社会制约性和规定性,从而突出了原文文本的中心性,追求同一性和一致性,最终堕入语言逻各斯中心"。① 语言学理论在翻译研究中一统天下的地位也受到挑战,翻译研究出现了"文化转向",语言学途径的翻译研究似乎出现式微的迹象。然而,从前几年开始,文化途径的翻译研究似乎逐渐失去了兴奋点和增长点,人们于是乎又回过头来重新反思翻译问题,有些学者开始探讨"翻译研究的语言学回归"。在编者看来,翻译研究中语言学回归绝不可能是一种简单的回归,历史的洪流不会逆转,翻译研究也绝不能简单地回到语言学途径。

　　文化途径的翻译研究丰富和发展了人们对于翻译活动的认识,使人们得出了这样的认识:翻译是多元的跨学科领域,没有哪一门学科理论可以解决翻译研究中的所有问题。语言学、文学、文化学、心理学等各个学科的理论对于翻译研究来说都是必不可少的,都会对翻译研究产生指导借鉴意义,而其中语言学无疑是最

---

① 《外语与外语教学》2008 年第 6 期。

为重要的。

其实语言学途径的翻译研究从来都没有停止过。即使在文化途径的翻译研究占据学术界的主流地位的时候，很多学者一直没有放弃他们的努力，从语言学的角度出发，在翻译研究领域进行了踏实、深入的研究，并且吸收了文化途径翻译研究的成果，取得了令人瞩目的成就，对于我们进一步认识翻译活动的本质规律做出了贡献。

为帮助读者了解语言学对于翻译活动和翻译研究的意义，了解翻译理论建设中语言学所扮演的角色，了解当前语言学的研究成果在翻译研究中的具体应用，以及语言学途径翻译研究的所产生的激动人心的成果，编者精选了语言学途径的翻译研究学术论文，汇编成《语言学与翻译研究导引》这本研究型教材。

为凸显本教材的研究性，编者首先以语言学的不同流派为线索，选择各个语言学途径翻译研究方面的重要学术文章。其次，在决定相关学术论文的取舍时，编者重视选文的代表性和经典性。需要指出的是，我们选材的范围局限于英文和中文两种文献，英文文献为主，也有个别中文文献。这并不是说其他的语言文化中没有这方面的研究成果，只是由于编者的阅读范围的限制以及要让大多数读者理解的宗旨使然。教材还提供了具体研究案例，帮助读者通过研读这些文章了解相关领域的研究动态，掌握相关课题的研究方法及学术论文的写作方法。除此之外，在选择研究案例的时候，我们特别选择了一些以英汉、汉英翻译为研究语料和研究对象的论文，从而能够为更多的研究者所理解，接受起来也更容易些。

本书共分九章，每章由"导论"、"选文"、"研究实践"等三大部分组成，选文后还有"延伸阅读"和"问题与思考"。"导论"部分简要介绍特定流派的语言学理论如何从独特的研究视角出发审视翻译问题的，力争概括出该理论流派的整体情况、研究脉络和前沿思想。"选文"部分是相关流派的代表性论述。这些文章绝大多数选自学术期刊，少量文章选自学术专著或百科全书。每篇选文配有"导言"，位于选文的正文之前，介绍作者的学术背景、所选文章的来源及其主要内容。"研究实践"部分是根据选文所讨论的研究课题和研究内容，选择一些学者的研究案例，力图帮助读者从这些研究案例中得到启发，找到研究的模式与方法，通过学习和模仿，创造性地开展具体的课题研究，培养读者的学术研究能力。

本书在编写过程中得到了南京大学博士生导师张柏然教授和南京大学出版社领导的大力支持，编者在此表示衷心的谢意。另外，许伟和徐铭远在书稿排版过程中都牺牲了自己的休息时间给予我们很大的帮助，郑贞也热情地提供了一些珍贵的资料，在此一并表示感谢。

由于时间和水平的限制，书中的疏漏之处，还敬请广大读者批评指正。

编者

2012 年 11 月

目　　录

第一章 绪论：语言、语言学与翻译研究

导　论

　　翻译是用一种语言的文本来代替另外一种语言文本的过程，在操作过程中必然要涉及语言。因此，对于语言本质的认识，对于语言使用规律的理解是有效进行翻译的必由之路，而语言学理论与翻译理论有着天然的联系。

　　起初有关翻译的研究只是语言学研究中的一个组成部分，或者说是语言学的一个分支，翻译研究可以说起源于语言学研究，并在很大程度上依赖于语言学的研究成果。

　　虽然翻译的过程涉及与两种相关语言有关的大量非语言问题，但是如果没有语言学理论的输入，翻译理论就很难实现系统化、理论化。正如罗杰·贝尔（Roger Bell）在他的专著《翻译与翻译过程》（*Translation and Translating*，Introduction，xv，1991）的序言部分所指出的那样，"翻译理论家们如果不利用语言学的研究成果，他们对于文本的评说就难免失之主观，难免会带有规定性的色彩"。语言学的发展及其对于翻译理论研究的介入，使翻译理论得以摆脱以往点评式、印象式的特点，变得越来越科学、系统。20 世纪中叶，语言学理论的发展继续带动翻译研究的发展，人们对于翻译研究的兴趣越来越浓厚。以至于每当语言学的理论有所发展，就会有人尝试将其应用到翻译理论研究中去，从而使翻译研究得以发展、深化。这一时期从语言学的视角探讨翻译问题的学者有加拿大的维内（Jean-Paul Vinay）和达贝尔内（Jean Darbelnet），他们于 1958 年发表了著名的《法英比较文体学：翻译方法论》（*Comparative Stylistics of French and English：A Methodology for Translation*）。另外一个较早从语言学的角度来考察翻译问题的学者是雅各布逊（Roman Jacobson），他 1959 年发表的《语言学视角下的翻译面面观》（"On Linguistic Aspects of Translation）是从语言学视角考察翻译现象的经典之作。接下来从语言学角度研究翻译问题的是美国翻译理论家奈达（Eugine Nida），他先后发表了他影响巨大的著作：《翻译科学探索》（*Toward a Science of Translating*，1964）以及《翻译理论与实践》（*The Theory and Practice of Translation*，1969，with C. R. Taber）。同时期，英国学者卡特福德（J. C. Catford）出版的著名的《翻译的语言学理论》（*A Linguistic Theory of Translation*，1965）也具有重要意义。这些学者都借助语言学理论，对翻译进行学理上的思考和系统的研究，并取得了具有里程碑意义的研究成果。从此，翻译研究从语言学研究中独立出来，并有可能逐渐发展成为一种独立的学科。

　　然而，这些研究远远不是语言学途径的翻译理论的全部，语言学的发展一直滋养着翻译研究。翻译研究领域出现"文化转向"以后，翻译理论家们把语境的因素（社会、历史、文化、心理学以及计算机技术）的发展都融入翻译理论的研究。仅就语言学而言，对比语言学、社会语言

学、系统功能语言学、语篇语言学、心理与认知语言学以及语料库语言学等都被纳入翻译研究中,使翻译研究这一学科的羽翼日渐丰满,并逐渐发展成为一门相对独立的学科。

选文一　On Linguistic Aspects of Translation

Roman Jakobson

导　言

罗曼·雅各布逊(Roman Jakobson,1896—1982),著名文学理论家和语言学家,出生于莫斯科,从小接受良好的教育,结交很多有才华的艺术家、诗人和学者。莫斯科语言学界以及布拉格语言学界都是他与他人合作先后于 1915 年和 1926 年创建起来的。他的论文"On Linguistic Aspects of Translation"拓展了翻译的内涵,除了语际翻译之外,他还将语内翻译和符际翻译纳入翻译的范畴。这篇论文在 1959 年首次发表,收录在哈佛大学出版社出版的、由 Reuben Brower 主编的具有里程碑意义的《论翻译》(*On Translation*)一书中。这篇文章是最早从语言学角度探讨翻译问题的文章之一,一直被视为翻译研究领域的经典之作。

According to Bertrand Russell, "no one can understand the word 'cheese' unless he has a nonlinguistic acquaintance with cheese"(Rusell, 1950:3). If, however, we follow Russell's fundamental precept and place our "emphasis upon the linguistic aspects of traditional philosophical problems," then we are obliged to state that no one can understand the word "cheese" unless he has an acquaintance with the meaning assigned to this word in the lexical code of English. Any representative of a cheese-less culinary culture will understand the English word "cheese" if he is aware that in this language it means "food made of pressed curds" and if he has at least a linguistic acquaintance with "curds." We never consumed ambrosia or nectar and have only a linguistic acquaintance with the words "ambrosia," "nectar," and "gods"—the name of their mythical users; nonetheless, we understand these words and know in what contexts each of them may be used.

The meaning of the words "cheese," "apple," "nectar," "acquaintance," "but," "mere," and of any word or phrase whatsoever is definitely a linguistic—or to be more precise and less narrow—a semiotic fact. Against those who assign meaning (*signatum*) not to the sign, but to the thing itself, the simplest and truest argument would be that nobody has ever smelled or tasted the meaning of "cheese" or of "apple." There is no *signatum* without *signum*. The meaning of the word "cheese" cannot be inferred from a nonlinguistic acquaintance with cheddar or with camembert without the assistance of the verbal code. An array of linguistic signs is needed to introduce an unfamiliar word. Mere pointing will not teach us whether "cheese" is the name of the given specimen, or of any box of camembert, or of camembert in general or of any cheese, any milk product, any food, any refreshment, or perhaps any box irrespective of contents. Finally, does a word simply name the thing in question, or does it imply a meaning such as offering, sale, prohibition, or malediction? (Pointing actually may mean malediction; in some cultures, particularly in Africa, it is an ominous gesture.)

For us, both as linguists and as ordinary word-users, the meaning of any linguistic sign is its translation into some further, alternative sign, especially a sign "in which it is more fully developed" as Peirce, the deepest inquirer into the essence of signs, insistently stated (Dewey, 1946: 91). The term "bachelor" may be converted into a more explicit designation, "unmarried man," whenever higher explicitness is required. We distinguish three ways of interpreting a verbal sign: it may be translated into other signs of the same language, into another language, or into another, nonverbal system of symbols. These three kinds of translation are to be differently labeled:

1. Intralingual translation or *rewording* is an interpretation of verbal signs by means of other signs of the same language.

2. Interlingual translation or *translation proper* is an interpretation of verbal signs by means of some other language.

3. Intersemiotic translation or *transmutation* is an interpretation of verbal signs by means of signs of nonverbal sign systems.

The intralingual translation of a word uses either another, more or less synonymous, word or resorts to a circumlocution. Yet synonymy, as a rule, is not complete equivalence: for example, "every celibate is a bachelor, but not every bachelor is a celibate." A word or an idiomatic phrase-word, briefly a code-unit of the highest level, may be fully interpreted only by means of an equivalent combination of code-units, i. e. , a message referring to this code-unit: "every bachelor is an unmarried man, and every unmarried man is a bachelor," or "every celibate is bound not to marry, and everyone who is bound not to marry is a celibate."

Likewise, on the level of interlingual translation, there is ordinarily no full equivalence between code-units, while messages may serve as adequate interpretations of alien code-units or messages. The English word "cheese" cannot be completely identified with its standard Russian heteronym "сыр," because cottage cheese is a cheese but not a сыр. Russians say: принеси сыру и творогу "bring cheese and [sic] cottage cheese." In standard Russian, the food made of pressed curds is called сыр only if ferment is used.

Most frequently, however, translation from one language into another substitutes messages in one language not for separate code-units but for entire messages in some other language. Such a translation is a reported speech; the translator recodes and transmits a message received from another source. Thus translation involves two equivalent messages in two different codes.

Equivalence in difference is the cardinal problem of language and the pivotal concern of linguistics. Like any receiver of verbal messages, the linguist acts as their interpreter. No linguistic specimen may be interpreted by the science of language without a translation of its signs into other signs of the same system or into signs of another system. Any comparison of two languages implies an examination of their mutual translatability; widespread practice of interlingual communication, particularly translating activities, must be kept under constant scrutiny by linguistic science. It is difficult to overestimate the urgent need for and the theoretical and practical significance of differential bilingual dictionaries with careful comparative definition of all the corresponding units in their intention and extension. Likewise, differential bilingual grammars should define what unifies and what differentiates the two languages in their selection and delimitation of grammatical concepts.

Both the practice and the theory of translation abound with intricacies, and from time to time attempts are made to sever the Gordian knot by proclaiming the dogma of untranslatability. "Mr. Everyman, the natural logician," vividly imagined by B. L. Whorf, is supposed to have arrived at the following bit of reasoning: "Facts are unlike to speakers whose language background provides for unlike formulation of them"(Whorf, 1956: 235). In the first years of the Russian revolution there were fanatic visionaries who argued in Soviet periodicals for a radical revision of traditional language and particularly for the weeding out of such misleading expressions as "sunrise" or "sunset." Yet we still use this Ptolemaic imagery without implying a rejection of Copernican doctrine, and we can easily transform our customary talk about the rising and setting sun into a picture of the earth's rotation simply because any sign is translatable into a sign in which it appears to us more fully developed and precise.

A faculty of speaking a given language implies a faculty of talking about this language. Such a "metalinguistic" operation permits revision and redefinition of the vocabulary used. The complementarity of both levels—object-language and metalanguage—was brought out by Niels Bohr: all well-defined experimental evidence must be expressed in ordinary language, "in which the practical use of every word stands in complementary relation to attempts of its strict definition"(Bohr, 1948: 317f.).

All cognitive experience and its classification is conveyable in any existing language. Whenever there is deficiency, terminology may be qualified and amplified by loan-words or loan-translations, neologisms or semantic shifts, and finally, by circumlocutions. Thus in the newborn literary language of the Northeast Siberian Chukchees, "screw" is rendered as "rotating nail," "steel" as "hard iron," "tin" as "thin iron," "chalk" as "writing soap," "watch" as "hammering heart." Even seemingly contradictory circumlocutions, like "electrical horse-ear" (электрическая конка), the first Russian name of the horseless street ear, or "flying steamship" (*jena paragot*), the Koryak term for the airplane, simply designate the electrical analogue of the horse-ear and the flying analogue of the steamer and do not impede communication, just as there is no semantic "noise" and disturbance in the double oxymoron—"cold beef-and-pork hot dog."

No lack of grammatical device in the language translated into makes impossible a literal translation of the entire conceptual information contained in the original. The traditional conjunctions "and," "or" are now supplemented by a new connective—"and/or"—which was discussed a few years ago in the witty book *Federal Prose—How to Write in and/or for Washington* (Masterson & Phillips, 1948: 40f.). Of these three conjunctions, only the latter occurs in one of the Samoyed languages (Bergsland, 1949: 374f.). Despite these differences in the inventory of conjunctions, all three varieties of messages observed in "federal prose" may be distinctly translated both into traditional English and into this Samoyed language. Federal prose: (1) John and Peter, (2) John or Peter, (3) John and/or Peter will come. Traditional English: (3) John and Peter or one of them will come. Samoyed: John and/or Peter both will come, (2) John and/or Peter, one of them will come.

If some grammatical category is absent in a given language, its meaning may be translated into this language by lexical means. Dual forms like Old Russian брата are translated with the help of the numeral: "two brothers." It is more difficult to remain faithful to the original when we translate into a language provided with a certain grammatical category from a language devoid of such a category. When translating the English sentence "She has brothers" into a language which discriminates dual and plural, we are compelled either to make our own choice between two statements "She has two brothers"—"She has more than two" or to leave the decision to the listener and say: "She has either two or more than two brothers." Again in translating from a language without grammatical number into English one is obliged to select one of the two possibilities—"brother" or "brothers" or to confront the receiver of this message with a two-choice situation: "She has either one or more than one brother."

As Boas neatly observed, the grammatical pattern of a language (as opposed to its lexical stock) determines those aspects of each experience that must be expressed in the given language: "We have to choose between these aspects, and one or the other must be chosen" (Boas, 1938: 132f.). In order to translate accurately the English sentence "I hired a worker," a Russian needs supplementary information, whether this action was completed or not and whether the worker was a man or a woman, because he must make his choice between a verb of completive or noncompletive aspect—нанял or нанимал—and between a masculine and feminine noun—работника or работницу. If I ask the utterer of the English sentence whether the worker was male or female, my question may be judged irrelevant or indiscreet, whereas in the Russian version of this sentence an answer to this question is obligatory. On the other hand, whatever the choice of Russian grammatical forms to translate the quoted English message, the translation will give no answer to the question of whether I "hired" or "have hired" the worker, or whether he/she was an indefinite or definite worker ("a" or "the"). Because the information required by the English and Russian grammatical pattern is unlike, we face quite different sets of two-choice situations; therefore a chain of translations of one and the same isolated sentence from English into Russian and vice versa could entirely deprive such a message of its initial content. The Geneva linguist S. Karcevski used to compare such a gradual loss with a circular series of unfavourable currency transactions. But evidently the richer the context of a message, the smaller the loss of information.

Languages differ essentially in what they *must* convey and not in what they *may* convey. Each verb of a given language imperatively raises a set of specific yes-or-no questions, as for instance: is the narrated event conceived with or without reference to its completion? Is the narrated event presented as prior to the speed event or not? Naturally the attention of native speakers and listeners will be constantly focused on such items as are compulsory in their verbal code.

In its cognitive function, language is minimally dependent on the grammatical pattern because the definition of our experience stands in complementary relation to metalinguistic operations—the cognitive level of language not only admits but directly requires recoding interpretation, i. e., translation. Any assumption of ineffable or untranslatable cognitive data would be a contradiction in terms. But in jest, in dreams, in magic, briefly, in what one would call everyday verbal mythology and in poetry above all, the grammatical categories carry a high semantic import. In these conditions, the question of translation becomes much more entangled and controversial.

Even such a category as grammatical gender, often cited as merely formal, plays a great role in the mythological attitudes of a speech community. In Russian the feminine cannot designate a male person, nor the masculine specify a female. Ways of personifying or metaphorically interpreting inanimate nouns are prompted by their gender. A test in the Moscow Psychological Institute (1915) showed that Russians, prone to personify the weekdays, consistently represented Monday, Tuesday and Thursday as males and Wednesday, Friday and Saturday as females, without realizing that this distribution was due to the masculine gender of the first three names (понедельник, вторник, четверг) as against the feminine gender of the others (среда, пятница, суббота). The fact that the word for Friday is masculine in some Slavic languages and feminine in others is reflected in the folk traditions of the corresponding peoples, which differ in their Friday ritual. The widespread Russian superstition that a fallen knife presages a male guest and a fallen fork a female one is determined by the masculine gender of нож "knife" and the feminine of вилка "fork" in Russian. In Slavic and other languages where "day" is masculine and "night" feminine, day is represented by poets as the lover of night. The Russian painter Repin was baffled as to why Sin had been depicted as a woman by German artists: he did not realize that "sin" is feminine in German (*die Sünde*), but masculine in Russian (грех). Likewise a Russian child, while reading a translation of German tales, was astounded to find that Death, obviously a woman (Russian смерть, fem.), was pictured as an old man (German *der Tod*, masc.). *My Sister Life*, the title of a book of poems by Boris Pasternak, is quite natural in Russian, where "life" is feminine жизнь, but was enough to reduce to despair the Czech poet Josef Hora in his attempt to translate these poems, since in Czech this noun is masculine *život*.

What was the initial question which arose in Slavic literature at its very beginning? Curiously enough, the translator's difficulty in preserving the symbolism of genders, and the cognitive irrelevance of this difficulty, appears to be the main topic of the earliest Slavic original work, the preface to the first translation of the Evangeliarium, made in the early 1860's by the founder of Slavic letters and liturgy, Constantine the Philosopher, and recently restored and interpreted by A. Vaillant (Vaillant, 1948: 5f.). "Greek, when translated into another language, cannot always be reproduced identically, and that happens to each language being translated," the Slavic apostle states. "Masculine nouns 'river' and 'star' in Greek, are feminine in another language as река and звезда in Slavic." According to Vaillant's commentary, this divergence effaces the symbolic identification of the rivers with demons and of the stars with angels in the Slavic translation of two of Matthew's verses (7: 25 and 2: 9). But to this poetic obstacle, Saint Constantine resolutely opposes the precept of Dionysius the Areopagite, who called for chief attention to the cognitive values (силе разума) and not to the words themselves.

In poetry, verbal equations become a constructive principle of the text. Syntactic and morphological categories, roots, and affixes, phonemes and their components (distinctive features)—in short, any constituents of the verbal code are confronted, juxtaposed, brought into contiguous relation according to the principle of similarity and contrast and carry their own autonomous signification. Phonemic similarity is sensed as semantic relationship. The pull, or to use a more erudite, and perhaps more precise term—paronomasia, reigns over poetic art, and whether its rule is absolute or limited, poetry by definition is untranslatable. Only creative transposition is possible: either intralingual transposition—from one poetic shape into another, or interlingual transposition—from one language into another, or finally intersemiotic transposition—from one system of signs into another, e. g., from verbal art into music, dance, cinema, or painting.

If we were to translate into English the traditional formula *Traduttore, traditore* as "the translator is a betrayer," we would deprive the Italian rhyming epigram of all its paronomastic value. Hence a cognitive attitude would compel us to change this aphorism into a more explicit statement and to answer the questions: translator of what messages? Betrayer of what values?

选文二　Translation and Language：A Linguistic Approach to Translation Studies

Peter Fawcett

导　言

本文选自英国翻译理论家福西特（Peter Fawcett）的专著 *Translation and Language*：*Linguistic Theories Explained* 第一章开篇的部分。该书首先于 1997 年由英国圣哲罗姆出版有限公司出版，后于 2007 年被该公司授权给外语教学与研究出版社，在中国大陆出版。本文主要介绍了语言学与翻译理论之间爱恨交加的关系：对于翻译的研究离不开语言学，但是语言学家大多对翻译理论不感兴趣，而在很多翻译理论家看来，语言学对于翻译研究到底有多少借鉴意义是颇值得怀疑的。福西特既不完全赞同对语言学的怀疑态度，也不把语言学视为翻译研究的大救星。他认为语言学对于翻译的意义有二：第一，语言学的研究成果可以被应用到翻译实践中去；第二，人们可以用语言学理论观照翻译研究，建立起翻译的语言学理论，与翻译的文学理论、翻译的心理学理论、翻译的经济学理论等不同理论一起，从不同的角度出发，共同解释翻译活动不同方面及其本质规律。

Introduction：A Troubled Relationship

Modern linguistics began in the early twentieth century with the work of the Swiss linguist Ferdinand de Saussure. He focused on the notion of language as a system at a given moment in time (a synchronic approach) at a highly abstract level that uncovered powerful principles about the way in which language in general is structured. The structuralist model he produced was to prove immensely influential when, much later, it was taken up by anthropologists, literary critics and philosophers as the one model that would apparently explain what we had always wanted to know about life, the universe and everything.

Since linguistics is the study of language and has produced such powerful and productive theories about how language works, and since translation is a language activity, it would seem only common sense to think that the first had something to say about the second. Indeed in 1965 the British scholar John Catford opened his book *A Linguistic Theory of Translation* with the words："Clearly, then, any theory of translation must draw upon a theory of language—a general linguistic theory." In exactly the same year, however, the famous American theoretical linguist Noam Chomsky was rather more skeptical about the implications of his own theory for translation saying that his theory "does not, for example, imply that there must be some reasonable procedure for translating between languages" (1965: 30). Although no expert in translation, Chomsky nonetheless divined that there was something about the activity that put it beyond reason. Perhaps he had read what the academic Ivor Richards (1953: 250) said about translation: "We have here indeed what may very probably be the most complex type of event yet produced in the evolution of the cosmos."

This uncertain relationship between linguistics and translation theory continued to be reflected in the literature. Eight years after Catford's and Chomsky's pronouncements, the German theorist Jörn Albrechet (1973: 1) expressed regret and astonishment that linguists had not studied translation; yet the Soviet linguist Aleksandr Shveitser, writing in the same year (although quoted here from the later German translation), made the opposite claim: many linguists had long since decided translation could indeed be an object of linguistic study (1987: 13). He rejected the idea that linguistics can explain only the lowest levels of translation activity, saying this was based on too narrow a view of linguistics. He did, however, refer briefly to the furore caused by the first major attempt by a Russian scholar to produce a linguistic description of translation (Fedorov, 1953), which provoked lively polemic and liberal accusations of "deviation" (see Cary, 1957: 187).

The intervening years have not resolved the tension. Almost thirty years after the Catford-Chomskey declarations, the English academic Roger Bell (1991: xv) claimed that translation theorists and linguists were still going their own separate ways. The French scholar Maurice Pergnier has pointed out even though linguistics has developed in ways that make it much more relevant to the concerns of translation, there are still those who would like to liberate translation completely from its sway (1993: 9). Indeed, his compatriot Marianne Lederer is just one among many who dismisses linguistics from translation studies: "I hope in this way to bring out the reasons why translation must be dealt with on a level other than the linguistics" (1994: 87).

Such a position is provocatively extreme. Linguistics quite clearly does have something to offer the study of translation, and in these pages we shall be exploring what that is. At the same time, however, we shall be pointing out the limitations of the discipline, especially if people want to see translation as an entirely linguistic activity or want to use linguistics as a recipe giving ready-made solutions to specific translation problems rather than as a resource for extrapolating general problem-solving techniques from specific concrete problems.

The relationship of linguistics to translation can be twofold: one can apply the findings of linguistics to the practice of translation, and one can have a linguistic theory of translation, as opposed, say, to a literary, economic or psychological theory of translation.

In the first approach, a subdivision of linguistics such as sociolinguistics might have something to say about the way in which language varies in relation to social status, age, gender and so on. It will enable us to recognize these variations and describe them. And when we have to deal with sociolinguistic variation in a text to be translated, linguistics can provide one input in deciding how to cope with the situation.

In the second approach, rather than applying linguistic theory to elements within the text to be translated, one can apply it to the entire concept of translation itself. Thus the theory of dynamic equivalence put forward by the American scholar Eugene Nida, can actually be seen as nothing less than a sociolinguistics of translation, describing the way translators can adapt texts to the needs of a different audience in the same way we all adjust our language to suit the people we are talking to.

选文三　Linguistics and Translation

Gunilla Anderman

导　言

《语言学与翻译》一文节选自 Piotr Kuhiwczak 和 Karin Littau 两位学者主持编写的 *A Companion to Translation Studies*(2007, Multilingual Matters Ltd.)。这部书是继 Jeremy Munday 的 *Introducing Translation Studies* 之后的又一部系统探讨翻译问题的重要理论著作。全书共收录论文九篇,分别为《文化与翻译》、《哲学与翻译》、《语言学与翻译》、《历史与翻译》、《文学翻译》、《性别与翻译》、《戏剧翻译》、《屏幕翻译》以及《政治与翻译》。《语言学与翻译》作者为 Gunilla Anderman,系统地论述了历史上语言学领域的每一重要发展对翻译乃至翻译理论所产生的影响,使读者能够理解语言学与翻译研究之间的关系,把握语言学与翻译研究这两个学科互动交融的历史,深刻体会语言学在翻译研究中的作用和影响。

Throughout the ages, translation as well as linguistics, the formal study of language, has attracted comments and speculation. The need for practising translators is acknowledged as early as the Old Testament where, in the Book of Daniel 1: 4, reference is made to the need for mastery of "the tongue of the Chaldeans" for use in "the king's palace." And since time immemorial the nature and origin of human language has invited speculation. As late as the 17th century one view held that the primitive language of mankind was Chinese, which was spoken by Noah and his family in the Ark and survived the flood (Aitchison, 1996: 4). It was to take until the latter half of the 18th century before linguistics, then known as philology, started to emerge as a discipline in its own right; for translation studies to become an independent academic subject with established interdisciplinary links to other fields of study including linguistics was to take close to the dawn of a new millennium. In 1786, the first step was taken, nudging the study of language closer towards becoming a discipline in its own right. In a paper presented to the Royal Asiatic Society in Calcutta, Sir William Jones (1746—1794) of the East India Company declared that no philologist could examine the Sanskrit, Greek and Latin languages without believing them to have sprung from same, common, Indo-European source which perhaps no longer existed (Jones, 1970). Comparative and historical linguistics now became the focus of the attention of philologists, and, by the possession of distinctive, shared characteristics, languages were successively grouped together genealogically into families. While the similarity of cognates such as "hand" in English, hand in German and hand in Dutch, Danish, Norwegian and Swedish points to a related Germanic group of languages, French "main", Spanish "mano" and Italian "mano" constitute some of the languages belonging to the Romance language family while "ryka," "rêka" and "ruka" in Russian, Polish and Czech respectively suggest membership of the Slavonic group of languages. The implications for translation arising from the groundbreaking work of philologists of the 19th century in grouping together into families the Indo-European languages as we know them today were aptly illustrated a century later by the observation made by translation theorists Vinay and Darbelnet that "literal translation is a unique solution [...] It is most commonly found in translations between closely related languages (e. g. French/Italian)" (Vinay & Darbelnet, 1995: 34). Following the discovery of the common historical origin of the Indo-European languages, the interest of linguists began to focus on the historical development of languages to the extent that, during the latter half of the 19th century, a reaction was beginning to be felt to the preoccupation with the past and the rigorous analytical methods employed in linguistic analysis, which at times were less than rigorous. In particular, criticism was voiced by the Junggrammatiker, a group of German linguists centred round the University of Leipzig in the 1870s. The legacy left by these scholars, known in English as the "neo-grammarians," remains in currency today: a concern with the spoken language as an object of examination coupled with an insistence on statable principles and a theory capable of formulation as a prerequisite to empirically-based linguistic investigation. The focus on a more systematic approach to the study of language attracted the attention of linguists from other countries including the Swiss scholar Ferdinand de Saussure (1857—1913), who, following studies in Leipzig and Berlin returned to Switzerland to lecture at the University of Geneva. "The father of modern linguistics," de Saussure stressed the importance of a synchronic approach, the study of language at a given point in time, not related to its past, which is the pursuit of historical or diachronic linguistics.

Also of importance to de Saussure's theoretical framework was the distinction between *langue*, the underlying set of rules of a language and *parole*, the actual use made of language by individual speakers. This distinction is still not granted sufficient importance in translation theory, where serious attention has only recently started to be given to vernacular and dialect translation. Another key concept introduced by de Saussure was the sign, which he invested with two parts, the signifier and the signified (1916/1983). While the former is a mental image of the physical sound made when saying for instance "dog" in English, the latter is a mental concept or representation of dogs in the real world. The relationship between the signifier and the signified was, according to de Saussure, an arbitrary social construct, a potential problem for the translator as signs do not signify in isolation. Although "dog" in English translates into Spanish as "perro," the two words carry different sets of associations or connotations. In English, animals like humans have "legs," "backs" and "necks." In Spanish, on the other hand, human legs are known as piernas, their backs as espaldas and their necks as cuellos while animal legs are referred to as patas, their backs as lomos and their necks as pescuezos. These observations tell a different story of the place of animals in Hispanic culture from that of the dog as beloved pet and man's best friend in English-speaking parts of the world.

The first half of the 20th century also saw links established between translation and anthropologically-based linguistics. Through the Empire, English speakers had been brought into contact with a world beyond Europe and with speakers of vastly different languages. Through his fieldwork centred on the life of the Trobriand islanders of New Guinea in the southwest Pacific, Bronislaw Malinowski (1884—1942), holder of the first Chair of Anthropology at the University of London, was empirically confronted with the limits of translation. With no English terms available for concepts crucial to his description of the culture and religion of the islanders, Malinowski was left no choice but to become "[i]n the history of English linguistics [...] the first scholar to deal with the systematic use of translation in the statement of meaning in ethnographic texts" (Firth, 1968: 76). Previously undocumented languages also attracted the attention of linguists in the United States, where interest focused on the Native American languages. Rapidly facing extinction, these became the object of study of such linguists as Franz Boas (1858—1942) and Edward Sapir (1884—1939), both born in Europe and trained in neo-grammarian methodology. The observations of Sapir, and in turn Benjamin Whorf (1897—1944), found an expression in what has become known as the Sapir/Whorf hypothesis which, with its emphasis on disparity in world view between speakers of vastly different languages (Whorf, 1956), makes translation a near impossibility in its more extreme, "stronger" interpretation. In its "weaker" version, on the other hand, it does little more than confirm the experience of every practising translator that languages differ not so much with respect to what it is possible to say in them as to the degree of difficulty with which it can be said.

The European heritage of the neogrammarian insistence on rigour in methodology was at the time reinforced in the USA by the influence of behaviourist, mechanistic psychology on linguistics, which found its leading exponent in Leonard Bloomfield (1887—1949). With its strong emphasis on methodology and concern with the structure of language to the exclusion of meaning, Bloomfield's *Language* (1933) dominated the study of linguistics during the 1930s and 1940s, confining the scope of linguistic analysis of American "structuralists" to only the structure and rules of the language investigated.

Early views on the link between translation and linguistics are found in an often-quoted paper by the Czech-born American structuralist Roman Jakobson. In "On Linguistic Aspects of Translation," Jakobson (1959/2000) points to three different kinds of translation. While interlingual translation entails the transfer of content as well as of form from one language to another, intralingual translation entails the process of rewording in one and the same language for purposes of clarification. The third kind is intersemiotic translation, which is the method employed when a written text is transferred to another medium such as film or music. Acknowledging the need for the latter two types of translation, Roman Jakobson presciently anticipated recently-debated issues and developments in present-day translation studies. In an article in *The Independent* of 15 November 2001, Susan Bassnett provoked a lively debate with her proposal that, in order to maintain the interest of present-day school children, Shakespeare is in need of rewording (in other words, intralingual "translation") into modern English. And, as the need for expertise in audio-visual translation rockets between English and other lesser-used European languages for use in film and television, intersemiotic translation is becoming the subject of avid attention.

The behaviourist stronghold on American linguistics came to a hotly debated end in the middle of the 20th century when the work of Noam Chomsky challenged the undisputed reign of leading behaviourist exponent B. F. Skinner (1904—1990) and the emphasis shifted to conditioning as the sole explanation of verbal behaviour. The interest of linguists now shifted to the study of the intuitive knowledge that speakers possess about their language; instead of highlighting the differences between languages attention turned to a search for the properties that they might share.

The 1940s had seen the first systematic attempts at developing automated translation, and the problems now occupying the interest of linguists were already familiar to scientists engaged in the process of trying to overcome the obstacles inherent in the advancement of machine translation. One such problem to be solved in non-human translation was the difficulty posed by syntactic ambiguity. Depending on whether "the turkey" is the subject or object of "eat," the sentence "The turkey is ready to eat" may be interpreted either as "The turkey is ready to eat something" or "Someone is ready to eat the turkey. " In the former case, the application of a "transformation" (a set of operations that at the time formed part of Chomsky's theoretical framework) has moved the object of the underlying "core" or "kernel" sentence into sentence initial position resulting in one, ambiguous surface structure representation. Venturing beneath the surface structure and focusing on speakers' competence, the internalised set of rules that speakers have about their language (which are often at variance with their performance), the search was now on for underlying universals. These are more easily detectable in the early language of children, prior to the acquisition of the transformations subsequently learnt by speakers in order to gain syntactic and grammatical mastery of their language (Chomsky, 1957; 1965). In spite of the far-reaching claims of his transformational-generative (TG) grammar, Chomsky (1965: 30) was less than optimistic about its implications for translation: "The existence of deep-seated formal universals ... does not, for example, imply that there must be some reasonable procedure for translating between languages." Nevertheless, the tenets of Chomsky's thinking offered an opportunity for a theory of translation to be given a linguistic framework and to be provided with a "scientific" foundation. At the time, this demand was increasingly placed on the social sciences, as evidenced by the titles of two early works by linguist and anthropologist Eugene Nida, in which the principles of TG grammar are applied to translation: *Towards a Science of Translating* (Nida, 1964) and, co-authored with C. Taber, *The Theory and Practice of Translating* (Nida & Taber, 1969). Prior to the transfer of the text from source to receptor language (Nida's designated term for what is more commonly known as target language), two types of grammatical analysis are applied, grammatical and lexical. Drawing on Chomsky's framework as a mechanism to find solutions to the translation problems encountered by Bible translators for whom he acted as a consultant, Nida uses the concept of transformations and kernel sentences in order to account for the need for syntactic divergence from the source text in translation. If, for instance, a language uses nouns only to denote concrete objects, the transfer into another language of nouns denoting events would require the application of "back-transformations" in order to arrive at the kernel sentences to be used in translation. A biblical phrase such as "the creation of the world" from Ephesians 1: 4 would therefore need to be "transformed" into "God created the world" in order for the original English noun phrase to be translated (Nida, 1969: 83).

For the solution of problems of translation on the lexical level, one of Nida's immediate concerns is the difficulty of interpretation frequently encountered in Bible translation. In order to determine correctly the meaning of a word in the source text, whether it is synonymous with another word having a different connotative rather than denotative or referential meaning, Nida subjects it to componential analysis. Following the analysis the transfer of the text is undertaken; this process enables Nida to make use of a concept such as "synthesis of components" that, to use a contemporary European example, transforms "sister and brother" in English into "Geschwister" in translation into German. Nida also discusses the addition of explanatory information, in present-day parlance the technique of explicitation (Klaudy, 1998: 83)—as in the case of expanding the reference to Vilnius in a text written in Lithuanian into "Vilnius, the capital of Lithuania" in translation into English for ease of reader comprehension.

Critical voices raised against Nida's proposed model have fastened on the seemingly disparate step-like progression of the journey from source to receptor language, which is less likely to reflect the work of practising translators than an overall more closely synchronised approach. Nevertheless, Nida's linguistic training and his data (collected from long experience as a practising translator), in combination with his attempt to formalise his findings within a linguistic framework set the course for translation theorists to further advance the interrelationship between translation and linguistics in the years to come.

While Chomsky's approach to the formal study of language reflected his cognitively-based interest, in the UK Malinowski's legacy set English linguistics on a different course. As developed by J. R. Firth (1890—1960), Malinowski's concept of "context of culture" was turned into "meaning as function in context" and, as further advanced by the "neo-Firthian" Michael Halliday, the notion became a full-scale linguistic theory, known as Scale and Category Grammar or Systemic Grammar. In a Hallidayan theoretical framework, the notion of context is viewed as the function of language operating on a number of different levels. According to Halliday, a problem such as syntactic ambiguity finds an explanation in the notion of rank shift, as in: "The man came from the police station." In one reading the adverbial (from the police station) ranks as "group" answering the question "Where did the man come from?" In another interpretation, however, it has been "shifted" from the rank of "clause" (who was employed at the police station) and in its contracted form becomes a mirror image of the unshifted adverbial, ranking as "group."

As in the United States, the emergence of a new linguistic theory that attracted a following among linguists was quickly followed by attempts to apply its theoretical framework to translation. In *A Linguistic Theory of Translation*, J. C. Catford (1965) drew on Halliday's linguistic framework and applied it to translation, including the notion of shift to account for the departure from formal correspondence that takes place when the original text is translated into the target language. While in English the sentence "John loves Mary" may be sequentially described as subject, predicator and adjunct (SPA), in translation into Gaelic, it corresponds to the structure PSCA. "Tha gradh aig Iain air Mairi" is "love at John on Mary" where C stands for "complement." This in turn yields the translation equivalence—English: SPA, Gaelic: PSCA (Catford, 1965: 77).

The notion of equivalence was of paramount importance, not only to Catford, but also to other early translation theorists attempting to formulate a linguistically-based theory of translation. In Nida the concept was accounted for by giving formal correspondence second place in importance to dynamic equivalence, achieved if the impact of the translation produced the appropriate response from the receptor in the target language. Catford's theoretical framework carefully eschewed Nida's somewhat cavalier treatment of a concept of crucial importance to the development of automated translation, and Catford's shifts bear real similarity to notions of complex transfer in machine translation (MT), where formal correspondence continues to hold pride of place (Kenny, 1998: 78).

In addition to Nida and Catford, there was no shortage of attempts by other translation theorists in the 1950s and 1960s to define the concept of equivalence and its place in translation theory. In their detailed, contrastive analysis of English and French, Vinay & Darbelnet (1958/1977) proposed a set of procedures for the translator to use in order to account for the need for "indirect" translation involving instances when equivalence in the target language cannot be established. One such procedure, "chassé-croisé," turns "Blériot flew across the Channel" into "Blériot traversa la Manche en avion" (Vinay&Darbelnet, 1958/1977: 105). While in English, motion and manner are both contained in the verb "flew," in translation into French the two features cannot be expressed through the use of one verb. Instead the notion of "motion" is conveyed through the verb traversa (crossed) and that of "manner" expressed separately, in "en avion (by plane)."

Drawing a distinction between a number of different equivalence types, the approach to the problem of accounting for the lack of equivalence between source and target text in translation that is favoured by German translation theorist Werner Köller (1972/1979) implicitly acknowledged that the notion is not an undifferentiated one. While connotative equivalence entails a choice between synonymous expressions, text-normative equivalence concerns the usage norms for a given text type, pragmatic equivalence involves the receiver to whom the translation is directed and formal equivalence concerns formal-aesthetic features such as word play (1989).

In the framework used by Peter Newmark (1981), equivalence came in for yet another form of treatment; to account for departures from formal correspondence between source and target text, Peter Newmark introduced the concepts of semantic and communicative translation. While the French "Défense de marcher sur la gazon" in semantic translation into English yields "Walking on the turf is forbidden," in communicative translation it is normally rendered as the more familiar "Keep off the grass." Similarly, in translation from German "Frisch angestrichen" reads in semantic translation into English as "Recently painted" while in communicative translation it turns into the more easily recognisable "Wet paint!" (Newmark, 1981)

Although varying in the use of terminology and approach, the notion of equivalence and departure from close correspondence between source and target text remained an issue of prime concern to early translation theorists. This can be explained in part by the importance of the notion in the development of automated translation, and in part by the firmly established role of translation as a means of language learning and teaching in a wider, European educational context.

At the end of the 18th century, the grammar translation method had been devised for use in secondary school teaching in Prussia (Howatt, 1984: 131), based on the principles employed for the teaching of Greek and Latin. In the study of the classical languages, translation had always formed an important part, ranking high in popularity as a teaching exercise. As spoken varieties of Latin and Greek no longer existed, the sole focus was on the written mode of language, and the role of translation was frequently that of examining in writing the acquisition of vocabulary learnt by memorising from wordlists new lexical items in the target language, together with their "equivalents" in the source language. When, in the mid-19th century, the study of modern languages was first introduced as a serious pursuit, the high prestige in which Greek and Latin were held caused the teaching pattern to be replicated. The emphasis was on the written language, and grammar was learnt by means of translation into and out of the foreign language. Translation, as a result, came to be associated with the process of testing the knowledge of grammar and vocabulary in the foreign language and the "equivalents" found in dictionaries and vocabulary lists were viewed as constituting the authoritatively correct answers. Based on the model of a course in French by Johann Valentin Meidinger (1756—1822), the first so-called grammar-translation course appeared in English in 1793, devised by Johann Christian Fick (1763—1821) (Meidinger, 1783; Howatt, 1984; Malmkjær, 1998b). In 1858, a system of public examinations was introduced, monitored by the universities of Oxford and Cambridge, this further sanctioned the method that was to remain the prevailing approach to foreign language teaching in Europe from the late 18th century until the 1960s. As large numbers of immigrants started to arrive in the USA from all over Europe, more conversational methods were required and, in his directives issued to teachers steeped in the principles of the "natural method," Maximilian Berlitz (1852—1921) firmly ruled out the use of translation in language teaching (Malmkjær, 1998b: 4). The deathblow to the grammar-translation method was further reinforced by the need, during World War Ⅱ, for United States servicemen to rapidly acquire spoken command of foreign languages, which helped to trigger sweeping changes in language-teaching methodology.

The approach to translation in an educational context, whereby words and grammatical structures in the source language were replaced with their "correct" equivalents in the target language, did not fail to leave its mark on the generations of translators regularly subjected to the process. Translators continued to translate the way they had been taught to translate. In the case of translation from French, familiarity in Europe with the language and culture of France often facilitated the work of the translator while, in translation from other languages, lack of equivalence was accounted for through the use of detailed footnotes. This was, for example, the practice of Ibsen translator William Archer (1856—1924) in translation from Norwegian.

Commenting on translations of another 19th century European dramatist, playwright Tom Stoppard notes that early English translations of Chekhov's *The Seagull* reveal what he terms almost "a philosophy" towards translation. "They are as scrupulous as ledgers: everything on the Russian side of the line is accounted for on the English side, sentence by sentence, and the sentences themselves [...] faithfully carry over nouns, verbs and qualifiers" (Stoppard, 1997: vi).

In addition to the misrepresentations of the source text that may arise from such an over-religious adherence to Stoppard's "ledger principle," the approach may also make the translator more susceptible to the allure of "false friends." In English where historical factors led to an influx of French loanwords into the lexicon, the "philosophy" of the grammar-translation method has been of little help to the translator in steering clear of the pitfalls in rendering for instance prétendre ("intend") and luxure ("magnificence") into English as "pretend" and "luxury" as has been noted in English Sartre translations of the

1950s (Reed, 2000: 1237).

In addition to the part that it played in language teaching methodology, translation fulfilled yet another function for modern European linguists following in the footsteps of de Saussure. Unlike the UK and the USA, for many smaller nations in Europe knowledge of more than one language constitutes a lifeline with the outside world and contrastive studies of modern languages have traditionally been a pursuit of scholarly interest. In 1926, Vilém Mathesius (1882—1946), together with Roman Jakobson and Nikolai Trubetskoy and others, founded the Prague Linguistic Circle whose publications, in particular *Travaux du Cercle Linguistique de Prague*, belonged to the most important writings on linguistics of the epoch. Unlike the American structuralists, the approach of the Prague School was characterised by a three-level concept of syntax: every sentence was viewed as having a grammatical structure, a semantic structure and a structure of sentence organisation. Through contrastive analysis, often taking the form of translation, differences were pinpointed in what was termed functional sentence perspective (FSP). Take for example the translation between German and English of the sentence Das meine ich ("That mean I"). The first constituent of the sentence receives stress in German and is less likely to be replicated as "That I mean;" instead, a cleft construction of the type "That's what I mean" often takes the place of the stressed German constituent in translation into English (Kirkwood, 1969: 96).

Through systematic studies concerned with the textual dimensions of contrastive problems between languages as revealed through the use of translation, Prague School linguists succeeded in unearthing consistent differences between European languages. This provided the practising translator with a background against which translation problems might be viewed and options for suitable solutions sought. These options may in turn be analysed from the viewpoint of evaluation of translations, as in the more recent work by Brno-born linguist Jan Firbas. In a study of four different translations from Russian into Dutch, English, French and German of the opening paragraph of Boris Pasternak's *Dr Zhivago*, the application of the concept of FSP allows Firbas to assess the faithfulness of the translations in relation to the communicative purpose of the original (Firbas, 1999).

The relationship between translation and linguistics may take two different forms: in the case of Nida and Catford it expresses itself in an attempt to formulate a linguistic theory of translation. However, it may also take the less ambitious form of just an ongoing interaction between the two, each drawing on the findings of the other whenever this is mutually beneficial. For linguistics, such interaction might entail the use of translation as a form of contrastive analysis as in the work by linguists following the Prague School tradition. The gains on the part of translation theorists on the other hand have often been the findings resulting from the research undertaken by linguists engaged in the study of language above the level of the word and the sentence.

The study of the factors affecting the overall organisation of the text above sentence level increasingly attracted the attention of linguists during the 1970s and 1980s. While early application of linguistic findings to translation drew its influence from the field of stylistics (Enkvist, 1978), later impetus was provided by discourse analysis (Hatim & Mason, 1990). Again, as the focus of the interest of linguists began to centre on text linguistics, translation theorists closely followed in their footsteps, looking for new models of description. In a paper delivered at the 1981 conference of the Association International de Linguistique Appliqué titled "Translation, interpreting and text linguistics," Albrecht Neubert pointed to the importance of paying close attention to the textual features inherent in the source text. "It is a different text. It is couched in a different world of discourse" (Neubert, 1981: 132). Hence the translator needs to be sensitive to the type of discourse that target language readers are likely to expect under similar communicative circumstances, often revealed through a comparison with parallel texts. Parallel texts form the background texts with which translations often do not compare favourably; as its parallel text in French the British Highway Code has for comparison "le code de la route" and in German, "die Strassenverkehrsordnung" (Neubert, 1981: 135).

Following the legacy of the previous century and its scientifically-based approach to the study of language, the 1970s—1980s saw a number of German translation theorists apply text linguistics-based theories to translation. A major, early influence, Katharina Reiss' work on text types uses as her starting point Bühler's (1934) three functions of the linguistic sign, the informative, the expressive and the operative, to which, presciently, an audio-medial type is added, where verbal sparseness is of the essence. While primarily "informative" texts such as reports and operating manuals need to be translated in plain prose with, if necessary, explanations in the form of expansions, a basically "expressive" text such as a poem or a play requires a greater degree of identification between translator and originator. In the case of remaining types, operative texts such as those used in advertising, call for an "adaptive" translation while the translator of audiomedia texts needs only to supplement what is already expressed by another medium (Reiβ, 1976, 1977).

A Hallidayan approach involving three macro-functions of language accounting for content (ideational), the relationship between speaker and addressee (interpersonal) and the cohesive links necessary for text cohesion (textual) also enabled Juliane House to put forward one of the first models for evaluating translation quality, focusing on a retrospective comparison of source and target texts of German/English translations (House, 1977, 1981). The importance of the function of the translated text is further emphasised by Hans Vermeer, who views translation as action to which an aim must always be ascribed or, to use the Greek word "skopos." According to Vermeer's skopos theory, a translation is inevitably undertaken for a purpose laid down by a client or the translators themselves, and is always accompanied, implicitly or explicitly, by a set of specifications as to how the source text should be translated whether it needs to be translated faithfully, paraphrased or completely re-edited (Vermeer, 1983; 1989). The growing demand from industry during the last couple of decades for professional translation is also reflected in the curriculum design of European translation training programmes. In the translational action model put forward by Holz-Manttari, highly specialised translation commissions point to the need for attention to be paid to the different roles of the participants in the translational action. The translator may require information with respect to text type and advice from subject area experts as well as knowledge about the users and ultimate uses of the translated text (Holz-Manttari, 1984). The functionalist approach is further emphasised by Christiane Nord (1988, 1991, 1997), who also points to the importance in a programme of translators' training of the "translation brief," the problems resulting from the function assigned to the translation and the importance of close analysis of the source text.

Just as the study of language may be extended beyond the level of the sentence to include the overall organisation of the text, it may be widened even further to take into account extra-linguistic factors. In the 1970s, research projects began to appear that were concerned with the influence of social variables on language use. In the USA, William Labov (1972b) first investigated the speech patterns of the inhabitants of Martha's Vineyard, off the coast of New England, then turned his attention to a very different kind of community. Through a study of the variation in speakers' use of the linguistic variable [r], he was able to point to a prestige-linked relation between speech and social class amongst New Yorkers (Labov, 1972a). The Labovian method of structured interviews was also used in a pioneering study in the UK undertaken by Peter Trudgill, in which he examined the interaction between language and social structure in his native town of Norwich (Trudgill, 1974). Sociolinguistics-based studies were increasingly attracting the interest of linguists, and a number of systematic research projects were initiated with the aim of revealing the causes underlying language variation and the interaction between language and variables such as geographical origin and social class membership of speakers.

Henry Sweet (1845—1912), the first British linguist to pursue a scholarly interest in spoken English, studied German philological methods at the University of Heidelberg before returning to England to enter Balliol College, Oxford. While still an undergraduate, Sweet edited King Alfred's translation of the *Cura Pastoralis* for the *Early English Text Society*, his commentary laying the foundation of Old English dialectology. In 1877, Sweet's interest in spoken language found an expression in the publication of *A Handbook of Phonetics*; this was followed in 1890 by *A Primer of Spoken English*, the first scientifically-based description of educated London speech, received pronunciation (RP). Bernard Shaw, who knew Sweet personally and regarded him a man of genius, writes in the preface to *Pygmalion*, of his "Satanic contempt for all academic dignitaries and persons in general who thought more of Greek than phonetics." Sweet, sharing a number of characteristics with Professor Higgins in Shaw's play, was a member of the Reform Movement of the late 19th century which stressed the primacy of speech, and the priority of oral classroom methodology, running counter to the grammar-translation method (Howatt, 1984;

Malmkjær, 1998b).

Having studied under Henry Sweet, Daniel Jones (1881—1967) further advanced the study of speech sounds, rising to become the head of the first Department of Phonetics in Great Britain in 1912. Influential in spreading the use of the International Phonetic Alphabet (IPA), throughout the world, his efforts provided the mechanism for the use of transcription of speech sounds. However, the distinction between written/spoken and standard/dialect is frequently not reflected in translation and awareness amongst translation theorists of the problems involved in vernacular and dialect translation has been slow in coming. While social class-linked dialects are likely to be found in most urban environments, facilitating the transfer of a vernacular such as Eliza Doolittle's cockney in *Pygmalion* into other languages, the work of European dialect writers has frequently fared less well in translation into English. Part of the work written in Sicilian dialect by Italian writer Luigi Pirandello (1867—1936), the 1934 recipient of the Nobel Prize for Literature, still remains unavailable in English translation. Also largely ignored in English translation is the 1912 Nobel Prize laureate Gerhart Hauptmann (1862—1946). Written in northeast German dialect, his masterpiece, *The Weavers*, has only recently been translated by Bill Findlay into Scots in a translation where the relationship of standard English/Scots parallels that of German/Silesian. Together with his sometime co-translator, Canadian-based Martin Bowman, Findlay has also succeeded in finding an English voice for the Quebéc playwright Michel Tremblay who writes in *joual*, so called after the pronunciation of the word "cheval" amongst the speakers in the district of east-end Montreal. Again Scots may be viewed as existing in relation to standard English as *joual* does to international French. Translating in the opposite direction, from Scots into Quebécois, the use of non-standard French has also enabled Martin Bowman and Montreal playwright Wajdi Mouawad to adapt Irvine Welsh's novel *Trainspotting* for the French-speaking stage (Bowman, 2000). In addition, it has proved successful as a medium in transferring the works of American writers such as Tennessee Williams and Edward Albee onto the French-speaking stage as well as the muscular dialect use of Brecht's *Mother Courage* and Jean's sociolect in Strindberg's *Miss Julie*, a means of overcoming the linguistic void in the normative system of French literature with which the translation of sociolects into French has to contend (Brisset, 2000). On other occasions, the prescriptive norms imposed by the Académic Françise and the Bulletin Officiel, which rule out the use of dialects in works of literature, have seen the distinctive New York voice of Holden Caulfield in J. D. Salinger's *The Catcher in the Rye* disappear in translation into standard French (Mailhac, 2000) or the northern English dialect in *Kes* by Barry Hines replaced by a French sociolect (Fawcett, 1998: 120). In the absence of socially as well as geographically determined options, the translator may as a last resort decide on the use of an ideolect, the linguistic system favoured by individual speakers. In for instance the case of the translation into Swedish of *Educating Rita* by Liverpool playwright Willy Russell, the failure to find a match for Rita's scouse in an appropriate dialect or sociolect resulted in the eponymous protagonist being given a colourful ideolect, a language all of her own making.

In addition to studying language as determined by social and geographical factors, linguists have also begun to investigate other factors influencing its use. Now a discipline in its own right, the field of pragmatics is receiving increasing attention among linguists interested in examining the purposes for which sentences are used and the real-world conditions under which they are appropriately uttered. In an attempt to describe translation in terms of a general theory of human communication, Gutt (1991) uses as his basic premise the ability of humans to infer what is meant through the principle of relevance. In addition to the descriptive use of language, which is restricted to entities in the real world, the interpretative use of language also entails references to thoughts and mental processes. Translation, according to Gutt, is an instance of interpretative use, constrained by the principle of relevance; the translation "should be expressed in such a manner that it yields the intended interpretation without putting the audience to unnecessary processing effort" (Gutt, 1991: 101–102). However, in addition to the attempt to incorporate translation into a general theory as suggested by Gutt, who used as his framework Sperber and Wilson's *Relevance Communication and Cognition* (1986), there is also, as in other branches of linguistics, the possibility of translation theorists drawing on the insights provided by linguists working in the field of pragmatics and when relevant, applying them to translation. Problems may, for instance, arise when speech acts are transferred in translation; situations such as when we make a complaint or a request, offer an apology or give a compliment. While the sole purpose of a conversation is, in a summary of Grice's maxims (1975), to "be brief," "tell the truth," "be relevant" and "be clear," the intervening need for urbanity often makes necessary further, culture-bound embellishment. When making complaints and requests, speakers of some languages are likely to voice their discontent more directly than do English speakers, as has been shown in the case of German speakers (House & Kasper, 1981). As indirectness in English is a favoured politeness marker, the question "Would anyone like another cup of coffee?" put by an English hostess to her guests as a social evening is drawing to an end may be less of a question than a request that the visitors take their leave. In translation into a language using other kinds of politeness markers the question may, however, be interpreted at face value, achieving the opposite effect to that intended, which in turn places the translator in the position of having to consider the need for adjustments in translation. Awareness of the existence of such differences between languages is of particular importance in the translation of dialogue, which often lacks the clues needed for the interpretation of utterances that are more easily found in narrative text.

Another speech act that may require some consideration in translation is that of apologizing, as the formulas used to repair a situation caused by the violation of social norms may also differ between languages. In English, as in many other languages, the apology speech act normally starts with the use of a performative verb such as "Please, forgive me" or "Excuse me," and some form of explanation often follows (Brown & Levinson, 1987). It is not uncommon for an English speaker, late for an appointment, to offer as an apology "Please forgive me, but the traffic was just terrible." If, however, a language traditionally requires only an explanation in order to meet the demands of politeness—as appears to be the case in Russian and Hebrew (Ohlstain, 1983)—speakers of such a language may find their apologies somewhat be grudgingly accepted if, when arriving late for a meeting in the English-speaking world, they use only the second part of the formula and simply announce "The traffic was terrible."

Another recent but fast-growing field of linguistics that has already provided translation theorists with valuable information, is that of corpus linguistics. The study of language on the basis of text corpora can be traced back to around 1960 with the launch of the Survey of English Usage (SEU) at London University and the advent of computers which made it possible to store large amounts of material. The first machine-readable corpus compiled at Brown University in the early 1960s was soon followed by others such as the London-Oslo/Bergen (LOB) Corpus. Capitalizing on the combined strengths of the Brown and SEU corpora, starting in 1975, Jan Svartvik and his colleagues at Lund University in Sweden, rendered the unscripted spoken texts of the SEU corpus machine-readable. This resulted in the London-Lund Corpus (LLC), an unmatched resource for the study of spoken English. While the Brown Corpus and the LOB Corpus may have seemed vast at the time, their size has been easily surpassed as massive amounts of machine-readable texts have become available as a by-product of modern electronic communication systems. Since its beginning in the 1960s, the corpus as a source of systematically retrievable data, and as a test bed for hypotheses, has become widely used by linguists, resulting in findings that include some with obvious implications for translation. Using a corpus consisting of 75 novels published 1967—1977, half of which were novels originally written in Swedish and half were translations, Martin Gellerstam of the University of Gothenburg has systematically compared original texts with texts in translation. His early 1986 study as well as later ones (Gellerstam, 1996, 2005) point squarely to the influence in translation of the source on the target text and also revealed previously-unobserved cross-linguistic differences between the two languages involved in the translation process. Another early corpus study of the influence of English on lexical selection in Danish confirmed Gellerstam's findings, showing that modality, typically expressed in many Germanic languages through the use of modal particles (such as "jo" and "vel" in Danish), was greatly underrepresented in texts in translation. In their place instead appeared English-influenced modal verb constructions such as "I presume" or "I suppose," often resulting in a marked awkwardness of style (Jakobsen, 1986). More recently, translation corpora have investigated the fate of another kind of particle in translation, so called discourse particles such as "oh," "well" and "now," which tend to express emotional attitudes and contribute towards the coherence of the utterance. In translation into other languages, these discourse particles are frequently rendered in a multitude of different ways and the availability of translation corpora now makes possible a study of the semantic and contextual reasons underlying the translator's choice as shown by Aijmer (forthcoming) drawing on an English/Swedish Parallel Corpus. Other language pairs for which parallel corpora have been compiled include English/French, English/Italian, English/Norwegian and English/German.

Not only are translation theorists close on the heels of linguists as new fields of inquiry such as pragmatics and corpus linguistics become the focus of new research interest, well-established notions in linguistics are also frequently revisited and introduced anew to provide translation theory with conceptual tools. In the late 1970s, Gideon Toury introduced the concept of norms in order to account for the translation options favoured by translators at a particular time in a given socio-cultural setting (Toury, 1978, 1980). A set of three translations into Hebrew of Ernest Hemingway's *A Story of Three Killers* showed that readers possessed an intuitive awareness of their chronological order, the result of the different translations being the product of prevailing norms at a particular time (Toury, 1999). Toury's concept of norms has been viewed as representing an interlevel between "competence and performance in Noam Chomsky's terms" or "langue and parole in Ferdinand de Saussure's terms" which makes it possible according to Mona Baker "to investigate what is typical rather than simply what is or what can be" (Baker, 1998: 164). Another development in translation theory reminiscent of what at one time represented a departure from earlier product-orientated approaches to linguistic investigation, is found in the "think-aloud" method, which shares with Chomskyan linguistics the emphasis on introspection and reliance on speakers' intuitive knowledge about their language. The approach first came to attention in the 1980s when experimental methods drawn from psychology began to be used in order to investigate the translator's mind during the process of translating. Translators were invited to verbalise their thoughts as they were translating and the recorded think-aloud-protocols (TAPs) were then studied with the aim of revealing how translators go about their task (Jääskeläiner, 1998).

From the time linguistically-based observations on translation ceased to be ad hoc and anecdotal, linguistics has provided an impetus to translation theorists to apply their findings to translation. When, in 1963, Joseph Greenberg made public his findings that, although the vast majority of languages may have several variant word orders, they all have a single dominant one, his observations became a clarion call to linguists who now began to classify languages according to type. As a result, over the years findings resulting from research in typology have succeeded in complementing the knowledge about languages previously made available by genealogical classification. As the result of continued work in typology, Vinay and Darbelnet's procedure triggered by the need for "chassé-croisé" in translation between English and French, is now known to be a transposition that needs to be applied not only between English and French but equally applies to Spanish, Italian and to all languages belonging to the Romance family (Talmy, 1985: 62).

Early linguistically-based work in translation theory has also been further developed in order to meet new sets of interests and circumstances. As English grows more and more comfortable in its role as the global language and the lingua franca of Europe, the attention of translation theorists is increasingly being directed towards its impact on other European languages. As a result, the linguistic framework previously employed by Juliane House for the assessment of translation quality has recently been adjusted to apply to an investigation of the influence of English via translation and text production on German, French and Spanish (House, 2003).

In a review of Chomsky's (2000) *New Horizons in the Study of Language and Mind*, the lack of advancement in the search for the innate set of the rules of Universal Grammar (UG) was ascribed to the fact that "the sheer complexity of the different rule systems for the different languages was hard to square with the idea that they are really all variations on a single underlying set of rules of UG" (Searle, 2002). In their search for universals, translation theorists of the 21st century have now begun to tread where linguists trod before. On the basis of contrastive analyses of translations and their source texts, a number of features considered common to all languages now clamour for the status of universals. With a linguistic feature such as "distinctive distribution of lexical items" amongst potential candidates (Sara Laviosa-Braithwaite, 1998: 288), translation theorists would seem to have their work cut out for the foreseeable future. In their search for universals, the task facing early typologists of tackling the problem posed by the complexity of polysynthetic languages was made less unmanageable by their familiarity with Native American languages. The challenge facing contemporary translation theorists by Inuit, another such language where sikursuarsiurpugut translates into English as "we-sail-through-the-big-ice" can only be described as formidable.

As the American linguist Dwight Bolinger observes:

Translation may be viewed amorphously as the rendition of a text from one language to another. This is translation from the standpoint of la parole: the text, the act of speech or writing is the thing. Or it may be viewed as a systematic comparison of two languages: this is translation from the standpoint of la langue. (Bolinger, 1965/66: 130)

Given this inherent interrelationship between translation and linguistics, linguistics seems set to continue to provide translation theorists with new research avenues to explore for further advancement of translation studies while, in the contrastive study of languages, translation will also have a role to play in helping linguists in their search for shared features and similarities between languages.

选文四　翻译的语言学情结

袁筱一

导　言

《翻译的语言学情结》是我国较早探讨语言学与翻译研究的一篇论文,1997年发表在第四期的《外国语》上,引起了一定的反响。现在读来,仍然感觉是一篇很有见地的文章。

毫无疑问,翻译理论在得到系统讨论之初是被包容进语言学的范畴的:因为翻译首先是一种语言现象。后来出现了语言学派和文艺学派之争,但是翻译理论当然不可能成为语言学的分支(或者被我们叫做所谓的"应用语言学"),因为它与生俱来是跨学科的。实践也确实证明,将翻译理论纳入语言学的一章只维持了相当短的一段时间。翻译理论的语言学途径是否已经走入了一条死胡同呢?

我们也许并不急于给予一个肯定或否定的答案,关键在于我们有必要来看一看语言学曾经给翻译理论带来过什么,以及,也更为重要的是还能为我们带来些什么。

一、事物—思维—语言模式:翻译的可行性基础

从语言的生成角度来看,事情仿佛非常简单。所以翻译不计名分地存在了几千年也没有问过诸如存在的可能性这一类的问题。语言是应交流需要而产生的,它是人之所以区别于其他动物的根本特征。"事物—思维—语言"模式由是至今仍然影响着我们对于语言,进而对于翻译的看法。也就是说,我们的脑中或多或少总存在着这样的想法,认为"思想或者观念反映事物,而语言是思想或观念的外在表达符号或工具,语言的优缺点就在于它们是否准确地表达了思想或观念"(徐友渔等,1996:2)。

这种与现代把语言当作思想或存在本身大异其趣的语言观却是翻译存在的最好佐证。既而索绪尔又指出了所指和能指之间的任意性原理,翻译的可行性于是被更加完满地证实了,许钧教授在其《翻译层次论》一文中借助高名凯的语言学观点这样写道:

> 具有全人类性的思维是翻译活动的基础。由于思维是人脑的一种机能,思维的职能在于反映客观的规律,在共同的客观世界的决定之下,在人脑的共同的物质结构之下,思维进行的能力及思维进行的规律是全人类性的,而充当思维材料的语言是以声音为前提的物质现象,它的任意性和约定俗成性决定了它的多种形式。但是,当各民族的语言源起时,虽然处在不同的时间和空间,但对客观事物本质属性认识的思维活动则是一致的。正因为这同一性,各民族的语言在语音、词汇、语法千差万别的情况下,才可互译。由此看来,思维的活动便构成了翻译活动的基础层次。
> (Meschonnic,1982:331)

很显然,如果各民族的语言只是在"语音、词汇、语法"上有所差别,哪怕是"千差万别",那么事情远远没有这么复杂。因为索绪尔告诉我们所指与能指之间原本就是任意的。对于两种"任意符号"之间的转换,我们也许不必如此心惊肉跳。这正是在翻译理论上名噪一时的信息论的认识根源。因此我们不难明白为什么奈达会说"一切在一种语言中得到表达的东西都可以在另一种语言中得到表达,除非在该表达中,形式是信息的主要构成因素"(许钧,1992:2)。

由是早在1898年,或许还根本未料翻译理论为何物的严复就提出了译事的"信、达、雅"。所谓"达",不过是达意,增之一分则太多,减之一分则太少。信也是在这个基础上的。由是以口译的角度来看,"达意"仍然不失为一个令人信服的标准。我们完全可以在另一种语言里,用另一种形式将某种信息表达出来,从而达到传递、沟通、交流的目的。

我们无意在此讨论该模式的是非,问题只是这种模式在翻译理论得到系统讨论之初所起到的决定作用,它不仅使翻译成为可能而且使翻译理论成为可能。法国当代哲学家、语言学家阿热吉论及翻译问题时竟然也与许钧教授的思维基础层次论有着异曲同工的说法,他问"翻译的障碍何在呢"?"无非是两类差别所致,而这两类差别,在散文和诗歌里都同样存在。第一类与文本之外的具体实在的、文化的条件有关。正是在此决定下人类及其生活方式的某种不变基础上的这些条件组成了种种人文的,或者是其他方面的大相径庭的真实。但是,我们在翻译时,正是通过这类被指证出的事实。而另一类差别关系到语音、语法及词汇。"(Hagège,1986:61)

我们发现,在所谓的语言学派和文艺学之间,如果都用这个模式来打基础,并不存在着本质的对立。或许更为致命的在于,当语言学内部事实亦复如此,当文艺学向语言学派发难时,它自己也很难跳出"千差万别"的"语音、词汇、语法"的转换技巧及正误的圈子。它使所有的翻译理论研究者及实践者在其工作伊始都不得不定向地思考着同一个问题:"语音、词汇、语法"能否尽可能地贴近而内容不损?

失望是难以言喻的。也正是这种失望构筑了两个学派的分水岭,使双方往两个极端滑去。

或许更为致命的是,当语言学内部对这个模式发生质疑时,以此为基础的翻译理论(绝不仅仅是语言学派)陷入了措手不及的境地。

二、语言:存在的本身———翻译不可行性的由来

乔治·穆南在他的《翻译的理论问题》一书中也不得不承认,"如果我们接受现代语言学关于词汇、语法及句法的流行观念,我们几乎可以明白地说,翻译是不可能的"(Mounin,1963:8)。除了交流,人们发现语言有着工具之外更为本质的特征。语言越来越成为一个谜一般的"存在"(?)。当然,我们倘若真的溯源而上,纵观语言学的发展历程,我们会发现这种质疑并不是突如其来的,它只是,出于种种原因,在今天显得尤为突出。

语言的可传达性在古希腊的高尔吉亚处就遭到了怀疑。他说,"语言是随着外界刺激我们的事物而产生的,亦即随着感性事物而产生的,由于事物与体质的接触,才产生了转达这种性质的语言;由于颜色从外而来,才产生了转达这种颜色的语言。如果是这样的,那么,便不是语言转达我们之外的东西,而是我们之外的东西表达语言了"(1982:142-143)。

中世纪的奥古斯丁、托马斯,到近代的莱布尼茨、维柯,乃至康德、洪堡,一直到维特根斯坦、海德格尔、伽达默尔,所有的语言哲学家一再思考着世界、人、语言的关系,它的确不是我们

想象中的线性关系。语言的无可依托最终是会导致翻译的无可依托的：无可信，无可达，无所谓雅。一方面是随着现代科学的发展，人与人之间的距离越来越短，交流骤增要求翻译活动尽快合法化；另一方面，人们越来越怀疑语言是交流的媒介（至少不仅是），从而越来越怀疑交流的可能性。

现代语言学发展到解释学，更为翻译的存在浇了一瓢冷水：海德格尔得出了前有（Vorhaben）、前见（Vorsicht）和前设（Vorgriff）的概念，伽达默尔更是发展了成见（Vorurteil）的理论，告诉我们成见是不可避免的。翻译理论关于翻译能够在另一种语言体系中还原原作的梦想终于完全破灭了。

翻译只能作为一种成见存在。伽达默尔为我们留下的唯一一点余地便是这种成见与完全的误解仍有区别，它有可能——在自我克制的前提下——是合理的，姚斯接下去发展了接受美学的理论，使得接受者的合法地位得到了承认。

而解构主义的存在则使语言彻彻底底地从描述思维的工具发展成为人类最本质的游戏。翻译不得不参与这场游戏，但是它胆战心惊。不见了意义单元（unités de sens），文字成了"播撒出去的种子"，不朝着固定的方向，自由生长着。这就是所谓"书写与阅读之间的零度"，任何一种欲将文字模糊性圈囿在某一固定意义上的企图都有悖于文字本身，阅读如此，翻译更是如此。形而上学是一种无奈的选择。

翻译是不可能的，哪怕只是作为成见存在。有趣的是，翻译实践没有消亡。其实翻译理论的系统发展不过是近几十年的事，与语言学的今日状况几乎是同步的。于是我们不难理解为什么自其伊始就会出现这样的悖论，法国的翻译理论家拉德米拉尔问道："我们难道还能想象到有另外一种实践活动，与翻译同等重要，所涉范围同等广泛，持续时间同样长久，却如同翻译一般，无法确证其合法的存在，甚至让我们无视其业已在日常生活中存在的实际吗？"（Ladmiral，1994：85）

在不可行与可行已存在的张力作用下，也许我们倒能发现，不可能的只是某一种翻译，某一种我们预设过、追求过，但从来没有实际存在过的翻译？

我们的理想主义啊。

语言不是一种无往不胜的描述，它是和思维一样受到主体限制的存在。翻译也不是一张万能的透明薄膜，可以覆在任何一个文本上而不显象。我们在关注现代语言学发展轨迹的同时，或许有一个问题要问：如是说来，现代语言学是窒息了翻译的存在呢，还是要将它从记忆补偿工具的牢笼中释放出来？

萨特说，我们被判处了自由……

三、语言学与哲学的纠缠：一扇被忽略的洞开之门

我们都知道，在这个世纪，语言学几乎席卷了人文科学的所有领域。这绝非一个撞击性的偶发事件。正如张汝伦教授在其《历史与实践》一书中指出的，"语言作为人类生存最基本的特征与手段与人同在，它既是思维的工具，也是实践的媒介，又是历史的表达。同时，它又是存在的视界与人文视界的基础和界限所在。语言的这种本体论上的先在性与生存论上的基础性，决定了它必然会成为人们反思与探究的焦点"（张汝伦，1995：352）。

当我们仰望本世纪的哲人，惊叹他们对于语言问题的探索和挖掘时，我们触到了真实的原

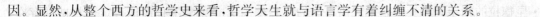

因。显然，从整个西方的哲学史来看，哲学天生就与语言学有着纠缠不清的关系。

语言与哲学一向在纠缠不清之中，因为哪怕是被罗兰·巴特、德里达消解为碎片，语言至少还是有"痕迹"的，可以为我们感受。哲学如果不借助语言，它永远也无法统领人类的精神领域。甚至在基督教的圣经教诲中，语言和世界的开端是合二为一的。

因为尽管源远流长、流派纷呈，语言学所致力解决的，实际上只是一个根本的问题，那就是语言究竟以何种方式连接了世界与人、主观与客观？语言究竟是在何种程度上成为洪堡所说的"从主观性到客观性的过渡点"（张汝伦，1995:352）？并且，这个过渡点又是怎样反过来——除却它的连接意义外——作用于主观与客观的关系之上的？

因为如果说翻译理论注定是一门跨学科的学科，如果说翻译决不仅仅是一个单纯的语言现象，它还牵连有更多的哲学、心理学、社会学等的文化意义上的因素，那么我们似乎早应该看到，决不是"单纯的语言现象"那么单纯，语言学的本身也注定是跨学科的。因为在这个世界上的所有"学"，都逃脱不了对一种对立关系的研究。翻译的语言学情结在这里：它研究的正是建立在语言关系之上的关系。翻译不能被语言学包容在内的原因也是在这里：它的关系比语言关系还要来得复杂。

也许在表达技巧的转换之外，语言学所提供给翻译的，应该是一种更为本质的东西。我们不妨借助其中一点，借助现代哲学与现代语言学共同探讨的核心问题之一——意义，来看看它有可能为我们的翻译理论带来怎样的暗示。

意义是什么，结论也许并不重要。重要的是围绕对这个问题的讨论，语言不可避免地从"单纯"的物质性的描摹中走了出来，语言的使用、接受及其在社会、历史、文化传统变迁中的遭遇都被语言学伸出手一把揽过。结构主义固然还怀揣着客观到底的痴想，较之近几十年才开始成形的翻译理论，语言学到底还是率先走向了跨学科的研究方法。

借助《语言与哲学》一书为我们所做的西方现代语言学的梳理，我们看到，意义一项下至少有以下五个子问题。

（一）意义和心理内容：意义是主观的心理体验还是公共性质的有效使用及共识？

（二）意义和对象：如果说意义和主观的心理经验无涉，那么它是否需要凭借指称对象来界定？

（三）意义和意向：能否用作者的意向或意图来说明本文的意义？

（四）语言的意义和讲话者的意义：是不是同时存在两个意义？如果不是，究竟哪一个意义是我们要追寻的？

（五）意义的整体论：语言的意义有没有基本的单位，如果有，应该定位在哪里？

（徐友渔等，1996:250-266）

翻译理论几乎无法不成为这场空前开阔的意义讨论的受益者。事实亦是如此。翻译理论步语言学之后，也最终开始寻找它林林总总的途径，融合在文化的大背景里。我们也可以相应地思考这样的五点：

（一）翻译所赖的真实可不可以到作者的主观心理体验中去找？《人在屋檐下》的译者永远都不可能对原作者的存在毫无顾忌，不能对米兰·昆德拉的绝对权威有所置辩，如是才胆战心惊地不知该把自己的手脚往哪里放——不是所有的译者都能那么幸运地聆听到他们的米兰·昆德拉的指手画脚！但是现代语言学的反心理主义立场毫不犹豫地否定了权威的存在，而心理学或精神分析方面的有限知识也还不够为我们提供足够的手段去还原原作者的心理体验，我们该用一种怎样的态度来划定原作者在译文当中的位置？

（二）文本倘若或多或少为我们留下真实的"痕迹"，我们能否通过对这些"痕迹"的客观分析重新建构——当然，是在另一个语言体系里——"重新表达话语的意义"？我们能否通过还原社会、历史、文化条件的方法还原一个客观存在？或者，像丹纳说的那样，通过重现"种族、环境、时代"的三大因素去考证原文本的真实？

（三）如果这不得不开口言说，那么这种言说合不合理？它有没有应该的限度？译者的立场与视角在怎样的程度上改变了文本的原意？

（四）语言（langue）本身作为一个社会的约定俗成有没有固有的意义？言语（parole）相较于语言的本身是否已经是一种背叛的存在？维特根斯坦否认了私人语言的存在，在他看来，"是人们说的东西对和错，人们在语言上一致，这不是观点的一致，而是生活形式的一致"（徐友渔等，1996：250－266）。然而自索绪尔区分了语言和言语之后，现代话语论一直孜孜不倦地强调翻译的不是语言而是话语。套用维特根斯坦的话来说，当生活状况出现了不一致的情况时，人们如何言说？翻译作为再一次的言说，它究竟是背叛了原文本的言语呢，还是背叛了作为原文本存在依据的语言？

（五）翻译单元究竟存不存在？是词语、句子、段落，亦或整个文本乃至由文本扩展出去的社会、文化、历史的环境，还是根本就是解构主义为我们论证的，这个单元并不存在？很显然，我们无法否认翻译实践有着最基本的操作单位：句或者段。然而在理论上，我们仿佛无法满足于这个单位，这究竟又是一个怎样的矛盾呢？

我们对于意义的思考于是不再重弹翻译理论上"忠实与背叛"的老调。它牵涉一个理解中的更为彻底的直面，那就是：如果我们不得不谈忠实，我们将忠实于谁？为了真理，我们准备牺牲一切，但是真理在谁的手里？

现代语言学要求我们重新理解。重新理解基础上的再创作，这个意义是空前的。问题看来不仅仅是在于两种语言体系中是否存在着同构异形的表达方式，回到我们在前文中业已涉及的观点，翻译的可能，或不可能，根本在理解中已经被决定下来了。我们一直以为我们懂得，并且因为懂得才爱。但是我们从来未曾想过，好像韩少功在译米兰·昆德拉时说的："我们只能理解我们理解中的……爱有时太过盲目，被我们放大成了虚设的真理所在，我们看来的确有必要向语言学借一点哲学的、冷静的、理智的头脑，走一条思辨的道路。"

翻译理论在西方，包括在中国几十年的系统发展，到了今天这个地位，在人文诸学科内确立下独立的、不可替代的一席，从我们上面的分析来看，语言学当然功不可没。谈到总结和展望，我们偏重于这样几个事实：

首先，（恰恰也是它难逃文艺学派攻讦的地方）正是语言学最初所包含的对于词汇、语音、句法的传统研究为翻译实践的操作、检验直至后来的无法自足提供了基础。尽管以今天的眼光来看，这种传统研究不免有其局限，甚至使翻译理论长期地停留在对"词汇、语音、句法"的比较之上，它却是翻译实践在几千年没有所谓"学"的状态下自我摸索着完成历史使命的根基所在。就像人类一直无法摆脱狮身人面的可怕纠结，在这个到处浸淫着人的主体精神的客观世界里，从语言到翻译理论，都决不会有彻底脱离物质一面的一天。

其次，语言学为翻译理论成为一门独立学科提供了必要的精神准备。或许的确是语言学为翻译理论划分了种种悖论存在的二元对立，可能与不可能，形式与内容，忠实与背叛，等等。语言的居中地位（不是时间上的居中）很容易把客体与主体截然区分开来，而对物自身一再提出疑问。翻译作为一种语言现象，似乎也理所当然地袭承了语言的这种居中地位，或者是"过渡点"。然而二元对立却是学科构建必不可少的阶段，它使理论的发展在不断的摇摆中更接近一个统一。而事实也真的发展到了这个程度。语言学自身对于二元对立的削减则必然会反射到翻译理论上。我们在这里仍然要举伽达默尔的观点，他对于语言思辨结构的贡献。他认为"主体、意志和客体、物自身之间存在着先天的统一"，"我们所能认识的事物就是在语言中表达的事物，事物就是如其在语言中所表达的"，但是"在语言中发生的关于事物的一致本身既不是说明事物的优点，也不说明使用相互理解的语言工具的人优先，倒不如说在语言的世界经验中具体化的这种符合一致本身是绝对优先的"，所谓的"词之光"使一切凸现出来，自身也是昭明而可理解的（徐友渔等，1996：415）。语言学这条从二元对立通向对立统一的历程也为翻译理论包容种种矛盾指出了道路。误解的不可避免性是一方面，主体的自我克制使"词之光"自我昭明又是另一方面。翻译的再创作于是可以被理解成语言的一种双重游戏。它消解规则而来，又遵循规则而去。

最后，也是最为重要的一点，语言学的发展方向永远都不会与翻译理论的发展方向相悖。翻译理论的发展前途就在于，它能够接受语言学对于世界与人的关系的思考，否则它永远只能是一门技术。如果说语言学不能够包容翻译理论，那么崇尚用文艺理论来包含翻译理论的文艺学派在坚持之下只有走进更为狭窄的胡同里。文学固然是在向外探视和接纳过程中最最敏感的触角，但它永远无法取代哲学而成为人文科学的精神领袖。文学的片面性就在于它可以将人文科学的科学性削弱到最低的程度，以至于在某种程度上不能维持一种平衡。由此它无论如何无法成为任何其他理论体系的基础，何况历史上它也曾经遭到过语言学的侵占。相反，就语言学的发展倾向来看，它倒并不是要把文艺理论置于对立的一面。

其实，如果说语言学有所沉默，它面对的不是别的——文艺学派的质疑更在其次——而是自己的诘难。从自己的诘难中挣脱出来是一个长久而痛苦的过程。诘难过后，便是语言学在今天流派纷呈的现状。也正是这种多流派不分主次的共存的状况，才有可能为翻译理论提供更多的视角与切入点。这就是我们所熟悉的语言的魅力。

无论如何，正如拉德米拉尔所说的，"语言学已经不再是它原来的模样了，那么纯粹，那么生硬"。而无论如何，习惯了大一统和分久必合的中国的理论界也应该认识到，翻译理论，凭借它天然的、对于几重关系的思考，也决不会停留在一个面目上。

更何况我们在这里所阐述的一切的理论基础，也还仅仅是语言学的一部分，是西方的、欧洲中心论的语言学。

选文五　翻译学研究中的语言学模式与方法

Mona Baker

导　言

　　本文是英国当代著名翻译理论家莫娜·贝克(Mona Baker)的力作,是作者为 2005 年在德国和美国同时出版的《翻译研究国际百科全书》撰写的一个词条。后经李尚杰翻译成中文,发表在 2005 年第 3 期的《外语研究》上。杨晓荣教授还为这篇文章写了编者按,很好地概括了这篇译文发表的背景和意义:"本刊今年第 1 期发表了刘世生教授的《语言与文学的接面关系研究》一文,涉及文体学研究在语言学和文学之间的桥梁作用。其实,翻译学和语言学的关系或许更为密切,更为天然,其间的'接面'更多,所以才会出现这样的现象:20 世纪当代翻译研究中的语言学途径一经进入我国,立刻引起了广泛的呼应,人们在基于中国传统文论和中国传统美学理论的传统译论之外看到了一片新天地,积极尝试以不同语言学派的观念、方法来探究、说明以往无法解释清楚的种种翻译现象。然而近年来,随着跨学科、多学科视野的不断开拓,特别是随着翻译文化批评的兴起,翻译研究的语言学途径似乎有点无所适从了。这条路还通吗? 翻译的语言学研究是不是除了套模式以外就无事可做了? 本期选登的当代英国著名翻译理论家莫娜·贝克教授的这篇文章,正是试图回答这些问题,相信会对我们有所启发。"[①]的确,莫娜·贝克的这篇论文,开宗明义,探讨了语言学途径的翻译研究可以采用的模式与方法,使我们能够对从语言学的角度从事翻译研究的模式和方法有清楚的认识和了解。

1　引言

　　语言学与翻译研究相结合,产生了许多积极成果,而且历史悠久,至少可以追溯到 20 世纪 40 年代末 50 年代初。那个时候,一些学者开始探讨如何将现代学术融入翻译理论和翻译教学研究,提出了一些新的理论模式。近年来,翻译研究的语言学视角这一悠久传统在本学科内遭到了一些批评。这些批评有些是有道理的,还有不少近来也引起了很大的关注。但同时也应该指出,现在依然对翻译研究语言学途径持批评意见者,也有许多人对相关信息的掌握是有问题的,他们心目中的语言学仍然是 60—70 年代的那些主流理论,已经不能代表今日语言学和翻译研究语言学途径的现状了。本文将回顾从 50 年代直到 90 年代语言学途径的发展历程,以期正确看待翻译研究语言学途径的得失,并回应对这一途径的一部分批评意见。

---

　　① 杨晓荣:《外语研究》,2005 年(3)。杨教授对这篇选文没有参考书目进行了解释:"需要说明的是,出于种种原因,和国内大多数同类期刊的做法一样,我刊一般也不发译作(尽管这的确是一件非常遗憾的事:好文章不管是谁写的,总比泡沫强),所以这里我们采用的是这篇文章的编译稿,作为全文最后一部分的一个精选书目也去掉了。"

Fawcett(1997a)对各种翻译语言学理论做了详细而公正的考察,同时介绍了这些理论的发展状况,比较了这些理论几十年来的功过,可资参考。

本文的回顾部分把研究者分为两类,一类是语言学者,他们感兴趣的是将自己推崇的语言学理论放在翻译领域里予以检验,因为翻译现象对语言学和哲学都可以说是一种很有分量的挑战(Firth,1956a:77);另一类是翻译学者,他们关心的是推动翻译研究的发展,希望语言学能为达到这一目标提供可靠的分析工具。前一类人如 Firth (1956a,1956b)、Haas (1962/1968)、Catford (1965,1994)、Halliday (1964)、de Beaugrande (1978),后一类人则有 Nida (1964,1969,1975a,1975b)、Delisle (1980,1993)、House (1977/1981,1997)、Blum-Kulka (1981,1986)、Wilss (1977/1982)、Hatim & Mason (1990,1997)、Mason (1994)、Bell (1991)、Baker (1992,1993,1995,1996b)、Neubert & Shreve(1992)、Harvey (1998,2001),等等。

2 语言学理论面对翻译的挑战

以 Noam Chomsky 为代表的转换生成语言学家从来都没有对翻译表示出太大的兴趣。相反,以 Firth 为理论渊源的语言学家却经常发表成篇的文章讨论翻译理论问题,Catford (1965/1980)则是写了一整本书。Firth 本人写过一些文章,其中对翻译的兴趣点在于把它看成一种"交际活动"(communicative event),这和当代翻译理论中 Hatim & Mason (1990,1997)以及 House (1977/1981,1997)等人的交际模式基本上是一致的。比如在《语言分析与翻译》一文中,Firth 反对用"赤裸裸的思想"(naked ideas)作为等值的衡量手段,认为不能以它为参照来判断翻译中意思是否已经得到转换;他认为"劳心费力地把一个词的意思全部都说出来是无益的"(1956a:78)。下面是他在翻译问题上的基本立场:

> 我想说明,语言的系统和结构,与事件的系统和结构,与相关的物、人及其活动中的系统和结构都是有关系的。你可以把语言结构和系统与思维结构和系统联系起来,也可以把它与情景中的结构和系统联系起来,构成情景的要素包括参与其中的人、人的非语言行为、相关的物以及其他活动。在这两种选择中,我认为——尽管看起来可能很难——情景要素系统更好把握,也更容易与翻译问题扯上关系。(Firth,1956b:91)

Firth 经常谈到的一个话题是意义的方式或层次,即音位层次、语法层次、情景层次(参见 Catford,1965/1980),他明确地说,与翻译行为相关,而且有可能把翻译行为解释清楚的是情景层次。因此,就翻译研究语言学途径而言,强调翻译是一种交际活动的观念可以追溯到 50 年代中期,一直到 60—70 年代,这种观念在相关文献中仍然占据着主流位置,尽管今天很少有人认识到这个事实。比如在 1962 年,Haas 重申了 Firth 的立场,虽然没有直接提及 Firth。Haas 说,"我们从不同表达法中抽象出来的'意义相似性',其实是这些表达法所发挥的不同功能之间的一种对应(correspondence)。不这样解释翻译,我们就无法解开中性意义上的纯粹事实(bare and neutral fact)这个谜团"(Haas,1962/1968:104)。Haas 认为"意义对等"(correspondence of meaning)的概念并不能有效地解释翻译,不仅如此,他还明确指出,"译者自己选择用什么单位来翻译","面对'自由结构'的译者就会自由地组织语言结构","译者使用的语言就是他手中的粘土"(Haas,1962/1968:107 - 108)。80—90 年代发展起来的一些理论,比如"目的论"和文化学派,对语言学提出批评,认为语言学的"意义"概念过于简单化,还认为语言学否定了译者做出选择的自由,等等。从以上引用的论述来看,这些批评在回顾文献时是各取所需、很不全面的,没有注意到语言学界有关翻译本质的重要讨论,而这些讨论至少在当时来看就已经非常深入了。Firth 等语言学家对意义的认识是非常复杂的,他们十分关注意义的社会性,对这一点予以认可的翻译学者为数不多,Bassnett-McGuire 就是其中一位,虽然她后来对语言学途径持批评态度(Lefevere & Bassnett,1990:4)。

尽管如此,公平地说,许多语言学家,包括承袭 Firth 传统的学者,虽然起步就提出了和60—70 年代 Firth,Haas 等人相似的假设,实际上最终都没有回应 Firth 提出来的挑战。有的时候,他们好像出于一种自我要求而转移了注意力,全神贯注于为每一种类型的翻译行为建立一套无懈可击的语言学范畴,必要时还会牺牲自己所提出的理论模式的有效性。Catford(1965/1980)就是一个典型的例子。和 Halliday(1964)不同,他把翻译看作一种语言现象而不是一种语言教学方法。Catford 的著作的确是最著名的翻译语言学理论著作,人们在质疑翻译语言学途径时,总是提及这部作品。甚至语言学界也公认,Catford 的理论反映出一个特定时期内语言学本身的局限性(de Beaugrande,1978:11)。

和 60—70 年代许多讨论翻译现象的语言学家一样,Catford 基本上也是把翻译看作对不同语言的操作,所涉及的活动就是将一种语言的文本材料替换为另一种语言的文本材料。他的重点始终是探索语言在这方面的潜能。因此,一方面,他根据语言层次划分翻译类型(由此产生了两个广为人知的范畴,即完全翻译和有限翻译,后者又进一步划分为语法、词汇、音位和字形翻译);另一方面,他根据(他所认为的)翻译等值关系得以建立的语法等级划分翻译类型(结果产生了"等级限制翻译"和"无界限翻译"等范畴)。这种重视潜能、不重视翻译实际行为的做法,现在语言学途径的学者已经不再青睐,但是将之全盘否定也没有道理。比如音位翻译的例子就确实存在,证明 Catford 提出的范畴中至少有一部分是有用的。

Catford 还创建了一套翻译转换(translation shifts)类型体系。这套体系吸引了不少学者,其中有些人后来又提出自己的、更为合理的转换类型体系[如 Popovič(1970)以及 Leuven-Zwart(1984,1989,1990)]。其实,80—90 年代翻译研究领域最著名的人物之一 Gideon Toury 在自己的著作中就大量地使用了"转换"这个概念[如 Toury(1980);在 Toury(1995)的个案分析中,这个概念又出现了]。Catford 的贡献之一就是第一次明确地讨论了"转换"这个概念,而且做了比较详细的阐述。如果不像 Catford 那样将"转换"局限于结构层的改变,我们就会清楚地看到,只要是将原作和译作进行比较,其中就隐含着"转换"这个概念,因此,它实际上存在于所有以产品为出发点的描述性翻译研究之中,而且居于中心位置,包括那些非语言学途径的研究。唯一的例外可能是近年基于对比语料库所做的研究,这种研究比较的是源语言和目标语言,而非源文本与目标文本,因此没有使用转换概念。不管怎么说,Catford 的理论模式有许多弱点,其中之一是没有区分"必要转换"和"任选转换"(做出这个区分的是后来的一些学者,如 Toury)。这恰恰是因为 Catford 所代表的那一代语言学家,其兴趣所在是把翻译当作语言形式分析的工具,而不是把翻译看作一种语言和社会现象来予以解释。

虽然 Catford 在翻译学领域内受到了严厉的批评,但是不应忘记,正是他的著作第一个尝试对一般意义上的翻译(而不仅限于文学翻译或圣经翻译)所涉及的语言问题做出详细而系统的理论阐述。Catford 的理论在许多方面都与翻译活动的实际情况脱节,他把分析的最高单位局限于句子,这也是不合适的。尽管如此,他的理论内在结构统一,定义严谨,自有一种典雅。

3　翻译学内部的语言学理论

早在 40 年代末 50 年代初,刚刚兴起的翻译学科中就已经有许多学者开始关注语言学,希望在其中找到能够有效地运用于翻译研究的理论及教学模式[如 Nida(1945);Casagrande (1954)]。对语言学的兴趣在当时是有道理的,现在也仍然如此,虽然对此不无争议。首先,一个明显的事实是,语言是翻译的原材料,因此一门说明语言行为的学科自然就应该可以为研究翻译的学者提供很多的东西。但是在那个时候,借用语言学模式也还有许多技术上的原因。40—50 年代,语言学本身也开始成为一门"科学"的学问,其标志是用严谨而高度形式化的方式来描述语言,结果是提高了语言学在学术界的地位。"科学"方式这一点正是近年来翻译学内部激烈批评的一个对象,语言学途径有时就被轻蔑地贴上"科学主义"的标签。然而在那个时期,努力跻身于科学性学科之列以确保自己在学术界的地位,对语言学和翻译学显然都具有莫大的吸引力。语言学在语言教学和词典编纂等领域里成功地解决了许多问题,改进了有关工作,这使它更加成为翻译学效仿的榜样。

翻译研究的语言学途径起初眼界是比较狭窄的(现在有一些理论仍是如此),目光局限于句子以下的单位,从语言学那里借鉴而来的理论概念也是零零碎碎[如 Nida(1975b)对成分分析法的应用,以及 Newmark(1988)对格语法和成分分析法的应用]。早期语言学途径的另一个特点就是倾向于认为意义和"现实"能够从语言中分割出来,然后在翻译过程中完整无缺地进行转换,这一点和 Firth,Malinowski,Halliday,Sinclair 等主流语言学家的立场形成鲜明的对比。比如,Rabin 将翻译描述为"一种语言中的某段口头或书面话语为了传达与另一种语言中已经存在的某段话语相同的意义而产生的过程"(Rabin, 1958:23)。有些语言学理论和翻译语言学理论至今仍然认为,语言中至少有一大部分都能够以独立的"意义"做出明确的定位,但是多数学者认为,"不存在意义,只有代码","翻译的本质是符号指代问题"(an essential problem of semiosis)(Frawley, 1984:164)。以语言学范式为背景的重要的口笔译理论家,或明或暗,所持的几乎全都是这个立场,包括 Hatim & Mason, House, Bell, Baker, Delisle, Sager, Shlesinger, Blum-Kulka 以及其他许多人。

早期翻译研究的另一个特点是主要为教学服务,少有描述性研究,几乎没人构建理论模式[Jakobson(1959)是个例外,值得一提]。这一时期占主导地位的是两类研究:一类是对特定的两种语言做对比分析,目的是指出翻译中可能出现问题的地方[如 Vinay & Darbelnet(1958)的英法语言对比分析],另一类是试图归纳翻译的一般性策略,不限定于具体的语言。《圣经》译者的著作大部分属于第二类。两类研究的主要目标都是要为解决翻译中的结构问题寻求明确的指导原则。

从 70 年代末开始,特别是到了 90 年代,翻译研究"语言学派"内部出现了一些具有鲜明特点但又互为补充的研究方法。有些研究者,如 House(1977/1981,1997)和 Bell(1991),主要以某一种语言理论为背景(House 和 Bell 用的都是 Halliday 的系统理论)。有些人探索如何在翻译中处理特定的语言型式(linguistic patterning)。比如 Blum-Kulka (1986)和 Shlesinger (1996)分别探讨了笔译和同声传译中衔接方式的转换问题。Baker (1992)研究了翻译中不同种类的语言型式,包括词汇型式、主-述位组织和衔接。还有些人尝试在大部分或主要借鉴语言学某一特定分支(而不是某一种特定的语言理论)的基础上创建自己的翻译理论,比如

Hatim & Mason(1990,1997)对批评语言学的借鉴。Gutt（1990,1991）是一个很有趣的例子。他借鉴关联理论的方式和 Bell 借鉴系统语言学的方式是一样的,但他明确表示,没有必要搞出一套独立的翻译理论,关联理论完全可以说明与翻译行为有关的所有问题[Malmkjer(1992)对这一观点做了详细的批评]。

总体来看,可以说翻译研究语言学途径这些年来已经发展得相当成熟了。一方面,这是自然发展的结果,特别是现代语言学本身已经扩大了视野,越来越关注实际应用中的语言,而不是把语言仅仅看作由各种关系组成的一个抽象系统;另一方面,这也得益于非语言学途径翻译学者提出来的批评意见。Hatim & Mason 和 House 在 1997 年分别出版了各自理论模式的修订版,修订的幅度相当大,而且明确认可了诸如意识形态、政治氛围、市场力量等因素的重要性,Hatim & Mason 甚至尝试将其中一些因素纳入自己的理论之中。对于近年来质疑翻译语言学研究之有效性的批评意见,House 给予了正面回应,她承认非语言因素的确对翻译行为产生影响,同时强调从语言学角度研究翻译仍然可以取得成果:选择显性翻译还是隐性翻译不仅仅取决于译者自身,或文本,或译者个人对文本的阐释,同时在很大程度上也取决于翻译的动因,取决于隐含的读者,以及出版政策和市场政策。换句话说,翻译中存在着许多译者无法控制的因素,这些因素与作为语言过程的翻译以及译者的语言文化能力是毫不相干的。这些因素是社会因素,与中介人、与社会政治甚至意识形态约束都有关系,其力量和影响一般来说比译者要大得多。尽管如此,翻译仍然是一种语言-文本现象,从这个角度来描述、分析和评价翻译仍然是合情合理的。（House,1997：118-119）下面要谈到的其他一些著作则明确地在语言学框架之内更为详细地讨论意识形态的问题。

4　近年来的发展

80 年代末以来,以语言学为背景的几位学者开始强调世界观、意识形态和权力运作对翻译行为的影响[Saadeddin(1989,1990)；Ireland(1989)；Williams(1992)；Fawcett(1995)]。这意味着译者不再被看作仅仅是运输管道,只是在忠实而客观地传递源语文本或话语中包含的信息。尤其是对法庭口译和社会生活口译(community interpreting)的研究表明,译员在交际中确实起到了非常积极的作用,影响他们(以及其他参与者如陪审员)行为的,是活跃于特定情景中的权力关系[Roy（1989,1993）；Berk-Seligson（1988,1990）；Wadensj（1992）；Hale(1997)]。这些研究在很大程度上借鉴了社会语言学、口语文化人类学和 Halliday 语言学的研究成果。同样,手语口译研究也借鉴了语言学在很多研究领域里的成果,并且也很重视意识形态和权力运作的作用。

不过,在这个方向上最具有发展潜力的成果源自批评语言学,有时也叫做批评话语分析。批评语言学和以它为背景的翻译研究认为,语言既是交际的工具,也是控制的工具,而意识形态则是"从某一特定视角出发系统地组合起来的一套观念"（Hodge & Kress,1979/1993：6）。语言学的这一支和其他派别对意识形态的认识的区别在于,他们坚持认为,"意识形态无需作为一种有意识或有目的的偏见来起作用"（Stubbs,1996：93）。比如,Mason(1994)原本是要分析一篇关于墨西哥历史的原文及其译文,考察系统的意识形态转换在其语言中留下的痕迹,以说明"意识形态是如何以微妙的方式在翻译过程中留下印迹的"（Mason,1994：23）,但是出于其批评语言学背景,他认为,译文中出现的意识形态偏离可能并不是有意而为：妥协在很大程度上往往是一个下意识的过程，我们所有的人都要受各自世界观的约束。Fawcett（1997b）用同样的方法揭示了 Stuart Gilbert 翻译的 André Malraux 的《王家大道》（*La Voie Royale*）中的种族主义成分，但他的结论是，Gilbert 未必就是一个种族主义者，他那样做只不过是因为"在他所生活和写作的那个年代，主流话语的压力使人几乎无法回避这种语言，就好像它是周围墙纸的一部分一样"（Fawcett，1997b：264）。

这种对"话语习惯化"（Fowler，1991：89）的认识意味着，语言学背景的学者很重视对语言型式进行详尽的分析，希望能借此让那些正因为"习惯化"而通常不为人知的种种关系显现出来。因此，和那些非语言学途径的研究相比，Mason（1994）对意识形态偏离类型的分析更为详细，所涉及的语言层次也更多，包括具体的词汇选择，词汇衔接和搭配衔接，主位安排，以及文本的总体结构。这和那些未借鉴语言学理论的研究形成了鲜明的反差，那些研究往往局限于很少几个范畴，涉及的语言层次最多一两个。例如，Venuti（1995；1996）用到的范畴就很少，只有古语、方言、个人语言、句法倒装，等等。在语言学，尤其是批评语言学看来，这些范畴数量太少，又过于宽泛，因此就语言型式而言，解释力有限。

宏观一些来看，语言学途径另一个重要的发展与翻译作为语言现象这一本质有关。在偶尔想到翻译的时候，大部分语言学家倾向于把翻译看作应用语言学的一个分支，如此而已。然而有趣的是，语言学本身提供了一些最有力的工具，可以用来证明事实正好相反：翻译是一种独具特色的现象，足以成为一个独立学科即翻译学的研究对象。

有两个具体的因素可以表明，翻译作为一种语言应用变体是非常独特的，显示出鲜明的型式特征。首先，翻译文本或翻译话语通常受制于用另一种语言已经全部表达出来的文本或话语，而其他类型的语言产出并没有这个限制。其次，译者会注意正在制作的文本将要处于什么样的社会环境，并有意无意地做出反应。他们知道，译作和原作被接受的方式通常是不一样的，至少在当代社会中一般来说是如此。这可以解释学术界认为翻译文本所具有的一个特点，即翻译文本一般倾向于遵从甚至夸张地使用译入语的典型结构。

所以，必须认识到，翻译就是"一种在其自身目的及产出的压力和语境制约下形成的交际活动"（Baker，1996b：175）。如果我们承认，所有的语言形式都会受到语言使用环境中当时正在起作用的那些制约因素的影响，那么就得接受这样的观点，即翻译文本的形式应该不同于源语文本产出的形式。换言之，翻译的性质和压力必然在译者产出的语言中留下痕迹（Baker，1996b：176）。问题是在实践中如何来探寻这样的痕迹。这里使用的方法并不是将原作和它的译本作比较，而是将同一种语言的语域相近的原创文本和翻译文本作比较。这两类文本都以机器可以阅读的形式出现，因此可以进行自动或半自动分析，这就是"比较语料库"（Baker，1995）。

语料库翻译研究框架内外近年来取得的成果显示出，翻译确实是一种独特的交际活动，和原创文本的产出性质不同。比如，与同一语言具有可比性的原创文本相比，翻译文本的词汇密度较低（即翻译文本中实词比例低于原创文本，而虚词比例较高），类型标记（type-token）比率也较低（即使用的词汇范围比较窄）（Laviosa-Braithwaite，1995，1996）。这表明，译者可能是在下意识地简化所使用的语言，以便把来自异域的信息传达给新的受众：第一个比率是提高冗余度，第二个比率是限制词汇的范围。出于同样的原因，译者还倾向于将标点符号规范化，即便原文中标点符号的使用方式并不规范而只是尝试性的（May，1997；Malmkjær，1997）；口译员还会补全断句，改变不合语法的说法使之符合语法，舍弃迟疑的部分和开头说错了的部分，即便说话者原本是有意为之(Shlesinger,1991:150;Berk-Seligson,1990)。这种将翻译语言"规范化"以及严格遵守译入语常规的倾向再次表明,译者会注意自己产出的文本或话语所处的文本地位,并下意识地做出反应。

5　目前状况

今日的翻译研究以多元化为主要特点,一是引起学者关注的课题多元,二是用来研究这些课题所使用的视角和方法多元。翻译学者越来越倾向于"四处采购"分析工具,不论其源自何方。结果就是,翻译研究的语言学途径与非语言学途径之间已经不像过去那样泾渭分明了。有些学者,特别是以文化研究为背景的人,现在仍然认为,凡是借用语言学分析工具或未将翻译研究政治化的研究方法都应该属于语言学途径,但是我们发现,很多大量采用语言学分析工具的人同时也很重视利用文学理论、批评规范、文化规划理论以及其他许多研究领域的成果,这就使我们很难(如果不是徒劳的话)把他们的研究归为"语言学途径"还是"非语言学途径"。比如Tymoczko(1985,1999)和Delabastita(1993)。甚至于有些学者虽然公开表示自己不属于语言学派,并从各个角度对之提出批评,但是一旦开始做描述性研究或讨论教学问题,他们就不由自主地要大量采用语言学分析工具。因为,要分析译文,要培训译员,不这样做如何入手?

比如,已故的André Lefevere就曾直言不讳地批评语言学途径(Lefevere & Bassnett,1990:4),但在他自己的著作里,他广泛使用了诸如言内之力和言外之力等主流语言学概念(Lefevere,1992)。他偶尔也会采用一种人们一向以为应该是语言学派学者才会有的口气说话。Lefevere告诉我们,译者应该能够把在总体语篇层次和言外语言使用层次上所做出的战术性决策与为了解决上述问题而设计的战略联系起来。如果他们做不到,那么这些决策就是错误的,反映出译者没有正确地理解源语文本(Lefevere,1992:111)。这类专横的断言有时会被误认为是语言学类著作的特点,其实,70年代末以来语言学研究就很少有这种口气了。

Venuti(1996)使用了诸如"句法倒装"、"词汇"和"方言"等概念,这些概念虽然其他学科的学者也开始经常性地使用,但却都是经语言学予以阐发的。有趣的是,Venuti使用这些概念的同时,又在极力反对语言学,他声称,语言学途径会"阻碍"(block)他倡导的伦理和政治方面的研究,让翻译研究成为少数人的事,而且还说,格赖斯的原则会"有力地抑制(repress)其他原则在翻译中起作用"(Venuti,1996:105,104)。

这种强硬的说法在任何时候都很难站得住脚,尤其是在当前,翻译研究从批评语言学等领域汲取营养取得了不少成就,而且自从80—90年代以来已经形成了一种多元的、跨学科的局面。Venuti最后提出,不管怎么说,语言学途径还是可以"在培训译员和分析译作中发挥作用的"(Venuti,1996:109),但这个建议延续了翻译学学科内不同理论途径之间可以划分得泾渭分明这种神话,似乎抑制了(用他自己的话来说)翻译研究的跨学科性质。

在Keith Harvey的著作中可以看到这种朝跨学科方向迈进的努力(Harvey,1998,2001)。他从形式和功能两个角度出发,研究了译者在翻译Gore Vidal,Genet,Kramer,Kushner等人作品的过程中处理"营地"语言(男同性恋者使用的一种言语风格)时所采用的翻译策略。Harvey证明,要解释这些翻译策略,就必须把"营地"语言的形式特征与其在一个更大范围内所承当的文化角色联系起来,这就是它的边缘化和同性恋身份的象征作用。同时,这种语言层面上的形式/功能分析还必须辅之以其他一些方面的考察,如:源语和译语文化大背景中是否存在同性恋亚文化符号,其可见程度如何,译语文化中是否已经存在某种"同性恋文学",译者对同性恋亚文化群体的认同状态,等等。Harvey 代表了新一代翻译学者,他们不愿意把自己拘囿于语言学或别的什么途径。他的研究表明,翻译的语言学分析不见得必须脱离其文化背景,实际上,完全可以借鉴其他学科的方法和观点,进行更有成效的工作,对翻译行为的描述也会比以往任何时候都更加全面。关于后殖民背景下翻译的语言和文化环境,Tymoczko(1999)有同样细致的研究,可供参考。

　　翻译研究语言学途径的确有过局限性,但是近些年来,这一途径已经极大地拓展了视野,改进了方法。在当前这种跨学科的氛围下,如果说还能谈得上比较清晰的理论途径的话,那么语言学途径就仍然是翻译研究最富有成效的理论途径之一,理由很简单:只要开始研究翻译问题,起码要从某个层面上的语言分析入手,大部分翻译学研究都绕不开这一步。翻译的语言学途径之所以如此灵活,它的无所不在之所以有时会在翻译界引起这么多的沮丧,原因正在于此。

选文六　试析翻译的语言学研究

张柏然

导　言

　　前面的几篇选文都从正面阐述了语言学理论对于翻译研究的指导意义。但是,早期语言学途径的翻译理论也在一定程度上存在着理论偏向,这也是语言学途径的翻译理论遭到质疑和批评的原因,因此特别需要引起读者的注意和警醒。这就是为什么我们在这一章即将结束的时候选取南京大学张柏然教授的这篇文章,希望读者在注意到普通语言学或结构语言学基础上的翻译研究产生积极理论成果的同时,也对于这一个研究"范式"保持清醒的认识,更好地体会新一代的语言学派途径的翻译研究学者在走出这些误区、突破固有局限方面取得了哪些成绩,从而继续努力,探索利用包括语言学理论在内的所有理论资源进行翻译研究的新途径。本文原载于《外语与外语教学》2008 年第 6 期。

　　翻译思想史表明,随着现代语言学的形成与日臻完善,20 世纪中叶以来,建立在语言学——普通语言学或结构主义语言学基础上的翻译研究获得了长足的发展,产生了许多积极的理论成果,在翻译研究领域逐步形成了独具"范式"的语言学派。由于语言学派的努力,翻译研究在学科化进程中迈出了坚实的一步,摆脱了"经验陈述"的模式而更具有科学的特性。多年来,国内外学者就翻译的语言学研究取得的成就所作介绍或论述,虽说不汗牛充栋,却也是林林总总,举不胜举了,在此就不赘述了。

然而,在对语言学派的研究文献作详尽的观察之后,我们就会发现,这一学派的翻译研究还存在着理论偏向。虽然交际理论、社会符号学等的介入使这一理论偏向在一定程度上得到修正,比如,纽马克(Peter Newmark)运用语义学理论分析了思维、言语与翻译的关系,阐述了语义翻译与交际翻译的特点,在其成名作《翻译研究途径》中所提出的"语义翻译"与"交际翻译"在理论上与实践上至今仍为人们所引用(Newmark,1981/1998),但是,翻译的语言学研究的偏向始终存在着。

纵观语言学派研究文献,我们可以将它们分为两类:一类是结构主义语言学家关于翻译的论述;另一类是以现代语言学理论为基础专门从事翻译问题研究的学者的论述。前者立足于结构主义语言学自身的研究,仅将翻译问题作为语言结构分析的个例或个别途径,其有关翻译的论述与其说是翻译研究,不如说是借助翻译来探索语言研究的方法论;而后者在前者范式的指导下,对翻译过程、翻译方法等范畴进行描述,以期得出具有普适性的翻译模式——语言学模式。

布拉格学派的创始人雅可布逊(Roman Jakobson)较早注意到翻译问题与普通语言学理论的关系。他认为,语言符号的意义在于将一种符号翻译为另一种的符号,翻译实际上就是语符和信息的诠释,因此翻译是语言学方法不可分割的组成部分。雅可布逊在其著名论文《翻译的语言观》中列举了诠释语符的三种方式:语内翻译、语际翻译和符际翻译。其中,语际翻译涉及一般意义上的翻译概念。在此雅可布逊意在强调在诠释语言现象时语言学对翻译行为的依赖性(Jakobson,1959)。

同样,英国语言学家弗斯(J. R. Firth)在《语言分析和翻译》一文中详尽地阐述了结合翻译进行语言分析的观点。弗斯肯定了翻译理论本身在语言学中的地位。他认为,把翻译作为语言分析的一种形式,用来阐明语义,这具有一定的可行性。弗斯指出,在英国语言学史上马林诺夫斯基首次系统地把翻译用于阐明某些民族话语的意义,并把这种方法称之为"语言分析"。弗斯提出了"全面翻译"(total translation)的概念,即要全面运用一切可能的手段传达意义,在语法、词汇、词的搭配和语境等四个层次上进行语言分析。弗斯将翻译的意义归纳为:其存在这一事实的本身就是对语言理论和语言哲学的挑战;语言分析与翻译结合可以为语言学家和社会学家提供广阔的研究空间(Firth,1957)。

在语言学翻译研究的第一类文献中,韩礼德(M. A. Halliday)的观点较为著名。他指出句子是翻译的基本单位,翻译过程包括三个阶段:寻找等值物、检验等值物以及调整译语结构。然而,韩礼德对翻译的论述,其出发点是外语教学。他认为利用母语进行语言对比可以使学生注意到两种语言的异同,因为他认为翻译是一种特殊的语言对比形式,它包括两个方面:语际等值和语法结构的全面对比。因此,他得出结论:翻译理论是普通语言学的重要组成部分(Halliday,1985)。

通过上述研究我们可以发现,语言学家在讨论翻译问题时,首先将翻译研究纳入语言学理论研究的框架,以结构主义语言学的理论与方法来描述翻译现象。他们研究翻译的根本目的在于将翻译研究作为语言研究的重要途径。因此,将翻译研究作为个例以补证语言学理论、突出翻译研究的工具性功能是第一类翻译研究的共同特征。

这类翻译研究由于其语言研究功利的前设性,直接导致其研究的理论偏向——研究的工具性目的,因而影响了其分析结论的普适性,给翻译研究带来了一定的局限。海德格尔认为,前设和前有、前见一样,是任何解释的基础,它们一起构成了理解的前结构,事物的作为结构出自理解的前结构。前设即运用一个观念来弄清作为结构。当我们面对研究对象时,总是对它预先做出假设,然后才能把它解释成"作为"某物(刘放桐等,1990:759 - 760)。前设就是研究翻译前我们预先已有的假设。任何解释都包含了某种假设,问题在于这种前设的客观性。上述语言学家从普通语言学出发,以结构主义范式观照翻译问题,其理论视角本身无可厚非。然而,这种研究具有明确的功利性:将翻译研究视为对结构主义语言学结论的补证,将翻译理论视为语言学研究的途径或手段。这种以工具性为目的的翻译研究必然导致研究结论的理论偏向,从而从根本上否定了翻译理论作为学科的建构。或许法国语言学翻译理论的代表人物穆南(G. Mounin)从另一侧面揭示出语言学翻译研究第一类文献的特性:他主张研究翻译问题的语言学家至少在最初阶段不要将翻译作为弄清某些普通语言学问题的手段,而应该运用语言学,特别是现代语言学的理论和方法,为译者解决翻译问题提出可能性(许钧、袁筱一,2001)。

如果说语言学翻译研究的第一类文献是基于语言学自身研究的需要,即功利性目的而对翻译现象进行分析,其结论给翻译研究带来极大的局限,从而从根本上否定了翻译理论作为学科的地位;那么,语言学翻译研究的第二类文献则是基于又一功利性:在为实现译文"等值"或"等效"的实用性目标的观照下,同样得出具有理论偏向的模式。

语言学翻译理论的第二类文献,其理论基础是普通语言学理论或结构主义语言学理论。该理论基础的选定是根据这样一个常识:翻译是特定形式的言语行为,而语言学则是研究语言的科学,它能够提供关于语言研究的基本概念、理论模式和方法,因此翻译理论无法回避语言学。对翻译性质、过程和方法的分析和描述必然要用语言学的基本概念、范畴和方法。

从广义上看,索绪尔是结构主义语言学的创始人。他认为,语言是一个体系(或系统),即一种结构。语言的特点并非由语音和意义本身所构成,而是由语音和意义之间的关系构成的一个网络,即成为一个体系,也就是语言的结构。这种语言体系被视为一个符号体系。索绪尔认为,一切符号都可以分为能指和所指,语言的研究可分为共时性研究和历时性研究。共时性研究是对特定时期语言横断面的研究。索绪尔十分重视语言的共时性研究。他还指出,由词结合成一个结构有两种关系:组合关系和聚合关系。总之,索绪尔的语言学模式是以共时性研究为基础的、将语言与言语加以区别的语言体系,这个体系由组合关系和聚合关系构成语言中的差别体系(索绪尔,高名凯译,1982:100 - 176)。

继索绪尔之后,美国语言学家乔姆斯基(Noam Chomsky)则强调语言学研究对象为语言能力而非语言现象。它将语言分为深层结构和表层结构。乔姆斯基提出的短语结构规则和推导模式说明了他的结构与转换的方法。短语结构规则是形成句子的一整套规则。这个规则先有一整套短语结构改写规则(Chomsky,1968)。

在实践上,语言学翻译研究的第二类文献均以结构主义语言学理论的某种语言模式作为其理论基础,如奈达(E. A. Nida)就以乔姆斯基转换生成语法为基础,提出由源语结构转换成译语结构的核心句模式,而卡特福德(J. C. Catford)则以韩礼德的系统语法理论为其翻译研究的基础。

奈达认为,一般意义上翻译过程包括以下几个阶段:分析、转移和重组(analysis, transfer and reconstruct),即首先分析原作语言的信息,将其剖析成结构上最简单明了的形式,在此基础上转移,然后再重新组织成正常的译作语言。分析阶段包括三个方面,即各成分之间的语法关系,语义单位的外延意义以及语法结构和语义单位的内涵值。转移阶段:将事件名词从一种语言转移成另一种语言时，一般先将它转换成动词形式；同理，通常先将抽象名词转换成形容词和副词。奈达认为，在将表层结构的各种表达形式转换成核心结构时，产生了四种基本的结构单位，即事物单位（thing）、事件单位（event）、抽象单位（abstract）和表示关系的单位（relation）。另外，奈达提出了限制和确立词汇单位在特定上下文中的含义的方法，即通过句法结构限定词义，以及通过语义结构辨别含义。词义相近的关系有三种，即邻近关系、内涵关系和重叠关系（Nida，1964，1969/1982）。

奈达强调，对源语语言进行分析时，不能局限于研究语言单位间的句法关系和这些语言单位的外延意义，文体风格在传达信息中具有更为重要的意义，在转移阶段，奈达就语言的意义非对应现象——喻体差异、喻体缺省、语义缺省等现象，提出了翻译对策。翻译时应注意内涵结构和外延结构，为此奈达提出了转移外延内容的三种方法：全新组合、分解组合和综合组合。奈达认为，重组过程涉及两个主要范畴：形式范畴和功能范畴。前者要求根据文体风格和文学体裁进行重组，后者则要求译者关注读者的接受效果。由此可见，奈达所谓的翻译时对源、译语两种语言的语法结构、语义单位、文体风格进行分析，在传达风格、功能的基础上为处理语义非对应现象设定语义层面上的对策，其核心在于语言对比分析和寻找语义对应（谭载喜，2002）。

卡特福德关于翻译理论的论述同样遵循与奈达相同的研究模式。他在其《翻译的语言学理论》一书中开宗明义地指出："翻译是用语言进行操作的工作，即把一种语言的文本转换成另一种语言的文本。因此，任何翻译理论都必然利用语言理论和普通语言学理论。"他还认为，翻译的中心问题是在译语中寻找等值物，而翻译理论的中心任务则是描述翻译等值的本质以及达到翻译等值的条件。卡特福德的理论核心在于它提出实现等值关系的途径：等值关系可以由"层面"（语法形式和词汇形式、语音实体和字形实体、语境）到"等级"（句子、子句、词组、单词、词素）在任何一个交叉点上建立。如果在较低的某一等级上不能确立等值关系，可以在较高等级上求得。与奈达相同，卡特福德翻译研究的中心仍然立足于语言分析，即界定等值成分的本质和条件（Catford，1965）。

语言学翻译研究的第二类文献表明，这种研究一般始于语言（双语）的结构分析，诸如语言各层次的划分、话语实用关系类别以及话语功能类别的确定，经由翻译单位的选定，最终规定翻译具体操作方法。这种方法在语言学翻译研究中通常表述为模式、方法和步骤等。

然而，我们应当指出，首先，翻译作为特定形式的文化活动，是以双语（源语和译语）的互动性转换为其表征的，但这并不意味着翻译仅仅局限于某种语言操作或语言活动。这种以语言为中介的双语互动或文化互动现象，以及由此导致的语音、语词、语法、文体等变异现象，绝非语言学理论所能涵盖的。所以，现代语言学理论必然为翻译研究带来空白，从而造成语言学翻译研究的理论偏向。翻译研究的基点应为语言的差异性，亦即双语的非等值性。结构主义语言学对翻译中源语和译语之间并合现象（不同语言的共同之处）的认同表明，该研究偏离了翻译研究的本质问题；同时，它对源、译语这一现象及其对策的解释和选定则又使该理论由于强烈的功利性而成为教学研究或应用研究，其结论的偏向性是不言而喻的。

包括语言学翻译研究在内，世界范围内多数学派对翻译研究的核心是如何实现等值或等效。这表明，翻译研究始终停留在对翻译方法（翻译模式）的探索和选定上。语言学翻译研究以其对翻译过程的描述而获得了科学性或客观性，因为"过程"与"现象"总是联系在一起的。应当指出，这种对"过程"的考察，其实质是对方法以及模式的操作程序的设定，和所有规范选择一样,它的研究结论带有浓重的经验色彩。

其次,语言学翻译研究的第二类文献认为,在具体翻译过程中,翻译家对源语本文接受的结果——深层结构的表述最初是由核心结构(核心句)来实现的。而所谓核心结构则指对特定深层结构最基本、最具代表性的表述形式。这类研究忽略了一个基本事实,即核心结构在其完形的初始,已经导致意义的缺省。事实上,在具体的翻译过程中,翻译家对深层结构的把握是通过"统觉"来实现的。然后,翻译家直接在译语中找寻与这种"非语言"或"超语言"的结构相对应的译语表层结构。再后,根据原文的深层结构对译语表层结构进行语义修正,以完成译语本文的建构。所谓的语体风格在此应列为语义构成。而"非语言"或"超语言"的结构通常表现为意义指向(在应用性文本中)和心理意象(在艺术性文本中)。总之,翻译家的基本任务是通过译语语言对意义指向和心理意象进行表述和修正。因此,对于奈达所谓的深层结构和表层结构之说,尽管他在分析阶段和转移阶段表现出结构特性——层级性或步骤性,然而,这并未使翻译过程得到客观的、经验性的描述,同时也使得这种翻译模式即使作为教学型模式也失去了可操作性。同样,卡特福德的理论也缺乏得以实现翻译等值的可操作性。他的翻译模式的核心在于界定等值成分的本质和条件,认为,等值关系可以在由"层面"到"等级"的任何交叉点上建立。这表明:他的论述与其说是对翻译模式的设定,不如说是在比较语言学范式中探求源、译语双语对应的可能性,只是卡特福德在此将双语对应表述为等值而已。换句话说,卡特福德虽然在主观上力求以结构主义语言学为基础对翻译问题进行详尽的探讨,但是,实际上在探讨翻译的过程中,他不自觉地偏离了翻译研究,而展开了源、译语双语的静态分析与比较。所以,卡特福德的翻译模式又可以界定为以翻译的语言学研究的第二类文献为表征的第一类文献。

翻译的语言学研究的第一类文献以及建立在这种范式基础上的第二类文献,他们或以翻译研究作为结构主义语言学理论研究自身的途径和手段,或在结构主义语言学观照下对翻译过程作语言学的静态分析。特别是由后者设定的翻译模式,他们或由于其层级性或步骤性使得自身失去了应用价值(可操作性),或以对双语言静态比较分析为转移,最终偏离了翻译研究而归于对比语言学范畴。

综上所述,17世纪以来,随着当时社会的文化转型,在逻辑实证主义和唯理论的刺激和推动之下,新型的语言理论受到青睐,西方译学的语言学范式亦随之渐露雏形。语言学家、翻译理论家们开始对语言分析、语篇分析产生浓厚兴趣,对从前一些零散的争论也开始了系统的整体性思考,既关注文本的结构层次,又重视形式本身,从而破除了语文学范式的"得意忘形"的陈规。语言学范式强调意义的构成特征和语言结构,努力制定对等转换的规则,以语言分析代替直觉感受,克服了语文学派的主观主义,使翻译活动具有一定的科学性和客观性。因此,根茨勒把翻译的语言学派也称之为翻译的"科学派"。布龙菲尔德的结构语言学、乔姆斯基的转换生成语法、韩礼德的系统功能语法等为翻译语言学派提供了理论基础。以雅可布逊、奈达、卡特福特、威尔斯、纽马克、斯坦纳、弗斯、弗米尔、费道罗夫和巴尔胡达罗夫等为代表的翻译语言学派筚路蓝缕,为现代翻译研究奠定了学科和学理基础,翻译理论也开始走上了系统化、科学化、客观化的研究道路。然而,翻译研究的语言学派认为翻译只能是一门语言学学科,翻译活动究其实质来说是语言学的任务,重要的是对比原作和译作语言单位意义上的相同,以达到内容上的等值;认为语言是透明的,翻译是一种纯语言的转换过程,所涉及的只是两种不同语符中的两个对等信息;把翻译视为一门精确的科学,集中研究语言系统的差异和语言形式的转换,注意寻找语言转换规律以及语义的对等模式,迷信语言的共性;译者的任务只是按照语言规律去解码与编码。这样一来,整个翻译过程就被简单化、机械化、程序化了,而起作用的只是语言的工具理性及其规律性。翻译理论由于长期受语言学的影响,形成了一种思维定势,认为语言是一个规范的、同一的和稳定的符号系统,是人们认识世界和把握世界的工具,因此,语言被类比为数学符号系统,成了理性和规律性的象征。翻译的语言学范式给人们带来了理性思维,破除了原来语文学研究范式的神秘性和主观直觉的研究方式,从主观性走向客观性,使翻译研究取得了很大进展。但由于语言学范式使译者过多依赖于语言的规律性,忽视主体的主观能动性,排除言语活动的社会制约性和规定性,从而突出了原文文本的中心性,追求同一性和一致性,最终堕入语言逻各斯中心。

由此可见,语言学范式的翻译研究太拘泥于原文的信息层,不甚注意作品的美学功能,忽视文艺作品的艺术再现,忽视文本主题结构以及文本的话语和语篇结构,忽视更大范围的文化与这些因素对译文的生成和接受所产生的影响;没有考虑语用维度、语用意义和文本的社会与文化语境,对这些方面的理论描述比较薄弱。其范式是封闭的、静止的和自足的。随着语言学的发展,人们对语言的研究也由语言本身扩大到语言与社会、语言与心理、语言与生理等方面,后期的语言学翻译思想把原作、原作者、原文读者等因素都考虑进去了,所以也就更科学、更完整地描述了翻译过程,突破了微观语言学的文本模式,开始关注两种文化之间的交流。上述封闭的、静止的和自足的翻译研究范式被 20 世纪 90 年代中期兴起的翻译理论研究的文化转向所打破。

【延伸阅读】

[1] Baker, M. (1992). *In Other Words: A Coursebook on Translation*. London & New York: Routledge.

[2] Fawcett, P. (1997). *Translation and Language: Linguistic Theories Explained*. Manchester: St Jerome.

【问题与思考】

1. 语言与翻译的关系如何? 语言学与翻译研究的关系如何界定?
2. 语言学在哪些方面能够指导翻译活动和翻译研究?
3. 如何看待翻译研究中的语言学回归?

研究实践

重新审视现代语言学理论在翻译研究中的作用

——比利时"语言与翻译研究国际研讨会"专家访谈录

张美芳

导　言

　　本文是作者在比利时"语言与翻译研究国际研讨会"上的观察及对几位专家的访谈。根据作者观察:翻译研究领域出现"文化转向"以来,语言学途径的翻译研究不但没有停止,而是一直在扎扎实实地进行,并取得显著的成绩。这种事实本身也肯定了语言学理论与翻译研究的密切关系及其对翻译研究的重要借鉴作用。作者在文中介绍了几位受访专家对现代语言学理论对于翻译研究的重要性的看法,论述了翻译研究跨学科及多元化的性质、翻译研究的现状及存在问题,指出现在该是心平气和地反思和总结翻译研究中的问题、脚踏实地多做一些翻译理论构建和实证研究的时候了。

1　引言

　　2006 年 1 月 12 日—14 日,笔者参加了在比利时的中世纪之城根特(Ghent)市举行的"语言与翻译研究国际研讨会"。会议由根特翻译学院主办,比利时安特卫普大学、伦敦大学学院等单位协办,并得到比利时语言学会的资助。大会最引人注目之处是请来了多位世界级的翻译学者作主题发言,他们是被誉为翻译理论之父的奈达、德国功能主义翻译学派的代表人物诺德、走在翻译研究最前锋的贝克、较早推介各翻译理论流派的切斯特曼以及贝克的老师、英国米道士翻译学院院长科思婷。

　　会议令人关注的另一特点是其语言学特性。组织者在会议征文中说,"翻译研究可以说是起源于语言学,并在很大程度上依赖于语言学理论,例如机器翻译模式几乎完全是用语言学理论来描述翻译的任务与过程的。翻译研究经历了上世纪八九十年代文化转向(阐释运动、操纵学派、后殖民主义等),现在是重新审视翻译研究语言学转向(或回转)的有利之处的时候了。"(见 http://veto. hogent. be/slt06/EN/inhoud_themata_EN. htm)

　　"重新审视翻译研究语言学回转的有利之处"一说引起了笔者的兴趣。自 20 世纪 90 年代初以来,"文化转向"的概念传入我国,随之,沿文化途径的翻译研究活动就一直蓬勃发展至今,各种文化意义上的研究论文,例如翻译与意识形态、翻译与政治、翻译与性别、翻译与权利等不断见诸各种学术刊物。文化转向为翻译研究开辟了空前广阔的空间,拓宽了研究领域,在某种程度上提升了翻译学科的地位,使翻译研究成为一门多元化的跨学科领域。可是,正如有学者指出,"翻译学上文化这一环无边无际……现在方向是转了,眼下似乎很难深入下去。翻译学这部车在文化转向后速度似乎又慢了下来"(方梦之,2006)。可能是由于文化研究在过去十几年气势恢宏,以致令有些文化学者对语言学翻译理论不屑一顾,甚至是"以咄咄逼人之势,向语言学派发起了猛攻",指责语言学翻译研究"只局限于较低的语言层次之内",斥语言学理论为"一种忽视翻译中译者的主体性和翻译过程涉及的文化因素的静态的、过时的理论"(李德超,2005)。例如,帕格诺尔(Pagnoulle)在评论韦努蒂(L. Venuti)的著作时说,"翻译研究不再局限于语言研究之中。那本奇怪的书居然还胆敢采用语言学观(语用学和语义学)。他这么做应该要先预告一声或道个歉"[转引自(Baker,2005)]。贝克指出,"书评者用'胆敢'一词,令整段文字充斥着学术威胁的气氛"(出处同上)。翻译研究中的两大流派——语言学派和文化学派——之间的分歧与争论由此可见一斑。

本文无意卷入此类争论,只想客观地了解世界其他国家和地区翻译研究的发展情况及专家对文化转向和语言学转向等问题的看法,希望能给我国读者传递一个客观的信息。因此,笔者参加了比利时"语言与翻译国际研讨会"并在会议期间访问了会议主办者万德维格(Willy Vandeweghe)和其中三位主题发言人诺德、切斯特曼和贝克。

2 会议概况

据会议组委会介绍,他们共收到80多篇论文,选中其中63篇,有55篇在会上宣读。严格的筛选制度使会议办得有质量、有特色。除主题发言外,还有分组发言,分组专题包括"认知"、"语料库"、"语篇"、"翻译的普遍特质"、"语言对比研究"、"口译及媒体翻译"等。在所有分组发言中,"认知"和"语料库"两组占大约一半,听众也最多。"认知"论文有约三分之一是关于TAP(有声思维资料)的实证研究的,而"语料库"组论文研究的对象则包括了译者风格、文化对比、语言对比、叙事手段等多种角度的研究。整个会议洋溢着非常浓厚的学术气氛。

3 学者专访

3.1 万德维格:语言学理论在翻译研究中的重要性不言而喻

首先接受访问的是此次会议主办机构的主要负责人万德维格教授。他是一位地道的语言学者:1983年获语言学博士学位,专长于荷兰语研究,也从事德、法、英语的比较研究,90年代开始通过语言学途径研究翻译,现为根特翻译学院负责人:

(以下Z代表访问者,V代表受访者。)

Z:教授,您组织此次会议的初衷是什么?

V:是希望把语言学者和翻译学者更紧密地联系在一起,令翻译研究更好地为翻译实践、为跨文化交际服务。

Z:您在会议征文里指出,"现在是重新审视翻译研究语言学转向(或回转)的有利之处的时候了"。此话引起我和我的朋友们的兴趣,请您说说您的看法好吗?

V:语言学,尤其是当代语言学,跟翻译研究有很多共同点,例如,两者都是逐渐走向了跨学科的研究,其视角都是从词法、句法扩大到文本分析、会话分析,从语言到语篇、语境、语用。语言学和翻译研究的另一共同点是,两者都乐于接受可能出现的新技术,并用于建立大型语料库来研究假设的问题。此外,认知途径也把两者联系起来,语言学家们利用认知理论已经取得很多成果,翻译研究者们也开始引入认知理论对翻译,尤其是对口译的过程进行研究。因此我们非常有必要认真总结一下语言学理论对翻译研究的作用。

Z:那么您本人如何看语言学转向或回转的问题呢? 您认为这个转向已经发生? 正在发生? 还是需要发生?

V:语言学回转到翻译研究早在90年代初就开始了。由于电脑的广泛应用,使个体和团体研究者们有可能利用大量的语料来研究各种平行文本。通过对大量原文和译文进行分析研究,我们可以更好地了解它们之间的关系以及译者在翻译过程中通常采取的措施:这种研究反过来也有助于翻译软件的改进与发展。目前,已有一些软件工具对译员颇有帮助,例如翻译记忆软件、词汇宝库、术语库等。

Z:我本人过去对比利时了解不多,本次会议的规模及质量让我对贵国刮目相看。请您介绍一下比利时翻译研究的情况好吗?

V:比利时是一个双语国家,大部分国民讲荷兰语和法语,也有一小部分地区讲德语,因此也可以说是三语国家吧。由于我们的首都布鲁塞尔地处欧盟的中心,因此从60年代就开始帮助欧盟培训译员了。比利时全国共有9个翻译学院(5个在德语地区,4个在法语地区)。这些学院原来只是专门培训译员,近年来纷纷跟当地的大学挂钩或合并,一是为了提高研究质量,拓宽研究范围,二是为了培养翻译研究生。本次会议就是我们翻译学院跟安特卫普大学合并后的学术活动之一。

Z:您对整体的翻译研究有什么展望?

V:随着欧盟的不断发展,世界全球一体化的进展,翻译的重要地位将越来越明显,翻译研究也随之增强。科学技术将在翻译工作和翻译研究中扮演越来越重要的角色,机器翻译和机助翻译将帮助我们分担部分重复性较高的艰巨工作:要提高机器翻译或翻译软件的质量,让译者更快更好更省力地完成翻译任务,就必须依靠可靠的语言学理论。因此,语言学理论在翻译研究中的重要性是不言而喻的。

3.2 诺德:翻译研究离不开语言及语言现象

第二位受访者是德国功能主义翻译学派的代表人物诺德(Christiane Nord)教授。她的著作《译有所为——功能翻译理论阐释》英、中文版已在我们国内出版并广被阅读,另一本代表作《翻译的文本分析模式——理论、方法及教学应用》修订版(2005)也即将在我国重印发行。笔者曾撰文评介过她的"功能加忠诚"理论(张美芳,2005),并应邀正在为她的新书写中文导读。

(以下 Z 代表访问者,N 代表受访者。)

Z:请谈谈您对翻译研究的文化转向和语言学转向的看法好吗?

N:过去的翻译研究一直都是以语言为焦点,甚至过分强调语言,文化转向拓宽了我们的视野。然而,从交际的本质来看,我们是需要语言的证据来证明文化的影响的。我认为,以文化为焦点的翻译研究从来都没有摒弃语言,因为语言是文化的组成部分。可以说,文化转向是研究者的视点从原来的自下而上转为自上而下,这同时也改变了人们对语言概念的认识。以前人们认为文本是指导与决定译者活动的主要因素,而现在人们认识到,译者及其他的文本使用者才是关键因素,因为是人决定如何按预定的目的进行翻译。过去说的"忠实"于原文的概念已被"忠诚于交际活动中的参与者"的概念所取代,这就是我说的转换或转向的一个例子。然而,无论是自下而上或是自上而下,翻译研究都离不开语言及语言现象。

Z:那您对目前翻译研究的状况如何评价呢?

N:我想,翻译研究经历了一个令人兴奋的时期之后,现在已经到了一个巩固的阶段:令人兴奋的时期我指的是过去 20 年,翻译学者们尝试引入各种相关学科的理论(例如解构主义、女性主义、后殖民主义等理论)研究翻译现象。据我观察,现在大家都有一种强烈的愿望,那就是要对专业翻译领域的翻译现象多做一些实证研究,包括文学翻译的和非文学翻译的研究。运用语料库进行研究是其中的一种方法,但我个人认为,语料库并不能解释翻译中非常复杂的现象,"人类分析者"是永远不可或缺的。此外,我也不认为近年流行的所谓的"普遍特质"(universals)研究会有什么特别的新发现。例如有研究证明"明晰化"(explicitation)即译文趋向于比原文更加明晰,似乎是翻译中的一种普遍现象。我认为这并不是什么新的发现。凡翻译必然包括阐释,原来陌生的东西、隐晦的表达,经阐释后就变得明晰,这是很自然的。

Z:如果请您对不同的翻译研究途径按主次顺序排列,您将如何排列呢?

N:我不会对它们进行排列。翻译研究的多样化确实令人惊讶,但是翻译研究的对象也确实是多样化的。据已有的研究结果显示,翻译研究的对象可能是翻译的参与者,其中包括译者及其社会角色的关系,也可以是翻译过程,其中涉及心理学、神经学等,还可以是过程的结果及其对目标语文化的影响。各种理论及方法都可能达到有意的研究结果,但是理论与方法必须经过验证才会有结果。

Z:您近年的研究兴趣、研究活动是什么?

N:近年来,除翻译教学(包括教材编撰、翻译评估与翻译批评)外,我主要的研究活动围绕着翻译规范及翻译惯例等论题进行。我最新的论著《德语和西班牙语之间如何有效地交际》(2003)是根据西-德平行文本小型语料库中所收集的实际使用中的例子进行比较分析的。分析工具是一种跨文化交际的功能模式,内含四个功能及其子功能。该模式可用于分析研究不同的语言对和文化对。我自己用它来做比较研究,对象包括德语、英语、法语和西班牙语,目的是探讨不同的语言如何实现各种交际功能。我已发表的几篇论文内容涉及学生用书中的交际元功能、广告正文的形式、同指、礼貌等。我目前对研究"寒暄功能"发生兴趣。寒暄功能指的是用于建立、维持、结束交际的话语形式及表达方式。寒暄交际可定义及形成交际各方之间的社会关系。在任何一种交际中,当指称、表情或感染功能尚未起作用时,寒暄功能就担当起开路先锋的角色。然而,无论是在语言学界还是在翻译学界,这方面的研究并不多见,因此我想在这方面从跨文化的角度做些探讨。

Z:您的著作《翻译的文本分析模式——理论、方法及教学应用》即将在中国发行了。能说说您当年为什么要研究设计"翻译的文本分析模式"吗?

N:那时我被安排在译员培训班教一门名为"文本分析与释义"的课程,我心里一直琢磨着应该教什么和如何教的问题。我想到,译员出去做翻译时,首先应该对要翻译的文本及其交际功能有所了解。于是,我开始阅读相关的文献,也因此开始了这方面的探讨。

Z:您的这本书在多大程度上受您的老师莱斯的影响呢?

N:莱斯当时是海德堡大学翻译学院英文系的主任,是她安排我教"文本分析与释义"这门课,令我有机会对此专题进行研究。但是可以说,书中的构思与理论并没有受她太多的影响。70年代中期是篇章语言学初露锋芒的时期,我阅读了此方面的很多论著,从中寻找灵感。此外,我先生是位神学家。他那时也开始借用篇章语言学的理论与方法研究《新约全书》。因此我们常常一起讨论,从而发展了现在的"翻译的文本分析模式"。

Z:您在您的教学中使用过这一模式吗? 如有的话,该模式在课堂上的效果如何?

N:事实上,此模式是在我教书的过程中,以及在跟学生的讨论中逐渐形成的。我在课堂上反复实验,不断改进,大约十年之后我才想到把它成书出版。

Z:您的两本书《翻译的文本分析》和《译有所为》之间有什么联系吗?

N:两者都是沿功能主义途径,而且都是以实际教学经验为基础,此外就没有什么联系了。《译有所为》(1997)是直接用英文写成的,目的是让英语读者了解德国目的论及其他功能主义理论在翻译教学中的应用,而《翻译的文本分析》(1998)则是用德文写的,目标读者是德国学生。后来很多同行朋友,尤其是南美的同行朋友们向我表示,他们希望能读到此书的英文版并在课堂上使用这个分析模式,因此我和我的朋友思芭路(Penelope Sparrow)把它翻译成英文出版。当然,书中一些教学法方面的概念(例如翻译问题、文学翻译分析模式等)也在《译有所为》中出现过,我也在《翻译的文本分析》的最新版(2005)中对这些经典的问题进行了修订。

3.3 切斯特曼:翻译研究要多种途径

第三位接受访问的是赫尔辛基大学教授切斯特曼(Andrew Chesterman)。他主编的《翻译理论精选》(1989)和与人合著的《路线图——翻译研究方法入门》成为很多研究生的必读书目;此外,《对比功能分析》(1998)、《翻译研究的实证研究方法》(2000a)、《翻译研究的因果模式》(2000b)等,也是人们常参阅的论著。

(以下Z代表访问者,C代表受访者。)

Z:您在会上的发言"相似性分析与翻译研究模式"充满了人生及做学问的哲理,请您再说说您的观点好吗?

C:有一些人想突出翻译的差异时就拼命排斥对相似性的研究,或反之。我认为,相似与差异是一对不可分割的语言现象,翻译研究需要把两者都放在焦点上。其实两者也不是可以绝对地划清界限的,相似性包含了偏离的相似和融合的相似。无论是研究相似性或相异性,我们都需要对两种语言进行描述、比较、分析。研究需要异同并存,融会贯通。这就是为什么我在发言中提出了一个以语言描述为基础的相似性分析的研究模式。

Z:您如何看待翻译研究的文化转向或语言学转向之说?

C:我不认为语言学途径曾经从翻译研究中消失过。文化转向引导人们关注了语言以外的东西,而不是代替了语言学研究途径。正如Maria Tymoczko曾多次指出的,我们需要两种途径。文化分析有助于解释语言的选择,而翻译中的语言特征又具有文化的意义。我认为语言学将继续处于翻译研究的文本中心位置,然而,若要探讨语言决策的结果及其原因,就要到语言学范围以外寻找答案了。

3.4 贝克:现代语言学对翻译研究的重要性从来也没有停止过

最后一位接受我访问的是贝克(Mona Baker)。我形容贝克是走在翻译研究最前锋的领军人物应该不会引起太多的争议。自1992年她的成名作《换言之——翻译教程》问世以来,她在翻译研究方面一直努力开拓,勇往直前。现在,只要我们打开她的个人网页,尤其是她专门为翻译研究者设计的翻译研究资源网站,就可以发现她对翻译研究的热忱与专业(见 http://www.monabaker.com/tsresource/)。她的新作《翻译与冲突——叙述途径》也即将问世,此书借用了社会语言学的各种理论及研究方法来研究翻译现象及政治、意识形态等很多方面的问题。她的论著体现了她深厚的语言学功底,也反映了她那些远远超越语言和语言学的关注点。我想,这正是我们有必要借鉴的。

(以下 Z 代表访问者,B 代表受访者。)

Z:我拜读过您的文章和专著,到英国访问过您,也听过您在几个国际会议上的发言,但我好像不曾听您说过"文化转向"、"语言学转向"的字眼。您对"转向"有何看法?

B:你说得对,我从来不热衷任何"转向",所谓的文化转向也好,语言学转向也罢,全是把翻译研究的多元化及其活力简单化。其实正是多元化及渗透在整个翻译研究领域的活力,使研究丰富多彩,视点多种多样。

Z:那您认为语言学途径是不是曾经在翻译研究界消失或被忽视呢?

B:现代语言学跟其他相关理论一样对翻译研究是非常重要的,这种重要性从来没有停止过,将来也不会停止。

Z:但是翻译研究界似乎仍然有些人对语言学途径有偏见,认为凡沿语言学途径研究翻译都只是关注词法、句法,视角太窄,而文化研究途径才能解释翻译的一切问题。您对这种看法有什么建议吗?

B:我认为,要消除这种简单化的观念就要彻底摒弃各种二分法:我曾在 CTIS 第一期论文集里发表了一篇文章论述这个问题,这篇文章后来被翻译成西班牙语再次发表。我在文章中提到,自上世纪七八十年代以来,从事语言学研究的学者们也在不断地拓宽自己的研究范围,挑战已有的研究方法与目标,把视点拓宽到语言学以外的其他领域。语言学领域最基本的研究目标是语言、语篇和话语,但在过去一段时期以来,语言学的研究对象已经从其内部机制拓宽到文本在真实世界中的评价、接受及效果等问题:例如,伊莲(Eelen, 2001)在一篇批评布朗和莱文森(Brown and Levinson)关于礼貌理论的文章中指出,"礼貌行为并不是用文字或非文字特性可以解释的,而是在于人们如何评价那一个行为"。又如,布力格斯(Briggs)在《语用研究中的语用冲突及暴力》一书的前言中指出,"被分析的语篇并非简单地表述冲突及暴力,语篇本身在构建暴力行为和形成其政治效果方面也起着重要的作用"。在近年的语言学文献中,类似这样的评述并不鲜见,其实这种情况也同样出现在翻译研究领域。换句话说,在翻译研究领域中,越来越多的人不再认为翻译只是被动地、静止地反映或重现某些社会规范和意识形态,而是认为翻译在构建社会、文化和意识形态方面也起着重要的作用。因此可以说,语言学和翻译研究是两个紧密相关的学科,语言学者和翻译学者们在这方面有着共同的研究目标与兴趣,他们的共同兴趣也反映了不同学科领域都在乎自身对所处社会文化环境的作用。

Z:您在会上发表的论文《在翻译中重构叙述》("Reframing Narratives in Translation")是尝试运用社会语言学的建构理论及其方法,研究译者如何处理原文中带有争议性论题的叙述,用于分析的例子全部来自西方对中东地区,尤其是伊拉克战争的报道及翻译。在我看来,您的研究模式与方法是地地道道的社会语言学理论模式及方法,但从您所分析的例子来看,您实际上是在研究政治或意识形态问题,是吗?

B:你说得对,我用的是社会语言学理论和方法,举的例子是涉及政治及意识形态方面的,但是我希望这个分析模式可用来分析研究所有的翻译现象。翻译本身是一种意识形态的活动,但是研究意识形态不能空谈。好比说"打仗就是要用武力解决纷争"。然而,如果我们不研究打胜仗要根据具体情况使用什么武器,只是高谈阔论打仗的重要性,那又有什么意义呢?你怎么能给后人留下可借鉴的经验呢?

Z:您的意思是,研究文化差异、政治、意识形态等问题都要从语言入手,对吗?

B:是的,因为文化差异、政治问题、意识形态问题以及后殖民等问题都是要通过语言来体现的,因而借用现代语言学理论,建构翻译研究所形成的分析模式是非常有必要的。

Z:在这次会议中,很多与会者的论文是涉及认知和语料库两种研究途径的。您如何评价这两种途径对翻译研究的作用呢?

B:两种途径都可以帮助我们有效地发展各种研究方法,从不同的角度考察翻译的过程及产品。我在 CTIS 的文章中提到,发展研究方法是非常重要的。如何将研究者的主观性在研究中减到最低,也是目前我们关心的问题,这实际上是方法论的问题。要使研究结果令人信服,我们的研究就需要有非常明确的方法,而不是用主观的、随意的、点评的方式来评述所研究的现象。同时,我们也要认识到,真正做到客观也是不可能的,因为研究话语比研究语言结构更会出现主观性——分析的过程给研究者更多操作的空间。

Z:您认为目前翻译研究的形势如何?

B:我认为,翻译研究正在卓有成效地引人注目,世界开始对翻译研究刮目相看,世界各地大学的翻译课程的迅速增长、各种媒体对翻译相关问题的报道以及译者积极参与各种事件(例如关塔那摩湾事件)等都是最好的证明。美国的爱国主义条例中也有一整句是关于翻译的。

Z:能透露您近期的研究计划吗?

B:参与更多的笔译和口译者协会活动,例如继续关注笔译和口译中语言选择所反映的政治问题,通过成立诸如 IATIS(www.Iatis.org)那样的组织及活动,挑战翻译领域中以欧洲为中心的观念。

4　综述:重新审视现代语言学理论在翻译研究中的作用

以上所记录的几位专家在访谈中表达的部分观点印证了我们大多数人对翻译研究的理解:第一,翻译研究是个多元化的领域,正是多元化使翻译学科朝气蓬勃,充满生机。第二,翻译研究与现代语言学有很多共通点,两者都逐渐走向跨学科研究,研究目标从语言、语篇、语用到话语,研究对象拓宽到文本在真实世界中的评价、接受及效果等问题。第三,语言学和翻译研究都乐于接受新技术,并用于建立大型语料库来研究假设的问题,包括重新审视现代语言学理论在翻译研究中的作用问题,包括利用语料库和认知理论来研究语言使用者翻译者在工作中的思维过程。第四,语言学途径和文化途径研究的视点虽然各有不同,但是两者并非各走各路,而是你中有我,我中有你,相互联系且互相弥补。不过,贝克直率的话语也令我们耳目一新,那就是,她从来不认同“文化转向”、“语言学转向”之说,因为这种“二分法”会把翻译研究的多元化及其活力简单化。她的说法打破了很多人一贯的思维方式,否定了很多人已认同的“文化转向”与“语言学转向”的概念,听起来颇有些“解构转向”的味道。如果观察贝克本人近年来的研究,尤其是最近的新作,我们不得不相信,她一直在努力尝试把语言学理论及其研究方法与翻译研究中的文化概念结合起来,而不是力图去区分或分化它们。她的观点是,要研究文化差异、政治问题、意识形态问题以及后殖民等问题,都离不开语言,因为所有这些问题都是要通过语言来体现的。因此借用现代语言学理论,建构翻译研究所需的分析模式是非常有必要的。贝克这一观点实际上也是以上几位受访者的观点。几位教授都认为,翻译研究发展到今天,虽然已经取得很显著的成果,但是也面临着一些需要解决的问题:① 要对专业翻译领域的翻译现象(包括文学的与非文学的翻译产品和翻译过程)多做一些实证研究;② 要发展有效的研究模式及方法。实证研究及发展有效的研究模式和方法是翻译研究领域目前面临的两大课题。但是,究竟什么样的理论模式及其方法适用于翻译研究? 翻译学是一门年轻的学科,又是一门开放性、综合性的学科,需要借助相关学科的理论与研究成果来加强与发展自己的学术领域及研究方法。贝克在十几年前就指出,“语言学,尤其是现代语言学,与翻译学的关系息息相关。因为语言学不再限定于研究语言本身,而是欣然接受一些子学科,例如语篇语言学(把文本视为交际活动而不是一串串一定形式的文字与结构)和语用学(研究语言的使用而不是把语言作为一个抽象的系统)。翻译工作者要研究语言,了解语言的基本结构,明白语言如何在实际中运作,就可更清楚语言的本质及其功能。”哈提姆也提醒我们,“几乎是在文化转向的同时,语言学领域也发生‘语境转向’(contextual turn)。到 80 年代中期,语言学家已进入语篇的语境研究,并思考这一转向对翻译研究的启示。”翻译研究是一个跨学科的多元化的领域,需要有多种途径,建立多种研究模式。纽伯特和舒勒弗(A. Neubert & G. Shreve)对翻译研究做过一个生动的比喻,他们说,“我们坚信,翻译好比‘一间屋子里有很多房间’,不同房间里的人往往是从不同的视角用不同的话语对共同感兴趣的话题——翻译——进行评述”(Hartim,2001:8)。“不同的视角”意味着不同的思想方式及意识形态,而“用不同的话语……进行评述”就是用语言来表现不同的思想方式及意识形态。由此可见,无论是翻译操作还是翻译研究,语言学理论都是非常重要的。很多翻译研究者在运用语言学理论方面已经做了大量工作,诺德和贝克就是其中的佼佼者。

诺德的《翻译的文本分析模式——理论、方法及教学应用》和贝克的《换言之——翻译教程》问世以来,一直受到读者的欢迎,原因之一就是她们善于利用语言学理论建立翻译研究模式与方法。诺德的《翻译的文本分析模式》以篇章语言学和语言哲学为主要理论基础,把语篇定义为一种交际活动,可以通过语言的和非语言的因素来实现。因此,诺德的文本分析模式包含的是翻译过程中涉及的几个重要因素:顾客或发起人、译者、目标文本、目标接受者、目标语、原文、源语、原文作者、原文发送者和源语文化。这些语言的和非语言的因素使诺德的《翻译的文本分析模式》不同于一般的文本分析模式,从而成为翻译教学与研究的一个可借鉴的模式。

贝克的《换言之——翻译教程》中运用多种语言学研究模式，例如克鲁斯(Cruse,1986)的语义分类，韩礼德(Halliday,1978)的语域理论、主位/信息结构理论、衔接及连贯理论，格莱斯的会话原则等来建构适用于分析研究翻译问题的模式。她的书之所以一直热销到现在，成为很多大学翻译研究生的必读书，我相信主要原因是她引进的理论框架及分析模式被广大读者认同及仿效。如果说她的成名作主要是探讨翻译所涉及的文本内部及其语境因素的话，那么她另一部即将问世的新作《翻译与冲突——叙述途径》则是借用了社会语言学中的建构理论研究翻译文本在真实世界中的评价、接受及效果等问题，涉及文本以外的社会、政治、意识形态、译者意识等各种研究对象。

第二章　语言对比与翻译研究

导　论

语言对比与翻译的关系是显而易见的。

首先,语言对比离不开翻译。虽然西方对比学界在 20 世纪 80 年代以前几乎忌谈翻译,他们喜欢使用一个对比中间项(tertium comparationis)作为两种语言的比较基础,但正如潘文国教授所指出的那样,任何对比,本质上都是一种潜在的翻译(potential translation)。两个毫不相干的项目是无法进行比较的,不管是形式、意义,还是功能、风格,其实都是在潜意识里先进行了翻译,然后才能拿过来比较。因此有学者明确提出,要观察对比语言学是如何工作的,一个有效的方法是通过翻译。翻译被看成语言学的一个分支。卡特福德的《翻译的语言学理论》是第一部从语言学的角度来研究翻译的专著,甚至可以说是第一部关于翻译问题的专著。这部作品以系统功能语言学理论为基础,全面系统地讨论翻译问题。当然,卡特福德首先是个语言学家,他研究翻译的目的是以语言为目的的,把翻译看成比较语言学的一个分支(1965)。

反过来,对比对于翻译的意义就更加重要了。要开展翻译研究,一定不能离开语言学的理论支持,而在与翻译学邻近的语言学学科里,没有比对比语言学与翻译的关系更密切的了。正是在对比的基础上,人们才可以谈论所谓的"对应"、"对等"乃至"转换"。

加拿大学者维内和达贝尔内合著的《法英比较文体学:翻译方法论》一书,从词汇、句法结构、信息这三个平面对法语和英语做了全面、细致的比较和分析,详尽地区分了翻译方法和翻译过程,对西方翻译教学与研究有相当深远的影响,开启了以翻译为目的的语言对比研究的先河。

奈达是翻译研究领域很有成就的翻译理论家,他提出的"形式对应"、"动态对等"以及后来的"功能对等"等概念都成为翻译理论家的核心概念。而这些概念的提出无疑受到过美国著名语言学家乔姆斯基(Norm Chomsky)提出的关于语言的"表层结构"和"深层结构"的观念的影响。根据乔姆斯基的观点,句子的结构可以分为表层结构和深层结构,我们实际听到的句子的形式或是说话时发出的声音都是语言的表层结构,而说话者试图表达的意图构成句子的深层结构。奈达简化了乔姆斯基的理论,将之用于翻译理论。不同之处在于,奈达将其用于原文与译文之间的转换。他认为翻译不应该受到语言表面形式的束缚,应该努力传达出原文句子的实际意义或意图。他的这个观点实际上也是在语言对比的基础上提出来的。奈达之后,英国的纽马克(P. Newmark)提出了 Semantic Translation 和 Communicative Translation 的概念,德国的赖斯(K. Reiss)等人提出了根据文本类型来确定翻译方法的观点也都离不开文本对比这个比较的基础。而最先由卡特福德提出的 shift(转换)的概念更是语言对比的产物。通过语言对比，发现译文与原文在各个语言层次上的转换，即不对等的情况。

因此，在本章和接下来的一章中，我们将主要介绍维内和达贝尔内、奈达、赖斯、卡特福德的经典之作，介绍后继学者在继续研究"转换"的过程中所产生的研究成果，在"文化转向"之后，"对等"的概念颇受质疑，而"转换"这个概念则成为一个备受关注的概念，成为文化途径学者的研究热点。他们首先找出译作与原作在各个语言层次上的"转换"，然后从社会学、历史学和政治学等角度出发进行分析，并尝试给出自己的解释，大大拓展了翻译研究的角度与空间。

选文一 翻译与对比语言学

潘文国

导 言

作者潘文国为华东师范大学教授，中国英汉比较研究会会长，在汉英对比语言学和翻译研究领域都有广泛的涉猎和深入的研究，因而对于对比语言学与翻译研究之间的关系最有发言权。这里的这篇文章于2007年1月发表在《上海大学学报》（社会科学版）第一期上，在这一章的开头引用这篇文章，希望读者能够在这里对对比语言学与翻译研究的关系首先有一个提纲挈领式的了解。

在与翻译学邻近的学科里，大约没有比对比语言学与之关系更密切的了，对于汉外翻译来说尤其如此。许多研究生的专业方向就是对比与翻译研究，中国英汉语比较研究会的系列丛书名称就叫"英汉语比较与翻译"，已经出版了六集。不少对比研究者同时是翻译研究者，反之亦然。例如中国的刘宓庆、陈定安、杨自俭、邵志洪，国外的哈特曼（Reinhard R. K. Hartmann）、斯奈尔-杭贝（Mary Snell-Hornby）、切斯特曼（Andrew Chesterman）、哈蒂姆（Basil Hatim）等。但是我们也必须看到，对于更多的对比语言学研究者以及翻译研究与实践者来说，这两者似乎还是相距颇为遥远的两门学科，搞翻译的认为对比语言学研究不切实用的，或者搞对比的认为翻译的材料不足为据的，还大有人在。后面一种人还更多一些。因此，谈谈翻译与对比研究的关系还是很有必要的。有三个问题值得讨论。

第一，翻译与对比研究是否仅仅是理论与实践的关系？

认为翻译与对比研究无关或者关系不大的人有一个误解，即认为两者仅是理论与实践的关系。或者认为对比研究属于语言学的范围，是研究理论的，而翻译是具体处理语言应用的，是搞实践的;或者认为对比研究关心的是理论体系问题,而翻译要解决的是非常现实的字、词、句、段的处理问题;或者搬出索绪尔的术语,认为对比研究关心的是语言的问题,而翻译要解决的是言语问题。以上种种认识折射出的问题有两个是值得我们思考的:① 从抽象的层面看,把理论与实践两分,搞理论的不关心实践,或搞实践的不关心理论是不是合适? 搞对比的是否可以自认为在搞理论而不关注翻译等实践方面的需要,而搞翻译的自以为经验最重要而不关注理论方面的进展? ② 从具体的层面看,是否对比研究所涉及的就只是语言学的理论问题,而翻译研究所涉及的就只是语言应用的实践问题? 对比研究和翻译研究自身有没有理论与实践之分? 需要不需要有理论与实践之分? 叶斯柏森对索绪尔的批评也许可以对我们有所启示,他批评索绪尔的语言和言语之分。有人认为“语言”相当于理论,“言语”相当于实践,且认为语言和言语各有其理论与实践。同样,对比研究与翻译研究也各有其理论与实践。这样,对比研究与翻译研究之间就是一个错综复杂的关系:对比研究的理论可以对翻译研究的理论产生影响,也可以对翻译的实践产生影响;同样,翻译的理论研究可以对对比的理论研究产生影响,也可以对对比的应用研究产生影响。这种新的认识可以使我们对这两门学科之间的关系有一个新的理解。

第二,翻译与对比研究的关系如何定位?

那么,这两门学科之间到底是个什么样的关系呢? 曾经有学者说过,对比语言学是翻译的理论基础,而翻译是对比语言学的服务对象。很长时期我们都持这样的看法。现在看来,这一说法是欠妥当的。这无意中抬高了对比语言学的地位而贬低了翻译学的地位,对翻译学是不公正的。同时,这也是上面所说的“理论”、“实践”关系的翻版,不利于两门学科各自的建设和发展。如果从承认两者都具有独立学科地位的角度出发,我们应该对两者的关系有一个更高层次的思考。切斯特曼,一位身兼翻译理论家和对比语言学家身份的芬兰学者,在他的《功能对比分析》(*Functional Contrastive Analysis*,1998)一书里对两者关系做了比较深入的探索,可说是研究这一关系的最新成果。从他的研究我们可以看出,翻译和对比研究的关系,不仅仅在于它们研究的对象都是两种或两种以上的语言,还有更深层次的共同性。亦即,首先,无论在理论或在应用层面,它们都对两种语言的异同问题感兴趣,甚至可以说,都是专门处理语言异同问题的学科:对比语言学要面对相距或近或远的语言,解释同—异—同的问题,特别是同中之异、异中之同、个别与一般、普遍与特殊这些理论问题,而为外语教学、跨语言交际、语际翻译、双语辞典编纂等提供理论支撑;翻译学也要在理论特别是实践层面,处理和解决跨语言、跨文化交际问题。其次,翻译研究和对比研究,有一个共同的基础。这个基础,以前叫做 equivalence,有人译成“等值”,有人译成“等效”,也有人译成“对等”,这主要是从翻译研究角度提出的术语;后来对比语言学界有人提出 tertium comparationis,我把它译成“对比中立项”;现在又有人提出一个术语 starting point,“出发点”,我个人比较赞同。无论是 equivalence,还是 tertium comparationis,还是 starting point,都有过很多讨论,其中 equivalence 翻译界讨论得多一点,tertium comparationis 对比语言学界讨论得多一点,而且不同时期、不同人、不同学派所指的内容和侧重点都不一样。譬如有的指结构,有的指功能,有的指意义等。对翻译研究和对比语言学的发展也各自产生了不同的影响。但两门学科有个共同的基础,使两者之间的关系比别的学科之间要亲近许多。最后,这两个学科还有个共同的目标,简言之,可说是“化异为同”、“异中求同”。翻译学不用说,翻译本身就是在不同语言、不同文化间建立沟通的桥梁;对比语言学从表面上来看是强调求异(这就使它与比较语言学区别开来),但求异本身不是这一学科的根本目标,对比语言学的根本目的也是要通过求异的研究,最终在不同语言、不同文化间建立沟通的桥梁。因为求异不是为了使不同的语言变得更加遥远、更加不可互相理解,而是为了更好地寻找共同存在的基础。由于"对比研究"与"翻译研究"有这么多共同基础,因此有人说,从某种角度看,对比分析和翻译理论简直是可以互换的术语。(Contrastive Analysis and Translation Theory are in some respects terminological variants of each other.)

但是,当然,这两者还是不可互换的。因为在有共同点的同时,它们也有着各自不可取代的特点。除了尽管各有理论和实践的追求,但是在人们的印象中,一个似乎对理论的关注更多一点,另一个似乎更强调理论要运用到实践上之外,并且更在于方法论上。切斯特曼创造了两个术语,一个叫 divergent(我译作从合到分),一个叫 convergent(我译作从分到合)。前者是分离性的,一个原文文本可以产生不同的译文文本(即使只有一个译文文本,加上原文也有了两个文本);后者是聚合性的,从不同语言的语言事实出发,最终要找到统一合理的解释。他还使用了传统的 type(类)和 token(例)两个术语,说翻译研究是从 type 到 tokens 的过程,而对比研究是从 tokens 到 type 的过程。我们认为这个理解比较符合这两个学科的实际,也比较符合现代翻译学和现代对比语言学发展的精神。从翻译学来说,现在已没有人追求以往那种唯一、等值的译本,不同译本的存在是必然的事,因而翻译过程的本质是 selection 或者说选择,确实像一种发散性的过程;而对比语言学要透过纷繁复杂的语言事实,寻找对人类语言共性的合理解释,确实也具有汇合的性质。

综上所述,我们可以给这两个学科的关系下这么一句断语:这两门学科具有共同的基础、共同的性质,还有共同的追求目标,但是在方法论上有着明显的差别,可以起到互补的作用。

第三,翻译与对比研究的最新发展各自对对方产生什么影响?

说到翻译和对比研究的关系,我们还必须关注这两门学科新近的发展,我们发现,两门学科近年来的最新发展,使它们的关系变得更密切、更贴近了。如果说在以前特别是在国外,翻译研究和对比研究还被视为互不相干的两门学科的话,现在双方却越来越关注对方的存在和对本方的意义了。在翻译和对比学界,还有不少人习惯用老眼光去看对方,总觉得对方的研究与己无关。在翻译学者眼里,对比研究还停留在六七十年代为二语教学服务,而又做得不很成功,后来被偏误分析取代的阶段;而在对比学者眼里,翻译似乎总是囿于讨论直译、意译,或者信、达、雅、形似、神似的范围,因而总是看不到对方的发展,也看不到己方能从对方的发展中汲取什么东西。殊不知 20 世纪 80 年代以来,这两个领域的研究都发生了翻天覆地的变化,与往日早已不可同日而语了。这两个互邻互补的学科,正可以从对方的发展中,找到自己进一步发展的动力。

翻译研究的发展大体经过了语言学派、文艺学派、文化学派、解构主义和后殖民主义几个阶段。其最重要的成果是,原文的权威被消解了,唯一的译本不再存在,译入语的社会、文化以及译文读者受到了前所未有的重视,译者的主体性得到了肯定,翻译过程变成了一个开放、选择的过程,翻译成了多元文化建设的重要手段,等等。这一切对对比研究的冲击其实一点不亚于对翻译界自身的冲击。我们知道,西方对比学界在 80 年代以前几乎是忌谈翻译的,这是他们爱用 tertium comparationis 这个术语的原因;中国的一些对比学者虽不忌讳,但总觉得翻译作为对比的基础是不可靠的,[①]但他们却不肯承认或者说隐蔽了一个事实,即任何对比得以进行的基础,不管是叫 equivalence 也好,tertium comparationis 也好,starting point 也好,本质上都是一种 potential translation(潜在的翻译)。两个毫不相干的项目是无法进行比较的,不管是形式、意义、还是功能、风格，其实都是在潜意识里先进行了翻译然后才能拿过来比较。如果说，以前翻译对于对比的影响在于采用不同的翻译单位和翻译方法，[②]其基础是对一种完全对应的翻译的相信；那么现在否定了有完全对等的翻译，在此基础上的对比语言学理论也必然会发生重大变化。

同样，对比语言学在 20 多年来也发生了重大变化，它再也不是早先那种在结构主义语言学基础上进行形式对比，相信可以用这个办法找出第二语言学习重点、难点的幼稚的对比分析，也不是其后在转换生成语法指导下建立在共同的深层结构基础上的表层所谓"对比"。自 20 世纪 80 年代以后，在西方，对比研究经过了纵向（由句子扩展到篇章）、横向（由句法分析发展到话语分析、语用分析），[③]以及外向（即上述的纵向、横向）、内向（进入语言使用者的心理）[④]的拓展，不仅在理论上吸收了篇章语言学、话语语言学、社会语言学、心理语言学、认知语言学等的成果，在应用范围上也早已突破二语教学的狭窄天地，主动与翻译相结合。尤其是，对比语言学对于对比研究的一个核心概念相似性（similarity）的哲学探索，使他们找到了对比与翻译研究的更深层的共同性；对比语言学所说的"相似性"，也就是翻译理论探讨的"可译性"。对比语言学最新的相似性理论认为，相似性是个相对的概念，相似性既属于逻辑世界、社会世界、又属于认知世界；相似既有客观性，又有主观性；对相似性的判断归根到底是人们心中对世界的认识的重新理解和整合；相似性不只涉及两方或三方，而是涉及多方，说 A 与 B 相似，实则是说，A 与 B 在 C 的方面，根据 D 程序的比较，参照 E 标准的判断，根据 F 功能，为了 G 目的，两者是相似的（When we say that A is similar to B, what we really mean is that A is similar to B in respects C according to comparison process D, relative to some standard E mapped onto judgments by some function F for some purpose.）；还有，看出某两件事物是否相似归根到底是想象力的问题，因而判断事物是否相似的能力是人类认知的核心；等等。由于对比研究中的相似性就是翻译理论中的可译性，因而上述种种见解，也可能对翻译研究产生深刻的影响，使我们能更好地解释翻译的相对性、开放性、主体间性、多种译本和多种翻译风格的可能性，等等。

而 20 世纪 90 年代中国的对比研究走得比西方还要远。由于汉语与西方语言的巨大差异，汉外对比似乎更适合美国语言学家沃尔夫当初倡议建立对比语言学的初衷，即通过对比相距遥远的语言，旨在研究不同语言在语法、逻辑和对经验的一般分析上的重大区别。在西方，不论是欧洲还是美国，由于其所使用的语言均属均质印欧语（Standard Average European）[⑤]的历史背景，很难体会和验证沃尔夫所说的语言相对论以及在此基础上建立的对比语言学，而汉语恰好符合了这一条件。因而对比语言学在中国得到了更广泛的重视和更全面的发展，也形成了中国对比语言学不同于西方对比语言学的一些特点。例如更强调对比研究的哲学基础（语言世界观），更强调通过对比发掘汉语的特色，对比研究有三个层面（表层：结构；中层：表达法；深层：语言心理和语言哲学）的思想，等等。这一些对语言，特别是对汉语本质的新认识，无疑也促进了翻译，特别是汉外互译理论和实践的新发展。例如从"均质印欧语"的理解出发，我们就很能体会到印欧语内部各种语言间的翻译，与汉语和印欧语之间的互译，是两种不同的实践，因而也就需要不同的理论。这一认识反过来又会促使我们正确理解和对待从西方引进的各种现代化的翻译理论，决定我们的取舍。

总之，翻译学和对比语言学看来是两门难分难舍的兄弟学科，我们要关心彼此的发展，善于利用对方学科取得的成果和经验，这样一定能更好地促进自身学科的发展。

注：
1. 王力(1944;1945:5)就明确指出这一点,说一切的对译都是不能帮助词性或用途的确定的。
2. 如 Krzeszowski(1990:19)主张在逐字直译的基础上进行对比,而王力因为害怕意译会造成形式不对应而反对翻译。
3. Carl James(1980)的用语。
4. Andrew Chesterman(1988)的用语。
5. 沃尔夫用语,见 Whorf(1939:138)。

选文二　Comparative Stylistics of French and English:
A Methodology for Translation

Jean-Paul Vinay　Jean Darbelnet

导　言

　　维内和达贝尔内是加拿大学者,1958 年出版了他们合作完成的《法英比较文体学:翻译方法论》,原文是用法语写成的,后由 J. Sager 和 M.-J. Hamel 翻译成英文,于 1995 年在约翰·本雅明出版社出版。这是第一部以翻译为目的的法英比较文体学专著,在翻译研究领域占有非常重要的地位。作者采用描写的手段,总结了法语和英语两种语言在翻译转换过程中常用的翻译方法。首先,翻译的方法被粗略地分为两种:直接翻译(direct translation)和间接翻译(oblique translation),而直接翻译和间接翻译又分别由不同的翻译方法组成。他们所总结出来的这些方法并不仅仅局限于英法翻译研究,还可以广泛用于多种语言对之间的转换描述,直到现在仍然有借鉴价值。

Generally speaking, translators can choose from two methods of translating, namely direct (or literal) translation and oblique translation. In some translation tasks it may be possible to transpose the source language message element by element into the target language, because it is based on either (i) parallel categories, in which case we can speak of structural parallelism, or (ii) on parallel concepts, which are the result of metalinguistic parallelisms. But translators may also notice gaps, or "lacunae," in the TL which must be filled by corresponding elements, so that the overall impression is the same for the two messages.

It may, however, also happen that, because of structural or metalinguistic differences, certain stylistic effects cannot be transposed into the TL without upsetting the syntactic order, or even the lexis. In this case it is understood that more complex methods have to be used which at first may look unusual but which nevertheless can permit translators a strict control over the reliability of their work: these procedures are called oblique translation methods. In the listing which follows, the first three procedures are direct and the others are oblique.

Procedure 1: Borrowing

To overcome a lacuna, usually a metalinguistic one (e. g. a new technical process, an unknown concept), borrowing is the simplest of all translation methods. It would not even merit discussion in this context if translators did not occasionally need to use it in order to create a stylistic effect. For instance, in order to introduce the flavour of the SL culture into a translation, foreign terms may be used, e. g. such Russian words as "roubles," "datchas" and "apparatchik," "dollars" and "party" from American English, Mexican Spanish food names "tequila" and "tortillas," and so on. [...]

Procedure 2: Calque

A calque is a special kind of borrowing whereby a language borrows an expression form of another, but then translates literally each of its elements. The result is either

i. a lexical calque, as in the first example below, i. e. a calque which respects the syntactic structure of the TL, whilst introducing a new mode of expression; or

ii. a structural calque, as in the second example, below, which introduces a new construction into the language, e. g.

English-French calque

Compliments of the Season: Compliments de la saison!

Science-fiction: Science-fiction

Procedure 3: Literal Translation

Literal (or word for word) translation is the direct transfer of an SL text into a grammatically and idiomatically appropriate TL text in which the translators' task is limited to observing the adherence to the linguistic servitudes of the TL.

I left my spectacles on the table: J'ai laisse mes lunettes sur la table en bas.

If, after trying the first three procedures, translators regard a literal translation [as] unacceptable, they must turn to the methods of oblique translation. By unacceptable we mean that the message, when translated literally:

i. gives another meaning

ii. has no meaning, or

iii. is structurally impossible, or

iv. does not have a corresponding expression within the metalinguistic experience of the TL, or

v. has a corresponding expression, but not within the same register.

Procedure 4: Transposition

The method called transposition involves replacing one word class with another without changing the meaning of the message. Beside being a special translation procedure, transposition can also be applied within a language. For example, "*Il a annoncé qu'il reviendrait*" [*He announced he would return*], can be re-expressed by transposing a subordinate verb with a noun, thus: "Il a annoncé son retour" [He announced his return].

In contrast to the first expression, which we call the base expression, we refer to the second one as the transposed expression. From a stylistic point of view, the base and the transposed expression do not necessarily have the same value. Translators must, therefore, choose to carry out a transposition if the translation thus obtained fits better the utterance or allows a particular nuance of style to be retained. Indeed, the transposed form is generally more literary in character.

Procedure 5: Modulation

Modulation is a variation of the form of the message, obtained by a change in the point of view. This change can be justified when, although a literal, or even transposed, translation results in a grammatically correct utterance, it is considered unsuitable, unidiomatic or awkward in the TL.

As with transposition, we distinguish between free or optional modulation and those which are fixed or obligatory. A classical example of an obligatory modulation is the phrase, "The time when ... " which must be translated as "*le moment où ...* " [*the moment where ...*]. The type of modulation which turns a negative SL expression into a positive TL expression is more often than not optional, even though this is closely linked with the structure of each language, e. g.

It is not difficult to show ... : Il est facile de demontrer ...

[lit. It is easy to show ...]

Procedure 6: Equivalence

We have repeatedly stressed that one and the same situation can be rendered by two texts using completely different stylistic and structural methods. In such cases we are dealing with the method which produces equivalent texts. The classical example of equivalence is given by the reaction of an amateur who accidentally hits his finger with a hammer: if he were French his cry of pain would be transcribed as "Aie!" but if he were English this would be interpreted as "Ouch!"

Most equivalences are fixed and belong to a phraseological repertoire of idioms, cliches, proverbs, nominal or adjectival phrases, etc. In general, proverbs are perfect examples of equivalences, e. g.

Like a bull in a china shop: Comme un chien dans un jeu de quilles.

[lit. *Like a dog in a game of skittles*]

Too many cooks spoil the broth: Deux patrons font chavirer la barque.

[lit. *Two skippers make the boat capsize*]

The method of creating equivalences is also frequently applied to idioms. For example, "To talk through one's hat" and "as like as two peas" cannot be translated by means of a calque.

Procedure 7: Adaptation

With this seventh method we reach the extreme limit of translation: it is used in those cases where the type of situation being referred to by the SL message is unknown in the TL culture. In such cases translators have to create a new situation that can be considered as being equivalent. Adaptation can, therefore, be described as a special kind of equivalence, a situational equivalence. [They] are particularly frequent in the translation of book and film titles, e. g.

Trois hommes et un couffin: Three Men and a Baby

[*Three men and a Moses basket*]

Le grand Meaulne: The Wanderer

[The Big *Meaulne* a character's name]

选文三　Principles of Correspondence

Eugene Nida

导　言

奈达(November 11, 1914—August 25, 2011),美国学者,师从几位著名的结构主义语言大师,本身也是地位重要的语言学家,曾任美国语言学会主席。他在年纪很轻的时候就成为一名基督徒,1936 年加州大学毕业后加入威克理夫跨文化宣教营,接触到圣经翻译理论。

他在美国圣经协会供职半个多世纪,主要学术活动都围绕《圣经》翻译展开。在《圣经》翻译的过程中,奈达从实际出发,发展出了一套自己的翻译理论,最终成为翻译研究的经典理论。奈达理论的核心概念是"对等"。所谓"动态对等"或是"功能对等",都强调在翻译时不求文字表面的死板对应,而要在两种语言间达成功能上的对等。本文见于1964年奈达发表的专著《翻译科学探索》的第八章,是翻译理论界的经典之作。

Since no two languages are identical, either in the meanings given to corresponding symbols or in the ways in which such symbols are arranged in phrases and sentences, it stands to reason that there can be no absolute correspondence between languages. Hence there can be no fully exact translations. The total impact of a translation may be reasonably close to the original, but there can be no identity in detail. Constance B. West (1932: 344) clearly states the problem: "Whoever takes upon himself to translate contracts a debt, to discharge it, he must pay not with the same money, but the same sum." One must not imagine that the process of translation can avoid a certain degree of interpretation by the translator. In fact, as D. G. Rossetti stated in 1874 (Fang, 1953), "A translation remains perhaps the most direct form of commentary."

Different Types of Translations

No statement of the principles of correspondence in translating can be complete without recognizing the many different types of translations (Herbert P. Phillips, 1959). Traditionally, we have tended to think in terms of free or paraphrastic translations as contrasted with close or literal ones. Actually, there are many more grades of translating than these extremes imply. There are, for example, such ultra-literal translations as interlinears; while others involve highly concordant relationships, e. g. the same source-language word is always translated by one—and only one—receptor-language word. Still others may be quite devoid of artificial restrictions in form, but nevertheless may be over traditional and even archaizing. Some translations aim at very close formal and semantic correspondence, but are generously supplied with notes and commentary. Many are not so much concerned with giving information as with creating in the reader something of the same mood as was conveyed by the original.

Differences in translations can generally be accounted for by three basic factors in translating: (1) the nature of the message, (2) the purpose or purposes of the author and, by proxy, of the translator, and (3) the type of audience.

Messages differ primarily in the degree to which content or form is the dominant consideration. Of course, the content of a message can never be completely abstracted from the form, and form is nothing apart from content; but in some messages the content is of primary consideration, and in others the form must be given a higher priority. For example, in the Sermon on the Mount, despite certain important stylistic qualities, the importance of the message far exceeds considerations of form. On the other hand, some of the acrostic poems of the Old Testament are obviously designed to fit a very strict formal "strait jacket." But even the contents of a message may differ widely in applicability to the receptor language audience. For example, the folk tale of the Bauré Indians of Bolivia, about a giant who led the animals in a symbolic dance, is interesting to an English speaking audience, but to them it has not the same relevance as the Sermon on the Mount. And even the Bauré Indians themselves recognize the Sermon on the Mount as more significant than their favorite "how-it-happened" story. At the same time, of course, the Sermon on the Mount has greater relevance to these Indians than have some passages in Leviticus.

In poetry there is obviously a greater focus of attention upon formal elements than one normally finds in prose. Not that content is necessarily sacrificed in translation of a poem, but the content is necessarily constricted into certain formal molds. Only rarely can one reproduce both content and form in a translation, and hence in general the form is usually sacrificed for the sake of the content. On the other hand, a lyric poem translated as prose is not an adequate equivalent of the original. Though it may reproduce the conceptual content, it falls far short of reproducing the emotional intensity and flavour. However, the translating of some types of poetry by prose may be dictated by important cultural considerations. For example, Homer's epic poetry reproduced in English poetic form usually seems to us antique and queer—with nothing of the liveliness and spontaneity characteristic of Homer's style. One reason is that we are not accustomed to having stories told to us in poetic form. In our Western European tradition such epics are related in prose. For this reason E. V. Rieu chose prose rather than poetry as the more appropriate medium by which to render *The Iliad* and *The Odyssey*.

The particular purposes of the translator are also important factors in dictating the type of translation. Of course, it is assumed that the translator has purposes generally similar to, or at least compatible with, those of the original author, but this is not necessarily so. For example, a San Blas story-teller is interested only in amusing his audience, but an ethnographer who sets about translating such stories may be much more concerned in giving his audience an insight into San Blas personality structure. Since, however, the purposes of the translator are the primary ones to be considered in studying the types of translation which result, the principal purposes that underlie the choice of one or another way to render a particular message are important.

The primary purpose of the translator may be information as to both content and form. One intended type of response to such an informative type of translation is largely cognitive, e. g. an ethnographer's translation of texts from informants, or a philosopher's translation of Heidegger. A largely informative translation may, on the other hand, be designed to elicit an emotional response of pleasure from the reader or listener.

A translator's purposes may involve much more than information. He may, for example, want to suggest a particular type of behaviour by means of a translation. Under such circumstances he is likely to aim at full intelligibility, and to make certain minor adjustments in detail so that the reader may understand the full implications of the message for his own circumstances. In such a situation a translator is not content to have receptors say, "This is intelligible to us." Rather, he is looking for some such response as, "This is meaningful for us." In terms of Bible translating, the people might understand a phrase such as "to change one's mind about sin" as meaning "repentance." But if the indigenous way of talking about repentance is "spit on the ground in front of," as in Shilluk,[1] spoken in the Sudan, the translator will obviously aim at the more meaningful idiom. On a similar basis, "white as snow" may be rendered as "white as egret feathers," if the people of the receptor language are not acquainted with snow but speak of anything very white by this phrase.

A still greater degree of adaptation is likely to occur in a translation which has an imperative purpose. Here the translator feels constrained not merely to suggest a possible line of behaviour, but to make such an action explicit and compelling. He is not content to translate in such a way that the people are likely to understand; rather, he insists that the translation must be so clear that no one can possibly misunderstand.

In addition to the different types of messages and the diverse purposes of translators, one must also consider the extent to which prospective audiences differ both in decoding ability and in potential interest.

Decoding ability in any language involves at least four principal levels: (1) the capacity of children, whose vocabulary and cultural experience are limited; (2) the double-standard capacity of new literates, who can decode oral messages with facility but whose ability to decode written messages is limited; (3) the capacity of the average literate adult, who can handle both oral and written messages with relative ease; and (4) the unusually high capacity of specialists (doctors, theologians, philosophers, scientists, etc.), when they are decoding messages within their own area of specialization. Obviously a translation designed for children cannot be the same as one prepared for specialists, nor can a translation for children be the same as one for a newly literate adult.

Prospective audiences differ not only in decoding ability, but perhaps even more in their interests. For example, a translation designed to stimulate reading for pleasure will be quite different from one intended for a person anxious to learn how to assemble a complicated machine. Moreover, a translator of African myths for persons who simply want to satisfy their curiosity about strange peoples and places will produce a different piece of work from one who renders these same myths in a form acceptable to linguists, who are more interested in the linguistic structure underlying the translation than in cultural novelty.

Two Basic Orientations in Translating

Since "there are, properly speaking, no such things as identical equivalents" (Belloc, 1931:37), one must in translating seek to find the closest possible equivalent. However, there are fundamentally two different types of equivalence: one which may be called formal and another which is primarily dynamic.

Formal equivalence focuses attention on the message itself, in both form and content. In such a translation one is concerned with such correspondences as poetry to poetry, sentence to sentence, and concept to concept. Viewed from this formal orientation, one is concerned that the message in the receptor language should match as closely as possible the different elements in the source language. This means, for example, that the message in the receptor culture is constantly compared with the message in the source culture to determine standards of accuracy and correctness.

The type of translation which most completely typifies this structural equivalence might be called a "gloss translation," in which the translator attempts to reproduce as literally and meaningfully as possible the form and content of the original. Such a translation might be a rendering of some Medieval French text into English, intended for students of certain aspects of early French literature not requiring a knowledge of the original language of the text. Their needs call for a relatively close approximation to the structure of the early French text, both as to form (e. g. syntax and idioms) and content (e. g. themes and concepts). Such a translation would require numerous footnotes in order to make the text fully comprehensible. A gloss translation of this type is designed to permit the reader to identify himself as fully as possible with a person in the source-language context, and to understand as much as he can of the customs, manner of thought, and means of expression. For example, a phrase such as "holy kiss" (Romans, 16: 16) in a gloss translation would be rendered literally, and would probably be supplemented with a footnote explaining that this was a customary method of greeting in New Testament times. In contrast, a translation which attempts to produce a dynamic rather than a formal equivalence is based upon "the principle of equivalent effect" (Rieu & Phillips, 1954). In such a translation one is not so concerned with matching the receptor-language message with the source-language message, but with the dynamic relationship, that the relationship between receptor and message should be substantially the same as that which existed between the original receptors and the message.

A translation of dynamic equivalence aims at complete naturalness of expression, and tries to relate the receptor to modes of behaviour relevant within the context of his own culture; it does not insist that he understand the cultural patterns of the source-language context in order to comprehend the message. Of course, there are varying degrees of such dynamic-equivalence translations. One of the modern English translations which, perhaps more than any other, seeks for equivalent effect is J. B. Phillips' rendering of the New

Testament. In Romans 16: 16 he quite naturally translates "greet one another with a holy kiss" as "give one another a hearty handshake all around."

Between the two poles of translating (i. e. between strict formal equivalence and complete dynamic equivalence) there are a number of intervening grades, representing various acceptable standards of literary translating. During the past fifty years, however, there has been a marked shift of emphasis from the formal to the dynamic dimension. A recent summary of opinion on translating by literary artists, publishers, educators, and professional translators indicates clearly that the present direction is toward increasing emphasis on dynamic equivalences (Cary, 1959).

Linguistic and Cultural Distance

In any discussion of equivalences, whether structural or dynamic, one must always bear in mind three different types of relatedness, as determined by the linguistic and cultural distance between the codes used to convey the messages. In some instances, for example, a translation may involve comparatively closely related languages and cultures, e. g. translations from Frisian into English, or from Hebrew into Arabic. On the other hand, the languages may not be related, even though the cultures are closely parallel, e. g. as in translations from German into Hungarian, or from Swedish into Finnish (German and Swedish are Indo-European languages, while Hungarian and Finnish belong to the Finno-Ugrian family). In still other instances a translation may involve not only differences of linguistic affiliation but also highly diverse cultures, e. g. English into Zulu, or Greek into Javanese. [2]

Where the linguistic and cultural distances between source and receptor codes are least, one should expect to encounter the least number of serious problems, but as a matter of fact if languages are too closely related one is likely to be badly deceived by the superficial similarities, with the result that translations done under these circumstances are often quite poor. One of the serious dangers consists of so-called "false friends," i. e. borrowed or cognate words which seem to be equivalent but are not always so, e. g. English *demand* and French *demander*, English *ignore* and Spanish *ignorar*, English *virtue* and Latin *virtus*, and English *deacon* and Greek *diakonos*.

When the cultures are related but the languages are quite different, the translator is called upon to make a good many formal shifts in the translation. However, the cultural similarities in such instances usually provide a series of parallelisms of content that make the translation proportionately much less difficult than when both languages and cultures are disparate. In fact, differences between cultures cause many more severe complications for the translator than do differences in language structure.

Definitions of Translating

Definitions of proper translating are almost as numerous and varied as the persons who have undertaken to discuss the subject. This diversity is in a sense quite understandable; for there are vast differences in the materials translated, in the purposes of the publication, and in the needs of the prospective audience. Moreover, live languages are constantly changing and stylistic preferences undergo continual modification. Thus a translation acceptable in one period is often quite unacceptable at a later time.

A number of significant and relatively comprehensive definitions of translation have been offered. Procházka (Garvin, 1955: 111ff.) defines a good translation in terms of certain requirements which must be made of the translator, namely: (1)"He must understand the original word thematically and stylistically;" (2) "he must overcome the differences between the two linguistic structures;" and (3) "he must reconstruct the stylistic structures of the original work in his translation. "

In a description of proper translation of poetry, Jackson Mathews (1959: 67) states: "One thing seems clear: to translate a poem whole is to compose another poem. A whole translation will be faithful to the *matter*, and it will 'approximate the form' of the original; and it will have a life of its own, which is the voice of the translator. " Richmond Lattimore (1959, in Brower, 1959: 56) deals with the same basic problem of translating poetry. He describes the fundamental principles in terms of the way in which Greek poetry should be translated, namely: "to make from the Greek poem a poem in English which, while giving a high minimum of meaning of the Greek, is still a new English poem, which would not be the kind of poem it is if it were not translating the Greek which it translates. "

No proper definition of translation can avoid some of the basic difficulties. Especially in the rendering of poetry, the tension between form and content and the conflict between formal and dynamic equivalence are always acutely present. However, it seems to be increasingly recognized that adherence to the letter may indeed kill the spirit. William A. Cooper (1928: 484) deals with this problem rather realistically in his article on "Translating Goethe's Poems," in which he says: "If the language of the original employs word formations that give rise to insurmountable difficulties of direct translation, and figures of speech wholly foreign, and hence incomprehensible in the other tongue, it is better to cling to the spirit of the poem and clothe it in language and figures entirely free from awkwardness of speech and obscurity of picture. This might be called a translation from culture to culture. "

It must be recognized that in translating poetry there are very special problems involved, for the form of expression (rhythm, meter, assonance, etc.) is essential to communicating the spirit of the message to the audience. But all translating, whether of poetry or prose, must be concerned also with the response of the receptor; hence the ultimate purpose of the translation, in terms of its impact upon its intended audience, is a fundamental factor in any evaluation of translations. This reason underlies Leonard Forster's definition (1958: 6) of a good translation as "one which fulfills the same purpose in the new language as the original did in the language in which it was written."

The resolution of the conflict between literalness of form and equivalence of response seems increasingly to favour the latter, especially in the translating of poetic materials. C. W. Orr (1941: 318), for example, describes translating as somewhat equivalent to painting, for, as he says, "the painter does not reproduce every detail of the landscape"—he selects what seems best to him. Likewise for the translator, "It is the spirit, not only the letter, that he seeks to embody in his own version." Oliver Edwards (1957: 13) echoes the same point of view: "We expect approximate truth in a translation .... What we want to have is the truest possible *feel* of the original. The characters, the situations, the reflections must come to us as they were in the author's mind and heart, not necessarily precisely as he had them on his lips."

It is one thing, however, to produce a generalized definition of translating, whether of poetry or prose; it is often quite another to describe in some detail the significant characteristics of an adequate translation. This fact Savory (1957: 49 – 50) highlights by contrasting diametrically opposed opinions on a dozen important principles of translating. However, though some dissenting voices can be found on virtually all proposals as to what translating should consist of, there are several significant features of translating on which many of the most competent judges are increasingly in agreement.

Ezra Pound (1954: 273) states the case for translations making sense by declaring for "more sense and less syntax." But as early as 1789 George Campbell (1789: 445ff.) argued that translation should not be characterized by "obscure sense." E. E. Milligan (1957) also argues for sense rather than words, for he points out that unless a translation communicates, i. e. makes sense to the receptor, it has not justified its existence.

In addition to making sense, translations must also convey the "spirit and manner" of the original (Campbell, 1789: 445ff.). For the Bible translator, this means that the individual style of the various writers of the Scriptures should be reflected as far as possible (Campbell, 1789: 547). The same sentiment is clearly expressed by Ruth M. Underhill (1938: 16) in her treatment of certain problems of translating magic incantations of the Papago Indians of southern Arizona: "One can hope to make the translation exact only in spirit, not in letter." Francis Storr (1909) goes so far as to classify translators into "the literalist and the spiritualist schools," and in doing so takes his stand on the Biblical text, "The letter killeth but the spirit giveth life." As evidence for his thesis, Storr cites the difference between the Authorized Version, which he contends represents the spirit, and the English Revised Version, which sticks to the letter, with the result that the translation lacks a *Sprachgefühl*. The absence of literary stylists on the English Revised Committee was, however, corrected in the New English Bible (New Testament, 1961), in which one entire panel was composed of persons with special sensitivity to and competence in English style.

Closely related to the requirement of sensitivity to the style of the original is the need for a "natural and easy" form of expression in the language into which one is translating (Campbell, 1789: 445ff.). Max Beerbohm (1903: 75) considers that the cardinal fault of many who translate plays into English is the failure to be natural in expression; in fact, they make the reader "acutely conscious that their work is a translation … For the most part, their ingenuity consists in finding phrases that could not possibly be used by the average Englishman." Goodspeed (1945: 8) echoes the same sentiment with respect to Bible translating by declaring that: "The best translation is not one that keeps forever before the reader's mind the fact that this is a translation, not an original English composition, but one that makes the reader forget that it is a translation at all and makes him feel that he is looking into the ancient writer's mind, as he would into that of a contemporary. This is, indeed, no light matter to undertake or to execute, but it is, nevertheless, the task of any serious translator." J. B. Phillips (1953: 53) confirms the same viewpoint when he declares that: "The test of a real translation is that it should not read like translation at all." His second principle of translating reinforces the first, namely a translation into English should avoid "translator's English."

It must be recognized, however, that it is not easy to produce a completely natural translation, especially if the original writing is good literature, precisely because truly good writing intimately reflects and effectively exploits the total idiomatic capacities and special genius of the language in which the writing is done. A translator must therefore not only contend with the special difficulties resulting from such an effective exploitation of the total resources of the source language, but also seek to produce something relatively equivalent in the receptor language. In fact, Justin O'Brien (1959: 81) quotes Raymond Guérin to the effect that: "The most convincing criterion of the quality of a work is the fact that it can only be translated with difficulty, for if it passes readily into another language without losing its essence, then it must have no particular essence or at least not one of the rarest."

An easy and natural style in translating, despite the extreme difficulties of producing it—especially when translating an original of high quality—is nevertheless essential to producing in the ultimate receptors a response similar to that of the original receptors. In one way or another this principle of "similar response" has been widely held and effectively stated by a number of specialists in the field of translating. Even though Matthew Arnold (1861, as quoted in Savory, 1957: 45) himself rejected in actual practice the principle of "similar response," he at least seems to have thought he was producing a similar response, for he declares that: "A translation should affect us in the same way as the original may be supposed to have affected its first hearers." Despite Arnold's objection to some of the freer translations done by others, he was at least strongly opposed to the literalist views of such persons as F. W. Newman (1861: xiv). Jowett (1891), on the other hand, comes somewhat closer to a present-day conception of "similar response" in stating that: "An English translation ought to be idiomatic and interesting, not only to the scholar, but to the learned reader … The translator … seeks to produce on his reader an impression similar or nearly similar to that produced by the original."

Souter (1920: 7) expresses essentially this same view in stating that: "Our ideal in translation is to produce on the minds of our readers as nearly as possible the same effect as was produced by the original on its readers," and R. A. Knox (1957: 5) insists that a translation should be "read with the same interest and enjoyment which a reading of the original would have afforded."

In dealing with translating from an essentially linguistic point of view, Procházka (in Garvin 1955) re-enforces this same viewpoint, namely, that "the translation should make the same resultant impression on the reader as the original does on its reader." If a translation is to meet the four basic requirements of (1) making sense, (2) conveying the spirit and manner of the original, (3) having a natural and easy form of expression, and (4) producing a similar response, it is obvious that at certain points the conflict between content and form (or meaning and manner) will be acute, and that one or the other must give way. In general, translators are agreed that, when there is no happy compromise, meaning must have priority over style (Tancock, 1958: 29). What one must attempt, however, is an effective blend of "matter and manner," for these two aspects of any message are inseparably united. Adherence to content, without consideration of form, usually results in a flat mediocrity, with nothing of the sparkle and charm of the original. On the other hand, sacrifice of meaning for the sake of reproducing the style may produce only an impression, and fail to communicate the message. The form, however, may be changed more radically than the content and still be substantially equivalent in its effect upon the receptor. Accordingly, correspondence in meaning must have priority over correspondence in style. However, this assigning of priorities must never be done in a purely mechanical fashion, for what is ultimately required, especially in the translation of poetry, is "a recreation, not a reproduction" (Lattimore, in Brower, 1959: 55).

Any survey of opinions on translating serves to confirm the fact that definitions or descriptions of translating are not served by deterministic rules; rather, they depend on probabilistic rules. One cannot, therefore, state that a particular translation is good or bad without taking into consideration a myriad of factors, which in turn must be weighted in a number of different ways, with appreciably different answers. Hence there will always be a variety of valid answers to the question, "Is this a good translation?"

Principles Governing a Translation Oriented toward Formal Equivalence

In order to understand somewhat more fully the characteristics of different types of translations, it is important to analyze in more detail the principles that govern a translation which attempts to reproduce a formal equivalence. Such a formal equivalence (or F-E) translation is basically source-oriented; that is, it is designed to reveal as much as possible of the form and content of the original message.

In doing so, an F-E translation attempts to reproduce several formal elements, including: (1) grammatical units, (2) consistency in word usage, and (3) meanings in terms of the source context. The reproduction of grammatical units may consist in: (a) translating nouns by nouns, verbs by verbs, etc.; (b) keeping all phrases and sentences intact (i. e. not splitting up and readjusting the units); and (c) preserving all formal indicators, e. g. marks of punctuation, paragraph breaks, and poetic indentation.

In attempting to reproduce consistency in word usage, an F-E translation usually aims at so-called concordance of terminology; that is, it always renders a particular term in the source-language document by the corresponding term in the receptor document. Such a principle may, of course, be pushed to an absurd extent, with the result being relatively meaningless strings of words, as in some passages of the so-called Concordant Version of the New Testament. On the other hand, a certain degree of concordance may be highly desirable in certain types of F-E translating. For example, a reader of Plato's *Dialogues* in English may prefer rigid consistency in the rendering of key terms (as in Jowett's translation), so that he may have some comprehension of the way in which Plato uses certain word symbols to develop his philosophical system. An F-E translation may also make use of brackets, parentheses, or even italics (as in the King James Bible) for words added to make sense in the translation, but missing in the original document.

In order to reproduce meanings in terms of the source context, an F-E translation normally attempts not to make adjustments in idioms, but rather to reproduce such expressions more or less literally, so that the reader may be able to perceive something of the way in which the original document employed local cultural elements to convey meanings.

In many instances, however, one simply cannot reproduce certain formal elements of the source message. For example, there may be puns, chiasmic orders of words, instances of assonance, or acrostic features of line-initial sounds which completely defy equivalent rendering. In such instances one must employ certain types of marginal notes, if the feature in question merits an explanation. In some rare instances one does light upon a roughly equivalent pun or play on words. For example, in translating the Hebrew text of Genesis 2:23, in which the Hebrew word *isshah* "woman" is derived from *ish* "man," it is possible to use a corresponding English pair, *woman* and *man*. However, such formal correspondences are obviously rare, for languages generally differ radically in both content and form.

A consistent F-E translation will obviously contain much that is not readily intelligible to the average reader. One must therefore usually supplement such translations with marginal notes, not only to explain some of the formal features which could not be adequately represented, but also to make intelligible some of the formal equivalents employed, for such expressions may have significance only in terms of the source language or culture.

Some types of strictly F-E translations, e. g. interlinear renderings and completely concordant translations, are of limited value; others are of great value. For example, translations of foreign-language texts prepared especially for linguists rarely attempt anything but close F-E renderings. In such translations the wording is usually quite literal, and even the segments are often numbered so that the corresponding units may be readily compared.

From what has been said directly and indirectly about F-E translations in preceding sections, it might be supposed that such translations are categorically ruled out. To the contrary, they are often perfectly valid translations of certain types of messages for certain types of audiences. The relative value and effectiveness of particular types of translations for particular audiences pose another question, and must not be confused with a description of the nature of various kinds of translations. At this point we are concerned only with their essential features, not with their evaluation.

Principles Governing Translations Oriented toward Dynamic Equivalence

In contrast with formal-equivalence translations others are oriented toward dynamic equivalence. In such a translation the focus of attention is directed, not so much toward the source message, as toward the receptor response. A dynamic-equivalence (or D-E) translation may be described as one concerning which a bilingual and bicultural person can justifiably say, "That is just the way we would say it." It is important to realize, however, that a D-E translation is not merely another message which is more or less similar to that of the source.

It is a translation, and as such must clearly reflect the meaning and intent of the source. One way of defining a D-E translation is to describe it as "the closest natural equivalent to the source-language message." This type of definition contains three essential terms: (1) *equivalent*, which points toward the source-language message, (2) *natural*, which points toward the receptor language, and (3) *closest*, which binds the two orientations together on the basis of the highest degree of approximation.

However, since a D-E translation is directed primarily toward equivalence of response rather than equivalence of form, it is important to define more fully the implications of the word *natural* as applied to such translations. Basically, the word *natural* is applicable to three areas of the communication process; for a *natural* rendering must fit (1) the receptor language and culture as a whole, (2) the context of the particular message, and (3) the receptor-language audience.

The conformance of a translation to the receptor language and culture as a whole is an essential ingredient in any stylistically acceptable rendering. Actually this quality of linguistic appropriateness is usually noticeable only when it is absent. In a natural translation, therefore, those features which would mar it are conspicuous by their absence.

J. H. Frere (1820: 481) has described such a quality by stating, "the language of translation ought to, we think ... be a pure, impalpable and invisible element, the medium of thought and feeling and nothing more; it ought never to attract attention to itself .... All importations from foreign languages ... are ... to be avoided." Such an adjustment to the receptor language and culture must result in a translation that bears no obvious trace of foreign origin, so that, as G. A. Black (1936: 50) describes James Thomson's translations of Heine, such renderings are "a reproduction of the original, such as Heine himself, if master of the English language, would have given."

A natural translation involves two principal areas of adaptation, namely, grammar and lexicon. In general the grammatical modifications can be made the more readily, since many grammatical changes are dictated by the obligatory structures of the receptor language. That is to say, one is obliged to make such adjustments as shifting word order, using verbs in place of nouns, and substituting nouns for pronouns. The lexical structure of the source message is less readily adjusted to the semantic requirements of the receptor language, for instead of obvious rules to be followed, there are numerous alternative possibilities. There are in general three lexical levels to be considered: (1) terms for which there are readily available parallels, e. g. *river*, *tree*, *stone*, *knife*, etc.; (2) terms which identify culturally different objects, but with somewhat similar functions, e. g. *book*, which in English means an object with pages bound together into a unit, but which, in New Testament times, meant a long parchment or papyrus rolled up in the form of a scroll; and (3) terms which identify cultural specialties, e. g. *synagogue*, *homer*, *ephah*, *cherubim*, and *jubilee*, to cite only a few from the Bible. Usually the first set of terms involves no problem. In the second set of terms several confusions can arise; hence one must either use another term which reflects the form of the referent, though not the equivalent function, or which identifies the equivalent function at the expense of formal identity. In translating terms of the third class certain "foreign associations" can rarely be avoided. No translation that attempts to bridge a wide cultural gap can hope to eliminate all traces of the foreign setting. For example, in Bible translating it is quite impossible to remove such foreign "objects" as *Pharisees*, *Sadducees*, *Solomon's temple*, *cities of refuge*, or such Biblical themes as *anointing*, *adulterous generation*, *living sacrifice*, and *Lamb of God*, for these expressions are deeply imbedded in the very thought structure of the message.

It is inevitable also that when source and receptor languages represent very different cultures there should be many basic themes and accounts which cannot be "naturalized" by the process of translating. For example, the Jivaro Indians of Ecuador certainly do not understand Corinthians 11: 14, "Does not nature teach us that for a man to wear long hair is a dishonor to him?" for in general Jivaromen let their hair grow long, while Jivaro adult women usually cut theirs rather close. Similarly, in many areas of West Africa the behaviour of Jesus' disciples in spreading leaves and branches in his way as he rode into Jerusalem is regarded as reprehensible; for in accordance with West African custom the path to be walked on or ridden over by a chief is scrupulously cleaned of all litter, and anyone who throws a branch in such a person's way is guilty of grievous insult. Nevertheless, these cultural discrepancies offer less difficulty than might be imagined, especially if footnotes are used to point out the basis for the cultural diversity; for all people recognize that other peoples behave differently from themselves.

Naturalness of expression in the receptor language is essentially a problem of co-suitability—but on several levels, of which the most important are as follows: (1) word classes (e. g. if there is no noun for "love" one must often say, "God loves" instead of "God is love"); (2) grammatical categories (in some languages so-called predicate nominatives must agree in number with the subject, so that "the two shall be one" cannot be said, and accordingly, one must say "the two persons shall act just as though they are one person"); (3) semantic classes (swear words in one language may be based upon the perverted use of divine names, but in another language may be primarily excremental and anatomical); (4) discourse types (some languages may require direct quotation and others indirect); and (5) cultural contexts(in some societies the New Testament practice of sitting down to teach seems strange, if not unbecoming).

In addition to being appropriate to the receptor language and culture, a natural translation must be in accordance with the context of the particular message. The problems are thus not restricted to gross grammatical and lexical features, but may also involve such detailed matters as intonation and sentence rhythm (Pound, 1954: 298). The trouble is that, "Fettered to mere words, the translator loses the spirit of the original author" (Manchester, 1951: 68).

A truly natural translation can in some respects be described more easily in terms of what it avoids than in what it actually states; for it is the presence of serious anomalies, avoided in a successful translation, which immediately strike the reader as being out of place in the context. For example, crude vulgarities in a supposedly dignified type of discourse are inappropriate, and as a result are certainly not natural. But vulgarities are much less of a problem than slang or colloquialisms. Stanley Newman (1955) deals with this problem of levels of vocabulary in his analysis of sacred and slang language in Zuñi, and points out that a term such as *melika*, related to English *American*, is not appropriate for the religious atmosphere of the kiva. Rather, one must speak of Americans by means of a Zuñi expression meaning, literally, "broad-hats." For the Zuñis, uttering *melika* in a kiva ceremony would be as out of place as bringing a radio into such a meeting.

Onomatopoeic expressions are considered equivalent to slang by the speakers of some languages. In some languages in Africa, for example, certain highly imitative expressions (sometimes called ideophones) have been ruled out as inappropriate to the dignified context of the Bible. Undoubtedly the critical attitudes of some missionary translators toward such vivid, but highly colloquial, forms of expression have contributed to the feeling of many Africans that such words are inappropriate in Biblical contexts. In some languages, however, such onomatopoeic usages are not only highly developed, but are regarded as essential and becoming in any type of discourse. For example, Waiwai, a language of British Guiana, uses such expressions with great frequency, and without them one can scarcely communicate the emotional tone of the message, for they provide the basic signals for understanding the speaker's attitude toward the events he narrates.

Some translators are successful in avoiding vulgarisms and slang, but fall into the error of making a relatively straightforward message in the source language sound like a complicated legal document in the receptor language by trying too hard to be completely unambiguous; as a result such a translator spins out his definitions in long, technical phrases. In such a translation little is left of the grace and naturalness of the original.

Anachronisms are another means of violating the co-suitability of message and context. For example, a Bible translation into English which used "iron oxide" in place of "rust" would be technically correct, but certainly anachronistic. On the other hand, to translate "heavens and the earth" by "universe" in Genesis 1: 1 is not so radical a departure as one might think, for the people of the ancient world had a highly developed concept of an organized system comprising the "heavens and the earth," and hence "universe" is not inappropriate. Anachronisms involve two types of errors: (1) using contemporary words which falsify life at historically different periods, e. g. translating "demon possessed" as "mentally distressed," and (2) using old-fashioned language in the receptor language and hence giving an impression of unreality.

Appropriateness of the message within the context is not merely a matter of the referential content of the words. The total impression of a message consists not merely in the objects, events, abstractions, and relationships symbolized by the words, but also in the stylistic selection and arrangement of such symbols. Moreover, the standards of stylistic acceptability for various types of discourse differ radically from language to language. What is entirely appropriate in Spanish, for example, may turn out to be quite unacceptable "purple prose" in English, and the English prose we admire as dignified and effective often seems in Spanish to be colorless, insipid, and flat. Many Spanish literary artists take delight in the flowery elegance of their language, while most English writers prefer bold realism, precision, and movement.

It is essential not only that a translation avoid certain obvious failures to adjust the message to the context, but also that it incorporate certain positive elements of style which provide the proper emotional tone for the discourse. This emotional tone must accurately reflect the point of view of the author. Thus such elements as sarcasm, irony, or whimsical interest must all be accurately reflected in a D-E translation. Furthermore, it is essential that each participant introduced into the message be accurately represented. That is to say, individuals must be properly characterized by the appropriate selection and arrangement of words, so that such features as social class or geographical dialect will be immediately evident. Moreover, each character must be permitted to have the same kind of individuality and personality as the author himself gave them in the original message.

A third element in the naturalness of a D-E translation is the extent to which the message fits the receptor-language audience. This appropriateness must be judged on the basis of the level of experience and the capacity for decoding, if one is to aim at any real dynamic equivalence. On the other hand, one is not always sure how the original audience responded or were supposed to respond. Bible translators, for example, have often made quite a point of the fact that the language of the New Testament was Koine Greek, the language of "the man in the street," and hence a translation should speak to the man in the street. The truth of the matter is that many New Testament messages were not directed primarily to the man in the street, but to the man in the congregation. For this reason, such expressions as"Abba Father," *Maranatha*, and "baptized into Christ" could be used with reasonable expectation that they would be understood.

A translation which aims at dynamic equivalence inevitably involves a number of formal adjustments, for one cannot have his formal cake and eat it dynamically too. Something must give! In general, this limitation involves three principal areas: (1) special literary forms, (2) semantically exocentric expressions, and (3) intra-organismic meanings.

The translating of poetry obviously involves more adjustments in literary form than does prose, for rhythmic forms differ far more radically in form, and hence in esthetic appeal. As a result, certain rhythmic patterns must often be substituted for others, as when Greek dactylic hexameter is translated in iambic pentameter. Moreover, some of the most acceptable translating of rhymed verse is accomplished by substituting free verse. In Bible translating the usual procedure is to attempt a kind of dignified prose where the original employs poetry, since, in general, Biblical content is regarded as much more important than Biblical form.

When semantically exocentric phrases in the source language are meaningless or misleading if translated literally into the receptor language, one is obliged to make some adjustments in a D-E translation. For example, the Semitic idiom "gird up the loins of your mind" may mean nothing more than "put a belt around the hips of your thoughts" if translated literally. Under such circumstances one must change from an exocentric to an endocentric type of expression, e. g. "get ready in your thinking." Moreover, an idiom may not be merely meaningless, but may even convey quite the wrong meaning, in which case it must also be modified. Often, for example, a simile may be substituted for the original metaphor, e. g. "sons of thunder" may become "men like thunder."

Intra-organismic meanings suffer most in the process of translating, for they depend so largely upon the total cultural context of the language in which they are used, and hence are not readily transferable to other language-culture contexts. In the New Testament, for example, the word *tapeinos*, usually translated as "humble" or "lowly" in English, had very definite emotive connotations in the Greek world, where it carried the pejorative meanings of "low," "humiliated," "degraded," "mean," and "base." However, the Christians, who came principally from the lower strata of society, adopted as a symbol of an important Christian virtue this very term, which had been used derisively of the lower classes. Translations of the New Testament into English cannot expect to carry all the latent emotive meanings in the Greek word. Similarly, such translations as "anointed," "Messiah," and "Christ" cannot do full justice to the Greek *Christos*, which had associations intimately linked with the hopes and aspirations of the early Judeo-Christian community. Such emotive elements of meaning need not be related solely to terms of theological import. They apply to all levels of vocabulary. In French, for example, there is no term quite equivalent to English *home*, in contrast with *house*, and in English nothing quite like French *foyer*, which in many respect is like English *home*, but also means "hearth" and "fireside" as well as "focus" and "salon of a theater." Emotively, the English word *home* is close to French *foyer*, but referentially *home* is usually equivalent to *maison*, *habitation*, and *chez* (followed by an appropriate pronoun).

Notes:

1. This idiom is based upon the requirement that plaintiffs and defendants spit on the ground in front of each other when a case has been finally tried and punishment meted out. The spitting indicates that all is forgiven and that the accusations can never be brought into court again.

2. We also encounter certain rare situations in which the languages are related but the cultures are quite disparate. For example, in the case of Hindi and English one is dealing with two languages from the same language family, but the cultures in question are very different. In such instances, the languages are also likely to be so distantly related as to make their linguistic affiliation a matter of minor consequence.

选文四　Shifts of Translation

Matthijs Bakker　Cees Koster　Kitty Van Leuvent-Zwart

导　言

　　本文选自贝克主编的 *Routlege Encyclopeida of Translation Studies*（《翻译研究百科全书》，2001）中关于翻译转换的一个词条，对于转换这个概念进行了深入的探讨。

　　翻译转换（translation shift）这个概念的提出可以追溯到 1965 年，归功于英国著名学者卡特福德。那一年，卡特福德出版了他的专著《翻译的语言学理论》。所谓"转换"，指的是译自源发文本的目标文本中出现的细微的语言变化，换言之，就是译文与原文相比在语言层面上与原文不对应的情况。这个概念的提出,目的在于通过对翻译中出现的"译自源发文本的目标文本中出现的细微的语言变化"进行系统的描写和分类,来全面、科学地反映译文与原文之间在语言层面上的偏差,从而考察译文与原文之间在语义、文体、语用、衔接和美学等方面在多大程度上是对等的。从这个概念的提出至今,关于翻译转换的研究发展至今已有将近50年的历史。继卡特福德在1965年正式提出翻译转移的概念后,捷克学者利维(Levy)、波波维奇(Popovič)、米科(Miko)等学者又把这个概念运用于对具体翻译文学作品的研究之中,尤其是探讨语言上发生的翻译转移对译文文本的美学效果、文体风格的影响。这也是翻译转移研究首次在文学翻译中的运用。进入20世纪80年代之后,库尔卡(Blum Kulka)、兹瓦特(Leuven-Zwart)和图里(Toury)在这一领域进行了深入的研究,带动翻译研究进入了一个新阶段。这个概念和奈达提出的 equivalence(对等、等值)一样,成为翻译理论研究领域的一个核心概念。

The term **shifts** is used in the literature to refer to changes which occur or may occur in the process of translating. Since translating is a type of language use, the notion of shift belongs to the domain of linguistic performance, as apposed to that of theories of competence. Hence, shifts of translation can be distinguished from the systemic differences which exist between source and target languages and cultures. Systemic differences, which pertain to the level of competence, are part of the opening conditions for translation. Shifts, on the other land, result from attempts to deal with systemic differences. Translation involves the transfer of certain values of expression or content across a semiotic border; shifts are concomitant with this transfer. The relation between any two systems confronted in the process of translation is asymmetric, and the way the transfer is carried out is not determined a priori. It is because the translation operation performed on an initial semiotic entity can lead to different resultant entities that "shift" is not a category of competence. The description and explanation of shifts in translation as performance therefore ought to be concerned with the dynamics of culture rather than the static contrastive description of languages and cultures, which takes place within the framework of various comparative disciplines.

Shifts and Invariance

Translation, like every transfer operation, involves an "invariant under transformation" (cf Toury, 1980a: 12). The transformation which is occasioned by the translation process can be specified in terms of changes with respect to the original, changes which are termed "shifts." The two concepts of invariant and shift are therefore interdependent, such that any classification or definition of shifts entails a definition of the invariant (Baker & Naaijkens, 1991: 204 - 205). Definitions of the concept of invariant (i. e. those elements which remain unchanged in the process of translation) necessarily serve a certain theoretical purpose, while presupposing a certain point of view, a very rough and schematic division can be made between those conceptions of invariance in which the point of view lies "before" translation (be it actual or ideal), and those in which it lies "after" the fact. In accordance with this division, two classes of definitions of the invariant can be distinguished. The first consists of those definitions in which the invariant is postulated as a necessary condition to be met before the transfer operation can qualify as translation; here, the invariant coincides with the *tertium comparationis* of translation (cf. George Steiner, 1975: 319; Lefevere & Bassnett, 1990: 3). In definitions of the second type, the invariant is meant for use as a descriptive, purely heuristic construct; here, the *tertium comparationis* is a device in the methodology of the description.

Invariance Defined "Prior" to Translation

When a certain type of invariance is considered a requirement for appropriate translation behaviour, the corresponding notion of shift is likely to be a normative or prescriptive one. The directive statements in which this notion is found can be cast either in an affirmative form as *do*, or in a negative form as *don't* (Van Leuvent-Zwart, 1990b). The choice of either the positive or the negative formulation depends on the way the initial differences between source and target codes or systems are taken into account. In both types of statement the concept of shift is especially relevant to the applied branches of translation studies: translation DIDACTICS and criticism.

In negative formulations, shifts are looked upon as unwelcome results of the translation act, as something to be avoided: the implied performance instruction is *don't*. The term, then, refers to transformations of certain source text values or properties which out to remain, or have remained, unaltered; the result is described as an error or mistranslation. Since shifts are thus seen as unnecessary deviations from the due course of the translation process, the concept could be said to operate within a restricted theory of "translatability" (cf Toury, 1980a: 26 – 28). This theory, while being derived from the source text, to a certain, variable extent already allows for systemic differences between the source and target languages: the source-text-based theory is modified to accommodate target-language possibilities and impossibilities, whether only linguistic, or textual and cultural as well. Consequently, shifts are shifts with respect to a specific translation ideal and some postulated concept of "equivalence." If, for instance, it is stipulated as an invariance condition that the translation be (at least) the maximal reconstruction of the conceptual semantic meaning of the source text, any deviation from this potential reconstruction will be marked as a shift.

In positive formulations, on the other hand, shifts are seen as required, indispensable changes at specific semiotic levels, with regard to specific aspects of the source text. Their supposedly necessary, or desirable, occurrence is a consequence of systemic differences. Shifts are the means which allow the translator to overcome such differences. In other words, changes at a certain semiotic level with respect to a certain aspect of the source text benefit the invariance at other levels and with respect to other aspects. With this notion of shift, the focus is not on departures from a given normative concept of translatability but on the systemic differences which, in the projected translatability model, remain to be provided for. It is these systemic differences which are rewritten in terms of performance instructions (*do*). The concept of shift, then, is instrumental within a set of translation procedures. Examples of shifts postulated as *do's* include changes at the level of formal linguistic means which are brought about in favour of functional or text-pragmatic equivalence. For instance, Nida's notion of dynamic equivalence, where "the focus of attention is directed, not so much toward the source message, as toward the receptor response" (Nida, 1964: 166) adopts a functional-pragmatic concept of invariance and presupposes shifts away from static, or formal hierarchies of source-text properties. Two of the translation procedures discussed in Vinay & Darbelnet (1958) provide further examples of positive performance instructions: "transpositions, where an SL word is rendered by a TL word of a different word class, and modulation, [a] translation method consisting of changing a point of view, an evocation, and often a category of thought".

Invariance Defined "After" Translation

As a descriptive category, shifts are defined and identified retrospectively. They are reconstructed or established during the description of actual, existing translations. The descriptive focus may be on the reconstruction of the translation process, or on the product, particularly with respect to its relation to the source. However, the distinction between process-oriented and product-oriented description is not clear-cut. Process-related elements may play a role within the description of translation as a product, and the study of the product is the principal means for describing translation as a process.

When the focus is on the process, typologies of shifts generally attempt to account for the nature of translation operations and the considerations underlying certain decisions taken during the course of translation. Because the translation process is essentially a "black box," and any classification of shifts at this level has to be based on translation competence, that is, on the possible relationships and differences beween systems or codes. But, since the empirical testing of cognitive processes involved in translation is problematical, process-oriented typologies tend to reduce theoretical, general translation competence to a specific translation ideal. A distinction is often made between obligatory and optional shifts. Obligatory shifts are dictated by differences between linguistic systems, for example a lack of correspondence between related lexical items in the source and target languages. Optional shifts are those opted for by the translator for stylistic, ideological or cultural reasons. This distinction is similar to one made by Popovič between constitutive and individual shifts, but according to Popovič constitutive shifts are not exclusively linguistic.

As far as the product-oriented view of shifts is concerned, the following definition by Popovič (1970: 79) may serve as a starting point: "All that appears as new with respect to the original, or fails to appear where it might have been expected, may be interpreted as a shift." In this definition, three elements can be discerned: (a) a relationship between the source and target texts ("new with respect to the original"); (b) a relationship between the target text and its reception in the target system ("where it might have been expected); and (c) a descriptive point of view ("may be interpreted"). The descriptive focus can be either on (a) or on (b). For example, a zero-shift established at specific textual or linguistic levels in the source/target relationship (i. e. an instance of invariance, where nothing new appears) may still be interpreted as a shift in terms of (b): by violating the expectations of the target system, a target text may acquire a function other than that fulfilled by the source text in the source system. This double point of view implies that there is always the possibility of a description in which shifts are shown to occur in translation. For this reason, shifts are sometimes called a categorical quality (Van den Broeck, 1984 - 1985: 117) of the class of translation. This quality can be causally linked to the double status of the translation as a reconstruction of another text and a text functioning in its own right in the target culture.

Definition and Classification of Shifts in Product-oriented Descriptions

Any typology of shifts presupposes a descriptive point of view. This point of view can be made explicit in terms of criteria or parameters for comparative analysis. For any given parameter, the degree of correspondence that will be taken as invariance has to be established. In the following survey, several possible criteria for the classification and typology of shifts are distinguished.

Catford (1965) discusses shifts within the framework of a linguistic theory of translation. Within this framework, shifts occur on the grammatical and lexical levels, and their investigation is therefore pursued within the boundaries of the sentence as an upper rank. Catford distinguishes between a textual equivalent, "any TL text or portion of text which is observed on a particular occasion ... to be the equivalent of a given SL text or portion of text," and a formal correspondent, "any TL category (unit, class, structure, element of structure, etc.) which can be said to occupy, as nearly as possible" the "same" place in the economy of the TL as the given SL category occupies in the SL (Catford, 1965: 27). He limits his theory of shifts to instances of translation which satisfy the condition that the relationship between source and target utterances can be identified by a competent bilingual as textual equivalence. In invariant of comparison Catford employs is formal correspondence. Shifts, in his definition, are "departures from formal correspondence in the process of going from the SL to the TL" (ibid. : 73). If, from a descriptive point of view, a given TL instance is observed to be a textual equivalent of a given SL form, this does not entail that formal correspondence exists between the units under comparison, since the TL categories cannot necessarily "be said to occupy, as nearly as possible the 'same' place in the economy of the TL as the given SL category occupies in the SL" (ibid. : 32). The type and degree of divergence between formal correspondence and translation equivalence can be detailed in terms of shifts. Catford distinguishes two major types, level shifts (where an SL item at one linguistic level, for example grammar, has a TL equivalent at a different level, for instance lexis) and category shifts, which involve (a) changes of structure (structure shifts, for example a subject-predicate-object structure may be translated as a predicate-subject-object structure), (b) changes of rank (unit shifts, for example a word may be translated by a morpheme or a group by a clause), (c) changes of class (class shifts, for example an adjective may be translated by a noun or a verb), or (d) changes of term (intrasystem shifts, shifts which occur internally, within a system, when Source and target language systems have the same formal constitution but translation involves the selection of a non-corresponding term in the TL system) (Catford, 1965: 73ff.).

In Popovič (1970), the main concern is with literary translation, and shifts are therefore defined as a stylistic category and termed "shifts of expression. " For Popovič, "a systematic evaluation of the shifts of expression that occur in a translation," and hence "the objective classification of differences between the translation and its original" (ibid. : 84) should be based on a theory of expression, such as can be found in Miko (1970). The linguistic means employed in the source and target texts cannot be compared in isolation, but only "in relation to the entire system of expression" (Popovič, 1970: 84). It is this system of expression which allows us to determine the expressive values of the respective linguistic devices, a necessary precondition for the establishment of shifts "in the sphere of style" (ibid. : 83). Style, for Popvic, is a multilayered and hierarchically organized concept. It is because it covers abstract and general categories and qualities, as well as more specific stylistic means, that it can be used as an invariant for the comparison of source and target texts. For the evaluation of shifts, it is necessary to examine the respective differentiation of stylistic qualities in the source and target languages and texts. Popovič distinguishes between constitutive shifts and individual shifts. Constitutive shifts are system-bound, but the concept is wider than that of obligatory shifts. Popovič defines a constitutive shift as "an inevitable shift that takes place in the translation as a consequence of differences between the two languages, the two poetics, and the two styles of original and translation" (1976: 16). One might also conceive of these shifts as constitutive in the sense that they are constitutive for the style of the translation. According to Popovič, the style of the translation, conceived as the "integrative principle" in the development of its structure (1970: 79), is necessarily determined by shifts because of its "dual character" (ibid. : 82): it has to comply both with the norms of the original and with a given target "translation ideal. " Individual shifts differ from constitutive shifts in that they are prompted by the stylistic propensities and the subjective idiolect of the individual translator. When changes at the level of macrostylistics cause the translation to fit a literary genre different from that of the original, Popovič speaks of a generic shift.

Within the methodology of Toury (1980a: 89 - 121; 1985: 32), the invariant of the comparison is the Adequate Translation (AT) and the unit of comparison is the texteme. An Adequate Translation is a reconstruction of source text textemes and consists of an explicitation of the textual relations and functions of the source text. As such, it is not an actual text but a hypothetical construct, serving only methodological purposes (Seeing Hermans, 1995: 218 - 220 for a critical assessment of this concept). The degree correspondence taken as invariance within this method is adequacy at the textemic level, and shifts are defined as deviations from adequacy. The purpose of comparison is to determine the distance between the "actual equivalence" found between source and target texts and the maximal norm of adequate translation, inasmuch as this distance can be attributed to norm-governed translational behaviour. Since obligatory shifts are rule-governed, they cannot be taken to reflect translational norms and are therefore not taken into consideration; methodologically, they are accounted for in the invariant itself (the weak version of adequacy, see Toury, 1980a: 69). The comparative procedure starts by assuming equivalence at the texual-functional level, hence the parameter of comparison is textual-functional. When the dominant relationship between target-text unit is found at that level, the translational relationship is one of adequacy. When there is no textual-functional correspondence, the procedure is to look for correspondence at lower textual and linguistic levels. Norms determine the position of the actual translation equivalence between adequacy and acceptability, and the establishment of individual shifts ultimately leads to the establishment of the translational norms governing the text in question. When, after further generalization and expansion of the investigated corpus, shifts show a certain pattern or statistical regularities, they can be explained by the existence of a historically and culturally determined poetics of translation or translation ideal.

In later stages of Toury's thinking (1985, 1990), the above procedure became part of a larger one in which an additional unit of comparison was introduced: the "coupled pair of 'problem+solution'." The notion of shift gradually became less central in his method of descrption.

Within the methodology of van Leuven-Zwart, a distinction is made between shifts at the level of a text's microstructure (comparative model) and the effects of these shifts at the macrostructural level (descriptive mode). At the microstructural level, the invariant of the comparison is the architranseme (ATR), which expresses the common denominator(s) in the relation between specific textual units of the source and target texts; these textual units are called transemes. Inasmuch as the descriptive model is comparative, it works with an invariant at the macrostructural level as well. The invariant in this case is based on a theory of the genre to which the texts under comparison belong. Van Leuven-Zwart limits her methodology to the domain of narrative texts, and the invariant is therefore derived from specific narratological concepts such as "story level" and "focalization." The ATR has to be established separately for each pair of transemes, the invariant at the macrostructural level will be established a priori.

Essential to the method of van Leuven-Zwart is the priority given to the concept of relation. Any comparative description involves establishing the relation between elements as well as attributing certain features to those elements. According to van Leuven-Zwart, a comparison based on the prior attribution of features is only a "second degree" comparison, since it departs from a descriptive operation, and the relationship between the elements is established afterwards. In a direct comparison, the order is reversed. According to this scheme, a texteme, for instance, would be a unit of description rather than a unit of comparison. At the microstructural level, a relation of complete conjunction between the transemes and architransemes (in which case there is a relation of synonymy between transemes) is assumed as a starting point, and shifts occur when there are aspects of disjunction between transemes and the ATR. Van Leuven-Zwart distinguishes three main categories: modulation (where a source or target transeme shows one or more aspects of disjunction with the ATR; a relation of hyponymy between transemes), modification (where a source and target transeme show one or more aspects of disjunction with the ATR; a relation of contrast between transemes), and mutation (where there are no aspects of conjunction, and therefore no ATR can be established; no relation between transemes). The purpose of this method is to arrive at hypotheses about the interpretation and the strategy underlying the translation involved in the comparison. As a consequence, shifts that do not reflect a translator's interpretation or strategy underlying the translation involved in the comparison. As a consequence, shifts that do not reflect a translator's interpretation or strategy are not taken into account: only optional shifts and substantial shifts are considered. As far as the distinction between obligatory and optional shifts is concerned, van Leuven-Zwart expresses a reservation as to its applicability. In the first instance, the decision whether shifts are to be considered optional or obligatory is suspended. Not until the effects of the microstructural shifts on the macrostructural level have been established will it be possible to determine to what extent the shifts are due to other than purely linguistic factors. Initially, all substantial shifts are noted; that is, all the shifts that have some bearing on one of the substantial levels, namely the semantic, stylistic or pragmatic level. As to syntactic shifts, only those that affect these substantial levels are taken into account. Purely formal shifts are disregarded. On the distinction between formal and substantial shifts see also van den Broeck & Lefevere (1979).

选文五　Type, Kind and Individuality of Text: Decision Making in Translation

Katharina Reiss

导　言

本文选自劳伦斯·韦努蒂(Lawrence Venuti)主编的《翻译研究读本》(*The Translation Studies Reader*,2000 年出版)的第十二章。赖斯(Katharina Reiss)是德国功能主义翻译学派的创始人和领军人物,以发表《翻译批评》(*Translation Criticism—The Potentials and Limitations: Categories and Criteria for Translation Quality Assessment*)在翻译研究界引起关注。她最重要的思想来源于对语言学家布赫的观点的吸收,她认为,译者应该根据文本类型的不同,确定不同的翻译方法和策略,而翻译评论者也应该在此基础之上进行相应的翻译批评。

1　General Preliminary Remarks

1.1　Interlingual translation may be defined as a bilingual mediated process of communication, which ordinarily aims at the production of a TL [target language] text that is functionally equivalent to an SL text [source language] (2 media: SL and TL+1 medium: the translator, who becomes a secondary sender; thus translating: secondary communication).

1.1.1　The use of two natural languages as well as the employment of the medium of the translator necessarily and naturally result in a change of message during the communicative process. The theoretician of communication, Otto Haseloff (1969), has pointed out that an "ideal" communication is rare even when one single language is employed, because the receiver always brings his own knowledge and his own expectations, which are different from those of the sender. H. F. Plett (1975) calls this factor the "communicative difference." In translating, then, such differences are all the more to be expected. At this point I distinguish between "intentional" and "unintentional" changes affecting the translation.

Unintentional changes may arise from the different language structures as well as from differences in translating competence.

Ex. 1　Je suis allée à la gare (French: information about a female person; no information about the means of travel) Ich bin zum Bahnhof gegangen (German: no information about the person; information about the means of travel)

=Linguistically conditioned communicative difference.

Ex. 2　La France est veuve (Pompidou at the death of de Gaulle)

Frankreich ist Witwe—Frankreich ist Witwe geworden—

Frankreich ist verwitwet—Frankreich ist verwaist [orphaned]

Linguistically conditioned: La France—Witwe [Widow]

"Frankreich" is neuter in German. The image of "widow" is odd to a person ignorant of French. "Waise" [orphan] is also neuter; the image of an emotional attachment programmed differently.

Intentional changes frequently occur in translating, if the aims pursued in the translation are different from those of the original; if, besides the language difference of the TL readers, there is a change in the reading circle, etc. Since this will entail a change of function in the act of communication, there is now no attempt any more to strive for a functional equivalence between the SL and the TL text, but for adequacy of the TL reverbalization in accordance with the "foreign function." It follows that, besides a text typology relevant to translating, a translation typology should be worked out.

1.2　Communication comprises linguistic and non-linguistic action.

1.2.1　Written texts and texts put in writing (material for translating purposes) are to be characterized as "one-way communication" (Glinz, 1973). This means, on the one hand, that non-linguistic elements contributing to oral communication (gestures, facial expressions, speed of speech, intonation, etc.) are partly verbalized (=alleviation of the text analysis). On the other hand, the text analysis is made more difficult by the limitation of the possibilities of explicit verbalization of such elements as well as by the spatio-temporal separation between addresser and addressee and the lack of feedback during the act of communication; these factors lead, among other reasons, to a variable understanding of a given text.

1.2.2　Action is *intentional behaviour in a given situation* (Vermeer, 1972). "Intention" means here speech purpose, speech aim, motive leading to language communication (Lewandowski, 1973—1975: 288). Through the intention, verbalized by the author in his text, this text receives a communicative function for the process of communication. In order to be able to establish this intention the translator receives significant assistance if he determines to which text-type and text-variety (relevant for translating) any given text belongs.

Written texts may have single or plural intentions. Plural intentions may be of the same rank and order. Mostly, however, one intention (and, with it, the text function) is dominant.

Ex. 3　C vor o und u und a spricht man immer wie ein k; soll es wie ein c erklingen, lässt man die Cedille springen.

(mnemo-technical rhyme:

Intention 1—to convey a rule

Intention 2—to facilitate remembering by giving the text an artistic form

Intention 3—to "sweeten" the learning process by giving the text a pleasing form)

Counterexample 3a

Ein Wiesel/sass auf einem Kiesel/inmitten Bachgeriesel ...

(Christian Morgenstern)

Intention 1—the communication of an objective fact

Intention 2—artistic creation to convey an aesthetic impression

The dominance of intention 2 is established through the text itself: "Das raffinierte Tier/ Tat's um des Reimes Willen." Max Knight gives five English versions, and Jirí Levy regards all of them as equivalent (1969: 103 - 104):

A weasel	A ferret
perched on an easel	nibbling a carrot
within a patch of teasel	in a garret etc.

1.3　Language is (among other factors) a temporal phenomenon and thus subject to the conditions of time. This also applies to language in written texts and therefore to these texts themselves, a factor which is significant for translating.

1.3.1　A natural consequence of this fact is, firstly, the necessity of re-translating one and the same SL text, if the TL has changed to such an extent, that the TL version reflecting previous language conditions does not guarantee functional equivalence any more (e. g. , Bible translations, the translations of classical authors).

1.3.2　A further consequence of this fact may be the loss of understanding of the original SL text functions, because of a change in the situation, in which the SL text fulfilled its function, and/or because of the impossibility of reconstructing this situation (e. g. , Caesar, *Commentarii de bello gallico*—electioneering pamphlet＝operative text [see 2.1.1 below]. Torn out of its original social context—now a historical report and also translated as such＝informative text. Jonathan Swift, *Gulliver's Travels*—satire on contemporary social ills＝expressive text with an operative secondary function; today only recognizable in this function by the experts specializing in this period; for the ordinary reader (also of the original)—a fantastic adventure tale＝expressive text.

2　The Translating Process

Phase of analysis. In order to place a functionally equivalent TL text beside an SL text the translator should clarify the functions of the SL text. This may be done in a three-stage-process, which may, in principle, be carried out either by starting from the smallest textual unit and ending with the text as a whole, or by beginning with the text as a whole and ending with the analysis of the smallest textual unit. For practical as well as for text-theoretical considerations, I have chosen the process of proceeding from the largest to the smallest unit.

(In practice, the conscientious translator reads the whole text first to get an impression; from a text-linguistic point of view, the text is nowadays regarded as the primary language sign.) Below, this three-stage process will be presented as a temporal sequence for purely methodological reasons. In practice, the separate stages of analysis dovetail, particularly if the translator is experienced.

2.1 Total function in the framework of written forms of communication.

2.1.1 Establishment of the "*text-type*"—a phenomenon going beyond a single linguistic or cultural context, because the following essentially different forms of written communication may be regarded as being present in every speech community with a culture based on the written word and also because every author of a text ought to decide in principle on one of the three forms before beginning to formulate his text.

Question: Which basic communicative form is realized in the concrete text with the help of written texts?

a. The communication of content—informative type

b. The communication of artistically organized content—expressive type

c. The communication of content with a persuasive character—operative type

Aids in orientation: semantic as well as pragmatic ones (content and knowledge of the world), for instance, "pre-signals," i. e. , titles or headlines (novel, law, report of an accident, sonnet, strike call, etc.) or "meta-propositional expressions" at the beginning of a text (Grosse, 1976) (e. g. , "Herewith I authorize … " in the case of a general power of attorney, etc.); medium: professional periodicals, pamphlets, the news section of a newspaper, etc.

Use of language:

a. The particular frequency of words and phrases of evaluation (positive for the addresser or for the cause to which he has committed himself; negative for any obstacle to his commitment), the particular frequency of certain rhetorical figures may, among other factors, lead to the conclusion that the text is operative. Decisive question: are we dealing with a speech object capable of making an appeal?

b. "The feature that speech elements are capable of pointing beyond themselves to a significance of the whole" (Grosse, 1976), "the principle of linkage" (rhymes, leit-motifs, parallelisms, rhythm, etc.) and the "transformation of the material of reality" (Mukar Vovsky) may lead to the conclusion that the text belongs to the expressive type.

c. Should the elements quoted under a. and b. be absent, the conclusion may be that the text is informative. Thus a "rough grid" has been established for the analysis.

2.1.2 *Mixed forms*. If we accept the three text types, the informative, the expressive and the operative type, as the basic forms of written communication (intercultural), it should be taken into account that these types are not only realized in their "pure" form, that is, that they do not always appear in their "fully realized form;" and it should also be considered that, for a variety of reasons (change in the conventions of a text variety, or if we have to do with plural intentions) the communicative intention and communicative form cannot be unambiguously adapted to each other. In the first case: texts merely appealing to an affirmative attitude of the addressee without intending to trigger off impulses of behaviour, e. g., newspaper articles expressing opinions (no fully realized form of the operative text). In the second case: versified legal texts in the Middle Ages; in order for their content to be acceptable, they had to be presented in verse form=greater dignity of rhymed language! (Mixed form between informative and expressive text type.)

2.1.3 *Additional types*? Bühler's three functions of the linguistic sign, in analogy to which I have isolated the three main text functions, are extended by Roman Jakobson to include the phatic and the poetic functions. Would both of these functions be suitable to isolate text types relevant to the choice of a translating method? Not so, in my opinion! Related to entire texts and not only to single language elements, the phatic function (=the establishment and maintenance of contact) is realized in all three of the basic forms of communication, i. e., the phatic function does not lead to particulars of the text construction.

For instance

Picture postcard from a holiday: informative text with phatic function

Original birthday poem: expressive text with phatic function

Memory aid in an advertisement slogan: operative text with phatic function

The phatic function does not arise from the text form, but from the use to which the text is put. Likewise, the poetic function of the language signs is realized in all three of the basic communicative forms.

Soccer reportage: informative text, partly with poetic language elements, e. g., "der Mann im fahlgrünen Trikot," "Erstaunlich matt war Hölzenbein, fehlerlos Grabowski, eindrucksvoll Neuberger." (rhetorical triple figure)

Lyrical poem: expressive text—the poetic function determines the whole text

Sales promotion: (e. g., in verse form) operative text with elements of poetic language "loan structure" (Hantsch, 1972)

However, in view of the relevancy for translating purposes, an additional type, a "hyper-type," should be isolated as a super-structure for the three basic types: *the multi-medial text type*. The need for this arises from the fact that the translating material does not only consist of "autonomous" written texts, but also, to a large extent, firstly of verbal texts, which, though put down in writing, are presented orally, and, secondly, of verbal texts, which are only part of a larger whole and are phrased with a view to, and in consideration of, the "additional information" supplied by a sign system other than that of language (picture+text, music and text, gestures, facial expressions, built-up scenery on the stage, slides and text, etc.).

Thus, when the message is verbalized, the multi-medial type possesses its own regularities, which ought to be taken into account in translating, besides—and above—the regularities of the three basic forms of written communication. Therefore I now put this type above the three basic forms, though, formerly, I placed it beside them. However, we should also consider a suggestion made by a research group of the Philips concern, according to which these extra-linguistic conditions should be regarded as the basis for a typology of media relevant to translating.

2.2 The second stage of the analysis aims at the establishment of the *text variety*, i. e., the classification of a given text according to specifically structured sociocultural patterns of communication belonging to specific language communities. Text variety is still a controversial concept in linguistics. The denotation of text variety as well as that of text type is at present still used for the most variegated textual phenomena. Therefore, I meanwhile define text variety as super-individual acts of speech or writing, which are linked to recurrent actions of communications and in which particular patterns of language and structure have developed because of their recurrence in similar communicative constellations. The *phenomenon* of text variety is not confined to one language. The various kinds of text variety are partly not confined to one language or one culture, but the habits of textualization, the patterns of language and structure often differ from one another to a considerable extent. Hence, the establishment of the text variety is of decisive importance for the translator, so that he may not endanger the functional equivalence of the TL text by naively adopting SL conventions.

Examples

Es war einmal: textual opening signal in German for fairy tales

In the name of the people: for verdicts

2×4 lines $+2 \times 3$ lines: structural pattern for the sonnet

Directions for use in French and German: according to the specific text variety there is a distribution of structures common to both languages.

The passive form and impersonal expressions—conventions in German

The indefinite pronoun "on"+infinitive phrase—convention in French

One single example may not always suffice for the establishment of the text variety.

Ex. 4 English death notice:

> FRANCIS. On Thursday, March 17, Jenny, beloved wife of Tony Francis and mother of Anthony. Service at St. Mary's Church, Elloughton, 9. 50 a. m. , Tuesday, March 22, followed by cremation. No letters or flowers, please.

The translation into German would be more or less as follows (the italicized words and expressions characterize conventions observed in German).

Am 17. März *verstarb meine* geliebte Frau, *meine* liebe Mutter

JENNY *FRANCIS*

Elloughton *Im Namen der Angehörigen* (or: in tiefer Trauer)

Tony Francis

mit Anthony

Trauergottesdienst: Dienstag, den 22. 3, 9. 50 in St. Marien (Elloughton)

Anschliessend *erfolgt* die Feuerbestattung

Von Kondolenzschreiben und Kranzspenden *bitten wir* höflichst *Abstand zu nehmen*.

2. 3　Third stage of the analysis: the analysis of style (the analysis of a particular textual surface). Now the *text individual* is placed in the foreground. This analysis is of supreme importance, because the translator's "decisive battle" is fought on the level of the text individual, where strategy and tactics are directed by type and variety.

Let style in this connection be understood to mean the ad hoc selection of linguistic signs and of their possibilities of combination supplied by the language system. The use of language in a given SL text is investigated in order to clarify in detail, firstly, what linguistic means are used to realize specific communicative functions, and, secondly, how the text is constructed. This detailed semantic, syntactic and pragmatic analysis is necessary, because, as is well-known, not even in one single language do form and function show a 1 : 1 relation. The same phenomenon applies to the relation of SL to TL.

2. 4　At this point I see, as it were, a "juncture" between the first phase of the process of translation, the phase of analysis, and the second phase of the process of translation, the phase of reverbalization, for it is already here that the translator, at any rate the experienced translator, pays heed to possible contrasts.

The detailed semantic, syntactic and pragmatic analysis is carried out in small stages of analysis, proceeding from the word, the syntagma, the phrase, the sentence, the section (paragraph or chapter) up to the level of the entire text.

The process of reverbalization is a linear one constructing the TL text out of words, syntagmas, clauses, sentences, paragraphs, etc. During this process of reverbalization a decision has to be made for each element of the text whether the linguistic signs and sequences of linguistic signs selected in the TL in coordination with a sign form and sign function can guarantee the functional equivalence for which a translator should strive, by due consideration of text variety and text type.

3　Phase of Reverbalization

Relevance of the classification of text type and text variety to the translating process.

Thesis: The text type determines the general method of translating;

The text variety demands consideration for language and text structure conventions.

3. 1　Normal cases

If functional equivalence is sought during the process of translation, this means

a. If the SL text is written to convey contents, these contents should also be conveyed in the TL text.

Mode of translating—*translation according to the sense and meaning* in order to maintain the invariability of the content. To this end it may be necessary that what is conveyed implicitly in the SL text should be explicated in the TL and vice versa. This necessity arises, on the one hand, from structural differences in the two languages involved, and, on the other hand, from differences in the collective pragmatics of the two language communities involved.

Ex. 5a   Vous vous introduisez par l'étroite ouverture *en vous frottant contre ses ords* ... (＝explicit)

Sie *zwängen* sich *durch* die schmale Öffnung (*not* "by rubbing against its walls") (＝ implicit)

"durchzwängen" in German contains the image of rubbing against an edge.

Ex. 5b   (after Klaus Rülker) A report by a French press agency about the presidential elections in France: seulement huit départements franöais votèrent en majorité pour Poher.

Literal translation: Nur acht aller französischen Departements stimmten in ihrer Mehrheit für Poher.

Equivalent translation: Nur acht *der hundert* französischen Departements stimmten in ihrer Mehrheit für Poher.

b. If the SL text is written in order to convey artistic contents, then the contents in the TL should be conveyed in an analogously artistic organization. Mode of translating: *translating by identification* (not in the sense Goethe uses). The translator identifies with the artistic and creative intention of the SL author in order to maintain the artistic quality of the text.

Ex. 6   (Ortegay Gasset: *Miseriay Esplendor de la Traducción*)

Entreveo que es usted una especie de *último abencerraje*, ultimo superviviente de una fauna desaparecida, puesto que es usted capaz, frente a otro hombre, de creer que es el otro y no usted quien tiene razón.

Literal translation: "eine Art letzter Abencerraje" (without content for the German reader)

Content translation: "eine Art Ausnahmefall" (absence of the artistic components— metaphors and literary allusion)

Functionally equivalent translation: "eine Art letzter Ritter ohne Furcht and Tadel"

(One element of the artistic organization in Ortega's essay is the many verbs and nouns alluding to seafaring, either directly or in a figurative sense, in spite of the fact that the subject has nothing to do with seafaring. This is an indication that he is aware of Jakob Grimm's saying, according to which translating resembles a ship manned to sail the seas, but though it safely carries the goods, it must land at shore with a different soil under a different air. The metaphor is obvious because all the images presented by Ortega on the subject of translation derive from what Schleiermacher, Humboldt and Goethe have said about the problem. Thus, he must have known Grimm's metaphor as well. Hence, the translator is satisfied in choosing as shifted equivalents concepts from seafaring, where there are none in the original, if these are easily available in German. The reason is that at other times, when in the Spanish language the association with "seafaring" is implied, an equivalent German expression is not available: *arribar = ankommen*, instead of *llegar*. This is one of the examples I mean when referring to "the analogy of artistic form.")

c. If the SL text is written to convey persuasively structured contents in order to trigger off impulses of behaviour, then the contents conveyed in the TL must be capable of triggering off analogous impulses of behaviour in the TL reader.

Ex. 7　Black is beautiful

This slogan appearing in English in a German sales promotion could not be retained in the translation into English of a whole sales promoting text, if that text is intended for South African buyers.

Mode of translating: *adaptive translating*. The psychological mechanisms of the use of persuasive language should be adapted to the needs of the new language community.

3. 2　Since form and function of language signs do not show a relation of 1 : 1, the same SL sequence may be represented in the TL by any other language sequence depending on which text type and text variety they appear and which function they may have to fulfill there.

Ex. 8　El niño lloraba bajo *el agua del bautismo*.

Text variety: social news; text type: informative.

Das Kind weinte unter dem *Taufwasser*.

Ex. 9　Marcelino lloraba bajo *el agua del bautismo*, como antes callara al advertir *el sabor de la sal*. (Sánchez-Silva, Marcelino, Pan y vino)

Text variety: narrative. Text type: expressive (parallelisms; rhythm-elements of artistic organization—retained in the TL).

Marcelino weinte unter dem *Wasser der Taufe*, wie er zuvor beim *Geschmack des Salzes* geschwiegen hatte.

Ex. 10　*Souvent femme varie*, bien fol est qui s'y fie.

a. This saying of Francis I is mentioned in a history book.

Text variety: schoolbook; text type: informative.

Frauen ändern sich oft, wer ihnen traut, ist schön dumm.

b. Mentioned in a drama by Victor Hugo (transl. by Georg Büchner), *Maria Tudor*.

Text variety: drama; text type: expressive.

Ein Weib ändert sich jeden Tag, ein Narr ist, wer ihr trauen mag (several semantic shifts, rhyme and rhythm retained).

c. Item in an advertisement for wine: "Souvent femme varie. Les vins du Postillon ne varient jamais."

Literary allusion in conjunction with pun-memory aid and the arousal of sympathy in the "connoisseur." The allusion should be re-programmed.

Text variety: the advertising of products; text type: operative.

Frauenherzen sind trügerisch. Postillon-Weine betrügen nie.

3.3　Problematic cases

If the three basic forms of communication are not realized in their "pure" form (cf. mixed forms, 2.1.2), then the principles of translating for the three basic types serve as aids for a decision in cases of conflict. In principle, the mode of translating for the entire text applies to all text elements, even if they do not belong to the same type as the dominant type.

If, for instance, elements of poetic language are used when content is conveyed (informative type)—the so-called loan structures (Hantsch, 1972)—the translation ought to strive for an analogously poetic form for those elements. However, if this is not possible in the TL without loss of the unity of content and artistic form, then the retention of content is dominant in informative texts and is to be preferred to the maintenance of an artistic form.

Ex. 11　Nun gibt es freilich moderne Nomaden, für die ein Caravan nur der zweitschönste *Wahn* ist (*Süddeutsche Zeitung*, Streiflicht).

Text variety: newspaper item; text type: informative.

We have here an item referring to an opinion poll among owners of camping places as regards the behaviour of German holiday makers. The "Streiflichter" [a newspaper column] in the *Süddeutsche Zeitung* [a newspaper] are often distinguished by an abundance of entertaining puns and other kinds of play with language. At the same time, however, the subject is invariably a topical state of affairs, and the main function of the text is the communication of content. In translation puns and other kinds of play with language will have to be ignored to a great extent so as to keep the content invariant.

If, however, artistically structured contents in a text of the expressive type have to be conveyed and if, during this process, the artistic organization might be harmed by the retention of the same content elements, then the rule applies for expressive texts that the contents may be changed.

Ex. 12　... une pâquerette, ou une primevère, ou un coucou, ou un bouton d'or ... (Samuel Becket)

Literally: ... ein Gänse*blümchen*, oder ein Himmels*schlüssel chen*, oder eine *Schlüsselblume* oder eine Butter*blume* ... (invariance of content)

Elmar Tophoven: ... ein Tausendschönchen, eine Primel, eine Schlüsselblume, eine Butterrose ...

Finally, if, in conveying contents with a persuasive form intended to trigger off impulses of behaviour, the unchanged adoption of elements of content or (loaned) elements of artistic structure from the SL texts does not have an operative effect, these elements may be replaced by other elements fulfilling the desired function.

Ex. 13　Füchse fahren Fir es tone-Phoenix

Foxes use Firestone-Phoenix (falsification of association, loss of alliteration; important elements of the operative use of language) Pros prefer Firestone-Phoenix (change of content to retain positive association and alliteration)

If operative text elements appear in different text types, then the adapting method of translating also applies to these single elements as long as this is possible without any harm to either the content to be conveyed (in the case of the informative type) or to the artistic organization as a whole (in the case of the expressive text).

3.4 Special cases

If there is a difference between the original text function and the function of the translation, the text typology relevant to translation as well as the establishment of the given text variety are of no significance at all for the question what mode of translating should be adopted to attain functional equivalence. In that case a *typology of translation* should replace the text typology in order to supply suitable criteria for the mode of translating. As has been mentioned above, in changes of function the aim of the translating process is not anymore the attainment of a functionally TL text, but a TL text possessing a form which is adequate to the "foreign function." The criteria are not to be derived from the question "to what end and for whom has the text been *written*?" but from the question "to what end and for whom is the text *translated*?"

E.g., a "grammar translation"

—Aim of the translation: to examine whether the pupil is acquainted with vocabulary and grammatical structures of the foreign language; translated for the teacher. Regardless of which text type is realized by the SL text, only vocabulary and grammar are considered.

E.g., interlinear versions

—Aim of the translation: the reproduction of the SL text for research purposes; translated for the student ignorant of the SL.

E.g., summaries of content

—Aim of the translation: communication of contents relevant for a certain further use; translated upon somebody's order.

【延伸阅读】

[1] Newmark, P. (1977). Communicative and Semantic Translation. *Babel*, 23, 163 - 180.

[2] Nida, E. (1945). Linguistics and Ethnology in Translation Problems. *Word*, 1, 194 - 208.

[3] Nida, E. (1964). *Toward a Science of Translating, with Special Reference to Principles and Procedures Involved in Bible Translating*. Leiden, Holland: Brill.

[4] Nida, E. & Taber, C. (1969). *The Theory and Practice of Translation*. Leiden, Holland: Brill, reprinted in 1982.

[5] Reiss, K. (2000). *Translation Criticism—The Potentials and Limitations: Categories and Criteria for Translation Quality Assessment*. Manchester: St. Jerome Pub.

[6] Popovič, A. (1970). The Concept "Shift of Expression" in Translation Analysis. In Holmes de Haan & Popovič (eds.), *The Nature of Translation: Essays on the Theory and Practice of Translation*. Mouton: The Hague.

[7] Van den Broeck. (1984). Shifts in the Stylistics of Translated Literary Texts: A Semiotic Approach. *Linguistca Antverpiensia*, 18-19, 111-145.

【问题与思考】

1. 有没有放之四海而皆准的翻译标准?

2. 奈达的对等翻译标准更适合什么样的文本的翻译?

3. 赖斯关于翻译批评的主要观点是什么?

4. 举例说明形式对应和动态对等之间的不同。

5. 维内和达贝尔内提出哪些翻译方法? 请举例进行解释和说明。

6. "转换"的概念最早是由谁提出来的? 你是否能够在雅各布逊等人的论述中找到关于转换概念思想的雏形?

7. 比较"对等"、"等值"和"转换"概念,说明"转换"与前面两个概念之间的关系。

8. 文化途径的翻译学者在"转换"这个概念的使用上有什么发展创新?

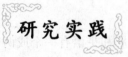

研究实践

汉语双主句英译初探

马 嘉

导 言

　　这篇文章涉及主题、主语的翻译问题,希望这篇文章不仅可以帮助读者进一步理解主题这一概念对于翻译的意义,同时能够促使读者对英汉两种语言转换过程中的一个突出问题——主语的翻译问题——有一个直观的了解和思考。

0 引言

　　语言类型学的研究表明,汉语是主题突出型语言,主题＋主语＋谓语的句子比较常见。例如:"那棵树叶子很大","这件事你不能光麻烦一个人","这本小说张三看完了"。为简便起见,我们把这种句型称为"双主句"。①而英语是主语突出型语言,主语+谓语的句子是其基本句型。例如:That tree has very big leaves. You can't deal with this matter by bothering only one person. Zhang San has finished this novel. ②虽然英语中也有与主题+主语+谓语类似的句型,如 Word-processors, I sometimes think they should be recycled into Space Invaders' machine,但并不常见。

与英语相比,双主句虽是汉语特有的句型,但在汉译英中并非难点,也很少引起研究者的注意。因为它并不难理解,而表达为英语时也往往可转换成英语的主谓结构,似乎没有讨论其英译的必要。如果孤立地看双主句的英译,事实确实如此。但不应忽视的是,主题与主语不同,并不属于句法层面,而是属于语用层面(徐昌火,1997;石毓智,2001)。它不仅表明句子的话题,还负载着许多语用功能,是语篇中不可或缺的"话语要素"(Li & Thompson,1981:100)。因此,本文将试图描述双主句的英译法,并从语用功能的角度比较其利弊,以期对日后翻译有所裨益。

1 双主句的分类

根据形式特点,双主句可分为显性双主句与隐性双主句;根据语序特点,又可分为无标记双主句与有标记双主句。

1.1 显性双主句与隐性双主句

显性双主句指主题与主语同时出现在句子中,而隐性双主句则指主题和主语有一个或两个在句中省略,但通过语境可以补充出来,且不会引起歧义。例如:

(1) <u>我</u>一张嘴吵不过他们十几张嘴。(茅盾,《林家铺子》)

(2) 天刚发白,林先生就起身,(他)眼圈儿有点红肿,(他)头里发昏。(茅盾,《林家铺子》)

(3) <u>那文章</u>(我)现在是一句也不记得了,总之是参康有为变法的;(那文章)(我)也不记得可曾抄了没有。(鲁迅,《朝花夕拾》)

之所以做此区分,是因为在汉译英中,通常以小句而不以句子为基本转换单位(罗选民,1992)。而小句在句中又多省略主题或主语,这样有助于识别隐性双主句,能较全面地考察双主句的英译。

1.2 无标记双主句与有标记双主句

仔细观察例(2)和例(3),不难发现即使补充省略部分,成为显性双主句后,二者在语序上还是有差别的:

(2′) <u>林先生</u>眼圈儿有点红肿。

(3′) <u>那文章</u>我现在是一句也不记得了。

例(2′)符合正常语序,可称之为无标记双主句,而例(3′)通过宾语提前打破了正常语序,

---

① 也有学者称之为"主题句"(申小龙,1986)或"双主语句"(严辰松,1997),但本文的"双主句"特指主题与主语不同,且主题为非时间短语或处所短语的该类句型。因为这样的"双主句"更具翻译研究价值。

② 例句引自 Li & Thompson (1981: 94—97),英文为笔者自译。

这种刻意主题化的双主句可称为有标记双主句。

根据以上两个分类标准,可得到四种双主句:显性无标记、隐性无标记、显性有标记、隐性有标记。从对大量双主句的观察中,我们发现一个有趣的现象,即在隐性无标记双主句中省略的通常是主题,而在隐性有标记双主句中省略的通常是主语。省略的成分不论是主题还是主语一般都是施动者,这也许是因为施动者往往可以从上下文中确定,出于简洁的需要而被省略。

2 双主句的语用功能

双主句无论属于哪种类型,主题都是其核心,在很大程度上,正是主题赋予了双主句特定的语用功能。主题与主语的差异在于,主语与谓语动词必须存在直接的语义关系,而主题则不必如此(Li & Thompson,1981:15)。语言学家们认为,汉语主题具有四个突出特点:① 居于句首位置;② 后加停顿或者语气词;③ 总是有定的,即表示已知信息;④ 是个话语概念,具有延续性,经常把它的语义辖域延伸到后面几个句子(石毓智,2001:83)。主题通常位于句首,表示已知信息,这决定了它在语篇中主要是承前,但也不排除在主题相同的句群中具备启后功能。据此,Li & Thompson(1981:100-101)认为主题具有以下四种功能:

第一,主题把它所在的句子与它前面的句子联系起来。① 例如:

(4)这些人都比一个月前瘦了许多,(他们)眼眶陷进了,(他们)嗓子也发沙,然而都很快活兴奋。(茅盾,《春蚕》)

第二,主题可以引出与前面的内容有关但略有不同的话题。例如:

(5)大约此后不到一月,就听到一种流言,说我已经偷了家里的东西去变卖了,这实在使我觉得有如掉在冷水里。流言的来源,我是明白的……(鲁迅,《朝花夕拾》)

第三,主题可以重提前面提过但中断的旧话题。例如:

(6)第二天早上,老通宝就到镇里去想法借钱来买叶。临走前,他和四大娘商量好,决定把他家那块出产十五担叶的桑地去抵押。这是他家最后的产业。……但这是最后五分钟了。再得两天,“宝宝”可以上山。人们把剩余的精力榨出来拼死命干。……他们钱都花光了,精力也绞尽了,可是有没有报酬呢,到此时还没有把握。② (茅盾,《春蚕》)

第四,主题还可以作为对比的焦点。例如:

(7)衣服,新的好;朋友,旧的好。(Li & Thompson,1981)

主题的这四种功能其实也是双主句的语用功能。此外,严辰松(1997:4)还列举了另外两种功能。

第五,表示由情景引发的凸显信息。例如:

(8)(长妈见年幼的鲁迅听了她讲的长毛杀门房的故事并不害怕,便说道)“像你似的小孩子,长毛也要掳的,掳去做小长毛。还有好看的姑娘,也要掳。”(鲁迅,《朝花夕拾》)

第六,表示强调。

(9)他呀,成绩不好,还怨老师没教好。(沈家煊,1999:236)

---

① 表述为“主题引出前面刚涉及的同一话题”似更恰当。

② 由此例可以看出主题并不总是位于句首,有时也会位于主语与谓语之间。

　　除此之外，我们认为主题通常居于句首，具有认知上的凸显性（perceptual salience），使得双主句还可以起到引起听话者注意，表达说话人激动、兴奋、气愤、迫不及待等心情的作用。例如：

　　（10）她穿着新的蓝布衫回来了，一见面，就将一包书递给我，高兴地说道："哥儿，<u>有画儿的'三哼经'</u>，我给你买来了！"（鲁迅，《朝花夕拾》）

　　（11）"三阿太，张家嫂，你们怎么坐在这里哭！<u>货色</u>，他们分完了！……"（茅盾，《林家铺子》）

　　以上是双主句常见的七种语用功能。据我们观察，无论是有标记还是无标记的双主句都具备前六种功能，最后一种功能似为有标记双主句所独有。尽管有标记与无标记双主句具备相同的功能，但有标记双主句的语用功能更加突出，因为有标记双主句毕竟有别于常规句型，更加容易引起受众对它的重视。以第一种功能为例，倒装句序往往使有标记双主句的主题与前一句最后的概念形成一种"顶真"结构，其承前性往往比无标记双主句要强。此外，有标记双主句往往会同时具备多种语用功能。如例（6）除了表示旧话重提外，还表示强调；例（10）既表示说话人激动的心情，也表示旧话重提。

　　下面我们探讨双主句的英译。首先需要说明的是，隐性双主句在理解时一般要根据上下文把它变为显性双主句，这通常不会给译者带来困难，因此我们重点讨论无标记和有标记双主句的英译。

3　无标记双主句的英译

　　英语是一种典型的 SVO 语言，所以汉语的无标记双主句译为英语时，多采用无标记的主谓结构。就汉语主题与主语的不同处理方法而言，大致有以下三种译法。

3.1　把主语译为主语，而主题译为主语之外的其他成分

　　（2″）（林先生）眼圈儿有点红肿。/His eyes were somewhat bloodshot and swollen.

　　（12）但是<u>老通宝他们</u>满心的欢喜却被这件事打消了。（茅盾，《春蚕》）/But the joy that old Tong Bao and his family had been feeling was dampened.

　　该译法比其他两种译法更易掌握，因为汉语双主句中的主语与谓语的语义联系比主题与谓语的联系更紧密。译者通常只需把源语的主谓搭配移植入译语，而把源语中的主题根据其与主语的关系译为相应的所有格形式［如例（2″）］、定语从句［如例（12）］或其他修饰限定成分即可。

3.2　把主题译为主语，而主语译为主语之外的其他成分

　　（13）<u>林先生</u>脸色变了。（茅盾，《林家铺子》）/Mr. Lin paled.

　　（14）可是<u>他们</u>那简单的头脑老是这么想。（茅盾，《春蚕》）/They had only one thought in their heads.

　　此种译法打破了汉语的主谓搭配，把双主句的主题译为英语的主语，而双主句的主语也只好译为其他成分：或者与谓语结合共同译为新的谓语［如例（13）］，或者译为状语［如例（14）］。

3.3 主题和主语都不译为主语,而是译为其他成分

(15) <u>常在那对蝴蝶门旁边看望的林小姐脸上</u>也有些笑意。(茅盾,《林家铺子》)/There was a pleased expression on the face of Miss Lin, who had been constantly watching from beside the swinging doors.

(16) <u>老通宝满脸恨意</u>,看着这小轮船来,看着它过去。(茅盾,《春蚕》)/Hatred burned in Old Tong Bao's eyes. He watched the boat approaching.

此种译法不以双主句的主题或主语为译文主语,而是选择新的主语。新主语或者是英语无人称主语 it 或 there be[如例(15)],或者是从谓语中确定[如例(16)]。

无标记双主句在汉语中本来就是一种常规句型,因此译为英语时如不考虑语用因素,译者不论采取何种译法,只要忠实、通顺即可。第一种译法相对最容易,第二种次之,第三种最难。从我们所掌握的语料看,第一种与第二种的译法较为普遍。

然而,从语用功能看,这三种译法得出的译文略有差别:第二种译法保留了主题的句首位,可以最大限度地保留双主句承前启后的功能;第一种译法也基本保留了主题的句首位(如把主题译为所有格),但有时也会失去句首的突出位置(如把主题译为定语从句),这时译文的承前性与原文相比略有减弱;第三种译法使主题完全脱离了句首,译文的承前性就比原文弱了很多,但这并不意味着译文存在瑕疵,如例(16)。然而,第三种译法有时会损害双主句的语用功能,如例(15),脱离语境很难发现译文有何不妥。但从其上下文:"虽然是累得那么着,林先生心里却很愉快。他冷眼偷看斜对门的裕昌祥,似乎赶不上自己铺子的'热闹'。<u>常在那对蝴蝶门旁边看望的林小姐脸上也有些笑意</u>,林大娘也少打几个嗝了。/Although he was worn out, he was very happy. He had been sneaking a look at the shop across the street. They didn't seem to be nearly so busy. <u>There was a pleased expression on the face of Miss Lin, who had been constantly watching from beside the swinging doors.</u> Mrs. Lin even jerked out a few less hiccups."可以发现该句主题"林小姐"在语篇中与其前后主题"林先生"、"林大娘"形成一定的"对比",文中的两个"也"字即是旁证。正是这一家三口各自的表现才共同描绘出生意上的起色给这个艰难的家庭带来了莫大欢乐。但是译文忽视了该功能,直接译为 there be 句型,使读者很难体察到原作中这一微妙的艺术效果。笔者试改译如下:

Miss Lin, who had been constantly watching from beside the swinging doors, had again a pleased expression on her face.

总之,无标记双主句的前两种译法通常对再现原文语用功能影响不大,但第三种译法有时会有不小的影响,需根据语境具体分析。

4 有标记双主句的英译

变换语序是汉语中最常见的话题化手段之一(石毓智,2001:88)。有标记双主句通常把宾语从谓语之后的无标记位置提到句首。英语中也有类似的标记化手段,如"This book I can't recommend","Weddings I just don't care for"(石毓智,2001:87)。因此,有标记双主句的英译主要有两种:标记化翻译与去标记化翻译,其中后者占了绝大多数。

4.1 去标记化翻译

把汉语有标记双主句进行去标记化翻译就是把它译为无标记的英语句型,其方法主要分为三种:

4.1.1 把主语译为主语,主题译为宾语

(3″) 那文章(我)现在是一句也不记得了。/I can't remember a single sentence of that article now.

(5′) 流言的来源,我是明白的。/I knew the source of the rumour.

(11′) 货色,他们分完了!/They've finished dividing up the property.

(17) 一元的银元日本早已废置不用了,又赔钱换了半元的银圆和纸票。(鲁迅,《朝花夕拾》)/And as they had long given up using silver coins of the one-*yuan* denomination in Japan,I changed mine at a loss into half-*yuan* coins and bank-notes.

(18) "都在这里了。栗市的那家黄茂记很可恶,这种户头,我们明年要留心!"(茅盾,《林家铺子》)/"It's all here," he said, "That Huang Shop in Lishi is rotten. We have to be careful of customers like that next year … "

有标记双主句的主题与主语之间通常存在受事与施事的语义关系,因此去标记化翻译最常见的方法就是先把它变为无标记的主谓宾句,然后再译为相同结构的英语。

4.1.2 把主题译为主语,主语译为谓语之外的其他成分

(6′) 他们钱都花光了,精力也绞尽了。/Both their money and their energy were completely spent.

(19) 他郑重地说:"日本的袜(你们)是万不能穿的,要多带些中国袜。"(鲁迅,《朝花夕拾》)/He told us earnestly:"Japanese socks are absolutely unwearable, so take plenty of Chinese socks."

该译法放弃了原句的句法结构,根据句子内的语义关系把原来的主题与谓语译为主系表结构,而原来的主语或者省略[如例(19)],或者译为定语[如例(6′)]等谓语之外的成分。

4.1.3 把主题译为主题,把主语译为主语

(20) 木刻的(我)却已经记不清是什么时候失掉了。(鲁迅,《朝花夕拾》)/As for the woodblock edition, I cannot remember now when that was lost.

(21) "图还是我画得不错;至于实在的情形,我心里自然记得的。"(鲁迅,《朝花夕拾》)/"My diagram was a good drawing. As for the true facts, of course I can remember them."

英语中通常把 as for 或 about 置于句首引出主题(Croft,2003:12),而在后面句子主干中再次提到主题时则用代词指代。这是一种常见句型,因此也是无标记的。汉语有标记双主句形式上与这类句型颇为接近,故可借用该句型进行去标记化翻译。但该句型的使用具有一定的语用条件,后文将谈到。

4.2 标记化翻译

标记化翻译就是把英语中本来在无标记位置上的宾语置于句首,而在宾语空缺的位置上不加任何指示代词,此译法形式上与汉语有标记双主句完全一致。例如:

(22) 洋鬼子怎样就骗了钱去,老通宝不很明白。(茅盾,《春蚕》)/How the foreign devils

had accomplished this, Old Tong Bao wasn't too clear.

（23）<u>别人不肯做，或不能做的事</u>，她却能够做成功。（鲁迅，《朝花夕拾》）/What others would not or could not do, she had been able to accomplish.

双主句的主题一般是名词短语，但有时动词或者动词短语，甚至一个完整的从句也可以充当主题(Li & Thompson, 1981: 96 - 99)。从我们所掌握的语料看，中外译者似乎都更倾向于当主题为从句（或称主谓短语）时采取标记化译法。一种可能的解释是，从句一般比短语语义更复杂，字数也更多，作为主题更容易引起译者对其标记化特征的重视。

有标记双主句在汉语中有别于无标记的汉语句型，其主题凸显，语用功能明显而丰富。去标记化与标记化译法得出的译文虽然都忠实于原文，但其语用效果还是略有差别。总的来说，标记化译法比去标记化译法更容易再现原文的语用功能，还可以表达强调、对比、凸现、特殊情感等去标记化译文难以传达的语用功能，增强译文的交际效果。以例（22）为例，该句位于段首，上一段最后一句为："可是他想起了'铜钿都被洋鬼子骗去了'这句话，就仿佛看见了老陈老爷捋着胡子摇头的神气。/But whenever Old Tong Bao thought of that remark—'The foreign devils have swindled our money away'—he could almost picture Old Master Chen, stroking his beard and wagging his head."由此可知，这个双主句既表示与前面相关的话题，又表示强调。如果把它去标记化译为 Old Tong Bao wasn't too clear about how the foreign devils had accomplished this，则功能减弱。

不同的去标记化译法在语用功能的再现上也有明显不同。第一种译法通常使主题由句首移到了句尾，在明显减弱了承前性的同时，也往往无法传达双主句所负载的多种语用功能。第二种译法把主题译为主语后，通常都保留了主题原有的句首位，较好地再现了有标记双主句的各种语用功能[如例（6）表示旧话重提，例（19）表示相关话题]。第三种译法既保留了主题的句首位，又如实传译了原句的主谓结构，但往往仅限于表达相关话题[如例（21）]和表示对比[如例（20）]。

汉语有标记双主句的不同英译多由语言表达差异造成，语用功能上的缺失是翻译之憾，非译者之责，而以上对各种译法的描写分析也为我们尝试不同语用效果的译法提供了思路。换言之，在可能的两种（甚至多种）译文表达上，译者可以选用效果更好的译法。例如，用标记化译法可以把例（3）、例（5）和例（18）分别译为：

（3‴）Not a single sentence of that article can I remember now.

（5″）The source of the rumour, I well knew.

（5‴）The source of the rumour, I did know.

（18′）That Huang Shop in Lishi is rotten. Such customers, we have to be careful next year!

即使标记化译法有时也行不通，可以尝试其他去标记化译法。如例（11）可以用第二种方法译为：

（11″）The property has been divided up by them!

再如，例（17）除了表示旧话重提外，还表示对比，可以用第二种和第三种方法分别译为：

（17′）And as the Japanese silver coins of the one-*yuan* denomination had no longer been in use there, I changed mine at a loss into half-*yuan* coins and bank-notes.

（17″）As for the silver coins of the one-*yuan* denomination, they had long given up using them in Japan. So I changed mine at a loss into half-*yuan* coins and bank-notes.

至于哪种译法更好,不同译者和读者会有不同的判定。

5 结语

长期以来,汉译英研究的重点是如何使译文规范,而较少探讨不同规范译文之间的差别。这也许是汉语双主句英译尚未引起学界关注的原因之一。本文重点考察了无标记双主句的三种主要无标记化译法,以及有标记双主句的标记化与去标记化译法,概括总结了各译法的规律,并从语用功能的角度分析比较了其利弊。我们认为,译者在酝酿汉语双主句的英译时,除了要考虑表达规范外,还应考虑译文能否尽可能地再现原文的语用功能。然而,双主句是否还有其他语用功能,无标记与有标记双主句是否还有其他译法等问题仍有待探讨。

标语翻译的文本分析和翻译策略
——以上海世博会标语的翻译为例

李德超　王克非

导　言

本文是香港理工大学李德超和北京外国语大学王克非两位学者在 2010 年《中国翻译》第一期上发表的论文。该论文对赖斯的观点既有继承也有质疑。在他们看来,在功能主义翻译观的影响下,强调意译、强调翻译效果而不注重形式的翻译策略通常被认为是标语翻译的最适合的方法,但是当今的不少标语越来越呈现出独特的文体特征。它不仅帮助标语实现语言的"呼唤功能",同时亦实现"表现功能",而后者正是赖斯所倡导的翻译策略在译文中无法复制的。在这篇文章中,作者以上海世博会标语的翻译为例,根据文体驱动型和非文体驱动型两种标语,提出一种更为精细的标语翻译策略模式,说明不同类型的标语需要用不同的翻译策略处理,在论文的细节上略有改动。

1 引言

上海世博会(Shanghai World Expo)将于 2010 年 5 月 1 日至 10 月 31 日在上海举行。世博会有世界第一展览美誉。上海举办这次盛会对中国的重要意义不亚于 2008 年北京举办的奥运会。全国上下对这次世博会都非常关心,世博会官方发布的一些标语(slogan)及译文也引起了不少讨论。

此届世博会的英文主题"Better city, better life"是数年前申办世博会时拟定的,相应的中文主题"城市,让生活更美好!"是后来依据英文译出。而上海世博会志愿者服务的标语却是先制定出中文"世界在你眼前,我们在你身边",再据此定出英文译文"At your service at Expo"。对于这两个标语的译文,褒贬不一。支持者认为两种译文都言简意赅,朗朗上口;反对者则认为原标语整饬的形式、美好的音效以及丰富的联想在相应的译文中流失。我们是否可以考虑尽量在形式上也保留这两个标语原文的美?如将"Better city, better life"译为"更美好的城市,更美好的生活",将"世界在你眼前,我们在你身边"译为"The world is before you, we are beside you",似乎同样甚至更能传达原文形义之美。

对上海世博会标语的这两种中译文应如何评价?标语通常都不长,但其翻译涉及的问题却并不简单。目前对标语翻译的研究往往只限于一些印象式、随感式的讨论,缺乏对标语原文和译文进行的详细的文本分析和讨论,往往令译文的认同性欠佳。本文拟反思传统标语翻译策略的不足,从文本分析与重构上对标语翻译加以考量,并以此为本,探讨有参照意义的可操作性的标语翻译的原则和方法。

2 传统重效果、轻形式的标语翻译策略的不足

标语(slogan)是人类在各种(如政治、商业、军事等)活动中表达活动目标、本质而使用的一些词、短语或句子,目的在于尽量吸引读者的注意力,其形式往往为读者喜闻乐见,从而使宣传效果彰显,使感染力增强。从语言形式来看,标语通常较简练,长度大多不超过一个句子,基本可以纳入 Quirk 所称的块式语言(block language)这一类别。标语的形式多样,可以是"一个独立存在的名词、名词词组或是名词性的小句(nominal clause)"(1985:845-847),或者是省略了某些句子成分(如主语、谓语等)或时态形式(对英文标语而言)的句子,亦可以是一个完整的、信息排列有特点的句子。如以下几例:

(1) A Kodak moment. (Kodak 广告,以名词词组形式出现,省略主语)

(2) Higher, Faster and Stronger. (宣扬奥林匹克运动会精神的标语,以形容词比较级形式出现,省略了主谓成分)

(3) One world, one dream. (北京奥运会标语,词语组合)

(4) 创一流服务,迎四海嘉宾。(常见饭店广告标语,省略主语)

(5) 丰顺龙归寨旅游度假区是您的投资宝地!(完整句子)

从语言功能来看,标语常用于表达发起人的某种意愿,希望读者能从中有所触动或行动。标语体现出德国心理学家和语言学家 Karl Bühler 所称的语言的"呼唤功能"(appellative function),主要以"读者"为中心,以影响"读者"的行动为目的。德国学者 Reiss 把具有这种功能的文本称之为"感染文本"(operative text, 亦称为 appeal-focused text),并认为判断这种文本的翻译是否成功在于译文能否再造"能够直接引发所希望的反应的文本形式"(1989:109)。她继而指出,"感染文本主要是要传递信息中所包含的非语言目的,其信息内容所采用的语言形式(linguistic form)仅仅是次要而已"(2000:38-39)。在 Reiss 的翻译类型学里,相对于翻译的效果而言,原文形式在"感染文本"的翻译中并非主要需考虑的因素。从理论上来说,只要译文对译语读者产生的效果能够与原文对原文读者产生的效果一致,原文形式无论在译文中怎么改变都可接受。这种翻译思想的精髓似乎可以用英谚"只要目的达到,任何手段无妨"

(the end justifies the means)来概括。按照这种思路,强调意译、强调翻译效果而不注重形式的"交际翻译"(Newmark,1988)和"动态对等"翻译策略(Nida & Taber,1969)长期以来都被认为是翻译标语的最佳方法之一。

Reiss提出以效果为中心的翻译"感染文本"的方法确实能够帮助译者快速地把握到该类文本的中心,从而围绕该中心有的放矢地组织译文,让译者能正确地把翻译重点放在传达原文的信息上,尽量使译文能够符合目的语的文本和文化规范,而不能拘泥于原文的形式和结构,以形害义,进而影响目的语读者对译文的接收。但这种强调用意译手法来翻译一切标语的提法会不会过于涵盖一切(a sweeping statement)?Reiss理论成立的前提就是标语的语言形式无关紧要,无需在译文中有所体现。但事实是否如此?

3 标语的语言和文体特点

若认真观察一下标语的语言形式,我们就会发现,有部分的标语确实如Reiss所言,相对于其表达的意思而言,语言形式只从属次要地位,例如某些国内常见的政治、政策和国情教育标语。计生标语例如"计划生育工作应常抓不懈!","为了国家富强家庭幸福,请您实行计划生育","一人结扎,全家光荣"等似乎都可以用"交际翻译"法意译为"family planning policy is of paramount importance for China",逐字逐句地直译既无必要,亦可能会效果不佳(如第三条标语)。

但除了这种信息内容重要于语言形式的标语外,亦有相当一部分的标语语言特点鲜明,与日常用语大相径庭。标语大都精炼,相对较短。正因为标语短,为了能让读者在瞬间领会标语的意图,好的标语都尽量在形式上具有独特的特点,让人一见难忘。所以用于商业用途的标语又称之为"击中要害之句"(punch line),即为具有压轴意味的句子。对于这种标语,表达的形式与表达的内容之间存在着紧密的联系。毫不夸张地说,这些标语的语言形式在相当程度上帮助实现标语内容的整体目标——激发读者作出标语发起人所期待的反应。这些语言形式或在语义、句法、词汇、修辞上有其显著的特点(统称为文体特点),造成或庄、或谐、或精警的效果。如京石段应急供水工程的标语"保京石通水,为奥运加油"用了对仗、双关的手法,节水标语"水是生命的源泉、工业的血液、城市的命脉"用了排比和比喻的手法,而美国海军陆战队的标语"The few, the proud, the Marines"则用了层进手法,句式的排列方式亦让人联想起罗马凯撒大帝的名言"I came, I saw, I conquered",读之令人豪气丛生。

面对这种语言形式经精心设计的标语,如译文不考虑原文文体特点,就无法传达原文的形式美,对译文读者的效果则很可能不如原文对原文读者的效果。译文即便能勉强达到原文表达的部分目的,也会不如原文那样能从多方面给予原文读者多重的阅读享受,比如让读者领会到原文文体特点所暗含的审美、期待、庄严、幽默、讽刺等意义。换句话说,在这种类型的标语里,形式已经成为其要传达的信息及效果不可或缺的一部分。用Karl Bühler的术语,这种标语不仅体现了语言的"呼唤功能",同时亦实现了语言的"表现功能"。

因此,对于形式与效果紧密结合的标语(以下称之为文体驱动式标语"stylistically motivated slogans"),我们在翻译时除了要了解标语传达的信息及预期意义外,还要对标语的语言形式作详尽的文体分析,确定其不同的文体特征对最终有效地传递标语的信息和意义所起到的作用,然后据此再来确定具体的翻译策略,如直译、改写、补偿等(对具体翻译策略的讨论见以下第5节)。

4 文体驱动式标语的分析——以上海市博会的标语翻译为例

如何才能全面地从文体角度分析标语语言？这里，我们可以借鉴 Leech 等（1981）提出的分析语言文体的一个清单（checklist）。该清单原为分析小说语言而设，但因为该清单考虑到语言文体的方方面面，也值得我们在分析非文学体裁时借鉴。具体而言，该清单提出考察文体时应注意文本的四大类特点，包括词汇、语法、修辞、衔接与语境（1981：75－80）。前三类是从以句子为单位的微观层面着手，而最后一类则是从以段落或语篇为单位的宏观层面着眼。这四类下面均有更详尽的划分，为研究者提供更为精细的考察角度，在此不赘。下面我们用 Leech 等（1981）提出的文体清单来研究前述上海世博会的标语原文的文体特点，并观察译文在多大程度上保留了原文的文体特点，从而在多大程度上在译文读者中实现了原文对原文读者的信息及语用功能。

回到开篇提及的"Better city, better life"及"世界在你眼前，我们在你身边"这两个标语。显然，它们均属于文体驱动式的标语。在"Better city, better life"这句中，从词汇角度看，整个句子的用词"Better, city, life"在词源（etymology）上均属盎格鲁-撒克逊（Anglo-Saxon）词汇。此类词汇是构成英语的基本词汇。与后期引入英语的拉丁语、法语等其他语言的借词相比，以盎格鲁-撒克逊为词源的词汇特点就是音节少（往往不超过 3 个音节）、构词简单，它们"构成了英语国家人民从小就认识的基本词汇，令他们感觉亲切，且词语还充满感情"（钱瑗，2006：88），这些词语如在文中适当运用的话可以造成一种朴实、粗犷和自然的效果。典型的例子如英国桂冠诗人 Ted Huges 写的《蓟草》（"Thistle"）一诗，通篇突出盎格鲁-撒克逊词汇，以蓟草这一在英国随处可见的野生植物来代表英伦岛上北欧海盗（Viking）后裔顽强、质朴和自强不息的精神。同样，"better"、"city"、"life"这些词在世博会的标语里亦构成了一种平实、平易近人的效果，拉近了与读者的距离。而这些词音节少（由两个双音节词和一个单音节词组成），阅读时就构成了一种节奏轻快又带紧迫之感，为此句标语带来了额外的如诗歌错落有致的音响节奏。而"better"一词为"good"的比较级，意指世博会将带来比如今更为美好的城市和生活，表达了一种更高层次上的展望和期盼。

从句子的组成上看，此标语由两个名词词组构成，均以 better 引导，各个名词词组包括的单词数量相同，音节相若，具有类似 ABAB 式的排比修辞效果。英语常被通俗地认为是"形合"（hypotaxis）语言，即句意的表达和理解在很大程度上依靠句中各个成分或有形的连接手段的帮助；中文则常被认为是"意合"（parataxis）语言，即句意的表达和理解主要靠人们对各个成分之间联系的意识和推测。但两者之间的划分并非绝对。如"Better city, better life"这句标语显然是一个意合的句子，在正常的英语书面语中，此句多半会以"we are building a better city so that we can live a better life"等类似的形合句子出现，用表示结果的连接词"so that"来连接前后两个小句，指明它们之间的逻辑关系。但在英语标语这种特定的语言场合里，受位置所限，同时为了让标语更为精练，"意合"特点这时反而成了英语标语的常态，成为"非标记性"（unmarked）的语言特征。

综上所述，这句标语音、形、义相结合，意义集中突出，读起来则朗朗上口、回环不绝。对于这种文体驱动式的标语，其目的并非只是让读者有所行动这么简单。它除了要激发起读者的反应，体现"呼唤功能"外，还希望读者从语言的形式中获得美的感受，也即"表现功能"

(expressive function)的体现。标语中表达的这两种功能很难如 Reiss 所说的那般，肯定有一种占统治地位(见 Reiss，2000：25)；相反，它们之间是一种有机结合、互为补充、互为强化的关系。没有"呼唤功能"，标语不成为标语；没有"表现功能"，标语的"呼唤功能"不能充分实现。因此，Reiss 在其翻译类型学中，强调在翻译以标语、广告为首的一众的"感染文本"时，译者只需对效果忠实，而无需对原文的形式负责这一论点(见 Reiss，2000：41)，在我们看来，显然是忽略了某些标语中"表现功能"的作用，把标语翻译的策略想得过于简单化。

我们再看看"Better city, better life"的两种译文。

译文一"更美好的城市，更美好的生活"直接复制了原文的排比修辞特点以及比较的词汇意义(用了"更美好的")，没有用上任何连接词，正符合中文"意合"的句式结构。在音响及节奏方面，译文亦简练，读起来铿锵有力，符合中文标语言简意赅的特点。同时，原标语的潜在之意，即随着城市变得越好，人们生活将不断改善的主题，也在译文之中得到强化，深入读者之心。当然，上述译文亦可简洁地改为"城市越好，生活越好"，或许更体现原文平实、朴素的风格。

译文二"城市，让生活更美好!"对原文句式做了很大的变动。原文的平行、排比结构在译文中变为普通的主谓宾结构，句子的组合上少了原文的修辞特点。原文的意合句式在中文译文里改成了用连接词"让"这一明显的言语标志来表达"城市"与"生活"这两个名词的关系，而不是让读者自己设想"意合"的连贯方式，少了想象空间。原文中城市与生活都用上了比较级，强调只有城市变得更好了，生活才会更美好。这两者当中都隐含着对当今城市和生活质量的比照。这种逻辑比较关系亦在译文中消失殆尽。但中译文因为在形式上对原文改动大，它亦有原文不具备的、从理论上而言更符合中文习惯的形式特点。具体而言，译文特意在城市之后加一非常规用法的逗号来起停顿作用，这除了让句子具有类似诗歌的节奏韵律外，还让句子具备了类似中文常用的"话题—评论"(topic-comment)结构(参见 Li，1976：469)。该结构的特点就是把句中要说的主题置于句子开始，以吸引读者或听众的注意，如句子"鱼，我们在乡下倒是经常吃的。"但在真正的"话题—评论"句中，主题并非主语(如上例中"鱼"非主语，"我们"才是主语)，而"城市，让生活更美好!"中"城市"却是真正的主语。因此，译文只是类似"话题—评论"句而已，并非真正的"话题—评论"句。从信息的轻重角度来看，在译文中，"城市"这个信息的重要性比原文得到放大，给人一种生活若要美好，则要依靠城市的感觉。而原文中，"城市"与"生活"这两个信息并没有孰重孰轻之分。

综合比较译文一与译文二，我们似乎可以得出这样的结论：虽然两种译文都能达到激发读者反应功能的目的，但程度却各有不同，且读者从中获得的对语言的美的感受也不一样。对于属于"感染文本"的原文，译文一与译文二采取了不同的翻译策略。译文一采用了直译的方法，尽量保持译文在形式与目的上与原文的一致，忠实复制了原文的文体特点，在充分反映了原文的"呼唤功能"的同时亦反映了原文的"表现功能"；译文二则基本遵循 Reiss 的重效果而不重形式，类似 Newmark 式的交际翻译或 Nida 的动态对等的策略，在形式上做了颇大的改动，虽然译文亦能部分反映原文的语用效果，即对世博会的美好期盼和展望，且译文在句式上做了某些创新以求补偿，但总体而言，在对读者的触动程度上却不如文体特点更为丰富的译文一。

5　建立标语翻译的翻译策略模式

综上所述，就标语这种"感染文本"而言，Reiss 把它们统一归为是重效果而轻形式的文本（见 2000：41），认为在翻译这种类型的文本时，形式并不重要，这显然是没有注意到当今标语亦愈来愈注意到形式与功能统一的趋势。在过去，标语的形式基本可称之为是"同质"的（homogenous），大多数运用"硬销"（hard sell）的手法来一味强调其最终希望的结果（如"严禁酒后驾车"，"坚决打击黄、赌、毒等"），口气僵硬。文体效果、表达形式所传达的阅读愉悦并非是过去标语的考虑对象。但在 21 世纪的今天，标语表现形式已经变得越来越多样化，很多标语的表现方向亦从原来的"硬销"表现手法转变成为更重视表达形式，强调内容与目的有机结合的新标语形式。新标语形式比以往的标语更具人性化，给读者以更多阅读的愉悦。对于当今标语更为"异质"（heterogeneous）的特点，相应的翻译策略亦应变得多样化。Reiss 提倡的那种"一刀切"翻译策略显然不适用于所有类型的现代标语，而有微调的必要。具体而言，在翻译标语时，我们除了要了解标语所要传达的信息内容及预期意义（intended meaning）外，还要对标语所用的语言形式作详尽的文体分析，确定该形式是否为文体驱动。若是，则需进一步了解其具体文体的特点，然后观察这些特点是否能直接在译文中保留。如果不保留，则又如何在可能的情况下，对译文在文体上做类似的补偿。

文体驱动型与非文体驱动型标语

下面我们仍以世博会志愿者的标语"城市有我更可爱"及"世界在你眼前，我们在你身边"的翻译为例，依照当今标语的特点，提出一种标语翻译策略模式，并阐述每种不同策略在不同场合的具体运用及其优缺点。

翻译标语之前，首先要确定原文的标语是否为文体驱动式。若否，基本上可以采取以下两种方法处理：一是改写法（paraphrasing），即采用 Reiss 提倡的重结果而不重形式的翻译方法，如交际翻译法及动态对等法，将原文的"呼唤功能"以符合目标语语言及文化习惯的方式改写，译文在形式上无需对原文亦步亦趋。注重译文的效果、注重译文在目标语文化的接受性是这种翻译方法最主要的考虑因素。理论上而言，这种翻译方法能让原文与译文在效果上基本一致，即译文等于原文。二是增强法（enhancing），即在翻译中除了保持原文的"呼唤功能"以外，还尽量在译文的语言中添加原文所不具备的文体特点，以传达标语的"表现功能"。这样一来，译文在形式和目的上都得到兼顾，译文胜于原文。

若原文标语为文体驱动式，则主要有以下三种处理方法。

一是简化（simplification），即忽略或仅保留原文部分形式特点，译文将重点放在重现原文的"呼唤功能"上，完全或部分放弃原文的"表现功能"。意译是常用于这一目的的翻译方法。采用这种译法，译文的效果小于原文。二是补偿（compensation），即译者在翻译时对多方面因素加以权衡，决定对原文的形式特点不予保留，但为了不让原文文体特点带有的"表现功能"在译文中完全丧失，译者在译文中保持原文"呼唤功能"的同时，对译文的形式进行不同于原文形式的文体建构，以期获得与原文类似的"表现功能"。换言之，译者采用这种方法时，完全摒弃原文的语言特点，在译文中另起炉灶。但这样一来，译者就要冒相当大的丧失原文语言效果的风险，除非译者能够在译文的其他文体特点方面做出补偿，正所谓"失之东隅，收之桑榆"，有失有得,殊途同归。这类似于翻译中的再创造的方法。这种译法最为灵活,其效果亦多样,译文效果差于原文、等于原文或胜于原文均有可能。三是移植法(transplantation),即译者采用直译的方法把原文的形式得到完全的保留,希望译文与原文在形式上的一致不仅能忠实地保留原文的"呼唤功能",亦能保持原文的"表现功能",让译文与原文一样达到形与义的统一。但保留有两个前提:其一是要对原文作详细的文体分析,弄清楚标语原文在词汇、语法、修辞和连贯(假如标语比较长的话)方面的特点以及它们在读者中引发的相应的表现意义。不彻底了解原文文本特点的话就根本谈不上全面移植原文有文体意义的形式。其二是译者要明确地衡量保持原文的语言形式在目标语文化系统里带来的利与弊。换言之,就是要确定这种保留能够符合目标语语言文化环境的惯例,保留后的译文不会引起译文读者在政治、文化、审美等其他社会文化层面上负面的联想。在这两种条件下,移植原文的形式就成为一个可行的翻译策略。通过这种方法得出的译文,其效果在理论上应与原文相等。除此三法之外,我们也可能会有优化(optimization)。这是标语翻译一种最理想的状态,即译者在译文中保留原文具有美学价值的表达形式及语用目的之余,能根据目标语的特点,在译文的表达形式上添加更多的文体特征,令"呼唤功能"在目标语内表达得更为彻底、更深入人心、更耐人寻味。换言之,译文相当于具有锦上添花的作用,即是译文胜于原文。不过这往往是可遇不可求的事。据此,我们提出标语翻译的翻译策略模式,用图1表示:

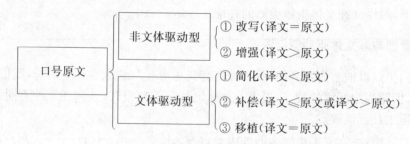

图1 标语翻译的翻译策略模式

从图1可以看出,无论是文体驱动式抑或是非文体驱动式的标语,其翻译方法均有多种。从理想的角度来看,对于非文体驱动式的标语,最佳的翻译方法应是"增强";而对于文体驱动式的标语,最佳的翻译方法应是"优化"。但这可以说是一种理想的状态,是译者追求的最终目标。在现实中,囿于译者的个人语言水平、翻译能力、时间和环境的限制、语言及文化上的差异,以及译者在衡量时间投入与译文产品效益后作出的决定,对于非文体驱动式的标语的翻译策略不少译者往往选择"改写",而对文体驱动式的标语的翻译策略往往选择"简化"及"补偿"。

下面我们用上海世博会志愿者的两个标语来阐释上述标语翻译策略模式。第一个标语的中文原文为"城市有我更可爱"。从语言特点来看,此标语为"非文体驱动式"标语,语言表达朴实无华,标语重点是其"呼唤功能",呼吁上海市民投入志愿者服务,令游人宾至如归,让世博会举办得更成功、更精彩。采用不同的翻译策略,我们可以得出以下两种不同侧重的译文。

译文1:Your volunteer work makes Shanghai Expo more attractive!(改写法译文)

译文2:A warm welcome to the world from willing hands!(增强法译文)

译文1直接将标语隐含的目的译出,呼吁大家来充当志愿者。从复制"呼唤功能"的这方面看,译文与原文是一致的,虽然原文与译文在形式上有出入。依照重功能而不重形式的改写翻译策略,我们还可以得出类似的译文,如"Thank you for being a volunteer in Shanghai

Expo!""Shanghai Expo wants you to be a volunteer!"上述这些译文配上合适的图案、绘画，亦能复现原文语用功能。这充分证明了 Reiss 强调的在翻译感染型文本时，要注重效果而非形式的翻译策略至少在翻译"非文体驱动式"标语时是有其运用价值的，因为它能让译者摆脱原文的桎梏，直接译出其言外之意。试设想上述标语如照字面直译，则会变为令人费解的"Your presence makes the city more beautiful"。这再次说明了在"非文体驱动式"的标语里，形式并不重要，重要的是其"呼唤功能"。译文 2 则在充分理解原文的"呼唤功能"的基础上对译文的形式作了精心的安排，句中"warm"、"welcome"、"world"和"willing"均以"w"开头，构成英语修辞中常用的头韵效果，读起来朗朗上口。译文表达的"志愿者重要，欢迎参加志愿者"的目的随着带有"表现功能"的语言形式的运用得到加强，两者互为促进，让人印象深刻，可称为是译文胜过原文。类似的增强性译法还有"You are needed to help Shanghai Expo succeed"，采用了音韵的手法，亦令人对表达方式印象深刻。

官方译文"Our city，your joy"也是用增强型译法，用两个长度相近的名词词组"our city"和"your joy"并列，造成强烈的对比，而"city"和"joy"亦有眼韵（eye rhyme）的效果；整个句子亦是用了"意合"方式，配合上图片，亦传递出志愿者帮助上海世博成为更美好城市的意思，可称得上译文胜过原文。但所嫌是太过简短，标语所指的志愿者工作过于隐晦，不容易令人立即联想到志愿者服务，当然这也正是"意合"标语的特点。

第二个要讨论的是上海世博会的志愿者标语"世界在你眼前，我们在你身边"的翻译。很明显，此为"文体驱动式"标语，语言表达整饬，两个短句字数相同，用了对比、对仗的手法，"前"与"边"还有音韵效果，结合整句的意思，将世博会面向世界的眼界以及志愿者起的作用有机地结合在一起，让读者的思维由大至小（"世界"与"眼前"对比），由远至近（"世界"与"身边"对比），整句用了汉语"意合"的特点，靠读者的意会来理解全文，读之令人回味无穷，令人既感受到标语的"呼唤功能"（即在世博会上随时可以向志愿者求助的隐含意思），亦感受到其"表现功能"。此标语可谓世博会上非常漂亮的志愿者标语之一，但亦为翻译增加了不少难度。根据以上提出的"文体驱动式"标语的翻译策略，我们大概可以得出以下几种译文。

译文 3：Turn to a volunteer for help at Shanghai Expo!（简化法译文）

译文 4：Our volunteers bring the world closer to you.（补偿法译文）

译文 5：Volunteers—your vital link to the world at Shanghai Expo!（补偿法译文）

译文 6：The world is before you；we are beside you.（移植法译文）

译文 3 摒弃了原文精心设计的语言形式，改用直接、平实的语言将其潜在的意思译出，虽然它保持了原文的语用目的，但优美的语言形式荡然无存，读者读了译文后无法获得像原文读者般美的享受，虽然明白其目的所在。类似的译法还可以有 Seek help from a volunteer at Shanghai Expo，等等。官方对此的翻译版本"At your service at Expo"亦属于简化译文这一类，译文完全没有任何原文形式的影子。这种类型的译文效果逊于原文。译文 4 没有完全复制原文语言表达形式的所有特点，而是另起炉灶，运用了拟人的形式（the world closer），把世界当成人似的可以亲近事物。相比译文 3 中只译出表面意思，译文 4 在表达方式上略胜一等。但与原文相比，译文的语言特点还是不够鲜明、突出，意义亦不及原文丰富。总体而言，译文 4 亦逊于原文。译文 5 则完全脱离原文形式的限制，巧妙利用头韵（"volunteers"、"vital"）来对原文的语言特点做另一方面的修辞补偿，指明志愿者对世博会的重要作用，其形式同样令人印象深刻，亦在一定程度上再创造了原文表达形式所带来的阅读愉悦。译文可说与原文各有千秋,难分高下。译文6尽量对原文亦步亦趋,亦用上对比、押韵、意合等组织方式,尽量保持原文形式,且译文形式在英国文化中亦可接受,可以说译文效果等于原文。

6　结语

从上述讨论可看出,标语虽然属于"感染文本"中的一种,但其翻译策略并非千篇一律地如Reiss所言只采用重功能而不重形式的方法。如今越来越多标语亦注重形式与功能方面相结合。为了在翻译中充分体现标语语言特点的时代变迁,我们设计了一种更为精细的标语翻译策略模式,并以上海世博会的标语翻译为例,说明标语翻译有不同层次的目标,这对我们提高标语翻译的教学和实践水平,以及提高对外宣传质量均有裨益。

第三章　系统功能语言学（SFL）与翻译研究

导　论

　　系统功能语言学是当今世界上最有影响的语言学流派之一，是在人类学的传统下发展起来的，与其他语言学流派的不同之处在于，他们强调语言使用者的社会性，着眼于语言在实际应用中的特点，以及语言的功能性。虽然系统功能语言学不是专门的翻译理论，但却被用于翻译理论研究，指导翻译理论的发展。系统功能语言学派的代表人物韩礼德（Halliday，1961：145-158）写过一篇有关语言学与机器翻译的文章，提出了建立翻译过程理论模式的设想。1964年，他又在《语言科学与语言教学》（*The Linguistic Sciences and Language Teaching*）一书中，专辟一章，探讨比较与翻译的关系问题。虽然他只是将文本的对比看作比较语言学的一个特例，而不同文本的对等在他看来只是为比较语言学提供了一个例证，但是在这篇文章中，他对翻译的本质提出了自己的看法，并在级阶与范畴语法的基础上建立了一个逐级选择的翻译模式。

　　早期受到系统功能理论影响的翻译理论家当数卡特福德。1965年，他写了《翻译的语言学理论》一书，利用韩礼德的范畴、层次和级阶的观点对翻译问题进行探讨。他把翻译理论中经常讨论的问题，如直译、意译、逐字翻译、全文翻译、部分翻译、完全翻译、有限翻译、音位翻译、词形翻译、语法翻译和词汇翻译等都置于语言学的理论框架中去探讨，使翻译理论研究趋于理论化、系统化。在韩礼德层次理论的基础上，卡特福德提出了级转换的观点，对于翻译的具体操作过程有一定的指导意义。继卡特福德之后，还有尤金·奈达和罗杰·贝尔。在奈达的许多论文和论著的参考书目中，一般都可以找到韩礼德的论文或著作。奈达在他的《语言、文化与翻译》（*Language，Culture and Translating*）一书中，对以韩礼德为代表的系统功能语言学理论作出了高度评价，认为该理论一改过去把着眼点放在静态结构上的传统，引入了动态的观点。系统功能理论倾向于把语言放到实际应用中加以考察，着眼于语言的功能。众所周知，奈达的对等概念的提出得益于乔姆斯基的转换生成语法，但韩礼德的社会的、功能的思想对于奈达的影响也是不容置疑的。奈达把从前提出过的动态对等改为功能对等。这样做，一方面是为了避免"动态"一词引起误解，另一方面则反映了他对功能这一概念的强调。因为——正如奈达（Nida，1993：124）自己所说，"功能"一词着眼于一个翻译过来的文本做了些什么，发挥了怎样的作用，实现了怎样的功能。从这点看来，奈达的观点与韩礼德的观点还是非常契合的。另外，奈达关于篇章的理论和语言作为社会符号的思想也都得益于系统功能理论的影响。另一位深受系统功能理论影响的翻译理论家是罗杰·贝尔。他的代表作《翻译与翻译过程》一书就是把翻译问题放到系统功能理论的框架中进行研究和探讨的。他试图建立的翻译模式是以系统的理论和认知理论为基石构建起来的,并用系统功能理论中语言的三个元功能来论述对于源语文本的意义的理解,而对于篇章问题的解释也完全是系统功能语言学派的篇章理论。

随着时间的推移,系统功能语言学与翻译研究的关系越走越近。可以说,当代最有影响的翻译理论家几乎都是从系统功能语言学中汲取营养从而取得成就的。除了卡特福德和贝尔之外,纽马克、贝克、哈蒂姆、梅森、豪斯等都将系统功能语言学的观点用于翻译研究,成就卓著,至少占据了当前翻译界的半壁江山。

贝克在她的专著《换言之:翻译教程》(*In Other Words:A Coursebook on Translation*)第五章、第六章两个章节中,主要运用了系统功能语言学的语篇分析模式讨论翻译问题,尤其关注如何运用主位、衔接、连贯等资源手段实现语篇对等。

哈蒂姆和梅森(Hatim & Mason)也主要运用系统功能语言学的语篇分析模式讨论翻译问题,从主位、述位、语篇的连贯性等层面考察译本与原文的对应情况。

而豪斯(Juliane House)则运用功能语言学的语篇分析,尤其是语域理论,从 8 个方面,即3 个涉及语言使用者的参数(地点、社会阶层、时代)和 5 个语言应用参数(媒介、参加者、社会角色关系、社会态度、领域),依据言语行为所涉及的形式、功能、情景要素及其彼此的互动关系,研究原文、译本在语境与言语形式方面在何种程度上是对应的,找出译文与原文在功能上对等或偏离的情况。

在本章中,我们主要从 Marina Manfredi 的专著《文本与语境的翻译:翻译研究和系统功能语言学》(*Translating Text and Context:Translation Studies and Systemic Functional Linguistics*)①中选取了一些章节,较为系统全面地介绍韩礼德、卡特福德、纽马克、哈蒂姆与梅森等人从系统功能语言学角度出发所进行的翻译研究。因为这些章节选自同一部作品,所以我们只在韩礼德的部分撰写了导言,其他几节不再赘述。另外,我们还选取了豪斯的一篇非常经典的作品,看她如何借用语域理论建立起翻译批评的框架。

选 文

选文一　M. A. K. Halliday and Translation

Marina Manfredi

导　言

这里关于系统功能语言学与翻译关系论述的一组文章都选自 Marina Manfredi 主编的

---

① http://amsacta.cib.unibo.it/2393/1/Manfredi_2008_Monografia.pdf.

《文本与语境的翻译：翻译研究和系统功能语言学》。全书分为上下两卷，上卷集中探讨理论问题，下卷"从理论到实践"，讨论理论如何被应用于翻译实践和翻译研究。

In this chapter we will not focus on M. A. K. Halliday's Systemic Functional model. Rather, what we wish to offer here is an outline of Halliday's own view on translation, as this emerges in particular from some articles where he offers his insights on the phenomenon. As we know, Halliday is not a translation scholar, but a linguist, or as he is fond of defining himself, a "grammarian," one who, however, has also shown interest in "[…] some aspects of linguistics which relate closely to the theory and practice of translation" (1992: 15).

We will focus in particular on three articles that Halliday wrote at different times. Back in the 1960s, he approached the topic of translation in the paper, "Linguistics and machine translation" (1966) [1960]. About thirty years later, at the beginning of the 1990s, his article "Language theory and translation practice" was hosted in the newly published Italian journal, *Rivista internazionale di tecnica della traduzione* (1992). At the beginning of the new millennium, he appeared as the first contributing author of the volume, *Exploring Translation and Multilingual Text Production: Beyond Content*, edited by E. Steiner and C. Yallop (2001), with the chapter, "Towards a theory of good translation."[①] Let us now look at the main issues raised by Halliday in these contributions.

Halliday's interest in translation thus goes back to the 1960s, the early days of experiments on, and enthusiasm for, machine translation. With "Linguistics and machine translation," he proposed a model for computer-assisted translation. Later he commented that, as far as he knew, that approach had never been adopted (Halliday, 2001: 16). However, what is relevant to our topic of translation is that there he defined translation equivalence with respect to the concept of "rank" (ibid.). In the article, he put forward the idea that

> it might be of interest to set up a linguistic model of the translation process,
> starting not from any preconceived notions from outside the field of language study,
> but on the basis of linguistic concepts such as are relevant to the description of
> languages as modes of activity in their own right (Halliday, 1966: 137).

Thus, as a linguist, he aimed at exploiting linguistics in order to construct an analytical model of the translation **process.**

In his study, based on examples from Russian and Chinese, Halliday's discussion

---

① Regarding Halliday's position on "Equivalence" in specific registers, set out in Halliday, M. A. K., "Comparison and translation," in M. A. K. Halliday, A. McIntosh & P. Strevens (1964), *The Linguistic Sciences and Language Teaching*, London: Longmans.

centred around grammatical hierarchies: in particular, he was looking for rank-bound correspondences. His idea was to list a set of equivalents at the lowest level of the rank scale (i. e. , the morpheme), ranged in order of probability, then to modify the choice by moving upwards, to the context① of the next higher unit, that is the word, then the group and phrase, and finally the clause. In other words, the context of any morpheme would have been the word in which it occurred, likewise, the word would have been put in a group, and so on.

With reference to his proposal for machine translation, his model was thus concerned with lexicogrammar only. He suggested that the process of translation be proceeded by three "stages":

(1) Selection of the "most probable translation equivalent" for each item at each rank.

(2) Reconsideration in the light of the lexicogrammatical features of the unit above.

(3) Final reconsideration in the light of the lexicogrammatical features of the TL. He specified that these "stages" were not meant as steps to be taken necessarily one after another, but rather only as abstractions which could be useful to understanding the process of translation (ibid. : 144).

It is, we think, noteworthy that the first issue of the translation journal, *Rivista internazionale di tecnica della traduzione*, published by the School for Translators and Interpreters of Trieste University (1992), included an article warmly solicited from Halliday on "Language theory and translation practice." The paper is rich with insights which we would examine by degrees.

At the beginning, Halliday makes the reason for his title, which avoids the expression "translation theory," clear. As a linguist, he means to offer a *language* theory that could be useful for the practice of translation, through an analytical model of the translation process, i. e. , of what happens when translating. In his view, the kind of linguistic theory which could serve this purpose is not a traditional formal grammar, one which offers prescriptive rules, but rather must be a functional grammar, conceived as an "explanation of potentiality." All this is strictly connected to his notion of "choice," which involves what is possible to mean, and, within this, what is more likely to be meant (Halliday, 1992: 15).

He immediately states that "[i]t is obviously a key feature of translation as a **process** that it is concerned with **meaning**," in other words, "[t]ranslation is a meaning-making activity, and we would not consider any activity to be translation if it did not result in the creation of meaning" (ibid.). Naturally, he acknowledges that the production of a meaningful text is also the goal of any kind of discourse. What distinguishes translation from

---

① Halliday uses the term "context" in this paper, but he is clearly talking about "co-text."

any other kind of discourse activity, he points out, is that it is not only a "creation of meaning," but rather a **"guided creation of meaning"** (ibid., emphasis added).

For Halliday, a language theory which is relevant to translation thus has to be "[...] a theory of meaning as choice" and, to be this, "[...] it must embody a **functional semantics**" (ibid.). And, by "functional," he specifies, he does not mean a vague sense of "use," but rather **"metafunction,"** i. e. "[...] function as the fundamental organizing concept around which all human language has evolved" (ibid.)—which brings us to a key point: "[a] linguistics for translation must be concerned with **functional semantics**"(ibid. : 16).

Halliday immediately makes clear that he does *not* mean to imply that he is *not* interested in formal patterns. Indeed he is, but he insists that these become relevant only through a functional semantics. If we recall the inextricable connection between wording and meaning posited in FG, this only makes sense.

Of course, he adds, **"semantic equivalence"** between languages and texts cannot be absolute. It can only be "contingent," or "with respect", i. e. , "[...] with respect to the **function** of the given item within some context or other" (ibid., emphasis added). And this takes us to the notion of context(co-text).

At this point, the key concepts of "meaning," "function" and "context" build up Halliday's own view of the concept of **"equivalence"**: "[i]f meaning is function in context, [...] then equivalence of meaning is equivalence of function in context" (ibid.). This means that the translator, when engaged in his or her activity of translating, "[...] is taking decisions all the time about what is the relevant context within which this functional equivalence is being established" (ibid.).

Any translator knows that if s/he is supposed to translate an SL"item"[①] into a TL one, it will have a range of potential equivalents in the TL, and these will be not "free variants;" they will be "contextually conditioned. " This does *not* imply that a translator must opt for one solution only, that s/he has *no* choice: it only means that if s/he chooses one option instead of another, then the meaning of that choice will inevitably differ, according to the kind of context s/he is dealing with. At that point s/he will have to decide what the relevant context which conditions his/her choice is, in order to translate the given "item" in the most relevant way.

But you may well now ask: what kind of context are we talking about?

The simplest case of an equivalent context (or context of equivalence) can be considered a word, as you can find it in a dictionary. But, the full meaning of any word is, of course, only *in use*, no dictionary, not even a good one, can hope to exhaust all the factors to be taken into consideration in order to choose a most appropriate translation! As Halliday notes, linguistics can offer a theory of context, but not of translation equivalence.

A first model of context that linguistics can offer the translator, he explains, derives

---

① By "item" Halliday means not necessarily a word, but also a morpheme or a phrase.

from the functional notion of "constituency" (ibid. : 17). In SFL, and as Halliday had explained with reference to his proposal for machine translation, "constituency" represents the part-whole relationship in grammar, according to which larger units are made up of smaller ones, along a hierarchy: the "rank scale" (Halliday, 1985/1994: 3ff).

Following this model, one could move up one or more levels in the scale, although sometimes, as he says, we do not need to go beyond the immediate grammatical environment, that is the context (co-text, once again) of wording. Nevertheless, Halliday points out, this modelling is not the whole story. Besides merely extending the grammatical environment, there are also other aspects of context that must be taken into account (ibid. : 20).

Firstly, even remaining within the level of lexicogrammar, metafunctional variation must be built in. A piece of discourse represents a mapping of three simultaneous structures realizing three different strands of meaning (i. e. ideational, interpersonal and textual). When faced with the translation of a text, as we have already mentioned, Halliday recommends examining all of them (ibid.), including, for example, the "[...] writer's construction of his or her own subjectivity and that of the audience, of attitude to and distance from the subject-matter and so on" (ibid.), that is, what he calls interpersonal meanings.

As the epigraph with which we began this volume demonstrates, we would appropriate Halliday's words and make them our maxim as translators: "[...] *we would not translate a personal diary as if it were a scientific article*" (ibid. , emphasis added). But all this is leading us out of grammar and into the level of **discourse semantics**. And indeed, "[...] we have to move outside the text altogether to engage with the '**context of situation**'" (ibid. : 21), or that of **culture** (ibid. : 23). What Halliday is calling for then is a "first order" and a "second order" context (ibid.), both of which the translator has to take into account.

At this point he takes us back to the key concept of his article, i. e. , translation as a "guided creation of meaning." Through what? Through the construction of the context of situation on the basis of the results of the analysis of the text. This context of situation will then be essential to—will "guide"—the creation of the new, translated, text. Halliday concludes this important article by summarizing what we see as being the fundamental process of translation with the following words:

> In each case, we are putting some particular item in the text under focus of attention, asking why it is as it is, how it might have been different, and what effect such other choices might have made (ibid. : 25).

In his "Towards a theory of good translation" (2001), he focuses in particular on the concept of translation equivalence, which, he argues, is "the central organizing concept" of translation (Halliday, 2001: 15). But, we might ask, with respect to what? In answer, he proposes a **typology of equivalences** (ibid.), in terms of a systemic functional theory, which centres on three "vectors":

（1）"Stratification;"

（2）"Metafunction;"

（3）"Rank."

These are detailed in figure below:

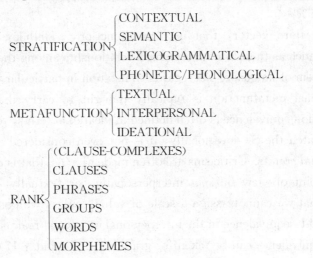

STRATIFICATION
- CONTEXTUAL
- SEMANTIC
- LEXICOGRAMMATICAL
- PHONETIC/PHONOLOGICAL

METAFUNCTION
- TEXTUAL
- INTERPERSONAL
- IDEATIONAL

RANK
- (CLAUSE-COMPLEXES)
- CLAUSES
- PHRASES
- GROUPS
- WORDS
- MORPHEMES

Figure 1　Parameters of Languages (Based on Halliday 2011)

（1）"Stratification," he explains, concerns "[...] the organization of language in **ordered** strata," which means the phonetic/phonological, lexicogrammatical, semantic and, outside of language "proper," contextual levels of the multi-coding system of language, each of which becomes accessible to us through the stratum above it.

（2）"Metafunction," a term we have already been introduced to above, regards the organization of the strata concerning **content**, that is, concerning lexicogrammar as realizing semantics, the (meta) functional components, i. e. ideational, interpersonal and textual.

（3）Finally, "Rank," as we've already seen, deals with "[...] the organization of the **formal** strata," i. e. phonology and lexicogrammar, in a hierarchy (remembering that, in the grammar of English, it is made up of: clause complexes, clauses, phrases, groups, words and morphemes).

This, as pointed out above, corresponds to the model adopted by Halliday when working on machine translation.

Halliday stresses that, as far as "stratification" is concerned, "[...] equivalence at different strata carries differential values" (ibid.). Generally, he says, the "value" is related to the highest stratum: for instance, semantic equivalence is usually granted more value than lexicogrammatical, and contextual perhaps more than anything else. However, he adds, these values need to be considered relative, since they will vary according to the specific translation task at hand.

Likewise, equivalence at different ranks will also carry different values; the highest value will tend to be assigned to the higher formal level: e. g. , the clause. That is, in a sense, to say, "[...] words can vary provided the clauses are kept constant" (ibid. : 17). However, again, particular circumstances can mean that equivalence at lower ranks may have a higher value (ibid. : 16). When, in stratal terms, equivalence is sought at the highest level, i. e. that of context, the ST will have "[...] equivalent function[...] in the context of situation" (ibid.).

As for the third vector, that is, "metafunction," Halliday warns that the case is different, insomuch as there is no hierarchical relationship among the three metafunctions, at least in the system of language. As regards translation in particular, he comments, it is true that the ideational metafunction is typically thought to carry the highest value, simply because translation equivalence is often defined in ideational terms, to such a degree that, if a TT does not match the ST ideationally, it is not even considered a translation. However, this is not all that counts. Criticisms are often made of a TT that is equivalent to an ST from an ideational point of view but *not* interpersonally, or textually, or both. In this case, Halliday says that we cannot assign a scale of value, unless we posit that "[...] high value may be accorded to equivalence in the interpersonal or textual realms—but usually only when the ideational equivalence can be taken for granted [...]" (ibid. : 17).

He concludes the paper by stating, rightly we think, what the actual value of a translation relies on: a "good" translation is a text which is a translation (i. e. is equivalent) in respect of those linguistic features which are most valued in the given translation context (ibid.).

选文二　J. C. Catford and SFL

Marina Manfredi

One of the first theorists to appear in many surveys of TS (see, e. g. , Hatim, 2001; Munday, 2001) is J. C. Catford, a British linguist and translation theorist who, in the 1960s, proposed a linguistic theory of translation where he acknowledged his debt to Firth and Halliday, both of whom he knew.

In his well-known book, *A Linguistic Theory of Translation* (1965), he became the first translation theorist to base a linguistic model on aspects of Halliday's early work on Scale and Category Grammar (such as Halliday, 1961). Indeed, he too considered language as working *functionally* on a range of different levels (i. e. phonology, graphology, grammar, lexis) and ranks (i. e. sentence, clause, group, word, morpheme).

Even though translation scholar Snell-Hornby later dismissed Catford's work as "[...]

now generally considered dated and of mere historical interest" (Snell-Hornby, 1988: 14 – 15), other scholars (like, e. g. , Hatim, 2001; Hatim & Mason, 1990; Taylor, 1993) showed that they recognized the value of his contribution to the theory of translation and his insights into some linguistic aspects which had not yet been taken properly into account.

Taylor (1993) suggests that possibly Catford's most important insights begin with his idea of "**unit**," i. e. "[...] a stretch of language activity which is the carrier of a pattern of some kind" (1965: 5), and continue with his own application of Halliday's notion of the hierarchical structure of units, in descending order: sentences, clauses, groups and words. Many languages are ranked in the same hierarchical way but, Taylor adds, it was Catford who first understood how the ranks at which translation equivalence occur are constantly shifting, from "word for word" to "group for group" (ibid. : 8). Furthermore, by suggesting that, when translation equivalence problems are generalized, they can provide translation rules that are applicable to other texts within the same variety or register (ibid. : 94), Catford was moving towards the important conclusion that "[...] for translation equivalence to occur, [...] both source language and target language texts must be relatable to the **functionally** relevant features of the situation" (1965: 94, emphasis added).

As Hatim & Munday point out (2004: 29), Catford seems to have been the first to use the term "shift" in translation. What are "**shifts**?" They are basically small linguistic changes that occur between ST and TT (ibid.). In his model, Catford distinguished between two kinds of translation shifts: level shift (occurring between the levels of grammar and lexis) and category shifts (unbounded and rank-bounded). He then moved outside the text to such higher-order concepts as variety and register (Taylor, 1993). As mentioned previously, Catford sees translation as a process of substituting a text in one language for a text in a different language. However, as Fawcett(1997) notes, according to Catford we do not "transfer" meaning between languages, but we rather *replace* an SL meaning by a TL meaning—one that can function in the same or a comparable way in that situation.

According to Catford, as we have already seen, one of the central tasks of translation theory is that of defining a theory of translation that is based on equivalence (Catford, 1965: 21), which he takes to be the basis upon which SL textual material is *replaced* by TL textual material. In Catford's model, this can be achieved through either "**formal correspondence**" or "**textual equivalence.** "

A formal correspondence is defined by Catford as "[...] any TL category (unit, class, structure, element of structure, etc.) which can be said to occupy, as nearly as possible, the 'same' place in the 'economy' of the TL as the given SL category occupies in the SL"(1965: 27). Thus, a noun such as *fenêtre* my be said generally to occupy a similar place in the French language system as the noun *window* does in English—and as *finestra* does in Italian. Formal correspondence, therefore, implies a comparison between the language systems but not of specific ST-TT pairs.

When "formal equivalence" is not possible, Catford suggests to aim for "textual equivalence," which can be carried out through the translation "shifts" we spoke of above. A textual equivalent is defined as "[...] any TL text or portion of text which is observed [...] to be the equivalent of a given SL text or portion of text" (ibid.: 27). In simple terms, "translation shifts" are "[...] departures from 'formal correspondence' in the process of going from the SL to the TL" (Catford, 1965: 73). Catford's book was sharply, and widely, criticized in the field of TS as being too highly theoretical and as putting forward what was essentially a "static" model. The main criticism lay in the nature of his examples, which were said to be for the most part abstract, idealized and decontextualized (Agorni, 2005: 15), and never related to whole texts (Munday, 2001). Venuti, for example, attacked his theory for being chiefly focused on the levels of word and sentence, and as using manufactured, i. e., unauthentic, examples (2000/2004: 327). Hatim also observes that, according to many critics, Catford saw equivalence as a phenomenon which is essentially quantifiable and thus was also criticized for what was called his "statistical touch" (Hatim, 2001: 16).

Newmark questioned specifically the ultimate usefulness of Catford's listings of, for instance, sets of words that are grammatically singular in one language and plural in another. In his estimation, by illustrating issues from contrastive linguistics he may have been giving helpful tips to students needing to translate, but he certainly was not offering a valuable contribution to translation theory (Newmark, 1981/82).

Fawcett remarks that even Catford himself was not unaware that his definition of textual equivalence could pose problems: the concept of sameness of situation (1997: 52), for example, is a thorny one, especially in those cases when very different cultures are involved. Nonetheless, other scholars, like Munday (2001) and Hatim (2001) point out his contribution to TS which remains, in the latter's words "[...] one of the very few original attempts to give a systematic description of translation from a linguistic point of view" (Fawcett, 1997: 121). That alone bears witness to the merit of his work. Moreover, as Fawcett notes, although certain scholars (Hatim, 2001) would censure him for decontextualizing the translation process, the accusation is not wholly a valid one. That is to say, Catford does make reference to context and even uses the concept of social contextual function to suggest solutions to dialect translation (Fawcett, 1997).

And Hatim himself admits that "[...] a glance at how Catford [...]uses the concept of social-contextual function in discussing **dialect translation** [...]" reveals that he is no stranger to a linguistics of **context** (Hatim, 2001: 17).

And indeed he is not. In his *Linguistic Theory of Translation* (1965), Catford devoted a chapter (n. 13) to the topic of "Language varieties in translation." He defined a "language variety" as "[...] a sub-set of formal and/or substantial features which correlates with a particular type of socio-situational feature" (84) and argued that in **dialect** translation "[...] the criterion [...] is the 'human' or 'social' geographical one [...] rather than a purely locational criterion" (86 – 87).

Catford distinguished varieties which he dubbed "more or less *permanent*," with reference to a given performer (or group) and other ones that for him were "more or less *transient*," i. e. that "[...] change with changes in the immediate situation of utterance" (ibid. : 84, emphasis in the original). Within the first group, he then identified "Idiolect" and "Dialect," sub-dividing the latter category into the following types: (proper) or geographical, temporal and social. By "Register," Catford means a variety"[...] related to the wider social role being played by the performer at the moment of utterance: e. g. , 'scientific,' 'religious,' 'civil-service,' etc. " (ibid. : 85). By "Style," on the other hand, he indicates a "[...] variety related to the number and nature of addressees and the performer's relation to them: e. g. 'formal,' 'colloquial,' 'intimate'" (ibid.). Catford includes in what he called "transient" varieties also the notion of "mode," related, in his view, to the medium of utterance, i. e. "spoken" or "written," what Halliday considers the "medium" of the message. Halliday of course would subsequently theorise register as language variation according to use, and dialect as variation according to user: his or her geographical and social provenance (1978: 35). Style, in a literary sense, he would see as a question of de-automatized grammar (1982). However, in the 1960s, Catford's contribution to a typology of language varieties, when applied to translation, could be considered as being quite instructive:

> The concept of a "whole language" is so vast and heterogeneous that it is not operationally useful for many linguistic purposes, descriptive, comparative and pedagogical. It is, therefore, desirable to have a framework of categories for the classification of "sub-languages," or varieties within a total language [...] (ibid. : 83).

And it will be from this same quotation that, twenty-five years later, Hatim and Mason will start their own investigation into language varieties.

选文三　Peter Newmark and SFL

Marina Manfredi

In the UK, translation scholar Peter Newmark referred to Catford in his early research, then was influenced by Fillmore and case grammar, and eventually turned his attention to SFL (Taylor, 1993).

In his 1987 paper, "The use of systemic linguistics in translation analysis and criticism," Newmark praised Halliday's work, declaring that since the appearance of his "Categories of the theory of grammar" (1961), a functional approach to linguistic phenomena had appeared to him to be useful to translation analysis, surely more than Chomsky's, Bloomfield's or the Montague Grammarians' theories (Newmark, 1987: 293). He expressed his admiration for Hallidayan linguistics, opening the article with the following remark:

> Since the translator is concerned exclusively and continuously with meaning, it is not surprising that Hallidayan linguistics, which sees language primarily as a meaning potential, should offer itself as a serviceable tool for determining the constituent parts of a source language text and its network of relations with its translation (ibid.). In particular, Newmark's closeness to Halliday is reflected in his approach to constituents, as well as to two specific aspects of grammatical analysis which, in his view, can offer valuable insights to both the translation analyst and the translator: Grammatical Metaphor and Cohesion. ①

Going back to Halliday's **hierarchical approach** (i. e., a "rank scale" made up of morphemes, words, groups and clauses), Newmark found that "[...] systemic grammar enables us to demonstrate the flexibility and multiplicity of grammatical variations" (1987: 294). On the basis of this, for instance, an SL nominal group may translate into a TL nominal group, but it may also be "rank-shifted"—upward into a clause or downward into a word. Even though Newmark argued that "literal translation" should be the first option of the translator (1981/82), he also admitted that there could be contextual reasons for preferring another solution. In his view, most "linguistic shifts" (Catford, 1965) or "transpositions" [as Vinay & Darbelnet (1958) call variations from a grammatical point of view] could be described in this way.

Newmark simply extended Halliday's descriptive hierarchy into: text, paragraph, sentence, clause, group, word, morpheme. In agreement with Halliday, Newmark asserted that, from an abstract point of view, none of these are more "important" than another, even though in practice, "[...] the text is the ultimate court of appeal, the sentence is the basic unit of *translating* (not of translation), and most of the problems are centered in the lexical units, if not the words" (Newmark, 1987, emphasis in the original). Thus, while Halliday's focus is on the clause as a representation of meaning in a communicative context, Newmark identified the **sentence** as the "natural" **unit of translation**. As Taylor observes, his "constituents boundaries" seem, therefore, to be marked by punctuation.

Newmark stated that "transpositions" and rearrangements may often occur, but that a sentence would *not* normally be divided unless there was good reason (1988: 165). He is careful to insist that any "rearrangements" or "recasting" must respect "Functional Sentence Perspective" (Firbas, 1992: 7b), what Halliday, following the Prague School of Linguists,

---

① The paper was first included in the volume *Language Topics: Essays in Honour of Michael Halliday*, edited by R. Steele and T. Threadgold (1987). A revised version was then integrated into Newmark's own monograph *About Translation* (1991) and became Chapter 5, entitled "The Use of Systemic Linguistics in Translation."

calls the clause's Thematic Structure (1994: 40).

In addition, he introduced the issue of text "authority," holding that "[...] the more authoritative the text, the smaller the unit of translation" (Newmark, 1988: 66), and made clear his agreement with Haas (1962) that "[t]he unit of translation should be as short as possible and as long as is necessary" (see Newmark, 1987: 295). As Taylor suggests (1993), Newmark's fundamental choice of the sentence as a basic unit of translation could be said to be linked to his admiration for the chapter on Cohesion in Halliday's *Introducing Functional Grammar* (1985). He is, of course, not alone.

As a matter of fact, with reference to *An Introduction to Functional Grammar* (1985), Newmark drew our attention to two chapters in particular, i. e. "Beyond the clause: metaphorical modes of expression" and "Around the clause: cohesion and discourse," since, he argued, these are very much related to the very nature of translation.

As regards the first of these two chapters, which deals specifically with the concept of "grammatical metaphor," Newmark went so far as to state that "[a]s I see it, this chapter could form a useful part of any translator's training course where English is the source or target language" (1987: 295).

According to Halliday, a "grammatical metaphor" is a "[...] variation in the expression of a given meaning" with reference to the more "congruent" realization, i. e. , "non-metaphorical" (Halliday, 1985/94: 342)[1]. Congruent does not mean "better;" nor does it mean "more frequent. " It simply means less metaphorical, and, perhaps, a more typical and also historically prior way of saying things. In the final analysis, it is an instance of language in which "[...] the speaker or writer has chosen to say things differently" (1994: 343). A typical example is represented by the phenomenon of "Nominalization," connected with what Newmark (1987: 294) calls a "[...] non-physical figurative use of verbs. "

According to Newmark, when translating metaphors translators always have a choice. He argues that the numerous examples of metaphorical forms and "congruent" rewordings included in Halliday's valuable chapter could sensitize a translator to the need for "recasting. "

An example from Halliday and his own rewording are provided:

(1) The argument to the contrary is basically an appeal to the lack of synonymy in mental language (1985: 331).

(1a) In order to argue that this is not so (we) simply point out that there are no synonyms in mental language (ibid.).

Newmark comments that the second, more "congruent" version could well be a "normal" translation of the same sentence into French or German.

The removal of verb-nouns such as "argument," "contrary," "appeal" and "lack,"

---

① For more illustration of Grammatical Metaphor, see Freddi (2006) and Lipson (2006) in this series.

especially when translating informative texts, is a common "shift" (Catford, 1965) or "transposition" (Vinay & Darbelnet, 1958), as Scarpa also points out (see Scarpa, 2001).

Thus according to Newmark, Halliday's advice to the linguist seeking to "de-metaphorise" grammatical metaphors, i. e. to unscramble as far as is needed (Halliday, 1994: 352 - 353), could even be more pertinent for a translator faced with such tasks.

In the same chapter, Halliday offers a further example of a grammatical metaphor, which, as Taylor notes, "[...] is superbly economic in English" (Taylor, 1993: 94):

(2) The fifth day saw them at the summit (1994: 346).

This is congruently reworded by Halliday as:

(2a) They arrived at the summit on the fifth day.

Newmark proposes a translation of the example above into French, where the "incongruent" form, i. e., the grammatical metaphor, has been turned into a more "congruent" one:

(2b) C'est au cinquième jour qu'ils sont arrivés au sommet (Newmark, 1987: 295).

Taylor proposes a congruent solution in Italian which "[...] could be arguably more concise," (1993: 94) adding that such a result is *not* however so common when translating into this language:

(2c) Al quinto giorno sono arrivati al vertice (ibid.).

The other chapter of Halliday's *Introducing to Functional Grammar* (1985), which Newmark recommended as useful for translators, is that on Cohesion. He stressed the relevance of the chapter with the following words:

> The topic of cohesion, which may have first appeared in Hasan (1968), was expanded in Halliday and Hasan (1976), and revised in Halliday (1985), has always appeared to me the most useful constituent of discourse analysis or text linguistics applicable to translation (1987: 295).

Although Halliday's account of cohesion is wide, including both structural (Thematic and Informational structure) and non-structural elements (reference, ellipsis/substitution, lexical relations and intersentential conjunction), Newmark was interested in particular in the examination of the use of connectives and, more to the point, in the phenomenon of "missing" connectives between sentences, which obliges the translator to interpret the logical connection. Connectors and prepositions cover a wide range of meanings and may thus often cause ambiguity (translating from English, *yet* and *as* are classic examples). Their meaning and function will clearly depend on the co-text they operate in. Newmark argued that, at least in the case of an "informative" or "social" text (i. e., as opposed to the expressive one), Halliday's treatment could offer translators a useful tool to guide them towards deciding how far to intervene.

Finally, Newmark's focus on the importance of grammar in translation should be remarked. In his *Approaches to Translation* (1981/82), in discussing the concept of "synonyms in grammar" (Newmark, 1981/82: 101), or what may be more easily glossed as grammatical equivalences, he states that they are "[...] often closer and more numerous than in lexis." Basically what he is warning against is a carefree overuse of lexical synonyms. As he notes: "[...] any replacements by lexical synonyms [...] are further from the sense than the grammatical synonyms. This becomes a plea for more grammatical dexterity and flexibility, and against lexical license, in translation practice." If we wish to relate this concept to Italian, we can think of the possibility of tackling the problem of translating Circumstances of Manner from English into Italian through a lexicogrammatical analysis of the ST following an SFL approach.

Newmark's appreciation of Halliday's work can be ultimately confirmed by his comment regarding his notion of **register**, a familiarity with which was recommended, as an "[...] invaluable [tool] both in analyzing a text, in criticizing a translation, and in training translators" (Newmark, 1987: 303)[①]. Again, we cannot but agree.

选文四 Basil Hatim, Ian Mason and SFL

Marina Manfredi

In the 1990s, translation scholars Basil Hatim and Ian Mason acknowledged Halliday's and, generally speaking, SFL's contribution to TS as follows: [...] a new approach developed by Michael Halliday and his colleagues in Britain in the 1960s and 1970s provided translation studies with an alternative view which approached language as text (Hatim & Mason, 1990: 36).

Working within a linguistic framework, they employ a Hallidayan model of language to analyse translation as communication within a sociocultural context. In particular, they offer influential insights on the issues of Register, Dialect and Ideology as applied to translation.

Their aim was to develop a theory of translation centred upon the role played by those "situational factors" that, they note, translators themselves had in fact been aware of for a long time (1990: 38). Employing a social theory of language and viewing texts as expressions of communicative events, they were particularly sensible to the issue of variation

---

① Newmark's comments on the translation of "restricted registers" (Halliday, 1973) will be given in volume 2 (chapter 11), when discussing the practical translation of different kinds of "Registers."

in language use, which they explored in relation to translation. They examined texts as expressions of such variation, according to two dimensions, that is, following Halliday's distinction between "Dialect" and "Register." Indeed, as we noted in discussing Catford's sub-divisions of the category of dialect, for Halliday language varies "according to the user" and "according to use" (see Halliday, 1978: 35, and also, in Halliday & Hasan, 1985/89: 41). Hatim and Mason represent the distinction as you can see in Figure 1.

LANGUAGE VARIATION	
USE	USER
Registers, etc.	Dialects, etc.
1. field of discourse	1. geographical
2. mode of discourse	2. temporal
3. tenor of discourse	3. social
	4. (non-)standard
	5. idiolectal

Figure 1   The Use-User Distinction (Adapted from Hatim & Mason, 1990: 46)

In their *Discourse and the Translator* (1990), Hatim and Mason deal with both kind of varieties, presenting illustrative examples connected with the activity of translation. As they clearly illustrate (Hatim & Mason, 1990: 39), **user-related varieties**, that is, "dialects," are linked to "who the speaker or writer is." According to the user, language can vary with respect to diverse aspects, including: geographical, temporal, social, (non-) standard or idiolectal factors(ibid.). Each of these features can inevitably pose problems for a translator having to tackle with it, not least because the linguistic aspect will be inextricably linked with sociocultural considerations and thus his or her decisions will have inevitable cultural implications.

Let us offer an illustrative example concerning a much-debated theme in TS, that is the translation of geographical dialects. We premise that, as Hatim and Mason unequivocally state, "[a]n awareness of **geographical variation**, and of the ideological and political implications that it may have, is [...] essential for translators" (1990: 40). They report a particular case which occurred in the field of TV drama translation, where the problem of rendering accents is particularly manifest, as it also is in the theatre. In Scotland, a controversy had been provoked by the adoption of a Scottish accent to convey the speech of Russian peasants (ibid.). Clearly, linking Scots pronunciation to lower social class Russians was not exactly appreciated by the local population.

In general, as Hatim and Mason clearly demonstrate, translating geographical accents into a TL is always problematic and "dialectal equivalence" is almost "impossible" to achieve (ibid.: 41). Which dialect in the TL should be chosen, if any? If the translator renders an

ST dialect into a standard variety, s/he will be taking the risk of losing the effect of the ST. If s/he translates an SL dialect into a selected TL one, the risk will be that of causing unintended effects (or resentment!) with respect to the target audience. A further option would be that of aiming at a sort of "functional" equivalence instead, modifying the standard itself, without necessarily adopting a particular regional variety: in this case a marked effect through different means would also be reproduced in the TT (ibid.: 43). Similar problems will be faced by a translator tackling other kinds of dialects, such as "social" or "non-standard" ones, with all of their socio-cultural implications.

The second dimension of language variation which Hatim and Mason theorise with reference to translation concerns **use-related varieties**, i. e. , "registers" (see ibid.: 45). As Halliday, McIntosh & Strevens (1964) had already pointed out back in the 1960s, language varies as its context varies and there is a relationship between a given situation and the linguistic choices which will be made within it. "Register" is the term adopted to indicate this kind of variety "according to use." Registers are defined according to their differences in lexicogrammar. Such differences are likely to be found in discursive activities as unlike each other as, for example, a sports commentary and a church service (ibid.: 46). As we have already seen with relation to the Hallidayan model of the context of situation, three main categories of register variation can be distinguished, that is: the Field of discourse, its Tenor and its Mode. Any discrepancy between any of these three contextual variables will make for diverse lexicogrammatical choices being made. From a translator's point of view, Hatim and Mason suggest, it is important to establish the conventions of the situation-use in the TL, to see if the linguistic choices being made are appropriate to that "use" (ibid.). But it is vital to consider *all* register variables; and with reference to this crucial point, Halliday comments:

> [...] they determine the register collectively, not piecemeal. There is not a great deal one can predict about the language that will be used if one knows *only* the field of discourse or *only* the tenor or the mode. But if we know all three, we can predict quite a lot (1978: 223). Hatim and Mason's register analysis also encompassed their investigation into the **hybrid nature of texts**, based on the assumption that, although texts are basically hybrid in their rhetorical purposes, one particular function always tends to predominate over the others (1990: 146 – 147)[①]. When faced with the multifunctional nature of texts, translators need to examine whether any shift might be substantially tipping the scales towards one function or another (see Hatim, 2001: 118).

In a wider perspective, Hatim and Mason also brought cultural considerations into their linguistic perspective, relating linguistic choices to ideology, their definition of which,

---

① The idea of communicative "functions" never being mutually exclusive goes back as least as far as R. Jakobson (1960) "Closing statement: linguistics and poetics," in T. A. Sebeok (ed.), *Style in Language* (pp. 350 – 377), Cambridge, Mass.: MIT Press, as does the notion of a "primary" function dominating.

following scholars who work in a Hallidayan framework (e. g. , Miller, 2005: 3), is a very broad one, having nothing to do with particular *-isms*. In their view, "ideology" embodies "[...]the tacit assumptions, beliefs and value systems which are shared collectively by social groups" (1997: 144). They interestingly distinguish between "the ideology of translating" and "the translation of ideology." The former refers to the kind of orientation followed by a translator when operating within a specific sociocultural context, while the latter concerns the extent of "mediation" (i. e. , intervention) carried out by a translator of what might be thought of as being ideologically "sensitive" texts (ibid. : 147).

In particular, they adopt a linguistic approach based on register analysis for the express purpose of getting insights into the all-important and interrelated cultural, social and ideological aspects of translation. For example, their invaluable investigation of a historical text concerning Mexican peoples (1997: 153 – 159), in which they probe the less than "neutral" lexicogrammatical choices made by the translator of the text—especially with reference to the experiential meanings enacted through transitivity and the textual ones constructed in and by cohesion—skillfully reveals the ideological assumptions which were the undeniable result of those choices, so often "hidden" from the untrained eye.

选文五　Translation Quality Assessment: Linguistic Description versus Social Evaluation

Juliane House

导　言

在翻译研究领域以研究翻译质量评估而为学界所关注的学者首推德国汉堡大学的学者豪斯。关于翻译质量评估的理论模式,豪斯发表了不止一部专著,不断修正和完善她的理论。这里选取的这篇文章,于 2001 年发表在 *Meta*(第 46 卷:243 - 257)上面,展示了豪斯在翻译质量评估方面的主要思想,其主要的理论框架是系统功能语言学当中的语域理论。

Introduction

How do we know when a translation is good? This simple question lies at the heart of all concerns with translation criticism. But not only that, in trying to assess the quality of a translation one also addresses the heart of any theory of translation, i. e. , the crucial question of the nature of translation or, more specifically, the nature of the relationship between a source text and its translation text. Given that translation is essentially an operation in which the meaning of linguistic units is to be kept equivalent across languages, one can distinguish at least three different views of meaning, each of which leads to different conceptions of translation evaluation. In a mentalist view of meaning as a concept residing in language users' heads, translation is likely to be intuitive and interpretative. If meaning is seen as developing in, and resulting from, an externally observable reaction, translation evaluation is likely to involve response-based methods. And if meaning is seen as emerging from larger textual stretches of language in use, involving both context and (situational and cultural) context surrounding individual linguistic units, a discourse approach is likely to be used in evaluating a translation.

In this paper I want to first elaborate briefly on these three approaches to translation evaluation; secondly, I will present my own views on the matter, and thirdly and most importantly, I will discuss the often blurred distinction between linguistic description and social evaluation.

1 Translation Evaluation in Different Schools of Thought

1.1 Mentalist Views

Subjective and intuitive evaluations of a translation have been undertaken since time immemorial by writers, philosophers, and many others, consisting more often than not of global judgements such as "the translation does justice to the original" or "the tone of the original is lost in the translation" and so forth. In a newer guise, such intuitive assessments are being propagated by neo-hermeneutic translation scholars who regard translation as an individual creative act depending exclusively on subjective interpretation and transfer decisions, artistic-literary intuitions and interpretive skills and knowledge. Texts have no core meanings at all, rather their meanings change depending on individual speakers' positions. I will not elaborate here my critique of the hermeneutic position (but see the recent lucid discussion by Bühler 1998), suffice to say that such a relativising stance, and especially the relativisation of "content" and "meaning" is particularly inappropriate for the evaluative business of making argued statements about when, how and why a translation is good.

1.2 Response-based Approaches

1.2.1 Behaviouristic Views

As opposed to subjective-intuitive approaches to translation evaluation, the behaviourist view aims at a more "scientific" way of evaluating translations dismissing the translator's mental actions as belonging to some in principle unknowable "black box." This tradition, influenced by American structuralism and behaviourism, is most famously associated with Nida's (1964) pioneering work. Nida took readers' reactions to a translation as the main yardstick for assessing a translation's quality, positing global behavioural criteria, such as intelligibility and informativeness and stating that a "good" translation is one leading to "equivalence of response"—a concept clearly linked to his principle of "dynamic equivalence of translation," i. e., that the manner in which receptors of a translation respond to the translation should be "equivalent" to the manner in which the source text's receptors respond to the original. Nida operationalized this equivalence as comprising equal "informativeness" and "intelligibility." Assuming that it is true that a "good" translation should elicit a response equivalent to the response to its original, we must immediately ask whether it evokes—using for instance reading aloud techniques, various close and rating procedures— have ultimately failed to provide the desired results, because they were unable to capture such a complex phenomenon as the "quality of a translation." Further, the source text is largely ignored in all these methods, which means that nothing can be said about the relationship between original and translation, nor about whether a translation is in fact a translation and not another secondary text derived via a different textual operation.

1.2.2 Functionalistic, "Skopos"-related Approach

Adherents of this approach (cf. Reiss & Vermeer, 1988: 4) claim that it is the "skopos" or purpose of a translation that is of overriding importance in judging a translation's quality. The way target culture norms are heeded or flouted by a translation is the crucial yardstick in evaluating a translation. It is the translator or more frequently the translation brief he is given by the person(s) commissioning the translation that decides on the function the translation is to fulfil in its new environment. The notion of "function," critical in this theory, is, however, never made explicit, let alone operationalized in any satisfactory way. It seems to be something very similar to the real-world effect of a text. How exactly one is to go about determining the (relative) equivalence and adequacy of a translation, let alone how exactly one is to go about determining the linguistic realization of the "skopos" of a translation, is not clear. Most importantly, however, it naturally follows from the crucial role assigned to the "purpose" of a translation that the original is reduced to a simple "offer of information," with the word "offer" making it immediately clear that this "information" can freely be accepted or rejected as the translator sees fit. But since any translation is simultaneously bound to its source text and to the presuppositions and conditions governing its reception in the new environment, Skopos theory cannot be said to be an adequate theory when it comes to tackling the evaluation of a translation in its fundamental bidirectionality.

1.3 Text and Discourse Based Approaches

1.3.1 Literature-oriented Approaches: Descriptive Translation Studies

This approach is oriented squarely towards the translation text: a translation is evaluated predominantly in terms of its forms and functions inside the system of the receiving culture and literature (cf. Toury, 1995). The original is of subordinate importance, the main focus—retrospective from translation to original—being "actual translations," and the textual phenomena that have come to be known in the target culture as translations.

The idea is to first of all attempt to "neutrally" describe the characteristics of that text as they are perceived on the basis of native (receptor) culture members' knowledge of comparable texts in the same genre. However, if one aims at judging a particular text which is plainly not an "independent," "new" product of one culture only, such a retrospective focus seems peculiarly inappropriate for making valid statements about how and why a translation qua translation is as it is. While the solid empirical-descriptive work and the emphasis put on contextualization at the micro-level of the reception situation and the macro-level of the receiving culture at large, as well as the inclusion of both a "longitudinal" (temporal, diachronic) and a (synchronic) systemic perspective (considering the polysystemic relations into which the translation enters with other texts in the receiving cultural system), is certainly commendable, the approach does fail to provide criteria for judging the merits and weaknesses of a particular "case." In other words, how are we to judge whether one text is a translation and another one not? And what are the criteria for judging merits and weaknesses of a given "translation text"?

1.3.2　Post-modernist and Deconstructionist Thinking

Scholars belonging to this approach (cf. Venuti, 1995) try to critically examine translation practices from a psycho-philosophical and socio-political stance in an attempt to unmask unequal power relations, which may appear as a certain skewing in the translation. In a plea for making translations (and especially translators as their "creators") "visible" and for revealing ideological and institutional manipulations, proponents of this approach aim to make politically pertinent (and "correct") statements about the relationship between features of the original text and the translation text. They focus on the hidden forces shaping both the process of selecting what gets translated in the first place and the procedures that result in the ways original texts are bent and twisted in the interests of powerful individuals and groups "pulling strings" when choosing texts for translation and adopting particular strategies of re-textualization. This is certainly a worthwhile undertaking, especially when it comes to explaining the influence translators can exert through their translation on the receiving national literature and its canon. Further, the application of currently influential lines of thinking such as post-colonial theory (Robinson, 1997) or feminist theory (von Flotow, 1997) to translation may not be uninteresting in itself. However, if comparative analyses of original and translation focus primarily on the shifts and skewings stemming from ideologically motivated manipulations, and if an agenda is given priority which stresses the theoretical, critical and textual means by which translations can be studied as loci of difference, one wonders how one can ever differentiate between a translation and any other text that may result from a textual operation which can no longer claim to be in a translation relationship with an original text.

1.3.3 Linguistically-oriented Approaches

Pioneering linguistic work in translation evaluation includes the programmatic suggestions by Catford (1965), the early Reiss (1971), Wilss (1974), Köller (1979) and the translation scholars of the Leipzig School. In this early work, however, no specific procedures for assessing the quality of a translation were offered. In more recent times, several linguistically oriented works on translation such as by Baker (1992), Doherty (1993), Hatim & Mason (1997), Hickey (1998), Gerzymisch-Arbogast & Mudersbach (1998) and Steiner (1998) have made valuable contributions to evaluating a translation by the very fact that all these authors—although not directly concerned with translation quality assessment—widened the scope of translation studies to include concerns with linguistics, pragmatics, sociolinguistics, stylistics and discourse analysis.

Linguistic approaches take the relationship between source and translation text seriously, but they differ in their capacity to provide detailed procedures for analysis and evaluation. Most promising are approaches which explicitly take account of the interconnectedness of context and text because the inextricable link between language and the real world is both definitive in meaning making and in translation. Such a view of translation as re-contextualization is the line taken by myself in a functional-pragmatic evaluation model first developed some 25 years ago and recently revised (House, 1981, 1997).

2 A Functional-Pragmatic Model of Translation Evaluation

2.1 An Analytic Framework for Analysing and Comparing Original and Translation Texts

The assessment model (House, 1997) is based on Hallidayan systemic-functional theory, but also draws eclectically on Prague School ideas, speech act theory, pragmatics, discourse analysis and corpus-based distinctions between spoken and written language. It provides for the analysis and comparison of an original and its translation on three different levels: the levels of Language/Text, Register (Field, Mode and Tenor) and Genre. One of the basic concepts underpinning the model is "translation equivalence"—a concept clearly reflected in conventional everyday understanding of translation, i. e. , the average "normal," i. e. , non-professionally trained person thinks of translation as a text that is some sort of "representation" or "reproduction" of another text originally produced in another language, with the "reproduction" being of comparable value, i. e. , equivalent. (This is the result of an informal interview study I conducted with thirty native speakers of German support staff as well as medical and economics students at the university of Hamburg.) Over and above its role as a concept constitutive of translation, "equivalence" is the fundamental criterion of translation quality. In an attempt to make "a case for linguistics in translation theory," Ivir expresses the inherent relativity of the equivalence relation very well: "Equivalence is … relative and not absolute … it emerges from the context of situation as defined by the interplay of (many different factors) and has no existence outside that context, and in particular it is not stipulated in advance by an algorithm for the conversion of linguistic units of L1 into linguistic units of L2" (1996: 155).

It is obvious that equivalence cannot be linked to formal, syntactic and lexical similarities alone because any two linguistic items in two different languages are multiply ambiguous, and because languages cut up reality in different ways. Further, language use is notoriously indirect necessitate inferencing to various degrees. This is why functional, pragmatic equivalence—a concept which has been accepted in contrastive linguistics for a long time—is the type of equivalence which is most appropriate for describing relations between original and translation. And it is this type of equivalence which is used in the Functional-Pragmatic model suggested by House (1997), where it is related to the preservation of "meaning" across two different languages and cultures. Three aspects of that "meaning" are particularly important for translation: a semantic, a pragmatic and a textual aspect, and translation is viewed as the re-contextualization of a text in L1 by a semantically and pragmatically equivalent text in L2. As a first requirement for this equivalence, it is posited that a translation text have a **function** equivalent to that of its original which—consisting of an ideational and an interpersonal functional component—is defined pragmatically as the application or use of the text in a particular context of situation, the basic idea being that "text" and "context of situation" should not be viewed as separate entities, rather the context of situation in which the text unfolds is encapsulated in the text through a systematic relationship between the social environment on the one hand and the functional organization of language on the other. The text must therefore refer to the particular situation enveloping it, and for this a way must be found for breaking down the broad notion of "context of situation" into manageable parts, i. e., particular features of the context of situation or "situational dimensions": for instance "Field," "Mode" and "Tenor."

Field captures social activity, subject matter or topic, including differentiations of degrees of generality, specificity or "granularity" in lexical items according to rubrics of specialized, general and popular. **Tenor** refers to the nature of the participants, the addresser and the addressees, and the relationship between them in terms of social power and social distance, as well as degree of emotional charge. Included here are the text producer's temporal, geographical and social provenance as well as his intellectual, emotional or affective stance (his "personal viewpoint") vis a vis the content she is portraying. Further, Tenor captures "social attitude," i. e. different styles (formal, consultative and informal). **Mode** refers to both the channel—spoken or written (which can be "simple," i. e., "written to be read" or "complex," e. g. "written to be spoken as if not written"), and the degree to which potential or real participation is allowed for between writer and reader. Participation can be "simple," i. e., a monologue with no addressee participation built into the text, or "complex" with various addressee-involving linguistic mechanisms characterizing the text. In taking account of (linguistically documentable) differences in texts between the spoken and written medium, reference is made to the empirically established (corpus-based) oral-literate dimensions hypothesized by Biber (1988). Biber suggests dimensions along which linguistic choices may reflect medium, i. e., involved vs. informational text production; explicit vs. situation-dependent reference; abstract vs. non-abstract presentation of information.

The type of linguistic-textual analysis in which linguistic features discovered in the original and the translation correlated with the categories Field, Tenor, Mode does not, however directly lead to a statement of the individual textual function. Rather, the concept of "Genre" is incorporated into the analytic scheme, "in between," as it were, the register categories Field, Tenor, Mode, and the textual function. Genre thus enables one to refer any single textual exemplar to the class of texts with which it shares a common purpose. The category of Genre is useful for the analysis and evaluation process because, although Register (Field, Tenor, Mode) descriptions are useful for accessing the relationship between text and context, they are basically limited to capturing individual features on the linguistic surface. In order to characterize " deeper " textual structures and patterns, a different conceptualization is needed. This is attempted via the use of "Genre." While register captures the connection between texts and their "micro context," Genre connects texts with the "macro context" of the linguistic and cultural community in which texts are embedded. Register and Genre are both semiotic systems realized by language such that the relationship between Genre, Register and language/text is one between semiotic planes which relate to one another in a Hjelmslevian "content-expression" type, i. e., the Genre is the content plane of Register, and the Register is the expression plane of Genre. Register in turn is the content plane of language, with language being the expression plane of Register.

The analytic model is displayed in Figure 1:

INDIVIDUAL TEXTUAL FUNCTION

REGISTER		GENRE
FIELD	TENOR	MODE
Subject matter	participant relationship and social action	medium
	author's provenance and stance	simple/complex
	participation	
	social role relationship	simple/complex
	social attitude	

LANGUAGE/TEXT

Figure 1　A Scheme for Analysing and Comparing Original and Translation Texts

Taken together, the analysis yields a textual profile characterizing the individual textual function. Whether and how this textual function can in fact be maintained, depends, however, on the type of translation sought for the original. I distinguish between two types: overt and covert translation, which I will briefly describe in the following section.

2. 2 Two Types of Translation: Overt and Covert Translation

The distinction between an "Overt Translation" and a "Covert Translation" goes back at least to Friedrich Schleiermacher's famous distinction between "verfremdende" and "einbürgernde" Übersetzungen, which has had many imitators using different terms. What sets the Overt-Covert distinction apart from other similar distinctions and concepts is the fact that it is integrated into a coherent theory of translation criticism, inside which the origin and function of the two types of translation are consistently described and explained. Translation involves text transfer across time and space, and whenever texts move, they also shift frames and discourse worlds. "Frame" is a psychological concept and it is thus, in a sense, the psychological pendant to the more "socially" conceived concept of context, delimiting a class of messages or meaningful actions. A frame often operates unconsciously as an explanatory principle, i. e., any message that defines a frame gives the receiver instructions in his interpretation of the message included in the frame. Similarly, the notion of a "discourse world" refers to a superordinate structure for interpreting meaning in a certain way just as a locutionary act acquires an illocutionary value by reference to an operant discourse world.

Applying the concepts of frame and discourse world to overt and covert translation, we can say that an overtly translated text is embedded in a new speech event, which also gives it a new frame. An overt translation is a case of "language mention"(as opposed to "language use"). Relating the concept of "overt translation" to the four-tiered analytical model (Function—Genre—Register—Language/Text), we can state that an original and its overt translation are to be equivalent at the level of Language/Text and Register as well as Genre. At the level of the individual textual function, functional equivalence, while still possible, is of a different nature: it can be described as enabling access to the function the original has in its discourse world or frame. As this access is to be realized in a different language and takes place in the target linguistic and cultural community, a switch in discourse world and frame becomes necessary, i. e., the translation is differently framed, it operates in its own frame and its own discourse world, and can thus reach at best second-level functional equivalence. As this type of equivalence is, however, achieved though equivalence at the levels of Language/Text, Register and Genre, the original's frame and discourse world are co-activated, such that members of the target culture may "eavesdrop," as it were, i. e., be enabled to appreciate the original textual function, albeit at a distance. In overt translation, the work of the translator is important and visible. Since it is the translator's task to give target culture members access to the original text and its cultural impact on source culture members, the translator puts target culture members in a position to observe and/or judge this text "from outside. "

In covert translation, which is a case of "language use," the translator must attempt to recreate an equivalent speech event. Consequently, the function of a covert translation is to reproduce in the target text the function the original has in its frame and discourse world. A covert translation operates therefore quite "overtly" in the frame and discourse world provided by the target culture, with no attempt being made to coactivate the discourse world in which the original unfolded. Covert translation is thus at the same time psycholinguistically less complex and more deceptive than overt translation. Since true functional equivalence is aimed at, the original may be manipulated at the levels of Language/Text and Register via the use of a "cultural filter." The result may be a very real distance from the original. While the original and its covert translation need thus not be equivalent at the levels of Language/Text and Register, they must be equivalent at the levels of Genre and the Individual Textual Function. Schematically, the theoretical distinction between overt and covert translation can be displayed as follows:

Figure 2　The Dimension of Overt-Covert Translation

Level	Is strict equivalence the translational goal?	
	Overt Translation	Covert Translation
Primary level function	NO	YES
Secondary level function	YES	N/A
Genre	YES	YES
Register	YES	NO
Language/Text	YES	NO

In evaluating a translation, it is thus essential that the fundamental differences between overt and covert translation be taken into account. These two types of translation make qualitatively different demands on translation criticism. The difficulty of evaluating an overt translation is generally reduced in that considerations of cultural filtering can be omitted. Overt translations are "more straightforward," as the original can be "taken over unfiltered," as it were. In evaluating covert translations, the translation assessor has to consider the application of a "cultural filter" in order to be able to differentiate between a covert translation and a covert version.

2.3　The Concept and Function of a Cultural Filter

The concept of a cultural filter is a means of capturing socio-cultural differences in shared conventions of behaviour and communication, preferred rhetorical styles and expectation norms in the two speech communities. These differences should not be left to individual intuition but should be based on empirical cross-cultural research. Given the goal of achieving functional equivalence in a covert translation, assumptions of cultural difference should be carefully examined before interventions in the original's meaning structure is undertaken. The unmarked assumption is one of cultural compatibility, unless there is evidence to the contrary. To take an example, in the case of the German and anglophone linguistic and cultural communities the concept of cultural filter has been given some substance through a number of empirical contrastive-pragmatic analyses, in which anglophone and German communicative priorities along a set of hypothesized dimensions were hypothesized. Converging evidence from a number of cross-cultural German-English studies conducted with different data, subjects and methodologies suggests that there are German preferences for rhetorical styles and conventions of communicative behaviour which differ from anglophone ones along a set of dimensions, among them directness, content focus, explicitness and routine-reliance (cf. House, 1996, 1998).

Given the distinction between overt and covert translation, it is obvious that cultural transfer is only possible in the case of overt translation, where cultural items are transported from L1 to L2 acting as a sort of "Verfremdung." In covert translation, however, there is no cultural transfer, but only a sort of "cultural compensation" for L1 cultural phenomena in L2 with the means of L2.

In speaking of a "cultural filter," we need to know, of course, what we mean by "culture." Given widespread post-modernist critiques of culture as an untenable idealization and as something outdatedly relating to the nation state of the nineteenth century, is it today still possible to talk of "the culture" of a language community? Has not the extension of culture to modern complex societies brought about a complexification and problematisation of "culture" which renders it useless as a methodological and conceptual entity? Should we therefore not follow the argumentation by Halliday (1999) who suggested substituting "non-essentialist" "non-reified" "small cultures" for "culture"? Obviously there is no such thing as a stable social group untouched by outside influences and group and personal idiosyncracies, and obviously it is wrong to assume a monolithic unified culture of which all differentness is idealized and cancelled out. Nevertheless, modernist relativation has in practice never yet led to its logical conclusion: the annihilation of research concerned with culture, nor has it prevented researchers from describing cultures as interpretive devices for understanding emergent behaviour. Further, we cannot ignore the experiences reported by "ordinary" members of a speech community, when they perceive members of another cultural group as behaving "differently" in particular situated discourse events.

2.4 Distinguishing between Different Types of Translations and Versions

Over and above distinguishing between covert and overt translation in translation criticism, it is necessary to make another theoretical distinction: between a translation and a version. This distinction is important in view of recent widespread attempts to indiscriminately view intentionally non-equivalent "versions" as translations—even though the new text may have a function different from the original text's function. Producing a version results from a deliberate turning away from the original, a reevaluation and often renunciation of the original. Versions are "freed" to become their own original, particularly in contexts where only intentions of clients and product specifications count, i. e., in highly practice-oriented, mostly technical translation activities, in which considerations of equivalence would only stand in the way of achieving client satisfaction and consumer service. While functionally equivalent covert translations may certainly look like new creations, it is still true that they would not have come into existence if there had not been an original text. And it is important to stress that despite the seemingly cavalier manner with which a translator may have dealt with linguistic correspondences at the word, group and sentence levels (i. e., below the levels of text and discourse), in a covert translation, her actions must be viewed as being subservient to producing correspondences that, each in their different ways, contribute to the overall functional equivalence of the entire translation to its original. This is what makes a translation a translation. It is only when new purposes are superimposed on the translation that a new product, i. e., a version results.

Overt versions are produced in two cases: firstly, whenever a special function is overtly added to a translation text, e. g. to reach a particular audience, as in special editions for children or second language learners with the resultant omissions, additions, simplifications or different accentuations of certain aspects of the original, or popularisations of specialist works designed for the lay public. And secondly, when the "translation" is given a special added purpose. Examples are interlingual versions, resumes and abstracts.

A covert version results whenever the translator—in order to preserve the function of the source text—has applied a cultural filter randomly manipulating the original.

In discussing different types of translations and versions, I do not want to imply, however, that a particular text may be adequately translated in only one particular way. For instance, the assumption that a particular text necessitates either a covert or an overt translation clearly does not hold in any simple way: any text may, for a specific purpose, require an overt translation, i. e., it may be viewed as a text of an "independent value" of its own, e. g. when its author has become, in the course of time, a distinguished figure, in which case the original text acquires the status of a sacrosanct document.

Further, while contrastive pragmatics has certainly made important contributions to assessing covert translations in a non-arbitrary way, it remains a challenge to assess the adequateness of applications of a cultural filter. Given the dynamic nature of socio-cultural and communicative norms and the way research necessarily lags behind, translation critics will have to struggle to remain abreast of new developments if they want to be able to fairly judge the appropriateness of changes through the application of a cultural filter in a translation between two given languages. One important new development that may affect social contexts today is the increasing importance of the English language.

3　English as a Global Lingua Franca in Cultural (Non) Filtering

With globalization and internationalization characterizing much of our life today, there is a concomitant rise in the demand for texts which are simultaneously meant for recipients in many different communities. In other words, ever more texts are needed that are either translated covertly or produced immediately as "parallel texts" in different languages. Until recently translators and text producers tended to routinely apply a cultural filter with which differences in culture-conditioned expectation norms and stylistic conventions were taken into account. However, due to the impact of English as a global lingua franca this situation may now be in a process of change leading to a conflict in translational processes between culture specificity and universality in textual norms and conventions, with "universality" really standing for North European/North American Anglo-Saxon norms. It is this hypothesized change in global translation conventions which has in fact motivated a research project which is presently being conducted in Hamburg inside a larger research undertaking (a Sonderforschungsbereich "Mehrsprachigkeit" funded by the *Deutsche Forschungsgemeinschaft*). Our main hypothesis in this project is that, instead of using a cultural filter in covert translations or parallel text production, increasingly many culturally universal (or rather culturally neutral translation) texts are created, and a species of "hybrid text" results, which is in reality a carrier of anglophone cultural norms "invading" other linguistic and cultural communities rendering, for example, German texts less content-focused, more interpersonally oriented, more emotionally involved, more situation-dependent and more concrete, to use Biber's (1988)dimensions of orality vs. writtenness in text production, than was the case before.

While the influence of the English language in the area of lexis has long been acknowledged and bemoaned by many linguistic "purists" in Germany and France, anglophone influence at the levels of syntax, pragmatics and discourse has hardly been researched. Rules of discourse, conventions of textualization and communicative preferences tend to remain hidden, operating stealthily at a deeper level of consciousness and thus presenting a particular challenge for translation evaluation.

In the Hamburg project which examines the influence of English as a lingua franca on covert translations into German (and later into French and Spanish), we are trying out a multi-method approach to translation evaluation, a method which goes beyond the procedure suggested in the assessment model by House (1997). As detailed above, this evaluation model provides for detailed qualitative case-study assessments of the quality of a translation. Just as the much maligned notion of equivalence cannot be taken to provide general guidelines for the translation process, because equivalence derives from the interaction of a particular text and a particular context, so the case-study approach adopted in the functional pragmatic evaluation model forbids any facile generalization, simply because the achievement of functional equivalence varies from translation to translation. In the case of covert translation, for example, equivalence must be achieved via the assessment of the specific communicative environments of the two texts and their linguistic correlates. The communicative environments of original and translation must therefore be compared in each individual case, and it is only through amassing evidence of similar textual exemplars that we can approximate generalizations. In order to validate both the hypothesized cross-cultural dimensions that substantiate the cultural filter and the results of the linguistic analysis, introspective methods may be used with which one may tap the translation process. While the evaluation of a translation is primarily product-based, it can thus be supplemented or "triangulated" by process-oriented work. Other ways of triangulating the primary analyses include interviews with commissioners of the translation, with editors and other persons involved in the making of a translation. In addition, background documentation, as well as comparisons of translations of the same original into different languages and comparisons of parallel texts and "monolingual" texts belonging to the same Genre can be taken into account. A further extension of the qualitative case-study approach consists of the use of computerized parallel and translation corpora suitable for quantitative analyses.

4 Linguistic Description versus Social Evaluation in Translation Criticism

In translation criticism it is important to be maximally aware of the difference between (linguistic) analysis and (social) judgement. In other words, a distinction must be made between describing and explaining linguistic features of the original text and comparing them with the relevant linguistic features of the translation text on the one hand and judging "how good a translation" is on the other hand. Instead of taking the complex psychological categories of translation receptors' intuitions, feelings, beliefs or the (equally vague) effect of a translation as a cornerstone for translation criticism, the functional-pragmatic approach outlined in the above model focuses on texts (validated by introspective accounts of their production). Such an approach, however, cannot ultimately enable the evaluator to pass judgements on what is a "good" or a "bad" translation. Judgements of the quality of a translation depend on a large variety of factors that enter into any social evaluative statement. Critical in the case of translation evaluation is the fact that evaluative judgements emanate from the analytic, comparative process of translation criticism, i.e., it is the linguistic analysis which provides grounds for arguing an evaluative judgement.

As mentioned above, the choice of an overt or a covert translation depends not on the text alone, or on the translator's subjective interpretation of the text, but also on the reasons for the translation, the implied readers, on a variety of publishing and marketing policies, i.e., on factors which clearly have nothing to do with translation as a **linguistic** procedure because these are social factors which concern human agents as well as socio-cultural, political or ideological constraints and which—in the reality of translation practice—turn out to be often more influential than linguistic considerations or the professional competence of the translator herself. However, it must be stressed that despite all these "external" influences, translation is at its core a linguistic-textual phenomenon, and it can be legitimately described, analysed and evaluated as such. It is for this reason that I would argue that the primary concern of translation criticism should be linguistic-textual analysis and comparison, and any consideration of social factors—if it is divorced from textual analysis—must be of secondary relevance in a scientific discipline such as translation studies. Linguistic description and explanation must not be confused with evaluative assertions made solely on the basis of social, political, ethical or individual grounds. It seems imperative to emphasize this distinction given the current climate in which the criteria of scientific validity and reliability are often usurped by criteria such as social acceptability, political correctness, vague emotional commitment or fleeting zeitgeist tastes. If we take translation seriously as an object of scientific inquiry, translation must be seen first and foremost for what it is, namely a phenomenon in its own right: a linguistic-textual operation. And the nature of translation as a linguistic-textual operation should not be confused with issues such as what the translation is for, what it should, might, or must be for. In approaches to translation criticism such as those squarely oriented towards the purpose and effect of a translation in a new cultural environment, it is unfortunately often the case that no clear line is drawn between translations and other (non-equivalence oriented) multilingual textual operations. One way out of this conceptual (and methodological) confusion seems to be to make a clear distinction between a translation and a version, a distinction which can, as I have tried to show above, only be made if one posits functional equivalence as an incontrovertible criterion for translation. Translation quality is a problematical concept if it is taken to involve individual and externally motivated value judgement alone. Obviously, passing any "final judgement" on the quality of a translation that fulfills the demands of scientific objectivity is very difficult indeed. However, this should not lead us to assume that translation criticism as a field of inquiry is worthless. As an evaluator one will always be forced to flexibly move from a macro-analytical focus to a micro-analytical one, from considerations of ideology, function, genre, register, to the communicative value of individual linguistic items. In taking such a multi-perspectival viewpoint, a responsible translation critic will arrive at a position where he or she can give a probabilistic reconstruction of the translator's choices, and with the support of the translator's own "voice," be able to throw some light on his or her decision processes in as objective a manner as possible. That this is an extremely complex undertaking which, in the end, yields but approximative outcomes, should not detract us from its usefulness. It is the task of the translation critic to work out, as far as possible, for each individual case, exactly where and with what types of consequences and (possibly) for which reasons (parts of) translated texts are what they are in relation to their "primary texts." Such a modest goal might guard the translation evaluator against making both prescriptive, apodictic and global judgements (of the "good" vs. "bad type") that are not intersubjectively verifiable.

In the field of translation criticism, it is unfortunately often the case, that the difference between linguistic analysis and value judgement is ignored when one talks about the quality of a translation. While it is true that both a linguistic and a judgemental component are implicit in translation evaluation, I would caution against mixing them up. I would also caution against using the evaluative component in isolation from the linguistic one.

Translation criticism, like language itself, has two basic functions, an ideational function and an interpersonal function. These two functions have their counterpart in two different methodological steps. The first and, in my estimation, the primary one, refers to linguistic-textual analysis, description, explanation, and comparison, and it is based on empirical research and on professsional knowledge of linguistic structures and norms of language use. The second step refers to value judgements, social, interpersonal and ethical questions of socio-political and socio-psychological relevance, ideological stance or individual persuasion. Without the first, the second is useless, in other words, to judge is easy, to understand less so. In other words, in translation criticism we have to make explicit the grounds for our judgement basing it on a theoretically sound and argued set of intersubjectively verifiable set of procedures. A detailed analysis of the "hows" and the "whys" of a translated text (i. e., its linguistic forms and functions) in comparison with the original from which it is derived, is the descriptive foundation for any valid, and argued assessment of whether, how, and to what degree a given translation can be taken to be (more or less) adequate. Clearly, this means recognizing the inevitable subjective part of any translation assessment by a human evaluator. However, this recognition does not invalidate the objective part of the assessment, it merely reinforces its necessity. Making a distinction between empirically motivated linguistic description and socially conditioned grounds for evaluating a translation, as I have tried to do in this paper, may lead us one step further towards solving the puzzling complexity of human translation.

选文六　系统功能语言学路向翻译研究述评

司显柱

导　言

本文选自 2007 年《外语研究》第四期,作者对中外系统功能语言学路向的翻译研究进行了较为全面的梳理。

1　引言

翻译是一项古老的活动,人们对翻译的认识和思考几乎与翻译活动本身一样久远。不过,对翻译现象的探索,无论中外,传统上是直观的、经验式居多,如严复的"信、达、雅"和英国泰特勒的翻译三原则。20世纪以来,尤其是霍姆斯(1972)在丹麦哥本哈根举行的第三届国际应用语言学大会上发表论文《翻译研究的名与实》(一般认为该文标志着翻译研究正式作为一门独立的学科的诞生)之后,人们更多地从科学的,特别是语言学的角度系统地探讨翻译问题,建构科学意义上的翻译理论。

由于翻译现象的复杂,对其描写和阐述自然不能囿于某一理论和单个视角。翻译研究,作为一门交叉性学科,需要从其他学科,如语言学、哲学、文学、人类文化学、认知科学、符号学、心理学、传播学、社会学等学科吸收营养和精华。事实也正是如此。回眸西方翻译理论发展的近百年历程,翻译研究之所以新的观点和流派层出不穷,异彩纷呈,如多元系统论、目的论、后殖民主义、后结构主义、解构主义、女性主义翻译理论等一幅色彩斑斓的多元化翻译理论景观,正是自觉地应用其他学科理论指导自身研究的结果。换言之,正如黄国文(1992)所说,"翻译学这块领地像是一个胸怀宽广的母亲,有海纳百川的气魄。她吸引着越来越多不同学科的学者在这个领域辛勤耕耘。"

2　系统功能语言学与翻译研究

在采纳其他学科理论开展翻译研究方面,语言学对翻译研究的指导最为直接,也因此贡献最大。这是不难理解的,因为无论如何翻译首先是一种语言活动。不仅如此,翻译的其他活动,如翻译研究文化学派所关注的翻译背后的后殖民主义、帝国主义等文化、政治活动最终也必然表现在语言层面的选择和操纵上。

另一方面,语言学派的翻译研究也是伴随着人们对语言认识的深化、语言学自身的发展而发展的。拿语言研究的两大流派形式语言学和功能语言学来说,代表前者的乔姆斯基(N. Chomsky)所创立的转换生成语法,特别是其中的深层结构理论曾强烈地吸引一批翻译学者如美国著名的翻译理论家奈达(E. Nida)研究翻译问题,推动了翻译研究朝科学化的方向前进,这在机器翻译领域尤其如此。不过,相比而言,韩礼德(M. A. K. Halliday)等建立和发展的系统功能语言学对翻译研究的贡献更大,影响更远。这不是偶然的!因为,系统功能语言学源于普罗塔哥拉(Protagoras)和柏拉图(Plato)等以人类学为本的语言研究传统,着眼于语言的人本性、社会性一面,自然更加重视语境、语用、会话含义、言外之意等,所以与以"意义"为本的翻译研究直接相关。

3　系统功能语言学路向翻译研究回顾

3.1　国外的情形

对这方面文献的搜集与梳理表明,系统功能语言学理论应用于翻译研究已有三十多年的历史。早在1965年,卡特福特(Catford,1965:20)就自觉地运用了韩礼德的级阶和范畴语法理论(系统功能语言学的早期形式),较为系统地探讨了翻译的性质、类型、方法、条件和限度,并运用层次(level)、范畴(category)以及级阶(rank)等语言学概念论述语际转换的根据,指出根据语言的"级阶",即词素、词、短语或意群、小句或句子,翻译可以分为逐词翻译、直译和意

语言学与翻译研究导引

译,逐词翻译是建立在单词"级"上的等值关系;意译"不受限制……可以在上下级之间变动,总是趋向较高级变动……甚至超越句子";直译则"介于逐字翻译与意译之间"。并提出翻译对等只能是话语对等和功能对等,开辟了翻译理论研究的新途径。

只要有翻译,就会有译评,可以说它与翻译活动本身伴随而生。但要对译文质量开展系统的评价,则一定要应用某个评估模式,所以建构这样的一个模式无疑是翻译理论家义不容辞的责任。德国翻译研究界著名的女学者豪斯(Juliane House)几乎毕其全部的研究精力来探索这样一个模式,近20年未曾停息:首先她将该题目作为自己博士学位研究的选题,并于1976年写成论文《翻译质量评估模式》而获得博士学位;之后,经过一年的加工,以专著的形式于1977年正式出版;到了1981年,经再次修改出了第二版;又过了11年,到了1997年以《翻译质量评估:修正的模式》出了第三版;而到了2001年,她又在国际翻译研究专业刊物 Meta 上撰文,发表对翻译评估的最新思考。

正如豪斯在其1997年的修订版里所明确声称的,她对翻译质量评估模式的探索,其理论基础就是韩礼德的系统功能语言学。具体地说,该书运用功能语言学的语篇分析,尤其是语域理论,从八个方面,即三个涉及语言使用者的参数:地点、社会阶层、时代和五个语言应用参数如媒介、参加者、社会角色关系、社会态度、领域,依据言语行为所涉及的形式、功能、情景三要素及其彼此的互动关系,通过对原文、译本各自的语境与形式(言语)特征的分析和互照,发现和确定译文是否与原文功能对等或偏离。因此假如译文在某个语境维度上与原文没有不匹配现象,就可判定译本在此维度上令人满意了,相应地表现为在措辞上的适切和功能/意义上的对等。(也可以反过来说,如果译文体现了与原文同样适切的措辞和对等的功能,也自然建构了与原文相应的语境维度。)换言之,豪斯对翻译对等所要做到的功能相符的基本标准是:译本与原本不仅应该功能相符,并且要运用对等的语境维度方式去获得这些功能。分析原本和译本时,就是要看她所提出那个模式的八个维度是否两两相符,是否用同样的方法获得同样的功能。二者相符程度越高,翻译质量越好。因此译本的最终质量判断包括对上述语境里的每个维度不匹配程度的陈述,即隐性错误(在语境维度上的错误)和显性错误(词语的所指意义与原文不对等或不符合目的语系统规范)的数量及类型的描述。

此外,她还把翻译分为两种类型:明译(overt translation)和暗译(covert translation)(House,1997:66-69)。她指出所谓明译是指译本必须明显是翻译的,而不是"第二原文"(second original);而暗译之所以如此命名,是因为从语用的角度看译本在目标语里并不呈现翻译的特征,而是像在用目标语进行创作,因此译本享有与原文在目标语文化中得以享受相同的地位。另外,她还认为等值应在语篇、语域、语类层面去寻找。

尽管该模式并非尽善尽美,尚存诸如"参数设置不够合理,运行步骤有待优化"(司显柱,2005a)以及"译本与原文的不对等或许并非是翻译上的差错而是由于译者采取诸如明晰化和补偿等翻译策略使然"(Gutt,1991:46-49)等不足和缺陷,但作为国际翻译批评界第一个系统、全面的翻译质量评估模式,其开拓性的历史性地位是否定不了的。

当代国际著名的翻译理论家贝克女士,1992年出版了《换言之:翻译教程》(Baker,1992/2000)。该书系统地探讨了现代语言学理论(主要是功能语言学、语用学等)中一些重要概念及其对处理翻译中诸多复杂难解问题的启示与指导意义,具有很强的理论性,名副其实地为一本培训翻译人员的教科书。全书采用从下到上(bottom-up)的方法,由易到难,从翻译中词的对等讲起,经过词、词组的搭配,句子的对等,直至篇章对等。在该书的主干"篇章对等"部分(几

乎占了全书一半的篇幅),贝克运用了韩礼德系统功能语言学里的主位结构和信息结构等概念以及词语连贯的所指、替代、省略、连接和词汇衔接五种黏着手段,全面论述了如何实现篇章层面的翻译对等的问题。

如果说贝克等运用系统功能语言学的语篇分析模式讨论翻译问题主要集中在语篇功能的层面,关注如何运用主位、衔接、连贯等资源手段实现语篇对等的话[另一在语篇的衔接、连贯层面讨论翻译问题的是柏偌莫-夸卡(Blum-Kulka,2000:302-303),她通过对选自品托(Pinter)的作品 Old Times 里一个情景案例的希伯来语译文的分析,描述了译本如何因在连贯方面发生改变而导致了译本功能变化的情形],哈蒂姆和梅森运用系统功能语言学语篇分析模式讨论翻译问题,除了在语篇的纬度,如主位、连贯性等方面考察译本与原文的匹配情形之外,还深入到了译本的概念、人际功能相对于原文的情形。如他们(Hatim & Mason,1997:7-10)通过对阿贝特·凯莫斯(Albert Camus)小说里的一段文字的及物性分析,揭示了英语译文中小句的及物性类型的改变如何导致了译文在概念功能上与原文偏离;又凭借语域分析这一工具(1997:21)剖析了译者如何在自身意识形态的作用下,怎样通过对目的语里词汇-语法资源的有目的操纵而改变了原文的人际功能,以此将原文原本所没有的意图编织进译本之中,从而充当了某个社会阶层利益代言人这样一个角色的情形。

由此,正如芒德(Munday,2001:100)所指出的,哈蒂姆和梅森(1997)的语篇分析模式体现并超越了豪斯的语域分析和贝克的语用分析范围,认为语言和语篇是社会文化信息和权势关系的体现,其最大特点在于将韩礼德关于语言的社会符号性和文化与意识形态的观点运用于翻译分析。

罗杰·贝尔是英国著名的语言学家,他较为系统地将语言学理论用于对翻译的探讨,写出翻译研究的专著《翻译与翻译过程:理论与实践》而成为翻译研究的语言学派的代表人物。韩礼德曾说过:"如果能用一个语言学模式来描写翻译过程,那会是非常有意义的。我们应根据语言活动本身来描写它,而不是以先入之见从语言研究领域外部去描写"(Bell,1991:ⅩⅥ)。贝尔就是试图从系统功能语言学和语篇语言学的角度来研究翻译问题,努力寻求一种"客观的"方法去描写翻译现象。他从系统功能语言学视角研究翻译,最集中地体现在书中的第四章,这里贝尔不仅较详细地介绍了系统功能语言学所论述的语言的三大元功能——概念功能、人际功能和语篇功能,而且凭借自己对多种语言学理论的融会贯通和对语言的洞悉,将系统功能语言学所概括的三种功能与语言的逻辑、语法和修辞等三大系统有机地连接起来,论述了语言的认知意义、交际意义和语篇意义,以及它们如何通过语言的及物性、情态、主位而获得体现。(事实上,这里的认知意义、交际意义与系统功能语言学所阐述的概念意义和人际意义系同一所指。)在这里,他对翻译研究的命脉——"意义"的探索已从静态转向动态,从语义学转向交际学,从脱离语境的词语和句子转向依赖语境的话语——翻译的实际单位。因此贯穿在系统功能语言学语言研究中的重视语境、语用和功能的理念成为他探索翻译问题、建构翻译理论的认识论和方法论。

芒德的博士论文《翻译的系统:对卡西亚·玛奎兹作品翻译文本基于机助的系统功能路向的分析》,通过对研究语料哥伦比亚籍诺贝尔文学奖作家卡西亚·玛奎兹(Garcia Marquez)的西班牙语小说 Doce cuentos peregrinos 和美国译者艾的斯·格汝斯曼(Edith Grossman)的英语译本的对照,研究翻译中的转移(shift)及其趋势。在对这一问题的探索和研究语料的文本分析过程中,他自觉地运用系统功能语言学的语言分析模式作为理论基础。之所以如此,据他

自己所言:"系统功能语言学的分析模式关注实际使用中的、作为交际行为的语言的功能,它视语言为'一套意义潜势的系统'(Halliday,1978:39)。也就是说,它将作者实际的选择与可能的选择进行对比而把握所实际选择的措辞表达的意义。因此用它来对翻译中转移和列维(Lèvy)所说的'作决定过程'进行分析似乎颇为适宜。况且,这一模式将语言层面的选择系统地与社会中个体的、社会的、文化的和意识形态的等诸多方面连接起来,从而提供了探索翻译中的转移所需的社会文化框架"(Munday,1997:3)。在《翻译研究入门》(Munday,2001)一书里,他还对豪斯、哈蒂姆和梅森、贝克等运用韩礼德语篇分析模式研究翻译的功过得失进行了分析。

3.2 国内的研究

在我国,最早运用韩礼德语言学理论讨论翻译问题的是胡壮麟。他(胡壮麟等,1989:188-189)运用系统功能语法关于语言三大元功能的论述对翻译研究的重要概念——"对等"的内涵作了深入挖掘和剖析,并由此论述了翻译的实质和标准:"翻译一般是寻求原文和译文在意义上的对等。……翻译应寻求两种语言的语篇在同一整体情景语境中具有相同的意义和相同的功能。""翻译的对等关系不能只建立在一种意义(通常是概念意义)的基础上;在寻求两种语言的语篇的概念意义对等的同时,还必须寻求两种语言的语篇在表达讲话者的态度、动机、判断、角色等人际意义,以及在表达媒介、渠道、修辞方式等语篇意义时的对等。在一般情况下,好的译文需在这三种意义上都与原文对等。"

但是胡壮麟等运用韩氏理论研究翻译问题却停留在对有限几个问题的一般而论,既未展开,又缺乏实证。这虽然不尽如人意,也是情有可原,因为作为一本介绍系统功能语言学的入门书籍,其初衷自然不是要详谈功能语言学与翻译研究,意图大概只是要向读者表明功能语言学的应用领域涵盖了翻译研究。

而比较系统、全面地运用韩礼德功能语言学探索翻译问题,既有理论阐述,又有实证支撑的是黄国文。他于2001—2004年连续在我国外语类核心期刊上发表了一系列从功能语言学角度讨论翻译的论文,其主要特点是运用韩礼德语篇分析模式探讨唐诗翻译问题,以其说明韩氏理论对翻译的实用性和可操作性,范围涉及唐诗的引述现象、语气、主位结构、信息结构、经验功能、人际功能、时态、形式对等、逻辑功能、功能语言学语境等,并从宏观角度阐述了功能语篇分析的可行性,为我国学者将韩礼德理论运用于翻译研究奠定了扎实的基础。

另一比较系统地从系统功能语言学视角研究翻译问题的是张美芳,她和黄国文(2003)合作的《语篇语言学与翻译研究》一文,着重阐述了功能翻译观,如:意义与其体现形式之间的关系,语篇特征、语境与语言选择、语篇体裁与情景语境等;《从语篇分析的角度看翻译中的对等》(张美芳,2001)则从语篇分析的角度,从语篇体裁和语域变体两方面对英汉翻译中出现的问题进行了分析;而《意图决定语篇制作的策略》一文则从原文和译文的情景语境视角分析了译本与原文功能的不同及其译者制订翻译策略的依据。

王东风近年也借用系统功能语言学里的一些重要概念探讨翻译理论与实践。在《小说翻译的语义连贯重构》(2005)一文中,他根据功能语言学中的连贯、衔接和衔接手段中的复现和同现等概念,从语篇分析角度,指出翻译是原文语篇连贯关系的重构理念,分析了语义连贯的构成及其翻译对策,并探讨了复现和同现两大衔接手段在语义连贯构成上的表现及其相应的翻译得失。在《小句物质过程被动语态的逆转式翻译所引起的功能亏损》里,他以英文小说《简

·爱》的片段作为主要分析语料,从诗学的角度探讨小句被动结构在逆转式翻译中的功能亏损,文章涉及系统功能语言学中的概念功能和语篇功能在翻译研究中的应用。

近年,尚媛媛、王鹏和李发根等也从系统功能语言学角度研究翻译。尚媛媛(2003)的博士学位论文《政治演讲词英汉翻译中的转移——从系统功能语言学阐释翻译中语言的应用》,对政治语篇英汉翻译中存在的翻译转换现象进行描述和探讨,拓展了系统功能语言学理论的运用领域,特别是作为一种语篇分析理论和工具在描述和分析翻译语篇中的作用,同时也为翻译现象的探讨提供了一种语言学角度的阐述。王鹏(2004)的学位论文《〈哈利·波特〉与其汉语翻译——以系统功能语言学理论分析情态系统》,则以说话者性别、年龄与情态动词 CAN,COULD 的情态系统(情态类别、情态指向、情态正反)之间的关系,调查《哈利·波特》英语原文及其汉语翻译之间是否存在翻译对等。李发根(2005)的论文《人际意义与等效翻译》,以唐代诗人李白的抒情诗《蜀道难》及其五种英译文为语篇分析素材,运用韩礼德的语篇分析模式和亨斯顿的评价局部语法探讨人际意义与翻译问题。该研究不仅证实了英汉语篇人际意义客观存在性和韩氏语言理论在翻译中的实用性和可操作性,而且构建了一个可用于分析唐诗人际意义翻译的模式,为研究人际意义提供了一个切实可行的依据,为翻译者提供了人际意义翻译的原则和方法。

另外,李运兴 2001 年出版的《语篇翻译引论》和萧立明的《新译学论稿》(2001)也主要是从语篇方面去讨论翻译问题,把翻译研究从以句子为研究单位扩大到语篇,涉及韩礼德的语境观、衔接连贯、语篇的语域、语篇的层次性等问题。

4　系统功能语言学路向翻译研究评述:成绩与不足

综上所述,愈来愈多的翻译理论家从功能语言学那里汲取营养,开展翻译研究,并已经一定程度上形成了翻译研究的韩礼德系统功能语言学派,推动了译学研究向前发展。

4.1　取得的成绩

概括起来,研究成果主要表现在以下几个方面:

4.1.1　建构了新的翻译理论体系和翻译质量评估模式

如前所述,英国语言学家卡特福特运用系统功能语法的早期形式韩礼德的级阶和范畴语法理论,勾纳了翻译理论体系,较为系统、全面地探讨了诸如翻译的性质、类型、方法、条件和限度等问题。哈蒂姆和梅森运用系统功能语言学语篇分析模式,应用其中的许多重要概念,如语境、语域、语言的三种元功能——概念、人际、语篇及其词汇-语法资源——及物性、情态、主位、连贯性等考察译本与原文,并将韩礼德的文化和意识形态观点运用于翻译分析。而豪斯则以系统功能语言学里的语域分析模式,建构了国际翻译批评界第一个系统、全面的翻译质量评估模式。

4.1.2　对翻译研究里的一些核心概念作出了新的阐释

豪斯根据系统功能语言学关于语言的元功能阐述,论述了翻译的实质是指包括语义的(semantic)、语用的(pragmatic)和语篇的(textual)在内的"意义"在从一种语言转移到另一种语言时保持不变。"翻译是用语义和语用对等的译语文本代替源语文本"(House,1977:30)。胡壮麟等(1989:188)则因此提出了翻译的标准。刘士聪、余东(2000)在论述翻译研究中另一核心问题翻译单位时,借助主/述位理论,指出在结构上,主/述位对句子有构建意义;语篇内,通过主/述位分析语篇衔接确定句内的信息及其交际功能将有助于更好地理解原文,进而提出"以主/述位作翻译的单位对原文进行分析和转换是有效的"。

4.1.3 对诸如"翻译转移"等现象作出了别开生面的描述与解释

柏偌莫-夸卡(2000)、芒德(1997)、尚媛媛(2003)、张美芳(2001)运用系统功能语言学理论或其中的重要概念深入探讨了翻译转移问题,哈蒂姆和梅森(1997)、张美芳(2000)等则从系统功能语言学的视角分析和揭示了译文与原文意图冲突及其背后的意识形态。

4.1.4 推进了对译本质量的评估研究

从系统功能语言学角度切入,研究译本质量的评价,可谓着力最多,涉及的语料也十分广泛,如英德翻译(豪斯)、英法翻译(哈蒂姆和梅森)、英西翻译(哈蒂姆)、英希翻译(柏偌莫-夸卡)等。在我国,尤以中国古诗英译质量研究的最多,成果也相对更为丰富,如黄国文、李发根、张晓春(2005)、郑元会和苗兴伟(2005)等。

4.2 缺陷与不足

虽然系统功能语言学之于翻译研究表现出广阔的发展前景,系统功能语言学路向的翻译研究取得了不菲的成绩,但也存在诸多问题和不足,主要表现在:

4.2.1 研究比较零散,涉及问题有限,缺乏大器之作

总体而言,目前的研究还处于"初始"阶段,表现在迄今尚未提出一个系统的、基于系统功能语言学的翻译理论框架,缺乏运用该语言学理论全面探索翻译问题的扛鼎之作。当下人们更多地只是应用该理论的一些原理、概念来阐释翻译研究中有限的几个问题,比较零散。如胡壮麟(1989)和贝尔(1991)都运用系统功能语法关于语言三大元功能的论述对翻译研究的重要概念"对等"的内涵作了深入挖掘和剖析,但却并未建构出基于系统功能语言学的翻译研究框架和写出从此视角系统地探索翻译问题的学术专著。

4.2.2 新瓶装旧酒

从系统功能语言学视角对翻译的探索和由此得出的一些看法与其他视角如传统译论的结论并无多少不同,没有多少新发现。如司显柱(2005b)在对一首诗歌几种汉语译本开展质量评价时,他从系统功能语言学的角度论述了虽然文学作品的翻译更关注对原文里"人际功能"的传递,但同样也不能不追求对原文本的概念功能对等,而这与传统译论的提法"文学翻译既需求真,也要求美"(许渊冲)并无什么实质上的区别。当然,另一方面,正如我们(司显柱,2006b)曾指出的:"虽然功能语言学对翻译的描述与结论,与传统译论比起来,不少是殊途同归。但视角不同,不能说就没有价值。"

4.2.3 较为烦琐,操作性不足

由于系统功能语言学的语言分析模式在语法范畴化方面的复杂性以及对结构和意义的一一匹配的规定性描写,这样到底要运用其中的哪些范畴来讨论翻译问题就颇费周折。如在评价译文时,如果要在体现语言的三个功能的所有词汇-语法资源层面分析译文既太过复杂,有时往往也没有必要;而要是作出取舍,那么哪些入选,哪些出局呢?这还只是一个方面的问题!根据系统功能语言学对包括翻译在内的言语行为的阐述,言语活动是在形式、功能和情景互动关系里运作的,由于情景决定意义,而意义是由形式体现的,因此必需考察翻译的情景。但情景又包含很多变量,这些变量不仅决定了译文将要发挥何种功能,也必然对翻译策略,进而对

译文的面貌发生作用。但到底要涉及哪些情景变量呢？这同样是一大问题。正是因为它的烦琐，所以用于翻译研究时也就难免显得操作性不足，关于这一点费施(Fish,1981：59-64)也有同感。

5　结语

对于系统功能语言学路向的翻译研究现状存在的不足和取得的成就,我们认为,要进行科学、理性的分析,既不能因此妄自菲薄,否定它对翻译研究的指导和启发意义,也不能沾沾自喜,而裹足不前。首先,对于系统功能语言学的翻译研究以上的不足,应当看到:由于社会本身包罗万象,基于社会符号学取向的,因而基于实际使用的言语而构建的系统功能语言学理论,自然要比形式语言学如转换生成语法只关注抽象的语言,只描写如何生成合乎语法的句子的语法理论,当然在语法的范畴化、框架结构等方面复杂得多,这虽然因此导致了前述应用于翻译研究时的选择的不便和操作性不足,但实践业已证明它比关乎如何生成语法合格句子而演绎出几条规则的转换生成语法对翻译研究更有指导性。

同时,翻译本身的复杂性以及研究者的视角、兴趣、能力、精力等因素也决定了系统功能语言学对翻译的探索,与其他语言学视角的翻译研究和文化学派的翻译研究一样,不可能解决翻译的所有问题。因此我们不能因为系统功能语言学没有触及翻译里的一些问题而责难或否定其价值。翻译本身的复杂性、翻译研究学科的属性决定了任一单一的理论都不可能解决其全部的问题。另一方面,虽然从系统功能语言学的视角对翻译里的一些问题的描述和探讨所得出的结论与从其他的角度而得出的结果在内容上没有多少不同或者说有不少雷同,但这同样不能说没有意义,因为方法的创新同样是学术的进步和繁荣的标志。

不过话说回来,缺陷是客观存在的,问题不容忽视！我们必须清醒地认识到研究的不足和存在的问题,下大气力在系统功能语言学对翻译研究的系统化、可操作性以及系统功能语言学与翻译研究的理论嫁接和移植等方面作出扎实、不懈的努力。唯有如此,系统功能语言学路向的翻译研究才可望获得长足的进展,系统功能语言学理论本身也有望在此过程中取得进一步的发展。

【延伸阅读】

[1] Catford，J. C. （1965）. *A Linguistic Theory of Translation*. Oxford：Oxford University Press.

[2] Halliday，M. A. K. （1961）. Linguistics and Machine Translation. In M. A. K. Halliday，A. McIntosh & P. Strevens.

[3] Halliday，M. A. K. et al. （1964）. Comparison and Translation. *The Linguistic Sciences and Language Teaching*. London：Longmans，Green and Co Ltd.

[4] Baker，M. （1992）. *In Other Words：A Coursebook on Translation*. London & New York：Routledge.

[5] Hatim，B. （1998）. Translation Quality Assessment：Setting and Maintaining a Trend. *Translator*，4，91-100.

【问题与思考】

1. 系统功能语言学在哪些方面对翻译活动和翻译研究有借鉴意义？
2. 豪斯应用了系统功能语言学的哪些理论思想来建构她的翻译批评模式？

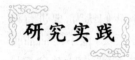

汉英部分语篇衔接手段的差异

左 岩

导 言

本文最早发表于 1995 年《外语教学与研究》第三期，对朱自清的散文《背影》及其英译文中部分语篇衔接手段作了统计及对比分析，发现汉英两种语言的部分语篇衔接手段在使用上各有所偏重，汉语更常用原词复现和省略，而英语则多用照应和替代。从表面看作者关注的焦点是英汉两种语言在谋篇布局中在衔接手段方面的差异，但也涉及了很多翻译实例，对于汉英翻译具有一定的启示意义。应该指出的是，作者认为译者的翻译过于拘泥于原文，因此在进行统计的时候，对一些译文的处理进行了改动，然后在此基础上进行比较研究，使她的讨论在客观性和可靠性方面留下了一点疑问，值得读者注意。

  功能语法学和语用学近二三十年来的兴起与发展，促使语言学家不再仅仅把语言看作代码(code)系统，而且视为交际手段(means of communication)，对语言的分析和研究也逐渐从以词素、词、短语、句子为单位扩大到以语段(paragraph)和话语(discourse)或篇章(text)为单位的超句研究。话语研究主要考察语言在日常生活中的具体使用；篇章学则更着重研究句子构成篇章这一超句统一体的各种手段。

  篇章并非是互不相关的句子的简单堆积，而是一些意义相联系的句子为达到一定交际目的，通过各种衔接手段(cohesive devices)而实现的有机结合。实际上，正如韩礼德和哈桑(Halliday & Hasan)在其论述语篇衔接的专著《英语中的衔接》(*Cohesion in English*)中所言，"篇章与非篇章(non-text)的根本区别在于是否具有篇章性(texture)，而篇章性是由衔接关系(cohesive relation)形成的"(1976：2)。因此，衔接手段自然成为篇章研究的重要对象之一。

  韩礼德和哈桑在上述著作中将英语的衔接手段概括成五种：a. 照应(reference)；b. 替代

(substitution);c. 省略(ellipsis);d. 连接词(conjunction);e. 词汇衔接(lexical cohesion)。笔者认为,尽管汉语与英语在篇章衔接手段上有诸多差异,但汉语篇章的衔接手段也大致可归于以上五种。这里有两点需作说明:① 汉语中没有确切地与英语中的替代相对应的衔接手段,我们不妨将汉语的"的"字结构和量词后省略名词的用法归为这种衔接性替代;② 词汇衔接分为两大类——复现关系(reiteration)和同现关系(collocation),我们在此仅考虑复现关系中最常见的一类,即通过原词的重复来达到语篇连贯。现对每一衔接手段各举汉英两例说明。

(1) 照应指用代词等语法手段来表示语义关系,可分为人称照应、指示照应和比较照应。如:

The Professor came in. *He* looked very serious.

觉新知道大祸临头了;<u>他</u>不敢多想。

(2) 替代指用替代形式去替代上下文出现的词语,可分为名词性替代、动词性替代和分句性替代。如:

My shoes are wet, so could you find me some dry *ones*?

这件上衣太小了,拿<u>那件</u>给我试试。

(3) 省略指省去句子中的某一成分。如:

I want some old newspaper. Have you got any Φ?

妈妈把孩子搂在怀里,紧紧地抱了一阵。然后,Φ往炉里加了点柴,推门出去了。

(4) 连接词指连接句子的各种连词、副词等。如:

It's a hard job. *But* I'll try.

眼睛是心灵的窗户。<u>因此</u>,诗人和画家都非常看重对眼睛的描绘。

(5) 词汇衔接如上所述,本文仅讨论词汇衔接中的原词复现。所谓原词复现,即通过重复上文已出现过的词来达到语篇的连贯。

The two men at the counter read the menu. From the other end of the counter Nick Adams watched them.

女人坐在小院当中,手指上缠绞着柔滑修长的<u>苇眉子</u>。<u>苇眉子</u>又薄又细,在她怀里跳跃着。

虽然汉英语篇衔接手段都可粗略划分为以上五种,但在具体运用上二者却各具特点。本文以现代著名作家朱自清的散文名篇《背影》及其英译文(参见张培基,1994)为语料,对汉英语篇衔接手段上的一些差异作一比较。《背影》一文文笔秀丽,细腻缜密,张培基先生的译文也忠实准确,但笔者认为译者因过于强调忠实于原文而将原文中出现"父亲"一词处,都对译为 Father,所以读来未免有重复拖沓、结构松散之感,译文的文采及风格也略受影响。笔者不揣冒昧,将其译文略加变化,在某些地方以代词 he 代替 Father,使之更为简洁流畅。

可以看到,在原文及这样处理后的译文(下略作译文)中,主要的语篇衔接手段有四种,即照应、替代、省略及词语复现,但四者在汉英文中的分布情况却差异很大,笔者对此作一统计,如表1所示。

表1　四种语篇衔接手段在汉英文中的分布

	汉	英
四种衔接手段总数	126	162
照应	51	132
所占比例	40.5%	81.5%
替代	1	5
所占比例	0.8%	3.1%
省略	40	2
所占比例	31.7%	1.2%
原词复现	34	23
所占比例	27%	14.2%
句子总数	54	42

另外,根据韩礼德和哈桑,照应可分为三类:人称照应、指示照应和比较照应,表1中的照应几乎全为前两类,比较照应在原文和译文中都很少。为便于下文分析,表2列出人称照应与指示照应各自的数目及所占比例。(人称照应是通过人称代词,所属限定词如 your,his 等和所属代词 mine,his 等实现的;指示照应可通过选择性名词性指示词:this,that,these,those,定冠词 the 及指示性副词 here,there,now,then 实现。)

表2　人称照应和指示照应在汉英文中的分布

		汉	英
人称照应	第三人称单数 he/his/him/himself	36	61
	比例	85.7%	76.25%
	其他人称	6	19
	比例	14.3%	23.75%
	人称照应总数	42	80
	占照应总数的比例	82.4%	60.6%
指示照应	这/那(儿、些、时) here, this, these, now, there, that, those, then	9	17
	比例	100%	32.7%
	定冠词 the	/	35
	比例	/	67.3%
	指示照应总数	9	52
	占照应总数的比例	17.6%	39.4%
照应总数		51	132

由表1可见,在原文和译文句子总数大致相当的情况下,汉语多用省略和原词复现来衔接

上下文以达到语篇连贯的目的,而英语则多用照应和替代。从表2可看出:① 由于本文内容侧重于描写父亲对儿子的爱,指代父亲时多用第三人称单数的各种形式,所以 he,his 及 him 在人称照应中占很大比例;② 汉语中没有定冠词的用法,而英语中的定冠词 the 却在语篇衔接中举足轻重,广为应用。下面我们对上述统计数字所反映出的汉英在语篇衔接手段上的不同,通过举例、对比加以进一步分析。为把问题说清楚,分析中的例子有时不限于《背影》及其译文。

三

1. 为使篇章连贯,汉语中广泛采用的一个衔接手段就是把原词重复一下,而英语则大量运用照应,用代词替代原词。请看《背影》及其译文中的情况。在原文中,"父亲"一词出现了13次,而在译文中只出现7次,原文其余6处出现的"父亲"一词均译为 he。如第一段后半部分的原文及译文。

原文:

(1) 那年冬天,祖母死了,父亲的差使也交卸了,正是祸不单行的日子,我从北京到徐州,打算跟着父亲奔丧回家。到徐州见到父亲,看见满院狼藉的东西,又想起祖母,不禁簌簌地流下眼泪。父亲说:"事已如此,不必难过,好在天无绝人之路!"

译文:

(2) In that winter, my grandma died and my father lost his job. I left Beijing for Xuzhou to join him in hastening home to attend my grandma's funeral. When I met him in Xuzhou, the sight of the disorderly mess in our courtyard and the thought of my grandma started tears trickling down my cheeks. He said, "Now that things've come to such a pass, it's no use crying. Fortunately, Heaven always leaves one a way out."

译文仅在第一句使用了名词 my father,接下来的几句都用 he 来代替,而原文却四处都用"父亲",一处也未用代词。这固然主要是由于汉英语法的不同所致,但这是一篇饱含感情的文章,所写亲情,催人泪下,原文中多处用"父亲"而少用代词"他",可能还有文体方面的考虑——通过多次重复"父亲"这一庄重正式的称呼可以使文章显得凝重深情,而若多用"他"则读来似略感轻狎随便,与此相对,英文中使用 he 代替 father,却并不使读者产生同样的感觉。英语中人称照应除通过人称代词(I,you,he,she 等)实现外,还可以由所属限定词和所属代词来实现,而汉语在此情况下仍多用原词复现的手段。《背影》及其译文也不乏这样的例子:

(3) 这些日子,家中光景很是惨淡,一半为了丧事,一半为了父亲的赋闲。

(4) Between my grandma's funeral and *his* unemployment, our family was then in reduced circumstances.

又如:

(5) You have your opinion about this matter; Mary has *hers*.

(6) 你有你的观点,玛丽有玛丽的。

在指示照应中,由选择性名词性指示词(如英语的 this,that,these,those 和汉语的"这、那、这些、那些")和指示性副词[here,there,now,then;这儿(边、里),那儿(边、里);现在、当时、那时]所实现的照应汉英用法差异不大,但涉及定冠词实现的指示照应时,二者则有天壤之别,直接原因在于汉语无定冠词或相当于英语定冠词 the 的指示词。英语中定冠词 the 本身虽无词义,但在语篇衔接中却用得很广并起举足轻重的作用,这一点由表2可看出。The 与名词连用,指定上文已出现的物或人(少数情况下也指定下文将要出现的),以其照应作用使语篇衔接紧凑。在这种情况下,汉语只能依靠原词复现来衔接上下文。如《背影》一文中:

(7) 我再向外看时,他已抱了朱红的橘子往回走了。过铁道时,他先将橘子散放在地上,自己慢慢爬下,再抱起橘子走。

译文如下:

(8) The next moment when I looked out of the window again, he was already on the way back, holding bright red tangerines in both hands. In crossing the railway track, he first put the tangerines on the ground, climbed down slowly and then picked them up again.

在该句的英译中,"tangerines"(橘子)第一次出现时因是不定指,故用无冠词复数,第二次出现时便冠以定冠词 the,至第三次出现时,又改用代词 them 与前两处 tangerines 照应,而在原文中,三次都重复使用"橘子"一词。汉英在指示照应这一语篇衔接手段上的差别可见一斑。

在比较照应中,汉英这种差别虽不及人称照应和由定冠词 the 所实现的指示照应那样悬殊,却也客观存在,这里不再赘述。

2. 除照应外,英语中另外一种常用的语篇衔接手段是替代,与之相应,汉语仍大量采用原词复现以达到衔接上下文的目的。

韩礼德和哈桑把英语的替代分为三类:名词性替代、动词性替代和分句性替代,其中最常见的是名词性替代。英语中可用作名词替代词的主要有 one 和 ones,汉语中没有与之相等的替代词,故用原词复现法。如:

(9) This book is a good one.

(10) 这本书是本好书。

另外,汉语有时出于简洁,尤其在口语中,并不重复整个原词,而常用重复部分(如量词)或"的"字结构的办法来衔接上下文。正如本文第一部分所述,"的"字结构和重复量词而省略名词中心词的用法也可被看作汉语中的名词性替代,但不可否认的是,这实际上是一种部分重复。如:

(11) He goes about interviewing eye-witnesses of the accident. The *one* that he met yesterday was a fascinating storyteller.

(12) 他四处采访事故的目击者,他昨天遇到的那位是个讲故事的高手。

除名词性替代外,英语中还有动词性替代和分句性替代。这两种情况下,汉语也偏重于用原词复现法。如:

(13) She sings better than she did last year.

(14) 她唱歌比去年唱得好些。

(15) John speaks French and *so* does his brother.

(16) 约翰说法语,他哥哥也说法语。

(17) A: Do you think John will win?

B: Yes, I think *so*.

(18) A: 你觉得约翰会赢吗?

B: 嗯,我觉得他会赢。

此外,英语中还可以由关系代词或关系副词引导一个定语从句,先行词是上文中的某词或句子的某一部分。关系代词或副词在此也起替代作用,而汉语没有与英语定语从句相等的用法,仍使用原词复现法衔接上下文。如《背影》中:

(19) 又嘱托茶房好好照应我。我心里暗笑他的迂,他们只认得钱,托他们直是白托!

(20) He also asked the train attendants to take good care of me. I sniggered at him for being so impractical,for it was utterly useless to entrust me to those attendants,who cared for nothing but money.

原文中虽不是重复名词,但因"他们"已是对前句中"茶房"的人称照应,所以实际仍是原词复现。

3. 原词复现是汉语中最常见的一种语篇衔接手段,而英语中最常用的是照应与替代,上文已将其做了粗略比较。此外,省略也是汉语中用得很广的语篇衔接手段之一。许多语法学家认为可将省略看作一种特殊的照应即零照应(zero reference)或一种特殊的替代即零替代(zero substitution)。为避免概念混淆,我们不妨按韩礼德与哈桑,将之划分出来,独成一类,对之进行简要分析并与英语的照应和替代这两种最常用的衔接手段略加对比。

如果说原词复现在一定意义上是词语的重复,那么省略的使用则是为了避免重复(包括代词的重复),同时使上下文相互联系,衔接紧凑。一个句子中的被省略成分往往隐含在上下文中,所以省略在句与句间,即语篇平面上起到了纽带作用。

英语中为避免原词复现而多采用照应或替代衔接上下文,而汉语则一方面广用原词复现使语篇连贯,一方面为了避免过多的重复(包括代词重复),又大量使用省略法,通过省略某些词或短语的办法来实现前后语句间的紧密联系。当然,省略也是英语的一种语篇衔接手段,但其应用远不及在汉语中广,这一点由表1即可看出。

汉语中最常见的省略是主语省略。如果两个句子的动作或状态的主体是同一个人或事物,那么,前面的语句保留该主体作主语,而后面语句的主语则往往省略不用。这样一来,后面的句子在意思和结构上要受前句的制约,不能脱离上文而单独存在,句与句间因此而联系起来。这属于后省略,也有前省略,即前面句子省略去的某一成分(通常也为主语)在后一句中出现,但前省略远不及后省略多见,所以我们着重分析后省略。

英语中独立的句子一般都有主语,所以当前后句主语相同时,后面句子通常以人称照应,即使用人称代词来连接上下文。以《背影》为例:

(21) 我从北京到徐州,打算跟着父亲奔丧回家。到徐州见着父亲,看见满院狼藉的东西,又想起祖母,不禁簌簌地流下眼泪。

英译为:

(22) I left Beijing for Xuzhou to join him in hastening home to attend my grandma's funeral. When I met him in Xuzhou, the sight of the disorderly mess in our courtyard and the thought of my grandma started tears trickling down _my_ cheeks.

原文只在第一句用了主语"我",后面句子中均省略主语;而英译中第一句用了"I",后一句中也用了代词"I"及所属限定词"my"。又如原文中:

(23) 回家变卖典质,父亲还了亏空;又借钱办了丧事。

译为:

(24) My father paid off debts by selling or pawning things. _He_ also borrowed money to

meet the funeral expenses.

汉语中不但可省略主语,在有些地方还可省略宾语。在此情况下,英语一般用相应的代词来照应上文。如《背影》原文:

(25) 等他的背影混入来来往往的人里,再也找不着了,我便进来坐下,我的眼泪又来了。

译文为:

(26) I, however, did not go back to my seat until his figure was lost among crowds of people hurrying to and fro and I could no longer find *it*. My eyes were again wet with tears.

又如一个很常见的例子:

(27) He took a knife in his hand, turned it over, laid it down and took it up again.

(28) 他拿了一把小刀,把它翻过来,放下去,再拿起来。

如前所述,英语中名词中心词前用所属代词或所属限定词进行照应时,汉语不用代词而将原词重复。除此以外,汉语还可在英语使用所属限定词或所属代词这一人称照应手段时,干脆省去不用。如《背影》中:

(29) 他用两手攀着上面,两腿再向上缩……

译为:

(30) His hands held onto the upper part of the platform, his legs huddled up ...

原文中不说"他的两手"、"他的两腿"。又如:

(31) 于是扑扑衣上的泥土……

(32) ... and patting the dirt off his clothes…

原文中既省略了主语"他"或"父亲",又省去了限定词"他的"(衣上)。这里所举的英文例句中几乎全是使用照应手段与汉语的省略相对应,同样,英语中用替代衔接语篇时,汉语也常用省略,尽管不如照应常见。如:

(33) John has passed the exam. He told me so yesterday.

(34) 约翰考试及格了。他昨天告诉我的。

(35) Joan has a birthday next month. Elizabeth has one too.

(36) 琼下月过生日。伊丽莎白也过。

综上所述,汉英两种语言的部分语篇衔接手段在使用中各有所重:汉语更常用原词复现和省略,而英语则更常用照应和替代。这一结论是基于对语料的统计分析和实例比较而得出的。当然,汉英在衔接手段上的这些区别只是相对而言,不能绝对化,因为英语中也不乏省略和原词复现的例子,而汉语中以照应、替代为主要衔接手段的语篇也非少数。

另外需要指出,语篇中有无衔接手段只是鉴别其篇章性的因素之一,是语篇表层结构上的,是"形式"连贯。除此以外,语篇连贯与否,或者说是否具有篇章性,更大程度上还取决于语义的连贯,只有语篇中的深层语义连贯,才具有真正的黏合力(cohesive power),只有这种语义连贯具有逻辑联系时,表层的衔接手段方有可能和有用。没有意义上的联系,诸如连词之类的衔接手段很难增强语篇的连贯。至于深层语义的连贯,本文不再讨论。

第四章　文体学与翻译研究

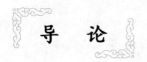

导　论

　　人们对于文体学的理解主要有两个,第一是对不同文类(genre)的语言特征的研究,比如对新闻语言、法律语言、文学语言、医学语言等不同文类的语言特征的研究;第二是对某个作家或是某个时代的作家、某个流派的作家的语言风格的研究。

　　无论文体类型如何,文本都是对语言的使用,都反映出独特的语言使用特点,都是语言艺术的结晶,而文体学的主要目的是借用语言学理论对文本在语言形式方面的特征进行分析研究,因而可以被借用过来进行文体分析,加深我们对于文本的语言特征的认识和了解。

　　奈达曾经说过,所谓"翻译",首先要再现原作的信息,然后要再现原作的风格,使译文读者读完译作之后的感受和原文读者读完原作之后的感受大致相同。文本翻译水平的高低在很大程度上取决于译者的文体意识以及对于某一个特定文类,某个作家或每个作家群体流派的作品在语言形式上的了解和欣赏。如果对于原作文本的文体特征没有感觉、无法欣赏,那么我们很难想象译者能够在文体上再现原作的风格。而文体学所提出的文体分析方法,可以用来分析文本翻译所涉及的原文和译文的语言形式特征或表达技巧问题。在分析方法方面,早期的文体学一般不关注文本以外因素对于文体和风格的影响,认为风格和文体是作品的内在特征,可以通过文本分析和细读进行研究和把握,而文本以外可能影响文本文体和风格的因素都被排除在文体分析之外。但文体学后来逐渐修正了这种纯粹的形式主义的分析方法,逐渐将读者的因素、社会历史和文化的因素也纳入研究视野当中,用这些文本外的因素来分析和解释语言层面的特征。

　　文体学与翻译研究的结合不仅仅体现在文体学对于以翻译为目的的文本的欣赏和分析,还体现在人们对于译者的翻译风格的研究。比如贝克在讨论了文本中的风格之后,又探讨了翻译作品在语言使用上的特点。另外她还尝试用语料库手段对翻译家所表现出来的翻译风格进行分析和研究,研究成果给学者们以很大的启发。

　　申丹在将文体学应用于文学翻译方面作出了可贵的努力,她的《文学文体学与小说翻译》(*Literary Stylistics and Fictional Translation*)就是这一方面的一个力作。因为小说是语言的艺术,与日常语言的使用相比,往往更多地体现出独特的语言文体特征。在小说文体中,由于作家的"语不惊人死不休"倾向,前景化的、脱离日常语言的死板模式的语言表达比比皆是。因而,文体学在文学翻译,特别是小说翻译中有着更加广阔的施展空间。

　　文体学途径的翻译研究的最新进展当属文体翻译学领域的认知转向。这种观点在最近英国学者琼·博厄斯-贝耶尔(Jean Boase-Beier)的专著 *Stylistic Approaches to Translation*(上海外语教育出版社,2011)中得到了阐发。博厄斯-贝耶尔系英国东安吉利大学(University of East Anglia)教授,一直从事翻译和文体学的教学和研究工作。她的这部作品首先追溯了早期的文体观,阐明文体对翻译的影响,然后又分别从读者和译者的不同视角考察文体的作用及其再创造过程中的选择。作者随之提出了翻译研究中的认知转向,以及文体学的认知观,最后对翻译研究的文体学途径进行了全面的总结。由此可以看出,不同语言学途径的翻译研究也不是壁垒森严的,它们之间也出现相互融合和借鉴的趋势,反映出翻译研究的跨学科特点。

 选 文

选文一　The Place of Literary Stylistics in the Translation of Fiction
申　丹

> **导 言**
>
> 把文体学与文学翻译,尤其是小说翻译的研究结合,并在这一领域有所著述的首推申丹。她的《文学文体学与小说翻译》(*Literary Stylistics and Fictional Translation*)至今仍被视为这一领域最重要的学术研究成果。《文学文体学与小说翻译》系统而深入地论述了文学文体学的性质和功能、词语表达、句法及其选择;另一方面又探讨了将文学文体学应用于小说翻译的可行性和必要性,并认为两者之间互为补充。我们这里推荐的这篇文章就选自这部专著,主要论述了将文体学应用于小说翻译和小说翻译研究的合理性和必要性。作者在北美和欧洲发表文体学、翻译学、叙事理论以及文学领域学术论文30多篇,也正是因为她在这些领域的成就,作者目前成为 *Style*(美国)、*The Translator*:*Studies in Intercultural Communication*(英国)、*Language and Literature*(英国)和 *JLS*:*Journal of Literary Semantics*(欧洲)等多个国际学术期刊的编委。

The discussion in this chapter centres on the justification of and, particularly, the necessity for applying literary stylistics to the translation of prose fiction. Basically, three factors combine to make such an application necessary. The first is that general translation studies, which have received much impetus from recent developments in linguistics and some related disciplines, are seen to be insufficient when applied to the translation of literary discourse. The second, which is no less obvious, arises from within the theory and criticism of literary translation itself, where attention has been focused on poetry with little time spent studying the problems characteristic of the translation of fiction, particularly of the traditional realistic kind. The third factor, one that is more immediately relevant, is the fact that many specific problems posed by fictional translation, which may be subsumed under the heading "deceptive equivalence," can be, and at present can only be, quite effectively solved by the introduction of stylistic analysis.

0　The Insufficiency of General Translation Studies

By "general" translation studies I mean translation studies that operate on the level of ordinary or natural language. During the past two or three decades, developments in the fields of transformational grammar, general and contrastive linguistics, semantics, information theory, anthropology, semiotics, psychology, and discourse analysis etc. have exerted great influence on translation theory and criticism, enabling the discipline to broaden the areas of investigation and to offer fresh insights into correspondence or transference between linguistic and cultural systems (see, for instance, Rabin, 1958; Nida, 1964, 1982; Nida & Taber, 1969; Catford, 1965; Newmark, 1981; Duff, 1981).

The traditionally-much-debated dichotomy between literal and free translation has been replaced by various linguistically-informed modern distinctions, like Nida's "formal" versus "dynamic" correspondence, Catford's "formal correspondence" versus "textual equivalence," or Newmark's "semantic" as opposed to "communicative" translation. In general, more attention has been paid to the translating process and greater emphasis placed on "equal-response" of the target language readers (see Shen, 1985). Such new perspectives on the theoretical front as well as the fairly extensive developments in specific interlingual contrastive studies have promoted considerably the understanding and mastery of the nature and skill of translation.

Given that literary translation primarily involves the transference of linguistic and cultural elements, developments in general translation studies are no doubt of relevance to a literary translator. But the point holds that this kind of study, which usually operates on the level of linguistic correspondence (including general stylistic norms), does not deal with problems intrinsic to or characteristic of literary discourse. One such problem, which is particularly significant in fictional translation, is how to make the appropriate choice(s) from grammatically correct "referential equivalents" or "stylistic variants" taking on different values or effects that tend to go unnoticed in ordinary discourse. If finding a grammatically-acceptable referential equivalent for the original is a matter of linguistic competence, the choice of a stylistically-optimal correspondent depends, by contrast, primarily on the understanding of the nature and function of literary texts.

It seems that some translation theorists have rather naïve notions about what literary style involves. In Alan Duff's *The Third Language*, the problem of register in literature is put on a par with that in non-literary writing. Duff focuses on the necessity of achieving consistency in register in translation, illustrating this necessity by translations of both non-literary and fictional texts. Duff contends that:

It would be a mistake, I think, to assume that only the literary translator is concerned with problems of style. Whatever discipline he may be working in ... he will have to decide on the *register* (formal—informal, official—unofficial) and to maintain this register consistently throughout (1981:7). Every text, has a *register*, i. e. , it is written at a level of formality or informality which is partly determined by the readers for whom the text is intended.

However, it would also be a mistake to think of the treatment of register in fictional translation as merely a matter of achieving consistency. Register in fictional discourse has to be seen as being of a more complex nature, and as integrated within the structure of the work. In many novels, variations in register operate to characterize different mind styles, to generate effects of parody or comedy, to convey the implied author's sympathetic identification or ironic distance and, not least, to indicate the mingling of voices or subtle shifts in point of view between various participants involved (see Fowler, 1977; Leech & Short, 1981; Bakhtin, 1981). Thus, rather than a superficial consistency in register (which a non-literary translator could be content with), a fictional translator would, or rather, should be concerned with thematically-motivated shifts in register, for it is in such deliberately-wrought variations that artistic significance inheres. In fact, many translation-critics are conscious of the essential difference in terms of style or expression between the translation of ordinary and literary discourse (see, for instance, Procházka, 1964; Popovič, 1970; Brisling, 1976; Cluysenaar, 1976; Holmes, 1978; Bassnett-McGuire, 1980). Indeed, in contrast with a non-literary translation,

for a literary translation the criterion for the functional equivalence of its structural elements cannot lie in the linguistic system in its usual sense, as it will be determined by the specific regularities of structuring of the text as an artistic construct. If the textual element of a literary translation is to possess a literary value equivalent to that of the original, a decisive part will be played by the functional equivalence of such categories, as for instance, the thematic means, the means to build up characters, contextual procedures, the prosodic elements in lyric poetry—all of them categories implying the notion of a literary tradition and aesthetic conventions which depend largely on historical and socio-cultural circumstances. (Broeck, 1978:39)

Apart from linguistic systems, in other words, literary translation also involves the encounter between literary polysystems and aesthetic conventions, including the conventions of artistic creation, of interpretation and criticism. In discussing problems concerning equivalence in translating poetry, Robert de Beaugrande justifiably draws a distinction between the general level (A) where one finds problems pertaining to "the relationships within or between language systems" (a level that "can be studied with the methods of linguistics and contrastive linguistics") and the more specific level (B) which "contains the more specific properties of poetic use of language and can be studied with the methods of poetics and literary analysis." Now since linguistically-oriented general translation studies only deal with the basic level (A), they are apparently insufficient when applied to literary translation. It is true that there has been a substantial amount of research into the translation of literary discourse. But most attention has been focused on the translation of poetry with little time spent studying the problems characteristic of the translation of prose fiction.

1　Characteristics of Fictional (vs. Poetic) Translation

This section directs attention to the fact that the problem of formal constraints, which has been much discussed in the criticism of poetic translation, does not, generally speaking, feature in fictional translation and, further, that the translation of fiction—particularly of the traditional realistic kind—presents its distinctive problems, many of which could be subsumed under the heading "deceptive equivalence."

1.1　Less Formal Constraints

In the large body of work discussing the translation of poetry, the weight of the argument often bears on the difficulties posed by the transference of such conventional peotic devices as verse form, stanzaic patterning, metre, line length, or rhyme scheme. The preservation of such formal features—either by "homologue" or "analogue" (see Holmes, 1978:75)—usually involves various losses or distortions of content (see Goodman, 1954: 227; Savory, 1968: 84; Nida, 1964:157). In fact, the constraint is not limited to the relation between form and content and may be found acting upon the association between formal devices themselves. More specifically, the choice of a particular corresponding formal device could render, as observed by Holmes (1978:76), correspondence for certain further formal features in the source-text unfeasible or even unattainable. Thus it is not surprising that the English translations of Catullus' Poem Sixty-Four display seven different modes of presentation, namely, (a) Phonemic translation, (b) Literal translation, (c) Metrical translation, (d) Poetry into prose, (e) Rhymed translation, (f) Blank verse translation, and (g) Interpretation (see Lefevere, 1975); each mode is seen to overemphasize one or more elements of the poem at the expense of the whole (Bassnett-McGuire, 1980:82; cf. Goodman, 1954:227). In connection with but distinct from this is the much-discussed formal constraint arising from the meaningful interaction between sound and sense, an element that features prominently in poetry as a genre and that significantly underlies the extreme difficulties of poetic translation (see Savory, 1968: 77 - 78; Widdowson, 1975:36 - 37; de Beaugrande, 1978:102).

When it comes to the translation of prose fiction, not only is a constraint of the preceding kind nonexistent, but also the constraint resulting from the interaction between sound and sense is very much more limited (with some exceptions like Woolf or Joyce). It is obvious that rhythmic, phonetic, or phonological properties are much less essential to the genre of fiction. This is just another way of saying that a large part of the criticism of poetic translation does not apply to the translation of prose fiction, which—particularly the traditional realistic kind—poses its distinctive problems to the translator. Many of these problems could, I think, be subsumed under the heading "deceptive equivalence."

1.2 Deceptive Equivalence

While the distinction between scientific translation and poetic translation is undoubtedly clear, the distinction between scientific translation and narrative translation tends to be blurred by an inadequate awareness of the function of language in realistic fiction. If a translator is sure to take account of the aesthetic effects of language in a poem, when it comes to translating realistic fiction, the translator is inclined to establish equivalence at the level of "paraphrasable material content" (Bassnett-McGuire, 1980: 115). This is hardly surprising since the writer's artistic manipulation of language in realistic fiction is much less obtrusive than in poetry; and also since the iso-morphic relation between the fictional world and the real world, allied to the resultant suspension of disbelief, can easily lead the translator to focus on the represented events or characters and to overlook the artistry involved in the use of the medium.

Such a neglect of the novelist's artistic manipulation of language is also found in some literary critics, as demonstrated by Philip Rahv's statement:

> All that we can legitimately ask of a novelist in the manner of language is that it be appropriate to the matter in hand. What is said, for that would be to dispel the illusion of life, and with it the credibility of fiction. (1956: 297)

This view misleadingly confines aesthetic significance in the novel to the portrayed fictional reality and does injustice to many great realistic writers (like those referred to in the following analysis) who are distinguished not only "by a vital capacity for experience, a kind of reverent openness before life, and a marked moral intensity" (Leavis, 1948: 9) but also by their skillful manipulation of language for aesthetic effects or by their use of language to create a certain texture and tone which serve to reinforce or modify themes and meanings. In translating Jane Austen, for instance, if one fails to capture the impact of her voice as conveyed by her subtle linguistic choices, there is sure to occur the loss of a substantial part of her artistry.

It is worth noting that, as far as a reader is concerned, even if s/he does not pay special attention to the effects of the writer's style, s/he could still be affected, though perhaps only unconsciously, by the writer's stylistic or rhetorical devices during the process of extracting the fictional reality from the linguistic medium. But if a translator does not consciously take account of such devices, s/he is bound to fail to represent them in the target language. Thus various kinds of deceptive equivalence may emerge in narrative translation, which convey approximately the same fictional "facts" but fail to capture the aesthetic effects generated by the original author's formal operations.

As already noted, "deceptive equivalence" in narrative translation also occurs at the level of fictional "facts," taking the shape of a distortion of fictional reality, which is mistaken by the translator as some form of equivalence. Theoretically, the boundary between the two kinds of deceptive equivalence in question is quite clear: one kind affects the represented fictional "facts" while the other only bears on the formal operations over and above the experience depicted. But in actual cases, one may find ambiguity or indeterminacy concerning which of the two dimensions of narrative structure is involved. Yet despite this tendency to overlap in practice, I would like to discuss the two kinds of deceptive equivalence separately, so as to see things in a clear theoretical perspective. (As this is only a preliminary theoretical discussion, some statements may be found rather vague, but they will be duly substantiated and clarified by the following practical analysis.)

1.2.1 At the Level of Fictional "Facts"

"Linguistically, this could be taken as the level of mere sense or the referential use of words. The stylistic interest here comes from the aesthetic motive underlying, or the aesthetic effect pertaining to the novelist's creation of fictional reality per se.

The deceptive equivalence in some cases can be accounted for on the one hand by what I consider "conceptual deviation" found in the original (i. e. violation of the relevant stereotypic conceptual frames in the translator's mind concerning human characteristics or behaviour under given circumstances) and, on the other, by the translator's failure to realize the larger structural or thematic functions of the fictional "facts" involved. What frequently happens is that the translator alters the fictional "fact(s) according to his/her normal or conventional ways of conceiving things, probably with the assumption that his/her rendering, which appears to be more logical or sensible than the original in the immediate context, is what the author ought to have said, but failed to say, and so is therefore a reasonable form of correspondence to the source language text." Although strictly or locally speaking, this is a matter of the translator's falling short of the novelist's "capacity for experience," it is in effect, on a larger structural scale, frequently a matter of the translator's failure to realize the function of the narrator's withholding information, suppressing explanation or immediate contextual substantiation: factors which make for "conceptual deviation" as such. As will be revealed by the analysis below, "conceptual deviation" of this kind may have a significant role to play in characterization or plot construction, giving rise to desirable stylistic effects such as irony, intensity or suspense: effects which regrettably disappear in the process of the translator's "normalization."

In fictional translation, the translator's emotional involvement—typically with certain characters—may also lead to deceptive equivalence at this level. Interestingly, the alteration of fictional "facts" here, which is characteristically motivated by "practical interests" coupled with "primacy effect," is usually carried out quite unconsciously (hence *deceptive equivalence*). In such cases, while the translator's emotional involvement constitutes the primary factor, his/her inadequate literary competence (in terms of, say the familiarity with the relevant novelistic conventions or the ability to perceive the larger structural or thematic functions of the fictional "facts" involved), may also have a significant part to play. In the next chapter, we shall examine in some detail the causes underlying, and the aesthetic losses resulting from, the translator's distortions as such.

Earlier, I made it clear that, in discussing deceptive equivalence, I do not concern myself with errors caused merely by inadequate linguistic competence (which is the concern of general translation studies) and I have been focusing on factors over and above that level: failure to realize the structural or thematic functions of the fictional "facts" involved, normal or conventional ways of conceiving or perceiving things, and emotional involvement. But in some special circumstances, the issue may be complicated by "traps" laid by differences in linguistic conventions between the source language and the target language. We shall see, in some examples, how deceptive equivalence is caused by a joint function of the translator's lack of awareness of the intended dramatic irony and his failure to detect a trap associated with the frequent omission of subjects and determiners peculiar to Chinese.

Before turning to the level of the narrative discourse, I would like to bring in one aspect of fictional reality, namely, the speech and thought proper of characters, which differs fundamentally from the rest of the purported reality in that it is in itself verbal. In this area, deceptive equivalence may arise at two contrastive levels. One is the level of mere sense, where deceptive equivalence typically takes the shape of the translator's regrettable normalization of certain illogical or unreliable elements in the original speech or thought; elements deliberately encoded by the author for given purposes of characterization. But more often, deceptive equivalence in this verbal reality arises paradoxically at the level of linguistic form. Now, as far as monologic fiction is concerned, artistic significance in this verbal reality inheres very much in the novelist's successful differentiation between speech (or thought) types or idiolectal features (like the crude distinctions between formal and informal, vulgar and elevated, or simple and sophisticated) as a way of creating different objectivized and finalized images of people (Bakhtin, 1973: 150). Being a matter of linguistic differentiation in terms of, say, register or dialect, it is only natural that the artistic significance here lies in the choices of given linguistic forms as opposed to others which convey approximately the same cognitive meaning (but one needs to bear in mind that, in this verbal reality, the change from, say, a character's informal expression into a more formal one is an alteration of the experience depicted). Basically, the translator's successful representation of this verbal reality in the target language depends on (i) the ability to differentiate the diversified speech or thought types in both the source language and the target language and to determine the general or specific correspondences between them; (ii) the understanding of the relation between the chosen speech or thought type and the given social or thematic role(s) of the character concerned; and (iii) the grasp on every single occasion of the relation between the characteristics, if any, of which the linguistic expression is found. If the translator falls short in any aspect, s/he can easily produce cases of deceptive equivalence, which convey approximately the same cognitive meaning but fail to correspond to the particular speech or thought type chosen by the original author, leading as a consequence to various losses of the function of the original speech or thought in terms of characterization. In the following practical analysis, I shall only touch occasionally on this verbal reality but I shall devote a whole chapter to the formal operations carried out on it, i. e. , to the different modes of speech and thought presentation, which pertain to the level of narrative discourse.

1. 2. 2　At the Level of Narrative Discourse

At this level, we are concerned with the authorial (and/or the dramatized) narrator's formal operations carried out on the purported fictional "facts" or, to put it another way, with the writer's exploitation of the resources or advantages of the linguistic medium in the representation of fictional reality. As far as the more or less "monologic" novel is concerned, the relation between fictional reality and formal operations as such is essentially a relation between fictional happening and the bearing brought on it by the all-encompassing authorial consciousness (in all types of narration). While fictional reality is in itself objectivized, represented by the implied author to fulfill certain thematic purposes, the way that linguistic form is manipulated to reinforce or modify that reality is a way of conveying the authorial vision of that reality (either directly or derivatively as in the case of first-person narration) and a way of making that reality function more effectively in the thematic unity constituted according to the author's artistic design. It is, however, understood that even in such authorial narrative discourse, there may be found a variety of characters' voices or social registers introduced typically through "speech allusion," i. e. , "the selective imitation of a style of speech by the author" (Leech & Short, 1981: 349–350; see also Bakhtin, 1981:298ff.).

In realistic fiction, deceptive equivalence at this level usually, as noted above, takes the form of cases which convey approximately the same fictional "facts" but fail to capture the aesthetic effects generated by stylistic or rhetorical devices in the original. The true equivalentce that one should aim for here is functional equivalence (which conveys similar aesthetic effects of both content and form) or "expressive identity" (see Bassnett-McGuire, 1980:25). But once we go beyond the solid ground of fictional "facts," the problems of determining translation equivalence begin to emerge. Indeed, in the translation of realistic fiction, questions as to what constitutes a free variation on the original and what involves stylistic losses are more difficult to deal with than either in the translation of newspaper reports (where any version which conveys approximately the same amount of information with an acceptable style may be regarded as a translation equivalent) or in the rendering of poetry (where stylistic losses are often more detectable).

It seems to me that, in determining functional equivalence in somewhat monologic realistic fiction, the following two closely related aspects deserve particular attention: one is authorial vision, stance or point of view; the other is the function of the linguistic form in the thematic unity of the work. Now, in order to see things in perspective, we may make a comparison in terms of these two aspects between newspaper reports and such realistic fiction. In the case of a newspaper report, the reader, whose purpose is usually to extract information, does not purposefully seek the vision, stance or point of view of the reporters. In the case of a novel as a work of art and dominated by authorial consciousness, the reader is by contrast, constantly seeking the authorial or narratorial vision or viewpoint which takes on aesthetic significance; which forms a crucial guide for the reader's interpretation; and the search for which constitutes an essential part of the reading activity.

Since, in describing the same event, the difference in point of view between different encoders lies mainly in the different choices of linguistic form at the level of narrative discourse (as opposed to the narrated story), in the case of a newspaper report, where the encoder's point of view does not really count, the difference between, say, surface syntactic choices may well be overlooked. But precisely for the same reason, the differences in choice between linguistic forms matter a great deal in prose fiction. Thus, given the two different surface choices: "after doing X, he did Y" and "he did X and then did Y," one may find both forms equally acceptable in the translation of a newspaper report. In the translation of fiction, by contrast, one surface choice may be found more suitable than the other in that the difference between the two in terms of the narrator's viewpoint (emphasis; given vs. new; foregrounding vs. backgrounding) may bear on narratorial stance and on characterization, among other things.

Much more notable is the difference between a newspaper report and prose fiction in terms of the writer's irony or sympathy. In fictional discourse, the authorial irony or empathy, conveyable through choices, say, between words or between modes of speech, constitutes an important dimension of the narrative structure, playing a positive role in shaping the characters concerned (who are in themselves a creation of the writer's imagination). Indeed, the fictional reader, whatever his/her political beliefs, is conventionally expected to share—perhaps only in the process of reading—the author's irony or sympathy (cf. W. Booth, 1961: 137ff.). The translator's failure to use functionally-equivalent linguistic means to carry over the authorial stance may lead to significant aesthetic losses. By contrast, in the case of news reporting whose function is to communicate actual happenings (although, influenced or controlled by given ideologies, newspapers can distort facts), the reporter's irony or sympathy is not supposed to come into play; and if it is brought into play through certain choices of linguistic form, the translator will probably either overlook it or justifiably reject it. For, while such total property is undoubtedly significant in revealing the ideological stance of the reporter or newspaper concerned, it may not be of significance to the translator whose aim is usually to provide a piece of news for the general public in the target language rather than to demonstrate the ideological character of a given reporter/newspaper for some special purposes.

Interestingly, in fictional discourse, the authorial or narratorial vision as embodied by given choices of linguistic form tends to superimpose an additional meaning—either imitative or contrastive—on the fictional reality depicted. In the contrastive cases, there is usually found an attempt to use the value of the linguistic form(s) to "shape" (vs. to imitate) fictional meaning, or the imitating or "shaping" effects as such which pertain to the level of narrative discourse, may well be suppressed in the case of a newspaper report where the reader/translator's interest is usually limited to the narrated story and where the narrative discourse does not really count. In fact, underlying the aesthetic significance of the narrative discourse characteristic of fiction is, among other things, the convention of thematic unity of form and content, or more specifically, the convention of using linguistic form to reinforce or modify meanings and themes. With such conventions, it is natural for the writer to use the narrative discourse as semantic reinforcement or modification of the narrated story; and with such conventions, the reader is apt to look for thematic effects or values in the writer's choices of linguistic form. Thus, if a novelist uses the mode of direct speech instead of indirect speech, the fictional reader would consciously or unconsciously search for the underlying authorial intention in terms of characterization, for the possible connection between this choice of form and the role or attitude of the character concerned. But if a news reporter uses the mode of direct speech instead of indirect speech, the reader is unlikely to try to find out the mode's thematic value or its function in characterization. What we have here is an essential difference in the function of linguistic form between literary and ordinary discourse. Given the same linguistic form or pattern, its stylistic values become functional in fictional discourse but tend to be dormant in non-fictional discourse.

Although focusing on the difference in the function of the writer's (or narrator's) point of view between newspaper reports and prose fiction, I have already touched on the difference between the two in terms of the structural or thematic function of linguistic form. As distinct from a newspaper report, a work of prose fiction is often marked by a thematic unity deliberately wrought according to the author's artistic design. The constituent parts form objectivized means used to generate thematically-related effects; that is to say, their functions are determinable only in relation to the total structure of the work (see Kroeber, 1971:24 – 25). This forms a contrast to a newspaper report whose constituent part is responsible only to the specific event(s) involved. The thematically-unified structure characteristic of monologic fiction is surely a significant factor that conditions the author's ways of manipulating linguistic form. Given the thematic unity as such, it is not surprising to find in a novel's motif in the shape of the consistent use of a linguistic form or pattern over a long stretch of text. In John Fowles's *The Collector*, for instance, the contrast between the inferiority of the kidnapper and the dominance of the kidnapped girl is continuously reinforced by the contrast between the former's free direct speech and the latter's direct speech (the mode of direct speech, with the inverted commas serving as invitations to an auditory experience, functions to strengthen the auditory impact of the speech). More frequently found is the motif in the shape of the recurrent use of a given word or an expression. A case in point is the frequent references to "dark" or "darkness" in Lu Xun's "Remorse for the Past" ("Shangshi"). The failure to realize the significance of this thematic motif has led a translator to suppress unconsciously the symbolic meaning of "darkness." Clearly, to avoid such cases of deceptive equivalence in fictional translation, the translator needs to judge the function of the linguistic forms concerned in relation to the thematic unity of the work.

The necessity of taking account of the total structure of the fictional text in the translator's choices of linguistic form has been stressed by Bassnett-McGuire (1980: 110 – 118) whose analysis reveals that, if the translator renders the opening passage of a novel without relating it to the overall structure, s/he runs the risk of producing what we consider deceptive equivalence, where the paraphrasable content is translated at the cost of everything else. It will have become clear that the implied author's, or dramatized narrator's, stance/viewpoint and the structural or thematic function of the linguistic form are two significant criteria for determining deceptive equivalence at the level of narrative discourse.

Now, because of the differences in linguistic and literary conventions, different languages have different stylistic norms or means; the same linguistic form, that is to say, may have different expressive values in different languages (see Broeck, 1978; Popovič, 1970). Further, the differences may be complicated by the fact that the source text is often not contemporary. When confronted with such differences, the translator's task is essentially to match the intended stylistic effects in the source language with functionally-equivalent, though formally-different, linguistic means in the target language. Failure to do so can easily make for deceptive equivalence with various stylistic losses. In terms of the translation between Chinese and English, the differences in stylistic norms or means feature prominently in the area of syntax and of speech and thought presentation.

2 Literary Stylistics and Deceptive Equivalence

For anyone who is familiar with literary stylistics and who knows the poor state of the criticism of narrative translation, the necessity of introducing the values and emphases of literary stylistics into the latter area—as an effective means of dealing with deceptive equivalence as such—would be fairly obvious. The deplorably small body of existing work on narrative translation is marked by general and impressionistic comments on style (showing little or no concern with its thematic relevance) or by intuitive analysis with a notable lack of sensitivity to the subtle stylistic devices.

At the level of fictional "fact," attention has been focused by and large on distortions caused by inadequate linguistic and/or cultural competence (typically in the shape of mistranslations of idiomatic expressions or syntactic errors). What I referred to as "deceptive equivalence" has hardly been discussed. As already noted, failure to realize the larger structural or thematic functions of the fictional "facts" in the original constitutes a significant factor underlying deceptive equivalence at this level, a factor which could be effectively dealt with by stylistic analysis, characterized by close observation of the relation between the facts involved and the surrounding linguistic and textual features. The basic task of the analysis here is to elucidate those functions in the source language and the aesthetic losses in the target language, as a means of enhancing one's awareness of the aesthetic motive underlying, or aesthetic effects pertaining to, the author's choices of fictional "facts." Despite the obvious difference in the data, the analytical rationale or procedure here is in essence quite similar to the stylistic analysis operating at the level of narrative discourse where the issue is the relation between the author's choices of linguistic form and literary significance. Interestingly, because of the essential similarity between the analyses conducted at the two different levels, in intra-lingual stylistic analysis of narrative, the critic may also shift— probably quite unconsciously—from one level to the other (see, for instance, Kennedy, 1982). But of course, most attention in intra-lingual stylistic analysis is devoted to the level of the narrative discourse (also the choices of linguistic form in the verbal reality composed of character's speech, thought or mind-style).

It is at the level of narrative discourse that literary stylistics may contribute most to the criticism of narrative translation (the same applies to the verbal reality as such). Existing work in intra-lingual stylistic analysis has shed much light on the aesthetic significance of narrative discourse, which displays a descriptive precision and stylistic sensitivity (concerning syntactic form in particular) not found in traditional translation criticism. But such attempts are rare; and some subtle stylistic areas like modes of speech or thought presentation, which have been extensively investigated in Anglo-American stylistic analysis, have remained completely untouched in the criticism of fictional translation. In view of the fact that deceptive equivalence is on the whole unexposed (and therefore not consciously guarded against), constituting a great threat to the literary effects generated by the novelist's manipulation of the linguistic medium, there is surely an urgent need to make extensive stylistic analysis of deceptive equivalence as such. The major role of stylistic analysis is to sharpen the translator's sensitivity to the aesthetic function of linguistic form in prose fiction, helping the translator to produce functional equivalence rather than referential correspondence with various stylistic losses.

Clearly, as distinct from a non-literary translator, a fictional translator needs to be equipped with adequate literary and stylistic competence. In the translating process, one must start with adequate literary and stylistic competence. In the translating process, one must start with a detailed stylistic analysis of the original, trying to determine the aesthetic function of the individual component (be it a fictional fact or a choice of linguistic form) in the thematic unity of the work, otherwise deceptive equivalence may be unavoidable.

选文二　Towards a Methodology for Investigating the Style of a Literary Translator

Mona Baker

导　言

翻译研究从文学研究中继承了对个体作家的创作风格的研究成果,从语言学那里吸收了对于语言的使用者和社会团体的语言文体风格的研究路向。但是,对于翻译家或翻译团队的翻译风格的研究一直是一个空白,而这个空白就是由英国曼彻斯特大学翻译研究教授贝克来填补的。贝克是曼彻斯特大学翻译与国际研究中心的主任,圣杰罗姆出版社的奠基人、*The Translator* 主编,当代翻译研究领域的领军人物。主要著作包括《换言之:翻译教程》、《翻译研究百科全书》、《翻译与冲突》等。这篇文章是译者翻译风格研究方面的经典之作,具体介绍了如何利用语料库语言学这个工具来进行译者风格的研究,非常具有方法论方面的指导意义。由于篇幅有限,选文略有删节。

Style in Translation

A number of translation scholars have attempted to apply various interpretations of the notion of style to the study of translation, mostly with a view to elaborating criteria for quality assessment. The best known and most explicit treatment to date is House (1977/ 1981, 1997).

House sets out to develop a model for describing the linguistic and situational peculiarities of the source text, comparing source and translation texts, and making informed statements about the relative match of the two. These statements are meant to be evaluative, to say something about whether the translation is good, bad or indifferent. The evaluation is based on analyzing two sets of "situational dimensions": the dimensions of language user and the dimensions of language use. The first covers geographical origin, social class, and time; the second covers medium, participation, social role relationship, social attitude, province. These are all elements that figure prominently in many types of stylistic analyses, and indeed most of these categories are borrowed from Crystal and Davy's *Investigating English Style*

(1969). The definition of social attitude (under dimensions of language use) is based on the distinctions proposed formal, consultative, casual, and intimate styles. ①

House in effect combines two of the most common interpretations of the notion of style: as variation in the level of formality, hence the borrowing of the categories from Joos, and as patterned choices across all linguistic levels. ② She does not attempt a systematic treatment of the notion of style as such, since ultimately what she aims to describe is not so much the style of the original text or author, and certainly not the style of the translation or translator, but where the two texts diverge along the two dimensions of language user and language use, and only along those two dimensions. Hers then is essentially a checklist of features designed to allow the scholar to formulate a statement of the relative match of source and target texts and the relative success of the latter in reproducing the "style" of the original.

Apart from this extended study by House, there have been various attempts to use insights from both linguistic and literary studies of style to explain the choices made by specific translators or, more frequently, to prescribe guidelines for the selection of specific translation strategies on the basis of broad stylistic categories formalized as text types or registers. This reflects the fact that the notion of style in both linguistic and literary studies has traditionally been associated with one of three things: the style of an individual writer or speaker (e. g. the style of James Joyce, or Winston Churchill), linguistic features associated with texts produced by specific groups of language users and in a specific institutional setting (e. g. the style of newspaper editorials, patents, religious sermons), or stylistic features specific to texts produced in a particular historical period (e. g. Medieval English, Renaissance French).

Translation studies has specifically inherited from literary studies its preoccupation with the style of individual creative writers, but only insofar as describing the style of a writer can inform the process of translating his or her work. The most recent example is Tim Parks' *Translating Style* (1998), which includes chapters on *Women in Love*, *James Joyce*, *Mrs. Dalloway*, *Samuel Beckett*, etc. From linguistics, on the other hand, translation studies inherited the interest in studying the style of social groups of language users (more commonly known as register analysis), for similar reasons. The most recent example of this is *Text Typology and Translation* (Trosborg, 1997), which continues a long tradition in translation studies of using text type classifications as a shorthand for clusters to which the student or practitioner of translation should pay particular attention. The classifications may be based on different criteria: the context in which language is used (e. g. journal articles, radio broadcasts), subject matter (medical discourse, legal language), a combination of both

---

① Cf. Gleason's (1965) distinctions between oratorical, deliberative, consultative, casual, and intimate key.

② Enkvist (1964) remains one of the most thorough attempts at defining style from a variety of perspectives. See also Wales (1989).

(medical journal articles, law textbooks), or the nature of the message and addressor/addressee relationship (argumentative discourse, the language of instructions). Whatever the basis for the various classifications, the aim is generally to provide a starting point for identifying the distinctive features of the source text in order to reproduce in the translation either those same features or the typical features associated with the same text type in the target language.

It is worth pointing out that studying the style of social groups (register analysis) may be extended to studying the language shared by a group adhering to a certain poetics (including, in the case of translation, a certain tradition or programme in translating), in which case the possibility of any clusters of linguistic features identified being attributable to socially shared preferences for certain uses of language must be worth examining. In the study presented here, this particular line of investigation is not pursued. Such a study would have to involve calculating the deviation shown by individual translators against the percentage norm derived from an entire corpus of translations (and against the source text in each instance). We can then subsequently see if we can group translators showing certain manifest preferences together and suggest that their output in a sense realizes a certain "register" or "sociolect." To the best of my knowledge, Kenny (1999, in press) is the only study that attempts to pursue this line to some extent, using corpus methodology. ①

Style of Translation?

Translation studies then essentially inherited from both disciplines—literary studies and linguistics—the association of style with "original" writing. So far there has been little or no interest in studying the style of a translator, or a group of translators, or a corpus of translated material that belongs to a particular historical period. This is clearly because tradition has traditionally been viewed as a derivative rather than creative activity. The implication is that a translator cannot have, indeed should not have, a style of his or her own, the translator's task, possible the style of the original. We may well want to question the feasibility of these assumptions—given that it is as impossible to produce a stretch impersonal way as it is to handle an object without leaving one's fingerprints on it. Moreover, several theorists of translation have been calling in relatively recent years for more visibility for translators, whether as a professional group or in terms of an individual translator's presence in the text (see, in particular, Venuti [1995] and the growing literature on feminist translation strategies). And yet these calls have not been accompanied by any attempt to demonstrate that a translator does indeed leave his or her individual imprint on every text they produce.

---

① I am grateful to one of the anonymous referees of this paper for drawing my attention to the importance of pursuing this line of investigation.

The translator's presence in the text, or rather the traces that this presence leaves in the text, has received some attention in the literature, most notably in May (1994), Hermans (1996a, 1996b), and Gullin (1998). Here, the discussion has been largely restricted either to describing general tendencies for translators to, for example, focus on the semantics of the source text and ignore its idiosyncrasies (May 1994), or describing instances of open intervention by the translator, mainly in terms of adding paratextual material or glosses. The latter aspect of the translator's presence is developed in Hermans (1996a), where it is clearly acknowledged that "that other voice [i. e. the translator's] is there in the text itself, in every word of it" (1996a: 9). Hermans (1996b) pursues this issue at greater length and starts by asking whether "the translator, the manual labour done, disappear[s] without textual trace" (1996b: 26). One of his proposed answers is that the translator's voice "may remain entirely hidden behind that of the Narrator, rendering it impossible to detect in the translated text" (1996b: 27; emphasis added), a conclusion we may wish to revisit in the light of recent advances in corpus methodology, as I will attempt to demonstrate in this paper. At any rate, Hermans' main focus remains on those instances where the translator's voice "breaks through the surface of the text speaking for itself, in its own name, for example in a paratextual Translator's Note employing an autoreferential first person identifying the speaking subject" (1996b: 27).[1]

This is the nearest we have come in translation studies to the idea of studying the style of a translator, in presence in the text, which is to say we have little about the issue. Given not only the fact that the notion of style is very difficult to define even in established disciplines such as literary criticism and stylistics (Wales, 1989: 435), but also that, to my knowledge, no one seems to have tried to apply it specifically to translation so far, at least not in the way I propose here, it is at this point what I mean by "style" and what I think the notion might cover in an analysis of translated text specifically.

I understand style as a kind of thumb-print that is expressed in a range of linguistic—as well as non-linguistic—features. As such, it covers the notion of "voice" as defined by Hermans above, but also much more. In terms of translation, rather than original writing, the notion of style might include the (literary) translator's choice of the type of material to

---

① Gullin attempts to "demonstrate in what ways it is possible to discern the translator's voice" (1998: 261), but I only have access to the short summary in English at the end of this Swedish book and therefore cannot comment on the details of this particular study.

translate, where applicable,[①] and his or her consistent use of specific strategies, including the use of prefaces or afterwords, footnotes, glossing in the body of the text, etc. More crucially, a study of a translator's style must focus on the manner of expression that is typical of a translator, rather than simply instances of open intervention. It must attempt to capture the translator's characteristic use of language, his or her individual profile of linguistic habits, compared to other translators. Which means that style, as applied in this study, is a matter of patterning: it involves describing preferred or recurring patterns of linguistic behaviour, rather than individual or one-off instances of intervention.

I am particularly interested at this stage in linguistic features which are probably more in the domain of what is sometimes called "forensic stylistics" than literary stylistics (Leech & Short, 1981:14). Traditionally, literary stylistics has focused on what are assumed to be conscious linguistic choices on the part of the writer, because literary stylisticians are ultimately interested in the relationship between linguistic features and artistic function, in how a given writer achieves certain artistic effects. Forensic stylistics, on the other hand, tends to focus on quite subtle, unobtrusive linguistic habits which are largely beyond the conscious control of the writer and which we, as receivers, register mostly subliminally. But like both branches of stylistics, I am interested in patterns of choice (whether these choices are conscious or subconscious) rather than individual choices in isolation.

As things stand at the moment, we have no model to draw on for conducting stylistic analyses of translators or translated text specifically. We do not, for instance, have a methodology for isolating stylistic features which can reasonably be attributed to the translator from those which are simply a reflection of the stylistic features of the original. I will attempt to look at this issue in more detail in the discussion section of this article. More importantly, in my view, until very recently we had no readily available data for analysis, especially for analyzing linguistic habits which are beyond the conscious control of the translator and for capturing patterns of choice rather than individual choices. This type of study can be greatly aided by access to a large body of data and relevant software to process it at least semi-automatically, and hence ought to draw to some extent on the methodology used in corpus linguistics. Unfortunately, however, corpus linguists have traditionally

---

① The degree of choice (of material to translate) varies a great deal among individual translators and types of translation. Most non-literary translators do not have the luxury of choosing what to translate, though many do make a conscious choice of at least what not to translate, often for ethical reasons: many will not translate for the arms industry as a matter of principle, for instance. In literary and book translation generally, by contrast, it is possible and fairly common for translators to propose books to publishers, often because they feel they have a particular affinity with the writer. If we accept that the themes that a particular writer such as Virginia Woolf or Mark Twain chooses to write about constitute part of his or her "style," then the same principle must be applied to the study of style in translation. A translator may consistently choose authors who deal with themes such as alienation, or carnal desire, and this choice will be reflected in the style of the translation, just as it will have had an impact on the style of the original.

Although the definition of style as "choice" is now widely accepted, the idea of this choice extending to themes is not explicitly acknowledged in the literature. It is, however, an extension of the definition that seems plausible to me.

excluded translated text from their corpora, on the basis that it is not representative of the language being studied (see Baker, 1996; 1999), which meant that until very recently no one had access to a large corpus of translated material that could be used for stylistic analysis of the type I am proposing here. ①

The Translational English Corpus (TEC)

We have tried to address this problem at the Centre for Translation Studies, UMIST (Manchester), by building a large computerised corpus of English text translated from a variety of source languages, both European and non-European, and developing software for processing it semi-automatically. The overall size of the corpus at the time of writing is 6.5 million words; it should reach 20 million words by the end of 2001. The corpus consists largely of fiction and biography (with smaller subcorpora of news and inflight magazines). This is a resource that is made available to the research community worldwide on the web (see http://www.umist.ac.uk/ctis/research/research_overview.htm). ②

The Translational English Corpus is meticulously documented in terms of extra-linguistic features such as gender, nationality and occupation of the translator, direction of translation, source language, publisher of the translated text, etc. This information is held in a separate header file for each text. The concordancing software is designed to make the information in the header file available to the researcher at a glance, as can be seen in Figure 1.

The corpus (TEC) is specifically designed to include, among other things, several works by individual experienced literary translators. In many cases we have perhaps five or six translations by the same person, translating different writers and sometimes from different source languages. The idea is to have a snapshot of the work of individual translators as well as a snapshot of translated English in general. The corpus also includes several works by the same author, translated by different translators, thus allowing us to look at the issue of style from different perspectives.

---

① This is true of corpus linguists working with English specifically. In languages such as Finnish or Norwegian, where translations account for a very large percentage of all published material, it is simply not feasible to exclude translations.

② The software and the site are developed and maintained by Saturnino Luz (luzs@acm.org). The concordancing software does not work properly on all browsers. Users may receive a message to the effect that the server may be down, in which case they can download a separate piece of software, also available on the site, to ensure direct access to the concordancing software irrespective of the type of browser used. At the moment, it is not advisable to search for high frequency words online, partly because the web technology is slow. We are in the process of rewriting the concordancing software to improve speed of access. Users who require concordances of high frequency words such as say or tell should contact the author directly (mona.baker@umist.ac.uk).

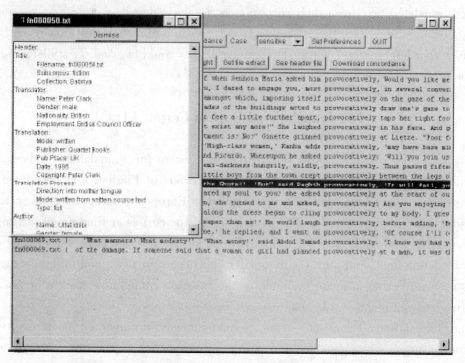

Figure 1   Screen Shot from the Translational English Corpus

Some Interesting Patterns

The overall question as far as the present study is concerned is whether individual literary translators can plausibly be assumed to use distinctive styles of their own, and if so how we might go about identifying what is distinctive about an individual translator's style. We need to explore the possibility that a literary translator might consistently show a preference for using specific lexical items, syntactic patterns, cohesive devices, or even style of punctuation, where other options may be equally available in the language. If there is sufficient evidence to suggest that this might be the case, we then need to address a number of questions, none of which can be answered satisfactorily on the basis of this exploratory study. The questions might include the following: (a) Is a translator's preference for specific linguistic options independent of the style of the original author? (b) Is it independent of general preferences of the source language, and possibly the norms or poetics of a given sociolect? (c) If the answer is yes in both cases, is it possible to explain those preferences in terms of the social, cultural or ideological positioning of the individual translator?

These are "large" questions which will take time to answer satisfactorily, especially given the current lack of large-scale descriptive studies in the discipline, a lack which inevitably means that we have little or no reliable data to use as a backdrop to some of the patterns we might identify. Nevertheless, I would like not only to raise these "large" questions but also to encourage other researchers to address them by exploring them in a very tentative way in the rest of this article. I will do so by looking at some aspects of linguistic patterning in a subset of the Translational English Corpus: the works of two British literary translators represented in the corpus, Peter Bush and Peter Clark. The subcorpus I have used for analysis at this stage consists of the following texts:

(a) Peter Bush: overall number of words in the corpus 296,146

Filename	Source Language	Author	Title
fn000003	Brazilian Portuguese	Chico Buarque	Turbulence
fn000028	Spanish (mainland)	Juan Goytisolo	Quarantine
fn000035	Spanish (South America)	Senel Paz	Strawberry and Chocolate
bb000002	Spanish (mainland)	Juan Goytisolo	Forbidden Territory
bb000004	Spanish (mainland)	Juan Goytisolo	Realms of Strife

(b) Peter Clark: overall number of words in the corpus 173,932

Filename	Source Language	Author	Title
fn000048	Arabic	Muhammad al Murr	Dubai Tales
fn000049	Arabic	Ulfat Idilbi	Grandfather's Tale
fn000050	Arabic	Ulfat Idilbi	Sabriya

Files beginning with fn are works of fiction, those beginning with bb are biographies or autobiographies. The files bb000002 and bb000004 are the autobiography of Juan Goytisolo, in two parts. All the authors translated by Peter Bush are male, but there are several source languages—or varieties of source language—represented, though all three (Brazilian Portuguese, mainland Spanish and South American Spanish) are closely related.

As for Peter Clark, there is only one source language represented and two authors, but the two authors are very different, and we might expect their writing to reflect this difference. Muhammad al Murr is a male writer from Dubai. Age-wise, he is in his mid-forties. Ulfat Idilbi is a Syrian woman writer, in her late eighties. Her life experiences and her style of writing are very different from al Murr's.

I will first describe some of the more interesting patterns I have identified so far and then offer a number of possible explanations for these patterns as a way of opening up the debate on methodology, which is the main focus of this article. The patterns relate to type/token ratio; average sentence length; variation across texts; frequency and patterning of SAY (the most frequent reporting verb in English). They are presented below as they are encountered in the translations, with little or no reference to the source texts to start with. The difficult issue of how we establish what is attributable to the translator and what is a direct reflection of the source text will be tackled in the discussion section.

Type/Token Ratio

One obvious difference between the two translators concerns the overall type/token ratio. In simple terms, type/token ratio is a measure of the range and diversity of vocabulary used by a writer, or in a given corpus. It is the ratio of different words to the overall number of words in a text or collection of texts. A high type-token ratio means that the writer uses a wider range of vocabulary. A low type-token ratio means that a writer draws on a more restricted set of vocabulary items. In studies of original English, texts addressed to non-native speakers of English (for example BBC World Service broadcasts) tend to have a lower type-token ratio than texts addressed to native speakers (for example Radio Four broadcasts). The relevant figures for Peter Bush and Peter Clark are as follows:

Bush	Overall	FT	RofS	Turb.	Quar.	S&C
Stnd. Type/Token	49.87	52.42	51.96	44.51	54.88	43.32

Clark	Overall	Dubai Tales	Grandfather	Sabriya
Stnd. Type/Token	41.00	42.34	39.53	41.07

First, a note about the procedure for calculating the above figures. Standardized type/token ratio figures are much more reliable than raw type/token figures, especially if the texts and subcorpora used are of different lengths, as in the present case. WordSmith Tools, the software used to obtain the above figures, computes type/token ratio (mean) every 1,000 words as it goes through each text file. In other words, the ratio is calculated for the first 1,000 running words, then calculated afresh for the next 1,000, and so on to the end of the text or corpus. A running average is then computed, which means that the final figure represents an average type/token ratio based on consecutive 1,000-word chunks of text.

The above figures show that the type/token ratio is lower overall for Peter Clark, with a very restricted range of variation among individual texts. It is higher overall for Peter Bush, with much more variation among individual texts.

Average Sentence Length

The average sentence length for all the texts in the corpus is as follows:

Bush	Overall	FT	RofS	Turb.	Quar.	S&C
Stnd. Sent. Length	23.76	31.82	28.49	10.34	19.64	10.85

Clark	Overall	Dubai Tales	Grandfather	Sabriya
Stnd. Sent. Length	8.07	8.45	7.91	7.87

Again, we see that average sentence length (using the same process of standardization used for calculating type/token ratio) is much lower for Peter Clark, and again with very much less variation among individual texts.

So far, I would tend to interpret these overall statistical findings as showing a stronger (probably largely subconscious) attempt on the part of Peter Clark to mediate the Arabic texts by making them, in a sense, less challenging linguistically. Perhaps he subconsciously realizes that the English reader faces sufficient challenges at the level of digesting the details of a very different world, with different values, priorities, and style of life. I will return to this point in the discussion.

Let us now look at some differences in actual language patterning.

Reporting Structures

Reporting structures in fiction and (auto)biography are both common and important in terms of providing a framework for dialogue and, consequently, for interpreting the role of the narrator and supporting characterization. We might expect a high level of variation here, given that different characters in a novel, for instance, are likely to speak in different ways, report others' speech in their own style, and so on. Within the scope of this initial study, it is not feasible to explore all or even several reporting verbs, given their very high frequency and the need to look closely at recurring patterns in a large number of concordances. I have chosen to look at SAY in all its forms (say, says, said, saying) because it is the reporting verb with the highest frequency in English.

Frequency-wise, it is immediately noticeable that Peter Clark makes much heavier use of this verb (bearing in mind especially that his is a smaller corpus), and particularly of the past tense of the verb. This may be explained by the overall tendency of writers in Arabic to make very heavy use (compared to English) of the "equivalent" verb qaal (see Sham'a, 1978: 168 – 171). I will return to the methodological implications of potential source language influence later in the discussion. In the meantime, here are the relevant frequencies:

	Bush	Clark
	(296,146 words overall)	(173,932 words overall)
say	218	168
says	145	18
said	210	905
saying	41	102
Total	614	1193

In terms of the predominance of the past tense form said in Clark, I looked briefly at the frequency of a few other reporting verbs and found that there does seem to be a tendency for Peter Clark to use the past tense more often than other forms, and to use the singular form of the present tense in particular very sparingly (says, tells, admits, advises, assures, begs, suggests, etc.). A very brief comparison of selected passages in the source and target texts also suggests that he sometimes opts for using the past tense even when the source and target texts also suggests that he sometimes opts for using the past tense even when the source text employs the present tense. This is quite revealing stylistically, because it has implications for the level of formality or informality in tone and for the sense of immediacy in the narration. There is also the question of whether a particular form is used in narration or in direct speech. Used in narration, rather than in direct speech or in proverb-style expressions for instance, a verb like says reflects a very different tone from said in the same function, heightening the sense of immediacy and drawing the reader closer to the narrator's world, giving the reader the impression that he or she is experiencing the event being narrated at first hand. Peter Bush tends to use says frequently in narration, as in the following examples.

> fn000035　As he passes by the Virgin he gives her a knowing smile and says in a low voice: DIEGO.

> fn000035　... of the opportunity to walk on. DIEGO says goodbye to the youth and then DAVID walks ...

> fn000035　... goes along with him, everybody is in the know but nobody says a word. So there are members ...

> fn000028　If the subject matter oppresses or disturbs you, she says, you can switch channels. But the ...

> fn000028　... knees, bitten by snakes. Oh, comme ils sont emmerdants says the Lady with the Parasol.

> fn000028　... the computer screen. Excusez-moi, she says as she finally turns to face you. Je suis toute à vous!

> fn000003　... ring of her broken bell. The porter says nothing, only nods, but does it with such solicitude ...

> fn000003　I'd end up ringing my ex-wife. Her answering machine says she's at the Custom House, on such ...

> fn000003　He covers one nostril in order to blow the other, and says he's only got the kids left.

> bb000002　... left again with me. That fellow says that my companion touched me up, the whole works ...

> bb000004　... and the one who is seen are one within yourself, says Mawlana; but the expatriate you now ...

Peter Clark's few uses of says, by contrast, are either in direct speech or proverbs, very rarely in narration.

> fn000048　... polite to say and replied, "Umm Kulthum says in her song from the Rubaiyat of Omar ...

> fn000048　... "without mixing it with other drinks." "Who says so?" "It's well known. Everybody drinks beer ... "

fn000049 ... was Umm Salih. " "Where has this man come from?" "He says he has come from Damascus ...

fn000049 ... the shop and stood before me. "Is what Abd al-Samad says true or is he joking?" said Ahmad ...

fn000050 ... you. Oh, you men! As the proverb says, "She who trusts a man is like one carrying water in a ... "

fn000050 ... again for as long as I live. " "Good riddance. Who says we want to see your face of ill omen? ...

Perhaps Clark subconsciously realizes that the worlds of his narrators and readers are too different, too removed from each other for him, as a translator, to "fake" a shared world and successfully introduce an element of immediacy. There also seems to be a clear preference for direct speech in Peter Clark's translations, clearly marked as such through the explicit use of quotation marks:

fn000048 And your family, how are they?" Rashid laughed and said, "A strange business. My father ... "

fn000048 ... will be with us before long. " Abdullah said, "Don't exaggerate, Sultan. I don't think things will ...

fn000048 She quickly withdrew her hand from his and said angrily, "You want to abandon me just like ... "

fn000048 Shopkeepers stand up when I pass and they all say, "Come in, my Arab lord. " I walk along as if ...

fn000049 "In the name of Allah Almighty," said her husband, "women are never satisfied. Now you are ... "

fn000049 "There's nobody more dishonest than these agents," said Abu Qasim. "I wouldn't have anything ... "

fn000049 ... for a moment. Then I found myself saying, I fear, my dear, that one day you would regret such ...

fn000049 I patted him on his shoulders and said with all courtesy, "But I am within reach of my seventies ... "

fn000050 She then opened her eyes, laughed and said derisively, "What's the matter with you? Aren't you ...

fn000050 "I testify that there is no God but Allah," said Father. "They are all men of virtue and of honour ... "

fn000050 "It's time for you to go home as well. " "Allah," said Mother, "we'd like to spend the night here ...

fn000050 ... a woman who was obviously well-to-do he would stop her and say, "Are you in need of a maid ... "

Peter Bush, on the other hand, tends to use indirect speech. He is relatively sparing in the use of direct speech, and where he does use it, it is often unmarked in terms of opening and closing quotes.

> bb000002　... ordered us to keep quiet about it. Above all, said my father, not one word to the servant.

> bb000002　... poem: read it slowly and you will understand, he said with a smile. But Gil de Biedma excuse ...

> bb000002　... Politics only brings unhappiness, my son, he would say suddenly, interrupting the conversa ...

> fn000035　... and with effeminate tone and gestures, says to her. DIEGO: Bye-bye, sweetie pie, big momma.

> fn000035　get it? Who gives it to you? DIEGO: (Upset) I can't say. DAVID: Yes, you can. DIEGO: It's a ...

> fn000028　Yes, he's here, his wife said after a while. Who's that? Sorry? She passed him the phone ...

> fn000028　... the transcendent? Nothing of the kind, she said. For Ibn Arabi, the multiplication of forms is ...

> fn000028　Your life is hardly exemplary, she finally said. You do agree with me, don't you? Absent ...

> fn000028　... from the baths. Arise, dress, and follow me, he said. You obeyed, trying to tiptoe over the floor ...

> fn000028　... indissoluble friendship. If I know you, she says as she presses the stop button on her remote ...

> fn000028　His wife had advised him to take the bus—the 93 from the Porte Saint-Martin will drop you right on the corner, she'd said—but his deep-rooted hankering for the métro won out and, ignoring the ...

Again, this is possibly an attempt to clarify and simplify the linguistic structure of the text on the part of Peter Clark. With unmarked direct speech, as in Peter Bush's data, it is often difficult to tell where the "quote" ends, and how much of what is said can be attributed to a particular character and how much to the narrator. [1] Moreover, the "fusion" of narrator and character speech also helps to reduce the distance between the reader and the world and events being narrated. There are no clear boundaries, no clear divide between the worlds, and worlds within worlds, so that the reader is encouraged not to separate him/herself from the fictional or autobiographical world.

There also seems to be a strong preference in Peter Clark's texts for modifying verbs of

---

① Leech & Short (1981:323) discuss James Joyce's tendency to run speech and narrative together by omitting the inverted quotes which signal direct speech. They suggest that "[b]y constantly removing the distinction between speech and narrative report, Joyce creates the impression that they are inseparable and relatively indistinguishable aspects of one state" (ibid.).

speech, for adding something about the manner in which something was said. Clark's world is one in which the focus is pretty much on people saying things to each other and reporting what they heard explicitly as direct speech. The characters frequently report things being said in a particular manner: angrily, apologetically, decisively, disapprovingly, in a shaky voice, in a strange voice, in amazement, in a voice trembling with genuine affection, in an alarmingly imperious way, indignantly, insistently, quickly, quietly, sympathetically, tenderly, gently, aggressively, affably, defiantly, with a mixture of bafflement and disapproval, with a slight foreign accent, with an air of condescension, with a smile, with a grin, with a laugh, with some asperity, with all courtesy ... Here are some examples:

fn000048 "Don't worry," he said. She said affectionately, "Promise me you'll write every day."

fn000048 "They say his slave killed him," Isa said cautiously. "Bilal was not the man to kill him," replied ...

fn000048 "He's older than Father." He said with disinterest, "That's life." When we returned to ...

fn000048 "How was that?" asked Isa. Shaikh Muhammad said dolefully, "He went where it was decreed ... "

fn000048 "That is not sandalwood perfume," he said disparagingly. "It is some obnoxious concoction ... "

fn000049 "We must go to Umm Ayub's house, my boys." the father said decisively, "however tiresome it is ... "

fn000049 ... we finally reached the outskirts of Damascus. Father said gently to me, as if he was pleading ...

fn000049 "A thousand congratulations, my son." he said affably. "I am very happy that this house, which ... "

fn000049 Father gave no answer to my questions. "I tell you." he said firmly. "Go at once before he gets ... "

fn000049 "It belongs to all of us," she said with a laugh. "We will not be paying for it, but Allah ... "

fn000050 ... would extend to the Ghuta? "But," said Raghib provocatively, "It will fail, just as the Hama ... "

fn000050 he was level with Father. "I love this woman," he said defiantly. "What's that got to do with you?"

fn000050 "... house is the day I leave it," she said in a way that did not invite challenge. "You know more ... "

fn000050 ... without hurting her. "I'm running away," she said automatically. "With my hairdresser, Wanis."

fn000050 Father turned to me. "I don't want any dinner," he said drily. "Bring me a cup of tea and a piece ... "

This pattern is not so noticeable in Peter Bush's translations. But perhaps what is noticeable, compared to Peter Clark, is a tendency to attribute opinions and thoughts to someone, or relate what is being said now to what was said by oneself or someone else on another occasion. This is most commonly expressed in the structure "as x said/says":

bb000002   As Albert Manent's friend had said at the university, "without those Andalusian guards the ...

bb000004   As Ibn Hazm beautifully said, I was exchanging a green and pleasant land "for one he ...

bb000004   ... few meters of land that, as Carlos Fuentes said, the Dutch reclaim patiently from the sea:...

bb000004   ... Marx, l'éternel voleur d'énergies! as Rimbaud would have said). Thus, I steeled myself for ...

fn000035   ... do so stridently. As Titón has said, the film isn't proselytising on behalf of homosexuality ...

fn000035   This wasn't what I should be doing, and, as I said, I didn't know any writers. But then I met ...

fn000035   ... to play the homosexual, I'm turning homosexual. " As I said, there was a blackmarket sale of ...

fn000035   ... people are very grateful that the film exists. As I said, people knew the story, they knew what ...

fn000035   If you ever get an opportunity, send them to me. As I said, they're Sèvres porcelain. But that's ...

bb000002   ... to eliminate them. As T. S. Eliot says in a quotation picked out from ... José Angel Valente's ...

bb000004   ... European predecessors. As Vargas Llosa rightly says, exposing the terrible consequences of ...

bb000004   ... of imagination and reason, as Malraux says of Goya, beneath the lying appearance of delirium.

There are also variations on this structure, as in the following example:

fn000028   ... the possibility of better things! Didn't Ibn Arabi once say that, if it were not so, heaven would ...

These structures are completely missing from Peter Clark's texts.

Discussion

It seems reasonable to suggest that the patterns discussed above, and any patterns we might similarly identify as distinctive on the basis of examining a translator's output, should next be compared directly with the source text in order to address the question of the potential influence of the source language and/or author style. I have no expertise in the source languages of Peter Bush's translations, and I do not propose to carry out a full-scale comparison of Peter Clark's translations against his source texts. My concern here is ultimately with developing a methodology, and for that purpose I can only tentatively propose, on the basis of a brief examination of selected passages, that some of the patterns identified above as distinctive in Peter Clark's corpus may be largely carried over from his Arabic source texts. This is true in particular of the heavy use of modifiers with the reporting verb SAY (said angrily, defiantly, with a slight foreign accent, etc.), though even these are not carried over consistently in all cases, and some are occasionally added at points where they do not appear in the source text. The same is largely true of the preference for direct speech, but not so much the preference for using the past tense in narration. There seem to be quite a few examples in Peter Clark of changes of the following type:

> Father became aware of an issue that should not have passed him by. He said severely to Mother, "This is your fault. Shouldn't you have brought her a veil that covers her face, as I suggested, rather than that coat which you got from the tailor's?"
>
> "But, Father," broke in Sami, "Sabriya is still young. She's only ten years old. It's not her fault if she was made tall, is it?"
>
> "Be quiet, you," Father snapped. "People who see her would suppose she was twelve or thirteen years old. Try and be like your elder brother, concerned with the honour and dignity of your sister."
>
> Sami held his tongue, but look[ed] annoyed.
>
> "I'll buy her a shawl," said Mother. "She can wear that over her coat and I'll get her a black veil which she can wear over her face. That's how young girls like her cover themselves up nowadays. The headscarf is no longer fashionable among girls of her age."
>
> "Whether it's fashionable or not, the important thing is that Sabriya does not go out from now on with her face uncovered."
>
> "As you wish, Sir," said Mother with her customary submissiveness.
>
> Raghib gave a smile of triumph and I felt perplexed. I was listening to things being said by my family that concerned me, but I didn't dare say anything myself.
>
> (Sabriya, p. 55)

In the Arabic original, the author uses the present tense to introduce each switch in argument and/or perspective among characters: all the highlighted elements above (and others in the same stretch which are not translated closely) are in the present tense in the original: "Father becomes aware ... wishes to cover up his mistake in front of us, so he says severely to Mother ..."; "Sami holds his tongue ..."; "Mother says ..."; "Raghib smiles a smile of triumph while I remain puzzled as I listen to things being said ... without daring to utter a single word" (literal back-translation of Arabic original, Dimashq, ya Basmat al-Huzn, pp. 92 - 93). The result is a heightened sense of immediacy in Arabic, and a more distanced portrayal of events in the English version.

All this needs to be examined more systematically, a task which is beyond the immediate scope of this study, especially given that building a computerised corpus of the Arabic originals to perform the same type of analysis automatically is currently not feasible, at least not without extensive investment in both scanning and analysis software. This problem does not apply to languages which use the Roman script, and scholars wishing to build corpora of, say, French or Spanish source texts to undertake analyses similar to those reported here would therefore be able to go much further in developing the proposed methodology than I am able to at this stage.

Going back to the question of methodology, one way in which we could explore the issue further might be to examine patterns which are less likely to be consciously reproduced on the basis of the source texts. One such pattern concerns the use of optional "that" in reporting structures, and particularly with the verb SAY already selected for examination here.

Earlier studies by Burnett (1999) and Olohan & Baker (in press) suggest that, compared to original English, translated English tends to show a marked preference for the use of optional "that" with various reporting verbs, including SAY. Table 1 shows the absolute values (i. e. raw figures) and percentages for each form of SAY as reported in Olohan & Baker:

Table 1　Distribution of Zero/That in Original (BNC) and Translated (TEC) English

	say		said		says		saying	
	(BNC)	(TEC)	(BNC)	(TEC)	(BNC)	(TEC)	(BNC)	(TEC)
that	323	316	183	267	64	116	76	142
	26. 5%	55. 5%	19. 2%	46. 5%	12. 8%	40. 4%	67. 2%	43. 0%
zero	895	253	771	307	435	171	37	188
	73. 5%	44. 5%	80. 8%	53. 5%	87. 2%	59. 6%	32. 7%	57. 0%

A close examination of this pattern in the two corpora which form the basis of the current study reveals a marked difference between the two translators in this respect, with Peter Bush being much closer to the patterning of "original" English and Peter Clark very close to the "normal" patterning of translated English. The figures are shown in Table 2. As with the studies reported in Burnett (1999) and Olohan & Baker (in press), only lines where the option of using or omitting "that" is available are counted. This means that lines such as the following, for instance, are discarded:[①]

---

① For a detailed discussion of the criteria for discarding irrelevant concordance lines, see Olohan & Baker (in press).

fn000049　very distressed，in spite of all the lovely things Father said about you. He was full of noble ...

fn000050　and went up to his room. Then Mother said, "After all that heavy burghul and lentils we had for ... "

bb000002　according to bets laid by people at the dinner，said the commentator，had just been eliminated ...

fn000028　She wasn't surprised to see him turn up, she said. Their separation had been so abrupt! She sen ...

bb000004　had the idea of talking to Sartre：he alone，she said，was sufficiently intelligent to argue convin ...

The figures in Table 2 suggest a marked overall preference for using a zero—rather than a that—connective in Peter Bush's corpus，as opposed to Peter Clark. This is interesting given that the option of deleting the equivalent of "that" is equally unavailable in all the source languages involved（Arabic，Spanish，Portuguese），so there is no question of source language influence here as far as I can see. In short then，one way to proceed with the study of style in translation is to look specifically at patterns which are less likely to be influenced by the source language and which are less amenable to conscious intervention on the part of the translator. This is in addition to，rather than instead of，looking for other patterns of the type discussed earlier in this study.

Table 2　Distribution of Zero/That in Translations by Peter Bush and Peter Clark

	say		said		says		saying	
	(Bush)	(Clark)	(Bush)	(Clark)	(Bush)	(Clark)	(Bush)	(Clark)
that	15	20	13	18	5	2	3	4
	31%	53%	27%	53%	13%	29%	30%	50%
zero	33	18	36	16	33	5	7	4
	69%	47%	73%	47%	87%	79%	70%	50%

On the Question of Motivation

Identifying linguistic habits and stylistic patterns is not an end in itself：it is only worthwhile if it tells us something about the cultural and ideological positioning of the translator，or of translators in general，or about the cognitive processes and mechanisms that contribute to shaping our translational behaviour. We need then to think of the potential motivation for the stylistic patterns that might emerge from this type of study，in addition to establishing a methodology for deciding what is attributable to the individual translator and what is simply carried over from the source text（whether what is carried over is a feature of the source language in general, the poetics of a particular social group, or the style of the author).① The two objectives are clearly interdependent; we cannot explain stylistic patterns without knowing who or what to attribute them to: the source language, the author, a given sociolect, or the translator. This is what makes the stylistic analysis of translated text particularly problematic: there are, in a sense, two "authors," two languages and two sociolects involved, and the analyst must find a way to disentangle these variables.

At any rate, whatever we manage to establish as attributable to the translator's own linguistic choices must be placed in the context of what we know about the translator in question and about the relevant positioning of the source and target cultures he or she has chosen to work with. Some of this information is readily accessible from the header files described above and of which we have a sample in the Appendix (omission). Other information has to be sought outside the corpus, perhaps by contacting the translators in question, as I have done in this instance.

Peter Bush and Peter Clark are both experienced professional translators and native speakers of English. They are both highly articulate and extremely well-educated: neither is likely to have only a narrow range of vocabulary or syntactic structures at his disposal, for instance. So why the apparent variation in the range and use of vocabulary and syntactic structures, assuming the variation is not a direct reflection of the relevant source texts? Let us assume, for the purposes of this initial exploration of methodology, that the variation is indeed attributable to the translators rather than the source language or author, given that no meaningful comparison between type/token ratio in English, Spanish, Portuguese and Arabic can be carried out,② and that such a comparison cannot be made between English and Arabic in relation to average sentence length either.③

Consider, for a start, that Peter Bush has always lived in Britain, whereas Peter Clark has worked most of his life for the British Council and spent most of his working (and translating) life in the Middle East, immersed in his source culture and language. The actual physical location of each translator and whether this might have any implications, not for their access to varieties or levels of languages as such but for their subconscious use of

---

① One could argue, nevertheless, that the decision to carry over or modify stylistic features of the source language/text/author is itself part of what constitutes the "style" of an individual literary translator.

② Any direct comparison of the type/token ratio of texts in different languages, especially languages as structurally diverse as English and Arabic, would clearly be meaningless, for obvious reasons. Zanettin (2000) proposes an ingenious method for overcoming this difficulty, but applying it requires access to large reference corpora of original texts in both languages.

③ English and Arabic have very different conventions of punctuation, and it is not uncommon for a whole paragraph in Arabic to consist of one long "sentence," if we follow the traditional definition of a sentence as ending in a full stop, question mark, or exclamation mark. Even more problematic in the present context is the fact that it is very difficult and costly at the moment to scan and analyze Arabic texts automatically, for a variety of technical reasons, which means that no corpus-based exploration of the Arabic originals can be undertaken, and a manual analysis would require a considerable amount of time to perform.

certain linguistic patterns or modes of interpretation, is an important issue here. The kind of environment that any language user is immersed in is known to have considerable impact on his or her linguistic habits. For instance, people who are used to working with non-native speakers develop certain linguistic strategies which respond to the need to accommodate listeners and readers with a different level of competence in the language, a phenomenon sometimes known as "accommodation." There is no reason to assume that translators are immune to social and cognitive processes of this type. We have to recognize that they too respond to their physical and linguistic environment in similar ways. Hence, perhaps, the tendency for Peter Clark's translations to be less challenging linguistically.

Consider also that Peter Bush is translating from Spanish and Portuguese, introducing into the English-speaking world the works of cultures with which the average reader of English has considerably more affinity than with Arab culture. Peter Clark arguably has a much tougher task in trying to promote a literature and culture widely viewed as more "alien" and associated with all kinds of negative stereotypes in the world of his English-speaking readers (terrorism, fanaticism, etc.). Indeed, relatively little Arabic literature manages to reach the English-speaking world via translation (see Said, 1990), and this both reflects and reinforces the gap between the two cultures. The two translators' positioning towards their implied reader then is very different indeed.

Another potentially important point to bear in mind is the nature of the texts that each translator has chosen to work with. At least some of the texts that Peter Bush has chosen to translate are, for lack of a better word, "difficult": they assume an educated, sometimes highly educated, reader. Quarantine is probably the best example. All three texts translated by Peter Clark, on the other hand, are pretty accessible to a lay reader (I refer here to the source reader in both cases). The Arabic texts are fairly ordinary narratives with a social message, fairly light on allusions and not philosophical in the way that Quarantine is for instance.

I would personally want to subsume under the notion of style the translator's choice of themes and literary genres to start with, and in this particular case I have ascertained (by speaking to Peter Bush and Peter Clark) that all but one text (Turbulence, translated by Peter Bush) were chosen by the translators, not the publishers. Sometimes the translator had to approach several publishers before he could secure a contract to translate his chosen book. However, whether we decide to treat the translator's choice of themes and literary genres as an aspect of his or her style or not, the nature of the material that is translated and the kind of implied target readers are undoubtedly an important factor to bear in mind when we are trying to find a motivation for the patterns we identify. Hence Peter Clark's extensive use of direct speech, clearly marked as such, and Peter Bush's heavier use of structures more typical of "learned" discourse, for example the "as x said" pattern, can be partly explained in terms of the material chosen for translation.

Conclusion

This small-scale, exploratory study suggests that, however methodologically difficult, it is possible in principle to identify patterns of choice which together form a particular thumb-print or style of an individual literary translator. It is also possible to use the description which emerges from a study of this type to elaborate the kind of world that each translator has chosen to recreate. Peter Clark's world is one in which ordinary, everyday people interact with each other directly, and quite elaborately in terms of telling each other exactly what they heard others saying, as well as describing how they said it, focusing very much on emotions. It is a highly vivid and passionate world within its own boundaries, but the reader is invited to watch it from a distance, a distance that perhaps reflects that felt to exist between the source and target cultures. The world Peter Bush recreates, on the other hand, is one where more learned, more intellectually sophisticated characters speak largely through the narrator, but where the boundaries between the narrator's and the individual characters' discourses are much less clear-cut, reflecting a more cultivated, self-reflexive milieu. It is a world in which people are not quite so preoccupied with the details of their daily existence: they have the time and luxury to reflect and make connections with events and characters outside the immediate context of narration. There is more emphasis on interpreting what is being said now in terms of what someone else said at another time and in another context (hence the use of structures such as "as x said"). Peter Bush is able to create a sense of immediacy, capitalizing on options offered by the English language (such as the more extensive use of the present tense of verbs like SAY), perhaps because he is conscious of the affinity that exists between his readers and the source culture with which he is inviting them to engage. He can confidently count on his readers to suspend disbelief and allow themselves to enter into the world he is recreating for them, for it is after all rather familiar world from the point of view of the English reader.

This type of study might therefore also help us to relate a description of linguistic habits to the social and cultural positioning of the translator, including his or her view of the relationship between the relevant cultures and his or her view of the implied reader. This in itself is valuable and worth pursuing in future studies. But we need to think more carefully about issues of methodology. How can we best distinguish stylistic elements which are attributable only to the translator from those which simply reflect the source author's style, general source language preferences, or the poetics and preferences of a particular subset of translators? Should we try to? And if we decide that it is important to distinguish between these elements, should we be looking at different data altogether? Instead of analyzing several translations by the same translator, should we perhaps be comparing different translations of the same source text into the same target language, by different translators, thus keeping the variables of author and source language constant? This is clearly one option，but it is with difficulties. Very few texts are translated more than once into the same target language and during the same period. Some texts are retranslated over a longer stretch of time，but then we could argue that the stylistic elements we identify may be explained in terms of the evolution of the target language or the poetics of a socially and historically defined group of translators. However much we try，it seems unlikely that we will ever be able to "fix" all the variables in order to tease out a set of features that can be totally and unambiguously attributed to the translator，and to the translator alone. Perhaps we should not even try，but the question does warrant more careful consideration. This study is no more than an attempt to raise questions of this type and to demonstrate that investigating the style of individual literary translators is in principle both feasible and interesting. Indeed，if theorists of translation wish to argue convincingly that translation is a creative and not only a reproductive activity，it is imperative that we begin to explore the issue of style，at least in literary translation，from the point of view of the translator rather than the author. If translation is a creative activity，as I believe it is，then translators cannot simply be "reproducing" what they find in the source text—somewhere along the line each translator must be leaving a personal imprint on the new text. Difficult as it may seem，it is the task of the analyst to develop a coherent methodology for capturing this imprint.

【延伸阅读】

[1] Boase-Beier，J.（2011）. *Stylistic Approaches to Translation*. Shanghai：Shanghai Foreign Language Educaiton Press.

【问题与思考】

1. 文体学如何能够指导翻译实践和翻译批评？
2. 如何通过平行语料库的建立进行译者风格的研究？
3. 如何理解翻译文体学领域的认知转向？

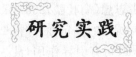

基于语料库的译者风格与翻译策略研究
——以《红楼梦》中报道动词及英译为例

刘泽权 闫继苗

导 言

这里推荐的这篇文章是国家社科基金项目"《红楼梦》中英文语料库的创建及应用研究"

的研究成果之一，两位作者来自河北燕山大学，他们通过对《红楼梦》三个英译本中对于报道动词"道"的翻译，考察三位译者的翻译风格和翻译策略。他们在研究过程中使用了语料库，研究方法借鉴了贝克提出的翻译风格的研究模式。

1 引言

中国古典小说《红楼梦》在文化、语言研究上的价值毋庸置疑。作为小说重要组成部分的人物话语是"曹雪芹这一文学巨著成功的主要因素"（刘泽权，2003：8），而《红楼梦》中引出人物话语的报道动词同样具有研究意义。"在传统文学批评中，人们一般仅注意人物话语本身——看其是否符合人物身份，是否具有个性特征，是否有力地刻画人物，等。1960 年代以来，随着文体学与叙述学的兴起，西方批评家愈来愈关注表达人物话语的不同方式"（申丹，1999：33）。然而，到目前为止，表达人物话语方式的报道动词研究不多，报道动词的翻译研究更是少人问津。

鉴于此，本文尝试对《红楼梦》中英文平行语料库中前 56 回的报道动词及其三个英译本的翻译进行系统的研究，借以探求译者风格和翻译策略。风格是一种"语言习惯的偏好，是不断重复出现而不是偶然出现一次或几次的语言现象"（Baker，2000：245）。语料库的使用，为译者风格的研究提供了便利。本文旨在围绕译者们的报道动词选择探讨以下三个问题：第一，汉语的报道动词［道］，无说话方式和内容的显示，译者是否根据具体语境翻译汉语中模糊的［道］？ 第二，译者对报道动词的选择是译者风格的彰显，还是翻译共性的体现？第三，这些选择与译者同时代英语小说中报道动词的使用有何差异，是否能体现出翻译的显化特征？

2 报道动词研究述评

按照系统功能语言学理论，复句小句之间的逻辑语义关系主要有扩展和投射两个类型。投射指第二个小句通过主句（第一个小句）得到投射，把它投射为话语或者思想（胡壮麟，2005：200）。在投射句中，引导出话语或思想的动词叫作"报道动词"。报道动词所在的小句称为"报道小句"，报道动词引出的话语或思想称为"被报道句"。报道小句对被报道句有引导作用，甚至直接进行说明、阐释等（贾中恒，2000：36）。

中国传统小说的报道方式比较单调，"间接引语"这种现代小说特有的表述方式极为少见。《红楼梦》中人物对话丰富，但表达人物话语的方式却很单一，并且没有现在通行的标点符号，因此人物话语与叙述语就需要频繁使用直接式的"某某道"，使两者能在人称和语气上区别开来。此外，中国古典小说由话本发展而来，说书人几乎无法面对听众用间接引语转述人物话语，而只能摹仿人物"原话"（马丁，1990：171）。中国旧有的标点符号只有句号和读号。20 世纪初，汪原放"大胆借鉴了英文图书的版式特点，开创性地做了古典小说的标点、分段与校勘工作，整理出来的《水浒》、《儒林外史》、《红楼梦》、《西游记》和《三国演义》成了亚东图书馆新文化运动时期的畅销书"（明清小说研究网，2009）。

由于《红楼梦》等白话小说行文中不得不在每一句人物话语、每一段人物对话之前加上引导性词句,这也成为白话小说与现当代小说最大的风格区别特征之一(卢惠惠,2007:243)。然而,英语小说中的报道小句位置很灵活,多出现在句尾,即句尾>句首>句中,并且还有省略报道小句的方式。一般被报道句是交流重点,在朗读时,报道小句一般不会重读。报道小句在句尾和句首时会有扩展现象;在句尾时,会通过诸如时间状语、方式状语、添加特定的受话者以及分词结构的方式进行扩展,而在小说中分词结构这种形式更为常见。在句首或代词作主语的报道小句多采用正常语序。在句尾时,正常语序和倒装现象普遍存在。当有具体受话者时,只出现正常语序,分词结构似乎对语序没有影响。在报道话语的时候,为了弄清话语的发出者,报道小句还有重复现象(Biber,2000:921),如:

So I *told him* the other day, *I said*, "Tony, you can't tell me that I'm too attentive to you."

另外,在西方写作实践中,词汇的丰富性是贵族阶级和精英文化的标志(Ben-Ari,1998: 1)。自然地,译者在翻译过程中有意无意地恪守"避免词汇重复"这一翻译规范(Toury, 1977)。与之形成鲜明对照的是《红楼梦》中相对单一的报道动词。因此,翻译《红楼梦》中的报道小句和报道动词无疑对译者提出了挑战。

报道动词的分类主要有语域和语言两个层面。一些学者(如 Swales,1987;Thompson & Ye,1991)对科技论文中的报道动词使用情况分类研究,为英语学习者提供借鉴。温特斯(Winters,2007)用言语行为理论对小说中的报道动词进行了系统的研究。韩礼德(Halliday, 2000:258)把报道动词分为四类:广义报道动词 say、提供和命令的动词(如 offer,request)、具有一定环境或其他语义特征的动词(如 threaten,agree)以及具有其他内涵与报道动词相关的动词(如 thunder,yell)。阿迪卡尼(Ardekani,2002)就话语内容、话语方式、话语本质以及隐性报道动词进行了系统的分类。从语言层面的分类来看,韩礼德并不针对引出话语的报道动词分类,不宜参考。阿迪卡尼基于话语的四种分类更适合本文研究需要并且列举了大量报道动词为实例。同时,由于译文中 said 的翻译形式出现频率最高,故单独列为一类。此外,由于省略报道句现象是一种翻译技巧,故单独归为一类。表 1 是本文采用的基于阿迪卡尼分类的译文报道动词归类方法。

表 1 《红楼梦》中报道动词的英译分类

	类别	例词		类别	例词
a	said	said	d	本质	answer, ask, tell
b	内容	argue, caution	e	隐性	nod, frown
c	方式	cry, interpose	f	省略	—

近年来,基于语料库的报道动词翻译研究呈上升趋势。贝克(Baker,2000)对翻译英语语料库(TEC)中出现频率最高的报道动词 say 进行了统计分析,证实了报道动词的选择可以反映译者的风格。温特斯(Winters,2007)通过研究小说中报道动词及其两个英译本的翻译也印证了译者风格的存在。叶常青(2003)从传统语法角度对《红楼梦》中的"笑道"进行了归纳和总结。目前对于《红楼梦》及其英译本中报道动词的研究比较全面的为 Liu & Hong(2004)的统计分析。然而,鲜有学者针对多个译本并结合具体语境对报道动词的翻译进行译者风格和翻

译策略的研究。

本文着眼于这两点，试图验证翻译普遍性假设之一"显化"现象，因为语料库翻译研究最突出的成就就是以真实、有效的数据来揭示翻译文本自身的特征与验证翻译的普遍性（胡显耀，2004）。翻译普遍性指"翻译文本而不是源语中出现的典型语言特征"（Baker，1993：243），主要有简单化、显化、规范化三个方面。目前对显化现象的探讨主要集中在两个方面：语际显化和类比显化。黄立波（2007：3）把"在译文中添加或明示原文中隐含语言成分的过程"称为语际显化，把"翻译文本相对于译语中的非翻译文本所表现出的显性程度提高"称为类比显化。《红楼梦》原文中报道动词是抽象、单调、模糊的[道]，根据显化假设，译文中的报道动词应该更加具体、丰富、清晰；并且，如果译文中的报道动词显性程度高于译入语原创小说，则翻译存在"显化"现象。

3　语料与研究方法

本文的语料来自于《红楼梦》120 回原文文本[①]、英国人乔利（Joly，1892—1893）的前 56 回译本（简称乔译）、英国汉学家霍克斯和闵福德（Hawkes & Minford，1973—1986）的 120 回全译本（简称霍译）以及我国杨宪益、戴乃迭夫妇（Yang & Yang，1978—1980）的 120 回全译本（简称杨译）。为了实现三个版本比较，本文只对前 56 回进行语料检索和数据提取。初步检测发现，《红楼梦》中报道方式结构单一，基本为[报道句："被报道句"]。依照这个规律，利用 ParaConc 检索工具对中文前 56 回的报道动词及其三个英译本的翻译进行检索并实现汉英对应。方法如下：

第一步，检索冒号，发现原文频率最高的报道动词及其结构。冒号不仅引出话语或思想，还有用在总括语之前以总结上文等其他作用（黄伯荣、廖序东，2002）。下图是分步实施的检索项目及按这些项目的检索结果所筛选出的频率最高的报道动词和方式。

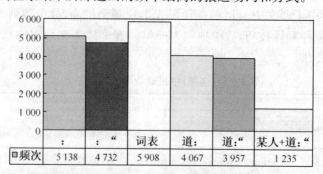

	:	: "	词表	道:	道:"	某人+道:"
□频次	5 138	4 732	5 908	4 067	3 957	1 235

图 1　《红楼梦》中报道动词检索项目及频次

基于该结果，人工整理出报道动词词表，再次检索原文。词表列出了 16 种报道动词，其中 83.62% 的报道动词以[道]结尾（见表 2），因此本文只对出现频率最高的报道动词[道]及其不同的翻译进行分析讨论。

---

① 由于《红楼梦》版本问题纷繁复杂，各译者所采用的底本也不尽相同，《红楼梦》中英文平行语料库选择了蔡义江校注本（曹雪芹，1993，876 000 字）作为语料库的中文底本。

第二步,用 EditPlus 工具提炼以[道]结尾的报道动词,手动删除[道]引出非话语的检索项。表 2 显示,频率最高的报道动词[(某人)道]占检索结果的三分之一。

表 2　以[道]结尾的报道动词频次表①

种类	频次	种类	频次
某人道	1 259	答道:	22
笑道	1 478	想道	22
说道	391	劝道	20
问道	104	骂道	20
又道	60	哭道	17
忙道	57	叫道	13
叹道	42	啐道	7
都道	35	其他	92
回道	32	合计	3 671

　　第三步,在 EditPlus 中对含有[(某人)道]的检索行进一步分类标注。每个独立行前标注⟨category⟩,手动对结构为[(某人)道]的独立行及对应译本标记为⟨category a⟩并另存为一个新的文本,然后按照表 1 分类在译文⟨category a⟩一栏手动修改为不同类别,再次插入两组尖括号标记译文中报道动词具体使用情况。如:

　　(721,1)⟨⟩⟨⟩:⟨Category="a"⟩ C3.txt145……黛玉道[[:]]"我自来是如此……

　　(722,1)⟨⟩⟨s⟩:⟨Category="d"⟩ H3.txt145. said Dai-yu.

　　(723,1)⟨⟩⟨exp⟩:⟨Category="b"⟩ J3.txt145. explained Tai-yu,

　　(724,1)⟨with⟩⟨s⟩:⟨Category="d"⟩ Y3.txt145. Daiyu said with a smile.②

　　第四步,对[道]及其不同翻译在 Excel 中按照表 1 的归类,分别建立文档。表 3 与表 4 为[道]的翻译及归类模型。

---

　　① 本表中,"笑道"中包含"冷笑道"、"憨笑道"等,故数量上超过了[某人道]。[向某人道]这种在[(某人)道]前添加介词的检索项计算机无法识别,需手动排除。

　　② 该检索中,[(724,1)]标示独立行位置。[C3.txt145]意为原文第三回 145 行,H,J,Y 分别代表三个译本。尖括号内分别表示报道动词结构和缩写:⟨with⟩意为使用 with 结构,⟨s⟩和⟨exp⟩分别是 said 和 explained 的缩写。

表3 ［某人道］的翻译频次①

类别	型次比	译者	频次
a	1/1 194	霍译	966
		乔译	48
		杨译	180
b	54/399	霍译	25
		乔译	215
		杨译	159

① said 出现频率最高,故单独列出;said 属于类别 d,故类别 d 也包含 said 的使用情况。4,(4):47-49.

黄伯荣、廖序东. 现代汉语下册[M]. 北京:高等教育出版社,2002,197.

黄立波. 基于汉英、英汉平行语料库的翻译共性研究[M]. 上海:复旦大学出版社,2007.

胡壮麟,等. 系统功能语言学概论[M]. 北京:北京大学出版社,2005.

贾中恒. 转述语及其语用功能初探[J]. 外国语,2000,(2):35-41.

刘泽权. 从称谓的翻译看文化内容的传播:以《红楼梦》的英译为例[Z]. 2003 年国际汉语教学研讨会论文,中国丽江,2003.

卢惠惠. 古代白话小说句式运用研究[M]. 北京:学林出版社,2007.

马丁. 当代叙事学[M]. 北京:北京大学出版社,1990.

申丹. 有关小说中人物话语表达形式的几点思考[J]. 外语与外语教学,1999,(1):33-38.

叶常青. 自建语料库在翻译教学中的应用:《红楼梦》中英文本用于翻译教学的课堂设计[J]. 外国语言文学,2003,(3):41-47.

明清小说研究[Z]. <http://www.mqxs.com/mqzg/xrjs/news 008.asp,2009.

Ardekani, M. A. M. The translation of reporting verbs in English and Persian [J]. *Babel*, 2002(2):125-134.

Baker, M. Corpus Linguistics and Translation Studies: Implications and Applications [A]. In M. Baker, G. Francis and E. Tognini-Bonelli (eds.), *Text and Technology: In Honour of John Sinclair* [C]. Amsterdam: John Benjamins, 1993:223-250.

Baker, M. Towards a methodology for investigating the style of a literary translator[J]. *Target*, 2000(2).

Ben-Ari, Nitsa. The Ambivalent case of repetitions in literary translation. Avoiding repetitions: a "universal" of translation? [J]. *Meta*, XIⅢ,1998(1).

Biber, D. *Longman Grammar in Spoken and Written English* [M]. Beijing: Foreign Language Teaching and Research Press, 2000.

Halliday, M. A. K. *An Introduction to Functional Grammar* [M]. Beijing: Foreign Language Teaching and Research Press,2000.

Hawkes, D. , Minford, J. (trans). *The Story of the Stone* [M]. Harmondsworth: Penguin, 1973—1986.

Joly, H. B. (trans). *Hong Lou Meng*; or, *The Dream of the Red Chamber: A Chinese Novel* [M]. Hong Kong: Kelly and Walsh, 1892—1893.

Liu, Z. , & Hong, H. A copus-based study of reporting verbs in fictions: a translational perspective [J]. *US-China Foreign Language*,2004(8):48-54.

Swales, J. Utilizing the literatures in teaching in research paper [J]. *TESOL Quarterly*, 1987(21):41-68.

Thompson, G. , & Ye, Y. Evaluation in the reporting verbs used in academic papers [J]. *Applied Linguistics*, 1991(4):365-382.

Toury, G. Translation Norms and Literary Translation into Hebrew, 1930—1945[D]. Tel Aviv University. The Porter Institute for Poetics Semiotics, 1977.

Winters, M. A corpus-based study of speech-act report verbs as a feature of translator's style [J]. *Meta*. L11, 2007(3).

Yang, Hsien-yi, & Yang, G. (trans.). *A Dream of Red Mansions* [M]. Beijing: Foreign Languages Press, 1978—1980.

(续表)

类别	型次比	译者	频次
c	20/207	霍译	13
		乔译	127
		杨译	67
d	40/2 305	霍译	1 015
		乔译	864
		杨译	426
e	19/33	霍译	8
		乔译	12
		杨译	13
f	1/750	霍译	175
		乔译	19
		杨译	556

表 4　[某人道]的翻译分类模型表

形式	例词	频次	霍译	乔译	杨译
said	*said*	1 194	966	48	180
话语内容	*explained*	60	1	53	6
	suggested	44	2	35	7
	protested	27	4	15	8
话语方式	*exclaimed*	85	1	68	16
	shouted	27	3	24	0
	cried	58	2	19	37
话语本质	*asked*	94	13	39	42
	replied	160	8	114	38
	told	32	6	0	26
隐含	*chuckled*	2	0	0	2
	smiled	8	0	6	2
	laughed	5	1	4	0
省略	—	—	—	—	—

4 分析讨论

4.1 源语影响下的报道动词翻译

经语料检索和分类后,[道]的翻译实现了数据的自由提取。经综合列表(见表5)我们发现,杨译使用的报道动词有 89 种之多,居《红楼梦》前 56 回翻译的三个版本之首;霍译使用报道动词种类最少,只有 54 种,其中 40 个报道动词只出现了一次;乔译报道动词省略情况最少(1.54%),杨译省略则近半数(45.50%),为三个版本最高。乔译的报道动词在数量上最接近原文,如果与其省略的个数相加,数量上则超过原文中报道动词的次数,其中一个原因在于乔译本有时使用两个报道动词来完成一个原文话语发出的任务,以便使读者在对话人数较多、话轮转换频繁的情况"弄清楚话语的发出者"(Biber,2000:1119)。如:

……宝玉道:"这算什么? 又不是账,又不是礼物,怎么个写法?"凤姐道[[:]]"你只管写上,横竖我自己明白就罢了。"……(第二十八回)

J28. txt … Lady Feng *remonstrated* with him. She *said* …

表5 三个译本所使用报道动词个数频数比较

译本	霍译	乔译	杨译
个数	54	63	89
频数	1 060	1 218	666
出现一次	40	17	36
10 次以上	2	29	15
省略	175	19	556

表6 直观显示了三位译者对报道动词的使用偏好。霍译和杨译使用最频繁的两个报道动词均为 said 和 asked,霍译大量重复使用 said,占其报道动词总数的 91.9%。相比之下,乔译仅使用 said 48 次,他更喜欢 replied, rejoined, observed, answered, added, exclaimed, remarked 这种书面化的"正规词"。杨译和乔译针对[道]使用了 15 种乃至 30 种以上不同的报道动词来明示原文中隐含的成分,似乎为译者有意无意恪守"避免重复使用同一词语"(Toury,1977)这一观点提供了实证,同时也在一定程度上体现了语际显化现象。

表6 三个译本报道动词使用情况一览表

报道动词	总频次	霍译	乔译	杨译
added	66	—	66	—
agreed	10	—	—	10
answered	87	—	70	17
asked	94	13	39	42
chimed in	10	—	10	—

（续表）

报道动词	总频次	霍译	乔译	杨译
continued	45	—	34	11
cried	56	—	19	37
demanded	12	—	—	12
ejaculated	12	—	12	—
exclaimed	84	—	68	16
explained	53	—	53	—
inquired	40	—	40	—
interposed	33	—	33	—
objected	15	—	—	15
observed	109	—	97	12
pleaded	11	—	11	—
proceeded	20	—	20	—
protested	15	—	15	—
pursued	18	—	18	—
put in	32	—	14	18
rejoined	106	—	106	—
remarked	89	—	66	23
remonstrated	10	—	10	—
replied	152	—	114	38
responded	12	—	12	—
resumed	24	—	24	—
retorted	42	—	23	19
said	1 194	966	48	180
shouted	24	—	24	—
suggested	35	—	35	—
told	26	—	—	26
urged	29	—	29	—
ventured	19	—	19	—
总 计	2 584	979	1 129	476

就乔译来说，其译文中出现10次以上报道动词的种类和数量均列三译本首位，达29个之多，而且有18个报道动词为他所独用，充分体现了被报道小句的话语内容、说话方式和话语本质。杨译三分之一以上的报道动词译为 said，达180个，其他词的出现频率均在40次以下。

他最频繁使用表现话语本质的报道动词,如 asked,replied 等,表现说话内容的有 demanded,objected 等。另外,有 4 个报道动词(told,objected,demanded,agreed)为杨译本独用。此外,杨译大量采取省略,这与译者大量综合原文话语内容是相关的。

同时,三个译本中均不同程度地使用了 asked 引导的报道小句,仔细分析发现其所对应的原文报道句均引出一个疑问句,可见译者还是在有意无意地结合原文语境,试图将话语本质与话语情境进行统一,属语际显化现象。

4.2 译入语影响下的报道动词翻译

三个译本中共有 1 194 处使用 said,霍译本出现频率最高,杨译居中,乔译频率最低。统计发现,said 的数量占译本所用报道动词的 46%,很明显,它的使用是受原文[道]千篇一律使用影响的结果。但是,三个译者的选择有何异同,其使用方法与译入语文体习惯有无关系?为了回答这一问题,我们进一步在 EditPlus 中检索〈s〉,发现近 1 100 处译例为倒装形式[said someone]。此外,三个译者均有译为[someone said]的顺序情况,杨译有 28 处,霍译 21 处,乔译最多,有 41 处。同时,我们发现大部分报道小句译文是出现在句尾,多采用正常语序,与"英文小说中报道动词在句尾时正常语序与倒装现象平分秋色"(Biber,2000:921)的结论有出入,说明译文更多受到译入语风格影响。《朗文英语口语和笔语语法》(Biber,2000)基于小说题材的语料库统计表明,代词作主语时多采用正常语序。这一特征在杨译本表现突出,基本为 *he/she* said 形式。霍译在使用顺序结构时,多明确主语对某个特定人说话时的情况,如:Baoyu said *to* someone 等。乔译使用顺序的情况最多,且多通过介词短语进行说话方式的补充,如:Hsiang-lien said *by way of response*。

另一方面,三个译者受译入语风格影响的程度和方式不同。霍译和杨译所受影响更明显,但杨译在处理报道小句顺序结构时注重搭配由代词构成的说话者,通过把直接引语转为间接引语的方式综合原文对话;霍译在顺译时习惯使用介词 to 来明确具体受话者,注重在表达报道方式的副词使用上进行调整,译者的风格可见一斑。乔译似乎更拘泥于原文的形式,顺序结构出现频率居三个版本之首,且精心挑选具有话语方式或反映说话内容的报道动词,这似乎进一步解释了乔译本中报道动词种类繁多的现象。同时,乔译倾向于使用从句来解释原文的被报道句,体现了翻译文本有异于原文的特性。

4.3 显化假设的验证

如上文所述,语际显化与类比显化是衡量译文显化现象的两把标尺。通过比较源语与译文报道动词使用的种类和频次已经初步印证了译语文本有明示原文中隐含语言成分的假设。为了进一步从语际显化角度验证翻译文本的特殊性,我们分别对〈ing〉、〈with〉、〈ly〉、〈clause〉和〈indirect〉的使用情况进行考察。检索分析发现,译者通过使用分词结构或副词作为方式状语修饰报道动词,使译文比原文更加明晰和直接。霍译使用分词结构的情况有 10 次,杨译 8 次,似乎证实了拜伯(Biber,2000:924)"小说中分词结构形式常见"的结论。相比之下,霍译更多使用副词,如 said patience indignantly,达 26 次之多。同时,三个版本均出现使用间接引语翻译原文直接引语的情况。在与读者距离上,直接引语比间接引语距离读者更近,而间接引语综合了译者的理解,暗含译者立场,是一种解释性翻译。另外,三个译者都有使用从句合并原文的现象,这都可以看作译文对原文进行明晰化处理的显化现象。

翻译文本的特殊性不仅在于其对源语的语际显化,还体现在对译入语非翻译文本的类比显化。为了印证这一现象,本文分别选取一部与三个译本同时代的非翻译英语小说进行比较:《苔丝》与乔译本出版年代接近,《飘》则与霍译本和杨译本创作年代相近,因此可以作为《红楼梦》的三个英译本在报道动词使用方面的对照本,从共时的角度来验证类比显化现象。我们分别把三个译本中出现的报道动词列成三个词表在《苔丝》和《飘》中进行检索。由于字数和情节差异,《苔丝》与《飘》中引出话语的报道动词数量与译本不可能相同,但通过比较报道动词使用情况的百分比可以较直观地发现其异同。

Liu & Hong (2004)曾将《红楼梦》中报道动词的翻译与《苔丝》中使用的报道动词按照 Ardekani 的分类方法进行统计比较,发现 say,ask,tell 在非翻译小说中出现频率很高,这说明译文和非翻译小说均多使用"隐含"性的、模糊的、抽象的词汇。本文通过对比发现,虽然非翻译小说报道动词种类繁多,但作者多使用少数报道动词(如 said)引出被报道句,这一特征在杨译与霍译中体现明显。就乔译而言,其使用的具有解释、明晰作用的报道动词,如 replied,rejoined,observed,answered 等,在《苔丝》、《飘》中均不多见,表明乔译的类比显化十分明显。

5 结论

本文借助语料库工具对《红楼梦》前 56 回中[(某人)道]在三个英译本中的翻译进行了系统检索和对比分析。研究发现,译者们对报道动词[道]的翻译确有规律可循,译者的选择不仅受到源语和译入语风格的影响,而且体现了译者的风格,但各译本风格迥异,翻译策略不尽相同。首先,三译者进行报道动词选择时在一定程度上受到源语单一报道方式[道]的影响,这在霍译中体现最为明显,其翻译几乎统一为 said,杨译次之,多省略,乔译最不明显。其次,译者们有意识地根据上下文语境来处理原文单一的报道方式,通过解释性报道动词对译文报道小句进行明晰化处理。乔译在这方面表现尤为突出,使用了种类最多的报道动词,显示了较强的译者主动性。再次,三译文均受到译入语风格的影响,报道小句多采用倒装形式和扩展结构,其中霍译和杨译表现较为明显,乔译则使用顺序情况较多,似乎更拘泥于源语报道的语序形式。这说明译者的风格在翻译文本的共性中得到彰显,验证了语际显化现象。此外,通过与非翻译文本对比,发现翻译文本的类比显化明显。总之,三译者对报道动词的翻译从词汇选择和句式结构上展示个人风格,同时也体现了翻译的普遍性。

第五章　语篇分析与翻译研究

導　論

　　翻译活动可以粗略地分为两个阶段,即分析理解阶段和翻译转换阶段。全面准确的分析理解离不开语篇分析。在这个过程中,译者以往大多根据自己的直觉进行文本的分析,以实现对原文的准确理解。随着语篇语言学的发展,越来越多的学者开始探索将语篇语言学应用于翻译活动的必要性和可能性。

　　把语篇分析思想应用于翻译研究的著作主要有:哈蒂姆和梅森合著的《语篇与译者》(*Discourse and the Translator*,1990),诺德(Christiane Nord)的《翻译中的语篇分析:以翻译为目的的文本分析的理论、方法和教学》(*Text Analysis in Translation*:*Theory,Methodology, and Didactic Application of a Model for Translation-Oriented Text Analysis*,1991),贝克的《换言之:翻译课程》和哈蒂姆的《跨文化交际:翻译理论与对比语篇语言学》(*Communication Across Cultures*:*Translation Theory and Contrastive Text Linguistics*,1997)。我国学者近年来在语篇与翻译方面也作了一些研究(如陈小慰,1998,2000;萧立明,1999;司显柱,1999;李运兴,2001;张美芳,1999,2000,2001;张美芳、黄国文,2002;王东风,2005)等。

　　语篇语言学区别于传统语言学的一个特点是,它的研究对象不仅仅是原文和译文两种语言体系,而且还涉及语言体系以外的各种制约因素,包括情景语境(context of situation)和文化语境(context of culture)。人们逐渐认识到,意义并非由语言结构本身决定,而是由整个语篇(包括它的语言体现形式和它的交际功能)来决定;翻译中传递的是原文的语言含义和语言使用(即交际)功能。

　　德国功能主义翻译学派的诺德在她的专著《翻译中的语篇分析:以翻译为目的的文本分析的理论、方法和教学》中探讨了以翻译为目的的语篇分析的必要性,并从理论、方法以及译者培训的角度进行了论述。在她看来,语篇语言学可以用于一般的文本分析,但是翻译研究学者的任务是如何建立一个以翻译为目的的语篇分析模式,从而指导翻译活动和译员培训。原文的语言因素以及原文的结构并不是最重要的,翻译的过程不是简单地用目的语中对等的语言因素去替换原文中的语言因素和结构模式,而是要实现翻译的目的(Skopos)。

　　贝克在她的《换言之:翻译教程》中探讨了语篇层面的对等问题。哈蒂姆和梅森在将语篇语言学与翻译研究相结合方面的研究成果最为引人注目。和贝克一样,他们主要借用韩礼德的系统功能语言学中的概念和理论框架进行文本的分析。语域理论中的语场、语式、语旨概念以及文本类型学的观点、文本的结构和组织、语篇的衔接与连贯等都是他们用来进行原文文本分析的重要理论工具。

　　在将语篇分析与翻译研究结合起来这方面,哈蒂姆作出了可贵的努力。在他的《跨文化交际:翻译理论与对比语篇语言学》中,哈蒂姆提出了一个语篇处理的理论模式。它包含语境、语篇结构和语篇组织这三大部分。在探讨语境时,哈蒂姆主要采用了语域理论(register theory)。该书围绕作者提出的语篇处理模式进行了充分讨论,哈蒂姆认为"规约性交际"、"语用行为"和"符号互动"这三种语境成分对于语篇类型、语篇结构和语篇组织起决定性的作用。他以该模式为框架,以英语与阿拉伯语之间的翻译为分析对象,对语篇类型、语篇结构和语篇组织进行了系统的探讨。就语篇类型来说,哈蒂姆区分了说明文和论证文这两大类。就语篇结构而言,哈蒂姆主要对段落划分、嵌入主文本中的次文本的作用等展开了讨论。至于语篇组织,哈蒂姆探讨了文本中的主谓递进、句间衔接手段、直接引语与间接引语等多种因素。这些语篇语言学思想的运用,不仅可以帮助译者更好地理解和分析原文,对于翻译教学和译者培训都有重要的意义。对于文本的语篇分析不再停留在直觉的印象,语篇语言学的这些理论工具提供的参数可以帮助翻译教师、译者对原文进行非常具体、客观的分析,使译者或者学生发现原文的篇章特征都具体可感,对于准确再现原作、实现翻译目的大有裨益。

选　文

选文一　Text Linguistics and Translation

Basil Hatim

导　言

　　本文选自贝克主编的 *Routlege Encyclopedia of Translation Studies*,是哈蒂姆撰写的一个词条,区分了话语和语篇之间的细微差别,介绍了语篇语言学的名与实,及其对于以翻译为目的的语篇分析的重要性。哈蒂姆从语域、语篇类型、语篇的层次、语篇的结构以及连贯等重要概念入手,探讨这些概念对于译者分析原文文本的价值和意义。在把语篇语言学用于翻译研究方面,哈蒂姆和梅森取得了令人瞩目的成就,发表了两部相关的专著:1990 年与梅森合作发表了《语篇与译者》,1997 年再次联手推出了《译者即交际者》。

　　Although invariably lumped together under the heading "discourse analysis," a considerable number of approaches to the analysis of language beyond the sentence would be more appropriately viewed as "text analysis." In terms of the distinction between text and discourse adopted here, text analysis is essentially concerned with the organization and mapping of texts rather than with social relationships and interaction through texts, the latter being, strictly speaking, a discourse analytic aim. A different distinction is sometimes made between discourse analysis as the study of spoken interaction and text linguistics as the study of written interaction, but this distinction is not adopted here.

Register Analysis in Translation Studies

Text analysis has largely been more concerned with characterizing than with explaining meaning. This is clear in an influential trend in applied text linguistics which has its way into the literature on translation. The study of language variation, or what has come to be known as register analysis, may be traced back to Halliday, McIntosh & Strevens' definition of register (1964:87): "Language varies as its function varies; it differs in different situations. The name given to a variety of a language distinguished according to use is 'register.'" A year later Catford (1965:38) set the tone for the variation debate in translation studies:

> The concept of a "whole language" is so vast and heterogeneous that it is not operationally useful for many linguistic purposes, descriptive, comparative, and pedagogical. It is therefore desirable to have a framework of categories for the classification of "sub-languages" or varieties within a total language.

Despite the usual time lag for theories of linguistics to be first accepted in applied linguistics and only then recognized in translation studies (Chau, 1984), translation theorists lost no time in making use of insights yielded by register analysis. A number of studies soon appeared, representing what turned out to be important landmarks in the development of a "science" of translation (Gregory & Carroll, 1978; Gregory, 1980). In the process, this new trend informed a number of textbooks and manuals in active use until today in many a translator-training programme around the world (Neubert, 1985; Nord, 1991).

The model of language variation to which this particular trend in translation theory subscribes focuses on two basic dimensions: one has to do with the "user," giving rise to an emphasis on dialectal meaning, and the other with "use" of language, leading to an emphasis on registers. User-related variation includes such factors as the geographical, historical and social provenance of the speaker, the standard language variable, as well as idiolectal meaning. Use-related variation subsumes aspects of message construction such as field or subject matter, tenor or level of formality, and mode or the basic distinction between speech and writing. Text analysis has specifically attended to the characterization of a level of meaning that is located within the latter type of variation, and translation theorists followed suit. Indeed, defining the register membership of the text came to be considered a prerequisite to successful translation. For example, an appreciation of register is important in translating and/or interpreting an utterance such as "She is sectioned in a hospital for 28 days and became one of those called specialled, which means you have a nurse following you everywhere you go. " In the initial stages of dealing with a text such as this, translators and interpreters are encouraged to work with a description of the user (in this case, dialectal variation would be important) and, perhaps more significantly in translation, with an account of the use to which language is put. Thus, the field of discourse (for which numerous glossaries and terminologies are developed), level of formality and mode would all ideally need to be identified prior to embarking on the translation task. In the present example, the medical field to which *sectioned* belongs, the semi-formal tenor and the spoken mode of the message would be considered crucial aspects of the meaning of the text, and the contribution of register analysis lies in systematizing such contextual variables for the benefit of language users in general and translators in particular.

This approach to text analysis has not gone unchallenged, however. It has been pointed out that anything beyond a superficial understanding of what register-membership involves would reveal that mere characterization (i. e. register specification) of meaning is far from adequate (Hatim & Mason, 1990, 1997). To do justice to intended meaning, it has been suggested, translators would have to consult a different kind of dictionary, one which lists pragmatic meanings and covers socio-textual practices such as irony, resentment and so on.

Text Typologies

Translation theorists have continued to assume that textual and discoursal meanings are closely bound up, and that any separation of the two could only be accepted as a convenience. In other words, text analysis has been seen as an initial exercise which has to be supplemented by the identification of other important levels of meaning that are primarily discoursal in origin. Recognizing this need, translation studies has not stagnated at the level of register rudimentaries, and notions such as text-typologies, which essentially extend the register-analytic framework thus became fashionable.

With the goal of siting the various interactive acts within some larger interactional frame, many attempts have been made to set up a typology of texts. A number of trends may be identified. First, texts have been classified according to criteria such as field of discourse, and statements were made about subject matter as the basis for lumping texts together, giving rise to types such as journalistic texts, religious texts, scientific texts and so on (Crystal & Davy, 1969). Despite the inherent lack of adequate predictive power, such typologies have indeed been influential, informing translators' decisions and forming the theoretical background of many a programme in translator training, to name but one area of applied translation studies.

Another trend in text-type research has taken domain as the basis for developing a different classification of texts into types such as literary, poetic and didactic (de Beaugrande & Davy, 1981). Text types identified in this approach, however, have exhibited an odd mixture of categories fluctuating between "field" in the sense of subject matter and "discourse" in the institutional sense. Didacticism, for example, is a domain of textual activity as well as a set of attitudinal meanings, an interlocking of contextual planes that is too complex and too over general to yield any meaningful categories with which translators can work. But, functional criteria such as these have, once again, formed the basis of a number of theories of translation and practical guide to the translator (see for example Picken, 1986; Anderman & Rogers, 1988). In addition to these two basic conceptions of text types, a number of functional typologies have been suggested. A few are based on the notion of "degree of translatability" (Gulich & Raible, 1975), but the majority adopt a three-way distinction between expressive, informative and vocative texts (e. g. Newmark, 1981; Robert, 1985). These points of orientation link up with Buhler's organon theory in which language is taken to be a tool for dealing with emotive meanings (where the producer is under focus), referential meaning (where the subject matter is under focus) and connotative meaning (where the receiver is under focus). The problem of overlap still remains unresolved, and such typologies could not therefore be said to have minimized reliance on intuition. However, a recognition of functional criteria has shed some useful light on the translation process; it has made possible an appreciation of the fact that texts are essentially hybrid and that, ultimately, text typologies can only account for predominant tendencies. To be exact, it was predominant textual focus which came to form the basis of a text typology that has made its mark not only on translation theory but also on the practice of translating and the training of translators (Werlich, 1976). Three major textual foci, subsuming a number of other subsidiary ones, are distinguished: a focus on states, events, entities, and relations (basic to the text-type conceptual, descriptive and narrative exposition), a focus on the evaluation of concepts (basic to the text-type argumentation) and a focus on the formation of future behaviour (basic to the text-type instruction). Various text forms are distinguished within each of these types, accounting for the influence of variables such as field, mode and tenor in message construction.

This text-in-context typology exhibits two basic strands, only the first of which may be appropriately considered here under text analysis, the other being more of a discoursal matter. The text analytic angle relates to texts as linguistic units, displaying strategic structure formats and patterns of cohesion. The discourse analytic aim, on the other hand, would text grammar and pragmatics (Zydatiss, 1983) and deal with issues such as the kinds of text available to particular groups of users and not to others, the ideological implications of such distribution and the socio-cultural implications of text-type deficit both within and across semiotic boundaries (Martin, 1985).

Hierarchical Text Structure

It has been argued that an important part of analysis, especially for the purpose of translation, involves the description of the suprasentential structure of the text or social transaction (Zydatiss, 1983; Tirkkonnen-Condit, 1986; Sa'adeddin, 1989). Basically, text structure analysis involves identifying interactive acts and siting them within some larger interactional frame. The compositional plan underlying this kind of text formatting includes a set of organizing principles which determine how written or spoken messages are moulded to fit particular structures. Linear progression from words to phrases and clauses, it has been suggested, does not account for the way we process text (de Beaugrande, 1978). In practice, we are conscious that each element of structure, whatever the analytic mode one happens to be working with, is ultimately active in fulfilling a particular function (for example, an event in a narrative or a step in an argument).

Within this functional slant on text analysis, models of text structure found to be particularly helpful to the translator have been those which can combine both mapping and negotiation, characterization, and interpretation of meaning, in dealing with the way texts are put together. Here, the basic assumption is that in the way texts are formatted, ideological meanings are read off and it is the interaction between this product and process of textuality which should form the focus of the translator at work (Bell, 1988). For example, text structure has been most usefully studied from the standpoint of cross-cultural differences in the utilization of persuasive strategy (Hatim, 1991), with reference to degree of oracy and literacy (Sa'adeddin, 1989) and in terms of macro-illocutionary force (Tirkkonen-Condit, 1986).

Texture

Another domain of text linguistics which has attracted much attention is texture, or structure-in-detail. Work on texture has occupied a prominent place in text linguistic research and has thus, albeit gradually found its way into translation studies, focusing in particular on two areas: cohesion and theme-rheme analysis.

Cohesion

From the perspective of text analysis, work on cohesion has been the single most important area to attract the attention not only of linguistics, from a variety of persuasions but also theorists and practitioners in the field of translation (see, for example, Blum-Kulka, 1986; Newmark, 1988; Baker, 1992). The principle on which cohesion studies are founded is a simple one: each sentence after the first is linked to the content and/or form of one or more preceding sentences by at least one "tie." These ties fall into five basic categories of cohesive relationships: reference, substitution, ellipsis, lexical cohesion, and conjunction. Although the majority of cohesion studies have been characterized by a surface bias, it is becoming increasingly more common in translation studies to assume that cohesion has to be examined in terms of underlying coherence if it is to yield any useful insights. For example, the analysis of ellipsis simply as deletion can be helpful only when supplemented by the various added meanings that the use of such a cohesive device takes on in context, meanings such as intimacy or intensity (Fowler, 1986). It is this search for underlying coherence, over and above surface manifestations of this or that cohesive tie, that has proven to be most relevant to the work of the translator. Numberous languages disallow or at least disprefer ellipsis as it is known, for example, in English, but the question is whether they also disallow or disprefer the expression of intensity or intimacy. Cohesion implies coherence, and it is the motivations behind the use of a particular cohesive device, rather than the device itself, that ought to be taken into consideration in the act of reworking a text (see for example Blum-Kulka, 1986).

Theme and Rheme

Theme and rheme analysis is another area that has attracted the attention of some translation scholars. The basic premise here is that sentences consist of themes, which present known, context-dependent information, and rhemes, which present new, context-independent information. Because they represent new information, it is rhemes rather than themes which push text development forward.

Just as coherence has been invoked to put soul back into the study of cohesion, the notion of thematic/rhematic progression has proved helpful in ridding basic theme-rheme analysis of its inherent sentence-orientedness. Thematic progression can be defined as the choice and ordering of utterance themes, their mutual concatenation and hierarchy, as well as their relationship to hyperthemes of the super text units " such as the paragraph, chapter ... to the whole text, and to the situation" (Danes, 1974: 113). Texts have been found to exhibit interesting patterns such as a simple linear progression, where Theme 2 redeploys Rheme 1, or a progression where a continuous theme is deployed, i. e. where the same theme is picked up again and again. A trend of theme-rheme analysis initiated by researchers like Deyes (1978) has successfully pointed translation theorists in the direction of a much more fruitful line of enquiry. This involves grafting text-typological considerations onto patters of thematic progression as these unfold. Thus, it has been argued that a so-called "simple TP" (where rheme becomes theme in subsequent discourse) is in fact a highly turbulent structure characteristic of argumentative texts. Continous themes, on the other hand, are typical of straightforward exposition, as in the case of news reporting (Hatim & Mason, 1990; Hatim, 1991).

Further Reading

Baker, 1992; de Beaugrande, 1978; Blum-Kulka, 1986; Gregory, 1980; Hatim, 1991; Hatim & Mason, 1990, 1997; Neubert, 1985; Nord, 1991; Roberts, 1985; Sa'adeddin, 1989; Tirkkonen-Condit, 1986; Zydatiss, 1982, 1983.

选文二 语篇语言学与翻译研究

张美芳 黄国文

导 言

本文 2002 年发表在《中国翻译》第三期,两位作者,前者是有语言学背景的翻译学者,而后者主要从事系统功能语言学研究。两位学者的合作,正折射出语篇语言学和翻译研究之间的密切关系以及语篇语言学对于翻译研究而言所具有的重要指导意义。

1 引言

美籍荷兰学者 James Holmes 在《翻译学的名与实》(1987)一文中,对翻译学的研究目标、研究范围以及学科内部的划分提出了详细的构想(张美芳,2000a);我们认同 Holmes 的观点,即翻译学实质上是以经验为依据的学科,其目标有二:① 描写客观翻译现象(翻译过程、翻译作品及其在译语文化中的作用);② 建立能够解释和预测这些现象的原则和参数体系。其基本研究方法是观察、描写和解释。

翻译学是一门年轻的学科,需要吸收其他相关学科的研究成果及其理论以发展和构建自己学科的研究方法。20 世纪 90 年代,西方学者纷纷把语篇语言学(也叫语篇分析)理论引进翻译研究领域(Bell,1991;Baker,1992;Hatim & Mason,1990,1997;Neubert,1995),这主要是因为语篇语言学不再限定于研究语言本身,而是把视野扩大到语境和语言的交际功能。例如,把文本视为交际活动,而不是一串串定型的文字与结构;研究语言的使用,而不是把语言作为一个抽象的系统(Baker,1992:4-5)。

本文主要探讨如何运用语篇语言学的理论来研究翻译中的问题。在下面的讨论中,我们将首先阐述语篇语言学的基本概念及其历史,然后简单比较它与传统语言学的异同,进而讨论翻译研究的语篇语言学方法以及语篇翻译研究的范围、研究重点以及研究方法。

2 关于语篇语言学

"语篇语言学"又称为"语篇分析"(discourse analysis)或"篇章分析"(textual analysis)。一般说来,英美国家的学者喜欢用 discourse analysis,而欧洲大陆的学者则喜欢用 textual analysis(黄国文,2002)。胡壮麟(1994:3)认为,"'语篇语言学'或'语篇分析'两种说法基本上是同义的"。在以下的讨论中,我们不对语篇语言学和语篇分析进行区分。语篇语言学是20 世纪 60 年代才逐渐发展起来的年轻的学科,很多学者的研究都促成了它的发展。例如,社会学家 Hymes 发表的题为"Towards Ethnographies of Communication"(1964)一文,从社会学的角度研究社会环境中的言语使用问题;语言哲学家 Austin(1962),Searl(1969)和 Grice(1975)等人从言语行为理论和会话含意等角度研究语言使用;Halliday 的功能语言学特别强调语言的社会功能和纯理功能(黄国文,2000);Labov(1972)对语言变异作了开创性的研究;Sacks,Schegloff & Jeferson(1974)和 Goffman(1976,1979)对会话常规(conversation norm)、话轮(turn)等口头交往的分析揭示了会话的结构规律;Gumperz & Hymes(1972)从社会语言学角度,对不同社会文化环境中的言语行为(如讲故事、问候语等)进行研究,探索了语篇分析的新路子;Sinclair & Coulthard(1975)对课堂上教师与学生的对话模式的研究揭示了话段与语篇之间的内在联系。总的说来,语篇语言学吸收了包括语言学、符号学、心理学、人类学、社会学、文学等学科的研究成果,慢慢形成了一个专门研究交际中语言使用情况的、涉及多个学科的学问。

语篇语言学的兴起和发展对翻译理论与实践的探讨起到了推动作用。在实际翻译中,已有不少人把语篇当作翻译对象和基本单位(司显柱,2001)。关于语篇的定义,目前有两种不同的观点。一是"形式/结构"派的看法:"语篇"是大于句子的语言单位;语篇由句子组成。一是"功能"派的看法:语篇是一个语义单位,它不是一个比句子大的语法单位;它与句子不属于同一类型(范畴),因此它们之间不是"大"与"小"的关系;语篇与句子之间的关系是"体现"(realization)关系,即语篇由句子体现,或者说句子(形式)体现了语篇(语义)。

3　语言学模式与语篇语言学方法

我们把语言学模式与语篇语言学方法进行比较,在某种程度上说是对传统语言学翻译研究模式与当代语言学翻译研究模式进行比较。翻译研究的语言学模式始于 20 世纪 60 年代。英国的 Catford(1965)提出了以"阶与范畴语法"(Scale and Category Grammar)为理论指导的翻译研究模式。他在书中阐述了语际间的层次转换(level shifts)和范畴转换(category shifts)问题;在这个模式中,层次转换指语法、词汇、语音、词形等,范畴转换包括语言结构、语言系统、语言单元、语言类别方面的转换,所有这些转换的核心概念是"对等"(或"等值")。简单说来,早期的语言学派视翻译为语言运用的一种特殊的形式,注重研究源语与目的语之间的异同及言内关系,把翻译过程视为把一种文字材料转换成另一种文字材料,把一种语言产物在保持内容(命题)不变的情况下改变成另一种语言产物的过程。因此,转换规则是翻译研究的重点对象,对等/等值是翻译研究的核心。正如 Neubert & Shreve(1992:19)所说,"语言学模式调查研究词与语言结构的转换潜势,力图建立语际间的对等规则,认为语际间的对等可在不同的语言层面实现。"

翻译研究的的语篇语言学方法(途径)是传统语言学途径的发展,它重视的是语篇分析和语用意义,其研究对象不仅仅是原文和译文两种语言体系,而且还涉及语言体系以外的各种制约因素,包括"情景语境"(contextual situation)和"文化语境"(context of culture)。这种模式认为,意义并非由语言结构本身决定,而是由整个语篇(包括它的语言体现形式和它的交际功能)来决定;翻译中传递的是原文的语言含义和语言使用(即交际)功能。

根据 Neubert & Shreve(1992:23)的观点,以传统语言学模式操作的翻译过程是一个从词及其互不关联的意思开始的自下而上(bottom-up)的过程,这种过程生产出来的译品,很难被目的语读者认同;而语篇语言学方法则把翻译看作一个自上而下(top-down)的过程,即先决定译文在目的语文化中的属性或类型及其交际功能,再通过一个个的语言结构来体现预定的语篇。在翻译实践中,要重组(建构)一个适用于目的语社会的语篇,并非取决于表层结构(如一个个句子)的转换,而是自上而下地、有目的地选择语言资源,对整个语篇进行重写。Neubert & Shreve(1992:23)认为,在动手翻译之前,译者的脑子里首先有一个"虚构的译本",在翻译的过程中,他"对语言的选择受控于脑子里的'虚构译本';目的语中的资源为虚构译本转变为真实译本提供了材料"。因此,翻译并不仅仅转移原文的意义,而是要转移原文的交际价值。

简言之,传统语言学翻译研究方法与语篇语言学翻译研究方法的差异至少有三点:① 前者的重点在句子,认为意义由词与句决定;而后者的重点是整个语篇,认为意义通过语言结构来体现;② 前者把翻译对等的概念建立在词、句层面上,而后者则认为翻译对等建立在语篇和交际层面上;③ 前者的研究对象只是语言,而后者的研究对象不仅是语言系统和言内因素,而且还包括言外因素(包括"情景语境"和"文化语境")。

4　功能翻译观

Halliday 在《功能语法入门》(*An Introduction to Functional Grammar*,1985)一书的前言中指出,他建构功能语法的目的是为语篇分析提供一个理论框架,这个框架可用来分析英语中任何口头语篇或书面语篇。从目前的状况看,越来越多的翻译研究者选择功能语言学理论作为分析和研究框架,因为功能语言学的最大关注点与翻译的目的一样,都是运用语言进行交际。

在我们看来,比较成功地把 Halliday 的语篇分析思想应用于翻译研究的著作有:Hatim & Mason 合著的《语篇与译者》(*Discourse and the Translator*,1990),Bell 的《翻译的理论与实践》(*Translation and Translating*,1991),Baker 的《换言之:翻译课程》(*In Other Words: A Coursebook on Translation*,1992),Hatim & Mason 合著的《译者是交际者》(*Translator As Communicator*,1997),以及 Hatim 的《跨文化交际:翻译理论与对比语篇语言学》(*Communication Across Cultures: Translation Theory and Contrastive Text Linguistics*,1997)。我国学者近年来在语篇与翻译方面也作了一些研究(如陈小慰,1998,2000;萧立明,1999;司显柱,1999;李运兴,2001;张美芳,1999,2000,2001),这些研究都是从功能语言学和语言使用的角度探讨翻译问题。

一般说来,语言是一个有规则的系统结构,是一种代码。它由不同的成分组合而成,可用来表达语义。同时,语言又是一个用于交际的系统,可以运用不同的代码形式来指称具体的和抽象的东西,并可创造具有交际价值的信号。语言可以用来描述主观世界和客观世界,也可以用来建立和保持人际关系,还可以用来组织信息,这三种功能分别属于 Halliday 所说的"概念功能"、"人际功能"、"语篇功能"(Halliday,1994)。

在翻译的过程中,译者有时不得不作出选择:一是放弃与语境息息相关的交际价值而保持形式上的等值;一是放弃与语境无关的纯语义等值而保持交际功能等值。这种选择事实上是在"直译"与"意译"之间作出的选择。如果选择前者,译文虽然在形式上忠实于原文,但在目的语读者眼里却可能是生硬、晦涩、难懂的译文,如果选择后者,译文虽然通顺易懂,却又可能被指责为"不准确、不忠实"。无论译者作出哪种选择,都无法做到面面俱到,都无法令各方满意。

译者应该怎么办？从功能语言学的角度看，选择就是意义（黄国文，1998，1999）。对于译者来说，在作出选择之前，必须弄清楚翻译的目的，同时要明白哪些语言形式可以使自己所希望达到的目的（功能）得以实现。在这一点上，Bell（1991）表达过一些很好的看法；他（Bell，1991：7）通过英国诗人 Kipling 一首诗中的第一段来给我们提出思考的切入点：

> 我有六位忠实的仆人，
>
> （他们教我运用我的知识）；
>
> 他们的名字是："什么"、"为什么"、"什么时候"、"怎么样"、"哪里"和"谁"。

这首诗中六个问题中的每一个都规定了一个（或多个）语篇参数（Bell，1991：9）："什么"指语篇所包含的信息，是信号的意义、言语行为的命题内容，也即语篇的范围（语场）。"为什么"指信息发送者的意图、产生语篇的目的、言语行为的施为作用等。"什么时候"所关心的是交际的时间背景。"怎么样"含有两种意思：① 交际者的态度，即语篇的基调（语旨），严肃的、一般的，还是冷淡的或是冷讽的，等等；② 交际的手段，即语篇方式（语式），文字的或是非文字的，口头的或是书面的。"哪里"所关心的是交际的地点（语场）。"谁"指的是交际者的身份和他们之间的关系，这些决定了语篇的基调（语旨）。

语言是一种具有各种特征的代码，包括语音、文字、语法、词汇、语义等方面的特征。语言的使用就是从这些代码特征系统中作出选择，创造出可以传递意义的语篇。另外，每一种语言都有其方言特征（dialect features）和使用标记（markers of the use）。对于译者来说，了解语言特征，尤其是了解语言的使用标记，是非常必要的。因为翻译过程的第一步就是要对语篇进行分析，而语篇参数是分析的重要依据。译者首先要辨认出语言使用的各种标记，即信息发送者和接收者之间的关系（语旨）、发送信息的渠道（语式）和语篇的范围与目的（语场）（张美芳，2001b）。译者碰到的问题是与社会因素紧密联系的：① 交际者的身份及其之间的关系；② 根据语篇的目的（功能）选择语篇的表现方式；③ 语篇所涉及的（发生在社会上某个领域的）事情。此外，译者还要对两种语言的（语音、文字、句法、词汇、语义的）特征了如指掌，才能根据语篇的参数在语言的特征系统中作出选择，创造出一个和原文等值的语篇来。

5 语篇翻译研究的几个重点

我们认为，从语篇语言学的角度看，在翻译研究中有几个方面是探讨的重点。下面我们对这些重点逐一进行讨论。

5.1 重点一：意义与其体现形式之间的关系

人们在交际过程中一般是通过形式来体现意义、目的与意图的。这种用于体现意义的形式既可能是言语性的，也可以是非言语性的，还可以是非言语性伴随言语性的形式。例如，要表示"要求某人关门"这一意义，在汉语中可以说"请把门关上"、"请你把门关上"、"请您把门关上"、"请把门关上，好吗？"、"请你把门关上，好吗？"、"请您把门关上，好吗？"，等等；在英语中则可以说"Close the door."、"Close the door, please."、"Please close the door."、"Can you close the door?"、"Will you close the door?"、"Would you close the door?"，等等。无论是用汉语还是用英语来表达"要求某人关门"这一意义都可以有非言语性的形式伴随。这些可能被选择的形式除了表示"要求某人关门"这一基本的"概念"（命题）意义（ideational/propositional meaning）外,它们还因各自的不同形式表达了不同的人际意义（interpersonal meaning）和语篇意义（textual meaning）。这三种意义与前面讲的"语场"、"语旨"和"语式"是属于同一类情形的。

5.2　重点二:语篇持证

Nubert & Shrevel（1992）认为,研究翻译模式有七种:① 批评模式;② 实践模式;③ 语言学模式;④ 语篇语言学模式;⑤ 社会文化学模式;⑥ 计算模式;⑦ 心理语言学模式。对于这七个模式,他们又着重阐述了语篇语言学模式。他们说,从语篇语言学初露端倪之时起,语言学家就一直在寻找一种导向性原则;而语篇特征原则（the principle of textuality）至今最具说服力,因为它把翻译过程、译者对外界的知识和语篇三者有机地结合在一起成为翻译成品（Nubert & Shrevel,1992:69）。他们认为,语篇特征指的是作为语篇必须具备的特征的复合体,是某个语言客体（linguistic object）在社会和交际制约中所折射出来的特质。一般说来,社会和交际制约可在语篇表层的语言结构中反映出来。他们所持的有关语篇特征的观点与de Beaugrounde & Dressler（1981）的看法是一致的。

在翻译研究中,语篇特征原则可用来解释如何获得原文和译文在语篇层面上的对等。但是,研究者必须清楚获得语篇对等的条件是什么。有哪些特别的因素使语篇有别于非语篇?是什么特别的东西结合在一起创造了语篇特征?de Beaugrounde & Dressler（1981）和Nubert & Shrevel（1992）都认为典型的语篇应具有以下七个语篇特征:意图性、可接受性、情景性、信息性、连贯性、衔接性、互文性。其他学者（如 Reiss,1989;Vermeer,1989;Hatim & Mason,1990,1997;Bell,1991）在谈论语篇翻译时,也提到了这些语篇特征。有些学者把语篇特征用作自己的分析框架,如 Reiss（1989）,Vermeer（1989）,Nord（1997）等翻译行动派（目的派）,而有些则把它作为研究对象,如 Hatim & Mason（1990,1997）,Bell（1991）,Baker（1992）等语篇分析派。

5.3　重点三:语境与语言选择

社会是一个文化系统,也是一个符号系统和意义系统,而语言是其中一种符号。语言之所以产生意义是因为它与社会文化中的其他符号相互联系,相互作用。研究语篇必须联系其语境,语境与语篇是互相依存的;特定的语境创造了特定的语篇,特定的语篇要求特定的语境。因此,非正式的语境导致人们使用非正式的语言,而正式的语境则要求人们使用正式的语言（Thompson,1996:9）。

在交际过程中,语言的意义通常是根据语境来确定的。同一个语言单位在不同的语境中有不同的意义。我们（黄国文,2001）曾举这么一个例子:book 在"He has written a book on discourse analysis."一句中是名词,它表示的意义是"书"（"他写了一本语篇分析方面的书。"）;它在"I will book a room for you."一句中是及物动词,表示的意义是"预订"（"我会给你预订一个房间。"）;在"He will book into a small hotel."句中,book 是不及物动词,表示的意义是"登记住入旅馆"（"他将住进一家小旅馆。"）;在"He speaks only the book variety of French."一句中,book 是形容词,它表示的意义是"按照书本的"（"他只能讲书本上学来的那种文绉绉的法语。"）。

Halliday & Hasan (1976:283)曾举以下例子以说明语篇衔接的一些特征：

There is a boy climbing the tree.

a. The boy's going to fall if he doesn't take care.

（这个男孩如不小心就会摔下来。）

b. The lad's going to fall if he doesn't take care.

（这个小伙子如不小心就会摔下来。）

c. The child's going to fall if he doesn't take care.

（这个小孩子如不小心就会摔下来。）

d. The idiot's going to fall if he doesn't take care.

（这个傻瓜如不小心就会摔下来。）

以上 a，b，c，d 四个小句都可以连接前面的小句，a 句中 the boy 是前面小句中 boy 的重复，b 句中 the lad 是 boy 的同义词，c 句中 child 是 boy 的上义词，d 句中 the idiot 是一个泛称。从功能语言学的角度看，选择就是意义。以上四个小句选择不同的词来指称前面提到的"男孩"，每个选择都有其特定的意义，因此在翻译中，要深刻理解原文的选择意义，才可以准确地把原意表达出来。虽然"衔接"主要指语篇内而不是语篇外的因素，但是它仍然会与语境有关系。选择什么字眼，既反映了说话者与听话者的关系，也说明了说话者的地位和身份特征（黄国文，1999）。

5.4　重点四：语篇体裁与情景语境

关于语篇体裁与情景语境问题，我们曾进行过专门的讨论（黄国文，2001；张美芳，2001b；张美芳，2001c）。我们认为，每一个语篇都是在特定的社会文化环境中起交际作用的，属于特定的社会文化背景的人通常都能看出其交际目的。例如，在中国，如果一个人在路上碰到一个熟人，可能会说，"你吃了饭没有？"、"去哪里？"、"去上班啊？"、"最近忙些什么？"。一般说来，这些话是中国人用来打招呼的，而不是想干涉别人的私事。但是，西方国家的人通常并不了解这一语言习惯，他们听到这些话后可能会误解，甚至还会恼怒。有些语篇的使用目的相同，语言行为所需的步骤也基本一致，例如到糖烟酒商店买香烟、到邮局买邮票或到市场去买菜，中国人和英国人的语言步骤基本上是一样的。这种有目的的语言活动在语篇分析中称为"语篇体裁"（genre），虽然属于"买卖"这个语篇体裁的语篇会有差异，但它们的基本结构是一样的。从文化语境的角度看，每个语篇都可看作属于特定的语篇体裁。语篇体裁是通过两种方式来体现的：一是"纲要式结构"（schematic structure），一是"体现样式"（realizational patterns）。

纲要式结构是指有阶段的、有步骤的结构。例如食谱的纲要式结构通常是：名称、简介、原料、配料、烹饪方法。而语篇体裁的体现样式通常是由特定的语言结构充当。例如，当一个英语语篇的正文的第一句是"Once upon a time…"时，它便表明这是一则关于童话或神话的叙事；当一则对话的第一句是"Can I help you？"时，在很多情况下它都是发生在服务行业中服务者与顾客的对话。

有些语篇体裁的纲要式结构和体现样式并不是十分独特，所以要经过"语域"（register）分析才能确定其语篇类型。Halliday（1994）认为，从语言的使用角度看，情景语境中有三个因素最为重要，它们影响着我们的语言使用。这三个因素是：语场（范围）、语旨（基调）、语式（方式）。这三个因素是情景语境的组成部分，称为语域变体（register variables）。语场指的是正在发生的事情及其性质、特点。语旨指的是交际者及其特点、地位、角色、关系等。语式指的是语言在交际中所起的作用,包括交际渠道和修饰方式。语场、语旨和语式跟语言的三个纯理功能(meta functions)相互联系:语场体现了语言的概念功能,语旨体现了语言的人际功能,而语式则是语篇功能的具体体现。语篇功能的作用主要在于联句成篇,它使语言与语境发生联系,使说话人生成与情景一致和相称的语篇。

5.5 重点五:蕴含意义的解释

在很多情况下,译者的难题并不在原文本身(因为他可以照字面意思译),而是能否让目的语读者明白原文的蕴含意义。Grice(1975)在其著名的"Logic and Conversation"一文中提出了会话含意的概念:为了使会话顺利进行,交际的双方都必须遵守一条原则,即"合作原则"。有了这条原则,交际双方所说的话语就不至于不连贯,因而双方就可以互相配合,达到成功交际的目的。

Grice认为,合作原则含有四条具体的准则:① 量准则(the Maxim of Quantity),② 质准则(the Maxim of Quality),③ 关系准则(the Maxim of Relevance),④ 方式准则(the Maxim of Manner)。在交际过程中,遵守这些准则就是遵守合作原则的具体体现。然而,在实际语言交际中,人们违反这些准则的情况比比皆是。Baker(1992:244)曾举以下例子说明人们在交际中故意不遵守合作原则:

A:What's Jane up to these days?

B:It's raining.

表面看来,B是答非所问。但实际上,他有可能是故意违反会话原则。因此A就要根据自己的判断去理解B的含意。在这里,其含意至少有两种:一是"我不想谈这个问题。"二是"你弄错了——你不该问我这个问题。"

对于故意违反合作原则的话语,在翻译中是比较容易处理的。但是,有时说话者并没有违反合作原则,只是话语不连贯,这时就需要译者遵循合作原则中的关系准则,对不连贯的话语作出连贯的解释。例如:Elizabeth is putting on a lot of weight. She smokes very heavily. (Baker,1992:226). Baker认为,如果把这两句话联系在一起,至少有四种解释:① 由于伊莉莎白吸烟吸得很厉害,因此胖了不少。② 由于伊莉莎白的体重猛增,所以她拼命地吸烟。③ 尽管伊莉莎白吸烟过多,她的体重还是增加了。④ 伊莉莎白体重猛增,而且还不断地吸烟。对原文两句话之间的语义关系的解释,一方面靠语境,另一方面靠它们之间可能存在的蕴含意义。当然,前面讲的语篇参数也可用来解释它们之间的关系;还可以从Halliday所说的"逻辑—语义关系"(logico-semantic relations)来寻找解释。

如何翻译出语言蕴含意义是译者的任务,而描述不同译者对此类问题的处理手法,并利用相关的理论去解释这些处理手法及其原则,就是翻译研究者的任务了。我们认为,语篇语言学的分析方法不但可以帮助我们正确地理解原文,而且还能为选择合适的语言去生产合理的译文提供理论上的依据。

6 结语

翻译学的目标是描写客观翻译现象和建立能够解释和预测这些现象的原则和参数体系。

翻译研究者要研究语言,掌握语言的基本结构,明白语言如何在实际中运作,了解语言的本质及其功能,才可以系统地、有效地对研究结果进行描述或解释,并为理论研究和应用研究提供具体的资料和依据。

本文探讨了描写翻译研究中的一种研究方法,即翻译研究的语篇语言学方法。我们在文中提出了语篇语言学方面的理论依据和研究重点,这些只是我们初步的设想和构思。语篇语言学方法给翻译的理论与实践带来的启示是很多的,本文限于讨论范围和篇幅,未能对其中一些问题展开讨论,对语篇翻译研究的重点也只是列举其中几点。我们相信,以后还有机会把我们关于翻译研究的语篇语言学方法方面的一些想法提出来与大家讨论。

【延伸阅读】

[1] Neubert, A. & Shreve, G. (1992). *Translation as Text*. Kent, Ohio: Kent State University Press.

[2] Hatim, B. (1997). *Communication Across Cultures: Translation Theory and Contrastive Text Linguistics*. Exeter, England: University of Exeter Press.

[3] Hatim, B. & Mason, I. (1990). *Discourse and the Translator*. London: Longman.

【问题与思考】

1. 如何能够使译文在语篇层次上与原文实现对等?这个目标是否总是能够实现?译者是否总是把语篇对等看作翻译的最终目的?

2. 为了实现既定的翻译目的,译者是否可以牺牲原文的连贯性,而只需保证译文自身的连贯性就可以了?

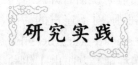

小说翻译的语义连贯重构

王东风

导　言

如何在译文中实现对原文语篇连贯关系的重构?这里选取的这篇文章可以很好地回答这个问题。该文章选自 2005 年《中国翻译》第三期。作者利用连贯、衔接和衔接手段中的复现和同现等概念,分析了语义连贯的构成及其翻译对策。作者在语篇与翻译领域进行了很多有益的尝试,主要观点散见于发表的学术论文和专著《连贯与翻译》和《功能语言学与翻译研究》等专著中。

1 引子

翻译是什么？谁都心知肚明，但就是不能说出来，一说出来就会出问题。那个心知肚明的东西就在那里，可就是说不清。古往今来，翻译已经有无数的定义，这无数的定义中的任何一个可以说都是对其他定义在某种意义上的否定。所谓定义，总是想用一句话定出被定义概念的本质，无数的定义其实都从某种角度上揭示出了翻译的某一个或几个侧面的本质，但始终还不是全部。本文无意在这众多定义中再加一个定义，只是想换个角度看翻译，这个角度就是关系。

翻译是一种关系的建构：翻译的过程即是建构与原文的互文关系的过程。这就意味着翻译是从一个原文派生而来的，符合这个条件的都是翻译，但与原文的关系有近有远。由于语言文化之间异质差异的存在，这种关系只能是一种近似。

翻译的过程是一种关系重构的过程：译者用目标语体现原文的意义和功能，实际上是对原文固有语篇关系的重构。无论是从语法学、语义学、语用学，还是从文体学、诗学、叙事学上看，意义就是一种关系，美也是一种关系，用语言体现意义、体现美，是对这种关系的建构，而用另一种语言来翻译这种关系，就是对这种关系的重构。本文的假说就是，只要以最优化的方式重构了这种关系，原文的意义和功能就能得到最优化的体现，译文对于原文的近似值也就会最高。

原文的语篇关系是什么？是连贯，分无标记连贯和有标记连贯两种。无标记连贯以良好的表层连接为标识，有标记连贯以不同程度的表层连接断裂为标识。判断表层连接断裂是有标记连贯还是不连贯要看这断裂的形成是否有深层的诗学促动，有则是有标记连贯，是积极性的，无则是不连贯的，是病句。在小说翻译中，我们一般对原文的表层连接断裂不做不连贯假定。这也符合斯坦纳的翻译四步的第一步：初始信任（initiative trust）（Steiner，1975：312），即译者在着手翻译原文时，已认定原文是有意义的。而意义其实就是一种关系效应，因此译者的任务就是要重构或隐或显地存在于原文中各个层次的各种关系。意义最佳的体现，是意义关系连贯的体现；那么，意义的最佳翻译，就是原文意义关系连贯的最优化重构。

连贯是一个多维概念，主要体现在语法层、语义层、语用层和文体层。本文选择语义层为切入点，探讨在翻译中语义连贯重构的意义。其他几个层次上的连贯问题将另文探讨。

在语言学界，提起连贯，人们马上就会想到衔接。这是两个意义相近但概念有所不同的术语。关于衔接与连贯的关系存在两种观点，一种观点认为衔接和连贯是两个平等的概念：衔接是表层连接，连贯是深层连接；另一种观点认为，衔接和连贯是两个"不平等"的概念：连贯是上义词，衔接是下义词，衔接服务于连贯，是连贯的重要条件之一，但绝不是必要条件。语篇是一个复杂的关系网络，连贯就是概括这所有关系的一个"伞状术语"（umbrella term）（Werth，1984：60）。本文采取第二种立场。由于篇幅原因，笔者不想把过多的精力放在对这两种观点的评判上，只是先简单地交代一下背景和本文的出发点。

2 词汇衔接的机制

语义连贯在系统功能语法的框架中，衔接是实现语篇功能的主要手段，分指称、替代、省略、连接和词汇衔接五种。衔接是一个句际连接概念。前四种衔接主要是通过语法手段来体现的；唯有第五种，按韩礼德和哈桑的话来说，是靠词汇手段来体现的。但并不是任何两个词之间都可以相互连接，词汇连接的机制归根到底是靠相关词语之间的语义关联。因此，词汇衔接的机制是一种语义上的连贯。韩礼德和哈桑也注意到了这一点，多次指出词汇衔接的语义价值。莫里斯(Morris)也指出，"词汇语义关系是存在于成对词语之间的个别关系，因此被用来创立词汇衔接"。

韩礼德和哈桑认为，句际语义关系主要是通过两种词汇衔接的方式建立起来的：一是复现(reiteration)，一是同现(collocation)。词语的复现无论是不是同义复现，其形式上相关的特征就注定了各复现项之间的同源性关系，衔接因此而生；"同现"也是一个语义概念，与习惯性同现的概率有关，如"菜单"常与"餐厅"同现，因此比较接近于语义场的概念。英语词汇的一个重要特征就是其多义性，一个词在语篇中的词义往往是建立在这个词和其他词的关系之上的，只有重构该词与相关词语之间的连贯关系，才可以成功地解读和体现该词的词义，而上述这两种关系就像是两条衔接链在语义的维面上把一个个词、一个个句子有序地连贯成了一个有机的语义整体。

一般说来，读者对语法关系的感知比对语义关系的感知更趋于程序化、自动化和规则化。在翻译过程中，语法特征往往是一种自动化的结构选择，译者只要能成功地解读原文的语法关系，一般很容易在目标语中找到近似体。但解读原文的语义特征就没有那么容易了，这往往是对译者理解和表达能力的挑战。尤其是在小说这样的文学语篇中，特定语境中的语义关系的不同体现方式往往具有不同的诗学价值，要求读者尽量在不损害原文表现方式的同时，保留原文的语义关系，因为原文的语义整体，也就是我们常说的"内容"，就是这语义关系的连贯体现。

3　复现关系

"复现关系是词汇衔接的一种形式，指在阶的一端对某一词项的重复；在阶的另一端用概括词对某一词项的回指；还有一些是处于中间地带的——或同义词、近义词或上义词的使用"(Halliday & Hasan,1976:275)，但韩礼德后来又认为，同义关系、近义关系、反义关系、上下义关系和部分整体关系其实都是同义关系(Halliday,1994:331-333)。因此概括起来，复现关系主要有两大类型：重复关系和同义关系。

3.1　重复性衔接

韩礼德认为，"词汇衔接最直接的方式就是词项的重复"(1994:330)。例如：

1. Algy met a bear. The bear was bulgy. (ibid.)

重复关系并不仅仅限于词语本身，它还可以是词根重复，如 pays, paying, paid, payment。韩礼德在例1的基础上稍作变化，给出了一个词根重复的例子：

2. Algy met a bear. Bears are bulgy. (ibid.)

例1和例2的区别并不仅仅在于前者是词语重复，后者是词根重复。二者的另一区别还在于例1中的第二个 bear 之前有定冠词 the，而定冠词本身具有指称意义，因此这里就有了两个衔接纽带：一个是指称(the)，另一个便是指称性词汇衔接(bear 的重复)。例2中的 bears 之前没有定冠词，本身不具指称意义，因此只有一个靠词根重复而建立起来的词汇衔接纽带。

由于指称性衔接一般要求被预设点和预设点之间的空间距离不能太大,因此多以近程纽带(immediate tie)为主,而非指称性衔接不存在指称上的预设与被预设的关系,因此多构成远程纽带(remote tie)。既然都是词汇衔接,二者的衔接功能都不能忽视,但实际情况是,非指称性重复由于不存在指称关系,因而在翻译中经常受到忽略。

例如,洛基指出,在小说《简·爱》中,有一个在不同的语境中不断被重复的词 fire。这个词有时明显被用作隐喻或象征,以体现主人公的某种情绪,但在很多情况下,其隐喻性或象征性并不明显,只有当我们意识到这是一个不断重复的意象时,我们才会发现这样的重复在有意或"无意"之间,在隐喻或非隐喻之间,总是具有某种象征指向,而这一感觉,或者说是这一诗学解读,正是被这不断重复的前景化意象所激活的。尽管这么多的"火"之间并没有多少是指称性的重复,但这丝毫不影响它的连贯功能,洛基的发现正是对这语义和"艺术连贯"(Lodge,1966:119)的重构。他认为,在这部小说中,"火"在很大程度上被赋予了隐喻和象征意义,"表达了为追求自我实现而表现出来的那充满激情、令人振奋而又让人望而生畏的内心生活,与此同时还体现了过于沉迷情感而带来的灾难和惩罚"(op. cit.:121)。他在《火与爱[爱是简·爱的爱,原文是 Fire and Eyre,作者注]:夏洛蒂·勃兰特尘缘未了的战争》一文中指出,"火"在《简·爱》中的重要性具有中心地位(op. cit.:121)。根据他的统计,整部小说中有一百多处"火"。这些"火"大部分都是非指称性重复,因而基本上都是远程纽带。根据文体学和话语分析的观点,由于"火"的重复出现,这个词本身的意象及其联想意义就被前景化了:"火"的物质能量便转化成了诗学能量。前景化的一个直接作用就是吸引读者的眼球,引起读者进一步的思考和探究,进而重构原文的语义和艺术连贯。在翻译中,"火"的一再重复而积累的诗学能量自然要求译者予以形式化的体现,但问题是如果译者没有发现这一处处"火"所构成的内在连贯,也就必定无法在主观上重构这一关系,因而必定会忽视这每一处"火"在重构那"火"的连贯中所起的集腋成裘的作用,最终导致一部分"火"由于意译的使用而流失。显然,"火"在此的翻译意义并不仅仅是形式上的,更重要的是这形式背后所蕴含的语义和诗学价值。但该小说几乎所有的中译本都没有完全体现出原文"火"的词汇衔接,各译本对这个词的翻译基本上没有体现出明确的目的性,好译的时候就译,不好译的时候就改。当英语中的 fire 与汉语中的"火"不共享同一喻意时,译者就成了"消防员"。以下是其中几例:

3. Strange energy was in his voice, strange *fire* in his look. (*Jane Eyre*, Chapter 15)

4. ... I saw a *glow* rise to that master's face. I saw his solemn eye melt with sudden *fire*, and *flicker* with resistless emotion. (op. cit.: Chap. 31)

5. ... but as his wife—at his side always, and always restrained, and always checked—forced to keep the *fire* of my nature continually low, to compel it to *burn* inwardly and never utter a cry, though the imprisoned *flame* consumed vital after vital ... (op. cit: Chap. 34)

3a. 他的声音里有一种奇特的力量,他的眼神中有一种奇特的激情。(《简·爱》长春版:137)

4a. 我看出那个主人的脸上升起一阵红光。我看到他庄严的目光被突如其来的热情软化了,带着无法抗拒的激情闪出了光芒。(op. cit.:344)

5a. 而一旦做了他的妻子——时时陪伴在他的左右,受他的限制、阻拦,被迫压低自己的天性,只得在内心燃烧而不敢外露,以致最后会被禁锢之火将五脏六腑烧光…… (op. cit.:386)

在以上三例译文中,原文的 fire 均被"扑灭"。显然译者没有发现"火"在原文中通过重复而建构的语义和诗学价值,否则的话他就不会这样轻易地去"灭火"了,因为这些"火"的翻译困难并不大。从局部看,译者的"灭火行动"还导致了例 4 和例 5 中的一条同现衔接链的断裂:例 4 的 glow—fire—flicker 被译成了"红光—热情—光芒";例 5 的 fire—burn—flame 被译成了"—燃烧—火"。由此不难看出,原文的"火"的语篇和诗学价值并不仅仅是构筑了一条孤立的"火"的重复衔接链,从局部看,每一处的"火"还有可能发挥其"物理"效应,呈局部放射状,因此把每一处"火"的放射区再串连起来,就会构成一个更大的"火场",形成一个重复与同现交错的语义连贯网,从而突出了整个小说底层隐含的"火"的主题意象,就像简·爱的姓氏 Eyre 的读音一样,不就是一个被刻意隐去了那 fire—flame—flicker(火—火苗—火光闪烁)中那"呼呼"作响的 F 音的余响吗?比较:fire[falr]和 Eyre[alr]。fire 的一个近义词是 ire(怒火)(小简·爱在被舅妈关起来时的内心独白中用过这个词),为此洛基指出,"ire 几乎就是一个双关"(Lodge:312)。既然 ire 可以因为在发音上与 fire 相近可以形成"几乎"双关,那么与 ire 发音完全相同的 Eyre 为什么就不可能呢?这是不是可以解释为什么作者要给女主人公起这么一个孤僻的姓氏。从这个角度上看,译者对"火"的改写在一定程度上破坏了原文的一条重要的意象连贯链。其实保留这一意象,并非是难事,只要微观语境设置得当,未必会造成局部语义亏损。以下三例来自另外一个译本:

3b. 在他的嗓音里有一种奇特的活力,在他的目光里有一种奇怪的火光。(上海译文版:172-173)

4b. 我看见主人的脸上升起了红晕,看见他严肃的目光,已被突如其来的火花所融化,闪烁着难以克制的激情。(op. cit.:421)

5b. 但是做他的妻子,永远在他身边,永远受到束缚,永远需要克制——不得不将天性之火压得很小……(op. cit.:470)

译者显然是感受到了"火"的意象在此的诗学价值,译文均保留了关键词"火",比 3a—5a 在语义上和文体上更接近原文的连贯模式。但必须指出的是,3b—5b 三句之间的"火"的连贯虽然都是词汇衔接,但原文的衔接模式是重复,而译文用词则分别是"火光"、"火花"和"火",其衔接模式是近义,属同现范畴,与原文的衔接模式还是有所区别的。这表明译者虽然对微观的诗学指向有所洞察,但并没有在宏观上重构起原文的这一意象的整体连贯。这一判断正确与否,也许可以在下一例中找到支持:

6. … a tale … narrated continuously; quickened with all of incident, life, fire, feeling, that I desired and had not in my actual existence. (*Jane Eyre*, Chap. 12)

6a. 这个故事还由于那些朝思暮想,却在我实际生活中所没有的事件、生活、激情和感觉,而显得更加生动。(《简·爱》上海译文版:121)

该例与 3b—5b 同出一个译本,但在这里已没有"火"的踪迹。笔者手头所有的《简·爱》中译本也都没有直译该例中的 fire。试在原译的基础上改译如下(5b 不变):

3c. 他的嗓音里有一种奇特的力,他的目光里有一团奇特的火。

4c. 我看见主人的脸上泛起红光一片,看见他严肃的目光,已被突如其来的火所融化,闪烁着难以克制的激情。

6b. 这个故事还由于那些我朝思暮想,却在我实际生活中所没有的事件、生活、火一样的激情和感觉,而显得更加生动。

改译尽量保留了原文的形式特征,但并没有以牺牲原文的语义为代价。这些例子证明了俄国形式主义的一个论断,即文学性并不是来自于内容本身,而是这内容的表达方式;而这样的表达方式并不仅仅只是微观层面上的遣词造句,宏观层面的变异和陌生化也同样有着深刻的诗学促动,而且更加挑战译者的诗学识别能力。

在狄更斯的小说《大卫·科波菲尔》中,也有那么一个远程的、非指称性的词汇衔接:书中有位叫米考伯(Micawber)的先生,此人说话有个口头禅,动不动就爱来个总结发言似的 in short(简言之),这个充满个性化的口头禅就成了这个人物的语言"指纹"——原本是一个再平常不过的短语,一经重复即被前景化,促使读者去解读它背后的诗学促动。在翻译中,要想体现这一特征,就必须要保留这个重复模式。如果译者没有识别这一连贯特征,而采用不同的表达方式来体现这个短语的概念意义,那么米考伯先生说话的信息内容虽不会受到损害,但他的个性特征就会因此而被消解。在该小说的第 11 和 12 章,也就是米考伯先生出场的那两章里,他在说话中共用了 10 次 in short,每章各 5 次。有一个译本是这样体现的:

第 11 章:简单地说吧——简单地说——简单地说吧——简单地说吧——简单言之

第 12 章:总而言之——简单地说吧——简单地说吧——简单地说吧——简单言之(《大卫·考坡菲》上海译文版:231,231,232,232,249,257,257,258,258,259)

译者分别用了四种表达方式,即"简单地说吧"、"简单地说"、"简单言之"和"总而言之"。虽然这四种表达方式的意思基本相同,但与原文相比,毕竟没有将重复进行到底。这只能说译者并没有意识到这简单的重复背后的诗学价值,因为这个短语的翻译本身不存在翻译困难。如果译者在阅读过程中重构了原文的语义和诗学连贯,在表达时只要选择那四个表达方式中的任何一个并把它重复到底就可以了。在另一个译本(人民文学版)中,译者就用"简而言之"一路到底,以不变对不变,体现了原文的这一连贯关系。

尽管原文重复性衔接的最佳翻译体现是形式对应,但我们不得不承认,在很多情况下,特别是同一个词用于不同意义的时候,如果目标语中的对应词与原文用词不共享相同的同义潜式时,就会出现翻译困难。

3.2 同义性衔接

复现关系的另一种形式是同义性衔接。这里所说的同义是个广义概念,包括(狭义的)同义关系、近义关系、反义关系、上下义关系和部分整体关系(Halliday,1994:331 – 333)。

同义性衔接是通过意义的相同、相近和相关来建构语义连贯的,也有指称性和非指称性之分(op. cit.:331 – 333)。

这种衔接的理想翻译仍然是形式对应,因此只要目标语具有相同的同义词资源,最佳的选择自然是以同义对同义,这样既可以保留原文的衔接功能,也不会损害其修辞价值。例如:

7. "Are there any *letters* for J. E. ?" I asked.

At last, having held *a document* before the glasses for nearly five minutes, she presented it across the counter, accompanying the act by another inquisitive and mistrustful glance—It was for J. E.

…

I now took out *my letter*, the seal was an initial F. ; I broke it; the contents were brief. (*Jane Eyre*, Chap. 10)

在该例中，letter 和 document 作为一对同义词出现。第二段的 document 因被不定冠词 a 限定，与第一段的 letter 形成非指称性词汇衔接。但第五段的 my letter 则是回指第二段的 document，二者指同一事物，具有同一性关系，因此构成指称性衔接。连贯模式是：letter—document—letter；这一规律在同一事件块的上文中已经出现，由于篇幅的关系，没有引用，相关上文的连贯模式也是 letter—document—letter，作者似乎是为了错开用词，避免机械重复。译者的任务就是要如实传达原文的语言痕迹，而这个痕迹对于译者来说应该是十分明显的，译者只需在原文的各衔接点上选择相应的同义词，就可以重构原文的连贯关系。在这个例子中，作为 letter 的同义词 document，一般多作"文件"解，在汉语里通常不作"信"的同义词用，因此在翻译中如果不作适当调整，可能会显得比较生硬。请看下例：

7a. "有 J. E. 的信吗？"

她把一个文件在眼镜前放了将近五分钟以后，终于隔着柜台把它递给了我，同时用好奇的、不信任的眼光又看了我一眼——信是给 J. E. 的。

……

于是我把我的信拿出来；封蜡上盖的是一个首字母 F.；我把信拆开，内容很简单。（《简·爱》上海译文版：82 - 83）

原文中的同义关系由于含了一个指称性衔接，因此比较容易识别，于是有的译者就干脆把 document 译成"信"（岳麓版：120 - 122）。这样处理的积极意义在于使衔接更紧密，也更直接，衔接功能不变，但缺陷也十分明显：作者所作的同义手段选择的修辞努力因此而被压制。原文的这一同义关系能否在目标语中得到理想的体现，关键就看"信"这个词项有没有同义词。"信"在汉语中并不是没有同义词，而且还不止一个，如"函件"、"邮件"、"信函"，可见"信"在汉语中的同义潜势也没有被译文释放出来。下面我们再来考察另一个案例：

8. **Stately**, plump Buck Mulligan came from the stairhead, bearing a bowl of lather on which a mirror and a razor lay crossed. A yellow dressing-gown, ungirdled, was sustained gently behind him by the mild morning air. He held the bowl aloft and intoned：

—*Introibo ad altare Dei.*

Halted, he peered down the dark winding stairs and called up coarsely：

—Come up, Kinch. Come up, you fearful Jesuit.

Solemnly he came forward and mounted the round gunrest. He faced about and blessed **gravely** thrice the tower, the surrounding country and the awaking mountains ... Then, catching sight of Stephen Dedalus, he bent towards him and made rapid crossed in the air. (*Ulysses*：1；斜体为原文所有，黑体为笔者所加)

这是《尤利西斯》一开始的几个段落。从文体学的角度一眼就可以看出，除了第二、四段的自由直接引语，其余三个叙事段均以状语，因而也就是有标记主位开头。第一段是副词 stately，第三段是过去分词 halted，第四段是副词 solemnly。这里的语境是 Mulligan 的出场，三个状语作为有标记主位强化了人物煞有介事的出场方式。连续的有标记主位所造成的强烈的变异必然会引起读者的关注和进一步解读。第一段和第四段的两个起首副词 stately 和 solemnly 实际上是一对同义词，放在一起看，还头尾押韵，两个词均表示"庄严的"、"庄重的"意思。在小说的一开始，就出现了 stately，显然是要把读者的注意力往庄严肃穆上去引，引起读者的期待，期待着一个什么神圣的、重要的事件的出现，然后紧接着出现的是什么呢？是无聊、琐碎、荒诞和滑稽。第三段故伎重演，再次以庄严肃穆开头，只不过这一回换了一个词 solemnly，再次故意误导读者的期待，接下来的内容同样猥琐、荒谬，与冠冕堂皇的 solemnly 相差甚远。

原文在语言材料调度上的妙处就在于用先入为主的方式故意误导读者的期待视野，然后再用与那期待视野形成巨大反差的猥琐和无聊造成滑稽的戏剧效果。但如果原文的这个妙处译者没有看出来，那无论有多么崇高的翻译理想，也无济于事。《尤利西斯》的两个译本是这样译的：

8a. 仪表堂堂、结实富态的壮鹿马利根从楼梯口走了上来。他端着一碗肥皂水，碗上十字交叉地架着一面镜子和一把剃刀。他披一件黄色梳妆袍，没有系腰带，被清晨的微风轻轻托起，在他身后飘着。他把碗捧得高高的，口中念念有词：

—Introibo ad altare Dei. *

他站住了，低头望看幽暗的盘旋式楼梯，粗鲁地喊道：

——上来，啃奇！上来吧，你这个怕人的耶稣会修士！

他庄严地跨步向前，登上了圆形的炮座。他环顾四周，神色凝重地对塔楼、周围的田野和正在苏醒过来的群山作了三次祝福。这时他看见了斯蒂汾·代达勒斯，便朝他弯下身去，迅速地在空中画了几个十字……

　　* 拉丁文："我登上天主的圣坛。"这是天主教神父主持弥撒开场用语。（译者注）（《尤利西斯》人民文学版：2）

8b. 神气十足、体态壮实的勃克·穆利根从楼梯口出现。他手里托着一钵肥皂沫，上面交叉放了一面镜子和一把剃须刀。他没系腰带，淡黄色浴衣被习习晨风吹得稍微向后蓬着。他把那只钵高高举起，吟诵道：

我要走上主的祭台。

他停下脚步，朝那昏暗的螺旋状楼梯下面瞥了一眼，粗声粗气地嚷道：

"上来，金赤！上来，你这敬畏天主的耶稣会士！"

他庄严地向前走去，登上圆形的炮座。他朝四下里望望，肃穆地对这座塔和四周的田野以及逐渐苏醒着的群山祝福了三遍。然后，他一瞧见斯蒂芬·迪达勒斯，喉咙里就发出咯咯声，摇着头，朝他弯下身去，往空中迅速地画了好几个十字。（《尤利西斯》译林版：47）

两个译本的黑体着重处与原文的几个主要有关不同点是：第一，都没有识别出 stately 是副词，把这个词看作了形容词；第二，由于 stately 的词类误断导致了其语义的变形，副词是修饰动作的，而形容词是修饰名词的，译文用其形容人物，必会使该词的语义向人物特征靠拢，变形由此而生；第三，语义变形的一个直接后果就是，stately 和 solemnly 之间的词汇衔接被截断；第四，两个被主位化的副词都失去了有标记主位的地位。显然，损失惨重。起因皆是因为 stately 词类误断所致，因为该词作形容词和作副词意思是不一样的。当然，笔者也不能武断地说这个词在此就一定是副词，像 Stately, plump Buck Mulligan came 这样的结构，也可以把 stately, plump 看作并列定语，如此说来，这就是一个歧义结构了。所谓歧义结构，就是两种解释都可以。解除歧义首要的原则就是分析哪一种解读更具合理性。笔者判断此处是副词的依据是，Stately, plump 如果是并列，中间为什么不用连词 and 隔开？在英语中二元并列不用连词是一种变异，而此处作变异解释，语境支持牵强；此外，这两个词的语义指向互斥，不具备同现条件，stately 有"帅气"的意思，而 plump 则指"肥胖"，如果硬要把这两个不沾边的词往一块扯的话,只能让一个词的语义迁就另一个词:8a 是让 plump 迁就 stately,未译成"肥胖"之类,而 8b 则是让 Stately 和 plump 相互迁就,译成了"神气十足、体态壮实",一个明显的语义变形是把一个"肥仔"译成了一个"壮汉"。而把 stately 看作副词,则没有任何结构上的疑问,且有下文的同类结构作支持。本人在与朱志瑜讨论这个案例时,他曾对把 stately 作副词解表示质疑,但在看完本文的分析时,表示同意本文的解读。为了慎重起见,本人又查阅了一些有关原作的论著,在比雷兹的一本关于《尤利西斯》的叙事策略的专著中看到了作者对这个案例有如下分析:

> 副词"stately"与形容词"plump"的混合很显眼,因为这两个词的字面意义在本质上是互相排斥的;肥胖和帅气通常是不同现的。此外,这两个词被逗号隔开,使句法范畴的副词和形容词变得难以分辨。如果不是因为这个逗号的话,stately 是可以做形容词解的。(Beeretz, 1998:20 - 21)

另一个学者哈特也认为:如果这个词是形容词,那么我们就不明白它和这个句子中的其他部分该怎么发生联系(Hart, 1993:428)。言下之意仍然是指 stately 和 plump 的语义互斥。而作副词解则除了有句法上的支持外,在语义和语境上也有一定的支持,因为相关文字所描述的是一种宗教仪式的滑稽模仿,以表现人物对宗教的轻视和故意亵渎,而宗教仪式与庄严肃穆构成社会语用连贯,甚至同现连贯。此外,作者在第四段的第二句还使用了另一个同义词 gravely,从而进一步强化了 stately 和 solemnly 的语义指向,并构成了一个由三个同义词组成的连贯链。有了合理的解读并不等于就有了适当的表达。英汉语状语语序差异表明,英语状语的句首殊位在汉语中对应率较低,如果把原文译成"庄严地,体态壮实的布克·穆利根出现在楼梯口",结构上显然不如原文自然。考虑到 stately 和 solemnly 之间还有头韵和尾韵的特征,不妨改译为:

8c. 带着庄重的神情,胖乎乎的布克·穆利根出现在楼梯口。……

停下脚步,他朝下看了一眼昏暗的螺旋状楼梯,粗声粗气地嚷道:

……

带着庄严的神情,他向前走去,登上圆形的炮座。

顺便一提的是,在例 8 中,除了这一同义性衔接之外,还"隐藏"着另一个重复性衔接纽带,即第一段的 crossed 和第四段的 crosses。在这段仿拟的宗教仪式中,这两个词都带有宗教色彩,但 crossed 的宗教含义由于是象征用法,因此比较隐蔽,不太容易识别。在译林版的译本中,这个重复纽带没有译出来。两个有关的句子被分别译成:"上面交叉放了一面镜子和一把剃须刀"和"往空中迅速画了好几个十字",而人民文学版的译本则成功地解读并体现了这一衔接纽带:"碗上十字交叉地架着一面镜子和一把剃刀"和"迅速在空中画了几个十字"。下面是另一个因同义关系识别失误而导致连贯亏损的案例:

9a. ……傍晚很潮湿,但是那些日子里白昼还长;我去了一两家铺子,再悄悄把信送进邮局,冒着大雨回来,衣服湿淋淋的,但是心里很轻松。(《简·爱》上海译文版:83)

敏感的读者可能会发现在这段文字中"潮湿"和"大雨"的同现有些勉强。生活中人们一般是把无雨而潮称为潮湿,因为潮湿和大雨在常识中是两个不同的等级。可能会有读者认为如此分析很勉强。我们还是来看看原文吧:

9. ... the evening was *wet*, but the days were still long; I visited a shop or two, slipped

the letter into the post office, and came back through heavy rain, with streaming garments, but with a relieved heart. (*Jane Eyre*, Chap. 10:119)

果然发现了问题。英语中的 wet 最常见的意思是"潮湿的",但它还有另外一个使用频率较低,但也比较常用的意思,即"下雨的",因此,原文的 wet 和 rain 构成远程同义性衔接。在汉语中,"潮湿"和"雨"不是一对同义词。如前所述,翻译中以同义对同义的前提是汉语中也存在同样的同义资源。"潮湿"不存在"大雨"的同义潜势。形式对应不行,只能采用功能对应的方式弥补:

9b. ……傍晚时分又下起了雨,不过白天仍很长。我逛了一两家店铺,又悄悄把信送进邮局,然后冒着大雨回家,衣服全淋湿了,但是心里却很舒畅。(《简·爱》浙江文艺版:99)

9b 将原文的同义关系改写为重复关系,但在衔接功能上仍属于复现关系范畴,语义价值和语篇功能都得到了最大的保留。

4. 同现关系

同现关系与复现关系的不同在于前者是一种"不依赖普通语义关系的词汇衔接","而是依赖于有关词项之间的一种特定的联系——一种同现的趋势"(Halliday,1994:33)。比如,"抽烟"和"打火机"、"寒冷"与"冬天"、"餐厅"与"菜单"等,就存在着这么一种同现趋势。在图式化的语境中,这些词的同现就会显得很自然,符合人们对世界的认识。而"抽烟"和"月球"、"寒冷"和"手提电脑"、"菜单"和"超生游击队"等之间就不存在这种当然的同现关系,除非有相关的语境支持。同现关系的识别和重构对于翻译有着重大的意义。由于英语是一种以多义词为主导的语言,因此英译汉的过程其实就是一个不断排除消极歧义的过程。消除歧义的一个重要参照就是语境,而语境参数在很大程度上就是由同现关系建立的。一个词出现消极歧义时,译者可以根据它的同现环境来确立它的语义指向。例如:

10. ... great grey *hills* heaved up round the horizon: as twilight deepened, we descended a valley, dark with *wood* ... (*Jane Eyre*, Chap. 5)

11. I wish to be a better man than I have been, than I am; as Job's leviathan broke the spear, the dart, and the habergeon, hindrances which others count as *iron* and *brass*, I will esteem but straw and rotten wood ... (op. cit., Chap. 15)

英语的 wood 是个多义词,词典释义包括"树林"、"森林"、"木头"、"木材",甚至"木桶"等。多义词在真实的语篇中除非是被用作双关(积极性歧义),否则一般要作单义化处理,语境参照是消除歧义最有效的方法,这个参照的一个主要语言特征就是同现关系,同现词项可以限制特定用词的语义范围,因而可以帮助译者对其进行准确的语义定位。在例 10 中,与 wood 相关的同现词项有 hills(山峦)和 valley(山谷),即把 wood 锁定在"树林"或"森林"之上。在例 11 中,与 wood 同现的词项是 iron(铁)、brass(铜)、straw(草),因此 wood 便被锁定在材料的范畴之内,在这一范围内的可选词项是"木头"或"木材"。例 10 中的 hills, valley 和 wood,以及例 11 中的 iron, brass, straw 和 wood 就构成了同现衔接。不同的同现关系决定不同的语义指向。请看以下译文:

10a. ……一座座灰色的大山耸立在地平线上。暮色渐浓,车子驶进一个山谷,那儿长着黑乎乎的一片森林。(《简·爱》上海译文版:44)

11a. 我希望做个比以往、比现在更好的人——就像约伯的海中怪兽那样,折断矛戟和标枪,刺破盔甲,扫除一切障碍,别人以为这些障碍坚如铜铁,而我却视之为干草、烂木。(op. cit.:163)

译文表达还是比较连贯的。比较一下张冠李戴的效果:

*10b. ……一座座灰色的大山耸立在地平线上。暮色渐浓,车子驶进一个山谷,那儿长着黑乎乎的一片木头。

*11b. 我希望做个比以往、比现在更好的人——就像约伯的海中怪兽那样,折断矛戟和标枪,刺破盔甲,扫除一切障碍,别人以为这些障碍坚如铜铁,而我却视之为干草、烂森林。

笔者不能断言,10b 和 11b 的现象就绝对不会发生,或者说绝对说不通,但相比较而言,还是 10a 和 11a 更符合语境和常识一些,因而也更连贯些。在歧义的消除中,当不同的语义选择处于同等水平的时候,选择是最困难的;而当不同的语义选择处于不同水平的时候,一般情况下是两害相权取其轻。尽管 10b 和 11b 是笔者的杜撰之例,但在实际翻译中,由于忽略同现衔接而导致的张冠李戴的现象还是很多的。请看下例:

12a. **遮棚上露出个秃头**,那是个精明而有怪癖的老头子。(《尤利西斯》译林版:139)

译文中的黑体着重处的意思十分怪异:遮棚上露出个秃头。"遮棚"是什么意思?词典上找不到,上 Google 网上搜索了一下,显示有两千多条,概括起来应该是"能遮阳挡雨的棚子"。那么"遮棚上露出个秃头"是什么意思呢? 大概只能是"遮棚破了,露出某人的秃头"吧。这个解读是很别扭,但只要有语境支持,也不是没有可能,只是原文中并没有这样的语境支持。原文是:

12. Bald head over the blind. Cute old codger. (*Ulysses*, Chap. 4:69)

解读此处症结的关键就是要破解 blind 的语义,英文词典上的两个相关释义分别是 a blind person(瞎子)和 a screen for shop window(商店橱窗的遮棚)。

12a. 选择的是后者。但一个人的头怎么无端会在"遮棚上露出"呢? 再看另一个译本:

12b. 秃子比瞎子强。精明的老家伙。(《尤利西斯》人民文学版:90)

这个译文看上去就很自然了。译者对原文的连贯重构思路十分清晰:bald head(秃子)和 blind(瞎子)均指人的生理现象,符合同现条件;此外,在英语俚语中,bald head 还可以表示"聪明"、"知识分子",这就与第二句中的 cute(聪明的)形成了同现。连贯之中见意义,由此可见一斑。本文介绍了语义连贯的构成机制,研究了在翻译中如何以词汇衔接为线索来识别和重构原文的语义连贯。表面上看,词汇衔接不过是五种衔接方式中的一种,但在笔者看来,语义的种种关联,翻译的种种难题,大多可以在这一范畴内得到解决。意义来自于连贯的关系在此得到了有力的证明。相对于语境理论而言,词汇衔接的进路更容易让我们把握词与词之间的各种关系,语篇中的每个词都是这纵横交错的关系网中的一个节点。一个词如果与语篇中本应相关的词失去了联系,它也就失去了意义,因此翻译说到底实际上就是这张关系网的重织。

第六章 语用学/社会语言学与翻译研究

导 论

语用学和社会语言学是两个不同的学科,但是两者之间有一个共同之处,那就是两者都强调语境对于语言使用的影响。这两个学科相互交叉渗透,有一些共同的议题,这也就是为什么我们把这两个学科对于翻译研究的影响放在一章里进行讨论的原因。当然,这两者还是有很多不同的。社会语言学主要考察各种相对确定或稳定的社会变量,如社会阶层、民族、性别、年龄等在说话人使用语言时所体现的系统化语言特征;而语用学则主要描述说话人使用语言时具有可变性特征的社会地位、社交角色等所体现的语言特征,以及研究说话人如何通过一定的言语行为去实施特定的交际目的。此外,社会语言学告诉人们说话人具有什么样的语言能力,语用学则关注说话人利用这些语言能力能做什么(冉永平,2003)。①

社会语言学之所以和翻译扯上关系,主要有三个原因:① 翻译是社会现实的反映;② 翻译是一个由社会因素决定的交际过程;③ 翻译的社会标准。从社会语言学视角进行翻译研究的学者主要有俄罗斯的什维策尔和科米萨罗夫,法国的莫里斯·贝尔尼埃、让·皮特斯,美国的尤金·奈达和英国的莫纳·贝克等。

奈达从社会语言学视角研究翻译问题,主要有 1986 年的论文《社会语言学与翻译》和 1996 年的专著《跨语际交际的社会语言学》(*The Sociolinguistics of Interlingual Communication*)等,《跨语际交际中的社会语言学》可以说是奈达的社会语言学翻译观的一个系统性的总结。

贝克的专著《翻译与冲突》(*Translation and Conflict*)列举了大量的实例,阐释了翻译与社会和政治的关系,认为翻译不是在真空中进行的,翻译本身就是政治的一部分,而且翻译本身也在创造政治。

从语用学角度来研究翻译的主要学者有古特(Gutt)、希基(Leo Hickey)、哈蒂姆和贝克等人。

语用学中的重要理论包括语境理论、言语行为理论、会话含义理论、预设理论和关联理论等。学者们尝试以这些理论为框架,对翻译问题进行探讨,其中希基主编的《翻译的语用学研究》(*The Pragmatics of Translation*)一书,是对这些研究成果的集中展示。

---

① 冉永平:《语用学与社会语言学之间的交叉研究》,《外语教学与研究》,2003 (1)。

选 文

选文一　Pragmatics and Translation

Basil Hatim

导　言

　　本文选自贝克主编的 *Routlege Encyclopedia of Translation Studies*。作者主要介绍了语用学中的几个热点问题：言语行为、隐含意义、合作原则、会话含义等，然后探讨了这些热点问题对于翻译和翻译研究的意义。

In 1955 at Harvard, the psychologists were buzzing with excitement about the lectures being given by Noam Chomsky on his theory of Transformational Generative Grammar. In the same year, the British philosopher John Austin was also at Harvard delivering the prestigious William James lectures and presenting what was to have an equally strong impact on a wide range of disciplines. This was a new perspective which was to radically reshape our view of language and the way it operates. Since then, the domain of pragmatic inquiry has emerged as a discipline in its own right, attending to such matters as the "study of the purposes for which sentences are used, of the real world conditions under which a sentence may be appropriately used as an utterance" (Stalnaker, 1972: 380). This new perspective, and some of its main findings, soon found their way into the literature on translation.

Speech Act

Speech acts are the acts we perform when, for example, we make a complaint or a request, apologize or pay someone a compliment. The pragmatic analysis of speech acts sees all utterances in terms of the dual function of "stating" and "doing things," of having a meaning and a force. An utterance, in this view has:

　　(a) a **sense** or reference to specific events, persons or objects;

　　(b) a **force** which may override literal sense and thus relay added effects such as those associated with, say, a request or an admonition;

　　(c) an overall **effect** or consequence which may or may not be of the kind conventionally associated with the linguistic expression or the functional force involved.

For example，"shut the door" is in a sense an imperative that could conceivably carry the force of a request，which in turn could be used simply to annoy the hearer. To these three aspects of message construction，Austin (1962) assigned the labels **locution，illocution** and **perlocution**，respectively.

In translation and interpreting，these distinctions have proved extremely important，particularly when force departs from conventional sense，or when the ultimate effect defies the expectations based on either facet. In pragmatics-oriented models of the translation process，the assumption generally entertained has been that the act of translation itself can be viewed as an attempt at the successful performance of speech acts. In their quest to achieve "sameness of meaning," it has been argued，translators constantly attempt to re-perform locutionary and illocutionary acts in the hope that the end-product will have the same perlocutionary force in the target language (Blum-Kulka，1981). Actual examples of pragmatics at work in the general domain of translation can be found in Baker (1992).

As far as interpreting is concerned，cases of communication breakdown due to misinterpretation of speech acts have also featured prominently in the literature. To take one practical example，in response to the question "What were the contents of the letter you handed to King Fahad?"，a Tunisian minister is reported to have replied rather curtly what should have been interpreted as "This is a matter solely for the Asudis to consider. " Not aware of the pragmatic meaning involved，the interpreter rendered the original Arabic sentence literally as "This matter concerns the Saudis. " The statement was obviously intended to carry the pragmatic gloss "Do not pursue this line of questioning any further," a meaning which the English journalist would have no doubt appreciated. However，lured by the kind of inviting answer he received through the interpreter，the journalist did pursue the initial line of questioning，only to be rebuked the second time round (Hatim，1986；Hatim & Mason，1997).

In assessing the potential of speech act analysis，translation theorists shared some of the misgivings expressed by critics of speech act theory. The theory was primarily more concerned with combating alternative philosophical views than with attending to the practical aspects of dealing with language use in natural situations. Naturalness is a key term for the practicing translator or interpreter，and actual use of language can and does throw up different kinds of problems from those that speech act theory would wish us to focus on. For example，there is a huge difference between acts such as "promising" or "threatening," on the one hand，and more diffuse acts such as "stating" or "describing," on the other. Yet，both lists are merged under the single heading of "illocutionary force" (cf. Searle，1969；see critique in de Beaugrande's 1978 study of poetic translating).

Appropriateness Conditions beyond the Single Speech Act

In attempting to apply speech act theory to translation and interpreting，mainstream translation theorists soon became aware of the fact that a text is not a one-dimensional, linear succession of elements glued one to the other evenly; rather it is a complexly constructed edifice with some elements enjoying a higher communicative status, some a less prominent one, within an emerging, evolving hierarchical organization (de Beaugrande, 1978). It is this insight into the way texts are perceived which underpins an influential body of work on the extension of speech act analysis. Both theoretically and in various domains of applied pragmatics, it has been demonstrated that the interpretation of speech acts depends crucially on their position and status within sequences. The variation in status which underlies the interrelationship of speech acts within sequences leads to the notion of the illocutionary structure of a text, determining its progression and defining its coherence (Ferrara, 1980).

In translation studies, it is now accepted that what needs to be relayed in the normal course of events is this overall picture and not a series of unstructured sequences whose equivalence in the target language is determined piecemeal (i. e. speech act for speech act). This sequence-oriented, global view of the force of action has been made possible by the emergence in pragmatics of the notion of the text act. Here, the force of a given speech act is assessed not only in terms of its contribution to the local sequence in which it is embedded, but also in terms of the contribution it makes via the local sequence to a more global sequence enveloping the entire text (Horner, 1975).

In an attempt to extend the analysis beyond the individual speech act, there has been a considerable shift of focus in the analysis of the translation process and entire text formats began to be considered from the view point of pragmatics. For example, argumentative texts have been found to display a global problem-solving structure, with the problem section being typically "assertive" in its illocutionary value, and the solution section typically "directive." Such global charactorizations are in formed by both functional and hierarchical criteria governing the various speech acts involved, and ought to be heeded in their globality by the translator (Tirkkonen-Condit, 1986).

In text type-oriented translation studies, a major issue addressed has been that of the indeterminacy which a particular speech act can exhibit and which can only be resolved by reference to the global organization of the text. For example, describing a given peace plan as *slightly better* than the previous ones could pragmatically mean "only slightly and therefore negligibly better," depending on whether the overall stance is pro- or anti-plan. The initial sequence is indeterminate and is settled only when we subsequently read *there are reasons for hope*. There are languages, such as Arabic, which have to mark such distinctions, and where a number of alternative lexico-grammatical structures are available to cater for the alternative readings involved (Hatim & Mason, 1990, 1997).

Implied Meaning and the Cooperative Principle

One of the basic assumtions of pragmatic analysis is that, in communication, being sincere is a social obligation (Austin, 1962; Searle, 1969). However, language users can evoke and interpret implied meanings by leaving certain things unsaid (as speakers) or interpreting what is said against the background of what could have been said (as hearers). Given this potential for generating and retrieving meanings other than those that are stated explicitly, Grice (1975) attempted to account for where, how and why the smooth ongoingness of interaction is intentionally thwarted, leading to various kinds of implicature. He stipulated a Cooperative Principle which guides human interaction on the basis of a number of Maxims to which language users conventionally adhere, unless there is a good reason for them not to do so. These Maxims are Quantity (Making your contribution as informative as is required), Quality (Do not say that for which you lack adequate evidence), Relevance (Be relevant), and Manner (Be communicatively orderly). The Maxims, Grice argued, may be obeyed or disturbed, and disturbance can take the form of flouting or disobeying the rules in a motivated, deliberate manner.

The notion of implicatures arising from the deliberate flouting of the cooperative Maxims has proven particularly helpful to practicing translators and interpreters. In purely receptive terms, appreciation of implied meaning facilitates comprehension which would otherwise be blurred. In terms of re-producing the message in the target language, on the other hand, the meanings which are implied and not stated could be the last court of appeal in assessing adequate equivalence. This last point is particularly relevant in working with languages which are both culturally and linguistically remote from each other, where different pragmatic means may have to be opted for to achieve a given ultimate effect.

Within this cross-cultural domain of pragmatic analysis as applied to translation, a plausible assumption entertained for some time now has been that, by examining the various rules that govern successful performance in any given language, it might be possible to make predictions regarding the possible to make predictions regarding the possibility or otherwise of reconstructing the same indirection in another language (Blum-Kulka, 1981). A case that springs to mind here is that, through failure to assess the effectiveness of target renderings in preserving implied meanings in the source text, Edward Said's *Orientalism* (1978) has certainly lost much of its irony in the published translation into Arabic (Hatim, 1997). For example, in the source text element *if these facts are facts*, at least one maxim has been flouted, that of quality, with the resultant implicature in the relevant context of "who is Balfour kidding, it is a pack of lies." In the Arabic translation, a literal rendering is opted for and a similar maxim is ostensibly flouted in the hope that an equivalent implicature would result. Regrettably, this has not been the case, and the pragmatic procedure adopted simply misfired. In such a context, flouting Quality could only produce the opposite effect in

Arabic, i. e. achieving emphasis and leading to a statement of conviction. To ensure that sarcasm, irony, etc. are optimally preserved, the translator could have more felicitously flouted the maxim of quality (by being unnecessarily verbose).

Politeness and Implicature

Motivated disobedience of any Maxim within the Cooperative Principle, then, gives rise to implicatures. Obeying the maxims, however, does not necessarily guarantee that implied meanings will not be generated. "Implying" as opposed to "explicitly stating" is possible even when a given maxim is adhered to, provided such adherence is opted for in contexts where non-adherence would be the expected norm. One such context may be illustrated by the following example from Act I of Bernard Shaw's *You Never Can Tell*, analysed in Leech (1992: 262 – 263).

> DENTIST:... Why didn't you let me give you gas?
> YOUNG LADY: Because you said it would be five shillings extra.
> DENTIST: [shocked] Oh, don't you say that. It makes me feel as if I had hurt you for the sake of five shillings.
> YOUNG LADY: [with cool insolence] Well, so you have.

Typical of Dolly's bluntness of character, the Maxim of quality is meticulously adhered to and truth is valued no matter what. It is speaking the truth when a white lie would do, however, that in its own way constitutes a flouting of some principle or other giving rise to an implicature all the same. What is being flouted here are norms of politeness, which sanction flouting Quality as a norm and deem not doing so a deviation from acceptable social behaviours (Leech, 1992).

This and similar examples raise important questions for a translation theory that seeks to confront cross-cultural pragmatics and account for the problems thrown up by this particular area of language use. In translating a play like Shaw's into Arabic or Japanese, for example, the hypothesis widely accepted in pragmatically-oriented theories of translation is that the more language-bound the rules governing the performance of any indirect speech act, the lower the degree of translatability (Blum-Kulka, 1981).

Relevance in Translation

Gutt (1991) tries to describe translation in terms of a general theory of human communications. This builds on the the basic premise that the ability of human beings to infer what is meant may be accounted for in terms of observing the principle of relevance, defined as achieving maximum benefit at minimum processing cost. Two basic kinds of language use are distinguished: descriptive use, involving reference only to entities in the real world, and interpretive use, involving reference to entities as well as to thoughts and expressions of thought. Gutt suggests that translation is an instance of interpretive use and that translations seek to resemble their originals interpretively. Translation is constrained by the principle of relevance in the sense that:

> If we ask in what respects the intended interpretation of the translation should resemble the original, the answer is: in respects that make it adequately relevant to the audience—that is, that offer adequate contextual effects; if we ask how the translation should be expressed in such a manner that it yields the intended interpretation without putting the audience to unnecessary processing effort. (Gutt, 1991:101 – 102)

Serious reservations about the value of relevance theory in translation have been expressed by a number of scholars on a number of grounds, including the vexed question of how and by whom the various "rankings of relevance" are to be determined in particular contexts of translation. But, perhaps a more relevant objection to Gutt's proposals relates to the contribution of Skopos Theory, which Gutt seems to undervalue. According to this theory, translations have sets of hierarchically-ordered purposes. It is these purposes, one variant of which may be the instructions attached to a request for translation, that determine the translation procedures and ultimately the process itself (Reiss & Vermeer, 1984). Tirkkonen-Condit (1992) questions Gutt's reliance on a general principle of relevance and asks: by what criteria, other than hierarchization of purposes, can a translator decide what must be retained and what can be legitimately sacrificed? Skopoi, together, with culture-specific conventions recognized by a given language community, are now seen as an important framework within which what readers expect of a translation is to be determined, making it incumbent on the translator to be loyal to the target audience by telling them why and how their expectations are defied when they are (Nord, 1991).

选文二　Perlocutionary Equivalence: Marking, Exegesis and Recontextualisation

Leo Hickey

导　言

利奥·希基(Leo Hickey)是英国索尔福德大学(University of Salford)研究员、教授,主要从事文体学、语用学和文体语用学的研究。这篇文章选自希基主编的《翻译的语用学研究》。

Perlocution

In distinguishing locutionary, illocutionary and perlocutionary acts, Ausin (1962) was referring to what a person says, does and brings about, or is likely to bring about, in or on somebody, respectively. In uttering a certain sentence, then, a speaker says something (thus performing a locutionary act, as in "Get Lost!"), does something (performing an illocutionary act, such as insulting or giving a command) and brings or may bring about some effect on somebody (performing a perlocutionary act, perhaps causing the hearer to feel upset and to go away). These three "acts" are so inextricably interrelated as to be regarded by some as no more than different perspectives of one and the same transaction (See Davis, 1980:37; Leech, 1983:201–203).

On perlocution Austin (1962:10) wrote:

> Saying something will often, or even normally, produce certain consequential effects upon the feelings, thoughts, or actions of the audience, or of the speaker, or of other persons; and it may be done with the design, intention, or purpose of producing them; and we may then say, thinking of this, that the speaker has performed an act … We shall call … the act performed, where suitable … a "perlocution."

He went on to describe a perlocutionary act as "what we bring about or achieve by saying something, such as convincing, persuading, deterring, or even, say, surprising or misleading" (ibid. :109).

Davis (1980:39) distinguishes the perlocutionary act (the speaker's causing the hearer to do something or something to be done to the hearer), the perlocutionary cause (the speaker's saying something) and the perlocutionary effect (the hearer's doing something or what happens in, on or to the hearer). Thus, for our purposes, an original or source text (ST) may perform a perlocutionary act and constitute a perlocutionary cause of certain perlocutionary effects.

Imagine that Paul has received a bill for a large sum which he cannot pay. It will probably worry him, send him scurrying to his bank manager and eventually get him to pay up. His wife happens to read the bill, she also gets worried and shows it to her friend to explain why she is worried; the friend feels and expresses sympathy for Paul's wife. One and the same text may thus bring about different reactions in different readers. Now imagine a similar bill comes to Ann, written in a language she does not understand, from an overseas supplier. She has it translated and the translation or target text (TT) worries her, gets her to scurry to her bank manager and eventually pay up. In this second case, clearly the ST and the TT produce different perlocutionary effects on Ann, and the ST does not directly cause any of the effects intended by the writer. Nevertheless the ST is capable of stimulating effects analogous to those that derive from Paul's bill and the TT must likewise be capable of stimulating all these effects; otherwise the translation is defective.

In studying perlocution in translation, let us keep in mind that a translator is not concerned with real effects (if any) produced on real readers (if any) of the TT, but only with the potential effects. Let us also be aware that the writer's subjective intentions are irrelevant and can be ignored, except in so far as they are objectively manifested in the ST (see Austin, 1962:106).

Following Austin's admission (1962: 110) that "any, or almost any, perlocutionary act is liable to be brought off, in sufficiently special circumstances, by the issuing, with or without calculation, of any utterance whatsoever," Gu (1993: 408) explains that "the utterance exerts *no binding force* on the effects produced," it may produce "an infinite and indefinite number" of effects and consequently it is impossible to infer, from what a speaker says, what consequences may ensue. Gu, therefore, rejects any strict line of causation between an utterance and its perlocutionary effects, stressing instead the hearer's "legitimate claim to agency" (ibid. :420) He argues that it is in fact the hearer who produces the reaction and that perlocutionary effects, psychological or mental events, are "response-acts" of which the hearer is the agent. A perlocutionary act then "is a joint endeavour between S(speaker) and H(hearer). It involves S's performance of speech acts and H's performance of response-acts" (ibid. : 422). In other words, the speaker's saying something plays (merely) a triggering role in the whole transaction and different individuals in different contexts may respond differently to one and the same trigger.

In accepting the broad thrust, though not the extreme details in all cases, of Gu's arguments, I will regard the speaker's locution and illocution as a trigger and I will deal here, not with the perlocutionary acts or even causes, but with perlocutionary effects potentially brought about in or on the hearer. To be practical, a translator must treat all such responses, however "infinite and indefinite," as being analogous to one another on the ground that they have at least their trigger or cause in common, even if the readers and their contexts may be different. Although such perlocutionary effects may fall outside the study of pragmatics and linguistic communication, as some argue (see Gu, 1993: 428; Leech, 1983: 203), in dealing as she thinks best with the locution (what the ST says) and the illocution (what the ST does), a translator must examine all potential perlocutions (the effects and responses reasonably predictable—on the basis of the common trigger or cause—in or on the mind, imagination, feelings or actions of a reader of the TT) as a check to ensure that perlocutionary equivalence—"perlocutionary analogy" might be a more accurate term—has been achieved.

My contention then is that, just as the ST is capable of producing or likely to produce or stimulate one or more analogically related perlocutionary effects on its original readers, so also any TT must, in turn, be capable of producing "analogous" rather than "similar," allows for the fact that, just as not all ST readers or their contexts are the same, so also the

TT readers may be quite different, and situated in different contexts, from any of the ST readers.

Perhaps I should recall here that philosophers have interpreted the concept of perlocution in varying ways. Grice (1957), for example, seems to believe that to say something and mean it is a matter of intending to perform a perlocutionary act, whereas Searle claims that saying something and meaning it is precisely a matter of intending to perform an illocutionary act; he argues that (simply to produce) understanding of what is said is not a perlocution (Searle, 1969: 46 - 47). With this divergence in mind, I wish to suggest that understanding or knowledge of what has been said—if such a reaction or effect is ever possible on its own in real life or if, to parody Austin, there is such an animal—comes under my (broadened) category of perlocution, on the grounds that it is something that takes place within the domain of the hearer's response allowing him to react further as he thinks best after the speaker has performed her part in the event.

Therefore by perlocutionary effect I mean, for the purposes of this study, any effect, result or response, which may range from (mere) understanding to being alarmed or frightened and even to shooting someone (Austin's example), produced in or on the hearer by a locution/illocution either alone or in combination with some relevant features of the context and the reader. It therefore extends to any change in the hearer's state of mind, emotion, actions etc.

Perhaps I have arrived, by circuitous route, at a position quite close to Nida's "dynamic" or "functional" equivalence (see de Waard & Nida, 1986: 36 - 40), OR TO Newmark's "equivalent effect" (see Newmark, 1988: 48), which the latter sees as a desirable result rather than as the aim of any translation. Yet my contention is that the concept of perlocution outlined here means that the translator must aim to provide a text capable of offering its readers the opportunity of experiencing an analoguous effect to that which the ST offered its own readers, that it must do this always and not just in certain cases, as Newmark seems to suggest, nor just allowing them to "comprehend the translated text to such an extent that they can understand how the original receptors must have understood the original text," as Nida requires (see de Waard & Nida, 1986:36).

Let us take a fairly realistic example. Suppose a commercial letter ends as follows: "Thanking you for the prompt settlement of your account," any translation of this phrase, however locutionarily (or literally) accurate or illocutionarily similar to the ST with regard to the linguistic level or the act of thanking the addressee, which gives the latter either a feeling of satisfaction at having paid the bill (if he has not) or convinces him that he must pay it (if he has already done so) will be inadequate from the perlocutionary point of view; the translator must produce a version that will be as perlocutionarily ambiguous as the original, which is locutionarily and illocutionarily clear (unless we wish to distinguish the speech act of "thanking an advance" from that of "thanking in arrears") but leaves the "prompt settlement of your account" perlocutionarily unclear as to whether the reader should feel satisfaction at having already paid or be convinced that he must now pay the bill.

I now wish to look at three factors that are closely involved with perlocution.

Marking

Whatever emerges from the pen of the translator, it seems certain that it will be, or have some connection with, reported speech. After all, a translator is *de facto* a mediator, a third person, intervening between the writer of the ST and the reader of the TT. Whether this mediation is quite "visible" (as in a word-processed document headed "Translation" and signed by the translator) or virtually "invisible" (as when a brief text on mathematics, consisting mainly of formulae, is translated from one language to another on an otherwise blank sheet of paper), the translator has accomplished a task that yields an output, the TT, which is one step away—in some real or metaphorical sense—from the original. The TT reader, consequently, will read something which is necessarily different from what the ST author wrote.

I suggest, therefore, that a TT is somehow "marked" in the sense that it may carry a kind of notice or signal, however notional, along the lines: "Read the following text as a translation," "The original text refers not to Britain but to Spain" or "An original text says, does and may cause you to ... " The result is that, at some level, the reader should or is bound to read the TT in a way that differs from the way in which the original text is read: for example, by imagining that he is in a "world" or society which he would not immediately imagine, by mentally adapting references, allusions or terms that he does not automatically recognize, or by simply making adjustments of the type "When the text says 'I' or 'my'," it doesn't mean the writer of what I am reading but rather some third person.

I am not referring necessarily to such overt marks as the translator's name on the title page of a work of literature, blatantly foreign names and addresses on word-processed sheets or even explicit references to foreign terms, currency, place-names or customs. I am referring, rather, to the reality interposed between the ST and the final reader, a textual operator which ensures that the reader is told what the original text says, does and may stimulate, rather than being obliged or permitted to experience the original for himself at first hand.

This is not to say that some translated texts may not themselves function as original texts: for example, multilingual public notices, Acts of Parliament passed in all relevant languages or other texts which are signed or validated by whatever person or process is competent to validate them, such as the President of the Republic, the Company Secretary or the author of a bilingual text in a multilingual or diglossic situation.

Exegesis

The view that translations are *ipso facto* mediated and marked to that effect leads easily to the question of exegesis or explanation of the ST. The difficulties readers may experience in understanding a TT may be due to the fact that it is not "about," does not "refer to" or "use" the culture, including the language or other realities, that would be accessible or known to them. A legal text is likely to be "about" certain concepts and realities (constituting, amending or discussing them), a literary text may "refer to" certain realities in order to stimulate a particular type of (aesthetic) experience, and humourous texts at most "make use of" certain realities which may be quite peripheral to what is being aimed at (usually to amuse the reader).

For example, if a Spanish text states that the "juez" visited the scene of a crime as part of his investigation, a translator will have to decide whether simply to translate "juez" as "judge" or perhaps "investigating judge" or to explain that some Spanish "judges" are more similar to English police officers than to English judges.

Since the TT will be marked as referring to Spain, the perlocutionary effect which it is capable of producing will be a function of the level of any exegesis provided. Perlocution derives from locutionary/illocutionary acts+context + reader, and TT context=ST context +exegesis+marking; therefore the perlocution will depend—among other factors—on the levels of marking and exegesis which operate to adjust the TT reader's context and his "suitability" as a reader, in order to make him a more "suitable" reader and situate him in a more "suitably fitted" context to the TT. The more strongly or visibly the text is marked as a translation of a text from a given source culture, the less exegesis will be appropriate; this is clear in the case of legal texts; the more weakly, invisibly or notionally the marking, the more exegesis may be required to make the text suitable to be read by a TT reader.

Recontextualisation

In discussing marking and exegesis I have posited a situation in which a translator may strongly mark a TT as deriving from an ST of a certain culture, leaving the cultural, linguistic and other references more or less intact or, alternatively, may give a strong exegesis or explanation of the ST background, thus requiring weaker marking. I now posit the possibility that an original context (including features of the language) may play such an essential part in the perlocution that no degree of exegesis or marking combined will achieve the desired effects. For example, humour frequently depends for its effect on some characteristic of the original language, which it may not share with the target language.

By recontextualisation I refer to a radical approach to the translation of a particular text, which consists of totally or partially abandoning the literal, propositional or locutionary level, while maintaining the illocutionary act (usually "telling") as far as possible and focusing strongly on the perlocutionary effect, directly or accurately reproducing it.

For example, a teacher is explaining proverbs to the class and asks one little boy: "Johnny, cleanliness is next to what?" "Impossible, Miss," replies Johnny. The humour here is caused by a one-word deviation from the well known proverb, which nevertheless makes perfect sense to an reader and makes more sense to a child than the expected "godliness." If a translator were to explain this (approximately as I have just done), he might achieve an exegesis but the perlocutionary effect (amusement) would be destroyed. Recontextualisation will involve finding a proverb in the target language and distorting it in the same way as the original: "En boca cerrada no entran caramelos," "De noche todos los gatos son ruidosos," "A quien madruga Dios le da sueno" etc. Here there is no marking or exegesis and the perlocutionary effect is virtually identical to that of the ST.

Perlocution in Practice

I now propose to exemplify how in some texts (legal) very strong marking and very weak exegesis may contribute to perlocutionary equivalence, in others (literary) weak marking and weak exegesis may achieve the same objective, while in yet others (humorous) very weak or no marking or exegesis together with recontextualisation may be effective. In Table 1 what I hope to show is as follows:

Table 1

Type	Perlocution	Marking	Exegesis	Recontextualisation
Legal	inform etc.	very strong	very weak	—
Literary	evoke etc.	weak	weak	—
Humorous	amuse etc.	—		very strong

The concept of marking, strictly speaking, conflicts with that of perlocution because, if we interpret marking literally, we reduce all TTs to the function of informing. If a text begins with a mark signaling: "The text of which the following is a translation says that ... " then it can literally or directly perform no speech act other than that of informing its readers of what the ST says, does and is capable of bringing about, just as a person who reports that a third party is performing, or has performed, a certain act is not, by doing so, herself performing any act other than reporting. Yet, of course, we are accustomed to being affected—and very deeply—by indirect speech, not to mention indirect speech acts. It still remains, however, that all the effects produced on the TT reader will be *de facto* at one remove from the ST. Just as an intended addressee's wife or casual visitor may react differently to a bill addressed to the intended addressee, so also—but no more so—a reader of a TT may react differently to the TT from the way in which the original ST readers reacted.

This, it seems to me, is an intrinsic feature of translation and is itself neither positive nor negative.

Legal Translation

Legal translation covers a wide range of texts, from a country's Constitution or Acts of Parliament, to a single-sentence fax from a client to a legal adviser, with all sorts of public and private documents, forms and paperwork in between, having in common only some link with the Law. However, we may generalize and say that legal texts usually make or amend the law or regulate relationships between persons, being informative, explicative and factual, rather than literary or humorous, often referring in specialized terminology and complex style to realities, concepts and distinctions that are not material, concrete or physical.

Any translation must, as I have said, be capable of potentially (that is, given an appropriate reader and context) affecting its readers in whatever way the ST was capable of doing to its readers: for example, moving them to take or refrain from taking some action, including feelings produced by illocutionary acts (such as thanking or promising) that some authorities explicitly argue are not perlocutionary and which, as it happens, frequently occur in legal documents (see Davis, 1980: 47).

Indexical or deictic expressions, which acquire their meaning directly from some features of the situation in which they are uttered (such as "I" or the first person singular of verbs), will usually appear in some very similar form in the TT, since this will normally produce analogous effects to those produced by the ST. However, some referring expressions (like "the Law," "the Constitution," "our Criminal Justice system" or "the Sale of Goods Act") may require "marking" to show that they refer to realities in the ST culture and not in the TT culture: "the Spanish Law," "the French Constitution," "the Senegalese Criminal Justice system," "the English Sale of Goods Act" etc. This is one form of marking and an alternative to labeling the whole text at or near the beginning.

We may assume that a translation of a translation, whether into a third language or back into the source language (in which case it will presumably be done either in ignorance of its TT status or as an attempt to recover the original, and in no case can it be attributed to the author of the ST, since it is highly unlikely to reproduce her words), is doubly marked. This would mean something like: "Another text says that an original text says that … " Interestingly, this indirectness reflects quite accurately the intuition that each translation takes the reader one step away from the original text, which is, in a way, the point I am treating under the heading of marking.

I come now to exemplify exegesis. Let us imagine that an English lawyer drafts a memo to his trainee saying: "Re So GA, see 1 All ER 135 1987 and advise." The intended reader understands that this concerns the Sale of Goods Act 1979 and he is to look up Volume I of *the All England Law Reports* 1987 and let his boss know whether the decision in the case reported on page 135 (Aswan Engineering Establishment Co. versus Lupdine Ltd.) is relevant to a case on which they are engaged at present. The TT must produce analoguous effects in a Spannish lawyer and this will be achieved by spelling out "Sale of Goods Act 1979" and "Volume I *All England Law Reports* 1987" and by translating "advise" as meaning "inform me of your findings." However, an English lawyer will be familiar with the Sale of Goods Act and will know whether, for example, if the thing to be sold is a crop of wheat growing in a field at the time the contract is made, this will be counted as "goods" for the purposes of the Act, whereas a Spanish lawyer might not know this or even see its relevance. Nevertheless, it is no part of the translator's task to provide an exegesis of this or any other substantive point of law. The translator must ask herself how the original text reader would have been affected and ensure that an analogical TT reader will be affected similarly by his reading of the text (hence his marking and spelling out) but not by any other means. She will thus be expected to explicate anything that is explicated in the text surface and nothing else.

Take another example: an English text about a Coroner's Court is to be translated into Spanish, Spain being a country which has nothing exactly like a coroner. Since it is no part of the translator's task to teach her TT reader about the English system relating to coroners, she will have fulfilled her function if she drafts a TT which can produce on a (notional) reader who knows what a coroner is an analogous effect to that which the ST was likely to have on the ST reader, using any term for "coroner" (including "coroner," "forense," "Juez," "juez correspondiente"... but perhaps not "medico foense," as this might lead to misunderstandings because of its similarities and differences from the coroner), which will trigger in the TT reader recognition without adding information not explicit in the ST: any information on the coroner's functions, methods of working, relationships with other officials or the legal system (and perhaps especially how he differs from the Spanish "medico forense") would constitute exegesis in my sense.

In particular, I suggest that a translator should not over-assimilate concepts or realities in the source and target cultures. This becomes relevant, for example, in cases of synecdoche or metonymy, where one system may use the name of part of something to refer to the whole and vice versa, or may simply name something closely associated with something else. In English to say that a car "passed its MOT" means that it passed its annual roadworthiness test, even though the Ministry of Transport (MOT) fulfils countless functions other than overseeing this test: so a phrase meaning "annual test" would provide a reasonable translation and it would be *ultra vires* if the translator were to give further information. Similarly, in Spanish "Hacienda" (referring to the Ministry of Finance, though containing no over mention of any ministry, and much less of any particular branch of the ministry) is the normal word corresponding to "Income Tex" or the "Inland Revenue," and these would provide reasonable translations without further explanation. In cases like these also, marking without exegesis might be the most appropriate translation procedure.

To sum up, then, legal texts being very culture-based or culture-specific, many of the concepts, realities and terms which condition them will not be readily accessible to readers of their translations. A TT should show therefore, by clear marking, that it is a translation, and this exonerates, indeed precludes, it from explaining the realities, concepts or terms; rather, it leaves them as they are, translated but unexplained, within the frame-work of the marked text so that the reader may seek legal advice or explanation exactly as he would if confronted by a technical text in his own language.

Literary Translation

Here I have in mind mainly novels and short stories which, according to Pratt (1977: 143, referring to Grice and Searle), "fall into the class whose primary point is thought-producing, representative or world-describing," rather than action-stimulating. The pragmatic status of such texts may be unsettled (see Pratt, 1977: 90; Searle, 1979: 58 - 75 for claims that fiction seems to pretend to perform speech acts), but in any case their perlocutionary effects must be safeguarded in translation.

Indeed, although Austin included under perlocution both overt, objective, actions on the hearer's part (like shooting someone) and although clearly some literary works may stimulate readers to take action, it is more normal and perhaps more essential that they induce or evoke in the reader some purely natural reaction: aesthetic experiences of pleasure, feelings of appreciation, enjoyment or admiration, images and mental activities such as relating singular characters or events to general or universal levels of meaning.

Although some aspects of literary texts, such as the story, characters, descriptions of places etc., usually "carry over" fairly easily from an ST to a TT, yet even these "transferable" realities will elicit somewhat different reactions in the TT reader: at some psychological or aesthetic level, any reader of a translation will react differently from a reader of the original. Nevertheless, the aspects of the ST which are more directly related to the language, including the stylistic choices, figures of speech and other language-specific features, tend to give translators more difficulty.

What kind of perlocution should the literary translator aim at? Should she try to adapt the whole work to the target culture, for example, situating a vovel originally set in Barcelona in Manchester and changing the Ramblas into Market Street or Deansgate? Should she replace original proper names with English ones? Should she, in short, present the TT as an original text, as if it had been written in English in the first place? The most realistic answer to these questions is that, in practice, this is not done: translators do not present translated literary works as originals (see Newmark, 1981:70 - 83). It is partly by marking the TT as such, signaling in effect, "The following is a translation of a Spanish novel," that the translator can offer the TT reader the opportunity of experiencing the aesthetic effects offered by the original. In fact, part of the marking may take the form of leaving names of characters and places, of institutions and other sociocultural realities, in the original language.

This differs from an original English work set in a foreign place in that the presuppositions, psychologies and values of such a work will be English and even the descriptions will be those selected by an English writer for English readers.

Within these constraints, a translator may make a list or inventory, however mental or approximate, of the strategies and features of the ST which seem to be directly transferable and then ask herself whether she can evoke in her TT readers effects analogous to all of those evoked in the ST by "reproducing" these features in the target language or whether some other steps are required.

The markings situate the reader in a context or situation foreign to him, thus compensating for any interstices that remain after the translator has done his best to provide—usually in the form of presupposition (see Hickey et al., 1993a, 1993b) or other style-preserving means—any relevant background information that an ST reader would be likely to possess but a TT reader might not. In other words, the fact that the intended readership is, and is marked as being, different from the original readership will tacitly justify the fact that certain features are "spelled out." For example, Hickey et al. (1993b) suggest that "Coronation Street" in an English novel might be translated into Spanish as "el culebron" "Coronation Street" (lit., "the soap opera 'Coronation Street'"); "suburban gardens" might become "jardines tipicos de aquellas zonas residenciales" (lit. "gardens typical of those residential areas," since "suburban" suggests to Spanish readers inner-city slums); and intertextual references to a "brave new world" might be elucidated as "Huxley reconoceria su Mundo feliz" (lit. "Huxley would recognize his brave new world").

The perlocution in these cases is effected by conveying to the TT reader just sufficient information about the "content" and "using a style that will evoke in him approximately the same reaction as would have been evoked in an ST reader," who would know that "Coronation Street" was a soap opera, that suburbn gardens are usually well kept and, perhaps, that *Brave New World* is the title of a book. When I say "style," I refer basically to the fact that no translator's note, additional sentence of explanation calling attention to itself need be used, but rather that the clarifications appear as brief presupposition-bearing adjectival or adverbial phrases.

In literary translation, as I have already suggested, the marking may be weak since the text is not essentially set in the ST world but is usually universal in its import. The exegesis may also be fairly weak because it will normally refer to realities that are "accidentally" culture-based but might have coincided with those of the target or any other culture. Unlike legal translation, where exegesis might well involve technical or professional explanations of concepts, institutionals and terminology, where such exegesis would be for denotational purposes only and would lie outside the competence of a translator who was not also a qualified lawyer, whose mistakes might have horrendous consequences, and where the text would make sense without exegesis, in literary translation, exegesis will involve only general world knowledge of realities and cultural concepts, it will be for detonational and, more crucially, connotational purposes, a normal translator will be qualified to provide it, if she gets it wrong, the consequences will be "purely" literary, not extraliterary, and the text will make little sense without it.

One aspect of literary exegesis that merits special mention is the question of time deixis. I refer to the fact that literary works remain for ever as they were originally drafted, whereas a translation may be done at any time after that date; consequently the language and all linguistic features may be chosen for the TT in relation to the moment either of the original composition, of the translation itself or of some moment in between. This is relevant to perlocution in that the effects caused on a reader of the ST will differ depending on, among other factors, when he is reading it, since as time elapses the context will become more and more distant from that of the original. A literary translation, therefore, being a weakly marked text, may attempt to replace a corresponding ST context with a later (for example, contemporary) TT context, arguing that a reader of the original ST would equally have been in a contemporary ST context. Since a translation can carry marks—such as diachronically significant language features—situating it in virtually any time relationship to the St, a translator will have to consider the perlocutionary effect potentially accessible to her TT readers.

My suggestion, then, is that literary translators consider the possibility of balancing some marking (situating the text openly in its original context, leaving proper names etc.) with some exegesis (conveying a degree of background information in a non-instrusive manner), thus offering the TT reader an aesthetic experience similar to that of the original readers' and evoking a perlocutionary effect or effects analogous to theirs.

Translation of Humour

The perlocutionary effect usually associated with humorous texts is recognition and appreciation of some kind of innocuous incongruity or non-threatening inappropriateness (see Chapman & Foot, 1976; McGhee, 1979; McGhee & Goldstein, 1983) either in the linguistic level of a text or in the positional content, with the reader's consequent amusement often manifested in a (more or less overtly articulated) laugh, smile or cringe, depending on the context, personality, mood and social manners of the reader. Three considerations of particular relevance to this type of translation deserve mention or reiteration.

First, if a translation of the ST is to arouse in a TT reader an effect analogous to that aroused or potentially aroused in an ST reader, it will not in the ST or to "explain the joke," for example, by presenting an analysis of the basis on which it is founded, such as an ambiguity or pun in the source language. In other words, no amount of exegesis is likely to bring about perlocutionary equivalence in this type of translation; on the contrary attempts to explain a humorous text usually end up boring the reader and killing the humour.

Second, the strength of the perlocutionary effect should be roughly similar in both texts; for example, the translation of a text which is likely to provoke only a cringe of embarrassment does not need—indeed, strictly speaking, should not, (though this will seldom be criticized)—provoke a hearty guffaw. Third, although a perlocution should be caused by a text that bears the closest possible similarity to the locution and illocution of the ST, in the case of humourous texts this is usually of secondary importance and is frequently impossible or irrelevant to the production of the desired perlocution (see Hickey, forthcoming). Of course, if the locution and illocution are, in the translator's opinion, capable of evoking a reaction in the TT reader analogous to that of the ST reader, then she can translate as she would a literary text, and in fact humourous texts share with literature many features: "tellability" (see Pratt, 1977: 136 – 147), narration and description of events and situations, dialogue etc.

If, however, the perlocution depends on a specifically linguistic or intertextual feature, then she could extricate the underlying formula on which the potential effect is based and there upon generate another, new, text or joke in the target language, keeping as close as possible, or relevant, to the propositional content of the original. Whether the new text will in itself provide sufficient similarity with the original text will depend on the overall desired perlocutionary effect: if the text was essentially about some topic that was central to the discourse, this topic will have to survive reformulation even at the cost of some other aspect of the perlocution, whereas if the text is relatively "free-standing" and independent of the discourse, then, so long as the formula is respected and maintained, the TT will count as a translation.

For example, in Sharpe (1982: 18) much of the reader's amusement derives from the protagonist's inability to distinguish the metaphorical from the literal meaning of language; when a teacher in anger tells him to get lost, the boy hides in a barn ten miles away and the police with Alsatians have to search for him. Here the "formula" consists of acting on the literal sense of an idiom which is normally understood only metaphorically; the perlocutionary effect derives from the double meaning and an inappropriate choice. In a TT, any similarly metaphorical idiom may be used: for example, in Spanish a companion of the boy may suggest to him "que de un sablazo al professor de ingles, y al dia siguiente le encuentran con un dedo de menos," but he is unable to claim the money he thinks he has been promised for groping the master, because the punishment meted out to him for such indecent intimacy has left him in the infirmary for three days.

Let us take an example of humour which is directly dependent on a lexical ambiguity. In San-Antonio (1991:19) the narrator says of his driver "Il a reçu des instructions (à défaut d'instruction)" a mild run on the word "instruction," meaning both instructions and education. A translator might decide to translate this as "He has received his far from holy orders," where the perlocutionary effect—mild amusement—is not transferred or conveyed but rather recreated on the basis of the same formula as the ST. On the same basis, and remembering that the potential perlocutionary effect (mild amusement) is the aim, other perlocutionary causes might have been set up: "He had not been well trained, or bussed either for that matter," "He was never properly taught, indeed he was quite lax," "The office floor was carpeted and so was he" etc.

Exegesis, therefore, is normally neither required nor appropriate in translating humour, at least in the sense of "explaining the joke," since the perlocution depends on "seeing" the fun or incongruity and enjoying it as a result of grasping both levels: the incongruity and an alternative congruity at the same time. Decontextualisation withdraws the text from its original setting in so far as may be necessary to reformulate it, or recycle the formula, either in a new context—more or less relevant to the discourse of the TT—or in a neutral context. This process or device also removes the need for marking: since the reader does not have to situate himself in a new context or culture, no very visible marking will serve any purpose.

It will be obvious that I have applied only to three types of translation the suggestion that a TT's effectiveness in bringing about perlocutionary effects analogous to those of the ST may depend directly on its strength of marking, degree of exegesis and use of decontextualisation. The validity or usefulness of the suggestion itself, not to mention its applicability to other types of translation, remains to be tested.

选文三　Pragmatic Aspects of Translation: Some Relevance-Theory Observations

Ernst-August Gutt

导　言

这里推荐的文章选自利奥·希基主编的《翻译的语用学研究》。作者古特(Ernst-August Gutt)是德国学者,最早将语言学中的关联理论用于翻译研究。他在其专著《翻译与关联》(*Translation and Relevance*)中指出,翻译是一种言语交际行为,是与大脑机制密切联系的推理过程,不仅涉及语码的转换,更重要的是根据动态的语境进行动态的推理,而推理所依据的就是关联性。作为交际的翻译,在源语的理解和翻译过程中,人们对语码的选择所依赖的也是关联性。他还指出,翻译中译文是否能提供最佳语境效果,寻求译文的最佳关联是翻译成功与否的关键。在翻译中,一是译文要与"译文读者产生充分的关联",或"提供充分的语境效果",二是译文表达的方式"让译文读者无须付出任何不必要的努力",在这一原则下,译者应该以寻求最佳的关联作为翻译的指南。

Introduction

This chapter focuses on two important aspects of translation: the notion of "translation" itself, and the significance of changes in context often involved in translation work. Both topics are looked at from the perspective of the relevance theory of communication as developed by Sperber & Wilson (1986, 1995), which I believe provides concepts that can help to better understand the nature of translation and some of the problems it typically involves.

Basics of Relevance Theory

Since this study is founded on the relevance-theory framework, a few essential concepts of relevance theory are briefly introduced here.

The Inferential Nature of Communication

According to relevance theory, communication not only requires encoding, transfer and decoding processes, but crucially involves inference in addition. Consider the following exchange:

Example 1

(a) Joe: "Will Sarah be long?"

(b) Pam: "She is with Frank now."

Pam does not answer Joe's question directly; rather, she informs Pam that Sarah is with Frank. Now as case A, let us assume that Frank is known to be very quick with people; usually he deals with a matter in a few minutes. In this case, Joe would gather from Pam's answer that Sarah will not be long.

Alternatively, let us imagine a case B where Frank is known to be someone whose office you could never leave in under half an hour. In this situation Joe would understand that Sarah would indeed be long.

How can the same utterance convey opposite meanings? The obvious reason is that its meaning depends, not only on its semantic content, but crucially on the context in which it is interpreted or, more technically, on the contextual information with which it is inferentially combined:

Case A

Premise 1	Utterance	Sarah is with Frank now.
Premise 2	Context A	Frank does not take long with people.
Conclusion	Implication	Frank will not take long with Sarah.

Case B

| Premise 1 | Utterance | Sarah is with Frank now. |

| Premise 2 | Context B | Frank keeps people a long time. |
| Conclusion | Implication | Frank will keep Sarah a long time. |

One rather obvious point of this illustration is that the success of communication can depend very much on whether the audience uses the right, that is, the speaker-intended, context. The use of wrong contextual information can lead to a complete failure of the communication attempt. This is in turn raises the question: if the use of the right context is so crucial, how can it be achieved? In preparation for addressing that question, something needs to be said about the notion of context as understood in relevance theory.

Context

In relevance theory, the notion of context of an utterancer is "a psychological construct, a subset of the hearer's assumptions about the world"; more specifically, it is "the set of premises used in interpreting [that] utterance (Sperber & Wilson, 1986:15)." Under this definition, "context" is a very wide notion that can include virtually any phenomenon entertainable by the human mind:

> A context in this sense is not limited to information about the immediately physical environment or the immediately preceding utterances: expectations about the future, scientific hypotheses or religious beliefs, anecdotal memories, general cultural assumptions, beliefs about the mental state of the speaker, may all play a role in interpretation. (Sperber & Wilson, 1986:15f.).

Note that this notion of context also includes the text surrounding an utterance, what has sometimes been called the "co-text."

A second important characteristic of context in relevance theory is that it is assumed to be organized, and that this organization affects the accessibility of a particular piece of contextual information on a particular occasion. For example, having just talked about childhood memories, information about some of your toys may be very easily accessible. On another occasion, though, it might take considerable effort required to recall it. With this clarification about context we now return to the question of how it is possible for hearers to find and use the contextual information which the speaker intended them to use and which is necessary for understanding her correctly.

Optimal Relevance

According to Sperber & Wilson (1986, 1995), the central factor that makes communication succeed is the pursuit of *optimal relevance* on the part of both the communicator and the addressee. An utterance is optimally relevant (a) when it enables the audience to find without unnecessary effort the meaning intended by the communicator and (b) when that intended meaning is worth the audience's effort, that is, when it provides adequate benefits to the audience. These benefits are psychological in nature; they consist in modifications of a person's knowledge and are referred to technically as "positive contextual effects." The function of optimal relevance in communication is captured in the principle of relevance, which is believed to be an innate constraint in our human psychological make up. According to this principle, whenever a person sets out to communicate something, she automatically communicates the presumption that what she is going to say is believed to be optimally relevant to the audience.

It is this claim to optimal relevance which guides the recipient in identifying the speaker-intended context for a given utterance in the following way. It makes him expect that the contextual information needed for the correct interpretation is readily accessible. Hence he begins the interpretation process from information most readily available to him at that time. Furthermore, he will assume that, when combined with the right context, the utterance will yield an interpretation that is worth the effort invested in processing it.

On these assumptions, the recipient will proceed with the interpretation process until he arrives at an interpretation that fulfils both conditions: it is derivable without unnecessary effort and yields adequate contextual effects. In other words, the claim to optimal relevance leads the hearer to accept the first interpretation consistent with the principle of relevance as the right, that is, the speaker-intended interpretation. Thus, the search for optimal relevance guides the hearer not only to the speaker-intended context but also to the speaker-intended interpretation. It should be added here that people are not usually aware of these interpretation processes in their minds; they take place subconsciously.

Interpretive and Descriptive Use of Language

One of the important claims of relevance theory is that there are two psychologically distinct modes of using language: the descriptive use and the interpretive use. Since these two terms are not necessarily self-explanatory they are now briefly introduced.

A language utterance is said to be used descriptively when it is intended to be taken as true of a state of affairs in some possible world.

An utterance is said to be used interpretively when it is intended to represent what someone said or thought.

Example 2

(a) Melody: "Fred and Judy have got a divorce."

(b) Melody: "Harry said, 'Fred and Judy have got a divorce'."

Both examples contain the utterance "Fred and Judy have got a divorce." In the first example Melody uses that utterance to claim that the state of affairs it describes is true. In other words, she maintains that it is true that Fred and Judy have got a divorce. She is using that utterance descriptively. She would be wrong if Fred and Judy were not divorced.

In example (2b), however, Melody does not (necessarily) claim that Fred and Judy have got a divorce; all she does is reporting what someone else said. Therefore, here the utterance is used interpretively. Melody's utterance in (2b) would not be wrong if Fred and Judy had not got a divorce, but it would be wrong if Harry had not, in fact, made that statement.

Interpretive Resemblance and Faithfulness

The crucial factor in interpretive use is that there be a relationship of interpretive resemblance between the original utterance and that used to represent it. Such interpretive resemblance between utterances consists in the sharing of explicatures and implicatures. This implies that resemblance is a matter of degree. Thus, two utterances interpretively resemble each other more closely, the more explicatures or implicatures they share. A direct quotation, as in example (2b), shows the highest degree of resemblance to the original: it shares all explicatures and implicatures of the original, though only under one important condition, to which we shall return below—that is, that the direct quotation is interpreted in the same context as the original.

By contrast, excerpts, paraphrases, summaries etc. can vary a great deal as to the degree and kind of resemblance they show. Thus if asked about the content of a particular lecture, the respondent or reporter would have a range of options open for her reply.

> This raises the important question of what will determine which kind of report the speaker will give? Being engaged in interpretive use, the speaker will aim at interpretive resemblance to the original; being constrained by the principle of relevance, she will aim at resemblance in those aspects which she believes will satisfy the expectation of optimal relevance. Thus, in interpretive use, the utterance of the speaker comes with a claim to faithfulness.
>
> The speaker guarantees that her utterance is a faithful enough representation of the original: that is, resembles it closely enough in relevant respects. (Wilson & Sperber, 1988: 137).

So if the reporter knows that the recipient is quite interested in the lecture as a whole, she will use option (3a), giving much detail. If she is aware that there is only one part which the recipient would find relevant, she is likely to choose option (3b), concentrating on that part of the lecture and so forth. Hence we find that relevance theory comes with a ready-made, context-sensitive concept of faithfulness, applying to the interpretive use of language in general.

The Pragmatic Role of the Notion of "Translation"

Translation as an Interpretive Use of Language

From the relevance-theory point of view, translation falls naturally under the interpretive use of language: the translation is intended to restate in one language what someone else said or wrote in another language. In principle it is, therefore, comparable to quoting or speech-reporting in intra-linguistic use. One of its primary distinctions setting it off from intra-lingual quoting or reporting is that original text and translation belong to different languages.

It follows that, as an instance of interpretive use, translation will also be constrained by the notion of faithfulness introduced above. In other words, the translator will design her translation in such a way that it "resembles [the original] closely enough in relevant respects"(Wilson & Sperber, 1988:137).

Up to here things might seem straightforward enough were it not for the term and concept called "translation." In order to understand the rather ambivalent function of this term, let us consider the role of labels for types of texts or acts of communication in general.

Text Typologies as Guides to Relevance

As for many other phenomena in our world, so also for communication people have coined particular terms to distinguish between particular kinds of texts or utterances. For example, we talk about eulogies and summaries, novels and comic strips, commentaries and abstracts, text books and hymn books and so forth.

From a general communication point of view, such terms can serve a significant purpose: they can help to coordinate the intentions of the communicator with the expectations of the audience. For example, when the communicator presents her utterance as a "report," this will trigger different expectations in the audience that if she called it a "satire" or a "curriculum vitae." In this way labels referring to different kinds of communication can fulfil an important pragmatic function in coordinating the activities of communicator and audience.

From the relevance-theory point of view, by the appropriate use of such labels the communicator can guide the audience in their search for optimal relevance; for example, when given something called "a novel" to read, one would be looking for the plot, for the way in which characters are portrayed, for values, attitudes and so forth. One would not necessarily seek the intended relevance of such a book to lie in historical accuracy, objectivity of presentation, quality and quantity of source materials used and the like, all of which would be of high relevance for a historical reference work, for example.

So, by labeling her work a "novel" rather than a "historical reference work," the author guides the potential audience to the ways in which she intends her work to achieve relevance. Hence, such typological labels can be helpful in guiding the audience towards the intended interpretation, and thus reducing the processing cost for the audience. In this sense, text-typological labels can serve to increase the relevance of a text or utterance, hence performing a pragmatic function.

Naturally, this relevance-increasing effect of text-type labels crucially depends on how well the types used by communicator and audience respectively agree with each other. The less they agree

253

the less helpful they will be in the communication process. For example, if your publisher's idea of an abstract significantly differs from your own, then the chances are that the abstract you have written of a paper of yours will not be satisfactory to him and vice versa.

The Notion of "Translation"

As a glance at the voluminous literature on translation shows, the terms "translation" appears to be a prime example of a text-typological lable which lacks a generally agreed definition. As a result, more often than not, it has caused confusion rather than aided the coordination of intentions and expectations. Over the centuries, scholars have tried time and again to define or settle what translation is, only to find that every new proposal has been doomed to be found inadequate or simply wrong by some school of critics. The resulting state of affairs is well summarized by Söll's dictum that "the history of translation theory [can] be thought of as a discussion of the polysemy of the word 'translation'"(1968: 161, quoted in Wilss, 1982:28).

When one meets an object of science as recalcitrant as this, an object which appears to defy all attempts at satisfactory definition or description, it may be best to stand back a little and ask some basic questions, such as what kind of reality there is in the object under investigation.

At a first glance, the answer to this question may seem obvious: there are thousands and thousands of books and articles that are all called "translations." So, surely, they are the reality we need to look at when we want to find out what translation is.

Unfortunately, matters are more complex than that. As soon as the scientist examines the speciments in front of him, he is likely to start sorting them out; removing some on the grounds that they are not translations and hence do not belong to the corpus. He may, on the other hand, include speciments that had not been considered part of the corpus before. In this way, the scientist finds himself in a vicious circle: his examination of the corpus will always be seen to support what his notion of translation was *a priori*.

As a result, not only has no generally accepted notion of translation emerged, but it seems difficult, in principle, to define the domain of this investigation in non-circular terms. Moreover, if relevance theory is right, there are no grounds to assume that such a naturally distinct domain should exist. As previously mentioned, the core relation between the translation and the original is one of interpretive resemblance, which we further defined as the sharing of explicatures and implicatures between the two texts. As such, interpretive resemblance appears as a scalar notion, ranging from zero-shared explicatures and implicatures, at the other. To the extent that this view is correct, there is no reason to assume that somewhere on that scale there is a non-arbitrary point that would separate translations from non-translations.

However, even this scalar view is still a gross oversimplification of the real situation since there can be variation not only in the number of shared explicatures and implicatures, but also in which particular ex- or implicatures are shared. Hence, there could be a large number of translations of the same original, all of which shared roughly the same number of explicatures and implicatures with the original, but which still would be quite different from each other in content since the particular ex- and implicatures shared would be rather different from one text to another.

Against this background, there appears to be very little reason to expect that one day a reasonably well-defined and generally accepted notion of translation will emerge.

This state of affairs might look deplorable until we ask ourselves: what does it matter? As far as explaining how and why translations work is concerned, relevance theory provides a fairly explicit account of translations as instances of the interpretive use of language across language boundaries, and it does so without needing to introduce theoretical notions that would presuppose a definition of translation. Then central concepts of interpretive resemblance and faithfulness already exist in the theory apart from translation.

What, then, is the significance of the term "translation"? The way we introduced it earlier was as a potential aid to facilitate that correct interpretation of the translated product by the target audience. In this way, the concept of translation is seen as playing a role similar to other text categories, such as "novel," "poem," "essay," "abstract" etc. Whatever their scientific status or otherwise might be, all these categories can be of value in pragmatic terms, coordinating the efforts of communicator and audience in their pursuit of optimal relevance—always provided that there is sufficient agreement about these terms between communicator and audience.

What successful communication does require is consistency with the principle of relevance and, as part of that, the use of the right contextual information when processing the utterance. The assignment of a particular act of communication to some category can be of help with this, but it is not necessary condition for communicative success; there are other ways in which the communicator can inform her audience of how she intends her text to be understood, for example, by means of introductory remarks, comments or the like. When there is any doubt whether the translator's notion of translation is sufficiently similar to that held by her audience, she would do well to sate clearly at an appropriate place how she has understood her task as translator.

Context-based Problems in Translation

Another primarily pragmatic aspect of translation has to do with context. It was shown earlier that the same utterance can have opposite interpretations, depending on the context in which it is processed. This means that the correct, that is, the speaker-intended, interpretation of an utterance, is highly context-dependent. The reason for this strong context-dependence lies in the inferential nature of human communication. Against this background, it is easy to understand why a change of context can change the whole meaning of an utterance and why, therefore, "quoting someone out of context" can be a rather serious matter.

Unfortunately, the process of translation often, though not necessarily always, involves this very situation: by translating a text for a target audience with a cultural background other than that envisioned by the original writer, the translator is, in effect, quoting the original author "out of context." Since the notion of "quoting out of context" usually has a negative ring to it, I prefer to call all instances where a text is presented to an audience with a context different from the one originally envisaged as "secondary communication situations" (cf. Gutt, 1991:72ff.).

The problems arising from differences in context have not gone unnoticed in the literature on translation. Best known is perhaps Schleiermacher's often-quoted distinction:

> The translator can either leave the writer in peace as much as possible and bring the reader to him, or he can leave the reader in peace as much as possible and bring the writer to him (Schleiermacher, 1838:47, as translated in Wilss, 1982: 33).

"Bringing the reader to the original text" would correspond to requiring him to process the translation in the context of the original: "[The translator] thus tries to transport [the reader] to its location, which, in all reality, is foreign to him"(Schleiermacher, 1838:219, as translated in Wilss, 1982:33). By contrast, "bringing the writer to the reader" would correspond to adapting the text to the context of the target readers.

While the difference between these two approaches to translation has been recognized, it seems that the nature of the problem and some of its ramifications have not been well understood.

Thus the supposed dilemma of translation, that it can either be faithful without being beautiful or beautiful but not faithful, is not limited to translation but can, in principle, affect all instances of the interpretive use of language. The use of verbally accurate quotations out of context, that is, in a context not envisaged by the original communicator, can occur, whether language barriers are crossed or not.

It may thus be helpful for the translator to realize that not all the problems she encounters in translating a text are problems peculiar to translation. Indeed, any text transferred from its original context to a different one is likely to be affected in its meaning by that change, even when there is no change of language involved. For example, when reading literature in our own language from a time period or setting other than our own, problems can arise due to differences in context.

We may then ask how such problems are usually addressed when they occur within the same language. With quotes out of context, the remedy is mostly to point out what the right context was. With problems in literary writings, it is usually seen as the reader's responsibility to familiarize himself with the historical and cultural background of a particular piece of literature to ensure correct understanding. This is one of the skills taught at school when dealing with literature. Sometimes the publisher intervenes and provides various explanatory notes to the text to help the reader overcome the problems. Very rarely, however, is the publisher expected or prepared to alter the text itself when it seems that the modern context could lead to a wrong understanding. Such alternations of the text are usually limited to special editions for children or other specified audiences, but then it is normally indicated that one is dealing with an adaptation of some kind rather than with the original itself.

Once made aware of the difference between context-based problems, on the one hand, and language-based problems, on the other, the translator may be in a better position to judge what a suitable solution might be.

When encountering a problem due to linguistic or lexical differences, these are peculiar to translation, arising when language barriers are crossed. Assuming that a central part of the translator's task is to help the audience overcome the language barrier, these problems need to be dealt with in the text by the translator. If the reader is expected to figure out problems in the translation that require knowledge of the lexicon or linguistic structure of the original language, then the question arises as to what the point of translating the text is.

However, when dealing with a problem caused by contextual differences, the translator should ask herself whether she could or even should address this problem by amending the translated text or whether other means need to be sought. This is especially true when the differences in context are extensive and would require major reworking of the text.

More importantly, perhaps, without a clear understanding of the nature of communication problems in translation, the translator may not be aware that significant mismatches in contextual information can not only lead to wrong meaning here and there, but can jeopardise the communicability of substantial parts of the original or even of the original as a whole.

The reason for this risk lies in the principle of relevance, which for successful communication requires consistency with the requirement of optimal relevance; such consistency, however, is always context-dependent. The writer of the original was concerned for her text to be optimally relevant in the context which she assumed the original audience to have. She would not normally be concerned with the question of whether her text would be optimally relevant in any other context.

To take a fairly drastic example, in the Bible the writer of the Epistle to the Hebrews devotes the first two chapters almost completely to the question of the position of Jesus Christ relative to that of the angels. From the evidence we have, this was apparently an important issue for the audience he was writing for at that time. It provided them with answers to burning questions they had in their day and age. Transfer this text to a present-day, Western-type audience, and most of them will find it difficult to process this text, no matter how well it is translated, the main reason being that the information provided there does not readily link up with the contextual information they bring to this text, and hence may not seem worth their while spending effort on. In this sense, the whole text may not be communicable to the receptor audience.

This is not to say that the text cannot be made sufficiently relevant to such an audience. Relevance can be increased, for example, by providing further background information, that is, by making accessible to them enough of the context of the original for them to appreciate its relevance. However, without such help the content of the original may well remain largely uncommunicable.

Once aware of the problems arising in secondary communication situations, translators can anticipate them and look for appropriate means to overcome them, which may well go beyond the usual task of translation and may require strategies for widening the contextual knowledge of the target audience by additional means.

As a caveat, I would like to point out clearly that this does not mean that it is possible in every case to draw a sharp distinction between communication problems as against language-based ones, just as it is not always possible to distinguish cognitive content from context. There will often be an overlap. Nevertheless, a greater awareness and better understanding of the different aspects of problems encountered while translating should help the translator to deal more appropriately with them.

Conclusion

To sum up, the two main claims made are, first, that translation itself is primarily a pragmatic notion, used to indicate the kind of communication intended by the communicator. Its communication-facilitating role will depend on how similar the notion of translation held by the translator and the notion held by the audience are to each other. If necessary, the translator may have to consider measures to bring those notions closer together.

Second, one of the main difficulties faced by the translator is again a pragmatic one: the fact, that very often in translation there is a difference, not only of language, but also of context. This problem is not peculiar to translation but occurs in all secondary communication situations. The translator needs to be aware of it in order to judge the degree of its effects correctly and to look for appropriate solutions.

It is hoped that a better understanding of these pragmatic problems will enable translators to increase the likelihood of success in their work.

【延伸阅读】

[1] Gutt, E.-A. (1991). *Translation and Relevance: Cognition and Context*. Oxford: Blackwell.

[2] Hickey, L. (2001). *The Pragmatics of Translation*. Shanghai: Shanghai Foreign Language Education Press.

【问题与思考】

1. 翻译这一选择过程中,关联对于译者来说起到怎样的作用? 请用古特的观点来阐述这一问题。

2. 什么是语境? 结合具体实例说明语境这一概念对于翻译的重要意义。

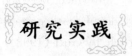

Contextualization in Translator
—And Interpreter-Mediated Events

Mona Baker

导 言

语境是语用学理论中的核心概念,语境理论是语用学理论中的重要组成部分。翻译不是在真空中进行的,译者在翻译的过程中必然要考虑到翻译这一交际行为面对新的读者和新的语境所引发的问题。这里推荐的文章首次发表在 2006 年 3 月《语用学》(*Journal of Pragmatics*,第 38 卷,第 3 期),主要探讨了语用学中两个相关概念"语境"和"语境化"在翻译研究中的应用。

Most of the central notions in the study of translation—at least the most illuminating—have always been rather elusive and difficult to pin down. This reflects the highly complex nature of the translation act. Like the very material in which it mostly takes shape, namely language, the act of translation is deeply embedded in wider social and cultural practices.

During periods and within scholarly traditions in which researchers focused on the internal mechanisms of language, the analysis of translation and interpreting events seemed relatively straightforward, if not particularly illuminating. The exclusive focus on internal mechanisms could not continue for long, however, and as scholars of both language and translation increasingly acknowledge the dynamic and negotiable aspects of both phenomena, they find that they inevitably have to draw on more fluid notions such as context, culture, power and ideology. Many have attempted to address the question of what the concept of culture means and how it impacts on translational behaviour; Katan (1999/2004) is the most recent and extensive treatment of this issue. Others have tried to tackle the notion of ideology in similar ways; the most recent treatment is by Calzada Pe′rez (2003). Very few have addressed the notion of power, among them Tymoczko (2000:31 - 34) and Tymoczko & Gentzler (2002). Yet, although the notion of context is routinely invoked in much of the literature on translation and interpreting, it is hardly ever subjected to scrutiny in its own right. In fact, no scholarly publication within linguistics or translation studies has yet attempted to explore the issue of context as it impacts on translational behaviour in any depth. [①] Even Hickey (1998), the only collection dedicated to the interface between translation and pragmatics, fails to address the issue of context in any detail or theorize it explicitly, except as part of the application of relevance theory in the article by Gutt (1998).

Within the limited scope of this paper, I will first outline a range of perspectives on context as elaborated in the recent literature in pragmatics and linguistic anthropology and offer examples of the various ways in which these perspectives relate to translation research and practice. My main interest ultimately lies in describing some of the active processes of contextualization in which translators and interpreters engage or to which they have to respond, and such processes are discussed and exemplified in the second part of the article. Rather than focusing on static descriptions of various components of context, I will argue, it is far more productive to examine contextualization as a dynamic process of negotiation and one that is constrained by the uneven distribution of power which characterizes all exchanges in society, including those that are mediated by translators and interpreters.

I start with the following broad distinctions in an attempt to explore the usefulness of various conceptions of context to the study of translation and interpreting: (1) cognitive versus social/interactive definitions of context; (2) static versus dynamic models and the shift from "context" to "contextualization;" and finally (3) neutral versus power-sensitive definitions of context. [②]

1 Cognitive versus Social/Interactive Definitions of Context

The notion of context has variously been conceptualized as an abstract, psychological construct that exists within rather than outside, or independently of, the mind of the language user, or as a concrete set of entities and parameters in the real world that allow us to make sense of verbal exchanges in actual instances of interaction.

---

① There have of course been some excellent attempts at exploring the notion of context in socio-pragmatics, linguistic anthropology and applied linguistics; see, especially, Auer & di Luzio (1992), Duranti & Goodwin (1992), Malmkjær & Williams (1998) and Dilley (1999). But none have addressed the issue in relation to translation and/or interpreting.

② Needless to say, the literature abounds with other types of distinction. Akman & Bazzanella (2003), for example, distinguish between local and global notions of context, the former relating to the immediate structural environment (context of the ongoing interaction) and the latter to external components of context. This is similar to Schegloff's (1992) distinction between proximate and distal variables of context. My first distinction between cognitive and social/interactional definitions of context is closer to Linell's (1998) distinction between cognitive and situational contexts.

Proponents of a cognition-driven approach argue that "contexts as such are not social situations but mental constructs" (Van Dijk, 2001a:582), that they are not "out there," but "inhere": "they are mental constructs of participants" (Van Dijk, 2001b:18). ① This is the approach adopted by the proponents of relevance theory, one of the few theories of pragmatics to have been applied in detail to the study of translation. Sperber & Wilson (1986/1995:15) insist that "[a]context is a psychological construct, a subset of the hearer's assumptions about the world. It is these assumptions … rather than the actual state of the world, that affect the interpretation of an utterance." When Gutt (1990, 1991, 1996, 1998, 2000) applies this conception of context in his writing on translation, what he ultimately takes as a point of departure in his analysis is not some readily identifiable and stable social reality but the assumptions of target readers. These assumptions are not "out there" for translators to recover; they are a product of our own cognitive processes, but they do guide us in making decisions about how to render a text from one language and social context into another. Ultimately, the question is one of interpretation, not of verifiable reality against which the truth or falsehood of a translation may be judged: "the focus of relevance-theory based translation is on the comparison of interpretations, not on the reproduction of words, linguistic constructions or textual features"(Gutt, 2000:233).

A cognitive view of context, then, will tend to draw a relatively clear line between what is in the world and what is in the mind of the language user or translator, stressing that it is the language user's assumptions about what is in the world, rather than what is actually in the world (assuming we have a reliable way of establishing the latter), that influences the way language is used and the kind of inferences that are drawn in a given situation. Thus, cognition-oriented definitions of context encourage us to see translational behaviour as motivated by a series of ultimately unverifiable assumptions on the part of the translator. And in this sense they are fairly similar to postmodern literary approaches which describe translation as "a process by which the chain of signifiers that constitutes the source-language text is replaced by a chain of signifiers in the target language which the translator provides on the strength of an interpretation" (Venuti,1995:17; emphasis added). The two approaches, however, differ markedly in terms of their resort to the notion of intention. Gutt's cognitive orientation does not preclude him from speaking of "the correct, that is, speaker-intended, interpretation of an utterance" (1998:49). Venuti and other scholars working within the postmodern literary tradition rarely, if ever, invoke the notion of "intention" in their discussions of translation.

Approaches that focus exclusively on social/interactive parameters, on the other hand, traditionally saw context in terms of a series of pre-existing entities and relations in the real world. The best known and one of the most elaborate is Hymes' SPEAKING model:

---

① Cf. the more anthropological and hermeneutic formulation by Holy (1999:50): "the context of the phenomenon does not exist out there for us to grasp but is itself, like the meaning, the result of our interpretation."

Situation, Participants, Ends (outcomes and goals), Act sequence (form and content), Key, Instrumentalities (channels and forms of speech), Norms of interaction, and Genres. Hymes' purpose in elaborating the notion of context in these terms is to stress that the linguistic form on its own supports a whole range of meanings, but in any given context (understood in terms of the SPEAKING model) many of these meanings are eliminated or downplayed (Hymes, 1964). In other words, the context restricts the range of relevant meanings of the form. On the other hand, a given context may support a whole range of meanings, and these in turn are restricted by the form used. Ultimately, Hymes was attempting to illuminate the process by which the actions of participants, including their verbal behaviour, interact in a given situation with social structures such as norms and genres to guide our interpretation of discourse.

This type of framework has been drawn on fairly extensively in translation studies, where scholars have sometimes found it useful to draw up a map of the context of situation of the source and target texts to anticipate potential problems in translation. Nord (1991) is a good example of this trend, as is much of the extensive literature on Bible translation. House's (1981,1997) well-known dimensions of language user and language use, which are employed to assess the quality of translation, offer another variant on this approach. Indeed, the application of systemic functional linguistics with its specific take on the context of situation (in terms of field, tenor and mode), which is ultimately a more elaborate instantiation of Hymes' model, has informed much work in translation studies, including Bell (1991) and House (1981, 1997). More recently, House (2002 and this volume) specifically described her "empirically derived" modes of translation—covert translation and overt translation—as "two fundamentally different types of contextualization" (2002:97). In another relatively recent development in translation studies, we can see the same general conception of context being applied in corpus-based research. For example, the header files that document extra-linguistic information on individual texts in the Translational English Corpus, as described in Laviosa (1997) and Baker (1999), are in some respects instantiations of Hymes' SPEAKING model or some variant of it, specifically giving details of situation and participants (see Figure 1).

To my mind, the two approaches—cognitive and social/interactive—are not mutually exclusive but can be applied at the same time, with varying degrees of emphasis, quite productively. For instance, we might want to explore how thinking of translation itself as a genre (the last component of Hymes' SPEAKING model) and situating this conception within a broader social framework may help explain the extent to which readers expect multiple cultural environments and voices to be invoked in a translation—and in turn how translators' own "assumptions" about such patterns of expectation may guide their decision-making process. Brief references to this potential line of research can be found in the literature, albeit very occasionally and largely only in passing, as in the following statement by Weizman & Blum-Kulka(1987:72):

TITLE
Filename: fn000009. txt
Subcorpus: Fiction
Collection: Memoirs of Leticia Valle
TRANSLATOR
Name: Carol Maier
Gender: female
Nationality: American
Employment: Lecturer
TRANSLATION
Mode: written
Extent: 55179
Publisher: University of Nebraska Press
Place: USA
Date: 1994
Copyright: University of Nebraska Press
Comments: Title in European Women Writers Series
TRANSLATION PROCESS
Direction: into mother tongue
Mode: written from written source text
Type: lull
AUTHOR
Name: Rosa Chacel
Gender: female
Nationality: Spanish
SOURCE TEXT
Language: Spanish
Mode: written
Status: original
Place: Spain
Date: 1945

Figure 1　Sample Header File from TEC Corpus

... it seems that the identification of a text as a translation, which is a meta-linguistic process in essence, "protects" the reader, as it were, from misinterpreting the writer's intentions. As is well-known, when looking for the implicit or indirect meanings of a text, the reader assumes that the writer indeed intended to convey them. The identification of a text as a translation product implies that deviations from cultural norms are not judged as intentional, and therefore are not assigned any "hidden" meanings. In this respect, the perception of "translationese" plays a significant role in the process of text interpretation.

There is also evidence in the literature (e. g. Shlesinger, 1989) that court interpreters tend to correct witnesses who sound confused, most probably because they believe this confusion maybe interpreted by other participants as an indication of their own incompetence. This type of behaviour, as well as Weizman & Blum-Kulka's argument above, further support the cognitive view of context in that they suggest that "we respond not to the context as it is in the world but to what we perceive as other participants' intentions as well as assumptions about the world."

2   Static versus Dynamic Models of Context

Thinking of context as a process of interaction between linguistic form and elements of the situation as outlined in Hymes' model can help account for creativity in language use. It is not the newness of words and structures that make an utterance creative (almost all our utterances are highly repetitive in this respect); creativity in language, and hence in translation, is more a question of the ability of the language user or translator to produce new meanings by extending the resources of language to new contexts of situation. However, defining context as a list of components of the type outlined by Hymes in his SPEAKING model or Scollon & Scollon (1995: 22 - 23) in their "grammar of context" suffers from serious limitations. The most serious weakness is that the components and entities are often treated as static phenomena that exist in a fairly stable environment which the analyst can simply document and use to generate an analysis of events and behaviour. For example, a participant is traditionally assumed to have a stable identity throughout the interaction, whereas more recent approaches in socio-pragmatics and linguistic anthropology would prefer to treat all elements of context as at least having the potential to shift and develop during the course of an event, to both shape and be shaped by the ongoing interaction. Another obvious problem with this approach is that "such open-ended lists suggest that the components are coordinate and independent, and they leave us with the nagging uncertainty of never knowing whether the list is complete or whether yet more components are needed" (Hanks, 1992: 47). A third problem concerns the difficulty of deciding which of the components on the list are relevant for the interpretation of a particular speech event. This is partly a question of whether we treat the components as static, taking the analyst's classification of the event as a given, or follow the perspective of the participants and find ways of establishing what they see as relevant by paying attention to those features that they themselves seem to attend to.

In terms of gender or profession for instance (if we were to consider either or both as aspects of a participant's profile), neither would be treated as purely a "given" within a dynamic conception of context: we "perform" our gender, we step in and out of professional and other roles numerous times during the course of a single conversation, and therefore, whether a participant behaves and responds as a woman, as a gay person, as a doctor, or as a professional interpreter at any moment depends on a variety of factors and can change during the course of a single interaction. Consider how a community interpreter will often shift back and forth between playing out the role of professional interpreter and other participant roles in a communication. In the following example, a community interpreter clearly switches into a different role—that of a caring adult—as she tries to comfort Clara, a 7-year-old child who is about to receive an injection (Wadensjö, 1992:159):

> Interpreter: I can sit—I can be here (.) yes. Clara, you know how many children I have seen already. who've had it done. and I haven't seen a single one that ... you know what. there have been those who cried like you. and afterwards they were so surprised that it was all over. this is what they say. is that all?

The "required" norm in interpreting is for the pronoun "I" to be strictly reserved for the speaker. But the interpreter here speaks in her own voice, not in her professional capacity as interpreter. It is not at all unusual for community interpreters to alternate between their professional and other roles in this way. Similar examples from a different domain can be found in Katan & Straniero-Sergio (2001), who discuss the shifting alignments of media interpreters in the context of talk shows on Italian television. Here are two particularly interesting demonstrations of the way in which an interpreter in this context switches participant roles in response to the unfolding dynamics of the show. English back-translations are provided in square brackets.

In the first example, the interpreter (Olga Fernando) signals the switch in participant roles clearly:

> Guest: I must say one thing
>
> Interpreter: posso dire una cosa? [May I say something?]
>
> Guest: *She is very shaken* (pointing lo Olga Fernando)
>
> Interpreter: *io s—... sta dicendo che (,) l'interprete (.) io é un po' sconvolta adesso spieghera perché* [*l shl—... she's saying that (.) the interpreter (.) me is a little shaken she'll explain why now*]
>
> Guest: Before the show we were sitting here and / *said to (.) Olga* "who is that lady there?"
>
> Interpreter: prima dell'inizio dello spettacolo eravamo seduti qui *e Rose ha chiesto a me parlo in prima persona adesso* chi era quella signora [before the beginning of the show we were sitting here *and Rose asked me I'm speaking in the first person now* who was that lady?]

(Maurizio Costanzo Show, Canale 5, 14. 05. 1998; adapted from Katan & Straniwro-Sergio, 2001:232-233)

In the next example, it is not entirely clear whether the interpreter has switched roles or not, and there is some confusion about the referent of the pronoun "I." The guest in this case is Asha Philips, the author of *Saying No: Why It's Important for You and Your Child*:

Guest: but I think culturally (.) because a lot of us I think were (.) young teenagers *in the sixties* (.) we find it very difficult (.) to: ehm agree to and to find a structure and rules that we don't want to fight against ourselves

Interpreter: poiche (.) noi eravamo = = adolescenti (.) molti di noi erano adolescenti negli anni sessanta (.) eh parlo anche per me per noi e difficile immaginarci (.) di strutturare ehm il =[*because* (.) *we were*= =*adolescents* (.) *many of us were adolescent in the sixties* (.) *eh I'm speaking also for myself* here (.) *for us it's difficult to imagine ourselves* (.) *structuring* ehm the=]

Host: beati voi [Lucky you (pi.)—referring to being adolescent in the sixties; notice in particular the plural "you"]

Interpreter: =nostro atteggiamento (.) in modo tale da dire no senza sentirci poi a nostra volta ribelli contro questa struttura [=*our behaviour* (.) *in such a way as to say no* without becoming *rebels* against this structure]

(Maurizio Costanzo Show, Canale 5, 30. 3. 2000; adapted from Katan & Straniero-Sergio, 2001;233)

There are many such examples in the literature and in real life, which highlight the dynamic nature of every aspect of the interpreting event. Translation studies scholars would therefore do well to adapt their methods of analysis to allow for the fact that participants in a translation event can themselves define rather than simply respond to the context that is sometimes assumed to surround them "statically. " And of course they can use language itself to do so.

Duranti & Goodwin (1992; 5) stress that " the dynamic mutability of context is complicated further by the ability of participants to rapidly invoke within the talk of the moment alternative contextual frames. " Indeed this is one of the key insights provided by Gumperz's notion of contextualization cues, which he uses "to refer to speakers' and listeners' use of verbal and non-verbal signs to relate what is said at any one time and in any one place to knowledge acquired through past experience, in order to retrieve the presuppositions they must rely on to maintain conversational involvement and assess what is intended" (Gumperz, 1992;230). Contextualization, within the Gumperzian framework, is achieved by means of cues at the levels of prosody, paralinguistic signs, code choice, and choice of lexical forms or formulaic expressions (1992;231). Other examples include code switching, the use of italics in writing, and discourse markers such as "let's be serious now. " When Venuti describes how at various points in his translation of Tarchetti's Fosca he alternated between British and American spelling or "made the combination of various lexicons more jarring to remind the reader that he or she is reading a translation in the present" (1998; 17), he offers us a good example of the use of code switching as a contextualization cue in translation. According to Gumperz (1992:232), contextualization cues "serve to highlight, foreground or make salient" certain interpretations or aspects of the communicative situation. We can safely assume that translators and interpreters make as much use of this dynamic aspect of interaction as everyone else.

Other examples of the dynamic process of contextualization include the way in which interpreters sometimes adopt linguistic strategies to redefine the context in which they are delivering their services, to make it clear to other participants—such as defendants and their families in court—that they are not to be held responsible for certain statements, i. e. that these statements do not represent their own views or wishes, perhaps as a way of protecting themselves from potential backlash when a harsh sentence is passed by the judge or an aggressive question posed by an attorney. Thus, as Berk-Seligson (1990:116) points out, when the judge says something like "I am now remanding you to the authority of the federal marshalls," interpreters will tend to render this either as "Yo, el juez (I, the judge), to make it absolutely clear who the 'I'refers to, or alternatively, they will use the noun phrase El juez by itself, thereby referring to the judge entirely in the third person." Another example, also from Berk-Seligson (1990:114 – 115), illustrates the use of different linguistic means to realize the same pragmatic strategy of recontextualizing the utterance to avoid the "I" of the speaker being confused with the "I" of the interpreter and hence holding the latter responsible for the utterance:

Attorney: As *I've indicated*, the defendant has pleaded "not guilty."
Interpreter: Como *se ha indicado* el aefendientee se ha declarado "no culpable" en esas acusaciones. [*as has been indicated*]

It is worth stressing again that none of the schematic approaches outlined here necessarily rules out the other perspectives. It is ultimately a question of emphasis. Thus, for example, while Basco et al. (2004) focus on elaborating categories of context and in that sense may be seen to approach the issue from a static, taxonomic perspective, they nevertheless embed their description within the dynamic notion of a "behaviour game." Moreover, they clearly inject their description with a dynamic view of context that acknowledges the agency of participants when they argue that:

The recognition of the behaviour game bid by the speaker does not bind the hearer to play a particular role in the game. On the contrary, the hearer can decide to accept or reject the proposed game, or to propose a different one, or to negotiate a specific one. (2004:471)

Similarly, an approach can be both cognitive and dynamic, as in the work of Van Dijk, who stresses that "context models are not static mental representations, but dynamic structures. They are ongoingly constructed and reconstructed by each participant in an event" (2001b:18). I would therefore argue that adopting a dynamic approach to context in the study of translation and interpreting does not mean that we do not need access to the type of ethnographic/extra-linguistic information documented in the TEC header in Figure 1, for instance, because in order for the researcher to appreciate whether someone is "doing" or "performing" the role of interpreter or friend or caring adult at any point, he or she first needs to know who the speaker is, in what capacity they are engaged in the interaction, and so on. The idea, then, is not to throw lists of apparently static situational components out altogether but to use them merely as a starting point for analysis, to acknowledge that they are not all necessarily relevant in every context and, more importantly, that every element is open to negotiation in the course of a given interaction.

3 Neutral versus Power-sensitive Definitions of Context

With the exception of more nuanced positions such as Basco et al. 's (2004), the various conceptualizations of context that I have surveyed so far, including the dynamic notion of contextualization cues, suggest a purely speaker-led form of communication as the norm, whereas it is of course not up to an individual participant alone to decide what is to count as context at any moment. Hence, Goodwin & Duranti (1992:6), among others, stress that "in so far as the processes to which context is relevant are social and interactive, one party's proposals as to what should constitute operative context might fail to achieve ratification by others" since "context is a socially constituted, interactively sustained, time-bound phenomenon. "

A related, and more important point, is that most treatments of context in the literature, including Hymes and even Gumperz, imply that context is a neutral field or framework in which we play out our social roles, and that in order to take control of it and shape it to our advantage all we need to do is to learn how to employ the appropriate contextualization cues. Lindstrom (1992:103) explains that "however plotted, these models of context often grant context an inert neutrality: context is a neutral field for the play of speech events, or is the cumulation of cognitive schemata that are cued to foreground past understanding. " These models clearly fail to explain much of what goes on in interaction. For example, as Shea (1994) points out, studies have shown that the simple association of an Asian face with standard English speech can be enough to make the speech of the Asian relatively incomprehensible to white US college students, which suggests that, however well the Asian speaker might master the use of contextualization cues, he or she remains seriously restricted in the way they are able to guide their interlocutors' interpretations of their behaviour. In the specific context of translation and interpreting, I would argue that an uncritical application of the notion of contextualization cues risks encouraging analysts and participants in an interaction to use the translator or interpreter as a scapegoat, an easy source of explanations for communication breakdown. The translator or interpreter can always be blamed for failing to adjust contextualization cues to target norms of interaction, when more often than not the failure or derailing of an interaction might lie in the cultural or political outlook of the participants, or in the conflicting agendas they bring to the speech event.

Dilley (2003:453) asks "[a]re the individuals captured in Afghanistan and now held at a US base in Cuba to be identified as 'prisoners' in the context of war or as 'criminals' in the context of criminal law?" His answer underlines the effect of power on determining what counts as context at any moment: "[t]he ability to define a context in a particular way or to initiate a set of contextualizing moves in a particular direction can be constructed as a political act in the light of other possible definitions or moves that could have been made" (2003: 453). Part of the power that an interpreter can exert in certain situations derives from the fact that he or she is normally the only participant with access to both languages and can therefore control the discourse to a large extent. This "power" is eroded in situations where monitoring① is possible and those doing the monitoring are in a more powerful position than the interpreter (socially, professionally, ethnically, etc.). Here is an example from court interpreting in the US, where many of the jurors and even the judge him- or herself often have some command of Spanish (Berk-Seligson, 1990:213):

Juror:	I understand the word *La Vado*—I thought it meant restroom. She translates it as bar.
Interpreter:	In the first place, the jurors are not to listen to the Spanish but to the English. I am a certified interpreter.
Juror:	You're an idiot.

Here, the interpreter's attempt to shape the context in ways that suit her own understanding of her role fails miserably, mainly because of the imbalance of power between her and other participants in this interaction. Other examples of the power relations encoded in the context of court interpreting concern the way in which court interpreters are prevented from seeing any documents relating to a case prior to the hearings, and the fact that they are normally not allowed to initiate turns or conversational sequences, except for the purpose of clarification—and very sparingly in this case.

Turning to another domain of interpreting, a more sinister exercise of power in determining the course of an interaction is evident at various points in Trevor McDonald's 1990 interview with Saddam Hussein, analysed in Baker (1997). Here, the exercise of power is not as overtly aggressive as in the example from Berk-Seligson above, but in real terms it is much more stressful for the interpreter and restrictive of his ability to participate actively in shaping the emerging context (adapted from Baker, 1997:121; back-translation

---

① I refer specifically here to linguistic monitoring, i. e. situations where one or more of the participants in an event is not linguistically handicapped and can therefore monitor the interpreter's performance and potentially intervene to "correct" him or her.

from Arabic in square brackets)①:

McDonald: Mr. President, these reports of atrocities you see are encouraged by the fact that you have sealed Kuwait off from the rest of the world. Why don't you let us go in and see for ourselves whether these reports are true?

Saddam: أنت محق في بعض ما ذكرت

      [You are right in part of what you say.]

Interpreter: Yes, you're right, you're partly right there.

Saddam (To Int.): في جانب مما ذكرت

      [*In part of what you say.*]

Interpreter: Partly right there.

In this excerpt, Saddam corrects the interpreter, making it clear that he expects a literal rendering of what he says. He repeats to the interpreter in Arabic, emphasizing every word: "In part of what you say." The interpreter repeats (presumably to reassure him): "Partly right there." Saddam's verbal instructions are accompanied by a stern look in the direction of the interpreter (who is not shown on the screen at that point).

But power also shapes the context of interpretation in more subtle ways in translation and interpreting, as in all instances of language use. One of its effects is to encourage the translator to evoke narratives that have currency within the dominant target culture in order to give voice to marginalized source-culture participants and enable a process of identification or empathy to ensue. Some of the interventions by the subtitlers of Mohamed Bakri's documentary *Jenin Jenin*, released in 2002 following the Israeli "incursions" into the Jenin camp in the West Bank,② demonstrate this quite clearly. At one point in the documentary, an old Palestinian man expresses his shock at what happened and the world's apparent indifference and reluctance to intervene. He ends his contribution by saying, literally in Arabic, "what can I say, by God, by God, our house/home③ is no longer a house/home."

أنا عارف والله العظيم، و الله العظيم، بيتنا ما صار بيت

The subtitle for this frame is:

What can I say? Not even Vietnam was as bad as this.

In order to communicate the gravity of the situation to a world public whose conception of gravity is conditioned by the political dominance of the US, the subtitlers recontextualize

---

① Saddam Hussein seems to have a good command of English and did not need Arabic translations of the questions posed in English during that interview. But he answered in Arabic throughout, and the interpreter therefore only interpreted his answers into English for the benefit of Trevor McDonald and the viewers.

② And the ensuing international controversy over what happened and the extent of the damage and loss of life in that area. Indeed, the term "incursion" itself was heavily contested in the media and by numerous pro-Palestinian

③ The Arabic word used (beit—beitna ma saar beit) can mean both "house" (in the physical sense) and "home," with all the connotations of the latter. It cannot, however, as in English, index a homeland or country.

the event by evoking a narrative which has moral resonances for those viewers. Indeed, the entire documentary is subtitled in such a way as to improve the chances of American and world public opinion, which is seen as holding the key to change in the area, empathizing with the Palestinian population. The subtitlers, for example, largely avoid translating the Arabic word shaheed and all its derivatives in the speech of Palestinian characters in the documentary into its standard equivalent martyr, presumably to suppress the associations of Islamic fundamentalism, terrorism and suicide bombing that this word readily evokes in the current political context, even though many Arab speakers who use it, including Palestinians interviewed in this documentary, may be totally opposed to any acts of violence on either side. Here is a typical example—original speech of Palestinian man:

"متخلفين عقليا استشهدو عندنا: معاقين استشهدوا عندنا، أطفال استشهدوا عندنا: نساء استشهدو عندنا"

[we have mentally retarded people who have been martyred; we have disabled people who have been martyred; we have children who have been martyred; we have women who have been martyred.]

English subtitles:
They killed some mentally disabled people, children and women in the camp.

In another shot, a Palestinian doctor describes how, as his area was being shelled by Israeli planes during the first intifada, he tended to many injured people and managed to save many lives, only to discover when the shelling stopped that his own son had been shot and was lying somewhere nearby bleeding to death. In one frame, he explains that when the shelling stopped he heard some of his neighbours shouting:

عميد استشهد، عميد استشهد

[Ameed (his son) has been martyred, Ameed has been martyred.]

The subtitles read as follows:
After the cease-fire the neighbours
started shouting that Ameed
my son was dead

Thus, the effects of power and dominance are always inscribed within processes of (re)contextualization. The dominant party generally dictates the terms of contextualization; even when the marginalized participant decides to contest the context as it were, they ultimately do so largely within the terms set by the dominant party. The tragedy of Jenin has to be compared to Vietnam, rather than any of the other tragedies suffered by other parts of the world in the recent past, in order to become meaningful in the context of American political dominance. But participants in most types of interaction are not totally powerless, and dominance is hardly ever absolute. In this context, the subtitlers could have evoked a more recent event which has even more currency among the target viewers, namely 9/11, but in opting for Vietnam they simultaneously identify the dominant political power as aggressor and perpetrator of violence even as the Jenin tragedy is recontextualized in terms that are relevant to that power.

4 Contextualizing Translation

Holy (1999:48) states that "[c]ontext is and always has been the key anthropological concept. " The same could be said of translation and interpreting, except that translation scholars have so far largely ignored the obvious centrality of the notion of context to their own discipline and failed to grant it sufficient scholarly attention. The question, of course, is what from this scholarly attention might productively take. We could, for instance, spend considerable time trying to enumerate all the possible elements that constitute context in any type of translational event and the various ways in which these elements constrain the behaviour (linguistic and non-linguistic) of translators and interpreters. But this approach can only take us so far. The problem is that the same complexity which "makes context a powerful device both in knowledge and cognition ... make[s] context difficult to define and study formally"(Akman & Bazzanella, 2003:322). More importantly, as Holy (1999:50) explains, "[t]he difficulties of specifying precisely what constitutes the relevant context and of marking the context's boundary, arise from the fact that the specification of the context is itself the result of interpretation. "

Instead of treating context as a constraint, a set of restrictions on what we can or cannot achieve in translation and other communicative events, and setting out to specify the numerous facts of that constraint, it might ultimately be more productive to recognize context as a resource, something that we selectively and strategically construct as we engage in any act of communication, including the act of translation. This suggests both an emphasis on the dynamic and ever changing nature of context and directing our attention to the strategic processes of contextualization in which translators and interpreters engage.

In terms of the dynamic nature of context, for example, a given source text will often have a "thicker" and possibly very different context in the target culture, partly through the sheer passing of time and the ensuing change in social and political environments. With the passage of time, a literary or scholarly text will have accumulated critical response and resonances, and both it and its translation(s) will be read and interpreted in a different context—politically, culturally, socially, aesthetically. Jones (2004) raises a related and important ethical issue. In deciding to translate the work of the Serbian author Vasko Popa during the war against Bosniain the 1990s, he was concerned that Popa drew on "Serbian atavistic images ... such as the Kosovo myth or the figure of the wolf as tribal totem" (2004: 719). Jones explains that Popa invoked these images positively in order to explore his cultural roots "in an age (the 1970s) when such explorations were relatively untainted" (2004:719). The question Jones poses as a translator who has to take an ethical decision is whether a text can "remain untainted by its social context" (2004:723), in this case the racially and ethnically torn Yugoslavia of the 1990s. The answer, I believe, is that it cannot, unless a serious effort is made to recontextualize the text in question. The success or failure of any such attempt a recontextualization will depend on many factors, most of which will be beyond the control of the translator as a single and not particularly powerful participant. I would nevertheless argue that such attempts at (re)contextualization are ultimately what we should be directing our attention to, and that processes of contextualization are far more revealing than any set of contextual constraints we might want to enumerate and describe in detail.

Holy (1999:53) argues that "meanings are subject to manipulation. And so are contexts because if meanings are intrinsically context-dependent, any manipulation of meaning involves, perforce, manipulation of its contextualization." More specifically, Mey (2003: 332) draws our attention to the problem of "an ambiguous utterance being wrongly interpreted in contexts that are decisive for the life or death of the utterer" and, I would add, that play an important part in heightening political or racial tension. A productive engagement with the notions of context and contextualization in the study of translation must be able to address the "politics of context definition" (Dilley, 2003:440) and explain how and why different parties to an interaction contextualize events and expressions in specific ways. A recent example from the so-called "war on terror" demonstrates how such processes of contextualization work in practice.

On 29 October 2004, in the thick of the US elections, Al-Jazeera aired a tape from Osama Bin Laden in Arabic. Its translation into English has been widely contested, especially the translation of a keyword used towards the end of the tape. The Arabic word wilaya can, in principle, mean either state in the sense of nation/country or state in the modern day sense of electoral region. Al-Jazeera translators opted broadly for the first sense, while the translators of MEMRI, a neo-conservative media institute which specializes in translating selected Arabic documents for Western consumption, opted for the second sense. Here are the two translations, respectively:

Translation 1 (Al-Jazeera)[①]

In conclusion, I tell you in truth, that your security is not in the hands of Kerry, nor Bush, nor al-Qaida. No.

Your security is not in the hands of Kerry or Bush or Al-Qa'ida. Your security is in your own hands, and any U.S. state that does not toy with our security automatically guarantees its own security.

Translation 2 (MEMRI)

Your security is not in the hands of Kerry or Bush or Al-Qa'ida. Your security is in your own hands, and any [U.S.] state [wilaya] that does not toy with our security automatically guarantees its own security.

---

① http://english.aljazeera.net/NR/exeres/79C6AF22-98FB-4A1C-B21F-2BC36E87F61F.htm

Shortly after MEMRI posted and publicized its version of the speech, other web sites and news agencies began to circulate this version, without the qualifying brackets and the original Arabic term, as in the following version posted on WorldNetDaily[1]:

> Your security is not in the hands of Kerry or Bush or Al-Qa'ida. Your security is in your own hands, and any U. S. state that does not toy with our security automatically guarantees its own security.

MEMRI and other like-minded media outlets insisted that Bin Laden "threatened each U. S. state, [and]... offered an election deal to the American voters—a sort of amnesty for states that don't vote for Bush," and that "[t]he U. S. media have mistranslated the words 'ay wilaya' (which means 'each U. S. state') to mean a 'country' or 'nation' other than the U. S... while in reality Bin Laden's threat was directed specifically at each individual U. S. state."[2] Juan Cole, Professor of History at the University of Michigan and owner of the activist web site Informed Comment (http://www.juancole.com) contested this interpretation[3]:

> MEMRI is claiming that the word used for "state"... means state as in Rhode Island and New Jersey.

> But while they are right to draw attention to the oddness of the diction, their conclusion is impossible.

> Bin Laden says that such a "state" should not trifle with Muslims' security. He cannot possibly mean that he thinks Rhode Island is in a position to do so. Nor can he be referring to which way a state votes, since he begins by saying that the security of Americans is not in the hands of Bush or Kerry. He has already dismissed them as equivalent and irrelevant, in and of themselves.

In contextualizing their interpretation of the potentially ambiguous word wilaya, MEMRI chose to appeal to the immediate political and temporal context (the elections and timing of Bin Laden's speech). Juan Cole, whose political views are very different from MEMRI's, chose to invoke a range of very different aspects of the context. He first posits that there is a logical problem with MEMRI's interpretation, by appealing partly to the immediate co-text (Bin Laden says that the security of Americans is not in the hands of Kerry or Bush) and partly to our knowledge of the world (a state like Rhode Island cannot possibly influence the security of Muslims, only nation states can). These aspects of the context are not sufficient to support his interpretation, however, since he has already acknowledged that Bin Laden's use of the word wilaya is unusual, and he goes on to admit that.

---

① http://www.worldnetdaily.com/news/article.asp? ARTICLE_ID=41211
② http://www.worldnetdaily.com/news/article.asp? ARTICLE_ID=41211
③ http://www.juancole.com/2004/11/bin-ladens-audio-threat-to-states.html

It is true that in modern standard Arabic, wilayah means "state" or "province" and that al-Wilayaat al-Muttahaddah is the phrase used to translate "United States." A state in the sense of government or international power would more likely nowadays be dawlah or hukumah.

So he goes on to suggest that there are "two possible explanations for Bin Laden's diction here." The first explanation is that Bin Laden "is simply using a fundamentalist archaism." This explanation invokes religious culture, linguistic culture, and history:

[Bin Laden] regularly uses archaisms. He has steeped himself in ancient, Koranic Arabic and the sayings of the Prophet, and he and his fellow cultists in Kandahar developed a peculiar subculture that rejected much of modernity.

... In classical Arabic, a ruler is a wali, who then rules over a wilayah or walayah. Wilayah can have connotations even in modern Arabic ... of sovereignty and it can mean "government." Bin Laden is attempting to revive ways of thinking he maintains were common among the first generation of Muslims, and to slough off centuries of accretions.

The second explanation Juan Cole offers relates to aspects of the personal history of the speaker (Bin Laden) and features of language contact, and further appeals to the specific political context of Pakistan to support the argument:

The other possibility is that Bin Laden has lived most of the past 25 years in Persian, Pashto, and Urdu-speaking environments and that he occasionally lapses into nonstandard usage. In Hindi-Urdu, I noticed that one meaning of vilayat is "the metro pole." At least in past generations, people going from British India to the UK said they were going to vilayat. More important, there is some evidence for fundamentalist Muslims using the word wilayah or walayah to mean "country." The Pakistani radical group Hizb al-Tahrir locates itself in "Walayah Pakistan," i. e. , the country of Pakistan.

As can be seen from this example, the same event can be strategically placed in a number of different contexts by different participants, depending on their relevant agendas. No model of contextual components, however detailed and comprehensive, can—on its own—explain what is happening here nor predict which of the two interpretations will be favoured by any given participant in an interaction that involves this text. But paying attention to the process of contextualization itself can tell us a great deal about the goals of each participant and what they hope to achieve by appealing to any set of contextual variables, given that contextualizing "is a form of social action" (Dilley, 2003:440). The way people construct contexts for the same phenomenon differs "because of the differences in roles, interests, purposes and power of those who do the contextualizing" (Holy, 1999:57).

5　Conclusion

The past decade or so has witnessed a general shift in scholarly discourse away from static concepts such as that of context and towards active processes of engagement, implied in notions such as contextualization, which underline the fluidity of interaction and the fact that it is socially and jointly constructed, partly in advance but also to a great extent at the point of interaction itself. Similar shifts have been taking place in translation studies, for example away from static concepts of equivalence and norms and towards recognition of the fact that the process of translation does not consist of passive responses to cultural, social and aesthetic conventions but of active negotiation among participants with shifting agendas and unequal levels of control over the interaction.

As we move towards a more explicit elaboration of how we engage in contextualizing discourses *in* and *about* translation, as well as our ethical and social responsibilities as translators, we would do well to acknowledge, as does Lindstrom (1992:102 – 103), that "... context is a field of power relations. It is not, however, a frozen field ... People can occasionally say the unsayable. They can contest the context, by evoking available alternative or competing discourses." This fluid, dynamic conceptualization of context should prove empowering for translators and scholars of translation, as well as more responsive to the political and cultural realities of what is proving to be one of the most conflictual phases of world history.

第七章 心理语言学/认知语言学 视域下的翻译研究

导 论

翻译研究领域取得进展的重要标志之一是翻译过程研究。这个从静态到动态的转变反映出人们对于翻译活动的本质特征的新认识：翻译是一个作决定、作选择的过程。那么在这个作决定的过程中，都有哪些心理和认知过程在期间发挥作用？ 翻译的心理和认知过程的研究从20世纪80年代开始受到西方学者的重视。用心理语言学和认知语言学的理论成果来考察译者在翻译过程中的心理活动和认知特点及其对于翻译过程和结果的影响是现代语言学理论与翻译实践相结合的一个新的视角。心理语言学和认知语言学基于体验哲学，对了解翻译者的思维模式、翻译过程都有重要的启示作用。从翻译的心理运作机制上以及认知的角度考察翻译的实际操作过程，为揭示译者的心理活动和认知特点，理解翻译的实际过程提供了充分的依据。心理语言学和认知语言学理论视角下的翻译研究解决了一些其他翻译理论无法解决的翻译问题，对翻译研究具有很强的解释力，为翻译研究注入了新的活力。

在本章中，编者选取了贝尔为《翻译研究百科全书》所写的"Psycholinguistic/Cognitive Approaches to Translation"一文，对心理语言学和认知语言学途径的翻译研究进行了全面的梳理和总结。由于翻译被视为"作决定的过程"，编者接下来选取了 Wolfram Wilss 对于这一问题的阐述："Decision Making in Translation"。该领域一个重要的研究成果是从"有声思维"的角度来研究翻译，尝试通过"有声思维"的方法解开译者翻译过程中大脑这个"黑匣子"的运作机制。编者因此选取了 Riitta Jääskeläinen 所撰写的"Think-Aloud Protocols"一文。这一方法实际上吸引了一些实践者，"研究实践"中选取的徐海铭的论文就是一个有代表性的研究案例。姜秋霞是国内最早从格式塔心理学的角度出发研究文学翻译的学者。而刘华文是国内近年来从认知语言学的角度研究文学翻译的一个代表性学者。他们的研究让我们看出从心理学、认知学的角度研究翻译取得的成果，对我们认识翻译的过程和本质具有怎样重要的启迪意义。

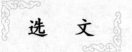

选文一　Psycholinguistic/Cognitive Approaches to Translation

Roger Bell

导　言

对翻译过程的研究由来已久,最早对翻译过程进行研究的学者当属英国学者贝尔。贝尔在 20 世纪 90 年代初结合认知心理学和语言学系统对翻译过程进行研究,并且构建了翻译过程模式,给后来学者科学地研究翻译过程和构建翻译过程模式以很大启示,即要将动态描述和静态研究、微观研究和宏观研究相结合;建立的模式应该能忠实地描绘翻译这一过程。他的研究对机器翻译、人工智能等领域意义重大。这里推荐的文章选自贝克主编的 *Routlege Encyclopedia of Translation Studies*,作者正是贝尔。

At it simplest, translation involves the transfer of meaning from a text in one language into another. This transfer constitutes a mental process which relies on sophisticated information processing skills. Since all human communication relies on the ability to process information, psycholinguistic studies of translation essentially set out to establish how translators and interpreters process information, both as distinct from other speakers and writers and as distinct from each other.

A psychologically plausible model of translation then must reflect what is currently known about human information processing and memory, taking monolingual communication as a starting point while recognizing that translation and interpreting are special instances of bilingual communication. It needs to address issues such as the extent to which translation-specific processes are embedded within a larger model of human communication, how the constraints under which translators operate differ from those which influence other communicators, the effects these constraints and differences have on the processes involved, and how we might gain access to the process in question in order to explain what translators actually do. In terms of variety of activities and process, a psycholinguistic model of translation needs to account for the translator's ability to shift from written text to written text(as in ordinary translation), from written text to spoken text(as in sight translation), from spoken text to written text(as in note-taking, prior to consecutive translation or to producing a written translation of a spoken source text), from written text to spoken text(as in consecutive interpreting), and from spoken text to spoken text (as in simultaneous interpreting).

Translation combines the activities of reading/listening and writing/speaking, and there is evidence to suggest that translators and interpreters listen and read (and speak and write) in a different way from other language users, basically because they operate under a different set of constraints. Three sets of constraints stand out as particularly significant in the context of translation (Danks, 1991):

> (a) **task**, the activity which the translator is required to carry out and the context in which this activity takes place;
> (b) **text**, the linguistic and discoursal structure of the source text;
> (c) **translator**, the linguistic and non-linguistic knowledge and skills of the person carrying out the translation.

Each of these constraints functions as an input condition to the process, and since they do not draw on the same cognitive resources, they exert different influences on the way the process functions. The task, for example, is carried out within severe time constraints, and these are different for translators and interpreters. Translating is, as it were, outside "real-time," since the translator has as much time as has been made available for processing the original text up to an agreed deadline (which might, in any case, be extended). Following United Nations norms of six to eight pages of translation per day, the professional translator typically produces about five words per minute or 300 words per hour. The simultaneous interpreter, in contrast, has to respond instantly to the incoming spoken text, typically at a rate some 30 times faster than the translator, i. e. 150 words per minute or 9,000 words per hour. While the translator is free, in principle, to weigh a range of alternatives before deciding on the "best" version, the interpreter has one chance and one only. These distinctions hold good for written translation and for simultaneous interpreting but fail to recognize the intermediate place of consecutive interpreting, where the interpreter takes notes and only interprets at the end of the original speaker's contribution, as well as much community interpreting where sight translation of written documents is a frequent requirement.

The lexical and stylistic structure of the source text poses further constraints on the translator, and there is evidence that monolinguals and bilinguals process texts rather differently. The monolingual communicator listens or reads for comprehension, while the translator listens or reads for translation. Both are engaged in gathering information from the text but, for the monolingual, that is the primary goal. The translator, on the other hand, has to be able to recognize translation-relevant elements of the text which may constitute problems or which signal significant variables, such as tenor, that ought to be reflected in the target text. For the monolingual, a particular turn of phrase may please, baffle or annoy; the translator may react in the same way but with the difference that such wording may well constitute a problem which has to be solved and, in the case of the simultaneous interpreter, solved instantly.

The roles of the two as receivers of messages also differ. The monolingual is essentially sender-oriented, paying attention to the speaker/writer's message in order to respond to it by agreeing/disagreeing, replying and so on. The translator, on the other hand, is essentially receiver-oriented, paying attention to the speaker/writer's message in order to re-transmit it to the receivers of the target text, and therefore suppressing, or at least controlling, personal reactions to the message. Translators tend to believe that they should discipline their understanding so as to exclude—as far as is possible—personal reactions to what is being said or written and privilege the expectations and assumptions of the client audience for whom the interpreting or translating is being provided(Seleskovitch, 1978).

So much for the receptive aspects of interpreting and translating. The productive aspects are also special instances of the general process of human communication but with differences which serve to distinguish translation as bilingual rather than monolingual communication. Compare, for example, a monolingual spoken dialogue with interpreting. In the first case, the "answering" turn would (a) be in the same language, and normally the same style as the previous speaker used, and(b) contain different semantic and, therefore, syntactic and pragmatic content. The translator's behaviour is the opposite on both counts: the turn(a) is taken in a different language—that of the target audience rather than the original speaker/writer, the latter being the normal audience for monolingual exchanges, and (b) contains the same semantic content as the original, as stored—with potential modifications—in the mental representation of the clause in the working memory of the translator.

A model of the translation process, then, inevitably replicates all the characteristics of a general model of human communication, with the addition of some components which are translation-specific, particularly components which represent problem-recognition and the strategies employed for problem-solving. In discussing any model of the translation process, terms like *next* may have to be used, but these are not to be taken literally as indications of a unidirectional, ballistic process which takes the source-language text and pushes it through each stage in a rigid order until it emerges at the end as the target-language text. Far from it, revision and backtracking (typically, but by no means exclusively, in translating) are the norm rather than the exception.

Stages, Problems and Strategies

There are two essential stages specific to the processes of translating and interpreting, and a further stage available only to the translator working with the written text. These are: **analysis**, **synthesis** and **revision**. During the analysis stage, the translator reads/listens to the source text, drawing on background, encyclopedic knowledge—including specialist domain knowledge and knowledge of text conventions—to comprehend features contained in the text. This requires processing at the syntactic, semantic and pragmatic levels, as well as in terms of micro- and macro-analysis of the actual text: monitoring for cohesion and coherence, and checking for coherence between the actual text and the potential text-type of which it is a token realization, respectively. There is, in other words, a trade-off between the micro-/bottom-up analysis of the text at clause level and the macro-/top-down analysis of text as an entity. During synthesis, the target text is produced, i. e. written, signed, spoken, and then evaluated in terms of the sender's meaning and intention (as interpreted by the translator), the translator's intention in translating the text, and the user's needs (as specified by the client and interpreted by the translator). On the basis of these evaluations the draft translation is revised/edited during the final stage of revision, and such things as clause linkage and the text's congruence with its text-type are adjusted.

All text processing is, to a large extent, a matter of problem-solving. Translators, just like other text-processors, encounter problems of comprehension, interpretation and expression and evolve strategies for coping with them. What a study of the translation process must investigate is the kind of problems which occur in translation and the frequency with which they occur, the specific strategies that translators employ in recognizing and resolving these problems, the frequency with which certain strategies are employed, and the kind of problem indicators which can be observed in the translation context(Krings, 1987).

A translation problem is some part of the process of transfer, whether deriving from the reception of the source text or the production of the target text, which makes analysis or synthesis non-automatic. Such problems may be anticipated at both the macro- and micro-levels. On the basis of this definition, a translation strategy is a potentially conscious procedure for solving a problem faced in translating a text, or any segment of it(Lörscher, 1991a:76). Clearly given the distinction between micro- and macro-level problems, strategies too can be divided between those which are local(dealing with text segments) and those which are global(dealing with whole texts). Equally, local and global strategies interact with relevant elements of the translator's background knowledge: critical awareness of the style and content of similar texts, of conventions of spelling, punctuation, and grammar, of compatibility of elements defining register, and intuitions about what constitutes the target language(Séguinot, 1989:39).

One of the fundamental problems the translator(and, in particular, the interpreter) faces is that of memory limitation. Text analysis and synthesis is carried on a clause at a time, and the major problem for the translator who wishes to increase the size of the unit of translation or reduce the pressure on the working memory, but the translator working with a written text tends to attempt to solve the problem by first reaching an understanding of the meaning of the source text before putting that meaning into words and then returning to the text as memory fades. There is a significant difference here between translating and interpreting, where the opposite takes place(Lederer, 1981: 129): interpreting operates at the level of the lexical item until a break occurs in the speaker's output—an actual silent pause or a point at which the interpreter is able to predict how the clause will be completed and then translate on the level of meaning(Isham & Lane [1993] provide empirical evidence in support of the clause as the unit of recall). Interpreters, particularly simultaneous interpreters, are especially sensitive to the influence of the "lag time," i. e. the delay between input and output. In simultaneous interpreting, this is normally between two and six seconds, though lags of up to 10 seconds have been recorded. Short lags tend to result in more errors(omissions, additions, changes) in form, while long lags tend to cause more omissions of content, because the working memory is overloaded with information(Isham & Lane, 1993: 243).

Translators appear to make use of at least three global strategies(Séguinot, 1989). They have a tendency to (a) translate without interruption for as long as possible, (b) correct surface efforts immediately(this is often marked by hesitation; typing at a slower rate than usual) but leave errors involving meaning until a natural break occurs, typically at the end of a clause or sentence, and (c) leave the monitoring for qualitative or stylistic errors in the text to the revision stage. The principle of least effort seems to be in force here. It is easier to correct errors as they come to consciousness than to attempt to hold them in short-term memory to be dealt with later. Many translators also approach the task of translating by reading the source text through once or several times, seeking potential problems and coming to a decision on how the translation should begin. Actual typing starts as soon as a decision has been reached on how to render the first part of the first sentence and continues, for at least four words, before a pause occurs.

Strategies of this type are investigated either by means of think-aloud protocols(where translators are asked to introspect and verbalize what they do as they do it) or they are inferred from translator behaviour. For example, indications of internal processing are frequently inferred from pauses(interruptions in the typing of the translation or breaks in speaking during interpreting) and hesitations(a slowing down of typing, note-taking or speaking speed), as well as from other markers. Some of these markers are verbalized, for example in the form of an explicit statement of the problem as in asides such as *I don't know how to translate that*, while others are ostensive and include the overall rate of production, the timing and duration of interruptions to production, as well as actions such as referring to a dictionary, marking problems in the text, editing, crossing out false starts, and correcting errors. Others still are signaled through the manner of articulation, as in slips, self-repairs, and so on.

Problems in Investigating the Process of Translation

Two main investigative strategies are used to overcome the inherent problem of investigating translator-behaviour, where the connection between the source and target texts is an indirect and covert one, linked by a process which is mental rather than physical.

Product-based studies proceed from a comparative analysis of source and target texts and use textual differences uncovered during the analysis as a means of accessing indirectly the mental processes employed during translation. Process-based studies use methods such as think-aloud protocols, measuring the eye-movements of translators as they read, videoing them as they work, asking them to fill in self report questionnaires on their attitudes to aspects of literary(König & Vernon, 1982) and non-literary: translating, as well as various techniques for developing personality profiles of professional translators and conference interpreters(Henderson, 1987). Danks(1991) offers a good survey of some of these methods.

Apart from the difficulty of observing what is essentially a mental activity, a further problem relates to the danger of lack of representativeness in the sample of informants or in the tasks they are asked to do. Fraser(1996) discusses various problems relating to the nature of the data used in process-oriented research. For example, most of the translators studied so far have been trainees, though Fraser's(1993) work with experience public service translators stands out as a particularly valuable exception. It is clear that different groups of bilinguals, including translation students and experienced professional translators, can differ markedly in the strategies they adopt. Similarly, there appears to be a considerable difference between the practices of the bilingual child engaging in interpreting and the professional translator/interpreter on the one hand, and the language student and non-professional translator on the other(Lörscher, 1992). According to Lörscher, the typical strategy of the bilingual child and the professional translator/interpreter is sense-oriented, making use of top-down processing, with the focus on function rather than form, and drawing on procedural knowledge. For these two groups, translation consists of the deconstruction of signs into sense and the reconstruction of sense into signs. The bilingualism is mediated by the possession of a single store of logical and encyclopedic entries for concepts but distinct language-specific stores of lexical entries for the languages involved. By contrast, the typical strategy of student and non-professional translators(on whom most empirical investigation has been carried out) is sign-oriented, making use of bottom-up processing which focuses on form rather than function, and drawing on factual, declarative knowledge. For them, translation consists of (semi-)automatic lexical transfer, and the sign in the target language is called by the sign in the source language rather than by the relevant concept.

Problems of representativeness of data and difficulty of accessing mental activities notwithstanding, the findings of empirical research, though far from uniform or conclusive, do suggest trends in the way translators translate, tackle problems and justify their decisions. It would, of course, be unwise to make exaggerated or unwarranted claims for the insights psychology can offer translation studies, since as Wilss(1982: 218) warns us, "neither psycholinguistics nor neurology can as yet provide reliable information on how linguistic data are stored in the brain, how linguistic matching procedures take place and what mental structures are active in recalling linguistic information. " However, a decade or more on, enough is now known to begin the task of creating a model of the process which reveals the logical underpinning of the act of translation itself: an analogy of the stages and steps which must be accounted for if we are to explain how translation is possible as a human activity. Such a model can help us reach beyond the notion of translation theory as "helpful hints for translator" to a range of consciousness-raising insights into a process which is paradoxically, at once both unique and typical. Indeed, some, such as George Steiner(1975) have gone so far as to claim that all human communication is tantamount to translation. The addition of a psychological perspective in translation studies can open the way not only for a greater understanding of translating and interpreting but also for a deepening of our understanding of human communication in general; a shift which can establish translation studies as a major and perhaps independent field of study linked symbiotically with all the human sciences, and in particular though by no means exclusively, with linguistics and psychology.

选文二 Decision Making in Translation

Wolfram Wilss

导 言

这里的这篇文章选自贝克主编的 *Routlege Encyclopedia of Translation Studies*，词条的撰写者 Wolfram Wilss 是德国著名翻译理论家，主要论著包括:《译者行为的知识与技巧》、《翻译科学:问题与方法》、《二十世纪的口译和笔译:以德语为研究重点》，对于翻译过程有着广泛的观察和深刻的研究。

Any discussion of decision making is clearly based on the assumption that human beings behave rationally. There is, however, ample proof that(primarily in their day-to-day activities, less so in their scientific undertakings) they also engage in irrational behaviour. This raises the question of how one should define rational behaviour or, for that matter, decision making. There is widespread consensus that any type of rational behaviour must satisfy four requirements: verifiability, plausibility, situational adequacy and value-orientedness(Wallsten, 1980). Beyond that, opinions vary considerably.

Decision Making: An Overview

A decision problem occurs when one is faced with an issue which demands some form of choice. Any non-trivial choice contains an element of risk, because most decision problems cannot be reduced to hard and fast rules involving "if/then" relations: if one handles a problem X this way, the result will be Y1; if one handles it that way, the outcome will be Y2. Comparing the solutions Y1 and Y2, one can often, but not always, state that one of the two solutions is more efficient than the other. Note, however, that in assessing a decision-making situation individual differences may play an important role and, as a consequence, different decision-making strategies may be employed.

Decision-making processes are inextricably connected with problem-solving activities. In order to solve a problem, a human being must basically possess two types of knowledge, declarative and procedural(Ryle, 1949). Declarative knowledge(knowing what) means that a person has available in his/her memory some pool of stored knowledge and experience. Hardly any problem-solving activity begins with a *tabula rasa*; it has to draw on stored knowledge. Procedural knowledge(knowing how) means that human beings have access to strategic knowledge: they know(or ought to know) in which situations they must apply which operative moves to attain the desired goal.

In translation, the decision-making issue is particularly complex, because translation is essentially a derived activity. "Derived" is understood here to mean that the purpose of a translation is not the creation of an original text but the transformation of a primary text into a secondary text. The task of the translator, it can be argued, is to reproduce a source text for a target-language readership, taking account of its semantic, functional, pragmatic, and stylistic dimension, in addition to the needs and expectations of the target-text readership. In view of the fact that professional translators have to handle semantically and stylistically difficult texts, they unquestionably engage in a great deal of problem-solving and decision-making activities. It is therefore surprising that in translation studies little has been said so far about problem solving in the sense of a systematic descriptive method, and the same is true, perhaps to an even larger extent, of decision making. Hardly any subject index of the current literature on translation contains a problem-solving or a decision-making entry. One important exception is an early attempt by Levy(1967) to apply game theory to decision making in translation; Levy states that every move "is influenced by the knowledge of previous decisions and by the situation which resulted from them"(1967:1172).

Macrocontext and Microcontext in Decision Making

In discussing problem solving or decision making in translation, it is important to distinguish between macrocontext and microcontext. In order to effect decisions at the level of macrocontext, a translator needs a strategy that is related to the totality of the text to be translated, thereby avoiding inconsistency in the use of strategies at the lower levels. Here, a rough orientation usually suffices, for which the Lasswell formula with its various determinants may be helpful: *who says what to whom*, *with what communicative intention*, *in what spatio-temporal setting*, *with what linguistic means*. Naturally, domain-specific texts such as technical reports or academic articles raise only minor problems at the level of macrocontext. It is rarely the case that texts of this type are assigned divergent perspectives by the participants in a translation event, namely the sender of the source text, the translator, and the recipient of the target text.

By contrast, handling microcontextual problems, particularly in literary texts, often necessitates time-consuming formulation and reformulation efforts, with frequent jumping back and forth between the source text and the emerging target text. Complicating factors include singular (episodic) phenomena of the source text, such as semantic vagueness, complex syntax, intricate rhetorical strategies, theme/rheme distribution, central vs. peripheral information, metaphors, wordplay, allusions, irony, lack of coherence, morphological idiosyncrasies or neologisms, adjective/noun collocations (Baker, 1992), prepositional phrases, string compounds, cultural lacunae, and so on.

Because of their lack of specificity, general problem-solving strategies of the type proposed by Miller et al. in their TOTE model(TOTE=test-operate-test-exit) are of limited help to translators when they encounter a concrete situation of conflict and start searching for optimal or near-optimal solutions. The reason is obvious: unlike grammatical rules for instance, microcontextual problems, and their solutions, can be generalized only to a very limited extent. The more unique a translation problem the less practicable the general problem-solving procedures and the less like a game of chess or an algorithmically organized flowchart the whole activity becomes.

Models of Decision Making and Their Applicability to Translation

In its early stages, the study of decision making concentrated on the development of formal models currently used in operations research. A good example of a formalist approach to decision making is presented in an article by Rachlin et al. (1986) who compare a cognitive model and a behavioural model of decision making and come to the conclusion that both approaches are "just two competing descriptions of a single fundamental process"(1986:33). Their argument suggests, at least implicitly, that formalist models of decision making are not applicable to translator performance; that is, incidentally, the same explanation given for the failure of fully automatic high-quality translation in Bar-Hillel's sense. Apart from very simple syntactic patterns such as Subject-Predicate-Object (he has read the book vs. *Er hat das Buch gelesen*), conventional expressions (in so doing vs. *dabei*) or otherwise highly standardized text configurations which exclude decision-making procedures anyway, translation, like any form of language use, is conditioned by a variety of messy factors, including memory limitations, knowledge and attentional gaps, vagueness, attitudinal factors, interference effects, and so on. The crux of the matter, both for the human translator and to a much higher degree for machine translation, is that language use simply cannot be treated in terms of binary oppositions, at least not exhaustively. Source text and target text normally stand in a one-to-many relation, i. e. translation is not a formal procedure of substitution on the basis of simple one-to-one correspondence. And this confirms the relevance of problem-solving and decision-making procedures in translator performance.

Wallsten, whose collection of articles on the nature of decision making has much to offer to translation studies, has shown that the outcomes and contingencies associated with a particular choice can be referred to a decision "frame" and that it is often possible to frame a given decision problem in more than one way(1980). The final decision depends on a host of factors, such as adequate knowledge bases, a sufficiently detailed characterization of the problem requiring decision-making strategies, and the individual's own preferences or value system. At the same time, Wallsten has, no doubt inadvertently, confirmed that choice behaviour in translator performance is not a well-integrated field of research in translation studies. So far, the decision-making aspect of translation has, except for a few isolated contributions, been relegated to the fringes of the discipline; concepts related to the process of discipline; concepts related to the process of decision making have rarely been invoked to support the findings and arguments of theorists, teachers, or practitioners with a view to explaining or guiding translator performance in a systematic way.

To make things worse, there is considerable uncertainty in translation studies as to whether the translator is in fact engaged in genuine decision-making procedures at all and, if so, to what extent decision making can be considered a recognizable and legitimate feature of translator behaviour. The clarification of this issue may become easier if we focus our attention on pre-choice behaviour, i. e. the factors that inhibit or promote choices, rather than on the choices themselves. Obviously, there is always a range of barriers that must be overcome prior to decision making, and it is arguably this clearing away of barriers which must be dealt with in future theoretical, empirical, and applied translation studies. We must "devote more attention to experimental situations in which the choice alternatives are not well defined, in which memory for information can be assessed, and in which individual differences can be systematically explored" (Wallsten, 1980: xiii). What we need is information not only on how translators perform in general but also on how they perform in a specific translation situation with all its inherent array of complex factors.

In order to come to terms with this issue, think-aloud protocols have been employed, particularly with students of translation, and may well prove useful in due course. They have become rather popular in recent years (Krings, 1986; Lörscher, 1991; Tirkkonen-Condit, 1993) because they offer a means of identifying the alternatives a student takes into consideration in executing a translation task and how s/he approaches a final solution. An important factor in decision making is trial and error: students randomly choose an option and observe the outcome(or should in the course of their education be made to observe and weigh the outcome of their performance). The process by which trial-and-error behaviour gradually leads to the development of internalized and internalizable decision-making strategies is at present only poorly understood. It is, however, reasonable to assume that the process of learning decision-making strategies is essentially inductive in nature: a student experiences individual problems and tries to develop decision-making heuristics with the aim of gradually establishing some general strategies for dealing with problems in a routine fashion.

Whether this procedure justifies the assumption of decision-making rules (Einhorn, 1990) is doubtful, because the concept of decision making and the notion of rule-governed behaviour are mutually exclusive. Of course, if decision-making procedures are learned through induction, it is necessary to group translation problems, as far as possible, on the basis of perceived similarity(Vinay & Darbelnet, 1958; Malblanc, 1961); otherwise there would be as many decision-making heuristics as there are translation situations. Hence, any type of decision-making heuristics has to be generalizable to some extent over an optimally wide range of translation problems. It is clearly the case that, faced with a novel translation problem, the translator cannot simply fall back on time-honoured decision-making strategies. In the course of time, however, what started out as a novel problem may become a standard feature of translator performance and, as a consequence, no longer require decision-making cognitive input.

Pre-decision Moves and Choice Behaviour

The issue of improving a translator's decision-making potential raises a number of questions, such as: why do choice situations occur in translator performance? What are the factors that determine which choices and which types of choices will occur in which surroundings? What are the possible alternatives to a decision-making move? Why are certain decisions, such as the translation of the title of a book, put off? How does one decide when to decide and which version to give preference to? Under what circumstances will decisions be partly or wholly avoided? What is the result of a decision-making procedure? At the moment, such questions seem to lie outside the domain of translation studies, relevant though they may be to this object of study. One way of bringing them into the realm of translation research is to adopt something like the following procedural pattern as a framework(modified from Corbin, 1980).

> problem identification
> problem clarification(description)
> information collection
> deliberation on how to proceed

moment of choice

post-choice behaviour(evaluation of translation results)

Obstruction may occur at almost any of these stages, halting or delaying the decision-making procedure, raising the question of stage boundaries or stage overlapping. Such boundaries are difficult to pin down in translation, a fact that may lead to what in decision theory has been called "not-choosing behaviour" (Corbin, 1980: 49). "Not-choosing behaviour" may be due to two reasons:

(a) Translators may be confronted with a long array of alternatives and may therefore find it difficult to make up their minds, especially if they are not trained to make fast decisions, with the almost inevitable consequence that their choices will draw on less than optimal decision-making strategies.

(b) As far as information collection is concerned, it is by no means certain that more information will automatically lead to better results. Nevertheless, a translator, especially an inexperienced one, may start accessing many possible alternatives in order to minimize subjective uncertainty.

It should be clear by now why pre-decision moves are so important. In addressing this issue, the discipline must deal not only with individual heuristics but with individual sequences of heuristics during which translators attempt to reduce complex problems to a form compatible with their limited processing capabilities. This procedure does not always work: often a translator is aware that a kind of problem exists, but does not know, or does not know immediately, how to specify the problem and make the necessary decision-making inferences. This is where research on decision making in translation is urgently needed. We need to be able to describe decision-making behaviour in terms of an interaction between the translator's cognitive system, his/her knowledge bases, task specifications, and, last but not least, the "problem space" which plays a decisive role in determining decision-making behaviour. All four factors profoundly influence decision-making performance in translation and require considerably more attention than we have given them so far.

选文三　Think-Aloud Protocols

Riitta Jääskeläinen

导　言

这篇文章选自贝克主编的 *Routlege Encyclopedia of Translation Studies*,词条的撰写

者 Jääskeläinen 为芬兰约恩苏大学(Joensuu University)英语教授,主要从事口笔译的教学和研究工作,近年来在利用有声思维进行翻译研究方面取得了不少的成果。2003 年他与 Sonja Tirkkonen-Condit 合作,选编了 *Tapping and Mapping the Processes of Translation and Interpreting* 一书,引起学界关注。

Interest in the "black box" of translation, i. e. the thought processes that take place when someone is translating a text, is probably as old as translating itself. Translators have also analyzed their own translation methods, for example the problems they encounter while translating a particular(literary) text and how they solve them. In the 1980s, experimental methods began to be borrowed from psychology to gain access to what goes on in the translator's mind. The most popular of these has been the "think-aloud" or "thinking-aloud" method, which involving asking a translator to translate a text and, at the same time, to verbalize as much of his or her thoughts as possible. Subjects involved in such experiments need special training to enable them to verbalize freely instead of analyzing and commenting on their thought process. Subjects' performances are generally recorded on audio- or video-tape; the term "think-aloud protocols" or TAPs for short, refers to the written transcripts of such recordings.

At the most general level, the purpose of TAP studies is to gain a better understanding of the psychological and linguistic mechanisms involved in the activity of translating. More specific areas of research have included, for example, problem-solving strategies(Krings, 1986; Lörscher, 1991), criteria for decision making (Tirkkonen-Condit, 1990), and creativity in translation(Kussmaul, 1991). At the early stages of process-oriented empirical research, the emphasis tended to be on formulating, testing, and refining hypothesis about what goes on in the "black box."

Thinking Aloud as a Method of Data Collection

The problem with investigating the processes of the human mind is that they are not available for direct observation. In psychological research, various methods have been developed to gain access, albeit indirectly, to mental processes. Thinking aloud is one of a large suite of data collection methods known as "verbal report procedures" or "introspective methods." These include, for example,(traditional) "introspection," where the subject of the experiment carries out a self-analysis of his or her own thought processes, and "retrospective verbal reporting," which takes place after rather than during the performance of a given task for the experiment. In contrast, thinking aloud is concurrent(takes place simultaneously with the task performance) and undirected(subjects are not asked to verbalize specific information). As a result, TAP data is considered more complete and more reliable than introspective or retrospective reports: more complete because there is less likelihood of forgetting or omitting information, and more reliable because there is less likelihood of distortion(Ericsson & Simon, 1984). In other words, the method of thinking aloud in data collection attempts, as far as possible, to elicit unedited data; it is then the task of experimenter to investigate whether—and if so which—regularities appear in the data. To facilitate verbalizing and to prevent subjects from analyzing their own thoughts (i. e. introspecting), some researchers have recommended that subjects should receive special training and be given warm-up tasks before the experiment proper(Ericsson & Simon, 1984; 1987).

Verbal reports have had a highly controversial history in psychology, ranging from unconditional acceptance by structuralists to total rejection by behaviourists. Contemporary assessment tend to be less extreme, most scholars now maintain that, when elicited with care and analyzed with sufficient awareness of their limitations, verbal reports can provide rich and useful data on human thought processes(Ericsson & Simon, 1984). One important and controversial question still remain though as to whether verbal report data provides access to mental processes or to(intermediate) products of these processes(sometimes called mental content; Nisbett & Wilson, 1977). The answer depends largely on the definition of "process." If mental processes are defined as neutral activities, they obviously have to be considered inaccessible by means of any method of verbal reporting. But Ericsson & Simon (1984), for example, view human thought processes as information processing. According to their theory of verbalization, that part of information process which takes place in working memory, i. e. which is the focus of conscious attention, is accessible to verbalization. However, making a clear distinction between mental processes and mental content—the latter comprising, for instance, prior experiences, focus of attention at any given moment, attitudes, emotions, and plans (Nisbett & Wilson, 1977)—may be less relevant to translation research. Verbalizations produced in the course of performing a translation task provide additional information about the otherwise hidden stage between understanding the source text and producing the target text. Whether this data reflects mental processes or mental content is, in some cases at least, of less importance.

There are, nevertheless, severe limitations on usefulness of TAPs. These include the inevitable incompleteness of the data. Because only that which is conscious can be verbalized, TAPs can provide no more plan than an incomplete account of the processing involved in any cognitive task. On the other hand, although the majority of mental processes take place at the unconscious level, many of them(for example basic perceptual processes) may not be of direct interest to translation studies despite being central to human behaviour in general. There is also the fact that the activity of translating tends to make those involved in it(i. e. translators) more conscious of certain phenomena, such as nuances of meaning, which in everyday language use require little or no conscious attention; this suggests that translation may be more amenable to verbalization than other forms of language use. In addition, tape-recording or video-taping an experiment enables the researcher to supplement verbal report data with observational data; for example intonation patterns, pauses and in the case of videotaping, eye-movements, gestures and facial expressions. The combination of verbalized and observational data can provide clues about what might be going on at the unconscious level. In the case of translation, the written end-product can also offer additional information. A second problem with the use of TAPs concerns the potential effect of verbalization on the process under investigation. Ericsson and Simon argue, on the basis of an extensive survey of research evidence, that verbal reporting does not change the course or structure of thought processes (1984: 78 - 107). However, in the absence of any methodological surveys of the effects of verbalization on translation processes in particular (rather than thought processes in general), it is difficult to determine whether a similar degree of optimism can be justified within translation studies. Until more research on methodological issues is carried out, we have to rely—cautiously—on the evidence from closely related areas, such as research on writing processes, where thinking aloud is regarded as a useful tool(see for example Hayes & Flower, 1980; Bereiter & Scardamalia, 1987).

In sum, although think-aloud protocols cannot help us unravel all the mysteries of translation, they do provide access to valuable information about the nature of translating. Other methods of acquiring such information include interviews, questionnaires and team translation(translators working in pairs or in small groups; House, 1988; Matrat, 1995). Complementary evidence collected from different sources is likely to provide the most complete and reliable picture of the contents of the "black box."

Overviews of TAP Studies

TAP studies of translation offer an excellent example of the interdisciplinary nature of translation research. Data collection methods were borrowed from psychology, and the methods used to describe and analyze TAP data came from a variety of disciplines such as psycholinguistics, translation studies and cognitive and social psychology. In fact, because methods of analysis usually have to be modified—even to the extent of being tailor-made—to describe a particular body of data, TAP studies have come to represent such a wide spectrum of research traditions that, instead of forming a clearly uniform approach within translation studies, many of them seem to share no more than the basic methodology of eliciting data.

Thus, for instance, the source and target languages have varied, as has the direction of translation(into or out of mother tongue). Usually subjects have produced a written translation of a written source text, except in Lörscher's study(1991), in which foreign-language students produced an oral translation of a written text. The source texts have represented different genres, ranging from travel brochures to political satire and from popularized science to government documents. Access to reference material has sometimes been allowed and sometimes denied, in the latter case in order to elicit richer inferencing strategies(as, for instance, in Gerloff, 1986). Subjects, in turn, have represented various levels of linguistic and translational competence and have included, for example, foreign language learners, translation students, competent bilinguals, as well as professional translators. The translation processes of language learners can of course be dismissed as not being representative of professional translation; on the other hand, it is useful to have control groups for comparison. More importantly, TAP researchers, seem to define the very notion of "translation" in different ways. For some, "the task of translating, by definition, demands a version as close to the original as possible" (Hölscher & Möhle, 1987:114), whereas others have adopted a broader functional definition which allows deviating from the original if necessary (see, for example, Jääskeläinen, 1990; Tirkkonen-Condit, 1990; Kussmaul, 1991). The definition of "translation" depends largely on the purpose of research, i. e. whether translation is used as a means of eliciting data on language processing or whether translation itself, as an activity, is the focus of investigation. The underlying definition of translation also seems to determine whether or not subjects are given a translation brief(description of the purpose of translation) at the start of the experiment.

Not surprisingly, such a multiplicity of approaches tends to create certain research problems. For instance, comparing the results and using the comparisons as a basis for generalization becomes highly complicated. Moreover, it is extremely important to be able to combine evidence from several studies, because subject populations have in general been rather small(ranging from one to twelve in most cases). On the other hand, the high level of variation within TAP studies has had its advantages too; different types of study have shed light on different aspects of the translation process and on different kinds of translation processes, thus illustrating the complexity of translational phenomena. In fact, the findings of TAP studies have so far offered indisputable evidence to support the view that there is no single monolithic translation process. The nature of the process varies considerably depending on several factors, including type of text, type of task and type of translator.

The evidence which has become gradually available from TAP studies has given rise to some intriguing hypothesis which merit further attention. In addition to some predictable results, for instance that language learners focus on the process of lexical transfer(Krings, 1986; Lörscher, 1993) whereas professional translators focus on style and the needs of the target audience (Jääskeläinen, 1990; Tirkkonen-Condit, 1990), TAP studies have also offered a few surprises. For example, one common assumption has been that for professional translators the translation process is highly automatized, with few problems and little conscious decision making(Börsch, 1986; Krings, 1986). Séguinot's case study(1989) of a Canadian government translator supported this hypothesis. However, further research has shown that professional translators often identify more problems and spend more time and energy on solving them than language learners(Krings, 1988; Jääskeläinen, 1990). On the basis of these findings, the automaticity hypothesis has been refined as follows: language learners are unaware of potential problems in translation, and a higher level of competence leads to heightened awareness of problems among professional translators (Krings, 1988; Jääskeläinen, 1990; Laukkanen, 1993). Finally, special attention is increasingly being paid to the role of affective factors such as attitude and of motivation (Kussmaul, 1991; Fraser, 1993). Preliminary results seem to imply that a positive attitude and a high level of motivation form part of professional competence and may even contribute to enhancing the quality of translation. These findings are supported by psychological research on expertise, where it is hypothesized that the decisive factor in the development of expertise may not be giftedness (nature) or extensive practice (nurture) alone: in order to sustain the long period of training required to gain the relevant expertise, a high level of motivation has to be created and maintained (Posner, 1988).

TAP research clearly still has a long way to go to establish itself within translation studies. More research is required to test the results and refine the hypothesis developed so far. The most important areas awaiting further research include refining the methodology, replicating earlier studies, and initiating longitudinal studies to map the development of translation competence in the same individual (or group of individuals) over a long period of time.

选文四　Aesthetic Progression in Literary Translation

姜秋霞

导　言

这里推荐的这篇文章最初发表在 2008 年第四期的 *Meta*，作者是国内最早的翻译学方向的博士，也是国内最早从格式塔心理学的角度研究翻译的学者，出版了专著《文学翻译中的审美过程：格式塔意象再造》。这里的这篇论文运用格式塔审美心理模式对文学翻译的审美过程进行动态的研究和认识，对于文学翻译过程中的格式塔意象的重建提出了自己的观点，给读者以很多启示。

1　Translation as an Aesthetic Progression

Progression instead of process is based on the conception that a literary text characterized by images as well as linguistic meanings inherently capable of multiple actualizations cannot be assigned a single correct translation, and that aesthetic experience is not a property of a finished product; it can never achieve a state of fixity but exists as continuously changing processes.

Aesthetic progression in literary translation is a psychological procedure acting on and building representations of what is described in the text. It is applied to denote the intermediary stage in literary translation, that is, how the image is mentally actualized. At the reading and interpreting stage, the translator is supposed to visualize images and consider possible linguistic means to reconstruct them in the target language. The act of image actualization is a cumulative process—the building of meaning upon meaning and experience upon meaning in order to establish finally an idea or an interpretation in the mind of the translator-reader.

Aesthetic experience in literary translation is a progression also in that the image of the translator is actualized in two languages and his mental actualization is integrated with transference into another language, for he is always operating between a source text and a target text. The image actualization of the translator is first of all a gradation from one version toward another like that of the ordinary reader, and on the other hand undergoes the further progression in transformation, since he has to represent it in another language.

What first appears in written form is very often not an adequate representation of the mental one, for the mental image is activated by two language schema simultaneously. The written representation has to obtain progression from ST-based schema to TT-based schema, and the production of T-text entails the application of regular and efficient transformations to a mental image. In this context, the mental representation of the text that is finally registered in the translator's mind may not be identical with the original text in formal structure. The syntactic or semantic elements are subject to constant reformulation and modification in accord with the TL rules and the gestalt image with TL schemata. For the translator, it is equally important to obtain the maximally text-based meaning representation of the original text, and obtain maximal realization of a new text in another language. The early versions of a translation would tend to correspond more closely to linguistic expressions of S-text, while the later versions would gradually approach the maximally appropriate representation which manifests a T-text schema. That is, an image would at first be characterized by S-text formulations, while the final realization would be adapted to fit the T-text organization. The translator has thus subjected the text to a process of rearrangement. And the aesthetic experience or image from ST to TT undergoes the progression from SL structured to TL structured.

Translation has been regarded as equivalent representation of linguistic structures, and translation studies have long been concerned with different levels of text equivalence. Ever since Eugene Nida presented his sentence-rank model to describe the translating process, researches in this field have devoted a great deal of thinking to the intermediary stage transfer(1964) and have then developed more adequate and sophisticated models. James S. Holmes developed on Nida's kernel-level by presenting a text-based model(1988). In his model, the stage of transfer has been expanded to a complex transference of map or mental conception.

Bell(1995) has gone even further by exploring the mental actualization, that is, how the translator processes Tsl information. He argues that the study of translation requires a double awareness, that of linguistic texture in terms of structure and of discourse, and of text processing in terms of construction and interpretation, linking linguistics with psychology in an attempt to understand what it is that translators do when they translate. Benefiting from information theory, he posited a translating process involving three processing stages with psychological faculties involved.

As is seen, translation studies have been more and more concerned with complexities of the mental operations at the intermediary stage. These models provided have doubtlessly made a great achievement in this area, especially Bell's model, which, closely related to theory of information processing, has explored cognitive factors involved in the mental processing. However, when applied to a highly complex entity of the literary text, the translating process still requires considerable development.

The literary text is universally recognized as work of art, which contains aesthetic essence within and beyond the linguistic structure. It is constituted by the possession of aesthetic qualities as a necessary though not perhaps a sufficient condition(Osborne, 1983; Mitias, 1988). These qualities as its defining characters are not given as ready made or finally formed realities, but as possibilities or inherent images for realization. They emerge as gestalt in the activity of aesthetic faculties, waiting to be actualized in the interaction with the translator. In reading and interpreting the literary work of art, the translator cognitively perceives a relatively stable linguistic structure and goes on to build artistic images which realize the aesthetic value that intrinsically belongs to the linguistic aspect of the work. This interaction between the text and the translator constitutes the aesthetic progression, which the translator, as a reader first of all, experiences in his interpretation of the literary text.

2　The Image Model

In literary translation, the text is not reproduced in the sense of linguistic structure but by way of meaning gestalt and image gestalt. Linguistic structure in the target text may come out as equivalent with that of the original text, which, however, does not rise from correspondence-finding of linguistic items. Rather, it is the result of psychological tendency and linguistic universals or coincidence. In his interpretation of the S-text, the translator formulates images, and represents them in a T-text. Just as de Beaugrande pointed out, the basis of the act of translation is not the original text, but rather the representation of the text that is eventually generated in the translator's mind. In the production of the T-text, the translator does not find individual linguistic items(words or sentences) correspondent to those in the S-text, but uses the image gestalt as a kind of general criterion against which to test each sentence. Translation does not mean to replace one linguistic text with another, or to find word-for-word, sentence-for-sentence equivalents, but to reproduce in linguistic forms the mental image constituted out of the ST. In the formulation of the new, translated text, there are no doubt equivalent linguistic structures, but they do not result from a direct or mechanical corresponding process, rather they are the necessary coincidences of two languages since there exist similarities between them. On the other hand, in the process of reproduction the psychological tendency of the translator would permit him to equate the linguistic items with the original ones. This processing result is quite different from mechanical corresponding translation in that, in the former action, the translator acts as a creative artist(like the author), while in the latter case, he is a mechanical simulator. In Holmes' translation model(1988), the translator as a reader abstracts a "map" of the original text(Map Tsl), then on the basis of this map he develops a second map(Map Ttl). The present study assumes an aesthetic image at the mental transferring stage without classifying it into Image-Tsl and Image-Ttl, for we further assume that the image-G is the interactive result of both SL and TL and its realization undergoes a progressive transference from one to the other.

The present study will therefore present an image-based literary translation model.

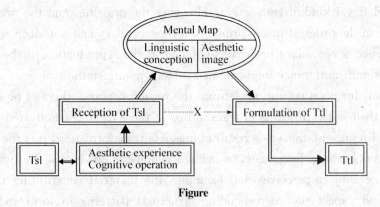

Figure

Main phases:

Phase I: to translate the written text into a mental map;

Phase II: to find goal-language exponents of the overall mental representation obtained in Phase I.

(The dotted line with x signifies an unsuccessful process.)

This is a macro model mainly concerned with the aesthetic progression in literary translation. The essential argument of this model rests on the following assumptions:

a. In literary translation, the translator's interpretation of the literary text undergoes an aesthetic progression.

b. The aesthetic progression is an image building process from ST to TT organization.

c. Successful literary translation results from image representation apart from text-representation, text in the sense of formal linguistic structure. The linguistic equivalents in the translation are mainly due to similarities in the two languages—ST and TT on the one hand, and the psychological tendency of the translator on the other hand.

Roger T. Bell, in his study of translating process(1995), has claimed that the translator translates with full resources of the semantic representations of the clauses available and with the unity of the text organized as a schema ready in memory. According to Bell, in this schema, all information about each clause and about the text as a whole is displayed and interconnected as a semantic representation. The mental process of the transformation of a source language text into a target language text is simplified as: (1) the analysis of one language-specific text(the source language text, the SLT) into a universal(non-language specific) semantic representation, and (2) the synthesis of this semantic representation into a second language-specific text(1995). Bell's schema focuses on semantic gestalt while our image model emphasizes aesthetic gestalt and significance, both promoting a unified conception and a gestalt transformation.

In literary translation, aesthetic properties derive from the dense restructuration of the artistic image presented in the original text. It follows that a translator has the duty of reflecting these qualities by means of a maximal preservation not only of the linguistically relevant information, but also of the image. Of course formal correspondence is also important in whatever kind of translation. However the priorities and the work sequence is supposed to be in the order of image primary, form secondary and not vice versa. Linguistic formal equivalence is secondary properties entailed in the reproduction of the texts but not independently significant. Since linguistic or syntactic manifestations of texts are themselves functional signals for creating and presenting the image in texts, there is no special motive for preserving their outward forms in translating. If the T-text is manifested in identical or invariant formal representations as a result of image-G transformation, it is the coincidentally equivalent aspects between languages, or is due to language universals. Naturally, when the translator as the subject perceives and examines the material constituting the pattern or image, he would expect the corresponding structural patterns in form and therefore in expression. Sometimes the coincidence would occur that both the form(the equivalent parts and expression) and the whole image are harmonized. But not always. The corresponding parts would most often add up to something that shows neither harmony nor conflict but a lack of unity or relatedness, which renders the whole meaningless, inexpressive. Therefore literary translation must be coordinated by a conscious establishment of images, especially in translations conducted between languages such as Chinese and English, which differ rather enormously in linguistic structures, and between which formal correspondence does not easily occur.

3　Aesthetic Progression and the Translator

As an artist, the translator must have a high degree of ability to represent, in the mind's eye, certain combinations of the S-text. Like a painter who has an uncommon visual imagery, the musician auditory imagery, the translator must have verbal imagery. As Zwaan claimed(1993:170), text comprehension is a process influenced by both textual and cognitive factors. That is, text comprehension does not just lie in the meaning the text conveys, but also in how the reader approaches and responds to it. In the process of meaning comprehension, or in this context, of image-actualization, the translator-reader has, apart from his cognitive mechanisms, his aesthetic faculties such as imagination, which operate to actualize the meaning and achieve certain aesthetic experience.

Different translators with different operations of psychological faculties might produce different comprehension of a literary text, hence different translated versions. This point is held by Iser who described the personalized aspect in the following way:

> In the same way two people gazing at the night sky may both be looking at the same collection of stars, but one will see the image of a plough and the other will make out a dipper. The stars in a literary text are fixed; the lines that join them are variable. (Viehoff, 1986)

Such a claim justifies the notion of dynamics in one's comprehension, which is also true in the comprehension of text meaning, thus the actualization of the aesthetic qualities of the image is dependent much on subjective perception and judgment. The artistic image is not a thing with a definite structure but a dynamic reality which becomes actual in aesthetic perception. First of all, the aesthetic quality originates in a creative process where the activity involved is vital and out of lived experience. The translator as an author in his re-creative activity has also to articulate the life of the mind. Hence if the reader is to actualize the image or quality, his dynamic activity is to be involved. It is for this reason that we will take into special account the translator's subjective role particularly his psychological operations in his image-actualization. The psychological operations are mainly constituted by passive synthesis and active operation, which can be further analyzed as imagination and reflection.

3.1 Imaginative Faculty

Imagination for the literary translator is the assistant operation of bringing together of elements which are not equivalently connected and organized or the operation of actualizing what is inherent in the source text. "As far as literature is concerned, the meaning of the literary work is not the same as the formulated aspects, but can only be built up in the imagination through continual shifting and reciprocal qualification of those aspects. The meaning of the literary work remains related to what the printed text says, but it requires the creative imagination of the reader to put it all together."(Iser, 1978: 142) As Richards puts it, the production of vivid images is the commonest and the least interesting thing which is referred to by imagination(1983:188). In the following translations, there involves obvious operation of imagination. When it works sufficiently and appropriately, it may result in a translation presenting a vivid picture.

Example 1

Arable lands are few and limited; with but slight exceptions the prospect is a broad rich mass of grass and trees, mantling minor hills and dales within the major. Such is the Vale of Blackmoor.

(Thomas Hardy: *Tess of the D'Urbervilles*)

Chinese pinyin:

Zheer de gengdi buduo, mianji ye shao, yiyan wangqu, chule jichu liwai, man shi lücao he shumu, fengmei qianmian, fugai zhe gaoshan dahe zhijian de zhepian qiuling xiaogu. Zhe jiushi heiyuangu de fengguang.

(By Sun Fali)

The phrase "minor hills and dales within the major" in the original calls for a mental picture of the translator, who has to actualize it through imagination and represent it out of a T-text schema. As a result, *gaoshan dahe zhijian de zhepian qiuling xiaogu* instead of *xiaoshan xiaogu zai dashan dagu zhong* is produced, which draws a clear outline of mountains and the hills, dales among them, and makes the picture in the translated version just as consistent. Imagination in literary translation is, first of all, an act of creation conceived as essentially and perpetually bringing of order out of chaos, or destroying chaos, chaos in the sense of a T-text schema, by making its parts intelligible by the assertion of the identity of the T-text schema.

Since the aesthetic experience did not happen in language, language per se can only communicate it symbolically; the power of language to symbolize experience depending on its power to stimulate imagination. Currie has also stressed imagination as a part of the mind's information processing system. The fictional status of didactic or motivating pieces, he stated, is secured when they are designed to instruct and exhort us by getting us to imagine. In order to symbolize experience as completely as possible, that is, to provoke the most complex imagination possible, literature makes appropriate use of every power language has of affecting the mind. The translator has the potentiality for image actualization, while psychological factors such as imagination might produce effects on the information processing of image qualities. Image qualities are manifestation of psychical processes, which are most often perceived in the aesthetic experience, for literally they are only suggested and not actually there. If all languages express the same ideas and feelings in all the same way, or if they express them with more words, it would become apparent that the image in question is actually present in the object of perception and not merely associated with it by imagination. But actually, aesthetic qualities are inherent hence experienced. Imagination is therefore necessary in formulating a gestalt image and experiencing the aesthetic qualities involved.

Example 2

The sky, now overcast and sullen, so changed from the early afternoon, and the steady insistent rain could not disturb the soft quietude of the valley; the rain and the rivulet mingled with one another, and the liquid note of the blackbird fell upon the damp air in harmony with them both.

(Daphne du Maurier: *Rebecca*)

Chinese pinyin:

Tiankong zheshi heiyun mibu, yinyinchenchen, he xiawu san si dianzhong de shihou buda yiyang, yu you buting di xiazhe, dan zhe que jingrao buliao shangu de jingmi; yu sheng he xishui sheng jiaorong zai yiqi, huamei de wanzhuan de qudiao zai chaoshi de kongqi zhong huidangzhe, he yu sheng, xishui sheng xiang yinghe.

The translator visualizes the picture, hearing all the sounds as if present at the scene. In reproduction he is able to use his image to recreate the vividness of the original, rendering "the rain and the rivulet" as *yu sheng*, *xishui sheng*, of which "sheng"(the sound) is not morphologically stated in the original, so that the T-text reader can experience the melody of what seems silent.

Example 3

It was a day as fresh as grass growing up and cloud going over and butterflies coming down can make it. It was a day compounded from silence of bee and flower and ocean and land, which were not silences at all, but motions, stirs, flutters, risings, fallings, each in its own time and matchless rhythm.

Chinese pinyin:

Lücao qiqi, baiyun ranran, caidie pianpian, zhe rizi shi ruci qingxin keai, mifeng wuyan, chunhua bu yu, haibo sheng xie, dadi yin ji, zhe rizi you ruci anjing, ran er bingfei anjing, yinwei wanwu ge yiqi teyoude jiezou, huo dong, huo yao, huo zhen, huo qi, huo fu.

(By Xi Yongji)

Out of imagination, the translator is able to associate *cao*(grass) with *lü*(green), *yun* (cloud) with *bai*(white), and *die*(butterflies) with *cai*(colourful) instead of *cao zhang qilaile* and so on. He can also transform all the nouns "motions," "stirs," "flutters," "risings," and "fallings" into correspondent Chinese verbs *dong*, *yao*, *zhen*, *qi*, *fu* to present the target readers with a vivid scene.

Imagination for the literary translator is the assistant operation, whose major function is to facilitate image-formulation, and helps to adjust the mental image, that is: (a) to experience the gestalt qualities and formulate a pictorial scene out of the linguistic schemata; (b) to organize mental image into a unified and T-text-oriented entity(structure).

However, in literary translation, a different operation of imagination may conjure up different images, or in other words, different versions may result from different imaginations of the original picture. Psychologically, this is most often due to a dissimilar perceptive schema.

Image perception for the translator is an automated process based on his linguistic and other comprehensive knowledge, and imagination is naturally involved in this process to supplement image-actualization. However, for the translator, who is sometimes confronted with syntactic and semantic deviations when two languages conflict in structure and dissimilar patterns emerge, this automated process will be impeded and expectations will be disturbed. Thus, more conscious and active imagination is integrated. Such imagination is what Coleridge has defined as secondary imagination which he classifies from the primary imagination. Primary imagination is what is involved in perception and what naturally operates unconsciously, an agency which enables us both to discriminate and to order, to separate and to synthesize, and thus makes gestalt organization possible, for without it we should have only a collection of meaningless sense data. The secondary imagination is the conscious human use of this power. When we employ our primary imagination in the very act of perception we are not doing so with our conscious will but are exercising the basic faculty of our awareness of ourselves and the external world; the second imagination is more conscious and less elemental. It projects and creates new harmonies of meaning. When its synthesizing, integrating powers are at work, bringing all aspects of a subject into a complex unity, then image-G in this larger sense results. Dewey once described the creative act of imagination and its conditioning factors, with reference to art in general:

> For to perceive, a beholder must create his own experience. And his creation must include relations comparable to those which the original producer underwent. They are not the same in any literal sense. But with the perceiver, as with the artist, there must be an ordering of the elements of the whole that is in form, although not in details, the same as the process of organization the creator of the work consciously experienced. (1958: 54)

This is closely related to secondary imagination in literary translation. That is, to perceive, the translator is to recreate but his imagination should remain as related as possible to what the text uncovers. Secondary imagination in literary translation, especially when it operates consciously, is a kind of relevant association. It is in such case not boundless, but is modified toward the author's perceptual patterns. It is simply association based on the context, rather than imaginative acts fully executed or given full play. The former would produce an image more equivalent to that underlying the original text, while the latter might reveal a product of one's own which might go astray from the SLT. For this reason, the translator often modulates his imagination, and reflection plays its role much more than an ordinary reader does. Thus the secondary imagination is imagination integrated with reflection in aesthetic perception.

3.2 Reflection or Accommodation

As perceptual patterns are particularly based on past experience and in most cases the interpretation of the perceived expression is influenced by what is known about the person or object in question and about the context in which it appears, reflection or accommodation comes into play when dissimilarity occurs in the perceptual patterns. Such active psychological operations will lead to more differentiated interpretations, which will take the particular context into account.

"Reflection" is illustrated by Dufrenne (1973) as "what to make perception and imagination as consciousness." It operates to control and, if necessary, restrain its spontaneity, and reduces the sense of confused totality which the translator experiences in the first reading of the text. It is thus capable of increasing the translator's comprehension of the work's meaning as an equivalent whole since the scene or character as an image is immanent in the linguistic sign, in contrast with external and conventional meaning of linguistic signs. The images he has built, the meaning he has obtained might be of self-identity(too much of the translator's own flavour), since the workings of his faculties are of occasional spontaneity, which can result in dissimilarities as discussed above. Rather than relying on intuition or spontaneity, the translator is to gather data and make analytical study, to supplement the inductive heuristics of actual reading, to organize elements and adjust his image according to the original. A translator is at first confronted with the parameters of choices made in the original text. Those parameters can serve as important criteria for making decisions about the translation, and serve as a standard for making appropriate choices and hence for reflection on the style of the work. We most often name an expression in accordance with the name of the creator of a work, because the characteristic quality of that work also appears to designate its creator. By reflective analysis we can identify the function of expression in the aesthetic object.

As an active operation, reflection is necessary in the aesthetic progression in literary translation, in a way to adjust the workings of his imaginative faculties and provide access to a more faithful meaning. Since emotion in aesthetic imagination may ravish and shatter us and prevent us from reading expression, since it may sometimes distort our proper understanding of the meaning, reflective analysis comes into play to define, or at least name expressions in a more correspondent sense.

On this point, "accommodation" by Piaget is also referential. According to Piaget's theory of cognition or perception, when confronted with a new stimulus, one tries to assimilate it into existing schemata. When sometimes a stimulus cannot be placed or assimilated into a schema because there are no schemata into which it readily fits, and when the characteristics of the stimulus do not approximate those required in any of one's available schemata, one can either create a new schema into which he can place the stimulus or he can modify an existing schema so that the stimulus will fit into it. These are two forms of accommodation in the cognitive sense, which means the creation of new schemata or the modification of old schemata. When applied to aesthetic perception, accommodation helps to modify or adjust the perceptual schema. In image-actualization in literary translation, the conscious accommodation of the translator can result in a change in, or development of perceptual schemata, that is, it can modify his passive perception of the image schema in the original, either adjusting his own to the original or the original to his own. Once accommodation has taken place, the image-G structure is readily assimilated, and a three-dimensional image is readily constructed in the mind of the translator.

With the supplementary aid of such active operation, sympatico can be relatively achieved, even when there occur perceptual dissimilarities between the translator and the author and even oppositions between their beliefs. The degree to which he accords with the relevant experience of the writer is a measure of the degree to which the image in S-text will arouse similar experiences in him. As Richards (1929: 255) has stated: poetry which has been built upon firm and definite beliefs about the world must appear differently to readers who do and readers who do not hold similar beliefs. Yet in fact most readers, and nearly all good readers, are very little disturbed by even a direct opposition between their own beliefs and the beliefs of the poet. Different readers, after due study, may respond in the same way to the poetry and arrive at similar judgments about it. Consequently, after due study, after active operation or an adjustment of his perceptual schema, the translator is likely to follow the writer in the writer's way. The operation of reflection or accommodation is a common operation agreed on by practising translators. But on how and how much it operates, there is still a lot to explore. This no longer concerns us at present due to limited space and time, but will be of much interest to be dealt with in future empirical studies. Here, however, we must mention a few factors the translator has to consider when his reflective analysis works to accommodate his schema. They are mainly: the context, the ideological component and the cultural diversity.

As is commonly known, the spatio-temporal context influences the way a phenomenon is perceived. "An object looks big or small depending on whether it is seen, spatially, in the company of smaller or larger objects" (Arnheim, 1949). The same is true for the temporal context. Mozart's music may appear serene and cheerful to a modern listener, who perceives it in the temporal context of twentieth-century music, whereas it conveyed the expression of violent passion and desperate suffering to his contemporaries against the background of the music they know. Shelley's poems might be difficult to comprehend if they are not related to the specific context of war or the fierce reality the poem is positioned against. The ignorance or irrelevance of the background knowledge may hinder a legitimate reception and production of meaning, even more an experience of the feeling. Such an example does not demonstrate that there is no intrinsic connection between perceptual patterns and the expression they convey but simply that experiences must not be merely evaluated in isolation from their temporal whole-context. Besides, there is also an ideological component, which acts as a constraint on the perceptual schema. Needless to say, "ideology" is taken here in a sense not limited to the political sphere; rather, "ideology would seem to be that grillwork of form, convention, and belief which orders our actions" (Jameson, 1974: 107). The translation usually projects a certain image in the service of a certain ideology. This fact is most apparent in the altered images in the translations. Some translators have tried to make the reproduced images fit their ideology by using all kinds of manipulative techniques, while other translators try to merge the poetics of the original with a poetics acceptable in their own ideology. What's more, the social and cultural diversities may make the pursuit of simpatico difficult if not impossible for the intra-lingual translator. Sometimes the translator does not activate the same image a native speaker of the language would activate, or the images the author intended, because the images realized by a linguistic frame are closely linked to a different socio-cultural background of the language user in question. Similar schema are more likely to be realized when the author and the translator live in the same historical moment, in the same ideological background. In such case they might share a common sensibility and enjoy a similar aesthetic experience.

All the above factors must be taken into account in the active operation for the translator to realize a similar schema and experience with the author.

Active operation is an indispensable facilitation to reach the point of simpatico at which author and translator converge, and this point marks the end of self-alienation which takes place while the translator is disregarding the author and his experience. Our discussion suggests that there are two kinds of simpatico or communion: one is operating unconsciously and the other consciously. By the unconscious one, we mean that which operates under the condition of similar patterns. And by the conscious one, we refer to that which operates when the translator voluntarily applies some psychological mechanisms under the condition when dissimilar patterns occur.

The need for access to the nature and function of aesthetic progression becomes more and more pressing and less and less deniable if translation theory is to set about providing a systematic and objective description of the process.

选文五　Cognitive Characteristics of Re-categorization in C-E Translation

刘华文

导　言

作者是国内近年来专门从认知语言学的角度研究文学翻译的学者,最近出版了他的研究专著《汉英翻译与跨语认知》(南京大学出版社,2009)。这部作品的前九章集中探讨汉英翻译过程中语义和句法两个层面的认知转化特征。第十章兼顾语义、句法和语用三个层面,通过考察包括形容词和副词这些修饰语的语义指向(semantic orientation)和句法位置(syntactic position)的跨语认知调整,透视修饰语因这些调整所连带的语用功能(pragmatic function)的变化。这里选取的是这部专著的第三章。

1　Re-categorization: A Cognitive Mechanism in Translation

Categorical system varies from language to language. A category does not necessarily have an absolutely corresponding category in another language. In translation, a categorical system in one language is more likely to undergo re-categorization in another language. Although the dislocated correspondence is inevitable between categories in two languages, the cross-lingual transfer can still be carried out. The information carried by the category in the ST can still be transferred into the TL, although some of the information is likely to be decreased or increased. As for Chinese-English translation, the equal-level or split-level transfer between categories is a cognitive process. In other words, the transfer involves the categorization, one of the basic human cognitive processes. Since the cross-lingual categorization occurs after the categorization which has taken place in the SL, we term it re-categorization. The most primitive categorization is actualized through brain by the interaction between human body and the external world. In a basic sense, it is "not a product of conscious reasoning."(Lakoff & Johnson, 1999: 18) With the deepening of the cognition about the things, the human cognitive categorical system is also maturing, and the categorization has become a conscious cognitive process. People make use of the names corresponding to the categories in human cognitive system for the purpose of categorizing in response to the stimulus from the external world. Nevertheless, when the stimulus received is fresh and original and its corresponding category does not yet exist in the conventional categorical system, people will take advantage of the existent categories to categorize the new thing. When people started to know platypus, the animal was quite confusing for its properties of simultaneously being egg-born and mammal. And thus it is hard to put it into a definite category. However, zoologist must categorize it. And then we have platypus as its categorical name. This category etymologically originates from flat-foot animal, which highlights the property of flat-footedness. Meanwhile, the animal also has such categorical names as duckbill or duckbill platypus, which figure its property of being flat-billed or both of the properties. However, when it enters into the corresponding categorical system in Chinese, 鸭嘴兽, its Chinese counterpart, has only reserved its property of being flat-billed while omitting its property of being flat-footed. Moreover, it has integrated 兽 into itself, suggesting that it is an ambivalent animal in both being egg-born and mammal. In this way, the category for platypus in English is different from its counterpart in Chinese as far as the categorical content is concerned. The difference results from the cognitive re-categorization in the process of cross-lingual transformation.

Generally speaking, the categorical system in a language has been conventionally inserted in the linguistic body and stored in the unconscious of human mind, waiting to be summoned up and surface onto the conscious of the language. But in the cross-lingual transformation, the differences between two categorical systems in two languages require the translator to consciously activate the two systems. If a category in SL has an exactly corresponding counterpart in TL, then the counterpart is adopted as the equivalent. If it is another case where the exactly corresponding equivalent is absent, the cross-lingual re-categorization needs to be implemented. Re-categorization is performed to play the role of matching a category in SL with its contingent category on a split level.

2 The Cognitive Characteristics of Re-categorization in C-E Translation

George Lakoff took categorization as the starting point in his study of cognitive philosophy. The purpose for doing this is to probe into where categorization starts as a "distinctive action." In accordance with the conventional philosophical viewpoints, "the categories of mind fit the categories of the world."(Lakoff, 1987:32) This philosophical doctrine has its version in cognitive linguistics: "doctrine of natural kind terms"(Lakoff, 1987: 32). In this light, the natural things exactly correspond to the categories in language. But in the actual process of naming, people do not necessarily perform naming by way of the supposed correspondence. Instead, things are categorized with reference to the "basic-level category," the point of departure for categorization. It is the same case with re-categorization in translation. Starting from the basic-level category, the re-categorization in translation is bi-directional: we have superordinate category upward, and we have subordinate downward. In Langacker's cognitive grammar(Langacker, 1987), these two-oriented categorizations are termed schematization and instantiation. For the reason that the re-categorization in translation do not necessarily occur on the same level as that of the SL. Rather it is performed on higher or lower level than that of the SL. In this way, the re-categorization in translation is characterized by split-levelness. However, as a type of cognitive conceptualization, re-categorization must take place within the same cognitive domain. Or, it would be the cross-domain conceptualization like mapping and mental space blending. Then, the re-categorization in translation is also characterized by the domain-confinedness. Finally, if the re-categorization in translation cannot be performed correspondingly, translator need look to the category on a level different from that of the SL. Anyway, this split level is not chosen at random. Rather, it is selected optimally. The optimally chosen category is often the schematic category or prototypical category. Then, the re-categorization in translation is quite parasitic as well as optimally chosen.

2.1 The Confinedness in Re-categorization

Categorization is a consciously or unconsciously defining act in perceiving objects outside in the world. Animals can identify the edible and the inedible, which is the most primitive categorizing act. Thus, "the categories we form are part of our experience! They are the structures that differentiate aspects of our experience into discernible kinds"(Lakoff & Johnson, 1999: 19). It can be said that categories and the way of identifying categories,

i. e. , categorization, play an important role in human experience. In the process of translation, translator need not categorize the direct experiential input. But what a translator categorizes is the verbalized categories, the result of the author's categorization. He or she is supposed to re-categorize what the author has categorized. Then re-categorization can be termed a cognitive processing of the indirectly perceived experiences derived from the categories in the SL.

The objects of re-categorization are categories. Both category and concept are two key terms in cognitive linguistics. They are related as well different in some ways. To deepen the understanding of category, it is necessary to make a distinction between them. If category is found in the perceptive experience and becomes part of it, concept is category on a higher level. In a certain sense, conceptualization is the extended categorization, which is performed within one cognitive domain. When we see a tree, we will subcategorize it further into sub-species. The categorization is executed within the domain of tree rather than beyond it. This cognitive process within one domain is categorization, the one-domain conceptualization. What makes a concept a concept is "their inferential ability, their ability to be bound together in ways that yield inferences"(Lakoff & Johnson, 1999: 20). In comparison to categorization, conceptualization can refer to the conceptualization within one domain. Moreover, it mainly refers to the categorizing of one thing with reference to the category of another thing within a domain different from that of the thing to be categorized. Then, conceptualization involves two domains. The forms of conceptualization are specified as metaphor and metonymy. Thus, in the eyes of Lakoff, conceptualization is either metaphoric or metonymic mapping. In terms of the range, categorization is one of the types of conceptualization, and conceptualization encases categorization. We thus can say "to conceptualize the category. " But we cannot say "categorize the concept. " In the same vein, we can say that "mind is conceptualized as body"(Lakoff & Johnson, 1999). But we cannot say that "mind is categorized as body," since mind and body do not belong to the same cognitive domain.

Categorization cannot be performed beyond the cognitive domain where the thing to be categorized finds itself. It is supposed to take place within one cognitive domain. For example, the categorizing of human being is to be performed with reference to the other categories within the domain of living thing, especially animal. Human being is categorized in two directions: upward the category it refers to is getting more and more abstract, and downward the referred category is becoming more and more specific. For the categories of the specific things in the world, categorization is easy to be carried out. But for such elusive categories as those concerned with time, mind, philosophy, and ethics, categorization is limited. Then conceptualization is employed to define the entities with reference to the categories in different domain (Lakoff & Johnson, 1999). Thus categorization is supposed to be performed within one domain while conceptualization is across at least two domains.

The theory of categorization is a way of cognitive organization within the same kind of categorical system. It is the substitution of the categories of the same kind in the process of translation. If the cross-lingual substitution involves the categories of different kinds, the conceptual mapping from one domain to another is to be employed. Then mapping is a way of substitution of one category or concept in a domain for that in another domain.

2.2　Split-levelness in Re-categorization

The categories of a same kind constitute a schema framework. The categorical members in the framework are aligned by levels. Starting from the basic level, upward there is superordinate level, and downward there is subordinate level. In Chinese-English translation, the category in the SL is the result of cognitive description of the category in the TL. This approach is allowed to be employed on different level. The two categories concerned belong to the same kind and find themselves in the same cognitive framework. However, they can be on different levels. The category in the TL is likely to be on the superordinate or subordinate level in comparison to its counterpart in the SL. For example, in the following translation:

(1) 在小学里，他是同学们玩笑的目标，因为这样庞大的箭垛子，放冷箭没有不中的道理。（钱钟书，2003：111）

In grade school he was the butt of his classmates' jokes; for with such a large *target*, no *shot* could ever miss the mark. (Kelly & Mao, 2003：111)

In the SL，箭垛子 cross-lingually share the same generic categorical system with "target" in the TL. But they are categories on different levels. Target is more abstract and thus less specific than 箭垛子 as far as the property is concerned, and then it is on the superordinate level. In comparison，箭垛子 is on the subordinate level. In same manner, for the translation of 放冷箭 in the latter part of the same sentence, its counterpart category in the TL is achieved in a split-level way. "shot" is also on a level upper to its counterpart in the SL. The split-level categorization that occurs between SL and TL is not performed at random. It must be carried out with reference to the basic level within the same cognitive framework the two categories share. The basic-level category is more often than not optimally chosen as the counterpart for the category in the SL. The choice of basic-level category can be justified by the fact that it is most easy to make distinction between two categories on the basic level. For instance, cow is easy to be told from horse, and elephant is easy to be identified as different from zebra. In contrast, buffalo is rather hard to be told from cow, and wild horse is difficult to be identified as different from tamed horse. In(1), target is identified as the basic-level category for its subordinate category 箭垛子. Similarly, "shot" can be pinned down as the basic-level category for 放冷箭. The basic-level categories are easy to be provoked by association. In conclusion, the split-level re-categorization in translational cognition is most likely to occur on the basic level, and the split-level category is to be optimally chosen for it has the following properties：

(1) The basic-level category has highly distinctive properties and thus easy to be identified. For instance, dog is easier to be distinguished from cat than greyhound is distinguished from a German shepherd, for dog and cat are basic-level categories.

(2) The image for the basic-level category can represent the properties of the category. For instance, the image of category dog can stand for the typical properties all the dogs possesses while animal cannot.

(3) The categories on the basic level have the priority to be identified, named, learned, grasped and memorized. In other words, they are to be most easily activated and used.

(4) The basic-level categories constitute the most fundamental elements of a person's knowledge body. (Lakoff, 1999: 27;赵艳芳,2001: 58 – 59)

Given these properties, the basic-level category is the category to be optimally selected in translation so as to curb the disordered categorization on split levels. Although the SL category and the category in the TL are on split levels, the fidelity principle also performing the guiding function in C-E translation. And the employment of basic-level category can guarantee the performance of the guiding function. In this way, the SL category is held back from derailing too far from its counterpart in the SL.

2.3 The Parasiticness of Re-categorization

In simple terms, categorization can be defined as the "mental process of classification" (Ungerer & Schmid, 2001: 2). Furthermore, categorization can also be reworded as "parasitic categorization." In this process, "you would 'borrow' the gestalt properties of the superordinate category from the basic level categories involved—a first case of what will be called parasitic categorization" (ibid.). This is termed as parasitic categorization. When furniture is to be categorized, people generally seek such categories as table or chair to serve as the reference category. The basic-level categories are borrowed to cognitively identify furniture. Furniture has no identifiable image. Only downward from the upper level to the lower level can we reach the category with imagistic properties that can be used to categorize furniture. The split-levelness and bi-directionalness in cross-lingual re-categorization are intended to find a reference category, similar to the seeking for the basic-level category in one-language cognition. The reader of the TL can indirectly perceive the category in the TL with resort to the reference category in the TL. Then, the re-categorization can be characterized as parasitic in a way similar to the categorization in single-language cognition.

2.4 The Bi-directionalness in Re-categorization

The re-categorization is mainly embodied in the transferring of generic noun or noun phrase into the TL. According to the parasitic property in translational re-categorization, when no corresponding same-level category in the TL can be found for the category in the

SL，schematic category or prototypical category is likely to be chosen by priority as the equivalent for the source category. As a conceptualizer, translator prefers to choose schema or prototype for the source category as its counterpart to be inserted into the TL. The schematic or prototypical category is attained by cross-lingual comparison.

If schematically oriented, the target category is the result of abstracting its source counterpart. As for the prototypically oriented re-categorization, the target category is achieved through the specification of its source counterpart. The two directions correspond to schematization and instantiation respectively. In terms of Langacker's cognitive grammar, the bi-directional re-categorization can be termed scanning, with the downward direction as elaboration and the upward direction as extension. The semantic of two categories overlap and cannot be correspondingly matched.

Here, we can look to Langacker's scanning formula for demonstrating cross-lingual re-categorization(Langacker, 1987: 102 - 103). When a category in the SL correspondingly matches up with a counterpart in the TL, a comparison of the two categories has been fulfilled. Langacker anchors the standard category as S while T stands for the target category. The categorization is carried out by following the algorithmic formula: $S>T=V$. In the context of cross-lingual re-categorization, S stands for the category in the SL and T stands for its counterpart in the TL. In the wake of scanning through schematization or prototypicalization, a value between S and T can be produced. Thus this formula represents the cognitive scanning in the translational re-categorization. In the formula, the relationship between S and T can be $<$ or $=$ as well.

2.4.1 Prototypical Re-categorization

If S and T is linked up by $>$ in the re-categorization formula, what translator adopts is the re-categorization by prototype, i. e. , the source category is schematic and its target counterpart is prototypical. The target category is the instantiation of the source category, just as illustrated by the translation of the following Chinese sentence:

> 只见宝钗手里托着一丸药走进来，向袭人说道："晚上把这药用酒研开，替他敷上，把那淤血的热毒散开，可以就好了。"(曹雪芹,1992:531)

In this sentence, 药 has appeared twice. The second 药 has the potential to be instantiated in translation. The instantiation is executed by prototype in view of the parasiticness of cross-lingual re-categorization:

> Bao-chai came in carrying a large tablet of some sort of solid medicine which she instructed Aroma to pound up in wine and apply to Bao-yu's injuries in the evening. "This is a *decongestant*." she said, handing it to her. "It will take away the inflammation by dispersing the bad blood in his bruises. After that, he should heal quite quickly."(Hawkes, 1977:155)

Obviously, the translator has come by the prototypical category for this medicine through inferring from the prototypical effect of the medicine. He performs the re-categorization with resort to the prototypical category for the source category. The direction of the re-categorization is downward from the upper level to the lower level. Otherwise, the re-categorization carried in opposite direction is the schematic categorization, which is also rather frequent in C-E translation.

2.4.2 The Schematic Re-categorization

The prototypical re-categorization from the upper level to the lower level can render the target category more specific. Otherwise, the schematic re-categorization from the lower level to the upper level can make the source category more abstract by omitting some contents of the original category. The example that follows up can illustrate the abstraction-oriented schematic re-categorization:

> 袭人看时，只见两个玻璃小瓶，却有三寸大小，上面螺丝银盖，鹅黄笺上写着"木樨清露"，那一个写道"玫瑰清露"。(曹雪芹,1992:535)

> Eventually she returned with two little glass bottles, each about three inches high, which she handed to Aroma. They had screw-on silver tops and *yellow* labels. One of them was labeled "Essence of Cassia Flower" and the other one "Essence of Roses."(Hawkes, 1977:162)

鹅黄 in the SL is translated into "yellow", or re-categorized as "yellow." "Yellow" as a category can be further subcategorized into a few subordinate categories, one of which "yellow" is. Although we cannot determine 鹅黄 as the prototype of "yellow," for "yellow's" prototype can sway from orange to apricot, yellow is undoubtedly the schematic category for 鹅黄. Thus, "yellow" in the TL is the result from the re-categorization of 鹅黄 in the TL by schematization.

2.4.3 Variation of Optimality in Re-categorization with Different Translators

The target category comes from the corresponding node in the schematic structure(See Langacker, 1987:388). A schematic system in one language cannot absolutely correspond to its counterpart in another language. Actually, they run parallel to each other and constitute a larger schematic system together. Thus comes into being a cross-lingual schematic system with the categorical nodes re-aligned in a certain order. A node in one language can be represented by its neighbouring node in another language. Despite that two absolutely equivalent categories in two languages are hard to find, it is also possible to find two categories that can be mutually substituted for. Nevertheless, the substitute category in the TL for that in the SL can vary from translator to translator. The individual difference exists in the choosing of substitute categories in translation. A re-categorization occurs in the following example:

> 王夫人坐在凉榻上，摇着芭蕉扇子……(曹雪芹,1992:534)

To render the sentence into English, translator is supposed to re-categorize 凉榻 and 芭蕉扇子. The former refers to a piece of furniture on which one can lie for coolness in summer. The two translators for the same sentence have applied two re-categorizing approaches to it. Yang's English version for 凉榻 is "couch":

> ... she found her fanning herself with a *palm-leaf* fan on the *couch*. (Translated by Yang Xianyi and Gladys Yang, 1978)

In this version, the translator takes 凉榻 as "couch," a piece of furniture between bed and sofa. Couch is brought about with resort to summoning up its two functions, i. e. , for lying and for sitting. The two prototypical categories in the schematic system of furniture are bed and sofa. The combination of the two prototypical categories presents the reader of the TL with couch. As a result, we can say the re-categorization in this version is a prototypical one. In comparison, we have the following version as well:

> She found Lady Wang sitting on a *cane summer-bed* and fanning herself with a *palm-leaf fan*. (Hawkes, 1977:160)

As seen from this version, the translator does not try to look for an in-between category for 凉榻. Otherwise, he attempts to seek the prototype of 凉榻. Then 凉榻 and *bed* are linked up by the common property they share. However, *bed* cannot fulfill the function of replacing 凉榻 in its full sense, although it can serve as its schema. Thus it needs to be refurbished into *cane summer-bed*, which is much closer to its source counterpart.

The two English versions for 凉榻 are achieved through a combination of two prototypes and a refinement of one of the prototypes. Two translators cannot necessarily reach an agreement about the target category for the same source category. This testifies to the individual differences in translational re-categorization.

Other than the individual difference in dealing with the same source category, two translators can coincide in their approaches to re-categorization. They can attain the same target category in translation. For 芭蕉扇 in the above Chinese sentence, both Yang and Hawkes have re-categorized it into "palm-leaf fan." The value between S and T in the re-categorizing formula $S>T=V$ is zero for the two categories in both SL and TL happen to be absolutely corresponding.

3 Conclusion: Translational Cognitive Re-categorization in the Light of Linguistic Philosophy

Two categories are linked up in a certain way and even can be replaced for each other to refer to a same entity. But the link-up is not necessarily ensured by the common properties they share. One of two categories can be substituted for another on the condition that they have some similarities, a doctrine advocated by Wittegenstein's theory of family resemblances (See Lakoff, 1987:32; Ugerer & Schmid, 2001:24 - 28). It is the same case with the cross-lingual re-categorization where a target category is substituted for a source category owing to the similarities they have rather than commonalities they share. The re-categorization by schema and that by prototype render it possible to match up a target category with its source counterpart in C-E translation.

【延伸阅读】

[1] Levy，J. (1967). Translation as a Decision Process. In *To Honor Roman Jakobson II* (pp. 1171 - 1182). The Hague：Mouton.

[2] Gutt，E.-A. (1991). *Translation and Relevance：Cognition and Context*. Oxford：Blackwell.

[3] 姜秋霞. 文学翻译中的审美过程:格式塔意象再造[M]. 北京:商务印书馆,2002.

[4] 刘华文. 汉英翻译与跨语认知[M]. 南京:南京大学出版社,2009.

【问题与思考】

1. 什么是意象？格式塔的概念对于文学翻译有什么意义？
2. 认知语言学对文学翻译有什么启示意义？
3. 有声思维的方法用于翻译过程的研究是否可靠？还有哪些问题需要克服？

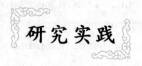

研究实践

汉英交替传译活动中译员的口译停顿现象实证研究
——以国际会议口译职业受训译员为例

徐海铭

导　言

　　这里推荐的这篇文章是徐海铭发表在《外语研究》2010 年第一期上的一篇文章。这篇文章是作者博士后项目的一部分,正是利用了"有声思维"的手段考察国际会议上汉英交替传译过程中译员的停顿现象,从而考察翻译过程中译者的心理活动和思维过程。

1　引言

　　言语产出过程既是说话人形成思想、组织思想和表达思想的过程,同时也是说话人不断利用自己的言语监控机制来克服或减少出错频率、确保言语产出准确和高效的过程。我们平均每分钟产出母语约 150 个词，但是在每 1 000 个词当中才会犯一个词汇错误（Slevc & Ferreira，2006：515）。人类犯错的频率如此之低，要归功于人类拥有一套独特的、能够有意识地利用言语理解和产出系统核查、校验和修正错误的内在机制。这个内在机制就是言语监控（monitoring）机制。监控行为和指导（supervised）行为不同。根据 Churland & Sejnowski 的看法，"如果学习活动得到系统自身内部检测错误装置的反馈，那么，这种学习就是监控式的。内部监控器是个非常精致、高向量的（high-dimensional）错误指示器。如果外部环境对学习行为做出反馈，那么，这种学习就是指导式的"（1993：98）。显然，言语活动过程中出现的错误，绝大多数是由说话人自己监控，然后自行纠正的，属于内部监控式类型，而不是外部指导类型。

但是，言语内部的监控活动有其外在表现。表现之一就是说话人在言语活动中表现出来的停顿。不同类型的言语活动可能会显示不同类型的停顿和特征（Postmas，2000）。例如，母语产出的停顿特征和外语产出监控的特征就有所不同（Kormos，2006）。不同语言间的口译活动出现的停顿特征无疑也会有所不同。长时间的口译教学经验和直觉以及大量的口译实践告诉我们，口译产出过程中，不同水平的译员停顿频率、停顿特征肯定与母语和二语产出时出现的停顿频率和特征不同，因为，一方面，口译是利用外语从事两种不同语言间的语码切换，译员的外语知识表征状态和行为的自动性程度[①]（automoticity）与母语不同，译员常常会碰到认知（如注意）资源不足，但是又面临着更多的语码需要加工等之类的困难；另一方面，口译活动本身发生的生态环境（requirements of ecological validity，Gile，2004）与一般直接利用母语或者直接利用外语交流的生态环境不同，译员面临心理紧张、信息传递方式不同、已经（高度）内化的职业意识和职业服务标准，以及外在的社会期待和要求等诸多压力，容易导致口译停顿，出现不流利情况。总而言之，口译这一特定言语产出活动决定了译员表现出的停顿类型和特征，相对于一般意义上的母语和外语产出停顿而言，肯定有所不同（徐海铭，2008）。

那么，译员口译过程中出现的停顿情况会是怎样？到底有哪些不同类型的停顿出现？不同类型的停顿又表现出哪些具体特征呢？导致停顿的会是哪些主要因素呢？本次实证研究尝试回答这些问题。本研究着重考察从汉语转换到英语的交替传译活动，详细描述译员在完成口译任务过程中表现出的停顿类型以及相关特征，力图揭示这一特定的双语切换活动中存在的一般停顿规律，为现有的言语产出非流利性（dysfluency）研究（Lickley，1994；关于非流利性研究的文献综述，参见杨军，2004）提供新的观察视角和分析内容。本研究共分三个部分：首先对国内外有关停顿的理论和口译活动中关于停顿的实证研究现状做简要回顾梳理；然后，交代本研究问题和设计；最后就本次分析结果对口译教学可能提供的启示做扼要探讨。

2　言语停顿和口译停顿的相关研究

2.1　关于言语产出过程中停顿现象的定义

停顿通常被看作考察外语流利性、流利性是否提高的一个参考指数。停顿本身是个时间概念，但是，停顿及其停顿长短往往受到各种因素的影响，既有语言因素，也有非语言因素。语

---

①　简单地说，自动性往往满足"快、不费力、与加工容量无关、无需有意注意、是长期实践的结果、无需监控"等标准。关于自动性的详细定义和讨论，参见 R. M. Dekeyser（2000：125 - 150）。

言因素主要包括语音表达、音位因素[重读、节奏、音律和整个语音曲拱形状(contour)的形成]的正确使用(Roelofs，2003)、词汇提取和选择、词汇形态的变化方式和选择、句法结构的选择和调整(Poulisse，1999；Meijer & Fox，2003)等诸多方面。就特定言语活动而言，非语言因素可能包括说话人对话题的熟稔程度不高，对交际场景的陌生而出现心理紧张并由此导致说话的犹豫迟疑，因为对说话内容的不确定或把握不准而导致的回复、修改、重述、修正错误，等等(Fulcher，2003)。停顿的长短常常被看成是言语流利和非流利界定的量化标准。

2.2 有关口语停顿的研究

关于外语口语停顿的研究不少。Raupach(1980)从时间量化[①]的角度分析停顿，将句内或者句间 0.3 秒以及更长的时间间隙界定为停顿；此外，他还从语速(speech rate)、发声时间比率(production time ratio)、平均语流长度(mean length of run)、起音速度(articulation rate)、平均停顿时长(mean length of pausing)等具体可操作指标考察停顿。这五个指标后来为许多外语流利性研究者所借鉴(Mehnert，1998；Ortega，1999；Freed，2000；Iwashita，Brown，McNamara & O'Hagan，2008)。除了从时间视角分析停顿之外，还有不少研究是从说话人的认知角度进行的。具体地说，就是从外语学习者外语水平发展的动态角度分析流利，积极地看待停顿现象，把停顿看作说话人采用言语策略或者有意识地监控和纠正自己的言语行为的结果(Postma & Kolk，1992；Wheeldon & Levelt，1995)，并且把停顿视为外语知识表征状态不全面以及语言使用能力没有达到自动性程度的体现(Kormos，2006)。

2.3 有关口译停顿和修正的研究

关于口译过程中停顿的专题研究我们目前尚未看到。但是，Petite(2005)首次利用同声传译语料库中译员修正口译产出的语料，探讨了口译活动的修正机制。她采用 5 个从英语翻译为法语和 3 个从英语翻译为德语的口译样本，参照 Levelt(1989)关于 L1 产出的修正框架[②]，[即把修正大致分为两大类：一类是言语恰当性(语用)方面的修正(appropriateness)，即 Levelt 框架中的 A 修正；一类是错误的修正(error)，即 Levelt 框架中的 E 修正]，然后分析同声传译活动的各种修正类型：按照由译入语产生的外显修正(input-generated overt repair)和由译出语产生的外显修正(output-generated overt repair)两大框架，来详细分析上述两类错误修正。这一研究，诚如 Petite 自己所言，是目前口译界唯一的实证分析(p. 31)。她指出：译员修正口译产出，出于不同的目的；不同译员之间的修正方式差异，表明了译员在线加工的过程差异、加工能力差异和决策过程差异(pp. 44－47)。

表面看来，修正与停顿似乎是两回事，似乎是两种不同的语言表现，其实，如果仔细观察和深究，我们会发现，停顿恰恰是形成思想和修正前的言语征兆；而形成思想和修正恰恰是停顿产生的原因，是停顿的动机和目的。简言之，口译中的停顿往往是由修正驱动。两者不仅仅在

---

① Fulcher(1993；2003：30－31)认为，流利是个更有弹性，也更难测量的测试构念。时间指标不应该成为衡量流利的一个纯粹指标。流利中的错误有时反而说明说话人进入了语言学习的高级阶段。即使是受过教育的本族人(educated native speaker)讲话也有不流利的现象。这一点，对于考察口译流利性是否有借鉴意义有待研究。

② Levelt(1983，1989)曾经根据说话人的动机分了五大类型的言语修正。(1) D 修正：说话者改变主意，决定说与当前正在言说的意向不同的话语；(2) A 修正：恰切性修正，使言语更适合语境；(3) E 修正：错误修正，包括发音错误的修正等等；(4) C 修正：隐性修正(covert)，其特征是表层句法结构没有改变，如停顿、重复等；(5) R 修正：其他各种形式的修正。

时间维度上存在先后关系，而且在因果维度上也是彼此关联。我们认为，为了能够更清楚地理解交替传译这一特定的语码转换的在线加工活动特征，揭示双语转换活动与纯粹母语或者纯粹外语活动的区别性特征，很有必要弄清停顿时间和停顿的深层原因，然后再来详细考察这两个方面与修正活动之间的相互关系，这样会更能够解释口译活动的实际本质。这是本次研究的出发点。

从方法论的角度看，Petite(ibid.)的分析完全是以静态的语料——口译产出结果为依据的，而不是以口译的动态过程——译员的口译活动(process)为依据，她的分析是基于语料的单向度(unilateral dimension)分析，没有对译员本人的瞬时思维和口译活动现象进行双向互动性(interactive)的深入探究。直白地说，她的研究没有深入讨论译员本人口译时的认知状态，没有考察译员修正活动的深层动机。毕竟，研究者的视角(*etic* perspective)和研究对象本人的视角(*emic* perspective)存在差异(Richards，2003：15)。此外，既然8个职业译员口译的材料不同，口译语境、口译听众和转换语言不同，他们采用的修正策略肯定有所不同，不同译员使用的不同策略似乎缺乏可比性。这是常识。要言之，她的比较其实犯了一个比较错误：比较译员的口译策略必须在同一语言层面上进行，这样才有可比性，也才能看出策略使用背后的真正动机。也就是说，针对不同语言层面出现的各种错误，译员使用的修正策略应该有所不同。鉴于此，本次研究力图动态地、互动式地接触"行为当事人"(即职业受训译员)，让他们在完成口译任务之后，即时反思自己停顿和修正行为背后的种种认知考虑。

3　本次研究问题和设计

3.1　研究问题

本次研究主要回答以下三个研究问题：

① 译员口译产出活动中出现哪些不同类型的停顿？② 不同类型的口译停顿又表现出什么样的时长和频数？导致不同停顿的原因是什么？③ 这些停顿现象对于口译理论和教学有何启发？

3.2　研究设计

鉴于前面提到的Petite(ibid.)研究未能探讨之处，本次研究首先采用统一的口译材料和统一的从汉语到英语这一语码转换方向；其次，采用研究者和被研究对象之间"互动(interactive)"的研究方法，也就是说，研究者不仅分析译员的外显口译产出，还要深入了解译员产出时的内隐认知状态，从而发现译员使用策略的内在原因或动机。基于这一考虑，我们采用"有提示回忆"(stimulated recall，Polio，Gass & Mackey，2001)这一研究方法，从而使研究方法"三角化"(triangulation of research methods)，尽可能增加研究有效性。

参与对象：5名男性职业受训口译人员，平均年龄23岁，接受国际会议口译职业训练时间已有3个月。

研究工具：

(1) 口译任务

让译员现场口译5段典型的官样文件的中文(共529个汉字)，具体为国际关系(2段)、就业政策说明(2段)和宏观发展政策(1段)。由研究者用正常语速面对面地读给受试对象听;测试现场的布置氛围与正式会议场合相似,力求最大限度地达到口译现场生态效度要求。学生边听边做笔记,并现场做交替传译口译任务(完成任务后支付报酬)。整个口译活动全程录音并摄像,然后由研究者转写录音。

(2) 有提示回忆(stimulated recall protocol)

有提示回忆作为一种数据收集手段,它的优点在于能够把研究对象在受试过程中的所感所思诱导出来,而不是研究者自己对受试者的行为做一些抽象的主观猜测(Ericsson & Simon, 1984：45-46;Susan & Mackey, 2000)。在口译研究中,有提示回忆作为一种有效的反思手段,它的优点和缺点早就被研究者讨论过(Vik-Tuovinen,2002：63-69)。最大的问题就是,有些受试对象在回答提问时,可能只报告自己所做的事情,而不是报告当时脑子里所思考的东西,容易把做(what he was actually doing)和想(what he was actually thinking about)混淆起来。因此,为了了解受试对象在某个口译瞬间的思维过程或思考目标,当每个人完成口译任务后,我们立刻播放他们完成任务的全过程录像,让受试观察自己的表现。研究者则根据他们的表情、停顿或犹豫等动作,提出问题,如“为何停顿?”“这里停顿这么长时间,碰到什么问题了?”“眉头皱,在考虑什么?”等(参见戴炜栋、徐海铭,2007)。通过这种即时反思,译员可以把自己当时的思维过程、决策过程(到底为何这样,而不是那样口译,决策的依据究竟是什么等)用语言表达出来。研究者完全按照译员的自然回答,对所有问答录音并转写。

数据采集与转写:转写好了录音之后,研究者反复阅读、核对整个数据与录音是否一致。

数据分析:

(1) 用 cooledit pro.(2.0)分析所有译员口译录音中的停顿时长

我们采用语音分析软件 cooledit pro.(2.0)系统对5名译员的口译产出文本进行分析。分析过程是:首先把摄像录音转换到软件系统中,然后软件按照提示自动分析停顿时长(见表2)。

(2) 根据有提示回忆结果,分析停顿原因

我们根据采集到的译员有提示回忆数据结果(参见徐海铭、柴明炯,2008),重点考察译员口译停顿的类型和详细原因。首先根据 Levelt(1989)关于一般母语言语活动过程的几个阶段,我们把口译活动分成信息生成、信息产出、产出策略使用等几个阶段。我们知道,口译产出毕竟不同于母语产出,比如监控,口译监控过程不可能像一般母语产出活动那样有很长时间来监控产出的言语表达质量、表达内容和表达的恰切性等诸多方面,更不可能像母语产出那样,采用各种各样的策略不断修正自己的产出。因此,我们反复阅读译员有提示回忆程序的转写文本,包括我们的提问和译员对问题的回答和自我解释,把停顿时长与录像中的停顿画面对比分析,然后再整理出“口译活动中的停顿类别分类表”和每个类别下面的子类别。详细见表1。

表1 口译活动中的停顿类型分类表

A 与口译信息有关的停顿	寻找笔记所致停顿;组织命题所致停顿;提取表达所致停顿
B 与口译产出有关的停顿	改述所致停顿;替代所致停顿;错误启动所致停顿;犹豫所致停顿;重复所致停顿
C 与口译策略有关的停顿	优化表达策略所致停顿;概括、总结策略所致停顿;填补、简化策略所致停顿;模糊表达策略所致停顿
D 由其他因素导致的停顿	个性因素;生理、心理因素;口译经验因素

（3）统计译员在不同类别停顿方面的时长、停顿频数和平均时长

根据上述不同类别的停顿分类，我们对每个译员的口译产出（5 个段落）进行逐一统计，统计内容包括：每个不同类别的停顿时长、停顿频数和平均时长。然后，对比不同类别的平均停顿时长，得到关于不同类别停顿时长的顺序排列表（见表 3）。

下面就不同类型的口译停顿的范例扼要举例注解（限于篇幅，不逐一举例说明），并把导致停顿的内在原因附录在每个范例之后。所有原因都来自使用"有提示回忆"调查工具得到的译员自己（当事人）的直接解释。因为译员对于个性、心理和生理因素的有提示回忆太少，仅一人提及，本文不作讨论。

A 与口译信息有关的停顿

1）寻找笔记所致停顿

描述：因为笔记格式和符号欠妥，在听完源语信息后寻找整理时有遗忘、辨认和解码困难而出现停顿。

例证（1）： "And we will coordinate all the aspects of this issue [0.39]-4-to ensure a sustainable development [4.29]-5-//"

受试对象的有提示回忆解释： "在对自己的笔记进行解码时，笔记上写的是'经'、'技'，但是原来写的符号代表什么意思，自己不太清楚了，因为笔迹上已经有了新的内容，这样解码时间长，自己要设法弄清楚符号是什么。"（受训译员♯4）

3）提取表达所致停顿

描述：知道信息内容但是在试图从长时记忆中提取目的语来组织表达时出现障碍而导致的停顿。

例证（2）： "During our economy the economy development，the employment [0.52]-6-issues will be addressed on [0.35]-7-both from the [1.42]-8-ideological [1.35]-9-perspective，also from our [1.35]-10-understanding perspective.//"

受试对象的有提示回忆解释： "'思想认识基础'表达很难，平时太少接触，我在思考如何表达翻译这个词，笔记上写得清楚，我也知道是'思想认识基础'。"（受训译员♯2）

B 与口译产出有关的停顿

5）替代所致停顿

描述：译员因为发音或者启动不正确，或者发现表达内容与突然想到的内容不吻合，重新表达。

例证（3）： "This has laid a solid foun-[0.85]-16-foundation [0.79]-17-for [0.48]-18-the [0.77]-19-so，for the final solution of [0.30]-20-the employment's problems.//"

受试对象的有提示回忆解释： "我一边翻译，一边在回忆，把内容回忆出来后，自己就改口，一下子把要说的说完。"（受训译员♯ 3）

C 与口译策略有关的停顿

11）简化策略所致停顿

描述：译员为了填补有些事前遗漏或者忘却的信息采取的消减口译内容的办法。

例证（4）： "And we have seen steady [2.24]-13-balanced development in our economy.//-[0.79]-14-our financial state is [0.91]-15-in the globe [0.30]-16-has also been quite stable."

受试对象的有提示回忆解释： "这里我就采用了一个 simplification 策略，因为有些内容记

不清楚,我强记也记不得了,就边翻译边考虑说得笼统一些。"(受训译员♯5)

4 研究结果与讨论

4.1 结果

表2是5个国际会议职业受训译员在不同类型的停顿方面表现出的停顿频数、停顿时长以及不同类型停顿的平均时长。

表2 5名受试对象口译活动中停顿类型、停顿频数和时长①

停顿类型 \ 受试	S1	S2	S3	S4	S5	平均停顿时长
1 寻找笔记所致停顿	4(6.10)(1.52)	31(24.33)(0.78)	20(22.38)(1.11)	26(20.99)(0.80)	28(26.11)(0.93)	1.02秒
2 组织命题所致停顿	4(3.61)(0.90)	16(17.03)(1.06)	24(17.70)(0.73)	21(14.08)(0.67)	19(18.08)(0.95)	0.86秒
3 提取表达所致停顿	3(3.79)(1.26)	21(27.76)(1.32)	18(21.29)(1.18)	23(17.80)(0.77)	15(14.13)(0.94)	1.09秒
4 改述所致停顿	1(0.41)(0.41)	2(1.01)(0.50)	6(5.99)(0.99)	1(0.30)(0.30)	1(0.84)(0.84)	0.60秒
5 替代所致停顿	1(0.41)(0.41)	2(0.68)(0.34)	1(0.74)(0.74)	1(0.34)(0.34)		0.46秒
6 错误启动所致停顿	2(2.11)(1.05)	1(1.03)(1.03)		1(0.51)(0.51)		0.86秒
7 犹豫所致停顿	5(3.29)(0.66)	3(2.07)(0.69)	2(1.31)(0.65)		4(2.33)(0.58)	0.64秒
8 重复所致停顿	1(0.41)(0.41)	8(7.32)(0.91)	5(5.15)(1.03)	2(0.94)(0.47)	2(1.31)(0.65)	0.69秒
9 优化策略所致停顿	2(2.15)(1.07)	—	—	3(5.70)(1.90)	2(1.56)(0.78)	1.27秒
10 概括策略所致停顿	1(0.50)(0.50)	—	1(0.35)(0.35)	4(3.28)(0.82)	—	0.55秒
11 简化策略所致停顿	—	6(3.33)(0.55)	2(1.34)(0.67)	2(0.87)(0.43)	4(5.71)(1.42)	0.77秒
12 模糊策略所致停顿	3(2.18)(0.72)			2(2.73)(1.31)	6(3.84)(0.64)	0.89秒

此外,我们以三个大的停顿类别为主题,把其中所包含的不同的子类别的平均停顿时长进行了排序,得到下表(表3),目的是为了能够更清楚地说明译员在哪个子类别上表现出的停顿时长和内在原因。

表3 不同类型的停顿频数、平均时长顺序排列表

停顿名称	频数	平均停顿时长
整理口译内容所致停顿	273	
1 寻找笔记所致停顿	109	91.02秒
2 提取表达所致停顿	80	1.09秒
3 组织命题所致停顿	84	0.86秒

---

① 说明:4(6.1)(1.52)表示,在口译5个段落时,因寻找笔记内容而导致的停顿次数共4次,4次总共停顿时长达6.1秒(即平均每次停顿为1.52秒)。表格中的其他数字解释亦如此。

（续表）

停顿名称	频数	平均停顿时长
修正口译产出所致停顿	51	
4 错误启动所致停顿	4	0.86 秒
5 重复所致停顿	18	0.69 秒
6 犹豫所致停顿	14	0.64 秒
7 改述所致停顿	11	0.60 秒
8 替代所致停顿	4	0.46 秒
使用口译策略所致停顿	38	
9 优化表达策略所致停顿	7	1.27 秒
10 模糊表达策略所致停顿	11	0.89 秒
11 简化策略所致停顿	14	0.77 秒
12 概括总结策略所致停顿	6	0.50 秒

4.2　讨论

根据受训译员"有提示回忆"数据中的自我解释和口译产出样本来看，停顿频数最多的以**"寻找笔记所致停顿"**这一类型最为明显，也就是说，译员因为"信息记忆不足、寻找笔记内容、解读自己笔记符号、整理笔记内容的逻辑关系"等所导致的停顿频数最多，5 个人的停顿总频数达到了 109 次；平均时长达到 1.02 秒，是一般口语停顿标准（0.3 秒）的 3 倍之多。徐海铭、柴明炯(2008)曾经专门对译员口译笔记困难和原因做过深度分析，结论是受训译员因为受训时间只有三个月，对课堂教授的笔记方法还没有能够熟练掌握和使用，因此，在做测试的过程中，存在"过分依赖笔记"的心理现象（同上，2008：124）。而利用大脑对所接受的信息进行临时深度加工表现出明显的不足。这一点，在 S1 译员身上就几乎没有出现，他因为整理口译内容导致的停顿频数只有 4 次，而 S2 译员却停顿了 31 次！S4 和 S5 两位译员也出现了多达 26 和 28 次的停顿。

停顿频数仅次于"寻找笔记内容"的是**"组织命题所致停顿"**(idea-formulation)这一类，总频数达到了 84 次，其中 S3、S4 和 S5 三个译员分别达到了 24、21 和 19 次。五位译员的停顿平均时长达到 0.86 秒，将近一般口语停顿时长的 3 倍。我们知道，一般口语中也有自然组织命题时出现的停顿或者犹豫(content-planning pause or hesitation，参见 Fulcher，2003：30)，但是口译停顿时间显得偏长，让人觉得不自然(Macias，2006：25 - 43)。而这一点对于听众来说感觉更为明显，他们甚至会怀疑译员的反应能力。导致这一问题的原因恰恰是和"寻找笔记内容"关联，两者环环相扣，紧密联系，具有前后连锁反应效应：前者找不到内容，组织命题当然会出现问题。因此，口译中的信息理解、记忆和组织命题，作为口译产出的开端，如果这个头开得不顺利，后面的产出必然受到影响。

再次是**"提取表达所致停顿"**。口译产出和二语产出相似，如果有了表达的内容或者命题，下一步就牵涉如何用外语来匹配命题内容，就是 Levelt(1989)所说的"语法编码"阶段，包括词项(lemma)选择和词体(lexemes)插入两步骤。这与语言生成能力有关。研究结果表明,译员在这个语言产出能力方面也表现出不少停顿,总频数达 80 次,S2、S3、S4 和 S5 四名译员出现了平均 20 次的停顿,人均停顿时长达 1.09 秒,也就是一般口语停顿时长的 3 倍多,是停顿时长最长的一项,高于"寻找笔记困难"(1.02 秒)类。看来,译员的语言能力或者迅速提取外语表达的能力尚待提高。S1、S2 和 S3 三位译员的停顿均超过了 1.26 秒,是口语停顿的 4 倍多。

从修正口译产出方面看,5 名译员都使用改述(11 频次)和重复(18 频次)等修正手段,平均停顿分别为 0.60 秒和 0.69 秒,是一般口语停顿的 2 倍。其他修正手段没有被每个人都使用,是因为每个译员的语言能力、表达习惯和口译经验不同所致。S2 译员的重复次数最多,达到 8 次,重复停顿的时长是 0.91 秒,大大超过口语停顿。**从使用口译策略方面看**,简化和补充策略使用频数达到 14 次,模糊策略达到 11 次,优化策略 7 次,而概括策略仅 6 次。口译策略一般是口译到了一定水平且口译经验较为丰富的译员才会使用的,因为策略通常是在认知资源较为充裕的情况下实施的一种解决问题的补救措施或者优化措施。以 S4 译员为例,他是所有译员中表现最为出色的,他使用的策略类型最多、频数最高。因为不是所有译员使用了每种类型的口译策略,因此,因为使用策略导致停顿的时长统计不够全面和准确,但是,总的趋向是:因优化表达策略导致的平均停顿时长为最长,1.27 秒(3 人使用),其次是模糊策略导致的停顿(3 人使用),平均时长为 0.89 秒;再次是因使用补充和简化策略导致的平均停顿时长为 0.77 秒(4 人使用);概括总结策略导致的停顿时长为最短 0.55 秒(3 人使用)。这一结果表明:译员希望把自己产出的语言说得更加地道、准确,有时反而会导致思维时间更长和流利性不足。原因可能是,译员的外语水平还未到达自动性程度,或者认知(注意资源)有限。

4.3 结论

口译产出过程中的停顿现象与译员的在线认知加工和策略使用高度关联。译员的工作记忆能量的大小决定了思想组织的顺畅与不顺畅,从而导致了产出的流利性和不流利性。从口译的社会效应来看,这又导致了听众对译员的印象好坏之别。因此,停顿的研究格外重要,它不纯粹是语言特征,有时还涉及社会影响(consequential backwash)。在本次研究中,我们分析了国际会议口译译员在汉英交替传译过程中表现出的停顿类型、停顿时长和停顿背后的不同原因。研究结果表明,译员常常在整理口译内容时出现较长的停顿时间,其中以寻找和解读笔记内容所耗时间最长,也就是说,因为表述内容问题,导致了主要停顿。其次是从长时记忆中提取信息和相应的外语表达导致了较长停顿。再次是把笔记内容和大脑所记内容合并起来所致停顿较长。这样类型的停顿显然与译员笔记能力和经验(参见徐海铭、柴明炯,2008)不足有关,亦与译员所接受的训练时间较短有关。这种类型的停顿给我们的教学启示是:口译活动中的听辨和记忆能力训练仍然应该成为教学活动的核心内容。没有了记忆内容,整个口译活动无从开展。而且,这样的停顿往往会给听众留下译员能力不足,甚至不能胜任的糟糕印象。此外,一开始就因为内容停顿,甚至"卡壳",给译员的心理会造成阴影,严重影响下一步的口译顺利进行。因此,在对口译内容进行笔记整理和大脑深度加工两个方面的训练再多也不为过(Nolan,2005;Lung,1996)。

本次研究还表明,译员在"表达"(articulation,Levelt,1989)过程中,也出现了不少停顿,如重复、错误启动、犹豫、改述、替代等类似二语口语产出的不流利现象(参见张文忠,2001;Fulcher,2003:30;Kurmos,2006:142 - 153)。这既有因紧张导致的口误,也有与语法和词汇关联的纯粹语言层面的错误。这似乎是任何言语活动过程中都会出现的停顿现象。不同的只是，在某一方面停顿的时长不同和频率有所差别。研究进一步表明，口译过程中因策略使用而导致的停顿具有更长的倾向（近乎是口语停顿时长的三倍，因为统计过程只涉及三个受试对象的样本，因此我们只能谨慎地说，具有这种倾向）。原因是，口译策略一般是在言语事件之后（post-utterance or post-production）口译者意识到要简化、补充或者优化语言表达时才发生的，因此，滞后性和停顿时间显得更长。但是，我们知道，这种"事后挽救或者事后优化"策略可能会影响到下一步的口译。因此，在口译过程中何时采用优化策略，是否有必要采用优化策略成为"度"的问题。本研究中译员的行为表现给予我们的教学和训练启示就是，就口译策略使用而言，如果因为使用策略而让人觉得口译不流利是个得不偿失的做法。

　　本研究的不足之处之一是：我们一次性地（one-shot observation）考察了译员的停顿现象，没有动态地跟踪性地研究译员的停顿表现。另外一个不足之处就是：限于篇幅，我们只是统计了口译停顿时长和频数，对于停顿比例与正常流利产出比例之间的比率等其他方面没有做更为详细的考察。同样，译员在哪一个语言层面上做出了修正，修正特征如何等具体细节问题还有待深究。此外，值得一提的是，对口译中的停顿时长测量，目前还没有任何研究提出具体的时间量化指标（temporal index），我们也只是参照一般二语口语的停顿测量指标（0.3秒）来分析口译停顿。未来的口译研究不妨在这个方面做出一些更加细腻的、实证性的探索（不是直觉式的主观印象描述），从而进一步揭示与停顿相关的口译产出过程中的认知加工（内隐知识和自动性）和策略使用（外显知识和有意控制）本质。

第八章　语料库语言学与翻译研究

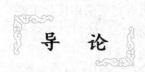

导　论

　　在当今的翻译研究领域,以语料库语言学为基础的翻译研究(CTS)已经被视为一种主要的研究范式。对于这一新的研究范式,学者们表现出日渐浓厚的兴趣,并越来越广泛地将其应用到具体的研究中去。语料库翻译研究这一新的范式并没有完全放弃以前的业已确立的研究模式,在很大程度上仍然在原来的理论框架内进行,但是引入了现代化的技术。新技术的使用不仅仅停留在增加一些看似科学的定量研究的数据的层面上,新技术的使用有效地改善了我们的研究手段,使研究更加可靠、客观。贝克是语料库翻译研究领域的倡导者和实践者,她所在的曼彻斯特大学的翻译研究中心在她带领下建立了大型的英语语料库,里面收录的既有英文原创作品,也有一些作品的英文译文,为翻译研究提供了大量的语料,开启了利用语料库进行翻译研究的先河。目前国内在语料库翻译研究领域也取得了一些成就,北京外国语大学和上海交通大学都是这一领域的领跑者。

选文一　语料库翻译学——新研究范式

王克非

导　言

　　王克非教授是北京外国语大学中国外语教育研究中心研究员,曾经主持教育部重大课题项目"双语平行语料库的创建及应用研究",随后又在2005年申报了国家社科基金项目"基于大型英汉对应语料库的翻译研究与翻译教学平台",建立双语对应语料库(parallel corpora)并以此开展语言、翻译研究,取得了令人瞩目的成果。这里选取了其两篇论文——《语料库翻译学——

新研究范式》,以及与黄立波合作完成的《语料库翻译学:课题与进展》。前者最初发表在 2006 年 5 月《中国外语》的第三期,后者是一篇综述性的文章,发表在 2011 年第六期的《外语教学与研究》,希望读者通过阅读这两篇文章,对语料库翻译学这一新的范式以及这一范式在国内外的课题研究及进展有一个全面的了解。

语料库语言学是近 20 年发展起来的新学科,它一方面提供了新的研究手段,另一方面则反映依据语料库大量语言事实所作的关于语言的理论思考。语料库翻译学同样如此,而且更加年轻,只有十几年研究史,包括方法论或工具层面上的应用研究和关于翻译特征的抽象性的理论研究。

语料库翻译学通常被称为"基于语料库的翻译研究"。鉴于基于语料库的语言学研究通称为语料库语言学,语料库翻译学也可以成立。既然是基于语料库的研究,语料库翻译学要借鉴语料库语言学的基本方法,包括语料的整理、标注、检索、统计等,但也有它独特之处。首先是所据语料库不同。语料库语言学依据单语语料库即可,语料库翻译学一般要依靠双语语料库,主要是翻译语料库(translational corpus)、对应语料库(parallel corpus)和类比语料库(comparable corpus)。其次是标注上双语语料库更加复杂。如翻译语料库需要对翻译、译者等要素加以详细标注,对应语料库需要对两种语料作句子或某种层级上的对齐处理,类比语料库需要对文体、主题、作者、译者等要素加以信息标注。再次是研究对象有别。语料库翻译学探究的是两种语言及其转换的过程、特征和规律。

传统的翻译研究是以源语文本为参照,以忠实程度为取向,主要探讨译文与原文之间的关系或对应关系。Even-Zohar 等人提出的多元系统理论,试图不仅从语言还要从翻译外部即社会文化层面上解释翻译现象,提升了目标语文化语境对于翻译的作用;Holmes 和 Toury 等人提出的描写性翻译研究法,一是重视翻译规范(translation norms)的研究,二是试图探究翻译的普遍性特征(universal features of translation)。语料库的发展,特别是双语语料库的研制,使描写性翻译研究得以充分展开,语料库翻译学基本上就是语料库语言学加描写性翻译研究。这也可以说是一种新的研究范式。因为基于语料库的翻译研究途径在逐步从方法论发展成为连贯、综合、丰富的范式,应用于翻译理论以及翻译的描写和实践等一系列问题的探讨。新的研究方法会促进研究范式的形成和发展,新的研究范式将带来研究思路的更新和研究重点的转移。这是特别值得注意的。

由此我们可以概括地说,语料库翻译学至少有三大应用的和理论的研究课题:

(1) 大范围的翻译调查,包括翻译教学、翻译文体的考察以及对应词搭配频率等统计数据的检索与分析;

(2) 自动翻译研究,将开展了半个世纪的机器翻译与语料库翻译结合起来,以期取得新的实质性突破;

(3) 更广泛更有效地描写性翻译研究,包括翻译规范的研究和翻译普遍特征或曰共性的研究。

Mona Baker 是最早进行语料库翻译学研究的学者之一。她在《语料库语言学和翻译研究》(1993)一文中对这两者的结合作了初步阐发。在大范围翻译调查方面,如翻译文体的考察,她(2000)也率先从语料库角度探讨译者的文体特征,特别是从类符—形符比、平均句长及词项使用特点等方面加以分析。

关于第二个研究指向,主要是将基于规则的研究方法(rule-based approach)同基于语料的研究方法(corpus-based approach)相结合,为自动翻译寻找出更便利可行的途径。

值得关注的是第三点,即语料库基础上的描写性翻译研究,特别是有关翻译普遍性问题的探讨。Baker 在前人研究成果的基础上,提出了翻译普遍特征(universal features of translation)的假设,主要内容是翻译文本中的① 显化(explicitation)现象;② 消歧(disambiguation)和简化(simplification)倾向;③ 范化(normalization)特点;④ 倾向于避免重复;⑤ 倾向于凸显目标语语言特征;⑥ 某些特征呈现特定类型的分布。此外,Laviosa 调查了英语翻译文本中的四种核心词汇运用模式;Kenny(1998)通过对原文、译文的语义韵比较,发现译文语言有净化(sanitisation)现象;Veras 考察了英语—挪威语翻译中衔接层面上的显化现象;王克非据大型对应语料库探讨了译本扩增情况;Laviosa 讨论译文与母语在词汇使用上的不同;柯飞通过语料库考察,发现翻译过程中对原文的模仿可能使译文变得复杂化、冗长化;Xiao & McEnery 发现在"体"标记的使用上,汉语译文比汉语原文多出约一倍;Ebeling 比较了英语和挪威语在存现句使用上的特点;Maia 通过双语对应语料库观察英语和葡萄牙语在人称主语使用频率上的差异等。

从这些文献可以看出,语料库翻译学在研究方法上以语言学理论为指导,以概率和统计为手段,以双语真实语料为对象,对翻译进行历时或共时的研究,代表了一种新的研究范式。

选文二　语料库翻译学:课题与进展

黄立波　王克非

导　言

这里选取的这篇文章介绍了近年来语料库翻译学所取得的成果。根据两位作者的总结,主要成果集中表现在两方面:一方面是对翻译共性、译者风格等原有课题的认识深化;另一方面则是基于翻译语料库的语言变化探索和多模态口译语料库建设等新课题的开拓。另外,两位作者还对该领域研究的发展趋势进行了预测:① 关注点从翻译本身转向翻译外部,从翻译文本转向制约翻译文本生成的各类因素以及翻译带来的语言互动与变化;② 从描写转向解释,实证性和跨学科性进一步增强;③ 打破了从前单语类比或单语类比加双语平行的综合研究模式,转变为根据实际研究需要建立的多重复合对比模式,并由对比模式向过程和因果模式过渡。

1 引言

语料库应用于翻译研究始于 20 世纪 80 年代中末期,主要是作为一种工具,进行语言对比和翻译批评方面的研究(参阅 Laviosa,2002:21)。90 年代初期,平行对齐的语料数据开始应用于机器翻译(McEnery & Wilson,1993:8)。同时,语料库语言学与描写翻译研究开始靠近,二者都以真实文本为研究对象,采用描写的方法,奠定了语料库翻译学的基础。1993 年,Mona Baker 发表了《语料库语言学和翻译研究:启示与应用》("Corpus Linguistics and Translation Studies:Implications and Applications")一文,倡导用语料库方法论来研究翻译,标志着基于语料库的翻译研究范式的诞生。自此,语料库翻译学开始了自己建立、完善和不断发展的历程。本世纪第一个十年是语料库翻译学大发展的时期,大量的语料库翻译学论著陆续出版。2003 年,在南非比勒陀利亚(Pretoria)召开了以"语料库翻译学:研究与应用"(Corpus-based Translation Studies:Research and Applications)为主题的国际会议,这是世界上首次纯粹以语料库翻译学为专题的国际会议。近年来,语料库翻译学研究内容更加丰富,对原有课题认识在深化,并不断有新课题产生。方法论也更为成熟,复合的对比模式逐渐取代了单纯的单语类比或双语平行模式。2007 年,在上海交通大学召开了"语料库与译学研究国际学术研讨会",这是第二个完全以语料库翻译学为主题的国际会议,语料库翻译学的实证性和跨学科性的特点愈来愈突出。本文以此为时间参照,集中关注近几年此领域研究的特点和动向。

2 近年语料库翻译学概况

2007 年的"语料库与译学研究国际学术研讨会"可以说是对语料库翻译学研究课题、方法论和动向的一个阶段性反思。Baker(2007:50)从资源、新技术、合作项目、研究日程、方法论以及解释力等方面讨论了语料库翻译学这一阶段的发展。值得注意的是,语料库翻译研究方法论不仅在适应本学科的性质与要求,还力图与其他学科所采用的方法从总体上保持一致;此外,注重方法论的解释力,即研究者如何选择研究对象、如何呈现研究发现以及如何对研究结果做出明确、详尽的解释(同上:53-54)。这说明语料库研究是一个不断检验和完善假设的过程,是在实证基础上的描写,但描写的最终目的是对翻译现象做出合理的解释。

2008 年,浙江大学主办了第一届"用语料库进行语言对比与翻译研究"(Using Corpora in Contrastive and Translation Studies,UCCTS)的国际会议。就翻译研究来看,这次研讨会体现出语料库翻译研究视角的多元化特征。从内容上看,虽然还是集中在翻译语言特征、语料库与词典学、专门用途语料库的翻译研究等课题,但研究切入点除形式方面的句法结构外,还延伸到了话语、修辞和准翻译文本等非形式方面。Rocha(2010)以多文类的英语-葡萄牙语平行语料库为基础,讨论了英语回指指示词 *this* 的葡萄牙语翻译,展示了基于平行语料库的话语分析在翻译研究中的应用。Ding 等(2010)借助语料库,尝试建立英汉语中的隐喻翻译模式。Miao & Salem(2010)以傅雷译《约翰·克里斯朵夫》为语料库,将关注点放在了译者注释上。此外,在内容上翻译共性研究已不再限于对假设的检验,而更多是集中在对方法论的反思方面,尤其讨论了基于英语和其他欧洲语言的翻译共性研究结果是否适用于汉语等非印欧语系的语言。在对比模式上，已不限于单纯的平行或类比，而是多类文本的复合对比，如平行加单语库的翻译语言和中介语的类比。从技术层面看，仍然以平行语料库构建、语料库的对齐、语言单位识别与自动提取为主。语料库口译研究所占比重依然较小，内容和方法上主要还是以笔译语料库的研究模式为依据。

同年，英国 Multilingual Matters 出版社出版了论文集《共用语料库：语言学家与译者》（*Incorporating Corpora：The Linguist and the Translator*），此文集展示了语料库基础上语言对比与翻译研究领域内的新发展，所使用语料库涉及英、法、汉、波兰、捷克、斯洛文尼亚、匈牙利、葡萄牙、西班牙语等多种语言，单从语种范围扩大这一点就可以看出语料库翻译研究发展之迅速。翻译共性依然是语料库翻译研究的一个重要课题，但主题是对方法论的反思，尤其是对相关概念的认识。Mauranen（2008）指出，"共性"这一概念被一些学者（如 Tymozko，1998 等）质疑，而且早先的某些假设与现有部分实证研究表现出一定矛盾和重复，但这些并不能否定翻译共性研究的价值。出现分歧的主要原因在于对研究对象的界定，如局部共性与整体共性、语际共性与语内共性（或源语型共性与目标语型共性）的划分等。Mauranen 认为"共性"并不一定意味着绝对法则，而在于对翻译语言的描写不仅有助于认识翻译的本质，双语加工语境下对语言的塑造更有助于理解其他类型的语言接触（language contact）。Malmkjær（2008）从社会学和理论语言学的角度指出，规范属于社会文化范畴，而共性则属于认知范畴。可以看出，这一阶段对翻译共性的认识已经超越语言或文本本身，开始转向文本之外的社会、文化和心理因素。

2009 年，比利时根特大学（University College Ghent）主办了"语料库翻译学方法论新发展"（Methodological Advances in Corpus-based Translation Studies）的国际会议。此研讨会的宗旨是"鼓励在较少被研究的语言中开展语料库相关研究，同时鼓励能够推进翻译研究方法论和概念边界的研究"。大会倡导的研究课题有：隐化、指示语转换、源文本与目标文本信息结构的不同对称性、翻译语言的语域差异等。2010 年，英国的艾吉西尔大学（Edgehill University）主办了第二届 UCCTS 会议。此次会议以翻译、语言对比和应用领域的语料库为关注焦点。就翻译方面的研究课题看，有以下几个特点：第一，翻译共性仍占据一席之地，但侧重于实证基础上对方法论的反思。第二，更加关注语料库的文类（genre）对研究结果的影响。语料已不仅限于文学与非文学的划分，而是涉及商业、旅游、医学以及航空等具体文类。第三，与翻译相关的语料库类型有所增加（如中介语语料库、多语语料库等），在此基础上的对比模式多样化。第四，在实证研究的基础上，从描写走向解释。2011 年，英国 Continuum 出版社出版了《语料库翻译学：研究与应用》（*Corpus-based Translation Studies：Research and Applications*）文集，展示了近年来此领域研究内容和研究方法方面取得的进展。在内容上，从纯形式的考察对象转向话语层面，进而关注翻译带来的语言变化；在方法论方面，最大的进展是建立复合式的对比模式，并向过程和因果模式过渡。

3　语料库翻译学的进展：深化原有课题和开拓新课题

语料库翻译学发展初期面临的首要问题是界定自己的研究对象。Baker 最初设想用语料库研究翻译主要是从翻译文本入手，从以下几方面展开：① 翻译语言普遍特征或翻译共性；② 特定社会-文化语境下的翻译规范；③ 翻译中介过程研究、翻译单位的大小与性质，以及对等的类型与层次等(1993:243-248)。可见,当时设想的课题,不仅针对翻译文本本身,还有对文本背后、翻译过程以及操作方式的关注,不仅包括语言,而且涉及社会、文化、认知等方面。但从后来的发展看,前两类课题得到了较为充分的关注,其中共性研究成果十分丰富。对第三类课题的关注则较少,原因在于:尽管语料库是一个丰富的资源,但由于语料自动标注的信息有限,数据提取主要侧重于语言形式方面,对语义、语用层面的数据只能通过间接的方式获取,限制了这方面的发展。当前语料库翻译学的内容,不仅深化原有课题,还拓展出新的课题。

3.1　翻译共性研究到底有没有价值

翻译共性是语料库翻译研究的一个传统课题。Baker(1993)提出的翻译共性具体包括:显化、消歧、简化、合乎语法性、避免重复、过度突显目标语语言特征,以及某些特征的特定分布七个方面。相关的实证讨论又增加了传统化、标准化、范化、中间化、净化等讨论,后来主要集中在显化、简化和范化三个方面,近年来又增加了独特项假设(unique items hypothesis)、干扰(interference)、非典型搭配(untypical collocations)、不对称假设(asymmetry hypothesis),等等。这些分别以不同语对或语种的语料库为基础,以语际对比或语内类比为模式的实证研究,既有对原有假设的支持,又有不同程度的背离,引起研究者们开始反思现有研究。

一些学者对共性研究持批评态度。Saldanha(2008:20)指出,现有关于显化的定义存在两个问题:第一,目标语文本中的显性程度并不一定与源文本中的隐形程度相对应。第二,目标文本"信息度"的增加并不一定是这种隐-显关系的结果;因此,要更全面认识翻译中的显化,就需要超越单纯的描写,来挖掘译者使用显化策略的动机。House(2008:11-12)认为,"对翻译共性的诉求从本质上讲是徒劳的,也就是说,翻译共性不存在,也不会存在"。她提出了五个理由:① 翻译同样是对语言的运作,因此一般语言共性也适用于翻译;② 翻译作为一种实践活动涉及的主要是言语(parole),即语言运用,因此本身受具体语对限制;③ 不同翻译方向上显化的表现并不一致,如英译德文本中表现出的显化并不一定出现在德译英文本中;④ 翻译受具体文类限制,如科普文本和经济类文本翻译中所表现出的显化程度并不一致;⑤ 从历时角度看,源文本某一文类语言的社会地位会影响翻译文本文类的性质以及具有类比关系的同类非翻译文本。Becher(2010)从定义、类型、理论和方法论几个方面讨论了"翻译内在"显化("translation-inherent" explicitation)的缺陷,指出 Olohan & Baker(2000)和Øverås(1998)各自显化研究存在的问题,如语料缺乏代表性、文类单一、未考虑源语言干涉、文本正式程度等,据此他建议研究者放弃对原有"翻译内在"显化假设的迷信,关注 Klaudy(2009)提出的"不对称假设"(Asymmetry Hypothesis),即 L1→L2 方向上的显化与 L2→L1 方向上的显化并不一定总是相对称,因为译者在有选择的情况下往往偏向于使用显化的语言操作,而往往不会去履行选择性的隐化。

以上这些批评不无道理,但也并不是很公平。首先,显化研究从对比模式上可以分为语际和语内/类比两种,前者是源文本与目标文本之间的对比,后者则是目标语内翻译文本与非翻译文本的比较。从影响因素方面,又可分为强制性和选择性两种,前者是语言系统影响的结果,后者则取决于译者、翻译过程、目标语规范等多种因素。从译者角度,又分为有意识的策略和下意识语言选择的结果。Saldanha 的切入点是源文本中的选择性连接词、自我指称和文化局限词在目标文本中的处理,因此她关注的是语际显化。其次,她将译者有意识的翻译"策略"与译者预期的读者群以及译者对自身作为文学或文化中介者的认识联系起来。但以此为标准来衡量其他不同类型的显化研究还不够充分。House 讨论的也是语际共性，但她的观点比较极端，直接否认翻译共性的存在。但 House 的理由也有值得商榷的地方，就第①条而言，语言共性是独立单语之间的比较，翻译共性研究中具体语对(language pair)表现出的属于"局部共性"(local universals)，不同语对都表现出的属于"总体共性"(global universals)，但两种共性都是从源语到目标语的转换过程或产品表现出的特征，因此语言共性可能部分适用于翻译共性，但翻译共性不一定全都是语言共性。第②、③、④、⑤条中的具体语对、翻译方向、文类和语言的相对社会地位都是翻译共性研究中的变量，不同变量控制的研究结果属于"局部共性"，而"局部共性"是我们认识"总体共性"的一条途径。Becher 的讨论对象是"翻译内在"显化，即由翻译过程而非源文本或语言系统差异造成的显化，属于译者下意识语言选择的结果。从其倡导的不对称假设看，他关注的也是语际显化。然而他所批评的两个研究却分属两个类别：Olohan & Baker(2000)讨论的是类比显化，Øverås(1998)则属于语际显化。前者主要针对译者下意识的语言模式，后者则集中讨论译者在语言转换中的策略；这样的批评站不住脚。

但上述讨论提出的一些观点也有值得肯定的地方，可供今后研究借鉴。第一，共性研究应该超越描写，将重点放在对现象的解释方面。下意识语言选择造成的显化可从心理语言学视角来探索，有意识的显化策略则可从社会、文化等视角来考察。例如 Pym(2005)指出，导致译者采用显化策略的一个社会性动机就是他们的交际风险意识，即要确保原作者和目标语读者的沟通，不惜一切代价避免误解。第二，共性研究中对具体语对、翻译方向、文类、源文本相对社会地位等变量的关注在一定程度上决定了研究结果的信度。其实，"翻译共性"像"忠实"、"对等"、"规范"等一样，都是翻译学研究的基本概念工具，与特定的研究取向对应，"忠实"对应语文翻译取向，"对等"对应语言学翻译，"规范"对应描写翻译学，"翻译共性"则对应语料库翻译学。正如不存在绝对的"对等"，也不一定有绝对的"共性"，但它们都是我们认识翻译现象的手段。Toury(2004:29)曾指出，翻译共性研究并非一个存在与否的问题，而是一个解释力问题，即如何借助各种概念工具对翻译现象进行更好的解释。这是对"翻译共性"概念的一个客观评估。Lavisoa(2007:57)认为，共性研究提出并检验了源自一般理论表述中的解释性和描写性假设，拓宽了人们对翻译的认识，表明解释性假设可以通过提出预测性假设而得到进一步的验证，预测性假设还可以通过因果或对比模式加以探究，基于此"共性研究提供了一个理论与描写互利互惠关系的典范"，将本学科的性质由描写推向实证，并且超越了实证，从认知等视角探究解释这些翻译行为的规律性。因此，翻译共性研究的价值不在于其存在与否，而在于是否有助于我们对翻译现象的认识，是否有助于翻译学科向前发展。Laviosa(2010:5)断言，未来翻译共性研究的发展取决于：第一，反思和改进方法论；第二，扩大所考察语言的范围；第三，将翻译视为一种双语加工情境和一种跨语言、跨文化交流的重要形式，开发并使其能有效地帮助我们认识其他形式的语言接触现象。

3.2 译者风格还是翻译风格

2000 年，Baker 发表了《文学作品译者风格考察方法论探索》("Toward a Methodology for Investigating the Style of a Literary Translator")一文，开创了语料库翻译学又一个重要课题——"译者风格"[translator('s) style]研究。此种研究不同于一般意义上以源文本/原作者文体/风格为关注焦点的翻译文体研究，而是以某一位(几位)译者所有的文学翻译文本为语料，从语言形式特征，如类符-形符比(type-token ratio)、平均句长(average sentence length)、叙述结构(reporting structure)等方面的语料库统计数据入手,关注文学翻译译者或译者群体独有的翻译语言特征。Baker 将这种风格理解为一种"指纹",即一位译者在翻译不同文学作品时,其译文所表现出的一些规律性语言模式(linguistic patterns),这些语言模式并非一次性的,而是为译者偏爱、反复出现、习惯性的语言行为模式,而且这些特征不完全是源文本或原作者语言风格影响的结果(2000,245)。严格地讲,Baker 倡导的基于语料库的译者风格研究有三个特点:第一,目标文本导向(target text-orientedness)。译者风格研究中,目标语文本整体是分析的焦点,分析过程通常忽略对应的源文本。第二,译者下意识的语言行为(subconscious linguistic behaviour)。译者风格考察的各类特征是译者下意识或习惯性选择的结果,而非针对源文本的有意识反应行为。第三,区别性(distinctiveness)。数据统计分析的结果能将该译者的风格与其他译者区分开来。

新的发展时期,研究者们对翻译中的文体有自己不同的诠释方式。Bosseaux(2007)考察了弗吉尼亚·伍尔夫小说《海浪》和《到灯塔去》(To the Lighthouse)法文译本中视点(point of view)的语言表现形式——自由间接引语(free indirect speech)、指示语(deixis)、情态(modality)和及物性(transitivity)——的翻译,从叙事学视角考察了译者的选择会对叙事结构转换产生什么样的影响。Bosseaux 在研究中使用的是双语库,关注的对象是翻译文本,但她的研究并未忽略源文本的角色。Winters(2007,2009)以菲茨杰拉德小说《美女和被诅咒的人》(The Beautiful and Damned)两个德文译本为语料,分别以情态小词(model particles)和言语行为转述动词为考察对象,讨论了两位德国译者的翻译风格。但其所使用的语料库为双语平行语料库,所考察的项目均与源文本相关联。Yu Ching-hua(2007)从英译汉的视角讨论了海明威小说《老人与海》(The Old Man and the Sea)两个中译本(余光中,1952 和张爱玲,1954)在译者文体方面的差异,具体考察了平均句长、类符-形符比率、汉语特有句末语气词和常用词几个方面。Wallaert(2010)通过对 Winters(2007)研究方法的不足之处进行批评,提出了利用文本与准文本结合的方法(textual and paratextual approach)对译者风格进行描写,即不仅要对原文和译文文本进行阅读,还要关注文本外的各类准文本。Pekkanen(2010)从翻译过程中的非强制性形式转换入手,考察了翻译小说作品中译者的个人印迹(translator's personal imprint),具体围绕根据译者的选择模式来区分不同译者或对个体译者的风格做个性化描写。Saldanha(2011)区分了两类翻译文体研究:翻译文体(translation style)和译者风格(translator style),指出前者将文体视为目标文本对源文本的应对方式,而译者风格则是译者特有的表达方式,并且在源文本不同的情况下也会保持一致。Saldanha 进一步通过对翻译文本中强调式斜体和外来词的使用进行统计分析,考察了两位英国译者 Peter Bush 和 Margaret Jull Costa 的译者风格。

上述研究大都没有完全根据 Baker(2000)的方法论,那么讨论译者风格时是否需要考虑源文本? 译者风格到底是有意识的语言行为还是下意识的语言习惯? 以这些问题为出发点,我们用同样的方法对葛浩文(Howard Goldblatt)和戴乃迭(Gladys Yang)两位译者翻译中国现当代小说的风格考察发现,两位译者在这几方面差异并不大,同时对照《红楼梦》几个英译本,以及英国"翻译英语语料库"(TEC)翻译小说子库在这几方面的统计数据发现,文学类翻译英语在类符-形符比、平均句长、叙述结构(这里指选择性 that 的使用)方面差异不明显,并不足以据此来区分不同译者的翻译风格。本文认为,这种脱离了源文本而仅对译文所做的纯形式的语料库统计对于翻译研究而言应该说意义不大。译者的选择可分为两类:一类是下意

语言学与翻译研究导引

识的选择;另一类则是译者面对原文的一些特定现象所做出的一些规律性的、有意识的选择。据此,译者风格研究可分为"目标文本型译者风格"(TT type,T-型)和"源文本型译者风格"(ST type,S-型)两大类,前者就是 Baker(2000)所说的"译者风格",类似于"作者风格"。后者与传统的翻译文体研究相似,主要关注译者如何在翻译文本中来表现源文本中的某些特征,不同以往的是关注对象是译者规律性的处理方式,用 Saldanha 的话来说,S-型译者风格研究关注的是译者"对源文本的反应方式"(2011:27),是一种有意识的语言行为。相比而言,以平行语料库为基础对 S-型译者风格的关注更有意义一些。

3.3 基于翻译语料库的语言变化探索

目标语语言变化的一个动因就是翻译带来的语言变化,这是一个历时的过程,大规模的语料库可以提供这方面研究的基础。近年来,除了翻译共性和译者风格外,通过语料库方法探索翻译对语言的影响开始成为语料库翻译研究的一个新课题。

Laviosa(2007)提出以 Hoey(2005)的"词汇启动"理论为基础考察翻译所导致目标语的变化,她具体关注了英语外来语(Anglicisms)在英语-意大利语翻译中的词汇启动现象,并提出三个假设:① 意大利语中英语外来语的词汇启动方式不同于其在英语中的方式,即英语外来语在源语和接受语之间发生了漂移(drift);② 译者可在使用目标语中的词汇启动、引入源语言的词汇启动和二者混用之间做出选择;③ 支配翻译文本的规范不同于支配同类型非翻译文本的规范。这应当说是语料库翻译学跳出翻译文本的局限,开始关注翻译与语言变化的关系这一新课题。Laviosa(2010)又以一个复合的类比与平行英语-意大利语语料库为基础,考察了经济类文本中英语外来语 business 的词汇启动模式,研究表明意大利语中的英语外来词 business 在两种语言之间转换时确实发生了语义漂流现象,具体表现在:business 在意大利语中共有五种意思,但用于表达其中两种意思时常带有贬义;英语中的 business 常用于指中小型企业,而意大利语中却用来指大公司;意大利语中 business 有时还被用于文章标题、字幕中的创造性表达,体现了其吸引注意力的语用功能。Hoey(2011)以三名母语为葡萄牙语的研究生翻译美国作家 Bill Bryson 的游记散文《不是故乡非客乡:旅欧纪游》(*Neither Here Nor There: Travels in Europe*,1991)的开篇句子为语料,对比了英语原文与三种葡萄牙语译文中的词汇启动现象,并以葡萄牙语语料库为参照库对相关词汇进行检索发现:在翻译中,是采用目标语中的词汇启动模式,还是引入源语言的词汇启动模式,都由译者来决定,但译者选择哪一种,则一方面取决于此种词汇启动模式是单个现象还是群体现象,另一方面就是看接受者的偏好。译者的选择倾向是语言变化的一个动因。Munday(2011)以英国国家语料库(BNC)和一个西班牙语语料库(CREA Spanish Real Academia Corpus)为参照库,考察了英语 *loom*(*large*)与其西班牙语对应词 *cernerse* 的语义韵律差异,指出语义韵律并非直觉性的,在翻译中译者往往会仿照源文本的韵律模式,但实际上源文本的模式在目标文本中并不一定得体,语料库检索可弥补此方面的不足。House(2011)的视角更广一些,她讨论了如何运用语料库方法,来考察作为世界通用语(lingua franca)的英语怎样通过翻译和多语文本生成等语言接触方式来引发并推动语言变化。她具体考察了英德翻译是否使德语表现出这样一些变化趋势:① 德语传统上强调语言的概念功能→英语强调语言的人际功能;② 德语文本强调信息的显性→英语强调推理得来的隐性和命题的不透明性;③ 词汇信息密集性、综合性、层级性的信息结构→松散、线性、句子的信息结构;④ 非连续的语序→连续的、并置的语序。考察结果有些支

332

持这些假设,有些则不支持。在此基础上,House 提出了未来此方面研究的三个模式。House 的研究告诉我们,翻译语料库不仅可以研究翻译现象,还可以透过翻译来探索翻译活动导致的语言变化,这是语料库翻译学研究的一个新路子。

3.4 语料库口译研究新动向——多模态口译语料库的建设

Setton(2011)指出,口译研究更多涉及的是认知和心理语言过程,在这个意义上口译语料库是一个丰富但尚未得到充分开发的资源库,因为现有研究主要遵循笔译语料库研究的模式,将主要关注点放在翻译产品上。从方法上来区分,有描写研究和过程研究两种。一方面,基于真实口译语料库(如欧洲议会口译语料库,EPIC)的描写研究有助于我们发现口译培训所需的专业技能,另一方面,心理语言学范式下的实验性研究却可以更多地揭示口译的语言心理过程。前者注重口译产品,后者则关注口译过程,两种模式各有各的优势。但到目前为止,后一种研究尚未取得实质性的发现,部分原因在于实验设计,主要原因在于用于阐释实验数据的理论基础不完善,导致对各类变量的控制与分析、抽样语料库的大小及代表性、实验环境与真实环境的差异没有统一的标准,使研究结果在信度方面存在一定问题。

多模态话语分析(Multimodal Discourse Analysis)是指从文本、声音、图像等多角度对语言交流活动进行描写的研究途径,这一方法正好适合口译研究的需要,因为口译研究中,仅对口译员的书面文本进行分析还不够。目前的口译语料可以对说话人和口译员的言语及说话过程中的停顿、口误等做标注,多模态的口译语料还会标出说话者或口译员的手势、节奏、声音大小、现场的各种环境因素等,真正实现对“使用中语言”(language in use)的多重描写,不仅从形式、语义,还能从语用方面达到对口译过程的全面分析,实现对口译过程而不仅仅是产品的分析研究,而且这些研究结果还可直接应用于口译培训,特别是实战训练。Setton(2011:49)提出,未来的研究可以有两大类:第一类是大规模语料库中可以统计的特征,这些特征可以作为口译员表现或口译文本的标志;第二类是局部微观过程,这类研究要求有共时的数据输入与输出和捕捉语用特征(如韵律)的研究框架。大规模多模态口译语料库的建设将为今后这方面的研究奠定基础。

4 语料库翻译学研究的趋势

第一,关注点从翻译本身转向翻译外部,从翻译文本转向制约翻译文本生成的各类因素,以及翻译带来的语言互动与变化。

语料库翻译学发展初期,研究重心主要集中在对翻译共性的考察方面,考察方式主要集中在类符-形符比、平均句长、词汇密度等纯形式方面。Baker(2000)提出用语料库的方法考察文学译者的翻译风格,也仅限于对翻译文本形式特征方面的统计。近年来的研究开始将翻译作为语言接触的一种形式,关注翻译活动中的语言互动和翻译带来的语言变化,即便是对翻译现象本身的描写,也将重点放在了从外部进行的解释方面,更多地将语境纳入了语料库研究方法的视野。如 House(2001)的研究对象就是通过翻译语料库来探究语言接触带给目标语的语言变化。

第二,从描写转向解释,实证性和跨学科性进一步增强。

对翻译共性的研究不再仅限于描写,而是将重点放在解释方面。按照 Chesterman(2004)

的观点,对翻译共性的解释可以从人类认知、翻译作为沟通行为的本质和译者对自身社会-文化角色的认识三个方面进行。这样一来,翻译共性研究将语言现象与社会、文化、认知等因素紧密结合,集中体现了翻译研究的跨学科性。Lavisoa(2007:57)在综述共性研究取得的成绩时指出,共性研究将语料库翻译学的性质由描写推向实证,并且超越了实证,从认知等视角探究解释这些规律性的翻译行为。实证研究提高了翻译研究的客观性,使其能够与其他学科在方法论方面达到一定的共享。House(2011)就方法论还进一步指出,尽管语料库研究方法有很大潜力,但其仍是众多研究方法的一种,需要与其他方法结合使用,不能仅局限于描写-分析模式,更要向探索-解释方向发展。社会学、心理语言学、认知研究等知识在语料库翻译学中的应用越来越广泛,研究的跨学科性可以进一步推动语料库语言学的发展。

第三,打破了从前单语类比或单语类比加双语平行的综合研究模式,转变为根据实际研究需要建立多重的复合对比模式,并由对比模式向过程和因果模式过渡。

Baker(1995;1996)正式提出了不同于传统对比模式的单语类比研究模式,主要应用于考察翻译共性。但 META(1998:43/4)专号中的许多研究由于对研究对象的界定不同,有的采用了双语平行的模式。Baker(2000)所倡导的文学翻译译者风格的语料库考察,在方法论上也是属于单语类比的模式。Kenny(2005)在此基础上,倡导将平行语料库重新引入翻译共性研究,重新考虑源文本在语料库翻译研究中的地位。但是,近年来语料库翻译研究的对比模式都不再是单纯的平行或对应,或是简单的平行加类比,大多都是复合式的对比模式,并向过程和因果模式过渡。如 House(2011)所使用的语料库有三类,既有平行,也有各种类型的类比;口译研究中的对比模式因为译者的身份差异、翻译模式等就更复杂一些。如 EPIC 中包含英语、意大利语和西班牙语以及每种语言同声传译的其他两种翻译语言,这样就构成了一个复合的平行或类比对应关系,研究者可以根据需要任意选取组合,对翻译现象进行三角考察,而且最终的落脚点都放在了对现象的解释上。

5　结语

语料库翻译学在短短三十年时间里,经历了从研究途径到一套方法论,再到一种新研究范式的发展过程,取得了相当可观的成绩。其对于翻译学科最大的贡献有三方面:第一,它所创造的"翻译共性"、"译者风格"等基本概念工具在很大程度上帮助我们更好地认识了研究对象;第二,多种类型语料库综合使用的多重复合对比模式为我们提供了更多的研究视角;第三,实证研究中的描写和解释过程拉近了翻译学科与其他相关学科的距离,跨学科的特点会进一步推动语料库翻译学向前发展。

选文三　Corpus-based Translation Studies in the Academy

Mona Baker

导　言

　　这里推荐的这篇文章的作者是利用语料库进行翻译研究的开创者、英国曼彻斯特大学的 Mona Baker 教授。该文于 2007 年 9 月发表在《外国语》的第五期上。作者认为，语料库语言学为翻译研究提供了一系列的工具和方法论，是对传统翻译研究方法的有效补充。在这篇文章中，作者着重介绍了语料库语言学如何具体应用于翻译研究。

The use of computerised corpora in translation research and education has attracted considerable attention in the past couple of decades, even from scholars who have not directly drawn on corpora in their own research or teaching. These include Maria Tymoczko, who recognised the importance and significance of this development as early as 1998, predicting then that "like large databases in the sciences, corpora will become a legacy of the present to the future, enabling future research to build upon that of the present"(Tymoczko, 1998: 652). Much of this attention has provided valuable critical assessment of the strengths and weaknesses of using corpora in translation research and education, and has explicitly recognised that what corpus-based research offers us is not a theoretical paradigm as such but a set of tools and methodologies which complement rather than replace traditional ways of researching and teaching translation. It is particularly important at this stage to reflect on this development, since it does not simply concern individual researchers working on their own but rather concerns creating resources for a whole generation of researchers, and these resources will inevitably contribute to the direction and orientation of research agendas in future. In this paper, I wish to contribute to the debate on corpus by attempting to place corpus-based research within the broader context of emerging trends and priorities in the academy.

Academic institutions have always had to respond to various priorities which are either generated from within the academic community or imposed from outside—by governments, funding bodies, industry, to name a few sources of influence—for a variety of political, financial and social reasons. These priorities include the creation of versatile resources, the introduction of new technologies, involvement in collaborative projects, clear articulation of research agendas, development of robust research methodologies, and demonstrating accountability and transparency in research. Below I deal with these in turn, outlining the strength of corpus-based research in relation to each set of priorities.

Versatile Resources

Among the current priorities of academic institutions in many parts of the world is the commitment to support research and methodologies that involve creating versatile resources for large communities of academics spread across regional and national boundaries. At the local level(of, say, a single academic institution), the quality of locally-held resources and the role played by the institution in providing resources for the wider academic community are often key factors in determining the level of support it attracts from government and other funding bodies. At a more specific level, an academic discipline similarly gains in credibility as it develops a range of resources that support research and teaching across the whole community rather than for the sole use of a local group academics.

Translation studies is a fairly young disciplines and is still regarded as part of their elementary research infrastructure. For example, we have only relatively recently started bringing out reference tools like dictionaries and encyclopedias of translation studies and abstracting services like Translation Studies Abstract Online (www. stjerome. co. uk/ tsaonline). These are elementary, traditional tools that have long been taken for granted in other disciplines. In addition to these, other disciplines also draw on a range of databases and archives. As we move into the 21st century, many of these resources are either set up as electronic databases or turned into electronic versions.

Corpora of translated texts fit very nicely into this contemporary picture of research infrastructure. They clearly do not preclude the need to develop other resources, both published and electronic. For example, a strong case can be made for the way the discipline is likely to develop. Unlike the individual research in the traditional model of academic scholarship, scholars working with corpora often create sets of data which are likely to feed into the work of numerous other scholars, if only because the very fact of their ready availability encourages others to draw on them. As I have argued elsewhere, "making large resources available to a community of researchers inevitably exercises some influence on the shape and direction of this community's research"(2002:7).

New Technologies & Collaborative Projects

Corpora also fit into the overall emerging academic culture in that they respond to the need(or in some cases ultimatum) to embrace new technologies. Academia in general has for some time been committed to deploy new technologies and has now largely ceased to support initiatives that involve manual processing of material, even in traditional areas of the humanities such as literature and theology. This is not necessarily a positive development, and no doubt has a number of negative consequences. But the fact remains that heavy reliance on new technologies is not only encouraged in the modern academy but is "expected," indeed "required," and the use of computerised corpora in translation research and teaching is in line with these expectations and requirements.

As academics and researchers, we naturally have to fit into this growing culture if we wish to be able to pursue our research and teaching objectives. This is pragmatic argument, though I also believe that technology has some very good, empowering aspects, and that these are evident in corpus work. Nevertheless, I would also argue that we must not embrace new technologies and developments like corpus-based translation research mechanistically, nor at the expense of other methodologies and resources. It would be unproductive and shortsighted to allow traditional methods of research to be marginalised in the process of responding to new imperatives in the academy. New technologies should not be embraced at the expense of human creativity and experience, especially since the most challenging aspect of any type of research especially in the humanities, still concerns the interpretation of results and data. This will always be dependent on the ingenuity of the human mind, ultimately the only "tool" we can employ for arriving at plausible explanations of whatever data we draw on, and however we decide to process this data.

Beyond embracing new technologies, today's academy also places considerable emphasis on collaborative team projects, made possible to a large extent by the availability of sophisticated technologies that allow us to overcome time and space limitations. For example, much of the research funding in the humanities in Britain is currently earmarked for projects that involve collaboration between "centres" (rather than individuals) located in different universities across the country. This provides an ideal environment for corpus work to flourish, because the typical agenda of a corpus-based research project cannot be pursued by a single individual working on their own, using local, traditional resources. Compiling a corpus requires time, commitment, funds, and the availability of different types of expertise. Moreover, the task is not accomplished once the corpus is created, for two reasons. First, corpora are typically open-ended affairs: a corpus project may set itself a target of reaching, say, 20 million words over a period of three years, but this target is always temporary, and is typically renegotiated even before it is met in full. There is no such thing as an ideal corpus size—practically all corpus builders adopt the moto "more is better." In addition, given that language use is not static, that language is always "in the making," corpora have to be continually updated in order to provide researchers with reliable data. Second, and beyond the question of compiling and continuously enlarging a collection of texts in machine-readable form, corpus work draws on a diverse range of expertise that cannot typically be provided by a single individual or a single academic department. It requires at least the following types of expertise:

Administrative expertise and commitment to handle communication with publishers and authors in order to secure permissions for the data to be included in the corpus;

Linguistic expertise for designing the structure of the corpus itself in relation to specific parameters of the language or languages involved;

Highly specialised computing expertise for designing software that allows researchers to run specific types of analyses on the corpus;

Less specialised computing/IT expertise for maintaining the integrity of the corpus itself on a regular basis, for example by ensuring that a robust daily or weekly back-up routine is in place.

By its very nature, then, corpus work requires continuity, a stable source of funding, and institutional rather than just individual commitment. These are precisely the qualities that national and international funding bodies value in academic projects. These funding bodies increasingly wish to invest in large scale, collaborative, relatively open-ended projects rather than limited, compact individual studies.

Articulating Research Agendas

Academic institutions around the world, but particularly in Europe and North America, are also increasingly expected to set and work to explicit goals and agendas. This is largely due to a growing preoccupation with regular monitoring of public expenditure, which gives rise to a culture that demands a high level of transparency and accountability. In both these respects, the use of computerised corpora in translation research and education scores very highly as a development that is very much in tune with the priorities of the academy in the 21st century.

In terms of setting explicit agendas, corpus work cannot proceed without a great deal of concrete planning, setting of agendas, and demonstrating that these agendas are being actively pursued in practice. This is partly because, as I have already indicated above, designing and compiling a corpus is no trivial matter; it requires the involvement of more than one researcher and hence is not a private undertaking that can proceed on the strength of personal conviction alone. Working with a team means that agendas have to be set and objectives defined and justified. Moreover, because compiling a corpus is not cheap, it usually involves applying for funds, whether internally within an institution or externally from research funding councils. Funds are naturally not granted unless explicit agendas and objectives are declared in detail. In this sense, corpus work is very much at home in the evolving culture of the academy.

Much has already been written about the agendas and objectives of corpus-based work, both in terms of outlining such objectives and in terms of querying them and drawing attention to their limitations(see for example Baker, 1993, 1996; Tymoczko, 1998; Olohan, 2004). There is therefore no need to address these issues again here. However we view these objectives—whether we agree with them or wish to reassess them—the main point here is that they have to be made explicit at every stage, and that it is this level of explicitness rather than the objectives themselves that is in line with current trends and priorities in the academy.

Critical assessment of individual objectives aside, it is fair to say that corpora have so far provided us with a number of plausible agendas. These agendas will continue to evolve and will become more refined as more researches begin to work with such large bodies of data, and as they design and compile different types of corpus: historical corpora, corpora of the output of individual translators, or of a specific group of translators, to name only a few.

Development Robust Methodologies and Demonstrating Accountability

The need to articulate research agendas goes hand in hand with the growing emphasis on issues of methodology in the academy. As with other disciplines, the credibility of translation studies in the academy is largely dependent on its ability to demonstrate that it can consciously and systematically draw on a range of robust methodologies. These methodologies have to be both broadly in line with the tried and tested methods employed in other areas of the humanities, and at the same time specifically fine-tuned to the nature and requirements of the discipline.

The attempt to articulate range of research methods for translation studies received its main impetus from the development of Descriptive Translation Studies. Corpus-based translation studies has drawn heavily on this tradition and has gone further in terms of elaborating very detailed methods of researching a range of features in translated text, for example in the work of Laviosa(1996, 1997), Olohan(2001, 2004), Kenny(2000a, 2000b, 2001), among others. More importantly, in the context of discussing the way in which corpus work responds to the new culture of the academy, it is worth noting that working with corpora forces researchers to engage directly with issues of methodology and allows them to demonstrate a very high degree of accountability. This is partly because the usual difficulties one encounters in any type of research are accentuated by the availability of vast amounts of data in the case of computerised corpora. Questions relating to how researchers select the features to be investigated, how the findings are presented, and how they may be interpreted all require more explicit and detailed treatment in this context. The accessibility of the same body of data to other researchers also means that the findings can be checked and challenged in other studies, and that other researchers can invoke different, and perhaps more plausible explanations of the same finds by appealing to parameters that may have been downplayed or ignored in previous studies. Taking the Translational English Corpus as an example (see Baker, 1999), it is perfectly feasible to scrutinize the claims made by any researcher drawing on this corpus, by checking them directly against the corpus itself, since it is publicly accessible on the web.

Concluding Remarks

Scholars in all disciplines are increasingly expected to function within a specific culture, one that is heavily dependent on the use of modern technology and views such dependence in highly positive terms; a culture that favours investing in large versatile resources and that values team work and collaboration across regional and national boundaries; a culture that insists on the articulation of research agendas, that no longer sees the elaboration of explicit and robust research methodologies as optional, and that demands a high level of accountability in research. Corpus-based translation studies is very much at home in this new environment, and researchers working in this area must make use of this fact in order to support further development in the field, without marginalising other research agendas. The culture of the academy may well change again, as it has done in the past, and what is considered a suitable form of research now may not be seen as worth supporting in future. As academics, we must both make use of what the institutional culture around us offers us at any given time, and be careful not to follow current institutional agendas too blindly.

Whatever the vagaries of institutional priorities, developing a strong research culture is not just a matter of pride but the only way to ensure survival in the long run. And developing corpora and building them into our research culture has the potential at least of helping us move in that direction, provided we do not underestimate the importance of other agendas and do not lose sight of our own long-term objectives for the discipline.

选文四　Corpus-based Interpreting Studies: Early Work and Future Prospects

Claudio Bendazzoli　Annalisa Sandrelli

导　言

这里推荐的这篇文章是两位意大利学者所撰写的论文,论文来自 http://www. fti. uab. es/tradumatica/revista/num7/articles/08/08central. htm。论文首先对在语料库基础上的笔译研究和口译研究进行了对比,然后将研究的重点放在语料库途径的口译研究上,介绍了口译语料库建立的历史和现状,最后详细介绍了两个正在建设当中的用于口译研究的平行语料库:DIRSI 和 FOOTIE。

1 Corpus-based Translation Studies(CTS) and Corpus-based Interpreting Studies(CIS): The Challenge

The idea of applying corpus linguistics techniques and methods to Translation Studies was put forward for the first time by Mona Baker, who predicted that "[t]he availability of large corpora of both original and translated text, together with the development of a corpus-driven methodology will enable scholars to uncover the nature of translated texts as a mediated communicative event"(Baker, 1993: 243). This intuition has had positive and fruitful implications amongst Translations scholars(Laviosa, 2004), as it opened up new research lines and methodologies(Baker, 1995) that could be used to "study translation as a variety of language behaviour that merits attention in its own right"(Baker, 1996: 175). Just a few years later, the "corpus-based approach" could already be considered a fully-fledged "new paradigm in Translation Studies," as testified by the many contributions gathered in the 1998 special issue of the Translation journal *Meta*(edited by Laviosa).

Those contributions gave insight into some of the key aspects of CTS, such as the possible types of corpora that can be created by using source and target texts(Baker, 1998), the problem of representativeness of one's data sample(Halverson, 1998), advantages and disadvantages of parallel corpora(Malmkjær, 1998), the potential benefits of using corpora in translator training(Zanettin, 1998; Bowker, 1998) and the need to correlate results to the context(and corpus with its specific features) from which the data are taken(Tymoczko, 1998). All but one of the remaining papers in the same issue concerned studies conducted on corpora made of written source and target texts.

The only exception was Miriam Shlesinger's paper, which addressed the application of a corpus-driven methodology to the study of interpreting, i. e. translation of oral discourse. A number of challenges and opportunities were mentioned in that paper, and these are considered in more detail in the following section. What is interesting to point out at this stage is that, clearly, the development of CTS(corpus-based studies on written translation) has been more advanced than the development of CIS(corpus-based interpreting studies) since the very beginning of this scholarly venture. There is still a considerable gap between the two, both in terms of corpus size and availability and in terms of number of studies and pedagogical applications(see, among others, Kenny, 2001; Laviosa, 2002; Zanettin et al., 2003; Kruger, 2004; Aston et al., 2004). This is probably due to the greater challenges and obstacles involved in setting up interpreting corpora, i. e. electronic corpora of transcribed speech events, which include an original(source language, hereafter SL) speech and its parallel(target language, hereafter TL) version into one or more foreign languages.

2 CIS: An Overview

2.1 General Obstacles

In corpus linguistics, corpus-based studies on spoken language are less advanced than studies on written language, mostly because of the time-consuming nature of data collection and transcription: "The recording and transcription of unscripted speech events is highly labour intensive in comparison to the work involved in collecting quantities of written text for analysis"(Thompson, 2005: 254).

Clearly, the same applies to CIS, since observational studies on interpreting necessarily involve the recording and transcribing of a communicative event (Gile, 1994, 2000; Shlesinger, 1998). However, an added difficulty is the limited access to authentic data, as was recently emphasised by Pöchhacker(2008): it is difficult to obtain collaboration from conference organisers and speakers(for confidentiality reasons) and even harder to obtain consent from professional interpreters, who tend to perceive scientific research as attempts to evaluate the quality of their work(Cencini, 2002; Gile, 1997; Kalina, 1994). This hurdle clearly makes it harder to collect sufficiently large samples of representative and homogeneous interpreting data.

Shlesinger(1998) points out that, given the complexity of the interpreting process, as many variables as possible must be controlled to obtain reliable results. The first variable is the type of interpreter-mediated event, since, clearly, interpreting in a medical conference is not the same as in court. The type of event determines participants and their roles, as well as the interpreter's role, and therefore has an impact on the interpreting service. Interpreting mode is also an issue, since consecutive, simultaneous and liaison interpreting all have their own specific characteristics. There is also high variability concerning speakers(their public speaking experience, their language skills, their accent, style, etc.) and speeches(topic, length, speed, degree of technicality, position along the written-to-spoken continuum, use of accompanying visual information, and so on). The target audience is also important, since the expectations of a small gathering of experts are different from those of the general public in a popular science lecture. Likewise, it is not possible to compare different interpreters, unless one tries to control certain factors, such as their training, expertise, language combination, preparation for a specific assignment, working conditions(equipment), and so on.

If, notwithstanding the above-mentioned practical and methodological hurdles, researchers manage to collect sufficiently homogeneous data which can be considered representative of a specific communicative situation, they are then faced with the problem of deciding how to transcribe the data. In other words, depending on the aims of the study, they have to decide what to transcribe and which conventions to use, and how to encode the data to make automatic or semi-automated analysis possible(see Armstrong, 1997; Cencini, 2002; Monti et al. , 2005; Bendazzoli & Sandrelli, 2005—2007; Bendazzoli, forthcoming [a] for a fuller discussion of these issues).

2. 2 "Manual" Corpora and Early Machine-readable Corpora

Despite this overall background, there have been a growing number of observational and experimental studies based on corpus data. However, until not long time ago most of these studies have been based on "traditional" or "manual" analyses, since they do not take advantage of computational linguistics or corpus linguistics methods; moreover, generally speaking, these studies are still based on relatively small samples, which are not available in electronic form. They also use different transcription conventions and the audio/video recordings and transcripts are not directly available to the scientific community(see Setton [forthcoming] for a comprehensive overview). For example, Vourikoski(2004) compiled a corpus of 122 speeches in four languages(English, Finnish, Swedish and German) recorded at the European Parliament. The transcripts of these speeches(together with their target versions) are in electronic form, and some of them feature a link to the relevant audio file. However, these transcripts would probably need further processing before they can be studied using corpus linguistics computer programs. Similarly, Straniero Sergio (2007) recorded a great number of interpreter-mediated events on Italian TV in order to study talk show interpreting from a Conversation Analysis perspective. Here again, the transcripts and the video recordings are there, but it is up to IT technicians, computational linguists and interpreting scholars to pool their expertise and work together to compile a machine-readable corpus.

There are very few studies which actually make use of corpus linguistics techniques and these are either student dissertations(which did not continue after the author's graduation) or small-scale projects carried out by individual researchers. For example Cencini(2000) created the Television Interpreting Corpus(TIC), a 36 000 word corpus with transcripts of interpreter-mediated TV programmes(the languages involved are English and Italian). The corpus is based on the TEI standard(see Web References) to transcribe, annotate and index the material, which can thus be queried using computer programs to automatically retrieve occurrences. As was commented in the previous section (§ 2. 1), this research work highlighted many critical issues in CIS. Regrettably, TIC is not available online and it is a closed project. Similarly, Fumagalli(1999—2000) created a parallel corpus of 18 English source speeches on international current affairs and corresponding Italian target speeches interpreted consecutively by interpreting trainees, and a comparable corpus of 15 Italian speeches.

The aim of the study was to verify whether the main trends of *translationese* (explicitation, simplification, normalisation and levelling; see Baker, 1996) could be identified in interpreted output too. The study was conducted by transcribing and aligning the source and target speeches by means of the *MultiConcord-Parallel Concordancer* application. Although the size of the corpora involved makes it impossible to generalize her conclusions, it is interesting to note that her starting hypothesis was confirmed: Fumagalli did find evidence of explicitation, simplification, normalisation and levelling in the interpreted speeches she analyzed. Unfortunately, like the other corpora mentioned in this section, the corpus is not openly available to the scientific community.

The same applies to another innovative corpus-based study(Shlesinger, 2008), which compared the output of different Translation modes(written translation and simultaneous interpreting), using the same SL text and the same group of subjects. By using corpus linguistics methods, it was possible to calculate type-token ratio and study a number of lexical and grammatical features with the aim of isolating any features of "interpreted language" or *interpretese*. Therefore, as well as parallel and comparable corpora, CIS can also include intermodal corpora, i. e. corpora "consisting solely of translations, in different modalities or in different modes" (Shlesinger, 2008: 240). Although this is surely a promising development to be further explored, to our knowledge there are no such corpora currently available to the scientific community at large.

It can be concluded that early attempts to develop CIS were first based on "manual" corpora, i. e. sample data and transcripts that could not be studied using corpus linguistics methods. Then, more steps were made towards fully-fledged machine-readable corpora, including easier (local) access to recordings. However, general accessibility to these electronic corpora was limited and most projects have remained isolated attempts.

2.3 Machine-readable Corpora

The current sub-section provides a brief overview of current projects based on machine-readable corpora that are already available to the scientific community. To our knowledge, the first corpus of this kind was EPIC, the European Parliament Interpreting Corpus(Monti et al. , 2005). In 2004 the Directionality Research Group in Forlì decided to create an interpreting corpus with speeches taken from the European Parliament plenary sessions, in order to bypass the practical and methodological problems mentioned in §2. 1. From a practical point of view, the EP plenary sessions are in the public domain and can be used for research and educational purposes. Moreover, homogeneity of the data is ensured by the institutionalized setting(the plenary debates, with their procedures and routines) and the interpreters' selection process and working environment. EPIC is a trilingual (English, Italian and Spanish) open corpus, with transcripts of SL speeches and corresponding TL versions in all the possible combinations and directions of the three languages involved(a total of 9 sub-corpora). In other words, it can be used both as a parallel and as a comparable corpus. The transcripts have been POS-tagged and indexed and the corpus can be queried online by means of a dedicated web interface. Currently, EPIC is the largest electronic corpus available in CIS, standing at almost 180 000 words in total. It has already been used to carry out research on lexical density and variety(Russo et al., 2006; Sandrelli et al., forthcoming) and on disfluencies in simultaneous interpreting (Bendazzoli et al., forthcoming), as well as for a number of graduation dissertations on various issues(Russo, forthcoming).

Another example of machine-readable interpreting corpus with its own freely available web interface is the K6 corpus compiled by Meyer(2008). This includes recordings(5 hours) and transcripts(35 000 words in total) of lectures originally given in Brazilian Portuguese and interpreted into German, using both simultaneous and consecutive interpreters. The speaker was invited to Germany by an environmentalist NGO and toured the country to give lectures on the Amazon in three different German cities. The talks were recorded and transcribed using the *EXMARaLDA* software; Meyer used the corpus to compare the treatment of proper names in consecutive and simultaneous interpreting.

The same researcher also created the K2 corpus for the "Interpreting in Hospitals (DiK)" project. This is a 160 000 word corpus including transcripts of monolingual and interpreted doctor-patient communication(in German, Turkish, Portuguese and Spanish). In total, about 25 hours of audio recordings and transcribed words are available from the same website as the K6 corpus.

3 CIS: Work-in-progress

In this last section, two ongoing CIS projects are briefly presented, namely DIRSI and FOOTIE. These two corpora share a number of features but, at the same time, they also have several differences. Both DIRSI and FOOTIE concern the same language pair(English and Italian) and the same interpreting mode, i. e. simultaneous interpreting(provided by means of technical equipment and a sound-proof booth). Permission to use the material(i. e. source and target speeches) for research and teaching purposes was obtained by the principal investigators, who were also directly involved as interpreters (in Gile's terms, *practisearchers*; see Gile, 2000) in most recorded assignments. However, the communicative situations under study are different in the two corpora, with DIRSI being based on international conferences about health-related subjects, and FOOTIE concerning football press conferences.

3.1 DIRSI

The first corpus is named DIRSI, i.e. Directionality in Simultaneous Interpreting (Bendazzoli, forthcoming[b]), since it includes interpreters' output into both their native language and their foreign working language. Notwithstanding the criticism which the latter language direction(A to B) has always received by interpreting scholars and professionals working in international institutions in the West, "working into B" is common practice in most domestic private markets and used to be the norm in Eastern Europe.

DIRSI is being created by using audio recordings from international conferences held in Italy over the last three years. These are always structured into different sessions(i. e. opening, presentation, debate and closing sessions) and involve more than one participant giving paper presentations or lectures. Five professional interpreters collaborated in this project by granting permission to be recorded(one English and four Italian native speakers). Their collaboration also had a positive influence in obtaining consent from conference organizers and other participants.

Debates and Q&A sessions are actually excluded from the corpus, owing to their high degree of interactivity in communication(dialogue), which strongly differentiates them from the "monologic" speech events delivered in all the other working sessions. At the time of writing, three conferences have been fully transcribed, POS-tagged, lemmatized and indexed, totalling more than 130 000 words. In particular, the SL sub-corpus includes approximately 70 000 words and the TL sub-corpus includes nearly 60 000 words from 20 hours of selected recordings overall. For this project, further material was collected from other conferences and this will be added as transcripts are completed. Text-to-sound alignment is also envisaged as a next step and the resulting corpus will be made accessible via a dedicated online web-interface. The creation of this new corpus has been possible thanks to the experience previously gained with the EPIC project.

3. 2 FOOTIE

FOOTIE is much more restricted in scope than either DIRSI or EPIC. The latter corpora include texts on various topics from different plenaries or conference sessions; by contrast, all the texts in FOOTIE come from the same setting and the same type of communicative event, namely the press conferences scheduled before and after every game played by Italy's national team during the 2008 European football championships(UEFA EURO 2008) held in Switzerland and Austria. This new project has just been started by Annalisa Sandrelli at LUSPIO University in Rome, where a number of undergraduate students are collaborating by transcribing portions of the available data for their dissertations on various aspects of interpreting.

As happened with data collection for DIRSI, once again it was possible to obtain the relevant recordings because the principal investigator was recruited to work as Italy's interpreter during EURO 2008; after the championship, UEFA granted permission to use the video and audio materials for research purposes. Clearly, this procedure may involve a degree of researcher bias, but, as was pointed out in § 2. 1, it is very hard to obtain authentic recordings of interpreter-mediated events and therefore the analysis of one's work is, unfortunately, rather common among *practisearchers*. In order to reduce the effect, permission is being sought from the other interpreters at work in the relevant games to use their recordings too.

During EURO 2008, Italy played Holland, Romania and France in the first round, and went out to Spain in the quarter finals. For each game there was one pre-match and one post-match press conference for Italy and the same for their opponents. Interpreters were "assigned" to a specific team and worked in all of the press conferences involving that particular team. Two interpreters were always at work in all the press conferences, each of them working in both translation directions(A to B and B to A) in his/her own booth. The official languages always included English(for the international press) and the two languages spoken in the countries of the two teams. English was also used by the interpreters as a *pivot* language whenever the foreign language used by the speakers was not one of their working languages. Overall, a total of 16 press conferences involving Italian, English, French and Spanish as SLs and TLs are available for transcription and analysis. However, in order to begin this project with an analysis of the more homogeneous part of the corpus, it has been decided to start by transcribing all of Italy's press conferences(in Italian) and corresponding English target versions. This part of the corpus corresponds to over two and a half hours of SL material and matching interpreted version produced by the same interpreter working from her A language(Italian) into her B language(English).

All the FOOTIE press conferences were interpreted simultaneously. Press conferences are an example of dialogic communication characterised by high interactivity, and in this sense the FOOTIE material can be said to resemble conference Q&A sessions. The type of dialogue is also specific to this setting, in that it features examples of one-to-one communication(interviewers posing questions to the interviewee/s, generally a football manager and sometimes a player) and of one-to-many communication(the interviewee replying to each question for the benefit of all the journalists present in the room). There is also a composite audience: there is a primary audience that is entirely made up of potential interviewers(only journalists were admitted to the press conference rooms) and a secondary audience that is not physically present, i. e. the football fans from all the countries involved (although the press conferences were not fully televised, excerpts were used by TV channels and information obtained during the press conferences was used by media people to write match reports and articles).

The project is still in its infancy and many aspects are still to be defined, including data encoding methods. However, the data certainly look interesting and it is hoped that their homogeneity will make it possible to carry out interesting studies on the corpus when it is ready for analysis.

4 Conclusions

Nearly two decades after the initial efforts to apply corpus linguistics to Translation Studies, Corpus-based Interpreting Studies are still at a less advanced stage of development than Corpus-based(written) Translation Studies. This is probably due to the many obstacles involved in creating spoken corpora in general and to the many variables at stake in setting up

Interpreting corpora.

Early attempts were based on small samples of data, which usually were not machine-readable. Over the last few years, technological advancements and greater collaboration between Translation scholars and IT experts have made it possible to obtain larger samples of data and store them in electronic form to create corpora. Unfortunately, once completed, many of these projects have not been made accessible to the scientific community at large. However, there are some exceptions, such as the European Parliament Interpreting Corpus (EPIC) and the K6 and K2 corpora, which are publicly available and can be accessed online.

The latest examples of ongoing CIS projects presented in this paper are called DIRSI and FOOTIE, two interpreting corpora based on health-related international conferences and football-related press conferences respectively. In particular, with these two corpora it will be possible to study the role played by directionality(i. e. whether interpreters work into their A or B language). Despite the principal investigators' direct involvement in data collection in both projects, we believe that *practisearchers* may have the key to accessing real life data. Although self-analysis is likely to be criticised, its limits are still to be demonstrated in most cases. If we really want CIS to catch up with CTS in terms of number of resources and contributions to research, closer collaboration between *practisearchers* and their colleagues in both academic and professional settings is vital and strongly called for.

【延伸阅读】

[1] Baker, M. (1993). Corpus Linguistics and Translations: Implications and Applications. In M. Baker, G. Francis & E. Tognini-Bonelli(eds.), *Text and Technology: In Honour of John Sinclair*(pp. 233 - 250). Amsterdam: Benjamins.

[2] 胡开宝. 语料库翻译学概论[M]. 上海:上海交通大学出版社,2011.

[3] 王克非. 双语对应语料库:研制与应用 [M]. 北京:外语教学与研究出版社,2004.

【问题与思考】

1. 你是否同意语料库翻译学代表了翻译研究的新范式？从何种意义上来说它代表了翻译研究的新范式？

2. 阅读了本章内容以及延伸阅读里面推荐的资料之后,你能否尝试建立一个小型的用于翻译批评的语料库？

研究实践

基于语料库的莎剧《哈姆雷特》
汉译文本中"把"字句应用及其动因研究

胡开宝

导　言

　　本文作者是国家哲学社会科学基金项目"基于语料库的莎士比亚戏剧汉译研究"以及上海交通大学 985 二期工程项目"历时性英汉平行语料库创建与应用研究"的主持者。这里推荐的论文为上海交通大学"985 工程"课题的一个子课题"莎士比亚戏剧翻译语料库的创建与应用研究",于 2009 年 1 月发表在《外语学刊》的第一期上。围绕语料库与翻译研究,作者相继发表了多项学术成果,除了这里推荐的一篇之外,为人们所熟悉的还有《莎士比亚戏剧英汉平行语料库的创建与应用》、《基于语料库的莎剧〈哈姆雷特〉汉译本中显化现象及动因研究》以及专著《语料库语言学概论》等。

0　引言

　　"把"字句一直是学界研究的热门课题。王力(1943)指出"把"字句的动词具有处置性。金立鑫(1997)和崔希亮(2001)分别从句法、语义和语用层面考察了"把"字句的本质特征及语用功能。李宁和王晓珊(2001)通过对三百多万字语料的调查,分析了"把"字句在话语中的具体语用功能。这些功能依次为阐述、指令、表达和宣告等。张旺熹(1991)分析了字数达 53 万字的汉语原创作品中"把"字句出现的频率,发现戏剧作品中"把"字出现次数多于小说,后者又比散文多。柯飞(2003)则对汉语原创语料和汉语翻译语料"把"字句出现的频率进行比较,发现后者高于前者。"把"字句是现代汉语中非常独特的句型,而汉语原创作品"把"字句使用频率却少于汉译文本,其动因是什么? 翻译英语语句时,译者选用"把"字句的依据何在? 同一英语作品的汉译文本中"把"字句的应用是否存在差异,其内在原因有哪些? 这些问题对于"把"字句研究以及翻译汉语语言的研究显然非常重要。然而,遗憾的是,迄今为止关于上述问题的研究还很鲜见。鉴此,本文基于自建的莎士比亚戏剧翻译语料库,采用自主开发的 ParaCorpus 英汉平行检索软件和 Concapp 等软件,系统研究梁实秋和朱生豪翻译的《哈姆雷特》汉译文本中"把"字句应用及其内在动因。(为方便起见,这两个译本分别简称为梁译本和朱译本。)

1 《哈姆雷特》梁译本和朱译本文体特征

1.1 梁译本和朱译本出版的时间

莎士比亚戏剧被誉为英国文学的瑰宝,世界文学的精品。自 20 世纪 30 年代以来,我国一些翻译家致力于莎士比亚戏剧的翻译,相继推出了莎士比亚戏剧全集的汉译文本。其中,最受欢迎且最具影响力的当属梁实秋译本和朱生豪译本。梁实秋自 1931 年开始从事莎士比亚戏剧的翻译,至 1968 年完成。1936 年 6 月至 1937 年 5 月,梁实秋翻译的莎士比亚戏剧《马克白》、《威尼斯商人》和《丹麦王子哈姆雷特之悲剧》等汉译本由上海商务印书馆先后出版。朱生豪则从 1935 年到 1942 年先后译出 31 部莎士比亚戏剧,如《威尼斯商人》、《皆大欢喜》和《哈姆莱特》等,不包括 6 部历史剧。1947 年世界书局出版了朱生豪翻译的《莎士比亚戏剧全集》。

1.2 梁译本和朱译本文体特征的定量分析

本文运用 Concapp 软件,对这两个翻译文本的文体特征进行量化分析,发现它们在许多方面存在差异。具体如表 1 所示:

表 1 梁译本和朱译本文体特征定量分析

	梁译本	朱译本
译本字数(不含注释部分)	55 427	62 290
类符数(不含注释部分)	3 058	2 790
类符-形符比	5.52%	4.48%
句子总数(不含注释部分)	2 239	2 409
平均句长(不含注释部分)	24.76	25.76
主要连接词出现次数	960	1 079
主要连接词使用频率	1.73%	1.73%
"被"字句出现次数	58	23
"被"字句使用频率(每万字)	10.825	4.013
"把"字句出现次数	117	223
"把"字句使用频率(每千字)	2.1	3.6

根据上表,朱译本的文字总数比梁译本超出近 7 000 字,其显化程度要高于后者。显化(explicitation)是翻译语言共性之一,也称为明朗化,是指译者为了便于读者理解译文,采用各种手段将原文隐含的但可以根据上下文推导的内容表达出来,如增加修饰词、连接词,重复先前提到的细节,插入额外的背景知识填补文化空缺等,采用重复和同义词代替省略,其结果导致译文文字总量超过原文。经统计,《哈姆雷特》英语原文文字总量为 32 154 词,与朱译本和梁译本文字总量之比分别为 1∶1.94 和 1∶1.72。英语原文句子总数为 2 055 句,平均句长为 15.65 字。朱译本和梁译本平均句长均大于原文平均句长。显见,从文字总量和平均句长角

度上看,这两个译本都在不同程度上存在显化,不过朱译本尤为突出。

由上表可知,朱译本的类符-形符比低于梁译本。类符是指文本一共有多少不同的词形,形符为文本的总字数。类符-形符比通常在一定程度上反映文本作者使用的词汇量大小和遣词的变化性。比率越高,作者用词的变化性越大。因此,可以认为梁译本所用的词汇量大于朱译本,且更富于变化。

一般而言,由于源语或目的语影响程度以及译者翻译策略等方面的差异,翻译文本常常表现为异化或归化趋向,前者为源语语言文化特征显著,后者则指目的语语言文化特征明显。毋庸讳言,《哈姆雷特》梁译本和朱译本具有异化或归化倾向,但它们在多大程度上,在哪个层面上趋于归化或异化?为此,本文根据"形合"与"意合"、"被动"与"主动"这些普遍认可的英汉语言之间差别,对梁译本和朱译本中主要连接词、"被"字句和"把"字句的应用进行定量分析,发现这两个译本中主要连接词使用的频率相同,均为 1.73%,远远低于《哈姆雷特》原著中主要连接词使用的频率。经统计,该原著中主要连接词出现次数为 1 765 次,使用频率为 5.49%。梁译本和朱译本中主要连接词出现次数分别比原著少 805 次和 686 次。很明显,原著中至少有 46% 和 39% 的连接词在这两个译本中没有译出。在这两个译本中,一些连接词并非译自原文,而是译者出于译文衔接自然的需要添加的。因此,就连词使用而言,梁译本和朱译本趋于归化。

在上表中,梁译本"被"字句使用频率为每万字 10.825 次,朱译本仅为 4.013 次,前者为后者的 2.7 倍。不过,梁译本中"把"字句每千字的使用频率只有朱译本的 58%。由此可见,就"把"字句和"被"字句的使用而言,梁译本显然更趋于异化,而朱译本更趋于归化。

2 梁译本和朱译本中"把"字句的应用与分布

如前所述,梁译本和朱译本中"把"字句使用频率分别为每千字 2.1 和 3.6 次。与汉语原创作品相比,这些频率居高还是偏低?这些译本中"把"字句的分布情况如何?"把"字句与哪些英语语句对应?为此,本文将对这些译本与汉语原创作品的"把"字句使用频率进行比较,并分析这些译本中"把"字句的分布和具体应用。

2.1 梁译本和朱译本与汉语原创作品中"把"字句使用频率比较

本文对曹禺戏剧《雷雨》和老舍戏剧《茶馆》中"把"字句使用进行定量分析,并对照李宁、王小珊(2001)和柯飞(2003)的研究成果,发现梁译本和朱译本的"把"字句使用频率高于许多汉语文学原创作品。请看表2:

表 2 汉语原创文学作品"把"字句使用频率

作品	字数	"把"字出现次数	"把"字句使用频率(每千字)
《雷雨》	74 187	154	1.9
《茶馆》	29 972	35	1.12
《四世同堂》第1部	317 000	521	1.6
《毕淑敏作品精选》	372 100	652	1.75

语言学与翻译研究导引

（续表）

作品	字数	"把"字出现次数	"把"字句使用频率（每千字）
《池莉小说近作选》	298 000	148	0.8
《骆驼祥子》	148 600	419	2.82
《林家铺子》	12 690	35	2.75

　　根据上表,朱译本"把"字句使用频率高于表中所列的所有汉语原创作品。其中,朱译本"把"字句使用频率比同类的汉语戏剧作品《雷雨》和《茶馆》分别高 47％ 和 69％,是《池莉小说近作选》的 4.5 倍。与《雷雨》和《茶馆》相比,梁译本"把"字句使用频率虽然要分别高出 10％ 和 47％,却比《骆驼祥子》和《林家铺子》低。

　　Mona Baker(1996)指出翻译语言"遵循,甚至夸大目标语中典型模式和做法"。前文所述的柯飞研究成果论证了这一假设。然而,表 2 数据表明,与《骆驼祥子》和《林家铺子》相比,梁译本并未过多使用"把"字句这一汉语特有的句式。我们认为判断某一目的语模式在翻译语言中是否显著,应考虑到相互比较的翻译文本和原创文本的文体类型是否相同或相似。

2.2　梁译本和朱译本中"把"字句的分布

　　《哈姆雷特》共有五幕。该剧的梁译本包括序言和注释在内共 141 页。朱译本没有序言,脚注不多,共 105 页。不包括注释部分在内,梁译本第一至第五幕分别为 24、21、28、21 和 21 页,朱译本第一至第五幕分别为 21、20、24、18 和 19 页。我们以戏剧的幕为单位,考察了"把"字句在这两个译本中的具体分布情况。请看下表：

表 3　梁译本和朱译本中"把"字句的分布

幕次	梁译本"把"字句出现次数	梁译本"把"字句每页使用频率	朱译本"把"字句出现次数	朱译本"把"字句每页使用频率
第一幕	10	0.42	34	1.62
第二幕	23	1.10	35	1.75
第三幕	31	1.12	62	2.59
第四幕	25	1.19	47	2.61
第五幕	28	1.33	45	2.37

　　从表 3 可见,这两个译本中"把"字句每页使用频率基本呈递增趋势。有趣的是,这一趋势与《哈姆雷特》剧情的发展相吻合。该剧主题为复仇,剧情逐步推进,人物冲突越来越激烈。第一幕为该剧情节发展的起始阶段,介绍交待事件发生的起由,开始交待有关人物之间的冲突。第四幕和第五幕是全剧的高潮阶段,讲述了篡取王位的叔叔两度设计除掉哈姆雷特,而后者最终以自己生命为代价完成了复仇计划。相应地,梁译本和朱译本中,第一幕"把"字句的使用频率较低,第四幕和第五幕则高出很多。在梁译本中,第四幕和第五幕"把"字句使用频率分别是第一幕的 2.83 倍和 3.17 倍。在朱译本中,第四幕和第五幕"把"字句使用频率分别是第一幕的 1.61 倍和 1.46 倍。就"把"字句出现次数而言,这两个译本"把"字句的使用主要集中于第三至第五幕。梁译本第三至第五幕"把"字句分别占该译本"把"字句总数的 26％、21％ 和

24％,而朱译本第三至第五幕"把"字句所占的百分比分别为 28％,21％和 20％。

2.3　梁译本和朱译本中"把"字句的具体应用

与汉语原创作品不同,翻译文本中"把"字句的应用均受到英语原文的影响。为此,我们提取梁译本和朱译本中所有"把"字句及其对应的英语语句,分析英语语句译为"把"字句的规律和特点。总体看来,译成"把"字句的英语句子结构主要为以下四大类。

2.3.1　动词＋宾语＋介词短语

(1) Upon my secure hour thy uncle stole,

With juice of cursed hebenon in a vial,

And in the porches of my ears did pour

The leperous distilment

梁译本:我那天正在园中睡熟的时候,你的叔叔偷偷的走来,拿着一瓶可恨的毒汁,把这毒汁倒在我的耳朵里。

朱译本:乘我不备,悄悄溜了进来,拿着一个盛着毒草汁的小瓶,把一种使人麻痹的药水注入我的耳腔之内。

(2) No such matter: I will not sort you with the rest

of my servants, for, to speak to you like an honest

man, I am most dreadfully attended.

梁译本:万无此理;我不能把你们当做我的侍从一类;我老实和你们说吧,我已经被伺候得难过透了。

朱译本:没有的事,我不愿把你们当作我的仆人一样看待。

2.3.2　动词＋宾语＋形容词/副词/分词

(3) What if this cursed hand

Were thicker than itself with brother's blood,

Is there not rain enough in the sweet heavens

To wash it white as snow?

梁译本:这该诅咒的手,纵然再沾厚一层我哥哥的血,天堂上就没有那么多的雨把它冲洗得雪一样的白吗?

朱译本:要是这一只可恶的手沾满一层比它本身还厚的兄弟的血,难道天上所有的甘霖,都不能把它洗涤得像雪一样洁白吗?

(4) It will be laid to us, whose providence

Should have kept short, restrain'd and out of haunt,

This mad young man

梁译本:这责任将在我身上,因为我事前就该把这疯狂的青年严加防范设法隔离才对。

朱译本:我们是不能辞其咎的,因为我们早该防患未然,把这个发疯的孩子关禁起来,不让他到处乱走。

2.3.3　动词＋名词＋名词/不定式

(5) I have a daughter—have while she is mine—

Who, in her duty and obedience, mark,

Hath given me this: now gather, and surmise.

梁译本：我有一个女儿，现在她还是我的——她激于孝心和服从之义，请注意，把这个
　　　　交给我了；请陛下来揣测一下。

朱译本：我有一个女儿，当她还不过是我的女儿的时候，她是属于我的——难得她一
　　　　片孝心，把这封信给了我。

(6) Since love our hearts and Hymen did our hands

Unite commutual in most sacred bands.

梁译本：自从两心相爱慕，月老缔良缘，一丝红线把我俩的手儿牵。

朱译本：自从爱把我们缔结良姻，许门替我们证下了鸳盟。

2.3.4　动词＋宾语

(7) And, in this brainish apprehension, kills

The unseen good old man.

梁译本：于是在狂妄迷惑之中，竟把里面藏着的老人刺死了。

朱译本：于是在一阵疯狂的恐惧之中，把那躲在幕后的好老人家杀死了。

(8) and we have done but greenly,

In hugger-mugger to inter him

梁译本：我的办法也未免太笨，竟悄悄的把他埋葬。

朱译本：我这样匆匆忙忙地把他秘密安葬，更加引起了外间的疑窦。

2.3.5　被动结构

(9) Let the foils be brought, the gentleman willing, and the

king hold his purpose, I will win for him as I can

梁译本：把比赛的剑拿来；假如那位先生愿意，国王依旧主张，我便尽力赢他。

朱译本：叫他们把比赛用的钝剑预备好了，要是这位绅士愿意，王上也不改变他的意
　　　　见的话，我愿意尽力为他博取一次胜利。

(10) and you from England,

Are here arrived give order that these bodies

High on a stage be placed to the view;

And let me speak to the yet unknowing world

How these things came about

梁译本：你们从英格兰奉使来朝，且令人把这些尸体高高的放在坛上由人瞻仰，容我
　　　　把这事的始末原由告诉你们不明真相的人听。

朱译本：有的刚从英国到来，恰好看见这一幕流血的惨剧，那么请你们叫人把这几个
　　　　尸体抬起来放在高台上面，让大家可以看见。

在梁译本和朱译本中，与以上英语语句对应的汉语"把"字句数量不等，具体情况如表 4
所示：

表 4　梁译本和朱译本中"把"字句的具体应用

英语语句结构	梁译本中对应的"把"字句数量	对应"把"字句占"把"字句总数的百分比	对应"把"字句出现频率（每万字）	朱译本中对应的"把"字句数量	对应"把"字句占"把"字句总数的百分比	对应"把"字句出现频率（每万字）
A：动词＋宾语＋介词短语	41	35％	7.39	67	30％	10.76
B：动词＋宾语＋形容词/副词/分词	8	6.8％	1.44	11	4.9％	1.76
C：动词＋名词＋名词/不定式	11	9.4％	1.98	20	8.9％	3.21
D：动词＋名词	33	28％	5.95	58	26％	9.31
E：被动结构	6	5.1％	1.08	12	5.3％	1.93

由上表可知,在梁译本和朱译本中,与 A 类语句对应的"把"字句数量最多,分别占梁译本和朱译本"把"字句总数的 35％和 30％。D 类英语句子结构次之,与这类结构对应的"把"字句分别占"把"字句总数的 28％和 26％。译自 C 类的"把"字句所占比例分别为 9.4％和 8.9％。在梁译本中,与 E 类语句对应的"把"字句数量最少,只占梁译本"把"字句的 5.1％;译自 B 类语句的"把"字句所占比例为 6.8％。在朱译本中,与 B 类和 E 类句子对应的"把"字句所占的比例为 4.9％和 5.3％。有必要指出,梁译本和朱译本中译自同一英语语句的"把"字句分别有 55 个。其中,与 A、B、C、D 和 E 类语句对应的"把"字句数量分别为 26、5、6、11 和 3 个不等。

比较梁译本和朱译本中"把"字句的出现频率,我们发现后者译自 A 类和 D 类语句的"把"字句居于前两位,分别是前者相应"把"字句的 1.46 倍和 1.56 倍。而前者与英语被动结构对应的"把"字句出现频率最低,只有后者相应"把"字句出现频率的 56％。

3　梁译本和朱译本中"把"字句应用的动因

根据认知语法,句法结构的外在形式是受内在认知因素驱动。"句法结构在相当程度上不是任意的、自主的,而是有自然的动因,其外形通常是由认知、功能、语用等句法之外的因素促成"(卢植,2006:219)。在翻译过程中,源语文本的认知、句法及语用等层面的信息,以及译者翻译策略和方法等都在不同程度上影响着译者对具体目的语句式结构的选择。因此,梁译本和朱译本中"把"字句应用的动因主要包括认知和句法动因、语用动因、翻译策略和方法动因等。

3.1　认知和句法动因

翻译本质上是由译者主体所进行的认知过程。A·切斯特曼(A. Chesterman)(1997)指出:"翻译从表面上看是两种不同语言体系之间进行的转换,而在形式的背后,却存在着极其复杂的认知活动,这项活动是通过认知主体即译者自身来完成的。"在这一过程中,源语文本所蕴含的事件图式会直接影响译者对目的语语言形式的选择。Langacker(1991:283)认为典型事件模型是形成语法构造和基本句型的基础。实质上,译者所选用的目的语语言结构是源语文本承载的事件图式的映射。译者常常自觉或不自觉地根据原文的事件图式,选用适当的目的语句式结构加以再现。

图式是指人作为主体所拥有的知识结构,是关于范畴的看法和认识,主要分为内容图式、语言图式和文本图式。根据 Cohen 的观点(1994:132),内容图式是指实际知识、价值观念和文化准则的表征体系。语言图式指句子结构、语法变化和曲折、文字拼写和标点符号使用、词汇和连贯结构。文本图式则为不同文本的修辞结构,如食谱、童话、研究性论文和教科书等。事件图式属于内容图式,也称为概念图式,它所反映的是参与者在某一行为或状态中最典型的组合,他们可能扮演主动或被动的角色。

在 2.3 小节,我们讨论了与"把"字句对应的主要英语语句结构。这些语句所蕴含的事件图式是空间位移图式。空间位移图式是指物体(包括抽象物体)在物理空间、时间、范围空间、心理空间和社会空间等不同空间内发生位移,或某一事物受到另一事物发出动作的影响,其所处位置、性质或状态发生变化。在上节所列的 A、B 和 C 三类句子中,宾语后的句子成分均用于说明受主语发出动作的影响,宾语所表示事物的位置、性质和状态所产生的变化。D 类句子也同样表示主语发出的动作使得某一事物的状态发生变化。不同的是,这一变化不是通过宾语后的成分来表示,而是蕴含于谓语动词意义之中。如例(7)中,动词"kill"的宾语"the unseen good old man"所发生的变化体现于"kill"之中,即"死去"。E 类句子中,主语是受事对象,动词被动式表示该事物所经历的变化,而动作发出者或施事对象虽然没有明确说明,但在具体语境中可以推出。

受上述英语语句所承载的位移图式制约,译者可以选择的汉语句式结构主要为动宾结构、动词+宾语+宾语补足语、"把"字句、"将"字句以及汉语被动句等。这些结构均表示由于外力的作用或影响,某一事物的状态或性质等发生变化。汉语动宾结构和动词+宾语+宾语补足语结构都比较常见。不过,由于汉语前端重心倾向的影响,除少数动词之外,如果宾语太长,宾语后成分复杂,或者为了强调宾语,人们大多使用"把"字句或"将"字句。"把"字句和"将"字句的语义特征基本相同,均表示"处置"和"致使"。"处置"是指主语有意识地对宾语施加作用并使之发生了变化。"致使"指主语致使宾语发生变化,对于事件的发生负有责任。"把"字句常用于口语之中,有时用于书面语言之中。而"将"字句多用于书面语言之中。石定栩(2006:131)基于对 18 世纪以来有关文学语料的考察,指出"将"字处置式结构大约在 19 世纪和 20 世纪之交从北方话口语之中消失,取而代之的是"把"字句。根据李宁、王小珊(2001)对 335 万字汉语语料中"把"字句应用调查的结果,"把"字句在电视谈话中的出现频率为 0.14%,在文学作品中出现频率为 0.09%。鉴于此,运用口语形式描述事物性质或状态所发生的变化,尤其是当汉语宾语后面成分复杂时,人们通常运用"把"字句。与其他文学体裁不同,戏剧主要由人物对白组成,并凭借这一口头语言形式塑造人物形象,交待人物之间的矛盾以及戏剧冲突。这些矛盾或冲突必然涉及说话人为了达到某一目的,通过行为或动作使事物发生变化。作为承载位移图式的主要汉语句式,"把"字句在梁译本和朱译本中的频繁使用当在情理之中。根据表3,"把"字句使用的频率随着剧情的推进逐渐上升,这与戏剧冲突愈来愈激烈不无关系。然而,"将"字句使用频率很低。在梁译本和朱译本中,"将"字句的出现次数分别为 2 次和 6 次。

还应指出,在《哈姆雷特》中,动词＋宾语结构和动词＋宾语＋宾语补足语结构十分常见。其中,许多宾语前往往使用若干前置定语,而宾语补足语常由介词、形容词、副词、动词不定式以及名词短语充当,补充说明宾语所发生的变化。这些结构若直译成汉语,汉语宾语或宾语后置成分则显得复杂、冗长,这与汉语前端重心趋势不符。因而,梁译本和朱译本常常将这些英语句式译为"把"字句。根据表4,梁译本和朱译本中,与这些语句对应的"把"字句分别占这两个译本中"把"字句总数的79.2％和69.87％。事实上,这些英语语句与汉语"把"字句之间存在显著的对应关系。为进一步了解这些英语句式的汉译情况,我们选取梁译本和朱译本均译作"把"字句的14个英语语句,要求19名英语专业硕士生在课堂上将这些句子译成汉语。这些语句均描述某一事物受外力影响所发生的变化。其中,7句为动词＋宾语＋介词短语结构,4句为动词＋宾语＋名词,3句为动词＋宾语＋副词短语。具体结果如表5所示:

表5　学生译文中"把"字句应用情况

学生译文序号	"把"字句/"将"字句出现次数	学生译文序号	"把"字句/"将"字句出现次数	学生译文序号	"把"字句/"将"字句出现次数	学生译文序号	"把"字句/"将"字句出现次数
1	7/2	6	7/5	11	10/0	16	5/3
2	8/1	7	3/2	12	5/0	17	6/1
3	0/5	8	2/7	13	11/0	18	7/3
4	3/7	9	3/1	14	12/0	19	6/2
5	12/2	10	7/4	15	7/1		

必须指出,"将"字句语义特征与"把"字句基本相同,"将"字句的应用是由于学生未曾意识到英语原文为口语语体的戏剧对白,故而本文将"把"字句和"将"字句合并考察。结果表明,学生译文中"把"字句使用频率较高。根据表5,"把"字句在所有学生译文中出现的次数为121次,每篇译文平均使用6.37次。"将"字句出现次数为46次,在每篇译文中平均出现2.42次。"把"字句和"将"字句在学生译文中出现次数为167次,平均每篇使用8.79次。由此可见,《哈姆雷特》人物语言中广泛存在蕴含位移图式的句式结构,尤其是动词＋若干前置定语＋宾语,以及动词＋宾语＋宾语补足语结构。这些句式结构的翻译,是梁译本和朱译本中"把"字句使用频率高于其他文体以及汉语戏剧原创文本的主要原因之一。

3.2　语用动因

语用动因是指源语文本语用信息对翻译的影响。在翻译过程中,译者通常自觉或不自觉地再现源语语句的语用特征和语用功能。语用特征是指源语语句在语气、态度或口吻等方面所表现出的不同特征,如客观中立或讽刺挖苦的语气等。语用功能,也称作言外行为,是指人们通过"说话"所实施的行为,如提出建议、发布命令等,是通过字面意义所表达的说话人的意图。根据 Searle(1976)的观点,言外行为可分成阐述类、指令类、承诺类、表达类和宣告类。阐述类是指说话人对于过去、现在或将来的客观现实进行陈述。指令类是指说话人命令、建议或要求听话人去做某一件事。承诺类指说话人对将来要做的某一行为作出许诺。表达类则是表达说话人的某种心理状态,如感激、悲伤等。宣告类则指客观事实按照说话人的话语发生变化。

抽样分析《哈姆雷特》原著第四幕第七景和第五幕第二景,我们发现蕴含位移图式的语句共 97 个。其中,语用功能为提出要求、建议或发布命令的语句计 40 个,15 个语句表示许诺。这类语句表示说话人的主观愿望、建议、要求或许诺等,具有明显的主观性。主观性是指语言不仅仅表达命题式思想,还表达说话人的观点、感情和态度以及说话人要实施的言语行为。(Langacker,1987;Lakoff & Johnson,1980)。陈述事实的语句有 42 个,这些语句虽然交待具体事实,但使用了表示说话人主观态度或有关价值判断的词语,同样具有主观性。如 2.3 小节的例(1)、例(3)、例(4)、例(5)、例(7)或例(8)均用于事实的陈述,它们分别使用了"cursed"、"mad"、"quaintly"、"sacred"、"wholesome"、"brandish"和"greenly"等表示价值判断的词语。

必须指出,蕴含位移图式的汉语语句均具有主观性,因为位置、性质或状态等变化实质上是人对变化的一种主观感知或判断,而"把"字句的主观性尤为突出。"把"字句可以表示主观处置,即某人对另一人或物施加影响,并使其发生变化,带有非常明显的主观体验成分。"把"字句还可用于表示说话人对某一动作承受者的主观情感。如"那些衣服把小姑娘洗怕了",反映了说话者对小姑娘的同情心。此外,"把"字句的语用功能主要为阐述类、指令类和表达类。根据李宁和王小珊对 300 万语料中"把"字句语用功能的调查,阐述类"把"字句占所有"把"字句总数的 85.99%,指令类"把"字句所占比例为 7.4%,表达类的比例为 5.75%。由于"把"字句与上述英语语句在语用特性和语用功能等方面的一致,梁译本和朱译本往往运用"把"字句翻译以上承载位移图式的英语语句。对照分析《哈姆雷特》原著第四幕第七景和第五幕第二景及其汉译文,可知梁译本和朱译本中"把"字句数量分别为 21 和 34 个,"把"字句与承载位移图式的英语语句的对应率分别为 22% 和 35%。

3.3 翻译策略和方法动因

翻译策略和方法动因指译者所采取的翻译策略和方法在很大程度上制约着"把"字句的应用。如果译者运用异化策略,根据源语句序或源语的其他语言文化特征来翻译,"把"字句使用的概率较低。相反,如果译者运用归化策略,力求译文符合目的语语言文化特性,"把"字句使用的概率较高。对比分析梁译本和朱译本中的"把"字句及其对应的英语原文,我们发现梁译本"把"字句数量之所以少于朱译本,其重要原因在于梁译本往往对原文亦步亦趋,拘泥于原文的词汇搭配和句序。翻译英语动词+宾语结构时,梁译本经常将汉语不及物动词误作及物动词使用。与之不同,朱译本则摆脱原文句法结构的桎梏,以汉语语言文化为依归。正如朱生豪在《莎士比亚戏剧全集・译者自序》中所指出的,"余译此书之宗旨,第一,在求于最大可能之范围内,保存原作之神韵……凡遇原文中与中国语法不合之处,往往再四咀嚼,不惜全部更易原文之结构……"

(11) Then if he says he loves you,

　　It fits your wisdom so far to believe it

　　As he in his particular act and place

　　May give his saying deed.

　　梁译本:所以他若是说他爱你,你只可相信他在身份所需的范围之内可以实践他的话。

　　朱译本:所以要是他说,他爱你,你要明白,以他的身份地位能够把自己的话实现多少。

该例原文为一主从复合句。梁译本完全按照原文词序来翻译,且将汉语不及物动词"实践"误作及物动词。而朱译本对该例主句部分的翻译调整了原文部分的词序和句序,并使用了"把"字句结构,译文与汉语句法要求吻合。

(12) O God, I could be bounded in a nut shell and count
　　　myself a king of infinite space, were it not that
　　　I have bad dreams.
　　梁译本:啊上帝哟,我若不做那一场噩梦,我即便是被关在胡桃核里,我也可自命为
　　　　　一个拥有广土的帝王。
　　朱译本:上帝啊! 倘不是因为我有了恶梦,那么即使把我关在一个果壳里,我也会把
　　　　　自己当作一个拥有无限空间的君王的。

该例原文为一被动句结构,梁译本将其译作汉语被动结构,而朱译本未受原文句式结构的束缚,将其译作"把"字句。

此外,朱译本频繁运用显化翻译方法,在一定程度上导致了"把"字句数量的增多。显化是指在目的语中将原文中隐含的信息明确表达出来。出于方便读者理解的考虑,朱译本常常在译文中交待英语原文中虽然没有明示但可以推导出来的动作承受者,这就意味着宾语的出现。众所周知,"把"字句运用的基本前提是必须存在宾语。因此,动作承受者的明示往往导致"把"字句使用频率的提高。

(13) But to my mind, though I am native here
　　　And to the manner born, it is a custom
　　　More honor'd in the breach than the observance.
　　梁译本:我虽然生长在此地,一切都已习惯,但是这种习俗,我却以为革除比遵守还
　　　　　体面些。
　　朱译本:可是我虽然从小就熟悉这种风俗,我却以为把它破坏了倒比遵守它还体
　　　　　面些。

(14) Haste me to know't, that I, with wings as swift
　　　As meditation or the thought of love,
　　　May sweep to my revenge.
　　梁译本:快令我知道,我好插上和默想爱念迅速的翅膀,去报仇。
　　朱译本:赶快告诉我,让我驾着像思想和爱情一样迅速的翅膀,飞去把仇人杀死。

(15) Slanders, sir: for the satirical rogue says here.
　　梁译本:一派诽谤的谣言,先生;这个善讽刺的坏人。
　　朱译本:一派诽谤,先生;这个专爱把人讥笑的坏蛋在这儿说着。

(16) My honor'd lord, I know right well you did.
　　梁译本:我尊荣的殿下,我清清楚楚地记得是你给的。
　　朱译本:殿下,我记得很清楚您把它们送给我。

在例(13)—(15)中,朱译本明确交待"breach"、"observance"、"revenge"和"satirical"等抽象词汇蕴含的动作承受者。在例(16)中,译者将"you did"内含的信息以及与其相关的动作承受者予以明示,并因此使用"把"字句。而梁译本只是根据上述词汇的字面意义翻译,未曾说明

有关动作的承受者,自然就没有必要运用"把"字句。

还应指出,与英语相比,汉语中代词零前指现象相当普遍。在汉语中,如果代词所指对象明确,作宾语的代词往往可以省略。然而,朱译本将充当英语动词宾语的代词或有关短语均译出,且往往使用"把"字句。梁译本则常常将这些宾语省译,其运用"把"字句的概率显然要低于朱译本。

(17) there is something in this more than

natural, if philosophy could find it out.

梁译本:哲学若能探索的话,这里面必有一点出乎人情的道理。

朱译本:这里面有些不是常可理解的地方,要是哲学能够把它推究出来的话。

(18) Fare you well, my liege:

I'll call upon you ere you go to bed,

And tell you what I know.

梁译本:叩别了,主上;陛下睡前我再来进竭,尽情禀告。

朱译本:再会,陛下;在您未睡以前,我还是要看您一次,把我探听到的事情告诉您。

在以上两例中,梁译本将动词后的宾语"it"和"what I know"省译,自然没有使用"把"字句的必要。而朱译本则将这些宾语均译出,且使用"把"字句。

4 结语

综上所述,作为交待人物之间矛盾冲突以及情节发展变化的主要手段,《哈姆雷特》人物对白中存在大量蕴含位移图式的语句结构,如动词+若干前置定语+宾语,以及动词+宾语+宾语补足语结构等。这些语句具有鲜明的主观性,其语用功能主要为陈述事实、提出建议和要求、发布命令或作出承诺等。由于"把"字句与这些句式结构在承载的位移图式、语用特性和语用功能等方面的契合,《哈姆雷特》梁译本和朱译本中"把"字句的使用频率高于其他文体以及汉语戏剧原创文本。然而,"把"字句的应用在很大程度上受到译者翻译策略和方法运用的制衡。相比较而言,梁译本更多地运用异化翻译策略,根据原文的句序和词汇字面意义翻译。朱译本则大多采用归化翻译策略和显化翻译方法,明示原文中隐含的动作承受者。因此,朱译本中"把"字句数量远远超过梁译本。

参考文献

[1] Anderman, G. & Rogers, M. (2008). *Incorporating Corpora: The Linguist and the Translator*[M]. Clevedon: Multilingual Matters.

[2] Baker, M. (1993). Corpus Linguistics and Translation Studies: Implications and Applications[A]. In M. Baker, G. Francis & E. Tognini-Bonelli (eds.), *Text and Technology: In Honour of John Sinclair* (pp. 233 – 250)[C]. Amsterdam: John Benjamins.

[3] Baker, M. (1995). Corpora in Translation Studies: An Overview and Some Suggestions for Future Research[J]. *Target*, 7(2), 223 – 243.

[4] Baker, M. (1996). Corpus-based Translation Studies: The Challenges That Lie Ahead [A]. In H. Somers (ed.), *Terminology, LSP and Translation* (pp. 175 – 186)[C]. Amsterdam: John Benjamins.

[5] Baker, M. (2000). Towards a Methodology for Investigating the Style of a Literary Translator[J]. *Target*, 12(2), 241 – 266.

[6] Baker, M. (2007). Corpus-based Translation Studies in the Academy[J]. *Journal of Foreign Languages*, (5), 50 – 55.

[7] Bencher, V. (2010). Abandoning the Notion of "Translation-Inherent" Explicitation: Against a Dogma of Translation Studies [J]. *Across Languages and Cultures*, 11(1), 1 – 28.

[8] Bosseaux, C. (2007). *How Does it Feel? Point of View in Translation: The Case of Virginia Woolf into French*[M]. Amsterdam: Rodopi.

[9] Chesterman, A. (2004). Beyond the Particular[A]. In A. Mauranen & P. Kujamäki (eds.), *Translation Universals: Do They Exist?* [C]. Amsterdam: John Benjamins.

[10] Ding, Y., D. Noël & Wolf, H. (2010). Patterns of Metaphor Translation: Translating FEAR Metaphors between English and Chinese [A]. In Xiao, R. (ed.), *Using Corpora in Contrastive and Translation Studies* (pp. 40 – 61)[C]. New Castle upon Tyne: Cambridge Scholars Publishing.

[11] Hoey, M. (2005). *Lexical Priming: A New Theory of Words and Language* [M]. London: Routledge.

[12] Hoey, M. (2011). Lexical Priming and Translation [A]. In A. Kruger, K. Wallmarch & J. Munday (eds.), *Corpus-based Translation Studies: Research and Applications* (pp. 153 – 168)[C]. London: Continuum.

[13] House, J. (2008). Beyond Intervention: Universals in Translation [J]. *Trans-Kom*, 1(1): 6 – 19.

［14］House，J.（2011）. Using Translation and Parallel Text Corpora to Investigate the Influence of Global English on Textual Norms in Other Languages［A］. In A. Kruger，K. Wallmarch & J. Munday（eds.），*Corpus-based Translation Studies：Research and Applications*（pp. 187 - 208）［C］. London：Continuum.

［15］Kenny，D.（2005）. Parallel Corpora and Translation Studies：Old questions，New Perspectives? Reporting *that* in Gepcolt：A Case Study［A］. In G. Barnbrook，P. Danielsson & M. Mahlberg（eds.），*Meaningful Texts：The Extraction of Semantic Information from Monolingual and Multilingual Corpora*（pp. 154 - 165）［C］. London：Continuum.

［16］Klaudy，K.（2009）. The Asymmetry Hypothesis in Translation Research［A］. In R. Dimitriu & M. Shlesinger（eds.），*Translators and Their Readers*（pp. 283 - 303）［C］. *In Homage to Eugene Nida*. Brussels：Les Editions du Hazard.

［17］Kruger，A.，Wallmarch，K. & Munday，J.（2011）. *Corpus-based Translation Studies：Research and Applications*［C］. London：Continuum.

［18］Laviosa，S.（2002）. *Corpus-based Translation Studies：Theory，Findings and Applications*［M］. Amsterdam：Rodopi.

［19］Laviosa，S.（2007）. Similarity and Differences in Corpus-based Translation Studies［J］. *Journal of Foreign Languages*，(5)，56 - 63.

［20］Laviosa，S.（2011）. Corpus-based Translation Studies 15 Years On：Theory，Findings，Applications［J］. *SYNAPS*，24，3 - 12.

［21］Laviosa，S.（2011）. Corpus-based Translation Studies：Where Does It Come From? Where Is It Going?［A］. In A. Kruger，K. Wallmarch & J. Munday（eds.），*Corpus-based Translation Studies：Research and Applications*（pp. 13 - 32）［C］. London：Continuum.

［22］Malmkjær，K.（2008）. Norms and Nature in Translation Studies［A］. In G. Anderman & M. Rogers（eds.），*Incorporating Corpora：The Linguist and the Translator*（pp. 49 - 59）［C］. Clevedon：Multilingual Matters.

［23］Mauranen，A.（2008）. Universal Tendencies in Translation［A］. In G. Anderman & M. Rogers（eds.），*Incorporating Corpora：The Linguist and the Translator*（pp. 32 - 48）［C］. Clevedon：Multilingual Matters.

［24］McEnery，T. & Wilson，A.（1993）. Corpora and Translation：Uses and Future Prospects. *UCREL Technical Papers*，1 - 11.

［25］Miao，J. & Salem，A.（2010）. The Specificity of Translator's Notes：Lexicometrical Analysis of Notes in Fu Lei's Translation of *Jean-Christophe* by Roman Rolland［A］. In Xiao，R.（ed.），*Using Corpora in Contrastive and Translation Studies*（pp. 79 - 108）［C］. New Castle upon Tyne：Cambridge Scholars Publishing.

［26］Munday，J.（2011）. Looming Large：A Cross-Linguistic Analysis of Semantic Prosodies in Comparable Corpora［A］. In A. Kruger，K. Wallmarch & J. Munday（eds.），*Corpus-based Translation Studies：Research and Applications*（pp. 169 - 186）［C］. London：Continuum.

[27] Olohan, M. & Baker, M. (2000). Reporting *That* in Translated English: Evidence for Subconscious Processes of Explicitation [J]. *Across Languages and Cultures*, 1 (2), 141 - 158.

[28] Øverås, L. (1998). In Search of the Third Code: An Investigation of Norms in Literary Translation[J]. *Meta*, 43(4), 557 - 570.

[29] Pekkanen, H. (2010). *The Duet between the Author and the Translator: An Analysis of Style through Shifts in Literary Translation* [M]. Helsinki: Helsinki University Print.

[30] Pym, A. (2005). Explaining Explicitation [A]. In K. Karoly & A. Fóris (eds.), *New Trends in Translation Studies: In Honor of Kinga Klaudy* (pp. 29 - 34) [C]. Budapest: Akadémiai Kiadó.

[31] Rocha, M. (2010). Translating Anaphoric *This* into Portuguese: A Corpus-based Study [A]. In Xiao, R. (ed.), *Using Corpora in Contrastive and Translation Studies* (pp. 11 - 39)[C]. New Castle upon Tyne: Cambridge Scholars Publishing.

[32] Saldanha, G. (2008). Explicitation Revisited: Bringing the Reader into the Picture [J]. *Trans-Kom*, 1(1), 20 - 35.

[33] Saldanha, G. (2011). Translator Style: Methodological Considerations [J]. *Translator*, 17(1), 25 - 50.

[34] Setton, R. (2011). Corpus-based Interpreting Studies (CIS): Overview and Prospects [A]. In A. Kruger, K. Wallmarch & J. Munday (eds.), *Corpus-based Translation Studies: Research and Applications* (pp. 33 - 75)[C]. London: Continuum.

[35] Toury, G. (2004). Probabilistic Explanations in Translation Studies: Welcome as They Are, Would They Qualify as Universals? [A]. In A. Mauranen & P. Kujamäki (eds.), *Translation Universals: Do They Exist?* (pp. 15 - 32)[C]. Amsterdam: John Benjamins.

[36] Tymoczko, M. (1998). Computerized Corpora and the Future of Translation Studies [J]. *Meta*, 43(2), 652 - 660.

[37] Vanderauwera, R. (1985). *Dutch Novels Translated Into English: The Transformation of a "Minority" Literature*[M]. Amsterdam: Rodopi.

[38] Wallaert, I. (2010). The Elephant in the Dark: Corpus-based Description of Translator's Style[A]. *Les Cahiers du GEPE*, N°2/2010. Outils de traduction-outils du traducteur? http://www.cahiersdugepe.fr/index1641.php (accessed 20/03/2011).

[39] Winters, M. (2007). F. Scott Fitzgerald's *Die Schönen und Verdammten*: A Corpus-based Study of Speech-act Report Verbs as a Feature of Translators' Style[J]. *Meta*, 52(3), 412 - 425.

[40] Winters, M. (2009). Modal Particles Explained: How Modal Particles Creep into Translations and Reveal Translators' Styles[J]. *Target*, 21(1), 74 - 97.

[41] Yu, Ching-hua. (2007). Similarity and Difference in Translator's Style: A Case Study of the Two Translations of Hemingway's Work[A]. Paper presented at Conference and Workshop on Corpora and Translation Studies. Mar. 30—Apr. 1, 2007, Shanghai, China.